P9-DYZ-917

SUPPLEMENT VII
Julia Alvarez to Tobias Wolff

AMERICAN WRITERS
A Collection of Literary Biographies

JAY PARINI
Editor in Chief

SUPPLEMENT VII
Julia Alvarez to Tobias Wolff

Charles Scribner's Sons
An Imprint of the Gale Group
New York

Copyright © 2001 by Charles Scribner's Sons, an imprint of the Gale Group

Charles Scribner's Sons
1633 Broadway
New York, New York 10019

All rights reserved. No part of this book may be reproduced or transmitted in any form or by any means, electronic or mechanical, including photocopying, recording, or by an information storage or retrieval system, without permission in writing from the publisher.

1   3   5   7   9   11   13   15   17   19   20   18   16   14   12   10   8   6   4   2

Library of Congress Cataloging-in-Publication Data

American writers; a collection of literary biographies. Leonard Unger, editor in chief.
    p.   cm.
    The 4 vol. main set consists of 97 of the pamphlets originally published as the University of Minnesota pamphlets on American writers; some have been rev. and updated. The supplements cover writers not included in the original series.
    Supplement 2, has editor in chief, A. Walton Litz; Retrospective suppl. 1, ©1998, was edited by A. Walton Litz & Molly Weigel; Suppl. 5 has editor-in-chief, Jay Parini.
    Includes bibliographies and index.
    Contents: v. 1. Henry Adams to T. S. Eliot — v. 2. Ralph Waldo Emerson to Carson McCullers — v. 3. Archibald MacLeish to George Santayana — v. 4. Isaac Bashevis Singer to Richard Wright — Supplement[s]: 1, pt. 1. Jane Addams to Sidney Lanier. 1, pt. 2. Vachel Lindsay to Elinor Wylie. 2, pt.1. W.H. Auden to O. Henry. 2, pt. 2. Robison Jeffers to Yvor Winters. — 4, pt. 1. Maya Angelou to Linda Hogan. 4, pt. 2. Susan Howe to Gore Vidal. 5. Russell Banks to Charles Wright.
    ISBN 0-684-19785-5 (set) — ISBN 0-684-13662-7
    1. American literature—History and criticism. 2. American literature—Bio-bibliography. 3. Authors, American—Biography. I. Unger, Leonard. II. Litz, A. Walton. III Weigel, Molly. IV. University of Minnesota pamphlets on American writers.

PS129 .A55
810′.9
[B]   73-001759

    ISBN 0-684-80624-X

Acknowledgment is gratefully made to those publishers and individuals who have permitted the use of the following material in copyright.

Julia Alvarez
Excerpts from "Memory is Already the Story You Made Up About the Past: An Interview with Julia Alvarez," by Catherine Wiley, in *The Bloomsbury Review,* March 1992, copyright © 1992 by Owaissa Communications Company, Inc., reprinted by permission of the author. Excerpts from *The Other Side/El Otro Lado,* by Julia Alvarez, Dutton, 1995, reprinted by permission of Dutton, a division of Penguin Putnam Inc. Excerpts from *Homecoming: New and Collected Poems,* by Julia Alvarez, Dutton, 1995, reprinted by permission of Susan Bergholz Literary Services.

A. R. Ammons
Excerpts from an interview with A. R. Ammons, in *Michigan Quarterly Review,* Winter 1989, copyright © 1989 by The University of Michigan, reprinted by permission of A. R. Ammons. Excerpts from *Ommateum,* by A. R. Ammons, Dorrance, 1955, reprinted by permission of A. R. Ammons. Excerpts from *Corsons Inlet,* by A. R. Ammons, Cornell University Press, 1965, reprinted by permission of W. W. Norton & Company, Inc. Excerpts from *Collected Poems: 1951–1971,* by A. R. Ammons, W. W. Norton, 1972, copyright © 1987, 1977, 1975, 1974, 1972, 1971, 1970, 1966, 1965, 1964, 1955 by A. R. Ammons, reprinted by permission of W. W. Norton & Company, Inc. Excerpts from *Sphere: The Form of a Motion,* by A. R. Ammons, Norton, 1974, copyright © 1974 by A. R. Ammons, reprinted by permission of W. W. Norton & Company, Inc. Excerpts from *The Snow Poems,* by A. R. Ammons, W. W. Norton, 1977, copyright © 1977 by A. R. Ammons, reprinted by permission of W. W. Norton & Company, Inc. Excerpts from *Tape for the Turn of a Year,* by A. R. Ammons, Cornell University Press, 1965, reprinted by permission of W. W. Norton & Company, Inc.

207703

BELMONT UNIVERSITY LIBRARY

Ref
PS
129
A55
sup.?

AAB-2564

Sandra Cisneros

Excerpts from *My Wicked Wicked Ways,* by Sandra Cisneros, Random House, 1987, reprinted by permission of the author. Excerpts from *Loose Woman,* by Sandra Cisneros, Random House, 1994, reprinted by permission of the author. Excerpts from *Woman Hollering Creek,* by Sandra Cisneros, Random House, 1991, reprinted by permission of the author.

Andre Dubus

Excerpts from *Book,* March/April, 1999, reprinted by permission. Excerpts from *Separate Flights,* by Andre Dubus, copyright © 1975 by David R. Godine, reprinted by permission of David R. Godine, Publisher, Inc. Excerpts from <http://www.english.swt.edu/excerpt.dir/excerpt1.dir/dubus1.htm>, reprinted by permission. Excerpts from *The New York Times Sunday Magazine,* November 20, 1988, copyright © 1988 by The New York Times Company, reprinted by permission.

George Garrett

Excerpts from *Death of the Fox,* by George Garrett, Doubleday, 1971, reprinted by permission of the author. Excerpts from *Days of Our Lives Lie in Fragments: New and Old Poems,* by George Garrett, Louisiana State University Press, 1998, copyright © 1998 by George Garrett, reprinted by permission of Louisiana State University Press. Excerpts from *For A Bitter Season,* by George Garrett, University of Missouri Press, 1967, reprinted by permission.

Donald Justice

Excerpts from *New and Selected Poems,* by Donald Justice, Alfred A. Knopf, 1995, copyright © 1995 by Donald Justice, reprinted by permission of Alfred A. Knopf, a Division of Random House Inc.

William Kennedy

Excerpts from a review of William Kennedy's works by Joel Conarroe, *The New York Times,* September 30, 1984, copyright © 1984 by The New York Times Company, reprinted by permission of the author. Excerpts from *The Ink Truck,* by William Kennedy, Penguin, 1984, copyright © 1969, renewed © 1997 by William Kennedy, reprinted by permission of Viking Penguin, a division of Penguin Putnam Inc. Excerpts from *Legs,* by William Kennedy, Penguin, 1983, copyright © 1975 by William Kennedy, reprinted by permission of Viking Penguin, a division of Penguin Putnam Inc. Excerpts from *The Flaming Corsage,* by William Kennedy, Viking, 1996, copyright © 1996 by WJK, Inc, reprinted by permission of Viking Penguin, a division of Penguin Putnam Inc. Excerpts from *Billy Phelan's Greatest Game,* by William Kennedy, Penguin, 1984, copyright © 1978 by William Kennedy, reprinted by permission of Viking Penguin, a division of Penguin Putnam Inc. Excerpts from *Ironweed,* by William Kennedy, Penguin, 1983, copyright © 1979, 1981, 1983 by William Kennedy, reprinted by permission of Viking Penguin, a division of Penguin Putnam Inc. Excerpts from *Quinn's Book,* by William Kennedy, Penguin, 1988, copyright © 1988 by WJK, Inc, reprinted by permission of Viking Penguin, a division of Penguin Putnam Inc. Excerpts from *Very Old Bones,* by William Kennedy, Penguin, 1992, copyright © 1992 by WJK, Inc, reprinted by permission of Viking Penguin, a division of Penguin Putnam Inc.

Jane Kenyon

Excerpts from *From Room to Room,* by Jane Kenyon, Alice James Books, 1978, reprinted by permission. Excerpts from an introduction to *Twenty Poems of Anna Akhmatova,* by Jane Kenyon, translated by Jane Kenyon with Vera Sandomirsky Dunham, Eighties Press and Ally Press, 1985, reprinted by permission. Excerpts from *The Boat of Quiet Hours,* by Jane Kenyon, Graywolf Press, 1986, reprinted by permission. Excerpts from *Constance,* by Jane Kenyon, Graywolf Press, 1993, reprinted by permission. Excerpts from *A Hundred White Daffodils: Essays, Interviews, Newspaper Columns, and One Poem,* by Jane Kenyon, Graywolf Press, 1999, reprinted by permission. Excerpts from *Let Evening Come,* by Jane Kenyon, Graywolf Press, 1990, reprinted by permission. Excerpts from *Otherwise,* by Jane Kenyon, Graywolf Press, 1996, reprinted by permission.

Jamaica Kincaid

Excerpts from "A Lot of Memory: An Interview with Jamaica Kincaid," by Moira Ferguson, in *The Kenyon Review* 16, Winter 1994, reprinted by permission of the author. Excerpts from *The Missouri Review* 20, copyright © 1991 by The American Audio Prose Library, Inc., reprinted by permission of the American Audio Prose Library.

Barbara Kingsolver

Excerpts from *Another America/Otra America,* by Barbara Kingsolver, Seal Press, 1998, reprinted by permission. Excerpts from *The New York Times Book Review,* September 2, 1990, copyright © 1990 by The New York Times Company, reprinted by permission.

Mary Oliver

Excerpts from *Dream Work,* by Mary Oliver, Atlantic Monthly Press, 1986, copyright © 1986 by Mary Oliver, reprinted by permission. Excerpts from *House of Light,* Mary Oliver, Beacon Press, 1990, reprinted by permission. Excerpts from *No Voyage and Other Poems,* Mary Oliver, Dent, 1963, reprinted by permission. Excerpts from "The Man on the Grass," by Mary Oliver, in *The Georgia Review* 35, 1981, copyright © 1981 by the University of Georgia, reprinted by permission of the author. Excerpts from *The River Styx Ohio, and Other Poems,* by Mary Oliver, Harcourt Brace & Company, 1972, reprinted by permission of the author. Excerpts from *White Pine,* by Mary Oliver, Harcourt Brace & Company, 1994, reprinted by permission of Harcourt, Inc. Excerpts from *West Wind: Poems and Prose Poems,* by Mary Oliver, Houghton Mifflin, 1997, reprinted by permission of Houghton Mifflin Company. Excerpts from *New and Selected Poems,* by Mary Oliver, Beacon Press, 1992, reprinted by permission. Excerpts from "Review of House of Light," by David Baker, *Kenyon Review* 13, 1991, copyright © 1991 by Kenyon College, reprinted by permission. Excerpts from *Twelve Moons,* by Mary Oliver, Little Brown, 1979, reprinted by permission of Little, Brown and Company. Excerpts from *American Primitive,* by Mary Oliver, Little Brown, 1983, reprinted by permission of Little, Brown and Company. Excerpts from *The Ohio Review* 38, 1987, copyright © 1987 by the editors of *The Ohio Review*, reprinted by permission. Excerpts from *Papers on Language and Literature* 30, Fall 1994, copyright © 1994 by the Board of Trustees, Southern Illinois University at Edwardsville, reprinted by permission. Excerpts from a review of *New and Selected Poems,* by David Barber, in *Poetry* 162, 1993, copyright © 1993 by the Modern Poetry Association, reprinted by permission of the poetry editor and the author. Excerpts from a review of *A Poetry Handbook and White Pine,* by Thomas R. Smith, in *The Bloomsbury Review* 15, 1995, copyright © 1995 by Owaissa Communications Company, Inc., reprinted by permission of the author. Excerpts from "Dialogues Between History and Dream," by Lisa Steinman, *Michigan Quarterly Review* 36, 1987, copyright © 1987 by The University of Michigan, reprinted by permission of the author. Excerpts from "The Language of Dreams: An Interview with Mary Oliver," by Eleanor Swanson, in *The Bloomsbury Review* 10, 1990, copyright © 1990 by Owaissa Communications Company, Inc., reprinted by permission of the author. Excerpts from *Women's Studies: An Interdisciplinary Journal* 21, 1992, copyright © 1992 by Gordon and Breach Science Publishers, reprinted by permission.

Annie Proulx

Excerpts from "Imagination is Everything," by Katie Bolick, in *Atlantic Unbound,* November 12, 1997, reprinted by permission of the author. Excerpts from *Publishers Weekly* 243, June 3, 1996, copyright © 1996 by Reed Publishing USA, reprinted by permission of the Bowker Magazine Group of Cahners Publishing Co., a division of Reed Publishing USA. Excerpts from *Heart Songs & Other Stories,* by Annie Proulx, Scribners, 1988, copyright © 1988, 1995 by Annie Proulx, reprinted by permission of Scribners, a division of Simon & Schuster. Excerpts from *Close Range: Wyoming Stories,* by Annie Proulx, Scribners, 1999, reprinted by permission of the Gale Group. Excerpts from *The New York Times Biographical Services* 25, June 1994, reprinted by permission.

James Purdy

Excerpts from *On the Rebound: A Story and Nine Poems,* by James Purdy, Black Sparrow Press, 1970, reprinted by permission.

Anne Rice

Excerpts from *New York Times Book Review,* March 28, 1999, copyright © 1999 by The New York Times Company, reprinted by permission. Excerpts from *New York Times Book Review,* August 11, 1999, copyright © 1999 by The New York Times Company, reprinted by permission. Excerpts from *New York Times Magazine,* October 14, 1990, reprinted by permission. Excerpts from *People Weekly,* December 5, 1988, reprinted by permission. Excerpts from *Rolling Stone,* July 13–27, 1995, copyright © 1995 by Straight Arrow Publishers Company, L.P., reprinted by permission. Excerpts from *Wall Street Journal,* June 17, 1976, reprinted by permission.

Carol Shields

Excerpt from "Interview with Carol Shields," by Marjorie Anderson, in *Prairie Fire* 16, 1995, reprinted by permission. Excerpts from *Coming to Canada,* by Carol Shields, Carleton University Press, 1995, reprinted by permission. Excerpts from *Intersect,* by Carol Shields, Carleton University Press, 1995, reprinted by permission. Excerpts from "Ordinary Pleasures (and Terrors): The Plays of Carol Shields," by Chris Johnson, in *Prairie Fire* 16, 1995, reprinted by permission of the author. Excerpts from "Interview with Carol Shields," by Eleanor Wachtel, in *Room of One's Own* 13, 1989, reprinted by permission. Excerpts from "An Epistolary Interview with Carol Shields," by Joan Thomas, in *Prairie Fire* 16, 1995, reprinted by permission of the author. Excerpts from "A Little Like Flying: An Interview with Carol Shields," by Harvey De Roo, in *West Coast Review* 23, 1988, reprinted by permission of the publisher and the author.

Tobias Wolff

Excerpts from *In the Garden of the North American Martyrs,* by Tobias Wolff, Ecco Press, 1981, copyright © 1981 by Tobias Wolff, reprinted by permission of HarperCollins, Inc. Excerpts from *Critique: Studies in Contemporary Fiction* 32, Summer 1991, copyright © 1991 by Helen Dwight Reid Educational Foundation, reprinted with permission of the Helen Dwight Reid Educational Foundation.

Editorial and Production Staff

Managing Editors
AMANDA MATERNE
ANNA SHEETS NESBITT

Copyediting
VISUAL EDUCATION CORPORATION

Proofreaders
KAREN C. BRANSTETTER
DANIEL J. HARVEY
PATRICIA A. ONORATO
CAROL PAGE
JANE E. SPEAR

Indexer
IMPRESSIONS BOOK AND JOURNAL SERVICES, INC.

Publisher
KAREN DAY

List of Subjects

Introduction

In an essay called "Spiritual Laws," Ralph Waldo Emerson wrote: "There is no luck in literary reputation. They who make up the final verdict upon every book are not the partial and noisy readers of the hour when it appears; but a court as of angels, a public not to be bribed, not to be entreated, and not to be overawed, decides upon every man's title to fame." This remains true, yet the work of criticism plays a role—the critic, in a sense, must act as a lawyer before this "court as of angels," making a case for various writers, new and old.

This series had its origin in a unique series of brief critical monographs that appeared between 1959 and 1972. The Minnesota Pamphlets on American Writers were elegantly written and informative, treating ninety-seven American writers in a format and style that attracted a devoted following of readers. The series proved invaluable to a generation of students and teachers, who could depend on these reliable and interesting critiques of major figures. The smart idea of reprinting these essays occurred to Charles Scribner Jr. (1921–1995). The series appeared in four volumes entitled *American Writers: A Collection of Literary Biographies* (1974).

Since then, seven supplements have appeared, covering over two hundred American writers: poets, novelists, playwrights, essayists, and autobiographers. The idea has been consistent with the original series: to provide crystalline, informative essays aimed at the general reader and intelligent student. These essays often rise to a high level of craft and critical vision, but they are meant to introduce a writer of some importance in the history of American literature, and to provide a sense of the scope and nature of the career under review. A certain amount of biographical and historical context for the work is also offered, so that readers can appreciate the ground that provided the texts under review with air and light, soil nutrients and water.

The authors of these critical articles are primarily teachers, scholars, and writers. Most have published books and articles in their field, and several are well-known writers of poetry, fiction, or criticism. As anyone glancing through this volume will see, they are held to the highest standards of good writing and sound scholarship. Each essay concludes with a select bibliography intended to direct the reading of those who may want to pursue the subject further.

Supplement VII is mostly about contemporary writers, many of whom have received little sustained attention from critics. For example, Julia Alvarez, Tobias Wolff, Sandra Cisneros, Annie Proulx, Jamaica Kincaid, Carol Shields, Richard Bausch, Andre Dubus, and Barbara Kingsolver have been written about in the review pages of newspapers and magazines, and their fiction has acquired a substantial following, but their work has yet to attract significant scholarship. That will certainly follow, but the essays included here constitute a beginning.

Some of the older generation of writers included here, such as George Garrett, William Kennedy, James Purdy, and Jerzy Kosinski, have already attracted a good deal of sustained attention, and their fiction has been slowly making its way onto the syllabi of college courses, but their work has not yet been discussed in *American Writers*. It is time they have been added to the series.

The poets included here—A. R. Ammons, Jane Kenyon, Donald Justice, and Mary Oliver—are well known in the poetry world, and their work has in each case been honored with major literary prizes. (Ammons, Justice, and Oliver, for example, have won Pulitzer Prizes.) These poets have been widely anthologized as well. Nevertheless, the real work of assimilation, of discovering the true place of each poet in the larger traditions of American poetry, has only begun. In each case, these poets are written about by critics who are themselves poets, and the depth and eloquence of their essays should be obvious even to casual readers.

The reader will also find Anne Rice among the subjects discussed in this collection. Like Stephen King, she has long had a vast reading public; only recently have critics begun to take a closer look at her work, finding resonances with earlier work in the American and British traditions of Gothic writing. It is, in fact, a goal of the American Writers Series to include critiques of popular writers such as Rice and King, who tend to work in a specific genre and are often overlooked.

Supplement VII is an abundant and heterogeneous collection that treats authors from a wide range of ethnic, social, and cultural backgrounds. Cisneros and Alvarez, for example, are Latina writers. Jamaica Kincaid is from the Caribbean. Kosinski was an emigrant from the world of Soviet-dominated Poland who escaped to the United States. Their work often (but not always) reflects their origins in fascinating ways.

The critics who contributed to this collection represent a catholic range of backgrounds and critical approaches, although the baseline for inclusion was that each essay should be accessible to the non-specialist reader or beginning student. The work of culture involves the continuous assessment and reassessment of major texts produced by its writers, and our belief is that this supplement performs a useful service here, providing substantial introductions to American writers who matter to readers, and who will be read well into the new century.

—*JAY PARINI*

Contributors

Bert Almon. Professor of English, University of Alberta. Author of eight collections of poetry and a critical biography, *William Humphrey: Destroyer of Myths*. RICHARD BAUSCH

Charles R. Baker. Poet, short story writer, and essayist. Author of *What Miss Johnson Taught* and *Christmas Frost*. ANDRE DUBUS

Jonathan N. Barron. Associate professor of English, University of Southern Mississippi. Editor (with Eric Murphy Selinger) of *Jewish American Poetry: Poems, Commentary, and Reflections* and forthcoming collections on the poetic movement New Formalism and on the poetry of Robert Frost. Editor in chief of *The Robert Frost Review*. MARY OLIVER

Philip E. Baruth. Associate Professor of English, University of Vermont. Editor of *Introducing Charlotte Charke: Actress, Author, Enigma,* a collection of essays, and author of short stories and novels, including *The Dream of the White Village: A Novel in Stories*. WILLIAM KENNEDY

Mary Ellen Bertolini. Lecturer, Middlebury College. SANDRA CISNEROS.

Susan L. Blake. Professor of English, Lafayette College. Author of *Letters from Togo* and critical essays on American literature and travel writing. CAROL SHIELDS

David Breithaupt. Poet, short story writer, essayist, and library worker. Author of numerous pieces of poetry and short fiction that have appeared in such journals as *Exquisite Corpse, Rant,* and *Beet.* JAMES PURDY

Philip Bufithis. Professor of English at Shepherd College. Author of *Norman Mailer,* a critical study, and articles on modern American literature in numerous publications. Associate Fiction Editor of the literary magazine *Antietam Review.* A. R. AMMONS

Laurie Champion. Assistant Professor of English, San Diego State University, Imperial Valley. Author of essays on American literature that have appeared in such journals *as Southern Literary Journal, Southern Quarterly, Mississippi Quarterly, Studies in Short Fiction,* and *Journal of the Short Story in English.* Editor (with Bruce A. Glasrud) of *African American West: A Century of Short Stories* and editor of *The Critical Response to Mark Twain's Huckleberry Finn, The Critical Response to Eudora Welty's Fiction,* and *American Women Writers, 1900–1945: A Bio-Bibliographical Critical Sourcebook.* ANNE RICE

Laban Hill. Author of more than twenty books, including a cultural history of the Harlem Renaissance. JANE KENYON

Robert Niemi. Associate Professor of English, St. Michael's College. Author of *Russell Banks* and (with Daniel Gillane) *The Bibliography of Weldon Kees.* ANNIE PROULX

Wyatt Prunty. Professor of English at Sewanee, where he directs the Sewanee Writers' Conference and edits the Sewanee Writers' Series. Author of *"Fallen from the Symboled World": Precedents for the New Formalism,* a study of contemporary poetry, and seven poetry collections, including *Unarmed and Dangerous: New* *and Selcted Poems.* Editor of *Sewanee Writers on Writing,* a collection of essays. DONALD JUSTICE

Andrea Schaefer. Visiting Lecturer in English and Theatre, Middlebury College. JULIA ALVAREZ

Donna Seaman. Editor for *Booklist* and author of reviews, essays, and articles in numerous publications, including the *Chicago Tribune,* the *Los Angeles Times,* the *Ruminator Review* (formerly the *Hungry Mind Review*), and the *Boston Review.* Editor of the anthology *In Our Nature: Stories of Wildness.* JAMAICA KINCAID

Stephen Soitos. Author of *The Blues Detective: A Study of African American Detective Fiction* and other works centering on German Expressionist painting, Brazilian art, and African American art and literature. JERZY KOSINSKI

Walter Sullivan. Professor of English and Director of the Program in Creative Writing, Emeritus, at Vanderbilt University. Author of three novels, three volumes of literary criticism, a memoir of Allen Tate, a collection of excerpts from women's civil war diaries, and numerous uncollected short stories and essays on literary themes. GEORGE GARRETT

Pauls Toutonghi. Poet and fiction writer who has published work in numerous journals. Recipient of a 2000 Pushcart Prize for his story "Regeneration," which appeared in the *Boston Review.* TOBIAS WOLFF

Dana Cairns Watson. Teacher of twentieth-century American literature at the University of California, Los Angeles. BARBARA KINGSOLVER

SUPPLEMENT VII
Julia Alvarez to Tobias Wolff

Julia Alvarez

1950–

"LANGUAGE IS THE only homeland." These words of the poet Czeslaw Milosz serve as the epigraph to the 1995 edition of *Homecoming*, Julia Alvarez's first collection of poems. The phrase also appears in her third novel, *¡Yo!* (1997), where the title character, Alvarez's alter ego, is complimented on her spoken English by her American landlady, to whom Yo responds, "Language is the only homeland . . . When there's no other ground under your feet, you learn quick, believe me." Language is a central issue in Alvarez's work, as is her experience as a Dominican-American navigating between two languages and two cultures. Although Spanish was her first language and its influence is felt throughout her work, it remains the language of her early childhood. The English language became the homeland in which Alvarez landed and where she has grown as a woman, teacher, poet, novelist, and essayist.

The author has repeatedly addressed her ability to shed the sense of herself that she describes in her book of essays *Something to Declare* (1998) as a "foreigner with no ground to stand on" through language (writing). The difficulty of doing so by other means has left her with a sense of not fully belonging to either her native Dominican homeland or her adopted American one. Language provides the means for Alvarez to negotiate her hyphenated existence as an immigrant and to shed light on such issues as acculturation, alienation, class, race, and politics. In a review of *In the Time of the Butterflies* (1994), Ilan Stavans quoted Alvarez as saying, "I am a Dominican, hyphen, American. As a fiction writer, I find the most exciting things happen in the realm of that hyphen—the place where two worlds collide or blend together."

Other issues central to Alvarez's work are family: patriarchy and the struggles of women against the circumscribed roles assigned to them within traditional Dominican culture, and relationships between men and women. Although her primary focus is on women and how all of these issues impact on their lives and her own, her later fictional work has broadened in a deliberate move to include men's voices as well. As Alvarez says in *Homecoming* (1984), all in all, the development of her voice as a writer reflects her maturation from a young poet "claiming [her] woman's voice" into a more versatile author who, in claiming her voice as a woman and a Dominican-American, deals head-on with "the further confusions of [her] bilingual, bicultural self."

CHILDHOOD AND BACKGROUND

Julia Alvarez was born to Eduardo and Julia Alvarez on March 27, 1950, in New York City. Her family lived in New York for just three weeks, however, before they returned to their native country, where Alvarez lived until she was ten years old. The family's return to the Dominican Republic was not without risk since her father had originally been forced to flee to Canada, where he lived for nine years, after his involvement in a failed student underground movement to overthrow the dictator, Rafael Leónidas Trujillo. Bloodthirsty and corrupt, Trujillo ruled over the Dominican people for more than thirty years until he was assassinated in 1961. The wealth and political connections of Alvarez's mother's family paved the way for her parents' return and, for a time, secured their safety. In contrast, Alvarez's father, a doctor, was "from a humble family" which, she has written, meant that they "had supported the wrong side of a revolution" and lost their wealth.

The second oldest of four sisters, Alvarez was raised among her large extended family and their servants in a house on property owned by her maternal grandfather. Alvarez's writing often addresses the benefits and drawbacks of being raised in this communal, closely knit familial environment. As Alvarez looks back on her early childhood, she notes that the immediate world in which she was raised was run by women: In *Something to Declare,* she says, "Every day, when my grandfather and father and my two uncles left for work, this complex of houses became a stronghold of women, my mother, my tias, and an army of maids." Alvarez is also quick to acknowledge the privileged nature of her early childhood.

Alvarez's maternal grandfather, who had attended an American university and spoke perfect English, had an appointment as cultural attaché to the United Nations and her grandparents resided in New York for several months out of the year. Keeping strong American ties was politically and personally prudent given the ruthlessness of the dictator, Trujillo. As Alvarez notes in the essay "An American Childhood in the Dominican Republic," which appeared in *The American Scholar* in 1987, "The one thing Trujillo still seemed to fear was losing American support of his regime." Thus, a tradition was established in her family of sending the children to boarding schools in the United States. Yet at an early age Alvarez was keenly aware of the limited set of expectations for girls' futures beyond a secondary level of education. Following graduation, the presumption was that the boys would continue on to good colleges while the girls would return home to prepare for marriage and motherhood. In *Something to Declare* Alvarez writes in her essay "Grandfather's Blessing" that she would leaf through her books in search of a kindred spirit, a model to "prove that I could become what I dreamed of becoming. I learned early to turn to books, movies, music, paintings, rather than to the family to find out what was possible."

Alvarez first learned English while attending the Carol Morgan School. It was her mother's idea to send her daughters to an American school on Dominican soil, influenced by her own education at a boarding school in the United States. In an essay from *Something to Declare* entitled "My English," Alvarez says that her mother would continually urge her daughters to learn "*your* English," instilling in her daughters a sense of language as inheritance. She captures the difficulties of having this bilingual "inheritance" imposed on her at such a young age, remarking, "Unfortunately, my English became all mixed up with our Spanish."

Feelings of insecurity about her native tongue were fostered early in Alvarez by her colonialist education and by the privileged status accorded to English at her school. Any mistaken use of Spanish words led to humiliation in front of her American classmates and the sense that her "native tongue was not quite as good as English, as if words like *columpio* were illegal immigrants trying to cross a border into another language."

Alvarez's use of the word *columpio,* which means a swing, underscores her sense of oscillating between two languages and two cultures at a tender age, even before her family ever emigrated from the Dominican Republic.

The Alvarezes immigrated to the United States in 1960 after her father became involved in a failed plot to overthrow Trujillo that was sponsored by the American government. When the United States withdrew its support for the plan and the SIM, the Dominican secret police, began rounding up plot participants, a well-placed American friend of Dr. Alvarez's arranged for him to receive a medical internship in the States. The family fled to New York City, settling in Jamaica Estates, Queens. As the only Latinas in a mostly German and Italian middle- to upper-middle-class neighborhood, Alvarez and her sisters encountered prejudice and general ignorance. When they were not being taunted as "spics" and "greaseballs" in the schoolyard, she writes that their "teachers and classmates at the local Catholic schools referred to us as 'Porto Ricans' or 'Spanish.' "

Alvarez was eventually sent to a New England boarding school, after which she attended Connecticut College from 1967 to 1969. Her early promise as a poet gained her a place at the Bread Loaf School of English Writers' Conference during the summer of 1969. She transferred to nearby Middlebury College in Vermont, from which she received a Bachelor of Arts, graduating summa cum laude, in 1971. She received a master of fine arts degree from Syracuse University in 1975. From 1975 to 1978 she was a Poet-in-the-Schools in Kentucky, Delaware, and North Carolina. She taught English at Phillips Andover Academy from 1979 to 1981. She also returned to the Bread Loaf School of English from 1979 to 1980. A series of college teaching stints followed at the University of Vermont (1981–1983), George Washington University (1984–1985), and the University of Illinois (1985–1988).

In 1988 Alvarez returned to Vermont to become an assistant professor of English at Middlebury College. Although she has since decided to stop teaching full-time and to relinquish her tenure in order to focus on her writing, she continues to live in Middlebury with her third husband, Bill Eichner, a doctor whom she married in 1989.

Awards received by Alvarez for her work include the Robert Frost Poetry fellowship from the Bread Loaf Writers' Conference (1986); an award for younger writers from the General Electric Foundation (1986); a grant from the National Endowment for the Arts (1987–1988); a grant from the Ingram Merrill Foundation (1990); and the 1991 PEN Oakland/Josephine Miles Award for works that represent a multicultural viewpoint, and selection as a Notable Book of 1992 by the American Library Association and the *New York Times,* all for *How the García Girls Lost Their Accents.* She also received a nomination for the 1995 National Book Critics Circle Award for *In the Time of the Butterflies,* which was also chosen as a Book-of-the-Month Club selection, and won the *American Poetry Review's* Jessica Nobel-Maxwell Poetry Prize in 1995.

HOMECOMING

Alvarez's first collection of poems, *Homecoming,* was published by Grove Press in 1984. The strongest aspect of the collection is a series of "Housekeeping" poems concerned with Alvarez's "housebound" upbringing, her relationship with her mother, and her struggle to forge her own identity apart from her "mami" and the traditional feminine role. A complete collection of the "Housekeeping" poems also came out in 1984 in a small, handmade edition, illustrated by the artists Carol MacDonald and Rene Schall, and funded by the Vermont Council on the Arts and the National Endowment for the Arts. Mounted panels of the book were on exhibit throughout the state of Vermont from 1984 to 1985.

The "Housekeeping" poems portray a young Alvarez engaged in household chores with her mother. In "How I Learned to Sweep," the poet implies that any dawning political awareness she may have had was nearly swept away by her mother. The television, which functions symbolically as Alvarez's window onto events outside the home such as news of the Vietnam War, is twice turned off by her mother: first when she tells her daughter to sweep the floor and then when she inspects the finished job. Like a general, her mother presides over the household inspection and like a ruthless dictator, prefers to sweep under the carpet that which she does not wish to see, including her daughter's rejection of the house-wife role.

In "Dusting" Alvarez's mother's domesticity threatens her daughter's identity as an independent woman and a writer with erasure. Yet even as Alvarez asserts her refusal "to be like her [mother], anonymous," she implicitly acknowledges that her mother's household work remains unrecognized in the eyes of society and her own family. The patriarchal structure of the household is reflected in the activity mother and daughter share of making up the "master bed" after her father leaves for work; the "black nose of his slip-per" peaking out from under the bed and the "long pillow with the sultan's tassel" serve as reminders of her father's role as head of the family.

Nonetheless, Alvarez's mother reigns over her daughters within the home in their father's absence. Even as Alvarez pays tribute to her mother, asking "Who says a woman's work isn't high art?," and acknowledges her moments of tenderness, the sense of the young poet's resentment and anger toward her mother grows in these poems. Storm windows are metaphors for their turbulent relationship and the activity of washing them is transformed into a desire to see beyond the limits of her mother's "reach, her house, her yard, her mothering." Alvarez clearly feels that her mother demanded too high a price for her love and saddled her daughter with feelings of guilt and self-doubt.

The key to transcendence for Alvarez lies in language. In one of the most effective poems, "Hanging the Wash," she mirrors the act of hanging wash on the line in the way in which she arranges words on the page. An analogy is drawn between the process of creating poetry ("She has in mind / a line in which / everything fits . . .") and the hanging of laundry on the clothesline, as she reshapes the domestic stuff of her childhood into the poetic material of her adulthood. But the sequence ends on an uncertain and somewhat bitter note in "Woman's Work." Alvarez observes that in releasing herself from being kept a "prisoner in her [mother's] housebound heart," the poet succeeded in building new walls around herself, "housekeeping paper as if it were her heart."

Her search for love and selfhood is explored further in the longer sonnet sequence, "33," so named to reflect both the author's age and the intended number of sonnets. Alvarez broaches the tension between her feminist awareness, her professional aspirations, and her romantic, "feminine" desires. She also addresses the pressure she feels from her immediate and extended family concerning marriage and motherhood. Again, the sonnets mark the emergence of her woman's voice as she asks, "Tell me what is it women want the most?" Mired as she is in fear, self-doubt, and frankly, at times, self-pity, she comes to recognize that finding an answer to that question lies in finding her voice. But this awareness is only tentative in these early poems. When she writes, "What kind of woman / are you? I wish I knew, I say, I wish I knew and could just put it into words," the sense the reader gets is of a woman who does not wholly believe in her ability to do just that.

This tentativeness is more qualified in a revised and expanded edition of *Homecoming* published in 1995. New poems include those that were added to the "33" sonnet sequence to reflect the author's age of forty-six at the edition's time of publication. Moreover, as Alvarez notes in the afterword, "These additions reflect a political awareness absent, for the most part, in the young women of thirty-three." In one sonnet she constructs the ABCs of modern atrocities: "A is for Auschwitz; B for Biafra; Chile. . . ." The personal, household dust kicked up by the thirty-three year old Alvarez is powerfully transfigured by her older self who brings her "modern primer" to a close with these lines: "An X to name the countless disappeared / when they are dust in Yemen or Zaire." Alvarez sees this heightened political consciousness as being inextricably linked to her discovery of her voice not just as a woman but as a Dominican-American woman. As such, the reader can take more heart from the last lines of the forty-sixth sonnet: "I once was in as many drafts as you. / But briefly, essentially, here I am. / Who touches this poem touches a woman."

The sense of wholeness that acknowledging her "bicultural, bilingual self" brings is also evident in the added sonnet sequence, "Redwing Sonnets," in which Alvarez further explores the themes of her voice taking flight and the power of language to effect personal and political change. These poems more explicitly address her Dominican roots and her "childhood in a dictatorship / when real talk was punishable by death." In the volume's final poem, "Last Night at Tía's," the poet confronts the fact that much of her connection to her Dominican relatives lies in the past and that deep divisions, political and otherwise, now exist between them. In the afterword, however, Alvarez emphasizes not what has been lost but what she has gained during the course of her life's journey: the knowledge of "where her roots really are—deep in the terra firma of language."

HOW THE GARCÍA GIRLS LOST THEIR ACCENTS

The autobiographical exploration in Alvarez's poems serves as the seed, planted in verse, of the fifteen interrelated stories that comprise her first novel, *How the García Girls Lost Their Accents,* published in 1991. The novel's title immediately signals a concern with language and the sense of loss inherent in the García family's immigrant journey and acculturation. Furthermore, as William Luis noted in 1997, the novel marks a shift in Alvarez's sense of her identity from the view of herself in "An American Childhood in the Dominican Republic." The essay contains stories that seem to have served as the basis for the novel and others that are not included in the full-length work; still other factual events recounted in the essay are rearranged in the fictionalized version. These include the events leading up to the Alvarez family's departure from the Dominican Republic. The essay also describes Alvarez's Americanized schooling; the allure of imported U.S. products in the local American-style supermarket; and Alvarez's fascination with her blond, blue-eyed American classmate, the daughter of the Chevrolet dealer. As the plane carrying her family touches down in New York City, Alvarez writes, "All my childhood I had longed for this moment of arrival. And here I was, an American girl, coming home at last."

Discussing "An American Childhood in the Dominican Republic" and *How The García Girls Lost Their Accents,* Luis notes, "In the essay, Alvarez finds her identity in her return home to the United States. In contrast, the novel begins [or ends] with Yolanda's return to the Dominican Republic." That said, Alvarez makes it clear in the essay that her Americanized upbringing in the Dominican Republic was rooted in a colonialist, repressive culture, dictated by Trujillo's racism and his desire to foster stronger economic ties with the United States in order to curry political favor for his regime. Nonetheless, it is fair to say that in the five years between the publication of the essay in 1987 and the novel in 1991, Alvarez grew into a fuller recognition and deeper acceptance of her Latina identity, with which she now identifies more closely. The measure of this, of course, is in her writing. Turning to *How the García Girls Lost Their Accents,* it becomes clear that the author writes the novel as a Dominican-American "girl," coming home at last to a richer, more complex sense of self that requires novel-length narrative expression.

Alvarez originally saw her first novel as the book that she simply hoped would get her tenure, never anticipating that it would become such a popular success and garner so much critical attention. The novel's vivid, heartfelt depiction of the lives of the four García sisters and their parents struck a chord with readers. The most fully dimensional character, not surprisingly, is that of Yolanda, the author's alter ego. The novel's fifteen chapters or stories are structured in three parts reflecting the sisters' lives in adulthood, adolescence, and childhood. The work also moves backward in time and, significantly, begins and ends in the Dominican Republic. The narrative's nonlinear structure reflects Alvarez's sense of herself as a woman and her interest in perspectives from outside of mainstream Anglo America.

In a 1992 interview with Catherine Wiley, Alvarez indicated that her thoughts about the plot of her novel and about the way women in general tell stories were shaped by a sense of women thinking relationally as opposed to directionally. She notes the influence of the novelist Louise Erdrich's thoughts on how Native American people experience truth on her own thinking about writing and women's issues: "It is something you get at, that's right there, but the truth is all the points around the truth, around the circle. Each little perspective somehow is what the truth is. . . ." The reader sees this approach to truth and the rendering of personal experience in Alvarez's use of multiple perspectives in all of her novels.

Alvarez related the figure of a circle even more directly to her own life when she said in her interview with Wiley,

A lot of what I have worked through has to do with coming to this country and losing a homeland and

a culture, as a way of making sense, and also it has to do with the sisterhood of my sisters and myself. They were the only people I really had as models. We were moving in a circle, because none of us knew any more than the other one but all we had was each other, not feeling part of this world and not really feeling part of the old world either.

This sense of being caught in between two worlds and of not really belonging to either one is embodied in Yo's character, who returns to the Dominican Republic for a visit with relatives at the beginning of *How the García Girls Lost Their Accents.* Yo makes the visit thinking that she may return permanently to live on the island. "Let this turn out to be my home," she wishes to herself as she regards her married female cousins, secure in their positions of authority within their households. Yet even as she yearns for security and stability, she chafes at the restrictions placed on Dominican women, such as the negative response that greets her desire to travel north in search of guava groves: "A woman just doesn't travel alone in this country." Yo rejects such advice and embarks on a journey of self-discovery.

The guavas Yo picks and relishes signify that her reward lies in tasting the fruits of her own independent labor. She feels threatened, though, by two workmen who come upon her as she waits alone in her car for help in fixing her flat tire. The irony is that Yo extricates herself from a potentially dangerous situation in part by pretending not to speak Spanish when the men interpret her frightened silence as evidence of her being "Americana." Yo's tourist pose is furthered when the young boy whom she sent in search of help returns and tells her that the *guardia* (police) would not believe his story: "No *dominicana* with a car would be out at this hour getting *guayabas.*" The story's ending implies that Yolanda has not found the home she was searching for, nor is she any closer to feeling like she belongs in the United States, whose culture is typified by the print advertisement referred to in the story's final lines: "the Palmolive woman's skin gleams a rich white . . . her mouth still opened as if she is calling someone over a great distance."

Alvarez looks to bridge that geographic and cultural distance with the stories she writes. But this open-mouthed image recurs, noticeably in the last story of the novel, and appears elsewhere as a gaping void also felt by Yolanda's sisters after emigrating from the island. As the family prepares to leave the Dominican Republic in the story "The Blood of the Conquistadores," Alvarez writes, "nothing quite filled the hole that was opening wide inside Sandi." And in the last story, "The Drum," Yolanda reveals that she was haunted for years by the image of a black cat, "her magenta mouth opening, wailing over some violation that lies at the center of my art."

This sense of violation may be read in a number of ways. There is the irreparable sense of loss that accompanied the family's sudden departure for the United States and the resulting years of struggle as immigrants. Alvarez may also be referring on some level to her conflicting emotions over having abandoned her original tongue for English, the language of colonizers and the American government which paved the way for and supported Trujillo's dictatorship. There is also the constant threat faced by all four sisters of personal violation through the loss of their individual identities. Alvarez binds the four sisters with what their old Haitian servant predicts will be an ability to "invent what they need to survive" in the new world.

In the third story, "The Four Girls," the sisters' efforts to individuate themselves are recounted. There is an emphasis throughout the story on language and on the power of words to wound and bind. Their relationships with their mother serve as the connective tissue of the story and she acts as the storyteller throughout it. The mother's self-defense against charges that she often lumped "the four girls" together or confused their names is that she has a particular story about each daughter that she likes to tell at special family gatherings.

Interestingly, the mother's total failure to understand her second oldest daughter, Sandi, is marked by the fact that she no longer tells a favorite story about her troubled daughter. She does talk about Sandi, though, with the girl's doctor, after she is hospitalized for anorexia and a nervous breakdown. Sandi is an intriguing character who begs for further development; she seems to represent some of the author's deepest fears and the dark side of her efforts to become a writer.

One of the features of Sandi's breakdown is compulsive reading. Her parents discover lists she has made of "all the great works of man," which she feels she must read before she ceases to be human and turns into a monkey. In the process of losing her sense of self, Sandi loses her fundamental connection to humanity. Her compulsive canonical reading only serves to damage her further as none of these dead, white "great men" speak directly to her own background, thoughts, and emotions. Nowhere does she find someone whose experience mirrors her own. Her feelings of isolation and rejection are compounded by the fact that she is the lightest skinned of her sisters, which only leaves her feeling further separated from those closest to her.

Even after her release from the hospital, Sandi appears fragile and edgy, and is reproved by her mother for using colorful language. This rebuke, aimed as it is at Sandi's use of language, underscores her tenuous state and again points to how Alvarez shapes her as the sister most closely linked to her alter ego, Yolanda. This becomes patently clear in the section titled "Joe," where language is the central theme even as the story itself is about the breakup of Yolanda's second marriage and her own ensuing nervous breakdown.

Alvarez crafts the story in pre- and postlapsarian terms: "In the beginning we were in love." Yo compares herself to Eve, creating the world anew in the wake of her divorce, healing herself through language. Reclaiming her name is one of the first steps toward renewal. The story begins with a litany of Yolanda's names: "nicknamed Yo in Spanish, misunderstood Joe in English, doubled and pronounced like the toy, Yoyo—or when forced to select from a rack of personalized key chain, Joey. . . ." The names signal the ways in which she feels torn by her various identities, is manipulated by others, and lacks a cohesive sense of self.

One of the first signs that her marriage is doomed is that Yo's husband, John, calls her "Joe." The gap between them widens as they play a word game where he fails to understand how her name can rhyme with "sky": " 'Yo rhymes with cielo in Spanish.' Yo's words fell into the dark, mute cavern of John's mouth . . . And Yo was running, like mad, into the safety of her first tongue, where the proudly monolingual John could not catch her, even if he tried." Her growing fears of losing her identity and being snapped up like the gingerbread man are underscored by the fact that "Yo" is not only her preferred nickname, but that it means "I" in Spanish.

As the relationship deteriorates, Yo finds herself taking on John's language and using words she hates in order to communicate with him. The end of the union comes when she finds that she is no longer able to understand a word he says; it is all babble to her. This precipitates a nervous breakdown where Alvarez further develops the connection between language, self, and emotional and mental stability that she introduced in Sandi's story.

Yo returns to live with her parents who worry about her incessant talking, which mirrors Sandi's compulsive reading. Yo's heartbreak, loss of identity, and anxiety about her as-yet-unfulfilled ambition to become a writer are marked by her constant yakking, consisting largely of quoting and misquoting from nursery rhymes and classic works by famous male authors. Even as she begins to recover, she develops "a random allergy to certain words" and worries about the fact that she does not know what the most important word

in her vocabulary is. Alvarez signifies that Yo is truly on the mend when she tests out saying the word "Love," develops a rash, but forges on, pairing "Love" with her name, "Yolanda." Loving herself by naming and thereby knowing herself opens the door to a flood of words. The gates have been opened and the story ends on a triumphant note that signals Yolanda's emerging discovery of her voice as a woman and a writer.

The stories in sections II and III of the novel, covering the sisters' adolescent and childhood years from 1970 to 1956, also do much to further the reader's understanding of their characters. The stories in section II concern the years 1970 to 1960, a turbulent period for both the United States and the Dominican Republic. The social and political turmoil of the time serves as a backdrop for the family's difficult first years of adjusting to life in the United States and the girls' growth into adolescence. The sisters note that "It was a regular revolution" in the García household during those years. Their acculturation may have eased some of their difficulties in fitting into American culture but in many respects it escalated tensions with their parents.

Inasmuch as the Garcías valued education and wanted their girls to succeed and be happy in the United States, the futures they envisioned for them were along traditional lines in terms of marriage to "homeland boys" and motherhood. Thus, the girls spent their summers in the Dominican Republic. Alvarez deals with the ensuing tensions between the girls' new world sense of themselves and the old world, patriarchal island culture in "A Regular Revolution."

What is striking about the story is that the coup staged against traditionalism is against their own sister or, rather, the macho Dominican that Fifi begins seeing after marijuana is discovered in her room and she is sent to live with relatives on the island. Her sisters are alarmed at Fifi's subsequent transformation into a heavily made-up, elaborately coiffed dominicana and at her submissiveness toward her beau, Manuel. Fearing an imminent wedding, her sisters plot to have the couple's secret, unchaperoned assignations revealed to the family. Their efforts succeed and their angry parents take Fifi back to live with them in the States. Fifi accuses her sisters of being "traitors," but they are steadfast in their belief that they have in fact rescued their youngest sister from "her fear of her own life."

The beginnings of Yolanda's love of language and interest in writing are explored in other stories such as "Daughter of Invention," one of the strongest in the novel. The story addresses the difficulty that Yolanda finds in developing her own voice when defining herself in American terms brings her into conflict with her family. In this case it is her mother who comes to the rescue. Moreover, it is her mother, portrayed here in a more sympathetic and multifaceted manner than elsewhere in the work, who is credited with fostering Yo's ability to invent herself through language.

After the family came to the United States, Mrs. García became a fledgling inventor. A correlation is made between her failed gadgets and her penchant for malapropisms when arguing with or lecturing her daughters in English: "her English was a mishmash of mixed-up idioms and sayings that showed that she was 'green behind the ears,' as she called it." Whereas her mother struggles with the new language, Yolanda finds strength and security in it. Surrounded by a foreign cultural landscape and unfriendly, even hostile schoolmates, Yo finds comfort in her writing and takes "root in the language."

While her frustrated mother eventually gives up her inventive brainstorming, Yo flourishes creatively and is asked to deliver the Teacher's Day address at school. She finds inspiration in Walt Whitman's poetry and incorporates his lines, "I celebrate myself and sing myself . . . He most honors my style who learns under it to destroy the teacher," into her speech. Her proud mother

asks her to read the speech to her father, who shocks them with his infuriated response, attacking Yo for being "insubordinate" and disrespectful of her teachers. The incident illustrates the culture clash in which Yo and her sisters repeatedly find themselves caught. Here it takes the form of a conflict between American individualism and the value placed in Dominican society on gratitude and respect for one's elders. The argument also underscores Dr. García's sense of being the ultimate authority in the home, for when his wife takes her daughter's side, he rips up the speech. The sense of her father as domestic tyrant is heightened by Yo's equally enraged response, which is to call him by "Trujillo's hated nickname, 'Chapita.' "

In the end, the family weathers the storm. Joined by her mother, Yo constructs a dutifully polite and respectful speech that pleases her teachers. Her chastened father asks for her forgiveness by giving her a typewriter and letting her know that he only wished to protect her. Yo recalls her mother's help with writing the speech as Mrs. García's last invention and a passing of the creative torch or in this case, pencil, to her daughter.

THE OTHER SIDE/EL OTRO LADO

Alvarez's first novel opened the door to the more integrated sense of self reflected in her second collection of poetry, entitled *The Other Side/El Otro Lado,* published in 1995. The title itself embodies her bilingualism and biculturalism and furthermore, the sense of othering/opposition between these "sides." Whereas the poems originally written for her first poetry collection, *Homecoming,* conveyed little sense of Alvarez as a Dominican-American woman, these poems are very much concerned with the cultural and linguistic dualities that shape her life. The title also refers to the work's recognition of other divides created by differences in class, race, politics, and education.

The first poem, "Bilingual Sestina," signals the collection's concern with both languages that have shaped Alvarez's writing. While written in English, the poem incorporates Spanish words in each of the six stanzas and the three-line envoi; the words "Spanish" and "English" themselves are also repeated in each stanza. The poem also reflects the shifting definition of "other side" throughout this collection and, indeed, throughout Alvarez's life and work. English is the "other side" in this work as Alvarez declares, "Some things I have to say aren't getting said in this snowy, blond, blue-eyed, gum-chewing English." In a partly ironic move, she rewrites the Third World status of the Dominican Republic as she observes that there are some words "from that first world I can't translate from Spanish."

In terms of language, cultural heritage, and personal history, Alvarez's first world remains the island where she spent her childhood and spoke her first words. Moreover, the teachers whom she credits for imparting a sense of wonder with those first vocabulary words are the family's maids. She repeats their names as a soothing litany, recalling the simpler days of her monolingual early childhood. The emphasis she places in her fiction on names and naming is explored throughout this poem in the repetition of the word "nombre(s)." By using the Spanish word for name(s), Alvarez again underscores her inability or unwillingness to translate certain words into English. She also connects the act of naming to the God-like status it gave to these simple country girls in her child's eyes, casting, in turn, an Edenic light on that Dominican first world: "Rosario, muse of *el patio*, sing in me and through me say / that world again, begin first with those first words / you put in my mouth as you pointed to the world— / not Adam, not God, but a country girl."

Yet even as Alvarez laments the confusion and complexity that came with learning English, she employs it to wondrous and beautiful effect, creating a bilingual duet out of her doubled world. For even as she writes in English, she believes that she can "almost hear my Spanish / heart beating, beating inside what I say en ingles." Again, the near tragic quality of the almost-but-not-quite nature of her connection to either culture, either tongue, is largely eclipsed by the beauty of these lines, among the finest in the collection.

"The Gladys Poems" which follow continue to uncover the hearts that beat in Alvarez's memory as her first muses. Gladys, one of the household maids, is a recurring figure in the author's poetry, fiction, and essays as a major early influence in her life. In "Audition," Alvarez recounts how her mother came to find Gladys and employ her. Gladys is not among those looking for an interview. Instead, the beautiful sound of her singing brings her to the attention of Alvarez's mother. Alvarez sees in Gladys a kindred artistic spirit. Her depiction of Gladys also reflects fears expressed in her earlier "Housekeeping" poems that domestic work and the added fact of Gladys' impoverished circumstances threaten to silence the young maid's beautiful singing. That Gladys serves as a kind of alter ego for young Julia is further reflected in the fact that it is Alvarez's mother who especially threatens the maid's self-expression. Alvarez writes that as soon as her mother left the house, Gladys would begin singing and dancing with her young charge. But on her mother's return, she says, "we fell silent, knowing the rules, / as the door opened upon / rooms sparkling like jewels / in a mummy's tomb."

Here again the reader sees the deadening effect of domesticity but with an added awareness of the social structure that compounds the silencing of both servant and daughter. As the embodiment of the domestic and social order, Alvarez's mother is seen as the villain, threatening to suffocate both Alvarez and her housebound muse. Nonetheless, Gladys is able to impart some important lessons, not the least of which is the power of self-expression, whether through singing, poetry, or any art, to breathe life into all things. Indeed, Alvarez credits Gladys with teaching her one of the most central themes explored in her work: that singing (art) makes everything else possible. In her essay, "Of Maids and Other Muses," from *Something to Declare,* Alvarez expounds further on the importance of Gladys and other real-life muses, returning the favors they did her by singing of them:

> When I read a page of my own writing, it's as if it were a palimpsest, and behind the more prominent, literary faces whose influence shows through the print (Scheherazade, George Eliot, Toni Morrison, Emily Dickinson, Maxine Hong Kingston), I see other faces: real-life ladies who traipsed through my imagination with broom and dusting rag, cookbook and garden scissors, Gladys (the family maid) . . . Of them I sing.

The sudden disappearance of Gladys left Alvarez feeling abandoned (she depicts the circumstances of Gladys' departure differently in *How the García Girls Lost Their Accents,* but its abrupt nature and the void it creates are the same). But the example the young maid provided of singing in the face of adversity and of believing in the power of self-expression remains with the author always.

Yet a sense of loss pervades the equally autobiographical poems that follow. "Sound Bites" is a poem that directly addresses language and bilingualism. Each "bite" of the poem takes us on a journey from Alvarez's first days in America, when she turns to her parents for help in understanding her strange, new surroundings ("What is a fire escape, Mami?") to the point where, as an adolescent, she "size[s] up *la situación*" and realizes only she can help herself by embracing English and turning to writing. But there is a sense of bitterness here, as if turning to English is a capitulation ("Give yourself over, girl") and the language itself seems inferior to her more vivid, native tongue ("Translate your *café con leche* into a glass of plain milk"). Yet the poem ends on a note of acceptance. A more resigned, adult Alvarez can now conclude with "*El* Round up," summing up the poem and her life's journey as "our family's grand adventure from one language to another."

The collection culminates in the twenty-one-canto title poem about Alvarez's stay at a Dominican artists' colony. The colonialist associations of the luxurious, walled-in setting of her artistic residency are not lost on Alvarez who soon ventures into a nearby fishing village and becomes enmeshed in the lives of its residents. The poet finds herself at a crossroads, struggling with a two-year-long case of writer's block. Looking back on her life, she again recounts how as a young, struggling immigrant she turned to poetry and in the English language "found the portable homeland where I wanted to belong." Yet a life lived on paper comes with a price, namely a sense of cultural alienation and personal isolation. Just as her alter ego, Yolanda, does in her novels, Alvarez returns to the Dominican Republic, hoping to find her place and voice again.

At first, being drawn into the lives of the people in Boca, a small, impoverished village full of hungry, begging children who follow Alvarez and her American lover through the streets, turns her attention away from her own troubles. Yet Alvarez soon realizes the emptiness of her current relationship with Mike, a pot-smoking aspiring hippie, whose function here seems primarily to illustrate the degree to which Alvarez has lost her way in life. At one point she turns to a Haitian *houngan,* a street-corner faith healer, for help as she asks which of his *santos* (statues of saints) will "help me make up my divided Dominican-American mind?" Despite his "cure-all body odor" and naked lust for her, she discloses her problems to him and finds herself bewitched by his healing performance, which is characterized in vivid, strongly sexual terms. Ultimately, the thrust of this encounter is that Alvarez must take the reins of her life into her trembling hands.

But Alvarez does not use the residents of Boca merely as projections of her own internal questioning. The villagers are drawn with great sensitivity and honestly recognized for the truths and lessons they have to offer. Yet even as Luisa, a spiritualist and wife of the bodega owner, urges Alvarez to simplify her life and return home to serve her own people, the poet realizes that this is not the path she must follow. Instead she recognizes "the *santéria* of the words I've chosen to serve in another tongue, another country." Alvarez arranges for a schoolhouse, a dispensary, and a new road for the village before she goes. The poem ends as she leaves "in search of a happier ending than what Boca affords, a life of choice, a life of words." Although this quest necessitates making her way back to the United States and the English language, to "the shore [she's] made up on the other side," Alvarez's deep connection to the Dominican Republic and its people is more evident than ever. It is not surprising, then, that her next novel is set there and fulfills the mission urged upon her by Luisa to serve the Dominican people and her own *santo* or spirit.

IN THE TIME OF THE BUTTERFLIES

In the Time of the Butterflies, published in 1994, is one of Alvarez's most ambitious and finest works. The novel is a fictionalized account of the lives of the four Mirabal sisters, three of whom became martyrs to the anti-Trujillo cause. Patria, Minerva, and María Teresa, whose underground code names were *Las Mariposas* ("The Butterflies"), were murdered by Trujillo's henchmen on November 25, 1960, a day now "observed in many Latin American countries as the International Day Against Violence Towards Women," as Alvarez notes in the afterword. The surviving sister, Dedé, to whom the novel is dedicated, continues to live in the Dominican Republic.

Although the work is a fictionalization of the sisters' lives and Alvarez admits to taking certain liberties with some of the facts and events pertaining to Trujillo's dictatorship, the book is literally wrapped in historical truths, calling attention to its factual basis. The book's inside cover lists the names of people who were murdered by Trujillo. Alvarez also fosters a sense of realism in her depiction of the sisters as she gives voices to them through letters, diary entries, and first- and third-person narration. The novel is divided into three sections, each consisting of four chapters (one for each of the four sisters). The progression of the work is chronological, beginning in 1938 and ending in 1960, the year of the women's murders, with interspersed references to the present, which is 1994. The narrative concludes with an epilogue concerning their deaths and Dedé's life in the present day. Lastly, there is a postscript in which Alvarez explains her long-held interest in the Mirabal sisters' story and her fictionalized approach to telling it. The author in fact inserts herself directly into the narrative in the form of a Dominican-American writer who interviews Dedé about her sisters.

There are correspondences between *In the Time of the Butterflies* and Alvarez's previous work such as her abiding concern with women finding a voice and coming into greater political and personal consciousness. The sisters struggle to free themselves from restraints placed on them by the patriarchal and politically repressive culture. An obvious parallel is created between their father, Enrique Mirabal, and Trujillo; later the reader sees shades of the dictator in Dedé's macho, conservative husband, Jaimito, whom she eventually divorces after many years of marriage. After a young Minerva successfully argues with her father over the opportunity to attend boarding school, she compares herself to a rabbit in a pen and observes, "I'd just left a small cage to go into a bigger one, the size of our whole country." When their father dies and María Teresa (nicknamed Mate) learns of the existence of his other, illegitimate family of four daughters, her disillusionment with her father mirrors the betrayal she feels toward the father of her country. Marching past Trujillo's daughter during the opening ceremony for the World's Fair, Mate wonders if the woman "knew how bad her father is or if she still thought, like I once did about Papa, that her father is God."

The growth of each sister's political consciousness is vividly depicted. A key moment for Minerva occurs after her very first encounter with Trujillo—a patriotic pageant that goes awry when one of her schoolmates, playing the part of Liberty, takes direct aim at the dictator with a crossbow. Minerva saves the day by deflecting attention away from her friend, whose father and brothers have been murdered by the regime, by leading the audience in a chant of "¡Viva Trujillo!" On the drive home, while a nun berates the girls for their conduct, Minerva notes, "As the road darkened, the beams of our headlights filled with hundreds of blinded moths. Where they hit the windshield, they left blurry marks, until it seemed like I was looking at the world through a curtain of tears." This haunting image conveys the degree to which so many of the Dominican people were either blind to Trujillo's tyranny, unable to see past the lies, or looked the other way. The passage also calls the reader's attention to the sisters' metamorphoses from blinded moths into visionary butterflies caught in the headlights of a murderous regime.

Minerva quickly emerges as the earliest revolutionary and leader among her sisters. Her chief characteristics are her bravery and artful intelligence, reflections of her mythological namesake. She takes Trujillo on directly in a series of encounters including a tension-filled dance that ends with her slapping him for his forwardness and a subsequent meeting where she challenges

him to a roll of the dice to determine whether she will agree to become his mistress or be granted her wish of attending law school. In the latter instance, Minerva uses loaded dice to roll a draw with the dictator. While her request is put on hold, underscoring the difficulty she encounters as a woman in achieving permission to pursue higher education, she does secure her father's release from prison.

María Teresa is depicted at first as following her older sister Minerva rather naively into the fight against Trujillo. Her portions of the narrative, written in the form of journal entries, are perhaps the most poignant because of their personal nature and the way Alvarez captures her youthful exuberance and awakening to love alongside of much wisdom, pain, and sorrow. Mate goes from asserting, "never in a million years would I take up a gun and force people to stop being mean," to being a full-fledged revolutionary and gunrunner who is imprisoned and tortured for her actions. Alvarez received some criticism for not realistically and fully developing this transition enough. But this is an inaccurate assessment. Mate, in particular, is still quite young even at the height of her participation in the movement (she is only twenty-five when she is killed), and Alvarez succeeds in honestly capturing her youthful and often naive perspective. Her politicization differs from that of her sisters, Minerva and Patria, who are also engaged in the struggle and, on the whole, Alvarez does demonstrate that the women have evolved in their understanding of themselves and the government they are trying to overthrow.

Mate is also the creative spirit in the group whose need for self-expression is essential; in this respect she mirrors Alvarez herself. When one of Minerva's revolutionary schoolgirl friends is caught by the secret police, Mate is forced to bury her diary along with all of Minerva's letters and papers. (These are eventually found by the police and used against the two sisters when they are imprisoned some years later.) As she bids her journal adieu, Mate writes, "my soul has gotten deeper since I started writing in you . . . What do I do to fill up that hole?" Mate's personal sense of loss is palpable, but more pointed is the correlation that is made between the suppression of freedom of speech and the deaths of the Dominican people, in body and spirit.

When Mate and Minerva are held in the infamous La Victoria prison from January to August 1960, the account the reader is given of their imprisonment is through Mate's eyes, in the form of secret journal entries kept in a notebook smuggled in by a kindly prison guard. Her writing, including an entry she secretly passes to the Organization of American States (OAS) Committee investigating Human Rights Abuses in the Dominican Republic, helps to keep her sane and to heal after she is subjected to torture and suffers a miscarriage. But Alvarez also makes it clear that Mate draws strength from the other women with whom she is imprisoned, despite their differences in class and education, and that words alone cannot comfort her in her darkest moments. Nonetheless, her written testimony is vital as Trujillo's fear of the OAS and international sanctions resulting from their findings leads to the sisters' release from prison.

As striking as Mate's development is, Patria's series of personal transformations are the most remarkable in the book. A deeply religious girl, she intended to become a nun until she met her future husband. Married at age sixteen and a mother of two in short order, she seems to be the least likely candidate for becoming a political radical and revolutionary martyr. Yet that is precisely the point of her story. She initially recognizes that Trujillo is no saint but is at least capable of building churches and schools and leading the country out of debt. Alvarez links Patria's maternity to her emerging sense of self apart from her role as a dutiful wife, mother, daughter of God, and citizen. Her third pregnancy ends in a mis-

carriage; the foreboding heaviness that she feels is directly connected to her dawning political awareness and questioning of her Catholic faith. (The Church is criticized in the novel for remaining silent about the regime for so long, although, as noted in the book, it did finally take a stand against Trujillo, who retaliated harshly against it.)

After Patria miscarries, she finds herself staring at the family's picture of the Good Shepherd, hung alongside the requisite portrait of Trujillo. Minerva's remark, "They're a pair, aren't they?," prompts Patria to question why God allows so much suffering and in her moment of challenging Him, she finds that His face and that of the dictator's had "merged." Patria turns away from God, the Father and toward Mary, the Holy Mother, embarking on a pilgrimage to a place where the *Virgencita* has been sighted. This journey culminates in a vision in which Patria realizes that the Mother of God may be found in the masses of people gathered all around her.

This sense of spiritual immanence does not fully flower into revolutionary action until some thirteen years later. Whereas Patria's nascent questionings of political and divine justice were marked by her miscarriage, the next stage in her development is manifested by the unexpected conception and birth of her third child, Ernesto. Notably, the boy is conceived on the night that news of Castro's revolution in Cuba reaches the Mirabals (the events in Cuba gave false hope to many Dominicans that their own revolution would follow shortly). The true change in Patria comes after she is unexpectedly caught in a battle between guerillas, inspired by Castro, and *guardias* joined by *campesinos* (laborers). During the fight, Patria sees a young boy about the age of her own daughter and shouts at him to get down, but he is shot and killed. In that moment she cries out, "my God, he's one of mine!" She is forever changed by this recognition of belonging to a human family and from here on is no longer willing to "sit back and watch my babies die." Thus Patria the traditional wife and mother becomes symbolic mother to the revolution and is venerated as such after her death.

Alvarez was criticized by some reviewers for relegating the sisters' deaths to a twenty-page epilogue. The events leading up to their deaths on November 25, 1960, are recounted in detail, though, in the final chapter, and told from Minerva's perspective. The narrative ends poignantly with Minerva's observation that as she and her two sisters headed up the mountain that would be the site of their martyrdom, "it was as if we were girls again, walking through the dark part of the yard, a little afraid, a little excited by our fears . . ." Her words remind the reader of the journey the novel takes, beginning with the sisters' youths, knowing all the while that it would end in death. The reality of their brutal deaths is not completely glossed over; Dedé says, "I saw the marks on Minerva's throat; fingerprints as clear as day on Mate's pale neck. They also clubbed them . . . They killed them good and dead."

Alvarez's decision not to dwell, however, on their deaths points to the fact that the book serves as a celebration of their lives. Her intent is to bring these very human women to life, rescuing them from disembodied untouchability as saints and martyrs. As real women who struggled through adolescence, fell in and out of love, grew into their political consciousness over time, and were filled with fears and doubts even as they bravely resisted a murderous dictatorship, they serve as more effective role models to all who suffer under oppression. Alvarez's novel is indeed a gift to the Dominican people, offering them the possibility of hope and healing. The figure who embodies the healing power of language and of storytelling is Dedé, whose martyrdom, as her husband puts it, is to be alive without her sisters. (Dedé was largely prevented from joining her sisters in their revolutionary activities by her husband, Jaimito, but she was also fearful of the

consequences of their actions.) Moreover, it is she who delivers the central message of the novel, that the necessity of storytelling, even when the story itself is painful and tells of terrible truths, is, as Dedé says, "so that it could be human, so that we could begin to forgive it."

The epilogue makes it clear that Dedé's life has served a vital purpose: it is she who has lived not only to tell the story of her sisters' lives but to listen to other people's stories about *las Mariposas*. In the aftermath of their deaths, those who saw them on that fateful day in the hours before they were murdered traveled as if on pilgrimages to Dedé's home to tell her what they had seen. Like a confessor, she listens to each visitor and although each account breaks her heart, she knows this is what she must do: "It was the least I could do, being the one who was saved." She in turn saves others in the process of transforming herself from the listener to the "oracle." When a close friend accuses her of still living in the past, thirty-four years after the deaths of her sisters, Dedé asserts that she is not living in the past, but has brought it with her into the present so that it may not be repeated: "we needed a story to understand what had happened to us."

¡YO!

Dedé's statement of the value of telling a story so that an understanding may be achieved of oneself, one's family, one's culture or cultures, as the case may be, resonates throughout the body of Alvarez's work. It is perhaps curious that after expanding her focus in *In the Time of the Butterflies,* Alvarez decided to follow it up with a return to more directly autobiographical terrain in the novel *¡Yo!,* a sequel to *How the García Girls Lost Their Accents,* published in 1997. Yet she clearly feels a need to flesh out her depiction of her fictional alter ego, Yolanda (Yo) García, and to continue the journey toward self-understanding begun in her first novel. Indeed, a good deal more is revealed about Yo's life and the bumpy path she has followed to becoming a now happily married, middle-aged writer and college professor, mirroring the author's own life. Like the author, Yo has also endured two divorces, a long period of indecision about whether to commit to her own writing, and many lean, lonely, and itinerant years.

Yet with this novel Alvarez also demonstrates her ability to craft a wide range of characters, including men, representing diverse cultural and socioeconomic backgrounds. As the title indicates, the focus of the novel is on Yolanda, using the same structure employed in the prequel: three sections of five stories each. But the stories themselves are told from many different perspectives, ranging from family members, a former teacher, and her third husband to her American landlady, a Dominican night watchman, and a stalker. The novel, in a sense, represents an opportunity for the subjects of Yo's work to write back and have their say about her.

The novel begins with a prologue, told from her sister Fifi's point of view, about the García family's angry reaction to the publication of Yolanda's first autobiographical novel. The episode of course reflects Alvarez's own situation of having to face her family following the successful publication of her first novel; she has written that her mother did not talk to her for months afterward. Yet here Yo's sisters come to accept their sister's need to write out of her own experiences, but as the story's subtitle, "fiction," indicates, they also begin to recognize her fictionalized versions of them as such. They discover too that not all roads in Yolanda's writing lead to her family. Ultimately, the birth of Sandi's first child brings the Garcías together and points to the novel's celebration of family. The focus on family broadens to include that of extended family members, the daughter of the Garcías' maid in the United States, and Yolanda's new family, consisting of her third husband and stepdaughter. But the novel significantly begins and ends with stories told, respectively, by Yo's mother and father; furthermore, the stories they tell attest to the power, both destructive and healing, of storytelling.

The novel also celebrates language. Each story or chapter is subtitled according to a literary genre or term that comments on the events being related. This strategy underscores that in addition to Yo herself, language serves as the thread that weaves together these characters and their stories about her. Her mother reveals in the first line of the first chapter that the hardest thing about coming to America was the English language. Her story is subtitled "nonfiction," reflecting its concern with definitions of truth and the mother's sense of revealing important truths about her daughter and their relationship.

Mrs. García relates how she used to frighten the children into behaving properly when they were small by throwing a fur coat over her head and pretending to be a bear. It was Yo who first fully understood that it was her mother beneath the coat. Later, Yo is found to have been rummaging around in the closet where her father hid his gun, which was illegal for him to own. Under questioning, Yo does not admit that she has seen it and instead, as her mother remembers, says, " 'Mami, the bear won't be coming anymore.' It was as if she were stating her part of our bargain."

A bargain made in silence and lies cannot end happily in Alvarez's world. Thus, the bear rears its ugly head again after the family immigrates to the United States. Her mother locks Yo in the closet one day as a punishment, forgetting that the fur coat is in there, and later finds the child in a nearly catatonic state of fear. A social worker shows up at their home soon afterward to investigate what lies behind the dark, unsettling stories that Yo has been writing in school. Mrs. García proceeds to tell the social worker about the difficulties of life in the Dominican Republic in an effort to gain her sympathy and understanding of the real-life terrors that their family would face if they were ever sent back there.

Mrs. García's storytelling is more than just a ploy: it breaks her own silence, which has been poisoning her relationship with her children and her ability to adjust to life in the United States. Moreover, it marks the first instance where she is told that she should be proud of her daughter's ability to express herself through writing, although the mother herself has a way to go before understanding Yo's need to invent things. The story seems to build on the nightmarish image of the "black furred thing lurking in the corners of my life," with which *How the García Girls Lost Their Accents* ends, further unpacking Yolanda's sense that "some violation lies at the center of [her] art." The black cat has been replaced by the bear, but the message remains the same: the importance of writing and of finding a voice in order to confront and overcome personal and political demons.

The significance of the bear episode is underlined by the bookend story that Dr. García tells in *¡Yo!*'s final chapter. His story serves a number of purposes. One is to reveal the close connection that exists between father and daughter. He admits, "Of all my girls, I always felt the closest to Yo." The reason, he reveals, is that she "understands [his] secret heart," an understanding gained largely through a regular written correspondence they share, which Yolanda uses to ask her father questions about his life and their family history. Yo stops writing to him after becoming upset by a lecture she attended where the speaker argues that baby boomers who never had children had effectively committed genetic suicide. Her father helps Yo by telling her that he is proud of her for following her destiny, which has been to tell stories, and that by doing so, she has "created books for the future generations."

The importance of parents telling their children that they are proud of them and giving them their blessing is threaded throughout Alvarez's work,

particularly in this novel and in her collected essays. But Dr. García goes even further by uncovering the guilt he feels over a time when he punished Yo and told her never to tell stories; this event, he suspects, lies at the heart of her feelings of self-doubt.

The gun episode is mentioned again in the story Dr. García shares. Five-year-old Yo actually finds her father's gun in its hiding place and soon mentions it in a story she invents and unfortunately shares with the family's neighbor, General Molino, a crony of Trujillo's. Her terrified parents decide they must teach her a lesson before she gets them all killed. They take her to the bathroom and turn on the shower to drown out her cries while her father beats her with a belt; but the most terrible aspect of the punishment, the father now believes, was his repeated instruction during the beating: "You must never ever tell stories!"

By giving his adult daughter his blessing, Dr. García hopes to heal the wounds of fear and insecurity that cut her far deeper than the physical scars that healed with time. The story ends with the father's desire to rewrite that terrible day and provide his daughter with an alternative, uplifting ending. The magic of fiction lies in Alvarez's ability to do just that, to write a beautiful story in which destructive secrets are replaced by blessings and familial connections are fostered by sharing secrets of the heart. The father's gun is replaced by the daughter's pen, making possible a brighter future.

SOMETHING TO DECLARE

It was fitting that Alvarez's next work was a collection of nonfiction essays entitled *Something to Declare,* published in 1998. (A number of these essays have already been referred to in this article.) Having begun her career as a poet seeking her woman's voice, she came full circle in her desire to proclaim her voice, to declare herself and her experiences. There is no doubt that Alvarez has something to say to her readers. In the foreword she writes that her aim is to provide answers to her readers' questions and to flesh out the information that may be gathered from her novels and poems concerning Alvarez's "experience of immigration, about switching languages, about the writing life, the teaching life, the family life, about all of those combined." These are familiar questions to which many familiar answers are given. But she does shed some new light on them and her sense of herself, particularly in relation to language, her writing, and family.

One of the strongest essays in the collection is "I Want to Be Miss América," a piece largely concerned with acculturation, told with much humor and not a little irony. Alvarez recounts her family's yearly tradition of watching the Miss America pageant. The event serves as a symbol of American cultural standards and the pressures the girls feel to adhere to them: "We would have to translate our looks into English . . . mold them into Made-in-the-USA beauty." What is ironic perhaps is that the Alvarez sisters also learned a valuable lesson from the pageant: "a girl could excel outside the home and still be a winner." The essay is also revealing in that Alvarez admits to still feeling like a stranger in the United States, as aware today as she was thirty years ago that the face of Miss America is not her own.

In "La Gringuita: On Losing a Native Language," Alvarez continues to explore issues of acculturation and language. The essay is an interesting extension of *How the García Girls Lost Their Accents;* whereas in the novel, the implication was that the girls lost their Spanish accents as they assimilated and bettered their English, here Alvarez notes that she now speaks Spanish with an American accent and has difficulty communicating in her native tongue. Once again, Alvarez wrestles with feelings of loss and guilt while acknowledging that her sisters' and her own "growing distance from Spanish" was a means of setting themselves free from restrictive "old world," Dominican values. She remembers a failed teenaged romance during a summer spent back in the Dominican Republic as the instance which demonstrated just how "unbridgeable that gap [between English and Spanish] had become."

Seventeen-year-old Alvarez spends the summer with relatives who speak only Spanish and who treat her like a child, probably, she admits, because she sounds like one when she speaks their language. She yearns to be a successful "hybrid" like her friend Dilita, who has lived in Puerto Rico and New York City and, unlike Alvarez, is not insecure or "tortured" by her hyphenated existence. Through Dilita, Alvarez meets her first boyfriend, Mangú. Alvarez wonders why she is not falling in love with her young beau and eventually realizes that the fault lies in the silences that exist between them. Intimacy is predicated on self-expression and, as Alvarez writes, "as English became my dominant tongue, too many parts of me were left out in Spanish" to achieve such intimacy with Mangú or any non-English speaker, although she often wonders what a life lived in Spanish would have been like. A chance encounter with Mangú in the Dominican Republic years later, while accompanied by her current husband, revives old memories and yearnings but ultimately affirms Alvarez's sense of herself as the "person I had become in English." Nonetheless, she decides to join her husband in taking Spanish lessons to close the gap between her two languages and countries.

Alvarez discusses her marriage in a number of essays and also deals with coming to terms with not being a mother. Self-affirmation is a thread that binds many of these writings as is seen, for instance, in Alvarez's ultimate acceptance of the fact that as a writer she gives herself to "a much larger *familia* than my own blood." This awareness also helps her in times of conflict with her family, particularly her mother. In "Genetics of Justice," she examines her relationship with her mother and her fears regarding her mother's reaction to her second novel, *In the Time of the Butterflies*. Alvarez imagines what life under Trujillo must have been like and considers the reasons for her mother's near-obsession with the man responsible for the disappearances of so many family friends and for atrocities such as the massacre of some eighteen thousand Haitian laborers in 1937. The essay reveals an important, adult understanding of her parents and the "habits of repression, censorship and terror" that were instilled in them by years of living under Trujillo's regime; these contributed to their difficulty in adjusting to life in America and believing in the reality of freedom of speech.

Alvarez's parents in fact tried to keep from their daughters the news about the murder of the three Mirabal sisters in November 1960, four months after the family's arrival in the States. This "mandate of silence," as seen throughout Alvarez's work, is often at the heart of clashes that occur between the author and her parents. As the publication of her novel neared, Alvarez was fearful of her mother's anger at the risk taken by her daughter in exposing herself and her family to retribution by former associates of Trujillo. Instead, her sobbing mother called to tell her daughter how proud she was of her for writing her book. A stunned Alvarez is for once at a loss for words, finding in this precious moment a kind of "genetic justice."

That Alvarez continues to see herself primarily in terms of her childhood family, despite the intervening years marked by conflict between *la familia* and her acculturated, strongly individuated self, is a subject considered in the essay titled "Family Matters." This essay offers some interesting insights into the author's writing, especially her awareness of the influence of Domini-

can culture, with its strong oral tradition. She also considers the "fictive cast of mind" among Dominicans, reflecting their years of living with lies perpetuated by their government. Alvarez recognizes how Spanish flavors her English prose, including her tendency to write longer sentences and what one editor characterized as her overuse of the word "little," reflecting the rhythms of Spanish and the habit of diminutizing names. Although she declares that her first allegiance is to her work and not her family, she admits to her need for their acceptance. It is a difficult balancing act—to stay true to herself and *la familia*—but one that leads to many rich and engaging contributions to the English language and the greater human family of Alvarez's readers, who now extend beyond the borders of the United States and the Dominican Republic.

CONCLUSION

In 1997 Alvarez and her husband purchased property located in the Dominican mountains, establishing an organic coffee farm/educational center called Alta Gracia (after the national *Virgencita*). According to their mission statement, one of their goals in establishing the farm is to maintain a "safe, healthy, and fair environment for workers"; the educational center is intended as a resource for students from the Dominican Republic and abroad who may come to learn about sustainable agriculture and the arts, and who will, in turn, teach the people living and working in the community. This valuable enterprise, rooted as it is in the soil of her native homeland, seems to be the perfect outgrowth of Alvarez's continuing efforts to more than just negotiate her hyphenated existence as a Dominican-American but to flourish as a successful "hybrid." Having landed in the "terra firma of language," Alvarez continues her fertile exploration of it, finding new ways to bridge the two languages and two cultures that have shaped her voice as a woman and as a vital force in contemporary literature.

Selected Bibliography

WORKS OF JULIA ALVAREZ

NOVELS

How the García Girls Lost Their Accents. Chapel Hill, N.C.: Algonquin Books of Chapel Hill, 1991.

In the Time of the Butterflies. Chapel Hill, N.C.: Algonquin Books of Chapel Hill, 1994.

¡Yo! Chapel Hill, N.C.: Algonquin Books of Chapel Hill, 1997.

SHORT FICTION

"Customs." In *Iguana Dreams: New Latino Fiction*. Edited by Delia Poey and Virgil Suarez. New York: Harper Collins, 1992. Pp. 1–16.

"Amor divino." *Ms*. January/February 1998, pp. 88–94.

POETRY

(Editor) *Old Age Ain't for Sissies*. N.p.: Crane Creek Press, 1979.

Homecoming. New York: Grove Press, 1984.

The Housekeeping Book. Illustrations by Carol Mac-Donald and Rene Schall. Burlington, Vt.: n.p., 1984.

The Other Side/El Otro Lado. New York: Dutton, 1995.

Homecoming: New and Collected Poems. New York: Dutton, 1995.

Seven Trees. Lithographs by Sara Eichner. North Andover, Mass.: Kat Ran Press, 1998. (Published in green cloth box, special edition limited to 50 books numbered 1–50.)

POEMS REPRESENTED IN ANTHOLOGIES

Cocco de Fillipis, Daisy, and Emma Jane Robinett, eds. *Poemas del exilio y otros inquietudes/Poems of Exile and Other Concerns*. New York: Ediciones Alcance, 1988.

Lehman, David. *The Best American Poetry 1991*. New York: Scribners, 1991.

Pack, Robert, and Jay Parini, eds. *Poems for a Small Planet: Contemporary American Nature Poetry*. Middletown, Conn.: Middlebury College Press, 1993.

Finch, Annie, ed. *A Formal Feeling Comes: Poems in Form by Contemporary Women*. Brownsville, Oreg.: Story Line Press, 1994.

Espada, Martin, ed. *El Coro: A Chorus of Latino and Latina Poetry*. Amherst, Mass.: University of Massachusetts Press, 1997.

COLLECTED ESSAYS

Something to Declare. Chapel Hill, N.C.: Algonquin Books of Chapel Hill, 1998.

OTHER WORKS

"An American Childhood in the Dominican Republic." *The American Scholar*, Winter 1987, pp. 71–85.

"Hold the Mayonnaise." *New York Times Magazine*, January 12, 1992, p. 14. (Later published in *New Worlds of Literature: Writings from America's Many Cultures*. Edited by Jerome Beaty and J. Paul Hunter. 2nd ed. New York: W.W. Norton & Co., 1994.)

"Black Behind the Ears." *Essence*, February 1993.

"An Unlikely Beginning for a Writer." *Mascaras*. Edited by Lucha Corpi. Berkeley: Third Woman Press, 1997.

CRITICAL AND BIOGRAPHICAL STUDIES

Barak, Julie. " 'Turning and Turning in the Widening Gyre': A Second Coming Into Language in Julia Alvarez's *How the García Girls Lost Their Accents*." *MELUS* 23, no. 1: 59–76 (Spring 1998).

Christian, Karen. "Invention of the Ethnic Self in Latina Immigrant Fiction: *The Line of Sun* and *How the García Girls Lost Their Accents*." In her *Show and Tell: Identity as Performance in U.S. Latina/o Fiction*. Albuquerque: University of New Mexico Press, 1997. Pp. 89–119.

Echevarria, Roberto Gonzalez. "Sisters in Death." *New York Times Book Review,* December 18, 1994, p.18. (Review of *In the Time of the Butterflies.*)

Frucht, Abby. "That García Girl." *New York Times Book Review,* February 9, 1997, p. 19. (Review of *¡Yo!*)

Gambone, Philip. "The Other Side/El Otro Lado." *New York Times Book Review,* July 16, 1995, p. 42.

Garner, Dwight. "A Writer's Revolution." *Hungry Mind Review* 32:23 (Winter 1994–1995). (Review of *In the Time of the Butterflies.*)

Hoffman, Joan M. " 'She Wants to Be Called Yolanda Now': Identity, Language and the Third Sister in *How the García Girls Lost Their Accents.*" *Bilingual Review/La Revista Bilingue* 23, no. 1: 21–27 (January–April 1998).

Luis, William. "A Search for Identity in Julia Alvarez's *How the García Girls Lost Their Accents.*" In *Dance Between Two Cultures: Latino Caribbean Literature Written in the United States.* Nashville, Tenn.: Vanderbilt University Press, 1997. Pp. 266–277.

Messud, Claire. "Conjured by Her Characters." *Book World—The Washington Post,* January 19, 1997, p. 9. (Review of *¡Yo!*)

Miller, Susan. "Caught Between Two Cultures." *Newsweek,* April 20, 1992, pp. 78–79. (Profiles Alvarez and other members of a new generation of Latino writers.)

———. "Family Spats, Urgent Prayers." *Newsweek,* October 17, 1994, pp. 77–78.

Muratori, Fred. "Homecoming." *New England Review and Bread Loaf Quarterly* IX, no. 2: 231–232 (Winter 1986).

Puleo, Gus. "Remembering and Reconstructing the Mirabal Sisters in Julia Alvarez's *In the Time of the Butterflies.*" *Bilingual Review/La Revista Bilingue* 23, no. 1: 11–20 (January–April 1998).

Rifkind, Donna. "*How the García Girls Lost Their Accents.*" *New York Times Book Review,* October 6, 1991, p. 14.

Stavans, Ilan. "*How the García Girls Lost Their Accents.*" *Commonweal,* April 10, 1992, pp. 23–25.

———. "Las Mariposas." In *Art and Anger: Essays on Politics and the Imagination.* Albuquerque: University of New Mexico Press, 1996. Pp. 35–40.

INTERVIEWS

Bing, Jonathan. "Julia Alvarez: Books That Cross Borders." *Publishers Weekly,* December 16, 1996, pp. 38–39.

Morales, Ed. "Madam Butterfly: How Julia Alvarez Found Her Accent." *Village Voice Literary Supplement,* November 1994, p. 13.

Wiley, Catherine. "Memory Is Already the Story You Made Up About the Past: An Interview with Julia Alvarez." *The Bloomsbury Review,* March 1992, pp. 9–10.

—ANDREA SCHAEFER

A. R. Ammons

1926–

ARCHIE RANDOLPH AMMONS was born February 18, 1926, the child of Willie M. and Lucy Della McKee Ammons, in a house built by his grandfather, on the Ammons family's small tobacco farm near Whiteville, North Carolina. Two sisters preceded him; of his two younger brothers, one died at birth and the other died at eighteen months. Growing up in the country during the Great Depression put Ammons in intimate contact with nature and the hardships that come with a life of economic stress. He fed the hogs and chickens, cut kindling, built the fire, called in the cow, plowed the rich black Carolina ground with his mule Silver, and he loved his favorite pig Sparkle to her dying day at the hog kill. He went racoon hunting with baying hounds and took pleasure in his aunt's stories of his ancestors from Green Sea County. School let out in early spring so children could plow. During a phone interview I conducted with Ammons on February 22, 2000, he said, "I was raised a farmer so I have no other reason than to feel down to earth, to see how things operate—so my native ground became conceptual." As for literature in his boyhood, the only book in the Ammons' house was the Bible.

A LIFE FROM SOUTH TO NORTH

Ammons attended New Hope Elementary School, an old wooden schoolhouse, and had excellent teachers. "Mabel Powell in seventh grade and in eighth grade Ruth Baldwin, who taught me how to parse sentences. I learned how a sentence worked. It's terribly inhibiting for a writer not to have that ability." He graduated in 1939 and gave the valedictory address.

After graduation from Whiteville High School in 1943, Ammons worked for a shipyard in Wilmington, North Carolina, installing fuel pumps in freighters; in less than a year he joined the U.S. Navy. While he was aboard a destroyer escort in the South Pacific, he began to write poetry during the long periods of idle quietness every seaman knows. According to Ammons, "It wasn't serious poetry, mostly rimes, jabs, gibes about my shipmates."

In 1946 Ammons attended Wake Forest College (now Wake Forest University) in Winston-Salem, North Carolina, on the G. I. Bill. "I was passionate about biology, chemistry, and comparative anatomy," he said. Ammons' interest in science stemmed directly from his farming background. In an interview with *Michigan Quarterly Review* (Winter 1989), he said:

I had wanted to stay a farmer, but my father sold the farm. So, that option was eliminated. I love the land and the terrible dependency on the weather and the rain and the wind. It betrays many a farmer, but makes the interests of the farmer's life tie in very immediately with everything that's going wrong meteorologically. I miss that. That's where I got my closeness and attention to the soil, weeds, plants, insects, and trees.

While at Wake Forest College, Ammons met and fell in love with Phyllis Plumbo, a Latin American specialist who had come down from Northfield, New Jersey, to teach for a semester. They married in 1949, the same year Ammons took a job as a principal and seventh- and eighth-grade teacher at a small elementary school in the island village of Cape Hatteras. There were only two other teachers. After two years Ammons entered the graduate English program at The University of California at Berkeley, where he studied with the poet Josephine Miles and completed the work for a Master of Arts degree except for his orals. Ammons explained, "My father became ill, so I left. It was a good thing I didn't get the Ph.D." which, he agreed, is not an attainment that fuels the poetic imagination.

For the next twelve years Ammons worked mainly in southern New Jersey as a sales executive for his father-in-law's company, which manufactured glass for laboratory equipment. He also did some magazine editing (*The Nation, Chelsea*) and worked in real estate: "I didn't sell one house. I hated it." During this period he published his first book of poems, *Ommateum, with Doxology* (1955). A vanity press publication, the volume sold sixteen copies in the first five years. It has since become a collector's item. Eight years after *Ommateum,* Ammons published another book of poems, *Expressions of Sea Level* (1963), which received strongly favorable reviews. Largely on the strength of this book, he was invited to Cornell University in Ithaca, New York, to give a poetry reading, and afterward members of the English Department offered him a faculty position to teach freshman English.

Ammons' appointment at Cornell rescued him from the time-consuming demands of the business world and provided him with a secure en-

vironment in which to write. In 1974, the year after he received the National Book Award for *Collected Poems: 1951–1971* (1972), he became the Goldwin Smith Professor of English at Cornell. The wide critical praise *Collected Poems* received began for Ammons a spate of successes that include virtually every major poetry prize in the United States: the Bolligen Prize in 1975 for his book-length poem *Sphere: The Form of a Motion* (1974), the National Book Critics Circle Award in 1981 for *A Coast of Trees* (1981), and the National Book Award again in 1994 for *Garbage* (1993). Other honors he has received are the Ruth Lilly Poetry Prize, a Lannan Foundation Award, a Guggenheim Fellowship, a MacArthur Prize Fellowship Award, the Levinson Prize, an American Academy of Arts and Letters Travelling Fellowship, the Frost Medal for Distinguished Achievement in Poetry over a Lifetime, given by the Poetry Society of America, and in 1998 the Tanning Prize, a $100,000 award for "outstanding and proven mastery in the art of poetry." Over a span of forty-two years Ammons has produced twenty-five books of poetry.

A professor emeritus, Archie Ammons lives in a retirement village near Cornell. He and Phyllis have been married for over fifty years; their son John lives in California with his wife and two children. Once or twice a week Ammons goes to campus and talks with students and friends. Despite failing health, he continues to write poetry. "Yesterday," he said during our interview, "I did a rewrite on my typewriter of a poem I've been working on. It was a good rewrite. I'm a little proud of it."

THE SELF AND NATURE

Ammons' first book of poems, *Ommateum* ("compound eye"), presents a poet—at once visionary, oracular, bardic, and Adamic—who matches his rhapsodic openness to nature with an open free verse form. "In the Wind My Rescue Is," for example, is an utterance of expansive imagining:

In the wind my rescue is
in whorls of it
    like winged tufts of dreams
bearing
   through the forms of nothingness
   the gyres and hurricane eyes
the seed safety
    of multiple origins

I set my task
. . . .
to mount upon the highest stone
a cardinal
chilled in the attitude of song

But the wind has sown loose dreams
in my eyes
    and telling unknown tongues
drawn me out beyond the land's end
    and rising in long
   parabolas of drift
borne me safely

As these lines show, nature infuses the self. However, just as often in Ammons' world, the reverse occurs. In "Having Been Interstellar" the poet melds with the firmament, then from "the earthless air" goes "out into the growths of rains." Nature/Self interfusion is the essential dynamic in Ammons' poetry from *Ommateum* and afterward.

This dynamic is usually expressed with no periods and no question marks. Reality in Ammons' poetry is infinite process; there cannot be closure. And there cannot be question marks because a question is the mind's desire to determine or to fix on. Any resultant answer is the illusion of control. An Ammons poem is the enactment of the mind unlocking itself from common consciousness and attaining a state of acute attentiveness to the processes of nature—its expansions, diminishments, disintegrations, and amplifications. These phenomena are reflexive—that is, they are the mind's processes. Informing Ammons' poetry, then, is "the doctrine of correspondences" propounded in the eighteenth century by the Swedish mystic and religious thinker Emanuel Swedenborg, who influenced Ralph Waldo Emerson, Ammons' direct literary forebear. The Creation is divine—it is the origin, the source, of value. Emerson wrote in his first major work, *Nature,* that the "sea-beaten rock" teaches firmness, the "azure sky" tranquility, and the "brutes" industry and affection. Exemplars of beauty, power, and peace are everywhere in the natural world. Nature is moral text.

Ammons' thought, however, is always speculative; to regard nature as what Emerson called "moral law" is a simplism. Correspondence is not truth; it is the avenue to truth. The truth is that the self is not in nature; it is not even as nature; it is *of* nature. Any thinking that supposes a true difference between self and nature is, Ammons contends, delusional, merely empirical. Perceiver/perceived, subject/object are false dichotomies. To operate on the basis of these dichotomies is the essence of alienation. Detachment from nature, not people, is alienation (the social sphere counts for very little in Ammons' poetry). In "Street Song," from Ammons' 1965 collection *Corsons Inlet,* the poet stands "Like an / eddying willow leaf," people "both ways coming / and going." He is "no stiller" than they, but he is "detached." The poem ends in revelation as he becomes the leaf: "gold is / coming into my veins." Detachment disappears. This is mysticism, not morality. Nature here is not Emerson's ethical expositor.

Recalling William Wordsworth, Ammons writes excursive poetry—walking poems. His lyric meditations are quests within the natural realm for the transempirical; and as the surroundings change, so does the poet. The poem "Corsons Inlet" is representative. The poet sets out across the dunes to the sea. The poem's structure—varied lineation and indentions—reflects the poet's fluctuant thought which, in turn, reflects the continuously shifting shoreline. To walk is to be unmoored.

> the walk liberating, I was released from forms,
> from the perpendiculars,
> > straight lines, blocks, boxes, binds
> of thought
> into the hues, shadings, rises, flowing bends and
> > blends
> > > of sight:
> > > > I allow myself eddies of meaning:
> yield to a direction of significance
> running
> like a stream through the geography of my work:
> > you can find
> in my sayings
> > > swerves of action
> > > like the inlet's cutting edge:

Always in search of the ultimate, of the one reality under which all other realities are subsumed, the poet says, "but Overall is beyond me." He knows that everything perceptible cannot be totaled. This is the philosophical cul-de-sac Ammons' reasoning imagination usually comes to. Particularities are everywhere—observed with the acumen of a gifted naturalist—but they are, as Ammons says, "eddies of meaning." By the poem's end—which for Ammons can never be a conclusion—reality is paradoxical and cannot be known. It can only be lived and embodied. The movements of nature are timeless, yet forever new. Orders collapse into larger orders, and the only constant is change. Of course these recognitions are as old as Hindu scripture. The freshness of Ammons' expression is the form it takes. "Corsons Inlet" moves—loosens, branches, expands, contracts, and loosens again—to become itself the organic energy the poet experiences.

COLLECTED POEMS

With the publication of *Collected Poems: 1951–1971* (1972), Ammons solidly establishes himself as a major American poet of his generation. The fusion he effects between science and poetry is especially remarkable. Without losing its power as fact, science—biology, botany, chemistry, geology, meteorology, astronomy, physics—becomes poetry. Ammons is a Romantic philosopher who uses empiricism to experience divine transcendence—the opposite of empiricism. A case in point is "Hibernaculum," which appears near the end of *Collected Poems,* a 27-page poem of 112 sections, each with three tercets that look hexametric but are actually free verse. The title means any natural cover for protecting an organism during the winter: for example, a bud or bulb for protecting a plant embryo, specifically a bud of a freshwater polyzoan that can develop into a colony in the spring. The protected organism is the poet; the colony in the spring is the poet's metaphor for the large, complex poem he is making. The poet reads nature reading him, and the polyzoan is a muse.

In a style that is, by turns, discursive, conversational, and veined with imagery, Ammons in "Hibernaculum" examines nature and the mind, those cognate realities. In Section 1, he speculates first on his favorite phenomenon—motion:

> A cud's a locus in time, a staying change, moving
> but holding through motions timeless relations,
> as of center to periphery, core-thought to
> > consideration,
>
> not especially, I'd say, goal directed, more
> a slime- and sublime-filled coasting, a repeating
> > of
> gently repeating motions, blissful slobber-spun
> > webs:
>
> today's paper says that rain falls on the desert and
> > makes
> it fertile: semen slips, jets, swims into wombs
> and makes them bulge: . . .

Motion is Ammons' philosophical *topos* throughout his career. Moving fluids such as cud, rain, and semen fructify. Every motion reflects every other motion. Such is the constancy and the timelessness of being. All motion repeats or transforms into other motion. There is no goal. Rather, a goal is merely a human idea and has nothing to do with the universe, which is not homocentric.

As motion yields to other motion, in a like manner people must give up what they have; nothing can be kept. Everything goes, including love, hate, and beauty. Even aging, for it too is but for a little while. Everything is a going out, a centrifugal force. Matter spending itself is Ammons' symbol for love. "I am not to be saved," says the poet in Section 12. "Fleshbody" translating itself to "wordbody" is how a poem, which is an act of love, is made. In Section 20 a poem is a soup with its "clarity of quintessential / consomme," which is its idea. Its imagery, which concretizes its idea, is "carrot cube, pea, rice grain."

Ammons' thought moves, as we see, from sublime meditation to eccentric, even facile, metaphorizing. "Hibernaculum" is a going along, his words stringing out where his speculation takes him; and one thing, however disparate from another, is only seemingly disparate. Ammons carries Aristotle's famous definition—"A poet is a man who has an eye for the resemblance of things"—to its outbound conclusion. Everything resembles or points to everything else, thus Ammons' continual use of the colon throughout his poetry. Every part of the universe—from the microscopic to the cosmic—is an effusion or, to use a favorite word of Ammons, a "suasion," that compares to every other part. Only from the unimaginative, unmetaphorizing perspective is the world composed of differences, of the many. Many is One, "so / that the universe seems available in the / gravity of a lady bug tipped down a blade of grass," as Ammons says in Section 70. Such is his integrative vision.

Ammons' thinking, however, is nothing if not shifting and deliberately working its own decon-

struction. His monistic vision, his apprehension of a unified whole, breaks down—as the universe in its divisions, devolvements, evolvements does—and in Section 87 Ammons absolutizes the particular: "gloriously every object in and on the earth becomes just / itself . . ." Mind/body, mind/nature, reality/appearance, fact/dream—whether they are equations or polarities—are illusions. The only reality is the thing: "the hollyhock, / what a marvel, complete in itself: the bee, / how particular, . . ." In Section 96 Ammons itemizes the bill on the repair of his car—parts and labor—starting with "1 push rod ($1.25)."

An apt word for Ammons' long meditative poems like "Hibernaculum" is his own—"scopy." He excludes nothing. Absorptive as his vision is, however, he is always sifting through experience and panning for gold. He is speculative but bent on determination. And finally—or as finally as the perpetual motion of his mind allows—Ammons agrees with the English biologist J. B. S. Haldane, who said: "My own suspicion is that the universe is not only queerer than we suppose, but queerer than we can suppose." "Hibernaculum"—this indulgent metaphysical treatise—concludes anticlimactically with a kick in the pants to cerebration and to artistic seriousness. Ammons is reading Xenophon's *Oeconomics,* enjoying it, and "saying so fills this stanza nicely." End of poem.

Understandably, in the more manageable form of the lyric Ammons exhibits craft, control, and clarity. The lyrics in *Collected Poems* show that after his debut with *Ommateum* he shifts his voice, starting with his second book of poems, *Expressions of Sea Level.* The voice of the *Ommateum* poems is hieratic, spiritual, and innocent, showing the poet unbounded by time and space and affined to all things in the natural world. Ammons' lyrics from *Ommateum* through his later poetry are often grounded in observable daily realities; experience becomes more natural than supernatural: though a religious impulse still propels the poet, he sanctifies the here and now: Jersey cedars, bay grass, a rock wall. The title itself, *Expressions of Sea Level,* signals a descent in altitude; sublimity will now be found in objects directly before the poet. Landscapes and sea-scapes as habitable places become his context, and vision gives way to cognition. There is a concentration, a luminosity, in the post-*Ommateum* lyrics that surpasses the best parts of Ammons' long meditative poems, for all their intelligence and flexibility. In *Expressions of Sea Level*'s poem "River," "the forsythia is out, / sprawling like / yellow amoebae, the long / uneven branches—pseudo / podia— / angling on the bottom / of air's spring-clear pool." In the grip of such rapt attention philosophy is not needed. The exultant poet goes down "to the moonwaters, / where the silver / willows are and the bay blossoms. . . ." The poem becomes a paean to the river, to "the great wooded silence / of flowing / forever . . . ," and to the water "silvered at the moon-singing of hidden birds."

The titles of *Collected Poems* indicate, however, that Ammons' perspective is as often rationalistic as Romantic. A few examples are: "Configurations," "The Unifying Principle," "Countering," "Convergence," "Locus," "Devising," "Mechanism," "Periphery," "Increment," and "Definition." These titles are abstract and academic. Ammons is, after all, a professor, albeit a professor of poetry writing.

"Countering" serves as a case in point. The poet likens crystal to reason, which "grows / down / into my loves and / terrors, halts / or muddles / flow, / casting me to /shine or break." Ammons opposes the Romantic dislike of reason here. The Romantic poets' antirationalism is renown, with examples such as William Blake's dark "Satanic Mills," Wordsworth's "We murder to dissect," Edgar Allan Poe's "To Science" who, he says, "alterest all things with thy peering eyes. / Why preyest thou upon the poet's heart, / Vulture whose wings are dull realities?" In fact,

Ammons' "Countering" counters the myth of the noble savage, a conceptual mainstay of Romanticism. Far from noble, the savage "peoples / wood slopes, shore rocks" with dream figures, born of superstition, who have the power to save or destroy human life. Ammons disassociates himself from the natural man the Romantics revered and says it is reason that preserves life. Reason forms a "sphere" that hides the poet's "contours" and "contains the war / of shape and loss / at rest." His reason holding contraries in abeyance, the poet of "Countering" becomes a man of Platonic aplomb.

When Ammons applies his intellectual imagination to the particularities of the natural world, as in "Countering," he creates the kind of lyric poem on which his critical reputation rests. But he writes, too, another kind of lyric, which is not typical of his oeuvre. "Visit," for example, is quiet and unperformative, an amalgam of Thoreau, Chinese pastoral poetry, and Robert Frost (the poem echoes Frost's invitational poem "The Pasture"). "Visit" appears on the first page of *Corsons Inlet* and beckons the reader into the volume.

> It is not far to my place:
> you can come smallboat,
> pausing under the shade in the eddies
>   or going ashore
>   to rest, regard the leaves
>
>   or talk with birds and
> shore weeds: hire a full grown man not
> late in years to oar you
>   and choose a canoe-like thin ship:
>   (a dumb man is better and no
>
>   costlier; he will attract
> the reflections and silences under leaves:)

Absent here is the toneless rationality typical of Ammons' poetry. Warmly humane, "Visit" talks to the reader. The poet will be at the landing and greet the reader "with some made / wine and a special verse." Wise and sequestered in nature, the poet has learned to value silence, which ties people to one another deeper than talk. He tells the reader to "keep still a dense reserve of silence" to "poise against / conversation." The welcoming poet is Thoreauvian, unworldly, and gathering nature's news, which is forever new: "I found last month a root with shape and / have heard a new sound among / the insects: come."

THE POETRY OF POETICS

Like other poets before him—Wordsworth, Gerard Manley Hopkins, Ezra Pound, T. S. Eliot, William Carlos Williams, and Wallace Stevens—who wrote poetry that was radically new, Ammons tries to justify his poetry by propounding his own poetics. Unlike his predecessors, however, who wrote mainly essays to explain their concept of poetry, Ammons presents his poetics mainly in his poems: examples are "Prodigal" from *Corsons Inlet,* "Muse" from *Northfield Poems* (1966), "Poetics" from *Briefings* (1971), and "Essay on Poetics" from *Collected Poems.* Primarily, Ammons wants his readers to understand that, for him, poetry is a kind of falling out, an expression that, by the very process of its being said, finds its own form. Such is Ammons' anti-formalist position, which he shares with his co-modernist Williams. Individual lines are not the basis of a poem, nor do they explain it or even total it. Rather, the whole exceeds the sum of its parts; a poem is a gestalt; its quality cannot be derived from its elements. This is an organicist view of art; the poem unfolds as a living thing. Ammons is in complete sympathy with Walt Whitman's title for his collected poems, *Leaves of Grass.*

"Prodigal" is an intense description, in the spirit of science, of various objects and people moving across the planet: foggy icebergs, "flotillas of ducks weathering the night," nomads set-

tling down at dusk in their tents. All and each are part of the orderings and disorderings, "dis- / continuities" and "congregations," the "molecules of meaning," that constitute the perpetual shifting that is the natural world. A poem is a tearing down and a building up or vice versa, depending on the "vectors" it takes. To compose a poetry that does not in its very form, in its lineations and thought processes, reflect such shifting is to compose poetry in a pre-established mode, thus inauthentic poetry.

In "Muse" Ammons takes his cue from Theodore Roethke, the modern American poet of botanical growth and fecund darkness, and admits that if his poetry is fragmentary and indeterminate, it is to show the very brokenness which is the "anguish of becoming," the "pain of moulting." The poet and poem remake themselves into "a wider / order, structures deepening, / inching rootlike into the dark!" The poet writes subconsciously, tapping into wellsprings within himself that he is not cognizant of but which nonetheless guide him and organically structure his poem. Primordial powers and precivilized urgings innate to everyone compel the poet.

In "Poetics" Ammons says, "I look for the forms / things want to come as." Poetry is galactic, centrifugal, in its formation. "I look for the way / things will turn / out spiralling from a center." Poetry emerges independently of him. Creativity is a force outside himself—many authors, painters, and composers have attested to the same—that expresses archetypal imaginings. The poet is a conduit "not so much looking for shape / as being available / to any shape that may be / summoning itself / through me / from the self not mine but ours." As contemporary as Ammons is, the meaning of his poetics is ancient and Orphic. The poet is demiurgic.

Ammons' fullest statement on his poetics is "Essay on Poetics," a twenty-one-page eccentric disquisition written in long tercets and various free verse forms. The poet begins by identifying poetry with vectors that cluster, "beefing up / and verging out" toward a boundary where movement stops, spreads, and takes shape: thus a poem is made. This aesthetic of kinesis is central to Ammons' theory of poetry.

Like Whitman, America's pioneering practitioner of free verse, Ammons notes what he sees before him and lets what it is be its meaning; what he sees he therefore equates with thought: "the way I think is / I think what I see." The world of natural objects is a language; it is tongued. Strings of syntax reaching rightward across the page catch in their path "saliences" (a favorite Ammons' word) that the seeking mind, knowing what it wants to see, never sees. These saliences do not include, however, what Ammons calls the "center," which exists at the heart of everything: "galaxies, systems, planets, asteroids, / moons, drifts, atoms, electrons." The center, as Ammons envisions it, is a seed, a pivot point, of concentrated pressure; but it is serene and empty, similar, then, to Eliot's mystical concept of "the still point," which is inexpressible, too considerable for consideration. The matter of Ammons' poetry is what spins off this center, what it produces— its meaning. Everything is a garment over the ineffable center. Ineffable, yes, but Ammons never stops explaining it. He is like Cotton Mather, Jonathan Edwards, and other Puritan theologians of Colonial America who said, in effect, God is inconceivable, but let me tell you about Him. The ineffable still point is located too, Ammons contends, in the center of a lyric poem—but is silent and unanalyzable, a ghostly reproof to critics. Prying professors, keep away.

Ammons' poetics is nothing if not epistemological. It asks questions such as: How do we know the world? How do we know? *Can* we know the world? With admirable lucidity Ammons tackles these questions in "Essay on Poetics." He uses a tree as representative of the world. One's knowledge of a tree is based on one's previous experience of trees, so that in perceiving a tree one is influenced by one's idea or imagining of trees. The idea of treeness has a reality, more than does the actual tree. One responds, then, to one's idea of the tree more than to the actual tree. One's fictionalizing ability, how one has imagined trees, transforms the tree. There is no other way of perceiving. To perceive is to transform through the alembic of our imagination. Perception can only be interpretation. Therefore the mind cannot know what is actually before it. So you "can't get mixed up with / an elm tree on anything / like a permanent basis." Ammons is the epistemological kin to Stevens who said that without fiction there is nothing.

Ammons' thinking leads him to refute Williams' famous dictum: "No ideas but in things." The interpreting mind relentlessly reforms the world; and that reformation becomes its own reality, the very thing the mind responds to. Ammons therefore reverses Williams' dictum and announces: "no things but in ideas." Indeed, he says, "no ideas but in ideas" would make equal sense. As for what the modern German philosopher Martin Heidegger called the *Ding in Sich* (the thing in itself)—yes, the thing in itself is out there, but it is not known for what it is; so there are, too, says Ammons, "no things but in things." But that is a proposition people will never know experientially.

The world in Ammons' poetry is a congeries of disparate particulars, of the infinite many, of multifarious uniquenesses. The poet's mission is imaginatively to cohere the world, to draw likenesses, to move, a godly traveler, toward the One. The things of the natural world are poems, and "the greatest poetry," says Ammons, is the sea with its waves, incoming and outgoing tides. The sea, like poetry, shapes itself by tides and currents and causes tensions at peripheries. And the reader, we could suppose, is a skiff.

In Ammons' view, poems are "verbal symbols" for biological and botanical forms—for the worm with its "coordinated construction" and "sequential arrangement," for plants with their "molecular components" and "structured cells." There is no telling where Ammons metaphorizing impulses might go, though at least we know they will almost always go to something in the natural world. At the conclusion of "Essay on Poetics" Ammons likens the risks and possibilities he ventures in composing a poem to the variable conditions—winds, floods, tidal currents, and temperature changes—in an estuary. Clearly, Ammons in his poetics regards making poetry as a preconscious and vitalistic process. His poetics, in other words, privileges his Romantic self while using his philosopher self to explain his Romantic self. Romantic Poet/Scientific Philosopher: this is the basic psychic split in Ammons poetry.

Since at least the time of Samuel Taylor Coleridge, poets who propound a poetics may think they are describing their poetry when, in fact, they usually are describing what they imagine their poetry is. T. S. Eliot, for example, advanced in his poetics a poetry detached from the emotions and subjectivities of the poet's personality. Eliot's actual poems, however, hardly correspond to what he recommends poetry should be. So too with Ammons' poetics, which describes more of a poetry imagined than the poetry Ammons actually delivers, which contains bardic rapture melded with strong intellection.

TAPE, SPHERE, SNOW

In November 1963 Ammons went to the House & Garden Store, bought a roll of adding machine tape, stuck one end in his typewriter, and composed "a long thin poem." *Tape for the Turn of the Year* (1965) is an interestingly odd daybook that runs from December 6, 1963, to January 9, 1965. It is witty, imaginative, and banal: a poem of "The man with bills to pay / [who] dreams with a Muse!" Ammons' perspective in this book is reflexive and therefore quite modernist, for he

takes as his subject the poem itself, continually commenting on what it is and how it is going. Consequently, *Tape* is somewhat airless.

To give Ammons his due, however, his avowed purpose is to avoid the high tones and themes of Romanticism. Indeed, he rejects a premise that undergirds much of his poetry before and after *Tape:* "the doctrine of correspondences." Early in the poem we have this annunciatory complaint:

> this is that & that is this
> & on and on: why can't
> every thing be just itself?
> what's the use of the
> vast mental burden
> of correspondence? doesn't
> contribute to the things
> resembled:
>
> except in the mind:

These lines reject not only the Romantic perspective but religion too, the root meaning of which is "to bind together." The drive of religious visionaries like Swedenborg and Emerson to harmonize the world, to make connections, and to create overarching meanings devalues the integrity of the particular. *Tape* contends that the mind's need for order is egocentric. Order is the result of myopia and exists only in the mind, which denies the disparities of reality. Organization, scheme, system, thesis—all cognitive models—should be avoided.

Typically in Ammons' long poems, this contention conflicts with an equally strong Romantic impulse, but in *Tape* Romanticism is trounced. No Coleridgean enchantment here, "no moonlight to loosen / shrubs into shapes that / never were:" No lending mystery to the familiar, only the familiar laid out flat: "lunch: / hot dogs and baked / beans again: swell:" The Muse Ammons recurringly addresses keeps her distance from this "poem." The result is an original book, but originality—that iconic value of Modernism—does not suffice to keep the reader engaged in *Tape*. Ammons declares that he hopes to achieve "clarity & simplicity!" and avoid "density" and the "talk of a posing man who / must talk / but who has nothing to / say." Ammons does avoid density and the talk of a posing man, but too often in *Tape for the Turn of the Year* he has nothing to say.

Sphere: The Form of a Motion (1974) is a book-length meditative poem of 155 sections, each with four long tercets. With characteristic wit and inventive imagery, Ammons explores the dualities that have become his ingrained themes—the tension between the one and the many, the universal and the particular, unity and diversity, and center and circumference. The immediate inspiration for *Sphere* is Ammons' vision of the earth in space, spinning, orbiting, maintaining its lands and waters in sublime equilibrium. The miraculous planet Earth, surrounded by black space, is solitary and magnificent—like the self. Ammons' tone is often prayerful. He is beholden to his Maker. For people to save themselves they must ". . . come to know / the works of the Most High . . ." Like *Essay on Man* (1733–1734), Alexander Pope's philosophic meditation in heroic couplets on the human's place in the universe, the purpose of *Sphere* is to justify the ways of God to man. Both poets affirm that blessedness and harmony lie in the recognition that people are finite, and if they "bend to cherish the greatness that rolls through / our sharp days," they will know "joy's surviving radiance." Transnational, Ammons goes beyond Whitman's epic embrace of America while retaining the great transcendentalist's loving spirit. With exhilarant sweep *Sphere* carries the reader from the western shore of Africa to Walvis Bay, Cape Palmas, Brest, Siberia, the Bering Strait, North America, the South Atlantic, Upper Volta, and Oran. The reader also travels outward from the atmosphere into the expanding universe and moves among blossoming nebulae.

Sphere keeps shifting from cosmic magnificence to the small and marvelously fictionalized; Ammons' readers can always expect in his poetry this strophe and antistrophe. He finds an inexplicable misprint in a newspaper—"repodepo"—and defines it for himself to make a new reality that will satisfy his hungry imagination: "let / [the word] stand for a made nothing, a pointer with no point: or / for anything about which the meaning is insecure:" Unlike Pope's formidable poem and Eliot's *Four Quartets, Sphere* has little philosophic coherence and structurally no compelling design. Yet it is a richly conceived work and genuinely spiritual. Also, for sheer play of mind, here—and throughout his oeuvre—Ammons has no equal among American poets living or dead.

The big aesthetic departure in Ammons' career is *The Snow Poems,* published in 1977. After the critical praise accorded *Collected Poems,* Ammons became such a prominent presence on the literary landscape that he could afford to produce a book of radical poetry five years later.

The Snow Poems is Ammons' only book of new poems that is not slim. The volume is 292 pages and contains 121 poems. Its reception was mixed. The negative critics were disdainful; the positive critics were merely warm. Seldom has a major contemporary American poet had to face such a strong front of critical attack. *The Snow Poems* were deemed undisciplined, garrulous, boringly confessional, tired, and diffuse.

The critical disdain was not so much a measure of the book's weakness as it was a demonstration of what can happen in the literary critical community when it applies criteria to a work which the work was never conceived to satisfy. *The Snow Poems* is anti-poetry in the same sense as Williams declared his poetry to be sixty years before—except more so. Ammons has engorged the antiformalist, antiliterary credo of High Modernism—the legacy, that is, of Pound, Eliot, and Williams—and presented poetry that is not only antipoetic in subject and theme but notational and seemingly unwrought in form. Of course, *The Snow Poems* did not appear to be new and full-fledged in 1977; poems like them had appeared in *Collected Poems,* but they are only preliminary in comparison.

Although Ammons says *The Snow Poems* can be read as one long poem, each is a set piece, a mode of being given articulation. Being that, like the reader's at any particular moment, may be intelligently aware or uninspiringly attentive to the mundane or intellectually overcurious or absorbed in puerility. What most people would call a poem, Ammons in *The Snow Poems* would say is a wrought, premeditated thing: a calcification. "Beauty," Williams said, "at its best seems truth incompletely realized."

The actual setting of *The Snow Poems* is late September 1975 to May 1976: a period of snow, threat of snow, rain, sleet, gray skies, intermittent sun, and more snow. In short: Ithaca, New York. Ammons is in his fiftieth year, a bourgeoise householder, husband, father, professor, intellectual woolgatherer, and watcher of inner and outer weather. *The Snow Poems,* then, is an extravagant eight-month daybook, the daybook that *Tape for the Turn of the Year,* thin in imagination, is not. Regarded this way, *The Snow Poems* can be appreciated on its own merits. "Ivy Winding," though not the book's first poem, should be because it describes, better than any critic has, what the book is.

imagine, a list, a
puzzler, sleeper, a tiresome business,
conglomeration, aggregation, etc.
nobody can make any sense of:
            a long poem, shindig,
fracas, uproar,
high shimmy uncompletable, hence like
paradise, hellish paradise,
not the one paradise where the points
& fringes of
perception sway in and out at once
in the free interlockings of
permanence:

"[F]ine-fannied friends!" is Ammons' inclusive phrase for people at Cornell, reviewers, and critics: these are the Arbiters of Taste every artist has had to deal with since art was first called "art." Ammons rebuts "art" with provisionary structures. Instead of the studied, adagio quality expected from poetry, the reader gets the poet, seemingly without preconception, waywardly taking in the world with such a variety of moods that *Sphere,* for all its richess of imagery, appears almost monochromatic. The image of winding ivy relates to academe, for centuries a bastion of formalist aesthetics. Ammons poses academe's own emblem against it: ivy is organic, its form is its growth, its growth is winding and sprawling.

The principal structural innovation Ammons produces in *The Snow Poems* is a diptych effect. A poem runs alongside his main poem to form a commentary on it or to supplement it.

. . . . imagine!
writing something that never forms a
complete thought, drags you
after it, spills you down, no barrier
describing you or dock lifting you up:
imagine writing something the CIA would
not read through,
the FBI not record or report,
a mishmash for the fun-loving,
one's fine-fannied friends!

if you caught a
duck-glimpse
as a first seeing
of the thin-tapering
hemlocks (a row   ringneck &
of raving beauties)   redwing
you'd think they'd   (redneck &
waggled and whipped,   ringwing)
worn off in the
wind that way

Ammons is showing that thoughts and things vie; meanings tie into each other and then disunite as birds fly out of a tree. Vertical letters border some poems; or a fragmentary poem, at first merely accompanying the main poem, will gain in amplitude and meaning or sometimes recede. When a poem is made, Ammons suggests, another poem is also produced which may be a revision, afterthought, or gloss—anything leftover. Whatever it is, he will get it on the page too. There is the poem and the poem's ghost. Ammons presents poetry as ready-made deconstruction. As much as they are poems, *The Snow Poems* are the making of poems. Years after their publication, they remain new and fascinating.

MASTER OF THE LYRIC

After the critically controversial *Snow Poems,* Ammons produced in the next ten years four volumes of poetry that arguably established him as the foremost practitioner of the antiformalist lyric among American poets of his generation: *A Coast of Trees* (1981), *Worldly Hopes* (1982), *Lake Effect Country* (1983), and *Sumerian Vistas* (1987).

The most accomplished poem in *A Coast of Trees* is the meditative lyric "Easter Morning," which is autobiographical and elegiac. The poet has returned to his ancestral homeland and visited his family graveyard, the hallowed ground of his brother, who died in early childhood, his mother, father, aunts, and uncles. He internalizes their burials. They are all "close, / close as burrowing / under skin." The dead brother is forever with the poet, and so a part of the poet will always be incomplete, scotched, a stump, in fact the very stump he stands on: his brother's grave that "will not heal." "Easter Morning" is about incompletion: the incompletion of a life that ended early and of life—the reader's and the poet's—that, because of early losses, can never truly know com-

pletion. The last third of this 105-line poem describes the flight of "two great birds, / maybe eagles . . ." They break from their pattern, seeking (as do poets) new patterns, and then return to their pattern. People break from the whole; and that breaking is life, a "dance sacred" and "fresh as the particular / flood of breaking across us now / from the sun." Life returns, as does the flight of the two great birds, to its original pattern, Ammons' symbol for the equilibrium of the universe. "Easter Morning" is Ammons' intimations of immortality prompted by recollections of early childhood.

"The Role of Society in the Artist" from *Worldly Hopes* is as penetrating a poem as any written in English—whether by William Butler Yeats, Eliot, or Stevens—on the problematic artist/public relationship. Because society does not understand the artist, it sends him an "invitation to go to / hell." Such rejection encourages the artist to care even less for societal approval and to forge an art even more original than before. Consequently, he creates art of greater fire and more radiance. Society likes this "bedazzlement," judges the art worthy, and, deeming itself perceptive and generous, bestows prizes. The artist, thankful for the appreciation, retreats again into the privacy of his fire-spewing, this time "blazon[ing] tree trunks" and setting "stumps afire . . ." Society warms itself with his flames and says it likes his "unconventional / verse best." Now the artist says, "& I invited society to go to hell." But surely, the reader must conclude, only in the privacy of his own mind. In public the artist's acceptance of society's gifts enables him to keep society at bay and to ply his trade, its subversion unacknowledged.

"Singing & Doubling Together" in *Lake Effect Country,* perhaps Ammons' greatest love poem, is addressed to a "you" which can be understood as nature or woman. The poet begins, "My nature in me is your nature singing." What nature or woman undergoes—her light and dark, her vitality and loss—the poet undergoes too. He shares with her "plunders down into the darkness" and tender risings. The theme of Ammons' poem recalls the spiritual sympathy Wordsworth felt for his beloved sister Dorothy and for wild nature—the realm in which she, even more than Wordsworth, found a true home. "Singing & Doubling Together" ends in dissolution, the poet becoming the song of the one he loves and therefore never again needing to sing himself.

In "The Hubbub" in *Sumerian Vistas,* Ammons takes the pagan concern with the conflict between sublunary life and the higher gods and opts for sublunary life: ". . . the lesser gods, local / imbalanced into activity" are clearer examples of how people should behave than people who sit immobilized in mystical apprehension of the One. The superior gods—Zeus, Jehovah—"can worsen / one" in the sense that when people transcend the world and obtain divine serenity, they exclude "empty stances, / paradisal with indolence," which "sweeten / to a sweetness savorless on high." Here Ammons, the Yankee transcendentalist—like Thoreau and Frost—implies that belief in heaven necessarily second-rates mortality and makes of human living merely a dress rehearsal for the life that supposedly really counts: eternal life with God in heaven. In "Birches" Frost said, ". . . Earth's the right place for love: / I don't know where it's likely to go better." Certainly not in bodiless heaven. Ammons brings us to the paradox that is transcendentalism: spirit is physical and heaven is on earth. The very style of "The Hubbub"—Ammons' typical colloquializing of the metaphysical—affirms his theme.

GARBAGE AND GLARE

Like *A Tape for the Turn of the Year, Garbage* (1993) and *Glare* (1997) are book-length medi- tative poems typed on a strip of continuous paper. Both poems are written in two line units that are, like all Ammons' meditative poems, heavily enjambed. In *Garbage* Ammons carries the modernist doctrine of the anti-poetic to its absurd conclusion, for the book's inspiration is a garbage dump off I-95 in Florida. Ammons dedicates his ruminative rummage to the great artists, animal and human: *to the bacteria, tumblebugs, scavengers, / wordsmiths—the transfigurers, restorers.* Actually, a titanic garbage dump quite appropriately suits what has always been thematically characteristic of Ammons' vision: the multifarious many that constitute the One. A dump is the exemplum of nature itself. Everything—from microscopic to macroscopic—is in the process of change. Yes, Ammons implies, change to the mundane mind, but transformation to the poetic mind—indeed transfiguration to the religious mind, the transfiguration that follows sin. For the dump is also a symbol of fallen man, his perishability and the disintegration of whatever passes through his hands. The world we make is "false matter" whose destiny is oblivion. Fallen man, as Buddha and Augustine aver, is always burning; the dump is an image of hell. But on another level its "eternal flame" is a "principle of the universe." The very stuff of the creating cosmos itself— "faraway / galactic slurs even, luminescences, plasmas"—burn in the same way as the dump. Mounds of decay, hell, Armageddon, the cosmos—the dump is at once foul, terrifying, apocalyptic, eternal.

Taking another tack, Ammons contends that humans have so polluted the environment that the earth itself is fast becoming garbage. Trash the size of mountains, leachments forming creeks, "meadows with oilslick": poetry has stopped none of it. However, when this world is choked to death by waste, all humans will have left is their language, their metaphorizing ability to make for themselves a new world.

we'll get off: we'll take it with us: our
equations will make any world we wish
   anywhere

we go: we'll take nothing away from here but
the equations, cool, lofty, eternal, that were

nowhere here to be found when we came: we are
a quite special species, as it were: . . .

The conclusion of *Garbage* is sacramental. After all, says the poet, garbage, in the long view,
is disintegrative and therefore "the cleansing of
decay." Everything is in the process of destruction on its way to a new form. A monument to
that proposition is the dump off I-95 in Florida,
its "digestive fire" a ritualistic radiance and its
smoke incense. Garbage, like all things decom-
posing so they may become something beyond
themselves, is holy.

Glare delivers everything Ammons' readers
have now come to expect from his book-length
poems: an ever-shifting, ever-probing perspective; philosophical wit; marvelously inventive
imagery; and diaristic descriptions of a conventional American life. A valedictory mood, however, prevails. A book of wisdom and humility,
of speculation on the fragility and finitude of human life and "the downward / slide of everything
toward entropy . . . ," *Glare* is a wry symphony
on the end of unnoticed things: for example, the
collapse of a dust cloud, "smegma flakes . . . off
the chilled penis," the cessation of birds' assertive
dawn song. At seventy-one Ammons candidly
discloses what happens to a man in old age, his
body and spirit wavering, edging toward peril.
Ammons' tone is mellow, accepting, his wit leisurely; he is less self-protective now; the reader
experiences more of him. And his mind is as ex-
ploratory as ever. In fact, *Glare,* compared to
Sphere, a book he wrote at age forty-seven and
celebrated for its breadth of vision, is even more
"scopy."

AN APPRAISAL:
THE POETRY OF NATURAL DESIGN

Ammons tries to make his poems idealities, "moments," he says in his article "Surfaces" for
American Poetry Review, "of such consonance
between the body, the will, the wish, the intellect
that we lose consciousness of any elements of
disharmony and feel that our own expressiveness
is inseparable from all expressiveness" (July/Au-
gust 1974). Ammons here accords his poetry a
Dionysiac ideal that no poetry can attain. His
greatest poems, however, approximate this ideal.
Each is like a natural force melded of sublime
imagination, scientism, and penetrating play of
mind. Ammons' long meditative poems sacrifice
direction and shape for range and depth; also they
are rhythmless. But his meditative lyrics, what
Ammons calls his walking poems (especially
those in *Ommateum, Expressions of Sea Level,* and
Corsons Inlet), constitute a unique poetic structure
that captures life in its vitalistic immediacy. In his
address, "A Poem Is a Walk," delivered to the International Poetry Forum in Pittsburgh (April
1967), Ammons describes with illuminating ac-
curacy the motion of his meditative lyrics: "The
motion may be lumbering, clipped, wavering, trip-
ping, mechanical, dance-like, awkward, stagger-
ing, slow, etc. But the motion occurs only in the
body of the walker or in the body of the words."
Ammons describes here a poem that is variously
kinetic, yes, but also a poem that reifies the environment it depicts. "There is only one way to
know [the poem]," says Ammons in his address,
"and that is to enter into it." The meaning of the
poem cannot really be determined; rather, A. R.
Ammons creates a poetry of living context.

Note: From "A Life From South to North" in this
essay, unattributed quotations are from my phone
interview with A. R. Ammons on February 22,
2000.

Selected Bibliography

WORKS OF A. R. AMMONS

POETRY

Ommateum, with Doxology. Philadelphia: Dorrance, 1955.

Expressions of Sea Level. Columbus: Ohio State University Press, 1963.

Corsons Inlet. Ithaca, N.Y.: Cornell University Press, 1965.

Tape for the Turn of the Year. Ithaca, N.Y.: Cornell University Press, 1965.

Northfield Poems. Ithaca, N.Y.: Cornell University Press, 1966.

Selected Poems. Ithaca, N.Y.: Cornell University Press, 1968.

Uplands. New York: Norton, 1970.

Briefings: Poems Small and Easy. New York: Norton, 1971.

Collected Poems: 1951–1971. New York: Norton, 1972.

Sphere: The Form of a Motion. New York: Norton, 1974.

Diversifications. New York: Norton, 1975.

The Snow Poems. New York: Norton, 1977.

Highgate Road. Ithaca, N.Y.: Inkling Press, 1977.

The Selected Poems: 1951–1977. New York: Norton, 1977.

Selected Longer Poems. New York: Norton, 1980.

A Coast of Trees. New York: Norton, 1981.

Worldly Hopes. New York: Norton, 1982.

Lake Effect Country. New York: Norton, 1983.

The Selected Poems: Expanded Edition. New York: Norton, 1986.

Sumerian Vistas. New York: Norton, 1987.

The Really Short Poems. New York: Norton, 1991.

Garbage. New York: Norton, 1993.

The North Carolina Poems. Rocky Mount: North Carolina Wesleyan College Press, 1994.

Brink Road. New York: Norton, 1996.

Glare. New York: Norton, 1997.

PROSE

Set in Motion: Essays, Interviews, and Dialogues. Edited by Zofia Burr. Ann Arbor, Mich.: University of Michigan Press, 1996.

"Surfaces." *American Poetry Review.* 3:53 (July/August 1974).

BIBLIOGRAPY

Wright, Stuart. *A. R. Ammons: A Bibliography, 1954–1979.* Winston-Salem, N.C.: Wake Forest University, 1980.

CRITICAL STUDIES

Bloom, Harold, ed. *The Ringers in the Tower: Studies in Romantic Tradition.* Chicago: University of Chicago Press, 1971.

———. *Figures of Capable Imagination.* New York: Seabury Press, 1976.

———. *A. R. Ammons.* New York: Chelsea, 1986.

Buell, Frederick. " 'To Be Quiet in the Hands of the Marvelous': The Poetry of A. R. Ammons." *Iowa Review* 8:67–85 (1977).

Bullis, Jerald. "In the Open: A. R. Ammons' Longer Poems." *Pembroke Magazine* 18:25–53 (1986).

Elder, John. *Imagining the Earth: Poetry and the Vision of Nature.* Chicago: University of Illinois Press, 1985.

Fink, Thomas. "The Problem of Freedom and Restriction in the Poetry of A. R. Ammons." *Modern Poetry Studies* 1–2:138–48 (1982).

Fishman, Charles. "A. R. Ammons: The One Place to Dwell." *The Hollins Critic* 19:2–11 (December 1982).

Gilbert, Roger. *Walks in the World: Representation and Experience in Modern American Poetry.* Princeton, N.J.: Princeton University Press, 1991.

Hans, James. *The Value(s) of Literature.* Albany, N.Y.: State University of New York Press, 1990.

Holder, Alan. *A. R. Ammons.* Boston, Twayne, 1978.

Kirschten, Robert, ed. *Critical Essays on A. R. Ammons.* New York: G. K. Hall, 1997.

Kober, Nancy. "Ammons: Poetry Is a Matter of Survival." *Cornell Daily Sun* 27:12–13 (March 1973).

Miles, Josephine. "Light, Wind, Motion." *Diacritics* 3:21–24 (Winter 1973).

Morgan, Robert. *Good Measure: Essays, Interview, Notes on Poetry.* Baton Rouge, La.: Louisiana State University Press, 1993.

Parker, Patricia A. "Configurations of Shape and Flow." *Diacritics* 3:25–33 (Winter 1973).

Schneider, Stephen P. *A. R. Ammons and the Poetry of Widening Scope.* Rutherford, N.J.: Fairleigh Dickinson University Press, 1994.

———, ed. *Complexities of Motion: New Essays on A. R. Ammons's Long Poems.* Rutherford, N.J.: Fairleigh Dickinson University Press, 1999.

Scigaj, Leonard M. *Sustainable Poetry: Four American Ecopoets.* Lexington: University Press of Kentucky, 1999.

Special Issue: The Work of A. R. Ammons. *Pembroke Magazine* 18:9–236 (1986).

Wolf, Thomas J. "A R. Ammons and William Carlos Williams: A Study in Style and Meaning." *Contemporary Poetry* 3:1–16 (1977).

—PHILIP BUFITHIS

Richard Bausch

1945—

RICHARD CARL BAUSCH was born in Fort Benning, Georgia, on April 18, 1945, to Robert Carl and Helen Simmons Bausch. He has a twin, Robert Bausch, who is also a novelist, an extraordinary circumstance. The Bausch family moved to Washington, D.C., when the brothers were three. Richard Baush has lived most of his life in Washington or in communities close to it: the family moved to Silver Spring, Maryland, in 1950, to Wheaton, Maryland, in 1954, and finally to Vienna, Virginia, in 1963. There were interruptions for service in the air force and graduate school at the University of Iowa, but he received his bachelor of arts from George Mason University, which considers itself part of Washington, in 1974 and has been a professor there since 1980. Bausch came of age during the Kennedy Administration, and he is haunted by the idealism of John F. Kennedy's presidency and by the sordid realities of it which became known later. Although he belongs to the Fellowship of Southern Writers and much of his work is set in the imaginary northern Virginia town of Point Royal, Virginia, proximity to Washington is a bigger factor than the South in his writing.

Bausch is not a southern writer in any strict regional sense. Reynolds Price said in a radio interview once that southerners are obsessed with place, race, and family. In an e-mail he sent me, Bausch by coincidence discussed his attitudes toward all three of those subjects, expressing scorn for "the cutsey southern writer, some of the young folks whose habit seems to be to pile on the quirks and the cornpone and the biscuits and gravy and the daddy drunk and have at it." He is not particularly interested in place because, he says "my terrain is interior, the landscapes are psychological, and the subject is shades of emotion as they give forth character and the nature of humans in terms of struggle. . . ." He points out that he uses landscape, as writers often do, to indicate states of mind. He also says he avoids race, "mostly because I hate the subject." He regards racism as "a disease, which is presently reaching plague proportions in the world." He goes on to observe wryly, "And having said this, I have of course begun to write about it lately." He says that "a wonderful professor" told him once that his interest in family made him a southerner, but nowhere do his characters show a genealogical obsession or trace their ancestry back to antebellum times. The reader of William Faulkner requires ancestral charts to keep relationships clear, but nothing like this is needed for Bausch. Indeed, antebellum times, the Civil War, and Reconstruction are not subjects of his work. Bausch feels great pride in being elected to the Fellowship of Southern Writers, but because he is honored to be in the company of writers like Shelby Foote, George Garrett (a close friend), Eudora

Welty, Elizabeth Spencer, and others. "Why, that is a list of the best writers in America."

Bausch observed in the same e-mail that he is often compared to Flannery O'Connor, usually to his disadvantage, and says he did read her once when he was twenty. But his real models, he says, are Anton Chekhov, Leo Tolstoy, Charles Dickens, and Shakespeare. He reads them repeatedly, and also Guy de Maupassant "for his meanness; and is he mean. He provides a balance." Chekhov's sense of the sadness in life and his ability to write short stories without plot contrivances have certainly influenced Bausch's stories, which generally convey their effects with restraint.

THE CHARMS OF AUTOBIOGRAPHY

Bausch wrote a long but reluctant account of his life for the *Contemporary Authors Autobiography* series (1991). His brother Robert has a substantial essay in the same volume and between the two a reader learns a great deal about the Bausch family. Richard Bausch's essay is a document remarkable for its distrust of autobiography. He declares that he reads biographies but not autobiographies: indeed, he says he has never been able to finish one. How can anyone claim to know what his first memory is, he asks, and he recounts one of his earliest in order to point out how inaccurate it turned out to be when he checked the facts later. Bausch does not provide the tales of family dysfunction and trauma that the recent participants in the "memoir boom" have dwelt on. He portrays his large family (there were six children, all with red hair) as close, sincerely Catholic but not fanatical, with a mother whose excellence as an amateur artist gave him an example of creativity. Family life is one of his basic themes, and the fictional families are usually unhappy. In "Truth and Trouble: A Conversation with Richard Bausch," an internet interview in *Atlantic Unbound,* Leslie Cauldwell asked Bausch about the

apparent inconsistency of his concern with suffering and violence in spite of his happy childhood and marriage. Bausch replies very reasonably that novels are about war, "interior or exterior, psychological or physical." He rejects "the fairly recent idea that fiction writers are always trying to exorcise inner ghosts by writing."

Twinship is an important biographical factor for Richard and Robert Bausch. In a lengthy profile for *The Washington Post,* "Twin Visions, Twin Lives," published in 1982, Curt Suplee recorded their strong admiration for each other's work and mentioned that occasionally they find that their imagery coincides. They resisted being classified as replicas of one another in a childhood that both declare was very happy. Richard wanted to become a priest, while Robert was always interested in politics. Richard's ambition to become a priest was thwarted by his poor marks in Wheaton High School. *The Washington Post* revisited Richard Bausch in a 1998 article on "Nature and Nurture; When It Comes to Twins, Sometimes It's Hard to Tell the Two Apart." On that occasion, he suggested that they have important differences and "have been profiled too often to really enjoy being a novelty act anymore." He also suggested that he was the more religious of the two and that Robert was more intellectual.

For all his distrust of autobiography, Bausch's 1991 essay provides ample detail for an outline of his life until that time. He and Robert entered the air force in 1965 under the buddy system. They became survival school instructors, preparing airmen for duty in Vietnam. Most of their time in the air force was spent at the Chanute Base in Illinois, where Richard met another serviceman, David Marmorstein, a guitarist and singer. They formed a group called The City Sounds. After Marmorstein went to Vietnam, Bausch became road manager for a band called The Luv'd Ones and had a brief romance with the lead singer/guitarist. He toured with the band on periods of leave from the air force, spending his time playing "the young depressed poet" and "reading William Carlos Williams' *Paterson* and Ernest Hemingway's *For Whom the Bell Tolls* at the same time." He used this period as background for Gordon Brinhart, the insurance salesman in *Take Me Back: A Novel* (1981). Bausch has also worked as a standup comedian and in an interview with Elizabeth Kastor, "The Author, Giving Rise to 'Violence,' " he mentions that his odd jobs have included driving a cab and writing and acting in "historical dramas produced by the National Parks Service."

Bausch married Karen Miller, a photographer, in 1969, and they have five children. After graduating from George Mason University in 1974, he attended the celebrated Writers' Workshop at the University of Iowa and received a master of fine arts in 1975. His classmates included Jane Smiley and Mark Jarman, and he studied with Vance Bourjaily and John Irving. Following graduate school, he began teaching English at George Mason University, where he is now a Heritage Professor. He knows an extraordinary number of American authors, and lists so many in the autobiography that the influence hunter would be discouraged rather than helped. George Garrett has a special position as a very close friend and mentor. Perhaps his clearest influence is F. Scott Fitzgerald. Bausch rereads *The Great Gatsby* every year. He shares a clear and precise style with Fitzgerald, but perhaps the most important similarity is the elegiac feeling about America that Bausch expresses in *Rebel Powers* (1993), and *Good Evening Mr. & Mrs. America, and All the Ships at Sea* (1996).

Bausch's autobiographical essay has much more information about when novels were written and the circumstances of their publication—career matters—than about his views of writing, but there are some important details. He is clearly an intuitive rather than theoretical writer: he says "you have to go with your subconscious." He

likes using terms such as "felt life" and "lived experience" to describe his fiction. In an entry for a 1981 volume of *Contemporary Authors*, Bausch says, "My vital subjects are family, fear, love, and anything that is irrecoverable and *missed;* but I'll dispense with all of that for a good story." Later in the same article, he states, "I have no literary creed and belong to no literary school; my only criterion is that fiction make feeling, that it deepen feeling," and he speaks slightingly of "elaborate crossword puzzles posing as fiction." He is essentially a realist in an age increasingly permeated with literary theory: he is not a generator of texts but a writer of stories. He is sometimes linked to the so-called "Dirty Realists" among his contemporaries, who include Raymond Carver, Jayne Anne Phillips, Ann Beattie, and Richard Ford, who often deal with life among the working poor. Like them, he has a fine sense of the American vernacular, which he employs in terse dialogue. His style is not "grungy," the term applied to the Dirty Realists, and he writes about the middle class more often than the working class.

At the end of his autobiographical essay, Bausch admits that it is basically a long "chronology of publications and arrivals of children, jobs, and friends," and he says that "the charms of autobiography elude me." But in 1999, he overcame some of his reservations about autobiography and contributed a powerful essay, "So Long Ago," to Charles Baxter's collection, *The Business of Memory: The Art of Remembering in an Age of Forgetting*. The essay ends with a pair of childhood scenes as compelling as anything in his fiction. Both incidents took place during the funeral of Bausch's great-grandmother. He experienced two moments of intense perception, one of a blue mark on the face of the corpse, the other of the mortician pushing his great-grandmother's head down into the coffin before shutting it. These memories, he says, are present and vivid. He suggests that such imagery seems to "drift toward the surface when I dream, or day-dream or write." Remembered life offers raw material to shape into the invented structures of fiction. He uses images he has experienced but does not describe his own life. Bausch's essay is a way of formulating his understanding of the almost instinctive basis of his work.

Bausch's work has won prizes and recognition. He was twice a finalist for the PEN/Faulkner Award, was a Guggenheim Fellow in 1984, and won the Lila Wallace–Reader's Digest Award (1992) and the Award in Literature from the American Academy of Arts and Letters (1993). His short stories have been included in *Prize Stories: The O. Henry Awards, The Best American Short Stories,* and *The Pushcart Prize Stories,* and he won the National Magazine Award for Fiction twice. A selection of his short fiction has been published in England as *Aren't You Happy for Me?* (1995) and The Modern Library has published *The Selected Stories of Richard Bausch.* In 1991, at the end of his autobiographical essay for *Contemporary Authors,* he suggested that his ambition at the start of his career was to write twenty books. Not counting the two retrospective volumes of stories, by the end of the twentieth century he had published twelve books.

THE EARLY WORK: PEOPLE TRYING TO GET USED TO THEIR PAIN

Bausch's first novel, *Real Presence: A Novel,* published in 1980, is a remarkably mature work. It was highly successful, gaining two particularly important signs of success for the period: it was a Book-of-the-Month Club Alternate Selection and it received a favorable review in *Time* magazine. This was not the traditional autobiographical first novel: Bausch chose as his protagonist an aging Catholic priest. Monsignor Vincent Shepherd, an ailing man who wants to withdraw from the world, takes a church in Demera, Vir-ginia, three hours away from his childhood home in Point Royal. Demera, like Point Royal, is an invented town, close to the North Carolina border. Father Shepherd has become a rather poor shepherd to his flock, but he is forced out of his detachment when a homeless family moves into the social hall of the church.

The family, which consists of Duck Bexley, his pregnant wife Elizabeth, and their five children, reminded more than one reviewer of Flannery O'Connor's characters, and the comparison seems in this case to be fair. Certainly the situation has some similarities to O'Connor's story "The Displaced Person," in which an elderly priest takes in an impoverished family from Poland. And a reader of southern fiction might be reminded as well of Abner Snopes and his family in "Barn Burning." Indeed, Duck Bexley's arrogance and bad temper, along with an act of arson before his coming to Demera, all give him a kinship with Abner Snopes. But Bausch does not traffic in southern "poor white trash" clichés. The novel brings Father Shepherd (and the reader) into an awareness of the humanity of the Bexleys. If they are rootless, it is because their roots have been cut by poverty and exclusion. Duck Bexley's anger comes from despair, and his moral collapse comes after the death of his father destabilizes his world. He also suffers from ambivalence about his war record, being aware that shooting North Korean soldiers in a ditch is not unequivocally heroic, and he has a serious physical ailment, lupus. Bexley, frantic for money, kills an old woman while attempting to rob her, but the death is not deliberate: he does not understand that his threats and rough treatment have been fatal. Even the Bexley children, who appear to be a crowd of little savages, are gradually individualized, and the mute child, Harvey, who takes and hides the priest's heirloom chalice, becomes an agent of the priest's redemption. Monsignor Shepherd feels love for the child, and the cup—which in the Mass would hold the blood of Christ—becomes insignificant, a physical object that the priest decides to give to the child. The novel has more Catholic atmosphere than any work by Bausch. Although many of his later characters are Catholics, the religion is part of their background rather than a subject of the work.

In "Body of Christ," a review of the *Real Presence* in *Time,* Mayo Mohs observes that the novel shows that redemption is to be found "in the world beyond the sanctuary, where the Real Presence must be sought among the lowliest of people and the darkest of hearts." The death of Duck Bexley, who provokes a policeman into shooting him, and the birth of his son in midwinter, are events with Christian overtones. But the power of the novel does not lie in its rather obvious symbolism, which includes the chalice and a series of bird images. Bausch's insight into character and his ability to shape a narrative are his strengths. He is not a daring stylist, but he has an eye for revealing detail. The novel shows that he has mastered such devices of modern fiction as multiple points of view, which is one of his favorite techniques. He also shifts into present tense narrative to give a sense of drama. More traditional is his use of dreams in the novel, a device found throughout his career as a means of revealing character and creating anticipation.

Bausch's second novel, *Take Me Back,* which was nominated for a PEN/Faulkner Award, is another exploration of ordinary lives. With it, he became an important novelist, not merely a good one, and he showed his ability to probe at the irredeemable losses in American life in a deeply moving way. The losses include any sense of history or nature. The novel is set in Point Royal and has three particular locales: an apartment complex, a trailer court adjoining it, and a shopping mall. The neon lights of the mall are visible in distorted form through the trees near the apartment complex where the chief characters, the Brinhart family, live. Their apartment is in the wing of the Winston Gardens complex nearest to the adjacent trailer court, and they pay lower rent because of the proximity to "an aggregate of railroad cars with a wild growth of TV antennas growing out of the metal." When *Take Me Back* first appeared, the term "trailer trash" (a national equivalent of the southern "poor white trash") had not been coined, but the attitudes involved in the term already existed. Bausch does not withhold his sympathy from characters because they live in mobile homes. When Gordon Brinhart attempts to express a kindly attitude toward the comfort of trailers, Red, the one southern good old boy in all of Bausch's fiction, replies, "That's all they are, cowboy, is trailers." Red laments the loss of the old south, noting that the town of Culpeper has become one big shopping mall. He has to switch his pronunciation of "Culpeppuh" to the American standard form, "Culpeper," before Brinhart, a southerner himself, can understand him. Red points out that he used to hunt in the very spot where the trailer park is built. He says of Virginia, "This ain't the South anymore—probably never was," which is a harsh comment on the Old Dominion, with its pride in being the first southern colony.

Gordon is an insurance salesman who once wanted to write poetry. He married a rock guitarist, Katherine, and adopted the child she had by a nihilistic drummer in the band. Bausch draws on his own experience for the background of the Brinharts, the days when he was associated with The Luv'd Ones and enamored of a guitarist. The Brinharts, like so many families in Bausch's stories, are deeply dysfunctional, another term not in general use when the novel was published, though we now seem to find it essential. Brinhart has become an alcoholic; Katherine, who has a history of mental illness, is on the edge of a mental collapse; and her eleven-year-old son, Alex, has no friends and takes refuge in being a baseball fan as a means of escaping his claustrophobic setting. Katherine's malaise seems tied up with her repudiation of her music: she tells a neighbor that she wanted to put away childish things, unconsciously echoing the Bible's I Corinthians 13:11: "When I was a child, I spake as a child, I understood as a child, I thought as a child: but when I became a man, I put away childish things." The next verse says "For now we see through a glass darkly," and Katherine has not cleared her vision. Her marriage was meant to create a normal life, but she has achieved that American specialty defined by Henry David Thoreau in *Walden,* a life of quiet desperation.

The occupants of two trailers force the Brinhart family into crisis and change. Gordon becomes smitten with Shirley, a single mother just short of eighteen who lives in an ambiguous relationship with a much older man, Red. The infatuation progresses eventually into an affair. More important is the arrival of Blanche and Stan and their thirteen-year-old daughter, Amy. Perhaps in the work of another novelist, the parents' very ordinary names and the mother's extraordinary obesity would type them as poor white trash, or anachronistically, trailer trash. Bausch's characters are deeply devoted to their daughter and live in a mobile home for easier access to the National Medical Center in nearby Washington. The possibility that the remission of Amy's leukemia will end hangs over the novel.

Just as Shirley, the sexy single mother, unsettles Gordon, his stepson, Alex, is forced into awareness by Amy, who is sexually precocious, claiming that she has already "done the deed." Her acting-out of sexual behavior (she undresses in front of Alex almost immediately) strains credibility, and her intellectual and emotional precocity are also a little unlikely, though her illness seems to have forced her into looking more deeply into life than Alex—or the adults in the novel.

Trailer parks and cheap apartments suggest transience, and the characters in the novel live precarious lives. The Brinhart marriage barely functions. Stan's bad joke early in the book, turn-

ing the name "Brinhart" into "Burn Heart," is appropriate: the Brinharts do in fact have burned-out hearts.

The character Shirley, whose mental limitations are not clear to Gordon but should be, is an orphan from Iowa, raised by an uncle who failed to tell her where her parents were buried. As if to redress that ignorance symbolically, she tends five nineteenth-century graves which she has discovered on an embankment by the service road behind the shopping mall. In a powerful scene she takes Gordon to see them, and he can simultaneously see the dumpsters behind the mall, which reflect its lights, and the mottled tombstones. One stone commemorates a daughter who died of a fever in 1859, a foreshadowing of Amy's fate. After the visit to the graves, Gordon and Shirley walk by a 7-Eleven store, where they see the "inevitable group of adolescents" in front. Bausch has a fine sense of the quotidian realities of American life, without attempting the exhaustive documentation of them that Don DeLillo uses in *White Noise.*

In *Take Me Back,* Bausch gives his fullest description of Point Royal. He seems to have no desire to create a rich history for it in the way that Faulkner turned his Yoknapatawpha County and Jefferson into a fictional universe. It has little left to distinguish it from other towns with a mall along the highway, and only a few historical buildings remain in the center of town. In a wry touch, Katherine's abortive suicide attempt takes place in the one historical hotel, a run-down place called The Andrew Johnson, after a remarkably unsuccessful and unpopular American president.

The new is represented by the Kmart store in the mall. When Katherine decides to kill herself, she goes to Kmart to buy sleeping pills. The huckster atmosphere of a discount store is superbly created, and Bausch creates a fine comic scene when Katherine becomes so exasperated with the check-cashing procedures that she seizes the microphone used to announce the blue light specials and loudly denounces the store. Later, in her distraught state, she drives along the highway and sees the marks of freeway culture:

> Before her there was a boundless landscape of asphalt lots and stores and motel signs and restaurants; a profusion of clashing color and insane cartoon figures vying for her eye—McDonald's, Burger King, Bob's Big Boy, the Exxon Tiger, the Michelin Tire doll. Everything smiled, everything. Lunatic faces. Faces that seemed to be straining to say there was no death.

In a passage like this one, Bausch has created a contemporary version of the Valley of Ashes in his beloved *The Great Gatsby*.

The cartoon figures may smile, but death is real. Katherine almost dies, and Gordon nearly destroys himself with alcohol. Amy suffers the fatal relapse of her leukemia and the reader is not surprised by this event. Mobile homes are indeed mobile: Blanche and Stan depart, as do Red and Shirley. Alex must cope with his mother's illness and his adoptive father's betrayal of the family. Gordon and Alex have a confrontation and make a kind of peace. The muted ending is typical of Bausch's novels: damaged people attempt to win a measure of peace and healing. This will be the resolution for some of the major characters in Baush's other novels. Such endings are perhaps very natural in an age of therapy and grief counseling. Bausch has inhaled the atmosphere of his era; he has also described his times with compassion and insight. In *Take Me Back,* he presents personal relationships and social change with equal clarity. The comparable achievement in his later work is *Rebel Powers.*

Bausch's third novel, *The Last Good Time* (1984), is set in an unnamed Ohio city that seems to be modeled on Cleveland. The most important characters are two elderly widowers, Edward Cakes, aged seventy-five, a retired symphony violinist, and Arthur Hagood, his eighty-nine-year-old friend who now lives in a nursing home called, ironically, The Homestead. The friendship of the two men is intricately worked out. Arthur has been a sensuous, impulsive man and believes that men achieve intimacy by discussing their sexual experiences. He constantly asks Edward to describe his great moment of passion, the weekend in Vermont in 1928, the moment when he became involved with—was seduced by—Ellen, who would become his wife. Edward, a prudish and compulsively orderly man, is often offended by Arthur's Rabelaisian attitudes. He cherishes memories of Ellen, whose picture (always referred to as The Flapper) is the only striking feature of Cakes' drab apartment. He is willing to talk about her, but within boundaries of propriety. Arthur, on the other hand, is happy to talk about his "last good time," when he was almost seventy and spent a night with a woman named Maxine, who was a little older than himself.

Cakes also has a last good time when a pregnant young woman, Mary Virginia Bellini, comes to look for a despicable man who once lived in the upstairs apartment after Arthur entered the nursing home. She winds up staying with Edward. The situation, a homeless young woman taken in by a benefactor who gives up his bed for her, is hackneyed, but the relative ages of the characters is a real twist. They have a brief affair, and Edward becomes preoccupied with her welfare. The young woman is a chronic liar (like Penny Holt in a later Bausch novel, *Rebel Powers*), and her life is a tangle of drug trafficking and casual prostitution. Her name, Mary Virginia, is clearly ironic, as is Arthur's name, Hagood: he has "had good" and is also "half good," a man who can be both kind and callous. In her review, "Redeemed by Love at 75," Nancy Forbes complains about the name symbolism, finding it contrived. The contrivance is there, and no doubt "Cakes" is meant to be symbolic as well, Edward being a somewhat stale delicacy for Mary Virginia (oral sex is a comic motif running through the novel). The dying kitten that Mary and Edward care for is clearly meant to be symbolic as well. It has little hope of survival and suggests Mary's precarious place in life.

The success of the novel proceeds not from its forced symbolism (the kitten is an unfortunate touch) but from the careful examination of the emotions of the characters. Mary is convincingly unstable and ambivalent toward both her elderly lover and the father of her child. But most admirable is the skill with which Bausch draws Edward and Arthur, creating their friendship in the present and exploring their memories of the past. Edward is forced by his experiences to admit to himself that his idyllic tryst in Vermont was not entirely successful, and he has to relive the loss of his wife and the death of his son, who had turned out very badly before his death in the Korean War. The complications of the marriage are handled with economy and power. Ellen gave up her faltering career as a dancer to marry Edward: like Katherine in *Take Me Back,* she renounced her art and never recovered from the decision.

Bausch's damaged people make compromises to save themselves, but the compromises can create further damage. Arthur's marriage was not bad, but his attempt to transform his life after his wife's death by giving up teaching school in Point Royal and starting a home repair business ended disastrously, and his "last good time" with Maxine was in part an attempt to get money to save his truck from repossession. Bausch does a fine job describing Arthur's complicated relationship with his daughter, who is now an old woman herself. In "The Way Things Are: Richard Bausch's Unadorned World," Paul Elie complains that the story of Edward is put aside in favor of his friend, but Arthur should be seen as a protagonist too. He opens up the novel and his enthusiasm for life balances the claustrophobic timidity of Edward.

Edward is remarkably like Mr. Duffy in James Joyce's great story "A Painful Case." He is not as inhibited as Duffy but he lives a similar life of loneliness and sterile order, eating in the same restaurant again and again, cutting himself off from the kind of human energy represented by the rowdy nurses across the hall, whose parties upset him. He has an overwhelming epiphany, recognizing the dismal condition of his life, standing outside himself and seeing "this wintry soul on a thousand afternoons at a window in a barren room, watching the progression of people on the street." At the end of the novel, after a last conversation with Mary Virginia, who plans to abort her baby (there is no glib happy ending for her), he goes to see the newest occupant of Arthur's old room, Ida Warren, an elderly woman who has been trying to offer herself to him. The conclusion is a little forced, but Bausch suggests that Cakes is going to choose life in the little time that he has left.

The actor and director Bob Balaban made *The Last Good Time* into a distinguished film in 1995. The setting was moved to Brooklyn and some plot complications were added, but the movie was faithful to the spirit and themes of the novel.

UNHAPPY FAMILIES

Bausch is one of America's finest living short story writers. His first collection, *Spirits, and Other Stories* (1987), was his second work nominated for a PEN/Faulkner Award, and one story, "What Feels Like the World," was an O. Henry Prize winner. In most of the stories he deals with the ordinary characters who so often appear in his novels. There are two notable exceptions. "The Man Who Knew Belle Star" deals with an ex-convict who picks up a hippie woman who turns out to be a serial killer. The story arouses suspense but lacks Bausch's usual psychological subtlety. The other story with unusual characters, "Spirits," is one of his best. Uniquely for Bausch's work, it treats a writer and academic life. The narrator, a novelist newly hired by a Virginia university, borrows the apartment of William Brooker, a one-time Kennedy Administration intellectual employed at the same university. The narrator finds and reads the letters of Helen, Brooker's beautiful wife, and this voyeurism is counterpointed brilliantly with the gradual revelation of a serial killer's crimes in the same town. The intertwined plots create a toxic atmosphere of duplicity and bad faith. Brooker's womanizing drives one of his lovers to suicide, putting him on a moral level similar to the killer's. Bausch's fascination with the Kennedy years would reach its height in *Good Evening Mr. & Mrs. America, and All the Ships at Sea,* but the Kennedy mystique already seems tarnished.

The rest of *Spirits* is more typical of Bausch's fiction and deals mostly with marriages and families. Tolstoy's claim at the opening of *Anna Karenina* comes to mind: "All happy families resemble one another, but each unhappy family is unhappy in its own way." But the reader of Bausch's stories can trace a number of causes for unhappiness: alcoholism, memories of childhood abuse, failures of parenting, or cumulative boredom in a relationship. One of the best stories is "All the Way in Flagstaff, Arizona," in which Walter sinks into alcoholism and loses his family because, ironically, he cannot escape the fear that he will batter his children as he was battered by his father. And "Police Dreams" uses one of Bausch's favorite devices, the symbolic dream, to trace the breakdown of a marriage. Casey's dreams of intruders in the house embody his fear that his wife will leave him, but he is powerless to intervene in the process.

Bausch can deal with family relationships other than marriage, such as mother-son relationships, the conflict of an elderly man and his daughter-in-law, a grandfather's love for a granddaughter; the range is impressive. Unlike the novels, his stories rarely depict people putting their lives back together. There is no space for such

developments in a brief narrative. He typically catches his characters at moments of crisis or collapse and leaves them there.

In Bausch's fourth novel, *Mr. Field's Daughter* (1989), the estrangement of father and daughter forms the theme. James Field is a widower who has raised his daughter alone in Duluth, Minnesota. Bausch's novel is set in the Midwest, but Field and his sister Ellen are both natives of Point Royal: Bausch seems compelled to touch his mythical earth to keep his strength. At nineteen, Field's daughter, Annie, elopes with the morally suspect Cole Gilbertson and goes with him to Savoy, Illinois, just south of Urbana-Champaign. When Field pursues them and shows up drunk and hostile, he alienates his daughter for years. But she eventually leaves Gilbertson, an increasingly dangerous cocaine addict, and returns with her child, Linda, to her father's house. The complex plot of the novel deals with the damaged but mended family life created in the Field household. Enormous suspense is created when Gilbertson's mother dies and he decides, in a drug-muddled state of mind, to go to Duluth, where he thinks he can recover his daughter and get revenge on Field for interfering in his life.

A further element in the plot is the relationship of Annie and a considerably older man, Louis Wolfe, who has retired from the air force. He runs a failing store, Star Dust Records, which specializes in nostalgia recordings. Louis' ne'er-do-well son, Roger, works in the store: his only real role in the novel seems to be to provide a victim for the deranged Gilbertson. While the relations of James and his daughter and granddaughter are rendered with great sensitivity, the romance of Louis and Annie is less compelling. She clearly settles for security and kindness, having learned the dangers of reckless passion: she is one of Bausch's compromisers. The reader is not likely to find this relationship convincing. Sometimes Bausch seems to run a twelve-step recovery program for his characters: they learn to change what they can and to accept what they cannot. One of the most interesting comments on Bausch's fiction comes from his wife, Karen, quoted in his autobiographical essay of 1991. At a time when he was trying to get the theme of a novel right, she said: "But don't you see, that's not what you do as a writer, all that intellectual stuff. You're like Tennessee Williams—you write about people trying to get used to their pain."

Bausch explores the relationship of father and daughter in meditative sections entitled "Certain Testimony," which show them mulling over their experiences and conflicts, explaining feelings that they would be uncomfortable expressing aloud. On the level of plot the *deus ex machina* is violence by Gilbertson, who murders Roger (intending to kill Louis) and shoots James before killing himself. James is left maimed for life, but the emotional upheaval of the events heals the alienation of James and Annie. The resolution is melodramatic, but Gilbertson's shooting spree is described brilliantly.

In his next book, *The Fireman's Wife and Other Stories* (1990), Bausch established himself as an outstanding contemporary short story writer. The one story that seems out of character for him is "Old West," an extravagant sequel to the famous Western novel, *Shane.* It is Bausch's only venture into deconstructive parody so far, and it sags under the weight of its own contrivances. Nearly all of the ten stories are about failed marriages or unhappy parent-child relationships. They are written in a lucid, understated style, and are emotionally powerful. Two have been particularly admired, the title story, and its sequel, "Consolation." They pack a great deal into a short space: marital discord, death, grief, and consolation. Comparable in quality is "The Brace," the story of a successful writer's visit to his son and daughter, who dislike him because he has exploited his marriage with their mother in his work. A fine story almost without plot ends the collection, "Letter to the Lady of the House," an epistle written by the husband in a long-married couple, who muses on the failures in their relationship and affirms his desire to remain with his "dear adversary." It succeeds without plot or interaction among characters.

STRESSES IN THE AMERICAN PSYCHE

Bausch's next novel, *Violence* (1992), probes into one of the deepest American anxieties, the fear of being attacked or even murdered. In an important *Washington Post* interview, "The Author, Giving Rise to 'Violence,' " Elizabeth Kastor talked with Bausch about this anxiety. Bausch was surprised when his bookstore readings from the book brought out people who behaved with verbal aggression toward the novelist, "as if he were somehow to blame for the blood and death filling the streets of this country, and would then storm from the store." Bausch found that others would talk to him at the readings about their own experiences with violence: how they had been "shot or attacked or frightened." He was troubled also by the assumption that he could give sociological explanations of violence in America. In a credo typical of his attitude toward writing, he told Kastor that "the book is about love and the obdurate force of love. That's what everything I write is about. I don't write my opinions, I tell stories." He does not diagnose endemic fear of violence; he conveys what it is like.

Love has to be obdurate in *Violence* to overcome the spiritual affliction that sets in after the central character, Charles Connally, is almost killed in a convenience store in Chicago. Charles and his pregnant wife, Carol, have come from Point Royal to visit his mother. Charles goes into a convenience store just as two men high on drugs enter to rob it. They kill three people in cold blood. The other survivor, a Chinese woman, thinks that Charles saved her life, though when he seized her hands during the rush of events he was momentarily thinking of using her body as a shield. He is acclaimed as a hero, and his disintegration through much of the novel is aggravated by the constant praise he receives, especially from reporters. The novel presents a highly negative view of television and newspaper reporters and their exploitative reports on violence.

Although the novel is not a sociological tract, it does capture the malaise of a violence-plagued society. During the ordeal in the convenience store, a black policeman (a genuine hero, who shoots one of the gunmen) says to Charles, "This is America, boy. This is what we got ourselves into now. At this time of the morning." In 1996, Bausch published "The Massacre and the Mastermind," an appreciative review of Philip Caputo's *Equation for Evil,* a novel about a massacre of school children. Bausch could be speaking of his own novel when he says that the massacre "provides Caputo with the opportunity to paint a very clear and lucid picture of the horrors we have come to in this country."

Charles' breakdown after his ordeal eventually forces him to confront his own scarred past. Here perhaps Bausch relies too much on one of our contemporary preoccupations: repressed memories and the kind of childhood abuse dealt with in "All the Way in Flagstaff, Arizona." In *Violence,* Charles was strangely disturbed by his wife's pregnancy even before the shootings, and afterward his repressed childhood memories cause the same anxiety about harming his family that destroyed Walter in the earlier work. Charles finally understands that he has been marked by abuse from his father, and that he resents his mother for not having intervened. This plot development seems to come out of the literature of the Recovery movement: by 1992, stories of childhood abuse and repressed memories had already become very familiar. To be fair to Bausch, the subject was not so familiar at the time of "All the Way in Flagstaff, Arizona." The resolution of *Violence* may seem too marked by the spirit of

the times: Charles begins to cope with his illness by a series of actions that bring him close to suicide but deal symbolically with his past. The pattern is rather tidy. His love for his wife is reaffirmed at the end of the novel and he decides to seek professional help. It appears that the persistent force of love will eventually lead Charles out of his emotional sickness.

Bausch's next novel, *Rebel Powers* (1993), is one of his finest, ranking with *Take Me Back*. It explores the American agony over the Vietnam War. Robert Bausch had published a novel about the war in 1982, *On the Way Home,* the story of a soldier who returns from Vietnam mentally shattered. In that novel, flashbacks provide scenes of the war. Richard Bausch deals with the war more obliquely in the later novel. In fact, his subject is not just the war but the social turmoil in the United States in the period. The title of the novel, from Shakespeare's Sonnet CXLVI, evokes a society on the brink of anarchy, though the epigraph has a particular meaning for the Boudreaux family:

Poor Soul, the center of my sinful earth,
Fool'd by these rebel powers that thee array,
Why dost thou pine within, and suffer dearth,
Painting thy outward walls so costly gay?
Why so large cost, having so short a lease,
Do thou upon thy fading mansion spend?

The novel's action is initiated by a crime: in 1967 Daniel Boudreaux, a noncommissioned officer in the air force and a war hero, is sent to prison for stealing a typewriter. His act proceeds from desperation over debts and bad checks that have accumulated as he attempts to keep his faltering marriage going by lavish spending. The sickness in the marriage results from the changes in his personality after his prisoner of war experiences. Daniel is pining within but he is painting the outward walls "so costly gay." The Boudreaux family functions as a microcosm of America in the

Vietnam War period, an era of unreal prosperity brought on by war spending.

This novel shows more geographical and artistic scope than any previous work by Bausch. Parts of *Rebel Powers* are set in Maryland, Virginia, North Dakota, and Wyoming. The novel has a leisurely pace: it begins with home movies of the narrator's first birthday in Alaska, and it eventually moves the characters to a brilliantly depicted town, Wilson's Creek, Wyoming, the site of a military prison. The narrator of the novel, Thomas Boudreaux, is writing from his idyllic refuge, Asquahawk Island, just beyond the mouth of Chesapeake Bay, where he runs a bookstore. In middle age he has become that quintessential sixties type, a dropout, and he is trying to understand the family conflicts that have left him at the margins of life. There are occasional reports on the life of his sister, Lisa, whose longing for stability leads her to marry a Mormon. Her memories do not always coincide with Thomas', which adds perspective to the novel, though his views are naturally privileged: he was older, he kept journals, and he tells the story. The work of memory is aided in the novel by the home movies the narrator analyzes, and by the journals. In *Rebel Powers,* Bausch's storytelling apparatus is unusually complex, but not for the sake of virtuosity. He has troubled times as well as a troubled family to depict.

Thomas Boudreaux's love for his father is clear, though he has some ambivalence. The generation gap so typical of the sixties gets attention early in the novel: Thomas, aged seventeen, lets his hair grow long and starts playing rock and roll. His father, a career airman, reacts by throwing his son's records into the yard, although he does in fact replace them: father and son are not bitter enemies. But Daniel has let the family down by his act of petty theft and fraud, leaving them penniless and fatherless. The theft and trial take place at Andrews Air Force Base near Washington—Bausch country. The mother, Connie, finds a job in Demera, the setting for *Real Presence,* but she soon decides to move with the children to Wyoming to be close to Daniel. They go to visit her father first, a North Dakota judge who has not approved of her marriage to an airman. The North Dakota scenes are precisely imagined and the characterization of the grandfather is a small triumph in the novel.

The journey enables Bausch to comment on the Vietnam War indirectly, as the train passes through Washington, D.C., during a turbulent demonstration in 1967. The pervasive war news on television colors the novel, and the climactic scene takes place on the night that Robert Kennedy was assassinated. Bausch may have been influenced by *The Man Who Knew Kennedy,* a novel published in 1967 by Vance Bourjaily, his teacher at the University of Iowa Writers' Workshop. Bourjaily counterpoints the domestic actions in his novel with the assassination and funeral of John F. Kennedy. Talk of the war is everywhere in *Rebel Powers.* On the train the family meets a Mr. Terpin, who is traveling to a different prison, Fort Leavenworth, where his brother Buddy is incarcerated, supposedly as a draft resister. An irony that emerges late in the novel is that Terpin's brother turns out to be a criminal himself, but he lacks the good qualities of Daniel. The system of military justice has put them on the same level. One of the masterful ironies of the novel is the assumption made by characters like Terpin that Daniel Boudreaux, a genuine war hero, is in prison for rejecting the war. Although he is a hero and has been a prisoner of war—a category of veteran particularly revered in America—Boudreaux's occupation has been the benign one of teaching survival techniques to airmen, and only chance put him into the control of the enemy, who subjected him to terrible treatment. His two-year prison sentence for a minor crime not only shames the family, it outrages them and engenders their own dislike for the war.

Terpin is accompanied by his brother's fiancée, the uncannily beautiful Penny Holt, one of Bausch's finest achievements in characterization.

Like Mary Bellini in *The Last Good Time,* she is a pathological liar. Her dishonesty is symbolized by her glass eye. She turns up in Wyoming and moves into the same boardinghouse as the Boudreax family. Thomas naturally falls in love with her, and his mother's increasing closeness to her is highly ambiguous, complicating family relationships. After Daniel's early release from prison in 1968, his wife refuses to let him sleep in her room, which reveals the discord in the marriage. Daniel eventually reasserts his authority as head of the family in a powerful and disturbing set of events the night of the Robert Kennedy assassination: it appears that the macrocosm of America and the microcosm of the family are both deeply shaken. The landlady says of the assassination: "What are we coming to—oh my Lord, what're we coming to, what're we coming to. . . ." In his rage at being excluded from his wife's bedroom, Daniel actually shoves Penny Holt down and tears open her pajama top, a kind of symbolic rape, and he strikes his own son for trying to intervene. Years later the son learns that his father had regained his place in the family by threatening to take custody of the children by accusing his wife of a lesbian relationship. But the father is a tragic figure, not a villain, and he soon abandons his patriarchal victory out of remorse for his behavior. He begins a downward spiral that ends years later in a car accident that may have been suicide.

The family and social themes are handled tactfully. Bausch does not pass easy judgments on the Vietnam War but rather reveals the strong feelings on both sides. The relationships of Connie and Daniel, Connie and Thomas, and of Connie and Penny are handled with subtlety and compassion. Bausch also looks carefully at the thematically less-important conflict between Thomas and his little sister, whom he lets down by reacting to her immaturity and failing to understand her grief over her father's absence. A number of minor characters are delineated briefly but indelibly, like the landlady, Mrs. Wilson, and

the sleazy boarder, Mr. Egan. *Rebel Powers* was Bausch's most elaborate work to date, and remarkably well-integrated for all its abundance.

SHADOWS ON THE AMERICAN DREAM

Bausch's productivity has been prodigious since the publication of *Mr. Field's Daughter* in 1989. A major grant from the Lila Wallace–Reader's Digest fund in 1992 probably helped. In 1994 he published *Rare & Endangered Species: A Novella & Short Stories,* a collection of stories and a novella. The stories are accomplished but not surprising, dealing as they do with marriage breakup or unemployment. In one of them, "Aren't You Happy for Me?" he provides more comedy than usual, as a couple tries to cope with their daughter's marriage to a professor who is older than they are. The novella is a complex work, a novel condensed into a long story, one that keeps several interrelated plots going: Bausch seems to want to braid rather than knot the stories together, which gives a spaciousness and open feeling to the work. The common element is the suicide of Andrea Brewer, who kills herself because she cannot endure leaving her beautiful house in the Point Royal area. She leaves no explanation, and the novella deals with the different ways that her husband, Harry, and her children, James and Maizie, react in the months after. He keeps a number of other plot strands going with other people whose lives impinged on Harry and Andrea's, as the novella form does not demand the relentless unity of the traditional short story. The story culminates, perhaps too predictably, with the birth of a daughter to Maizie and her husband Leo: it appears that the rift in the fabric of life will be mended. We are part of a rare and endangered species, but so far it has survived, even though individuals sometimes destroy themselves.

The Bausch twins were admirers of John F. Kennedy in their youth, as they make clear in their 1991 autobiographies. Kennedy's idealism, expressed in noble speeches, impressed Richard deeply, and after the assassination he drew a number of portraits of the president, one of which he brought to Robert Kennedy in McLean, Virginia. The younger Kennedy invited him for a conversation, and Bausch says in the autobiography that "I went on my way, feeling that I had stepped back out of history and into my life again." He also sent a portrait to Jacqueline Kennedy.

But the years have brought disillusioning facts to light about John F. Kennedy, and Bausch's 1996 novel *Good Evening Mr. & Mrs. America, and All the Ships at Sea* turns the facts to fictional use. Bausch's hapless hero, Walter Marshall, is comparable to Nathanael West's Lemuel Pitkin in *A Cool Million,* another idealist who gets taken in by a corrupt society. Walter has the same given name as the cynical gossip columnist Walter Winchell, whose famous opening line on his radio broadcasts provides the novel with its cumbersome title. The advantage of the title is that it identifies the work as a treatment of America. And it seems that poor Walter is symbolically at sea throughout the novel.

Walter attends the D'Allessandro School for Broadcasting in the fall of 1964. The school is a dubious operation run by Lawrence D'Allessandro and his English wife, Esther, who have a night school in the same building. The schools draw in victims of the American dream, who spend their limited money trying to better themselves. D'Allessandro gambles and is threatened by thugs employed by his bookie. Esther provides a corrupt version of the American Dream when she says, "The thing about my husband is his unlimited capacity for hope," an echo of the novel Bausch loves so much, *The Great Gatsby,* the definitive novel about the failure of the American Dream. D'Allessandro's hope involves both the exploitation of his naive students and a misguided confidence in his abilities to pick winners at the track. The students at his school represent a variety of ethnic backgrounds and social attitudes—

they're a microcosm of America—but none of them is likely to be a winner.

The novel is Bausch's first comic work, dark as it occasionally seems. Walter is so naive that he assumes he can be president of the United States by 1988, when he will be forty-three, as Kennedy was when elected, although he has no real plans for his life until then. He takes part in a sit-in demonstration (one of Bausch's few treatments of racism) out of a desire to help create Lyndon Johnson's Great Society. Ironically, his best friend at the school, Albert, is engaged to a woman who was blind from birth but turns out to be an embarrassing racist: the problem of racism will not be solved by singing "Ain't gonna let nobody turn me round"—not if someone who cannot perceive skin color dislikes black people. Mr. D'Allessandro integrates the broadcast school, but not out of idealism. He needs the money. The new student, Wilbur Soames, has a sardonic view of the politically naive integrationist sentiments he encounters in the class.

Walter is so eager to please that he winds up engaged to two somewhat older women: Alice Kane, whom he does not love, and the German student from the night school, Natalie Bowman, whom he can imagine as his First Lady. The scene in which he tries to explain his double engagement to his astounded priest is a superb piece of comic dialogue. At the end, Walter learns the truth about John F. Kennedy's morals from Natalie, who has in fact been a paid guest in the presidential bedroom. He solves his somewhat bigamous engagement situation by enlisting in the army: "He would ask to be sent to that place, Saigon, where the war was being fought for freedom, and where the conflict was definite, the enemy clear." The novel is often extremely funny for all its bitter undercurrents. It also seems overlong, and the historical ironies are sometimes too obvious.

Bausch's next novel, *In the Night Season: A Novel* (1998) received mixed reviews. It is a thriller with brilliantly executed action scenes. Andy Solomon's review in *The Boston Globe,* "Behind the Crime Mystery, the Mysteries of Marriage," suggests that the balance of literary and popular elements is a good one. A. O. Scott's review in *The New York Times* is entitled "The Desperate Hours," alluding to the 1955 Humphrey Bogart film as a way of pointing to the hackneyed situation of a family held hostage. In this case the family consists of Nora Michaelson and her eleven-year-old son, Jason, who live in Steel Run Creek, near Point Royal. The criminals, led by Reuther, a German mastermind, seek more than two million dollars' worth of stolen computer chips. They were double-crossed by Nora's husband, Jack, who kept the chips for himself. Jack has died in a traffic accident. Bausch has provided a high-tech updating of familiar plots in which criminals seek money or drugs kept by a double-crosser. Reuther sends his henchmen, two brothers named Travis and Bags, to search the Michaelson house. The thugs are stereotypes: Travis is the clever one, capable of quoting *Heart of Darkness,* while his brother is fat, stupid, and uncontrollably violent.

The physical action in the novel is abundant and brilliantly described. One problem is that the mother and son are improbably resourceful in their struggle with the criminals, and the improbability is compounded when Nora's parents in Seattle, who are rather unnecessarily being held hostage also, prove just as resourceful in coping with their captor. Evil destroys itself rather neatly in the novel: the death struggle of Reuther and Bags after a falling-out is so intricately described that it becomes comic. Scott suggests that the novel reads like a film treatment. It does have elements of genuine characterization when the grief of Nora and Jason for their husband and father is dealt with, and there is a moving subplot about the detective in the novel, Chief Investigator Shaw, who is divorced and worried about losing the affections of his daughter. Unfortu-

nately, the most sympathetic and original character, a black VCR repairman named Edward Bishop, is killed off very early in the novel. Bausch's skill in depicting action reaches a peak in this work, but the book reads like a thriller with serious overtones rather than as a serious novel with elements of a thriller. The balance is not quite right.

In 1999 Bausch had another collection of stories, *Someone to Watch Over Me: Stories,* published. This one has few surprises: most of the characters are damaged people, and the marriages have failed or appear to be wounded. In a long and perceptive review, "At the Edge of the Ordinary," the novelist Joan Silber says that "the sense of ineffectiveness is a secret and constant component of one kind of American life," and she points out that "Bausch's understanding of it is thorough and unerring. . . ." One story, "Glass Meadows," has an interesting twist. The narrator remembers life with his happy and irresponsible parents. Their pranks and carelessness have left him and his brother cautious and insecure in adulthood, but he is aware that his parents were very happy. In Bausch's fiction parents are often brutal or at least unhappy. Here the children were blighted by the loving but unstable ways of parents who would not take life seriously enough.

The title story is more typical, a snapshot of a failing marriage at its moment of collapse. The couple, Ted and Marlee, go to a pretentious restaurant to celebrate their first anniversary. She becomes increasingly uncomfortable with the world she has entered through her husband, a distinguished professor much older than herself, and she shows her distress by buying several doubles of a Napoleon brandy selling for $145 a glass. She becomes drunk and disorderly, and it is clear that the marriage is doomed. She realizes that she may, as the cloying George and Ira Gershwin song says, have someone to watch over her, but he has been attracted to her youth, not to any of her other qualities.

The number of failed marriages in the book is high. In "Riches," a man's enormous lottery win brings out greed in his wife and all his relatives and he drifts into despair. "Nobody in Hollywood," which was a *Best American Short Stories 1997* selection, takes a character into and out of a grotesque marriage in a few pages. A daughter's marriage in "Fatality" is so brutal that the father kills the abusing husband. The protagonist of "Valor" becomes a hero by rescuing the passengers in a school bus, but his act does not save his collapsing marriage. In "Par," Bausch presents the comic courtship of a couple who have both had failed relationships. The story ends with the man in bed after injuring his groin with a golf ball as he tried to demonstrate his prowess in the game to the woman. Symbolically, at least, the new relationship is not off to a good start, although the narrator assures the reader that "in spite of everything, this is a happy story." The experienced reader of Bausch may be skeptical.

Richard Bausch has made himself the laureate of unhappy families. He is at the height of his powers in narrating such stories, but at the same time he is in danger of becoming predictable. The extraordinary rate of marriage breakup in the United States certainly sustains his view of the family as a beleaguered and disappointing institution. His task is to convince his readers that he can show each unhappy family as unhappy in its own way, or at least in an interesting way.

CRITICAL RECEPTION

Considering his publishing record and awards, Richard Bausch has had very few critics aside from reviewers in newspapers and magazines. The reviews have often been perceptive, but their scope is limited. The best article was an early one in *Commonweal,* Paul Elie's "The Way Things Are: Richard Bausch's Unadorned World," which links him with the Dirty Realists and considers his moral vision. In his introduction to *Aren't You Happy for Me?* Richard Ford also praises Bausch's works "as morally vivid inquiries." Paul Lilly's article, "Richard Bausch," in *American Short Story Writers Since World War II,* in the *Dictionary of Literary Biography* offers commentary on almost every story in *Spirits* and *The Fireman's Wife.* Michael L. Gillespie's "Drugs and Thugs: The Aesthetic Roots of Violence," uses Bausch's *Violence* and works by two other writers to illustrate Joseph F. Kupfer's theory that acts of violence are committed by people who have no feeling of agency: violence becomes an aesthetic pleasure. Bausch's novel seems subordinated to this thesis in an article that misspells the name of his protagonist.

If there is a postmodern divide in American literature, a gulf between writers who write traditional novels and writers who create innovative texts, Bausch is definitely on the traditionalist side of the split, which may account for the lack of academic attention to his work. He talks of writing stories and creating characters rather than producing texts, and he assumes that fiction can represent life. The author's note to *Rare & Endangered Species* takes an aggressive and humorous stance on such matters. He declares that "there has been a tendency on the part of certain so-called schools of critical theory to make sociological constructs out of fictional characters." He humorously states that the resemblance of his characters to such constructs is entirely coincidental, but all "resemblances to actual persons— that is to recognizable, complicated human beings caught in their time and place—are exactly, wholly, and lovingly intended, even though I imagined them all."

As a dedicated storyteller and creator of human character, Bausch is not likely to catch the attention of critical theorists. His inquiry into the ways that people live today is not even as radical as Donald Barthelme, Don DeLillo, or Thomas Pynchon. His style is eloquent when it needs to be without calling attention to itself. His books are carefully structured and meticulously written but not innovative. The fact that he has been praised for his moral insight by Paul Elie and Richard Ford is significant. He is not didactic, but he looks with compassion and precision at how people treat each other and evokes how they feel. He gives a strong image of American life in the late twentieth century, with its anxieties, failures, and occasional moments of joy and reconciliation. These are the achievements of a realist; not a Dirty Realist, but a faithful one.

Note: I interviewed Richard Bausch via e-mail on February 28, 2000. I have cited excerpts from this e-mail in this essay.

Selected Bibliography

WORKS OF RICHARD BAUSCH

NOVELS

Real Presence. New York: The Dial Press, 1980; Baton Rouge: Louisiana State University Press, 1999.

Take Me Back. New York: The Dial Press, 1981; Baton Rouge: Louisiana State University Press, 1998.

The Last Good Time. Garden City, N.Y.: The Dial Press/Doubleday, 1984.

Mr. Field's Daughter. New York: Linden Press/Simon & Schuster, 1989.

Violence. Boston: Houghton Mifflin/Seymour Lawrence, 1992.

Rebel Powers. Boston: Houghton Mifflin/Seymour Lawrence, 1993.

Good Evening Mr. & Mrs. America, and All the Ships at Sea. New York: HarperCollins, 1996.

In the Night Season. New York: HarperCollins, 1998.

SHORT STORIES

Spirits, and Other Stories. New York: Linden Press/Simon & Schuster, 1987.

The Fireman's Wife and Other Stories. New York: W. W. Norton, 1990.

Rare & Endangered Species: A Novella & Stories. Boston: Houghton Mifflin/Seymour Lawrence, 1994.

Aren't You Happy for Me? and Other Stories. Introduction by Richard Ford. London: Macmillan, 1995. (Includes stories from *Spirits, The Fireman's Wife,* and *Rare and Endangered Species.*)

The Selected Stories. New York: The Modern Library, 1996. (Includes stories from *Spirits, The Fireman's Wife,* and *Rare & Endangered Species.*)

Someone to Watch Over Me. New York: Harper-Flamingo/HarperCollins, 1999.

AUTOBIOGRAPHICAL WRITINGS

"Richard Bausch." In *Contemporary Authors: A Bio-Bibliographical Guide.* Vol. 101. Edited by Frances C. Locher. Detroit: Gale Research, 1981. Pp. 42–43.

"Richard Bausch." In *Contemporary Authors: Autobiography Series.* Vol. 14. Edited by Joyce Nakamura. Detroit: Gale Research, 1991. Pp. 1–16.

"So Long Ago." In *The Business of Memory: The Art of Remembering in an Age of Forgetting.* Edited by Charles Baxter. St. Paul, Minn.: Graywolf, 1999. Pp. 3–10.

ESSAYS AND REVIEWS

"So Much Like a Lost Boy." *New York Times Book Review,* September 12, 1993, p. 15.

"Oh! Lucy Such a Loss." *New York Times Book Review,* June 12, 1994, p. 30.

"The Low Road to Gettysburg." *Civilization,* March/April 1995, p. 78.

"The Massacre and the Mastermind." *Washington Post,* March 17, 1996, p. OX3

"Representative Government: A Correspondence." *Harper's,* May 1999, pp. 19–21.

"Traveling North." *Meridian* 3:106–111 (Spring 1999).

"Charm." In *Eudora Welty: Writers' Reflections on First Reading Welty.* Edited by Pearl Amelia McHaney. Athens, Georgia: Hill Street Press, 1999. Pp. 1–3.

MANUSCRIPTS AND PAPERS

The papers of Richard Bausch are in the Special Collections Library of Duke University. The holdings include early published stories and four unpublished novels, manuscripts of published works, and all correspondence.

CRITICAL AND BIOGRAPHICAL STUDIES

Allen, Arthur. "Nature and Nurture: When It Comes to Twins, Sometimes It's Hard to Tell the Two Apart." *The Washington Post Magazine,* January 11, 1998, pp. 6–11, 21–25.

Bausch, Robert. "Life Thus Far." In *Contemporary Authors: Autobiography Series.* Vol. 14. Edited by Joyce Nakamura. Detroit: Gale Research, 1991. Pp. 17–31. (Memoir by Richard Bausch's twin brother.)

Bawer, Bruce. "Family Values." *The Hudson Review* 46, no. 3:593–599 (Autumn 1993).

Brickner, Richard P. "Troubled Lives." *The New York Times Book Review,* April 26, 1981, p. 14.

Budy, Andrea Hollander. Review of *Rare and Endangered Species. Georgia Review* 49, no. 3:751–752 (Fall 1995).

Busch, Frederick. "Contemporary American Short Fiction." *Southern Review* 27, no. 2:465–472 (Spring 1991).

Cahill, Thomas. "Fireworks Hidden and Deep." *Commonweal* 114, no. 17:568–569 (October 9, 1987).

Davenport, Gary. "The Novel of Despair." *Southern Review* 105, no. 3:440–446 (Summer 1997).

Desmond, John. F. "Catholicism in Contemporary American Fiction." *America* 170, no. 17:7–12 (May 14, 1994).

Elie, Paul. "The Way Things Are: Richard Bausch's Unadorned World." *Commonweal* 117, no. 19:642–646 (November 9, 1990).

Forbes, Nancy. "Redeemed by Love at 75." *New York Times Book Review,* December 23, 1984, p. 14.

Ford, Richard. Introduction to *Aren't You Happy for Me? and Other Stories,* by Richard Bausch. London: Macmillan, 1995. Pp. ix–xiv.

Gillespie, Michael L. "Drugs and Thugs: The Aesthetic Roots of Violence." In *The Image of Violence in Literature, the Media, and Society.* Pueblo: Society for the Interdisciplinary Study of Social Imagery, University of Southern Colorado, 1995. Pp. 363–370.

Lilly, Paul R., Jr. "Richard Bausch." In *Dictionary of Literary Biography.* Vol. 130, *American Short Story Writers Since World War II.* Edited by Patrick Meanor. Detroit: Gale Research, 1993.

Mohs, Mayo. "Body of Christ." *Time,* September 22, 1980, p. 81.

Scott, A. O. "The Desperate Hours." *New York Times Book Review,* June 7, 1998, p. 16.

Shields, Carol. "The Life You Lead May Be Your Own." *New York Times Book Review,* August 14, 1994, p. 6.

Silber, Joan. "At the Edge of the Ordinary." *The World and I,* 1410:282–285.

Solomon, Andy. "Behind the Crime Mystery, the Mysteries of Marriage." *Boston Globe,* May 31, 1998, p. N2.

Suplee, Curt. "Twin Visions, Twin Lives." *The Washington Post,* March 26, 1982, pp. C1, C6.

Tallent, Elizabeth. "So Easy to Fail at Love." *New York Times Book Review,* May 16, 1993, pp. 9–10.

Zeidner, Lisa. "Somebody I'm Longing to See." *New York Times Book Review,* August 29, 1999, pp. 11–12.

INTERVIEWS

Brainard, Dulcy. "Richard Bausch." *Publishers Weekly* 237:425–426 (August 10, 1990).

Cowgill, Michael. "An Inteview with Richard Bausch." *Meridian* 3:97–105 (Spring 1999).

Cauldwell, Leslie. "Truth and Trouble: A Conversation with Richard Bausch." *Atlantic Unbound.* www .theatlantic.com/unbound/factfict/ff9808.htm. (August 20, 1998).

Kastor, Elizabeth. "The Author, Giving Rise to 'Violence.' " *Washington Post,* March 2, 1992, pp. B1, B4.

FILM BASED ON THE WORK OF RICHARD BAUSCH

The Last Good Time. Screenplay by Bob Balaban and John C. McLaughlin. Directed by Bob Balaban. Samuel Goldwyn, 1995.

—*BERT ALMON*

Sandra Cisneros

1954–

JUST AS SANDRA Cisneros, the woman, is not bound by the conventional assumptions of culture, nation, or gender, so too Sandra Cisneros, the writer, breaks the traditional bounds of genre. Her prose spills over into poetry, and her poetry breaks freely into prose, while both teem with palpable images and rich narratives that cut across barriers of nation, culture, genre, and gender. Cisneros grew up traveling frequently between the United States and Mexico, and she has used the varied cultural influences of both countries in her work.

Not only did Cisneros grow up with two cultures—Mexican and American—but even the backgrounds of her Mexican grandparents varied vastly. While her mother's parents came from humble circumstances in rural Guanajuato, Mexico, Cisneros' father was born into a privileged, military family in Mexico City. Cisneros vacationed in Mexico with her father's family in their comfortable home in Oaxaca. This contrasted greatly with the series of Chicago apartments in neighborhoods with "empty lots and burned-out buildings" where the Cisneros family lived. She says in the *Desert News* web site, "I'm in a nice vantage point of being neither Mexican nor completely American. From the middle, I can see the places where the two don't fit. These interstices are always a rich place to write."

CISNEROS' BACKGROUND

Sandra Cisneros was born December 20, 1954, in Chicago to a Mexican-American mother and a Mexican father. As the only daughter in a family with six sons, Cisneros grew up feeling as if she had seven fathers—all telling her what to do. "I am the only daughter in a family of six sons," she says in a *Glamour* article, and according to her, "*That* explains everything." Her six brothers divided themselves into pairs of three, leaving her lonely in an apartment full of people. Forced to develop her own resources, she turned to books. In particular, Virginia Lee Burton's children's book, *The Little House,* planted in Cisneros the desire to have the perfect house.

Although moving back and forth between the United States and Mexico and from school to school and neighborhood to neighborhood in Chicago left Cisneros shy, introverted, and self-conscious, Cisneros' mother encouraged her independence by raising her in a nontraditional way and encouraging her to study at school and to pursue writing. Educated in both public and parochial schools in Chicago, Cisneros graduated from Loyola University in 1976 and enrolled in a University of Iowa Writers' Workshop Master of Fine Arts program in creative writing. While in this program, Cisneros began writing sketches for her novel in vignettes, *The House on Mango Street* (1984), and finished her master's thesis, "My Wicked Wicked Ways." She received her master of fine arts degree from the University of Iowa in 1978.

After receiving her degree, Cisneros returned to Chicago, where from 1978 to 1980 she taught and counseled students at the Latino Youth Alternative High School. During this time, she continued writing and began reading her poetry in coffeehouses in Chicago. The exposure she received from these readings soon led to a wide and diverse audience for her work in an unusual venue. The Poetry Society of America, sponsoring a project with the Chicago Transit Authority, chose the poetry of Cisneros as well as that of other poets to display in space on public transport usually devoted to advertisements. Soon thousands of commuters were reading and admiring the poetry of Sandra Cisneros.

When the Mexican-American writer Gary Soto became aware of Cisneros' work, he encouraged the publication of her chapbook *Bad Boys* by Mango Press in 1980. The poems from the chapbook have all been included in Cisneros' volume of poetry *My Wicked Wicked Ways* (1987). While her writing career continued to develop, she worked as an administrative assistant, recruiting and counseling minority students at Loyola University from 1981 to 1982. Although her work with high school and college students diminished her writing time, the stories of the young Latina students she worked with provided compelling material for her own work.

Receiving her first grant from the National Endowment for the Arts in 1982, Cisneros finally had the money and the time to devote to her own work, and she moved to Massachusetts to complete *The House on Mango Street*. In 1982–1983, the opportunity to travel came through arts residencies in France and Italy. Cisneros, gathering new material for her poetry, also traveled in Greece and spent a summer in Yugoslavia, where

she developed a deep friendship with Jasna, a woman from Sarajevo. The year 1984 changed Cisneros' life in two ways: *The House on Mango Street* was published to critical acclaim, and a job as the literary director of Guadalupe Cultural Arts Center San Antonio brought her to the geographic area she would claim as her own.

After the positive reception of *The House on Mango Street,* awards and increased recognition followed. In 1985, she received the Before Columbus American Book Award and a Paisano Dobie Fellowship, and in 1987, Third Woman Press published *My Wicked Wicked Ways.* In the same year, she sold *Woman Hollering Creek and Other Stories* (1991) and *The House on Mango Street* to Random House and Vintage, received a second NEA grant, and taught as a visiting professor at California State University. In the next few years, she had other visiting professorships, at the University of California at Berkeley in 1988, and in 1990 at both the University of California at Irvine and the University of Michigan at Ann Arbor. In 1991 Random House published *Woman Hollering Creek,* and Vintage reprinted *The House on Mango Street.* During this year Cisneros received the Lannan Literary Award and taught as guest professor at the University of New Mexico at Albuquerque. In 1992 Turtle Bay reissued *My Wicked Wicked Ways,* and Random House provided her with an advance for *Loose Woman: Poems,* a poetry collection, and for a novel, *Carmelito.* She completed *Loose Woman,* which Knopf published in 1994; the same year Knopf published *Hairs/Pelitos,* a children's book from one of her vignettes in *The House on Mango Street* in English and Spanish.

The MacArthur Foundation presented Cisneros with a $255,000 "genius" grant in 1995, the year that Random House published *La Casa en Mango Street,* a version of *The House on Mango Street* translated into Spanish by Elena Poniatowska. Cisneros, who lives in San Antonio, Texas, continues to write and to spend time encouraging young people, particularly Latinas, through frequent appearances at schools and community centers.

THE HOUSE ON MANGO STREET

The House on Mango Street, Cisneros' first work to receive critical acclaim, traces the coming of age of a young girl becoming a writer in a city barrio. Through poetic devices such as striking images, deliberate repetition, alliteration, metaphor, and simile, Cisneros' prose vignettes—told first through the voice of a child, later through the voice of a gradually maturing young woman—resonate with adult sensibility and wisdom. In these brief stories, the child, Esperanza, whose "name means hope" in English and "too many letters" in Spanish, struggles to cope with her feelings of displacement and the challenges of reconciling the twin tensions of emerging sexuality and increasing imagination. In doing so, she seeks to find herself, her identity, her place, and her home, but even the first and title story of this volume hints at the difficulty of Esperanza's finding any permanence.

In the story "The House on Mango Street," the narrator describes the house itself in terms of negatives. The story, not surprisingly, begins with the negative statement, "We didn't always live on Mango Street." Even what is positive about the house is described negatively: "we don't have to pay rent . . . or share the yard . . . or be careful not to make too much noise. . . ." This house with "no front yard" and a "small garage for the car we don't own yet" and "only four small elms" is not the house of Esperanza's dreams or what "Papa talked about" or "what Mama dreamed up." Instead, the repeated negatives describing what the house is not and what it does not have remind the reader of the threat to Esperanza's self-discovery and of her awareness of that threat.

The story concludes: "I knew then I had to have a house. A real house. One I could point to. But this isn't it. The house on Mango Street isn't it. . . . Temporary, says Papa. But I know how these things go."

The story "Cathy Queen of Cats" hints at the negative opinion some people hold of the neighborhood around Mango Street and perhaps of Esperanza's family for moving there, for Cathy offers to be her friend "only till next Tuesday . . . when we move away." Esperanza realizes that people like Cathy and her family feel they have to move "a little further north from Mango Street, a little further away every time people like us keep moving in." In contrast to the negative view of the house and the neighborhood, the second story in the volume, "Hairs," later published as children's book in Spanish and English, celebrates a warm view of the differences within the narrator's family. Family members have hair that is straight or slippery or described in similes, "like a broom" or "like fur" or "like little rosettes." The narrator dwells most lovingly on the description of her mother's hair, and repeats phrases such as "my mother's hair, my mother's hair" and "holding you, holding you" almost as in a lullaby or a prayer. Tucked up in bed with her mother, smelling her mother's hair, which smells like "the warm smell of bread before you bake it . . . sweet to put your nose into," Esperanza may seem to have found contentment and her place, but her own hair belies this sweet-smelling harmony. It shows signs of rebellion because it is lazy, and "never obeys barrettes or bands."

The images within these stories show the tension within Esperanza. In "Boys and Girls," the tension results from her female gender and the expectations her culture places on her because of that gender. Forced to be responsible for her sister Nenny, rather than able to play with her brothers, Esperanza feels like "a red balloon, a balloon tied to an anchor." To represent Esperanza's plight,

Cisneros creates emphasis by deliberate repetition of the word "balloon," a word that itself repeats two letters.

In "My Name," tension results from the narrator's conflicting emotions about the mix of her gender and her heritage. She likes the sound of her name, Esperanza, better in Spanish where it seems "made out of a softer something, like silver" rather than the way it is said in school "as if the syllables were made out of tin and hurt the roof of your mouth," but she fears that "Mexicans don't like their women strong." She does not want the fate of her great-grandmother and namesake who "looked out the window her whole life." Rather than "inherit her place by the window" or be one of the women who "sit their sadness on an elbow," Esperanza decides to "baptize herself under a new name, a name more like the real me, the one nobody sees."

In "Our Good Day" though, Esperanza's new friends, the sisters Rachel and Lucy who wear clothes that are "crooked and old," do not laugh when they hear her name. Instead, they urge Esperanza to find five dollars to help them buy a joint bike, and soon she is laughing and pedaling down Mango Street, beginning to find her own place within herself and her neighborhood. "Those Who Don't" finds Esperanza feeling solidarity in her neighborhood: "All brown all around, we are safe." Aware that those outsiders who stray into her neighborhood "think we're dangerous," she knows also that those on Mango Street fear a "neighborhood of another color."

In the accepting voice of a child, though, the narrator does see and relate the danger that can exist within the neighborhood, danger that comes from risky choices, neglect—and for young women—developing sexuality. In "Meme Ortiz," Meme, who moves into Cathy's old house, wins the "first annual Tarzan Jumping Contest" by jumping from a tree in his backyard and breaking both of his arms. The story centers on descriptions of the house, Meme's dog, the backyard, and the tree. Meme's fall would almost seem added as an afterthought but for the clipped final ironic sentences that emphasize the danger: "Meme won. And broke both arms."

Another episode revealing the dangers of the neighborhood takes place when Louie's cousin, who takes the children of Mango Street driving in his yellow Cadillac, ends up handcuffed in the back of a police car in "Louie, His Cousin & His Other Cousin." Esperanza's tone at the end of the story as she comments ". . . and we all waved as they drove away . . ." reveals the ordinariness with which the children view this event. When Angel, one of Rosa Vargas' too many children in "There Was an Old Woman She Had So Many Children She Didn't Know What to Do," falls "from the sky like a sugar donut, just like a falling star . . ." no one seems surprised that Mrs. Vargas, preoccupied with "buttoning and bottling and babysitting," cannot control or protect her children, or that Angel Vargas "exploded down to earth without even an 'Oh.' "

The danger lurking in the alliteration, "buttoning and bottling and babysitting," develops, of course, from the latent sexuality and possible maternity that threatens to derail Esperanza and the other young woman in the neighborhood. In "Alicia Who Sees Mice," motherless Alicia, who studies at the university, "must rise with the tortilla star" to make lunch for her family. Although she wants more from life, her responsibilities leave her sleepy and threaten her education.

On the other hand, in "Marin," the young woman, Marin, sees her sexuality as the means to escape. She wants to get a job downtown, so she can "look beautiful . . . wear nice clothes . . . meet someone in the subway" to marry and take her "to live in a big house far away." She smokes cigarettes, wears short skirts, and flirts, unafraid, with passing boys. In a later story in this volume, "Geraldo No Last Name," we see a brief portrait of one of the men Marin actually does meet while dancing uptown, a man killed in a car accident, a man without a last name, "just another *brazer* who didn't speak English. Just another wetback."

Still Marin waits hours in the emergency room for him, although she "can't explain why it mattered." At the end of "Marin," the narrator pictures her somewhere "under the street light, dancing by herself . . . waiting for a car to stop, a star to fall, someone to change her life." Marin waits for her sexual fulfillment as if it were a star, but since Cisneros has used the image of the star in the "tortilla star" that threatens Alicia's education as well as for the doomed Angel, "the falling star" child of Rosa Vargas, the reader can assume Marin's star probably will not fulfill her in the way she seeks or imagines.

"The Family of Little Feet" thrusts Esperanza and her friends feet-first into the danger of their own sexuality. When the girls are given a paper bag full of women's dress shoes, they think ". . . we are Cinderella because our feet fit exactly." As they try on shoes of lemon and red and pale blue, they particularly "laugh at Rachel's one foot with a girl's grey sock and a lady's high heel." The combination of the sock and the high heel symbolizes the transition between the worlds of innocent girlhood and mature female sexuality. Like an infant first discovering its fist, the girls soon discover their legs ". . . all our own, good to look at, and long." Later in "Hips" Esperanza and her friends will discover that part of their anatomy, "ready and waiting like a new Buick with the keys in the ignition." Ironically, Rachel, whose grey sock and high heeled foot the girls first laughed at, "learns to walk the best all strutted in these magic high heels," and, of course, Rachel is first at risk, and not Cinderella-like from Prince Charming but from the corner bum who offers her a dollar for a kiss. When her sister Lucy sees Rachel is "thinking about that dollar," she takes her hand and hustles her home. The narrator comments, "We are tired of being beautiful." Lucy hides the shoes, and no one complains when her mother throws them out. For the moment, the sexual threat has passed.

Shoes play a very different role in "Chanclas," however. Except for new dress shoes, Esperanza's mother has completely outfitted her in new clothes for her cousin's baptism party, so she must wear brown and white saddle shoes, practical school shoes, with her new party clothes. She cannot enjoy her new pink and white striped dress or her new slip with its little rose "with feet scuffed and round, and the heels all crooked that look dumb." When a boy asks her to dance, she says, "I shake my head no. My feet growing bigger and bigger." Finally, her uncle takes her to the dance floor where her "feet swell big and heavy like plungers," but he tells her she is "the prettiest girl here," spins her across the dance floor, and together they dance "like in the movies" while everyone watches, and she forgets her "ordinary shoes, brown and white, the kind my mother buys each year for school." What she does remember is her mother's pride in her, the "clapping when the music stops," and that "the man who is a boy" watched her dance. Here, art in the form of Esperanza's ability to dance overcomes her feelings of inferiority, and the very "scuffed and round" feet that brought her shame bring her glory.

Finding the transforming power of art in an unusual, unexpected place occurs also in the story "Gil's Furniture Bought & Sold" in which Esperanza discovers a special music box in a dark junk store. Just as she undervalues her feet in her school shoes, she at first thinks nothing of the music box because it is not "*pretty* with flowers painted on it, with a ballerina inside." Instead, it just looks like "a wood box that's old," but when the owner starts it up:

> . . . all sorts of things start happening. It's like . . . he let go a million moths all over the dusty furniture and swan-neck shadows and in our bones. It's like drops of water. Or like marimbas only with a funny little plucked sound to it like if you were running your fingers across the teeth of a metal comb.

The narrator conveys the effect of the sound of the music box, or the power of art, through images not only of sound, but also of sight and touch. Nenny, Esperanza's sister, responds conventionally and wants to buy the box, but the old man tells her it is not for sale. Esperanza, on the other hand, turns away and pretends not to care "so Nenny won't see how stupid I am," as if the box contained a meaning, a secret that Esperanza should have known.

In "Hips," as Esperanza wonders where her new hips will take her, the power of imagination and the power of sexual awareness separate Esperanza from Nenny. While Esperanza and her friends discover their hips and learn to create their own jump rope songs about having hips, they move farther away from Nenny who stays behind in girlhood "too many light years away . . . in a world we don't belong to anymore." Soon, in "Bums in the Attic," Esperanza does not want to accompany her family to see the beautiful houses on hills where her father works in the gardens. No longer content with riding past "staring out the window like the hungry," she vows that when she owns her own home, she "won't forget who I am or where I come from," but will, instead, invite passing bums in to live in her attic because she knows "how it is to be without a house."

As Esperanza's imagination begins to fuel her aspirations for a life beyond Mango Street, the stories begin to reveal the power of imagination to heal, to hurt, and to free. In "Papa Who Wakes Up Tired in the Dark," her father wakes her with the news of the death of her *abuelito* (grandfather), and she sees him "crumple . . . like a coat" and cry. Her imagination allows her to visualize in her own mind the scene that will follow: her father's trip to Mexico, the mourning aunts and uncles, the photo in front of the tomb "with flowers shaped like spears in a white vase." Imagining this scene makes her understand her own father's mortality: "And I think if my own Papa died what would I do," and so she reaches out to him, and her imagination kindles her love for him and pos-

sibly helps her father to heal. She concludes: "I hold my Papa in my arms. I hold and hold and hold him."

In the following story, "Born Bad," however, Esperanza's imagination leads her to feel shame. Every afternoon, Esperanza and her friends play a game in which they imitate someone, first famous people, then people in the neighborhood, and then, finally, Esperanza imitates the characteristic movements and voice of her blind Aunt Lupe who "had been dying such a long time, we forgot." Esperanza and her friends take turns playing Aunt Lupe and laughing at each other, but then feel ashamed when she dies the day they play the game. For Esperanza, her aunt's death, which seems a result of her imaginative play, particularly frightens her because Aunt Lupe had always listened to Esperanza's poems and encouraged her to keep writing because it would keep her free. Lupe's encouragement and the game Esperanza plays suggest both the power and the danger of her imaginative life.

Esperanza's aspirations and ambition open her also to the increased threat of sexuality. The vignette "The First Job" catapults Esperanza uncomfortably into the workplace to offset the expense of attending Catholic school. Ill at ease in the photo-finishing shop where she works, Esperanza feels grateful to an older "Oriental" man who befriends her, but when he asks for a birthday kiss and she tries to kiss him on the cheek, he grabs her face and kisses her "hard on the mouth and doesn't let go." For Esperanza, the threat of sexuality soon begins to come from within as well as from outside of herself, and the vignette "Sire" demonstrates Esperanza's growing sexual curiosity and rising desire.

When Sire, pitching pennies with his friends, repeatedly stares at her, Esperanza will not let him see that she is afraid, will not "cross the street like the other girls." Rather, to prove her bravery, she stares "back hard, just once, like he was glass." She attempts to control rather than be controlled, but like Cinderella who stays too long at the ball, she looks too long into the "dusty cat fur of his eyes," and finds herself transformed:

> Everything is holding its breath inside me. Everything is waiting to explode like Christmas. I want to be all new and shiny. I want to sit out bad at night, a boy around my neck . . . the wind under my skirt. Not . . . talking to the trees, leaning out my window, imagining what I can't see.

Ironically, the words repeated here "Everything . . . everything . . . I want . . . I want . . ." which emphasize longing, return the reader to the voice of the younger Esperanza. The phrase "leaning out my window" alludes to her great-grandmother, an Esperanza clearly controlled rather than controlling her own life, who "looked out the window her whole life . . ." after Esperanza's great-grandfather "threw a sack over her head and carried her off . . . as if she were a fancy chandelier."

While the sexually curious but still innocent Esperanza imagines "a boy around my neck" as a cure for "leaning out my window, imagining what I can't see," many women in her neighborhood that she can see are like Rafaela in "Rafaela Who Drinks Coconut & Papaya Juice on Tuesdays," who find themselves confined by marriage and sexual knowledge. Rafaela, "who is still young but getting old from leaning out the window so much," finds herself literally locked within her house on the nights her husband plays dominoes. Not surprisingly, Esperanza's description of the sexually active women in the neighborhood suggests they have been infantilized by their sexuality. Sire's girlfriend has "barefoot baby toenails all painted pale pale pink, like pink seashells, and she smells pink like babies do," and cannot tie her own shoes. Although *Mamacita,* in "No Speak English," weighs so much the taxi man must push as her husband pulls to squeeze her from the cab, she emerges still wearing "a tiny pink shoe" on "a foot soft as a rabbit's ear" with "little rosebuds of . . . toes."

The models of confined young woman who succumb to cultural and sexual pressures steer Esperanza to find other paths for herself, to discover and accept on her own terms her own sexuality, her own future, her own home, her own destiny, and her own self. First intrigued by Sally "with eyes like Egypt and nylons the color of smoke," Esperanza ultimately rejects the life of Sally who in the stories "Sally," "What Sally Said," "The Monkey Garden," and "Linoleum Roses" uses and is abused for her overt sexuality first by her father who beats her or forgets he is her father "between the buckle and the belt," then by the boys she teases and is used by in "The Monkey Garden," and finally by her husband, who breaks "the door down where his foot went through." Unlike the other confined women in these vignettes, Sally's husband "doesn't let her look out the window," so she can only look inside at "the linoleum roses on the floor, the ceiling smooth as a wedding cake."

In "Red Clowns," Esperanza is sexually attacked by young men as she waits by the red clowns for Sally, and decides for herself that Sally lied and that "all the books and magazines" that write about love and sex are wrong. From this sexual attack, Esperanza knows only "his dirty fingernails against my skin, only his sour smell again." Esperanza, warned by this encounter, rejects Sally's way, and in "Beautiful & Cruel" she sets out her own credo of sexual power. She will become like the one of the great women in the movies with "red red lips . . . who drives the men crazy and laughs them all away. Her power is her own. She will not give it her way." To gain this power, Esperanza rejects domesticity and the role of women in her culture by leaving "the table like a man" and not "putting back the chair or picking up the plate." Nor will she follow the path of Minerva in "Minerva Writes Poems" with whom she shares poems. Slightly older than Esperanza, but already with two children and a husband who comes and goes and "sends a big rock through the window," Minerva can only write when her children sleep.

If some women discourage Esperanza by their example, encouragement for the life of the imagination and the mind comes to Esperanza in the form of other women and in her own strength. Although one form the desire for sexuality takes for Esperanza in "Sire" is "imagining what I can't see," ironically Esperanza's blind Aunt Lupe first sees and tells her that it is writing that will keep her free. Just as Cisneros' own mother encouraged her, so Esperanza's mother in "A Smart Cookie" sparks her ambition and challenges her to make something of her life. Esperanza's mother can sing an opera "with velvety lungs powerful as morning glories." She seems as magical and as hidden as the wooden music box in "Gil's Furniture Bought & Sold," and she confesses to Esperanza that she "could've been somebody," but that shame over not having nice clothes influenced her to quit school. She warns Esperanza not to let shame keep her down. In "Four Skinny Trees," Esperanza finds her own source of strength in the trees "who grew despite concrete" and "send ferocious roots beneath the ground." Like herself and her ambition, the trees "reach and do not forget to reach."

One of Lucy and Rachel's aunts in the story "The Three Sisters" encourages Esperanza to look to a wider destiny for herself by urging her to "come back for the others . . . for the others who cannot leave as easily as you," reminding her that "you can't erase what you know. You can't forget who you are." Alicia of the tortilla star also tells her this when Esperanza laments about not having a house in "Alicia and I Talking on Edna's Steps." Alicia tells her, "Like it or not you are Mango Street, and one day you'll come back too." Esperanza has yet to see that the house she will have—her own home—already has been predicted for her by Elenita in "Elenita, Cards, Palm, Water," who lays Esperanza's "whole life on that kitchen table." As she reads her cards,

Elenita asks Esperanza if she has lost "an anchor of arms" and promises her "a home in the heart." If earlier in the book Esperanza was a balloon tied to an anchor of family, she is moving free of the anchor. Still, to find her destiny she must learn to find the home she dreams of in her heart.

In "A House of My Own," Esperanza begins to find the house in her heart. Because she rejects domesticity and patriarchy, it will not be "a man's house. Not a daddy's" with "nobody's garbage to pick up after." Because she has imagination and aspirations, it will have "my books and my stories." Because she is a poet, it will be "clean as paper before the poem." Finally, in "Mango Says Goodbye Sometimes," her own destiny becomes clear to her as she realizes the paradox about the house on Mango Street, which is where she belongs but feels she does "not belong to." As she becomes a writer and writes her story "down on paper," she finds that "the ghost does not ache so much." She realizes that she has to go away, but vows to return for those who cannot leave. Through her imagination and the power of art, she will build them all houses in her heart and invite all, even the bums, into the attic.

MY WICKED WICKED WAYS

Divided into four sections, *My Wicked Wicked Ways* covers life in the barrio, memories of childhood, life abroad, and a series of poems about a lover. To create narratives and still-life snapshots of characters in the poems, Cisneros plays with unexpected placement of parts of speech, deliberate manipulation of sound to convey meaning, internal rhyme, alliteration, and striking images. The title for this volume of poetry comes from the name of Errol Flynn's autobiography, and Cisneros specifically refers to Flynn in two of the poems in her book, first in her Preface poem and later in the title poem, "My Wicked Wicked Ways." The allusions to Flynn set the tone for this volume in which Cisneros turns on its head the traditional pattern of male writers describing their encounters with women. The poems in this volume fulfill the promise of the narrator of *The House on Mango Street* by celebrating the power the speaker has attained by wresting control of her life. Power of this sort comes at no small cost; still, as the Preface poem indicates, it is a cost the speaker has paid willingly.

In its first verse, the Preface calls attention to itself as a performance by directly addressing its audience, a theatrical audience that has to be interrupted: "Gentlemen, ladies. If you please— these / are my wicked poems from when. / The girl grief decade. My wicked nun / years, so to speak. I sinned." By beginning conventionally as if asking pardon of her audience, then surprising the reader by ending the second line and sentence with the adverb "when" and using it unexpectedly as the object of the preposition "from," the speaker warns her readers that she will shatter their expectations and challenge their conventions.

The speaker claims, at first, not to have been wicked in the same way as Flynn:

> not wicked like the captain of the bad
> boy blood, that Hollywood hood-
> lum who boozed and floozed it up,
> hell-bent on self-destruction. Not me

Then she undercuts her denial with, "Well. Not much . . ." Although she will describe her sexual encounters with a variety of men on various continents, her sexual adventures are not her real wickedness. Her most important crime, her "first felony," her sin, the reader learns, is writing poetry, a sin that challenges the cultural expectations her family has for her. "My first felony—I took up with poetry. / For this penalty, the rice burned. / Mother warned I'd never wife." By using "wife" as a verb, Cisneros again plays with syntax, and this inventive use of "wife" gives the

word a stronger connotation of choice; instead of choosing to wife, she "took up with poetry," and here, she refers to poetry in terms one would use to describe a sexual encounter.

The climax of the poem, the stanza that describes her leaving home, resonates with hard consonant sounds like *ch* and *ck,* contractions of hard *'d,* and verbs predominantly ending with the letters *d* or *t:*

> I chucked the life my father'd plucked for me.
> Leapt into the Salamander fire.
> A girl who'd never roamed
> beyond her father's rooster eye.
> Winched the door with poetry and fled.
> For good. And grieved I'd gone
> when I was so alone.

Not until she has left, "Winched the door with poetry and fled . . ." do we have softer sounds, "when I was so alone" that suggest some regret. The verb "Winched," which implies the use of a hand tool, is particularly apt as earlier in the poem the speaker describes herself as the daughter of a working man, "Daughter of / a daddy with a hammer and blistered feet . . ." Just as her father uses a hammer to do his work, so for the speaker "poetry" (as well as being her lover, "I took up with poetry . . .") is the tool that frees her.

But after she is free, she plays out her own version of Errol Flynn's "boozed and floozed it up" and wonders what she should really do with that freedom: "I took the crooked route and liked my badness. / Played at mistress. / Tattooed an ass. / Lapped up my happiness from a glass. / It was something, at least. / I hadn't a clue."

Living alone, the speaker finds, has two faces: "Sometimes the silence frightened me. / Sometimes the silence blessed me," but still it enables her to write. As she nears the end of her poem, she reveals what her work has cost her: "No six brothers with their Fellini racket. / No mother, father, / with their wise I told you."

She introduces her poems again, describing them with metaphors both of value ("pearls" and "jewels") and of annoyance ("itch," "colicky," "fussed"):

I tell you,
these are the pearls
from that ten-year itch,
my jewels, my colicky kids
who fussed and kept
me up the wicked nights
when all I wanted was . . .
With nothing in the texts to tell me.

Finally, the speaker concludes her Preface with a return to the first verse's inventive use of "when." "But that was then, / the who-I-was who would become the who-I-am. / These poems are from that hobbled when." The word "when" assumes a greater emphasis here as it not only end-rhymes with "then," but its *w* sound is repeated from the alliteration of the previous line, "the who-I-was who would become the who-I-am." Here, the addition of the words "that hobbled" before "when" suggests that the poems that follow in this volume come not only from a difficult time, but from a person in transition, "the who-I-was who would become the who-I-am," a person, perhaps, with the "wicked wicked" sin of writing poetry.

The first section of the volume, 1200 SOUTH / 2100 WEST, revisits several characters and situations from *The House on Mango Street.* In "Velorio," Lucy and Rachel, Esperanza's friends play outside in their backyard while inside their family mourns their baby sister. When their mother calls them inside, the juxtaposition of the playful outside world and the dark inside world is acute: "You laughing Lucy / and she calls us in / your mother / Rachel me you I remember / and the living room dark / for our eyes to get used to . . ." The vital, scruffy children seem, to the speaker, not quite fit before the beautified package of death: "The baby in a box like a valentine / and I thinking it is wrong / us in our raw red ankles / And mosquito legs / Rachel wanting to go back out again / you sticking one dirty finger in . . ."

"South Sangamon" recalls the plight of Minerva in "Minerva Writes Poems" whose come-again–leave-again husband also throws a rock through her window:

And just when we get those kids quiet,
and me, I shut my eyes again,
she laughing,
her cigarette lit,
just then
the big rock comes in.

Here, unlike in *The House on Mango Street,* the speaker is joined in camaraderie with another woman, "we get those kids quiet . . ." However, the "just when" that precedes the "we" returns in the "just then" rhyme before "the big rock comes in."

The "linoleum roses" in "Curtains" allude to the Cisneros story "Linoleum Roses" in which Sally, who has married young, is even denied the pleasure of looking out the window by her possessive husband. In the poem "Curtains," however, curtains prevent others from seeing what is inside: "the dinette set that isn't paid for, / floorboards the landlord needs to fix / raw wood, linoleum roses . . ." The poem ends with the paradox that sums up the inadequate domesticity confronting poor women, who never receive "the what you wanted but didn't get."

In section II, MY WICKED WICKED WAYS, the title poem returns to the Errol Flynn allusion, but now a photo of the speaker's father, rather than the speaker, is compared to Flynn: "He looks like Errol Flynn. / He is wearing a hat / that tips over one eye." Not only is the father physically compared to Flynn, but verses that come later in the poem suggest his comparison to Flynn's escapades with women. "The woman, / the one my father knows, / is not here. / She does not come till later." The Flynn connection between the speaker and her father suggests a familial connection to wickedness that will surface in other poems in this section. When the speaker describes her mother, she says, "That is me she is carrying, / I am a baby. / She does not know / I will turn out bad."

In "Six Brothers," which alludes to the Grimm's fairy tale "The Six Swans" and plays on the author's name Cisneros (which means "swan"), the theme of bad blood will recur. The speaker will be the "wicked" one, but she will not be completely alone in her wickedness. "Brothers, it is so hard to keep up with you. / I've got the bad blood in me I think, / the mad uncle, the bit of the bullet." Even among the brothers, perhaps, there is one, like her, who is not quite perfect, the ". . . little one-winged, / finding it as difficult as me / to keep the good name clean."

In "His Story," the speaker continues the themes of bad blood, "A family trait we trace back / to a great aunt no one mentions," and of leaving her family, but considers these themes from her father's point of view: "I was born under a crooked star. / So, says my father. / And this perhaps explains his sorrow." Recasting the main event of the Preface poem, the speaker's leaving home, from the father's point of view better enables the reader to appreciate the challenges the speaker has overcome, "An unlucky fate is mine / to be born woman in a family of men." It also better enables the reader to understand what the speaker's leaving has cost her and her father emotionally, "Six sons, my father groans, / all home. / And one female, / gone."

The poems in section III, OTHER COUNTRIES, recount the nomadic wanderings of the speaker after she leaves her family and country to write, love, and travel through France, Italy, Yugoslavia, and Greece. Among these, the poem "For a Southern Man," while rejecting domesticity, fulfills the independent female sexual credo Esperanza proposed in "Beautiful & Cruel" in

The House on Mango Street. "I've learned two things. / To let go / clean as a kite string. / And to never wash a man's clothes." The poem, "Peaches—Six in a Tin Box, Sarajevo," on the other hand, emphasizes the peace and warmth fulfilled sexuality and love can bring: "And if peaches could / they would sleep / with their dimpled head /on the other's / each to each. / Like you and me. / And sleep and sleep." Still for the speaker, human lovers cannot compete with art as a lover.

The poem "Ass" humorously plays with the idea of art as a lover, although this time rather than poetry, Michelangelo's David holds the speaker "victim," a role she rejects in her relationships with men: "Then / am I victim / of your spell, / bound since mine eyes / did first espy / that paradise of symmetry." In this poem, the speaker, wishing to play the Pygmalion rather than the Galatea part, embraces for herself the traditional roles of male artists.

And like Pygmalion transfixed,
who sincere believed
desire could unfix
that alabaster chastity,
grieved the enchantment
of those small cruel hips—
those hard twin bones—
that house such enormous
happiness.

The poems in section IV, THE RODRIGO POEMS, which make clever use of imagery, contain a cycle of poems devoted to several phases of a relationship with a married lover for whom she describes herself in "For All Tuesday Travelers" as "the middle-of-the-week wife." The cycle begins with the poem "A woman cutting celery" in which domestic images acknowledge the perspective of the lover's wife: "And she is cutting / celery and more celery . . ." The wife performs a domestic act "cutting celery," but one in which the knife in her hand indicates danger.

The line break between "cutting" and "celery" falls like the chop of a knife. The "more celery" she cuts indicates both her frustration and the passage of time. What she waits for " . . . no familiar stumble / of the key. Nor / crooked tug and coy / apology. No blurred kiss / to comfort this cruel / hour and quit those / sometimes fears to sleep . . ." hardly indicates a happy marriage. This seems a familiar scene to her, not unexpected, but still, unwelcome: "Surely / love has strayed before."

In "Sensuality Plunging Barefoot into Thorns," the speaker is drawn into the relationship with Rodrigo by the image of a red handkerchief: "you sneeze / and pull like a magician / from your sleeve— / a handkerchief. / Red." The effect of the red handkerchief on the speaker is as immediate as a red matador's cape to a bull. "Extraordinary. / Loud as timbales," but the effect is long-term. "Already it begins, / all the way home— / a slow smoke without warning." Cisneros emphasizes the importance of the color "Red." by isolating it on one line and by punctuating it as a complete sentence. The image of the red handkerchief unites harm or danger, symbolized by the color red, with domesticity, symbolized by the handkerchief, just as being a "middle-of-the-week wife" combines danger with domesticity:

> In a few weeks
> all you'll have to do is phone.
> By then
> the handkerchief
> will have done its harm.

Visual images, particularly domestic ones, continue in this cycle. In "The world without Rodrigo," the speaker, "does not mind to hesitate / undoes one button," and in "Rodrigo Returns to the Land and Linen Celebrates," bed sheets "puffed with air / the muslin and satin / the fitted and flat / the dizzy percale / and spun cotton," which can symbolize both domestic and sexual

spheres, herald Rodrigo's return: "billowing and snapping / sun-plumped and flapping / everywhere! everywhere!" Since the color red initiates the relationship, not surprisingly, in "Amé. Amo, Amaré," the speaker wears a "green green dress" when the relationship ends. In doing so, Cisneros, of course, depends on the idea that green represents jealousy, but she also plays with the traditional meaning of red-for-stop, green-for-go, and she subtly returns the reader to the green color of celery, the image that begins the cycle.

WOMAN HOLLERING CREEK

Although retaining much of the poetic language and imagery Cisneros used in *The House on Mango Street,* her second collection of fiction, covering a wider geographic area and time period, consists of bold, more fully conceived stories. In this collection, which draws on myths, legends, and history of Mexico and the American Southwest, she gives voice to the stories of many women and expands her point of view to include third-person narrative, the male point of view, and interview-structured fiction.

In the first section of this collection, "My Lucy Friend Who Smells Like Corn," the narrator re-explores the world of childhood, this time centering not on an urban barrio as in *The House on Mango Street,* but instead on both sides of the Texas-Mexico border. The title story contains poetic images

> . . . when we are squatting over marbles trading this pretty crystal that leaves a blue star on your hand for that giant cat-eye with a grasshopper green spiral in the center like the juice of bugs on the windshield when you drive to the border, like the yellow blood of butterflies.

and images that reveal the narrator and her friend Lucy jubilant in the messy beauty of girlhood:

"We're going to run home backwards and we're going to run home forwards, look twice under the house where the rats hide and I'll stick one foot in there because you dared me."

Shared cultural identity enhances the narrator's relationship with her friend:

> Lucy Anguiano, Texas girl who smells like corn, like Frito Bandito chips, like tortillas, something like that warm smell of *nixtamal* or bread the way her head smells when she's leaning close to you.

Rejecting Anglo patterns of beauty, the narrator wants to look more like Lucy. She sits in the sun even "if it's a million trillion degrees outside, so my skin can get so dark it's blue where it bends like Lucy's."

"Eleven," the next story in this section, deals with feelings of shame rather than jubilation. On the day that Rachel, the narrator, celebrates her eleventh birthday, her teacher thinks she is the owner of "an ugly sweater with red plastic buttons and a collar and sleeves all stretched out you could use for a jump rope," and forces her to wear the sweater in class. The shame of wearing an ugly sweater that is not even hers ruins her birthday and makes her want to be "far away like a runaway balloon, like a tiny *o* in the sky." Cisneros repeats here the "balloon as freedom" metaphor she used for Esperanza in "Boys and Girls."

Other stories in this section deal with finding a Mexican-American identity. In "Mericans," Mexican-American children in Mexico play outside a church while inside, "Like La Virgen de Guadalupe, the awful grandmother intercedes" on behalf of family members who have sinned. When American tourists speak to the children in Spanish, they answer in Spanish. Later, when they overhear the children speaking to each other in English, one of the surprised tourists remarks, "But you speak English!"

" 'Yeah,' my brother says, 'we're Mericans.' " The children seem to be neither American nor Mexican, yet at the same time, they are both. The fact that the tourists cannot culturally identify the bilingual children, whose identity expressed in the word "Mericans" so closely resembles the sound of the word "Mexicans," suggests the children's own ambivalence about their cultural identity.

A Mexican-American child in Mexico is also the narrator of "Tepeyac," this time as the voice of memory. The child visits grandparents in Tepeyac where, in twilight, the sky "opens its first thin stars and the dark comes down in an ink of Japanese blue above the bell towers." In the opening of the story, the narrator strings together a succession of visual images such as this one to describe the square where the child "who will leave soon for the borrowed country" goes to meet the grandfather to walk him back to "the house on La Fortuna, number 12" where "the Green iron gates . . . arabesque and scroll like the initials of my name." The story ends by relating the consequences of time. The house is sold. Businesses change. People die or move away. One particular memory the child recounts of the square is of "souvenir photographers and their Recuerdo de Tepeyac backdrops." Now, like a photograph, the adult child recalls the visual memory of Tepeyac and wonders, "Who would've guessed after all this time, it is me who will remember when everything else is forgotten."

"One Holy Night," the second section of this volume, contains two stories, the title story and "My *Tocaya,*" both of which deal with adolescent Latinas exploring love and facing the consequences of their sexuality. The title of the story "One Holy Night" refers to the Virgin birth, and Cisneros plays with this idea in the story. The narrator becomes pregnant after sleeping only one night with a man who claims to come from "an ancient line of Mayan kings." She describes her sexual encounter with him. "So I was initiated beneath an ancient sky by a great and mighty heir—Chaq Uuxmal Palouin. I, Ixchel, his queen."

Later she discovers he has no Mayan blood, "was born on a street with no name," and may be a mass murderer, and she is just one of many girls who have taken "the crooked walk."

In the third section, "There Was a Man, There Was a Woman," Cisneros includes, as well as shorter stories, several longer, more complex stories: "Woman Hollering Creek," "Never Marry a Mexican," "Eyes of Zapata," and "*Bien* Pretty." The longer stories, in particular, give voice to adult women who must learn to sort out the difference between myth and reality in love, who must—in some way—come to terms with their men and who, often, must learn to stand on their own and live without them.

In "Woman Hollering Creek," Cleófilas, a Mexican woman who thinks love resembles the *telenovelas* (soap operas), marries a Mexican-American and crosses the border to live with him. As she crosses the border, she travels over Woman Hollering Creek. She soon discovers that marriage does not resemble the *telenovelas* and that her husband "farts and belches and snores as well as laughs and kisses and holds her." After she becomes a mother and her husband begins to abuse her, she remembers her father's words: "I am your father, I will never abandon you," but shame and fear, at first, prevent her from returning home to Mexico. Finally, pregnant with a second child, she persuades her husband to let her visit a doctor who discovers her bruises and helps her to orchestrate an escape with her son.

The instrument of that escape, Felice, who drives Cleófilas to the bus station in San Antonio, is "like no woman she has ever met." She challenges Cleófilas' assumptions in two ways. First, she drives her own pickup that she is paying for herself, and second, as she drives over Woman Hollering Creek, she "opened her mouth and let out a yell as loud as any mariachi." She tells Cleófilas, "Every time I cross that bridge I do that. Because of the name you know. Woman Hollering . . . Makes you want to holler like Tarzan."

In this story, Felice gives a new voice to women like Cleófilas, a new way to "holler"—not just in "pain or rage," but freely in "a long ribbon of laughter, like water."

Cisneros uses a third-person narrator for "Woman Hollering Creek." This is unusual for her, but it enables the reader to hear the doctor's conversation with Felice and to see Cleófilas' reaction to Felice's hollering. Throughout the story, we know Cleófilas' thoughts, but we hardly hear her speak until she returns to Mexico and narrates the story of crossing the arroyo with Felice to her father and brothers. It is as if while crossing Woman Hollering Creek, Felice has given Cleófilas a voice.

The narrator of "*Bien* Pretty," a female professional artist painting in Texas, struggles to put a beautiful cockroach exterminator who poses for her as a model out of her thoughts. She remembers him with "skin sweet as burnt-milk candy, smooth as river water . . . *bien* pretty," and that he made love to her in Spanish:

> *That* language. That sweep of palm leaves and fringed shawls. That startled fluttering like the heart of a goldfinch or a fan . . . How could I think of making love in English again?

Finally, though, to free herself she burns "his letters and poems and photos and cards and all the sketches I'd ever done of him. . . ." In place of these, she starts watching the *telenovelas*. Unlike Cleófilas, however, she wants to "slap . . . the heroine to her senses because she wants the heroines "to be women who make things happen" rather than victims. She wants women to be, "Above all, fierce." The women whose stories are told in the last section of *Woman Hollering Creek* are often scarred by their dealings with both Anglo and Mexican men, but they are survivors, on their way to becoming "fierce," and Cisneros has given them a voice.

LOOSE WOMAN

If the poetry in *My Wicked Wicked Ways* casts one eye tentatively back to the speaker's past, the poetry in *Loose Woman* roars with the full frontal assault on life of a mature writer and woman who celebrates both her Mexican heritage and her American right to live life by her own rules. Consequently in this volume, many of Cisneros' poems expand with longer lines and longer length than her earlier poems.

In the first section of the volume, "Little Clown, My Heart," the speaker is self-assured and seems in control of her life. The strong rhythms in "You Bring Out the Mexican in Me" hurry the reader through a litany of pulsing appositives loaded with images that mix myths, politics, culture, history, Hollywood, anatomy, natural disasters, and sex.

> You bring out the Mexican in me,
> The hunkered thick dark spiral.
> The core of a heart howl.
> The bitter bile.

The rapid juxtaposition of such disparate images as "the Dolores del Rio in me," " The Aztec love of war in me," "The Mexico City '85 earthquake in me," and "the switchblade in the boot in me" conveys the full-throttled but mercurial nature of passion as well as the speaker's acceptance of her Mexican roots. In this tide of rhythm and images, the speaker seems to hold nothing back, yet at the end of most stanzas, she places a subtle qualifier, such as "Maybe. Maybe" or "Yes, you do. Yes, you do" or "Oh."

Although the poem "I Let Him Take Me" seems, at first, about male domination, in its last lines, "Husband, love, my life— / poems," it continues the theme of poetry as lover from *My Wicked Wicked Ways*. The language Cisneros uses in reference to her lover, poetry, reveals many aspects of her relationship with her art. As his bride, she lets him submissively take her "over the threshold and over the knee," even though the phrase "over / the knee" implies submission to the violence of a husband or father. Phrases with religious connotations such as "pilgrimed with him" and "vigiled that solitude" suggest her role as devout believer in his religion. The language in the sentence, "I labored love / fierce stitched / and fed him . . ." implies maternal care and solicitude, while "bedded and wifed him" conveys sexual love, and "He never disappointed, / hurt, abandoned" displays his fidelity. Most significantly, the language of the first and title line, "I Let Him Take Me" reminds the reader that the speaker's roles as bride, wife, lover, mother, child, and true believer are all her choice. She *lets* him take her.

In the second section, "The Heart Rounds Up the Usual Suspects," the speaker acknowledges that although some things may be beyond her control, she knows she can survive. In "I Want to Be a Father Like the Men," the speaker explores what it means to engender "like the men / I've loved" rather than as a woman. Such men have a "bold Arctic flag" like an explorer to claim what is theirs, and they have a power she seeks: "I'd like to give / without disgrace / my name." "Full Moon and You're Not Here" laments the absence of a married lover under a "Useless moon / too beautiful to waste." The images here that mix fairy tale and religion with domestic business suggest that the speaker doubts the seriousness of her lover:

> But you, my Cinderella,
> have the midnight curfew,
> a son waiting to be picked up from his den
>   meeting,
> and the fractured marriage weighing on your head
> like a crown of thorns.

Though she complains that she will go to bed alone, "Full moon and you're not here. / I take off the silk slip, / The silver bangles," first, she will, "smoke a cigar, / play a tango, / gulp my gin and tonic." She may suffer a setback in the absence of her lover, but she is not undone by him.

In the third and final section of the volume, "Heart, My Lovely Hobo," the speaker in "A Man in My Bed Like Cracker Crumbs" reasserts writing as the premier focus of her life. At the beginning of the poem, she strips the bed, shakes the sheets, and "slumped / those fat pillows like tired tongues / out the window for air and sun," to shake what is left of the man from her bed. She uses a string of quick-sounding past participles "punched . . . fluffed . . . billowed . . . snapped" to rid herself of male intrusiveness, so she can "sit down / to my typewriter and cup." In the last stanza, the image, "dust motes somersault and spin," suggests both a sunny place and space to work as well as the creative movement of the writer's mind. With a place to write and solitude to write in, the speaker ends the poem like a prayer: "Coffee's good. / Dust motes somersault and spin. / House clean. / I'm alone again. / Amen." At the end of this poem, Cisneros comes full circle by creating the space Esperanza wished for in "A House of My Own" in *The House on Mango Street:* "Only a house quiet as snow, a space for myself to go, clean as a paper before the poem."

Selected Bibliography

WORKS OF SANDRA CISNEROS

FICTION

The House on Mango Street. New York: Random House, 1991. Originally published by Arte Publico, Houston, Tex., 1984. Published in Spanish as *La Casa en Mango Street.* Translated by Elena Poniatowska. New York: Vintage Books, 1994.

Woman Hollering Creek. New York: Random House, 1991.

Hairs/Pelitos. Translated by Liliana Valenzuela. Illustrated by Terry Ybanez. New York: Knopf, 1994.

POETRY

My Wicked Wicked Ways. New York: Random House, 1987.

Loose Woman. New York: Random House, 1994.

ESSAYS

"Do You Know Me?: I Wrote the House on Mango Street." *The American Review* 15, no. 1:77–79 (Spring 1987).

"Ghosts and Voices: Writing from Obsession." *The American Review* 15, no. 1:69–73 (Spring 1987).

"Notes to a Young(er) Writer. *The American Review* 15, no. 1:74–76 (Spring 1987).

"Only Daughter." *Glamour,* November, 1990, pp. 256–258.

"Poem as Preface." *New York Times Book Review,* September 6, 1992, p. 1.

"Who Wants Stories Now." *New York Times Book Review,* March 14, 1993, pp. 4–17.

CRITICAL AND BIOGRAPHICAL STUDIES

Carbonell, Ana Maria. "From Llorona to Gritona: Coatlicue in feminist tales by Viramontes and Cisneros." *MELUS* 24:53–74 (Summer 1999).

Colby, Vineta, ed. "Sandra Cisneros." In *World Authors 1985–1990.* Bronx, N.Y.: H.W. Wilson, 1995.

Desert News Press Release. www.desertnews.com (January 23, 2000).

Doyle, Jacqueline. "More Room of Her Own: Sandra Cisneros's *The House on Mango Street.*" *MELUS* 19, no. 4:5–35 (Winter 1994).

Elias, Eduardo F. "Sandra Cisneros." In *Dictionary of Literary Biography.* Vol. 122. Edited by Karen Rood. Detroit: Gale Research, 1992. Pp. 77–81.

Fuentes, Carlos. "The Blending and Clashing of Cultures." *Christian Science Monitor,* June 1, 1992, p. 6.

González-Berry, Erlinda, and Tey Diana Rebolledo. "Growing Up Chicano: Tomás Rivera and Sandra Cisneros. *Revistas Chicano-Riqueña* 13, nos. 3–4: 109–119 (Fall–Winter 1985).

Ganz, Robin. "Sandra Cisneros: Border Crossings and Beyond." *MELUS* 19, no. 1:19 (Spring 1994).

Hoffert, Barbara. "Sandra Cisneros: Giving Back to Libraries." *Library Journal* 117, no. 1:55 (January 1992).

Kanoza, Theresa. "Esperanza's Mango Street: Home for Keeps." *Notes on Contemporary Literature* 25, no. 3:9 (May 1995).

Kingsolver, Barbara. "Poetic Fiction with a Tex-Mex Tilt." *Los Angeles Times Book Review,* April 28, 1991, p. 312.

Klein, Dianne. "Coming of Age in Novels by Rudolfo Anaya and Sandra Cisneros." *English Journal* 81, no. 5:21–26 (September 1992).

Lewis, L. M. "Ethnic and Gender Identity: Parallel Growth in Sandra Cisneros' *Woman Hollering Creek.*" *Short Story* 2, no. 2:69–78 (Fall 1994).

Olivares, Julián. "Sandra Cisneros' *The House on Mango Street* and the Poetics of Space." In *Chicana Creativity and Criticism: Charting New Frontiers in American Literature.* Edited by Helena Maria Viramontes. Arte Publico Press, 1988. Pp. 160–170.

Magill, Frank, ed. "Sandra Cisneros." In *Great Women Writers.* New York: Henry Holt, 1994. Pp. 102–105.

McCracken, Ellen. "Sandra Cisneros' *The House on Mango Street:* Community-Oriented Introspection and the Demystification of Patriarchal Violence." In *Breaking Boundaries: Latina Writing and Critical Readings.* Edited by Asunción Horno-Delgado et. al. Amherst: University of Massachusetts Press, 1989. Pp. 62–71.

Mirriam-Goldberg, Caryn. *Sandra Cisneros: Latina Writer and Activist.* Springfield, N.J.: Enslow Publishers, 1998.

Moore Campbell, Bebe. "Crossing Borders." *New York Times Book Review,* May 26, 1991, p. 6.

Prescott, Peter, and Karen Springten. "Seven for Summer." *Time,* June 3, 1991, p. 60.

Scalise Sugiyama, Michelle. "Of Woman Bondage: The Eroticism of Feet on Mango Street." *The Midwest Quarterly* 41:9–20 (Autumn 1999).

Soto, Gary. "Voices of Sadness & Science." *The Bloomsbury Review* 8, no. 4:21 (July–August 1988).

Tabor, Mary B. W. "A Solo Traveler in Two Words." *The New York Times Literary Review,* January 7, 1993, pp. 6–8.

Thompkins, Cynthia. "Sandra Cisneros." In *Dictionary of Literary Biography.* Vol. 152. Edited by James R. Giles and Wanda Giles. Detroit: Gale Research, 1995.

Valdes, Maria Elenade. "The Critical Receptions of Sandra Cisneros's *The House on Mango Street.*" In *Gender, Self, and Society.* Vol. 13. Edited by Renate von Bardelben. Frankfurt: Peter Lang, 1993. Pp. 287–300.

Yarbo-Bejarano, Yvonne. "Chicana Literature from a Chicana Feminist Perspective." In *Chicana Creativity and Criticism: Charting New Frontiers in American Literature.* Houston, Tex.: Arte Publico, 1988. Pp. 139–145.

INTERVIEWS

Bray, Rosemary. "A Deluge of Voices: Interview with Sandra Cisneros, author of *Woman Hollering Creek and Other Stories.*" *New York Times Book Review,* May 26, 1991, p. 6.

Rodríquez Aranda, Pilar E. "On the Solitary Fate of Being Mexican, Female and Wicked and Thirty-three: An Interview with Writer Sandra Cisneros." *The American Review* 18, no. 1:64–80 (Spring 1990).

Sagel, Jim. "Sandra Cisneros." *Publishers Weekly,* March 29, 1991, pp. 74–75.

—MARY ELLEN BERTOLINI

Andre Dubus

1936–1999

ONE OF THE many gifts Ernest Hemingway gave to the world in general and to writers in particular was his image. Though often ridiculed, lampooned, and dismissed, the Hemingway persona has survived. Indeed, in his centennial year, 1999, the commercialization of the man himself and to a lesser extent, his works, was seen everywhere. Aside from a major furniture company's splendid attempt to capture the spirit of the man in bedroom sets, writing desks, and objets d'art, it is the man himself who still captures the imagination long after his death in 1961. His example has spawned generations of two-fisted tough guys who can drink and fight and make loveless love until dawn and then, in solitude with pencil and paper, craft prose as delicately as medieval monks once applied gold decorations to illuminated manuscripts. In his life and works, Andre Dubus proved himself to be a full beneficiary of the Hemingway legacy.

YOUTH, COLLEGE, AND THE MARINE CORPS

Andre Jules Dubus (Dub-YOOSE) Jr. was born on August 11, 1936, in Lake Charles, Louisiana. Lake Charles is located in the southwestern part of Louisiana, between the capital, Baton Rouge, and the little town of Lafayette. This is the heart of bayou country where the summers are very hot, damp, and seemingly endless. Most of the population takes pride in its Cajun heritage and most are lower-middle class. This was certainly true of Dubus' parents. He was the youngest child and only son of Andre Jules Dubus, a civil engineer and district manager for the Gulf States Utilities Company, and Katherine (Burke) Dubus. They had two other children, Kathryn Claire Dubus, born in 1930, and Elizabeth Nell Dubus, born in 1933. In 1944 the family moved to Lafayette and Dubus was enrolled in the Christian Brothers' School. Although his father was an Episcopalian, his mother was a Roman Catholic, and Dubus was raised in her faith and remained a devout Roman Catholic to the end of his life. Indeed, Roman Catholicism forms the foundation of all of Dubus' work. Throughout his life, he identified himself as a Catholic writer who addressed the ethical questions of ordinary life. He said in an interview with Patrick J. Samway, "I've seen the whole of my fictive world through the eyes of someone who believes the main problem in the United States is that we have lost all spiritual values and not replaced them with anything comparable."

In 1954, Dubus graduated from the Christian Brothers' Cathedral High School and entered McNeese State College, a small liberal arts school in Lafayette. He graduated with a bachelor of arts degree in English in 1958. In February of that year he had married Patricia Lowe and, after graduation and with few prospects, he elected to join the United States Marine Corps. He entered with a commission as a second lieutenant.

Younger readers of Dubus who may be reluctant to approach the works of men who served in the military, writers such as Dubus, James Salter, J. D. Salinger and countless others, should understand that such service was not looked down upon in the era preceding America's involvement in Vietnam. Indeed, it was a respectable way for young men with limited prospects to provide for themselves and, in Dubus' case, a growing family. Four of Dubus' six children were born during his five and one-half years in the marines: Suzanne, born August 16, 1958; Andre III, born September 11, 1959; Jeb, born November 29, 1960; and Nicole, born February 3, 1963. Dubus was often asked if he ever regretted taking on so much responsibility so young. In response to such a question that was asked during an e-mail interview hosted by Barnes and Noble (June 12, 1998), Dubus said, "That is a good question. Friends of mine in their 30s have expressed astonishment that my first wife and I had four children before we were 25. I have never regretted it. . . . The responsibility was nothing. My generation of boys wanted that. That was manhood, to have a job and a home and support a family."

However, there is some curiosity regarding why Dubus chose the marines. After all, not every young man with a degree in English saw service in the armed forces as his only choice. Some clues to answering this question can be found in Dubus' short stories. Most of his marine stories feature characters who signed up with the hope, either their own or their father's, that the armed services would make men out of them. In Dubus' story "Over the Hill," Gale Castete's father says to his son, "So you joined the Army. Well, maybe they can make something out of you. I shore couldn't do no good." Perhaps this

was the case with Dubus since his service in the marines, onboard an aircraft carrier in the Pacific and on bases along the West Coast, lasted only until his father's death. When cancer claimed the life of his father at the age of fifty-nine in 1963, Dubus resigned his commission as a captain in the marines. As in the case of the writer Reynolds Price, whose father died of cancer at the age of fifty-four, this loss may have been what finally allowed Dubus to cross the threshold from prolonged adolescence into his own life as a writer and teacher.

FIRST PUBLISHED WORK, IOWA WRITERS' WORKSHOP, AND TEACHING

Another possible reason for Dubus' dramatic change in his life's direction could be his emergence as a published short story writer. *The Sewanee Review,* the literary journal of The University of the South and one of the oldest continuously published reviews of its kind in the United States, published his short story "The Intruder" in its April–June 1963 issue. Dubus long maintained that publication in such a prestigious journal did not influence his decision to leave the marines and pursue a career in letters. Clearly, however, such an early affirmation of his creative talent encouraged him to move in that direction.

"The Intruder," like most early short stories by American writers, is a coming-of-age story in which the blinders of a childhood fantasy life are abruptly removed by very real, very adult events. The story contains most of the basic ingredients found in all of Dubus' work: family, sex, violence, Catholic ritual, denial, and paternal protection. Kenneth Girard is spending the summer at his family's vacation cabin in Louisiana with his mother, father, and sixteen-year-old sister, Connie. They have been there six weeks; the father leaves for his job on Monday mornings, and returns the following Friday evenings. Kenneth, who is thirteen, gives free rein to his vivid imagination in the pastoral setting. Wandering the countryside with his twenty-two caliber rifle, he pretends to rescue villagers from Nazis, rid a town of outlaws in the Wild West, and, putting his rifle aside, pull a drowning girl from a raging river and then hit the game-winning home run. He also has a strong but guilt-ridden interest in a picture of a bikini-clad young girl he has found in a magazine.

On the day the events of this story take place, the parents have plans to go out for the evening and Connie is looking forward to entertaining her boyfriend, the high school football player Douglas Bakewell, in their absence and without their knowledge. Kenneth, who adores Connie, is clearly uncomfortable with her plan.

> He liked being alone, but, even more, he liked being alone with his sister. She was nearly seventeen; her skin was fair, her cheeks colored, and she had long black hair that came down to her shoulders; on the right side of her face, a wave of it reached the corner of her eye. She was the most beautiful girl he knew. She was also the only person with whom, for his entire life, he had been nearly perfectly at ease.

Kenneth resents Douglas' intrusion into what he had hoped would be a night of making fudge and watching television alone with Connie and makes a show of cleaning his rifle when the young man arrives. Kenneth, who does not perform well academically or athletically, wants to impress Douglas with the one talent he has—shooting.

Later, after Douglas leaves and Connie goes to bed, Kenneth is once again drawn to the girl in the magazine. However, guilt overcomes him. He puts the magazine away and seeks relief from his anxiety by reciting Hail Marys and doing pushups. Hearing a sound outside the cabin, he carefully peeks through a corner of his window. He sees the figure of a man approaching his sister's window. His fantasy role of rescuer takes over and he fires his rifle, hitting the man in the head. In the chaos that ensues, Kenneth is sure the man

he has killed is Douglas, whom he believes was returning to the cabin for a late-night assignation with Connie. His mother sits at his bedside and strokes his forehead and his father gives him a pill to help him sleep. They try to assure him that the man who was killed was a prowler, an intruder, and that he had done the right thing. Kenneth is not so sure and as he falls asleep, a vision comes to him. "He saw himself standing on the hill and throwing his rifle into the creek; then the creek became an ocean, and he stood on a high cliff and for a moment he was a mighty angel, throwing all guns and cruelty and sex and tears into the sea."

After the publication of "The Intruder," Dubus moved his young family to Iowa City, Iowa, and entered the University of Iowa's Writers' Workshop in 1964. An assistantship in this program paid Dubus $2,400 a year. To supplement this, Dubus stood in line every month for government surplus food, sold his blood for $25 a pint every three months, and earned $100 dollars a month teaching the Britannica Schools Correspondence Course. His assistantship was raised to $3,600 during his final year at Iowa. That was certainly welcome, but the increase made him ineligible for the surplus food program.

Dubus earned his master of fine arts degree from the Iowa Writers' Workshop in 1965. While there, he was fortunate enough to be taught and influenced by R. V. Cassill and Richard Yates. In an interview published in Southwest Texas State University's on-line journal, *Excerpt,* Dubus said of Cassill, "He pushed me and said to me once in a bar, 'You know, you are very good at describing people and writing down what they say, look like, and do. But you don't have the killer instinct of most Catholic novelists—you don't go down deep and find out why they do it.' I was pretty innocent and dumb. That was the first time I knew you were supposed to."

Richard Yates, whose first novel, *Revolutionary Road* (1961), was a finalist for the National Book Award, came to teach at the University of

Iowa in 1963, after the assassination of President Kennedy. Yates had been a speechwriter for the president's brother, Attorney General Robert Kennedy. Yates' fiction displays a lean, clear style and he has been compared to Anton Chekhov and F. Scott Fitzgerald. He found a kindred spirit in Dubus and they remained lifelong friends.

Upon completion of his master of fine arts degree, Dubus returned with his family to Louisiana. From 1965 until 1966, he taught English at Nichols State College in the small Louisiana town of Thibodaux. One summer of the searing heat and thick humidity of the bayou country was enough for Dubus, and in 1966 he moved his family to New England where he accepted a position teaching modern fiction and creative writing at Bradford College in Haverhill, Massachusetts—a school for women. These frequent changes of residence were remembered by Dubus' oldest son, Andre III, in an article by Jerome V. Kramer in an issue of the magazine *Book:* "I have always been a small guy," the younger Dubus says. "I am only a 165-pound man now. But in school I was very small. Went to a lot of schools, always the new kid. At age 15, I had such self-loathing that I would rather get stabbed to death than ever endure humiliation again, and I became a real brawler" (March/April 1999). In 1966, however, the regular uprooting of his family ceased and Dubus lived in Massachusetts for the rest of his life.

Bradford College, founded in 1803, was one of New England's first coeducational institutions. In 1836 it became exclusively a school for women. In 1971 Bradford, which had become a junior college in 1932, was authorized to grant bachelor's degrees and men were once again admitted to the school. The small liberal arts college, located an hour north of Boston, near the New Hampshire border, had a student body of 600 during the eighteen years Dubus taught there. It was in this idyllic setting near the Merrimack River that Dubus settled into a life of writing and teaching.

In 1967, Dial Press published Dubus' first novel, *The Lieutenant.* It was written while he was in Iowa and is drawn from his Marine Corps experiences. The novel tells the story of Lieutenant Dan Tierney, a commander of marines aboard an aircraft carrier, and his struggle to protect a young serviceman from harassment. Burt Lancaster bought the movie rights to the book, but it was never produced. The novel has long been out of print and Dubus maintained it ought to be. Its interest lies in what it shows of Dubus' earliest themes and abilities.

In 1970, Dubus' marriage to Pat Lowe ended in divorce. Although Dubus said that the divorce was somewhat friendly, the impact on his young children and the adjustments to a new way of being a family troubled Dubus enough that it became the focus of most of his stories. The harrowing effects of divorce on children, and the question of how to survive as a husband and father when those roles are drastically changed, are major themes in all of his later work.

SEPARATE FLIGHTS

Dubus' stories continued to be published in university literary journals such as the University of Northern Iowa's *North American Review* and the University of Oregon's *Northwest Review* through the early 1970s. In 1975 the Boston publishing house David R. Godine published Dubus' first collection, *Separate Flights.* The slim book contained seven short stories and one novella.

"We Don't Live Here Anymore" is the first of three novellas that chronicle the lives of two couples, the Linharts and the Allisons. Thirty-year-old Jack Linhart tells the story of his marriage to Terry and his affair with Edith, the wife of his friend and colleague Hank Allison. The setting is New England academia and the story closely resembles the marital and professional life led by Dubus. Jack is a teacher and Hank is a writer at a small university. They enjoy good beer, long runs, each other's company and, eventually, each other's wives. Hank has had an affair with an exchange student, whom Edith calls "that phony French bitch," and Edith, in search of comfort, reassurance, and revenge, seeks the solace that is eagerly offered by Jack. Jack feels trapped in his marriage to Terry and longs for the romantic and carefree love to which he feels entitled. Life with Terry is sheer tedium and his desire for her has been dulled by the everyday routine of housework and raising their two children. Jack's vision of paradise and escape is cold imported beer and outdoor sex. Edith supplies both. Hank is aware of his wife's unfaithfulness with his friend but displays a cold cynicism. He views marriage as a comfort zone, a place of rest and recuperation after adulterous dalliances. Indeed, he even thanks Jack for keeping Edith happy while he was putting the finishing touches on a novel, saying, "You even helped get it done. It's so much easier to live with a woman who feels loved."

Unaware of her husband's infidelity but feeling unloved, Terry begins her own affair with Hank. This proves unsatisfactory and she confesses to Jack. He in turn confesses his involvement with Edith. They are now faced with the question of how to continue their lives. No one in this story is strong enough to make a radical change; everyone stays put at this point. It is clear, however, that the code of marital conduct that is acceptable to Hank and Edith (Hank has taken up with a nineteen-year-old and Edith has a "new man") is unacceptable to Jack and Terry. Jack remains in his marriage not because of any love he feels for Terry but out of pity for her. Terry makes the commitment to regain her husband's love even if it means she must become a more conscientious housekeeper. The future looks grim for all of the characters. Their story continues in Dubus' next collection.

"Over The Hill" is Dubus' first short story that shows the influence of his Marine Corps experiences. Gale Castete, a twenty-four-year-old marine, is blowing his entire savings, $150, on Old Crow whiskey and a Japanese woman in a Yokosuka bar. He received a letter from his mother back home in Louisiana the day before and a telephone conversation with her to confirm its contents has sent him in search of physical and emotional numbness. Six months earlier, in June, Castete had met a nineteen-year-old girl, Dana. Two months later they were married and Dana is now reluctantly living with Castete's parents while he is away at sea. His mother's letter reaches him in December and relates the problems she and his father are having with Dana. Castete knew when he met Dana that he was not her first, or even fourth or fifth.

But most disturbing of all was her casual worldliness: giving herself that first time as easily as, years before, high school girls had given a kiss, and her apparent assumption that he did not expect a lengthy seduction any more than he expected to find that she was a virgin. It was an infectious quality, sweeping him up, making him feel older and smarter, as if he had reached the end of a prolonged childhood. But at the same time he sensed his destruction and, for moments, he looked fearfully into her eyes.

Certainly Castete hoped that life under his parents' roof and watchful eyes would control his bride's possible waywardness and provide an example of proper spousal behavior. This clearly has not happened. Dana is unfaithful and the knowledge of that is driving Castete "over the hill." He does not return to his ship at the appointed time and, instead, stays with the Japanese woman, Betty-san, thereby compounding his anxiety and despair. Mental pictures of Dana's betrayal torment him.

Then he thought of her face tilted back, the roots of her hair brown near the forehead when it was time for the Clairol again, the rest of it spreading pale blonde around her head, the eyes shut, the mouth half open, teeth visible, and the one who saw this now was not him—.

Drinking dark rum in Betty-san's apartment, Castete sees only one way to release the agonizing pain growing within him. He returns to his ship and is court-martialed and sentenced to three months' confinement, most of it to be served in the Yokosuko brig. Afterward, he will serve out his tour of duty at the marine barracks there in Yokosuko. The fact that he will not be returning to the United States for nearly a year deepens his hopelessness and strengthens his resolve to end his life. When he hands over his personal belongings prior to confinement, he hides a razor blade between his belt and waistband. His utter helplessness is highlighted by his inability to write a letter home to Dana or even properly make up the bed in his cell. He slashes his left wrist with the razor blade but immediately regrets it and calls for the officer in charge. Once he is patched up, the doctor asks him, "You didn't do a very good job, did you, son?" "No, sir." "Do you ever do a good job at anything?" "No, sir."

As he returns to his cell, Castete sees his life will be as long, empty, and dark as the passageway he walks. He is "conscious of the bandage on his wrist as though it were an emblem of his uncertainty and his inability to change his life." In his final acceptance of this, he walks away from the nothingness of death. One is reminded of the ending of Hemingway's *A Farewell to Arms,* which contains a brilliant scene of disillusionment and loss. In the final paragraph of that novel, Lieutenant Henry leaves the hospital where his stillborn child and dead wife lie and walks to his hotel, in the dark, in the rain. Castete, like Henry, has lost everything that gave his life meaning and purpose.

Another story in *Separate Flights,* "The Doctor," is a very short and haunting story. Art Cas-

tagnetto, an obstetrician, is out for a run on an idyllic Sunday morning and suddenly feels that something is terribly wrong. He runs back to a bridge where he had seen some boys playing. The guard walls of the bridge are made of large, rectangular concrete slabs and somehow one of these slabs has fallen, trapping a boy beneath it in the brook. The doctor tries desperately to lift the slab, but it is too heavy. He runs to a nearby home and tells the woman who lives there to call for help and returns to the brook. It seems impossible to him that this young boy could be drowning right before his eyes and there is nothing he can do about it. He continues to struggle with the slab and feels the boy's hands trying to push it off of his chest. Ten minutes later, four volunteer firemen arrive. It is too late.

All afternoon Art is haunted by fears for the safety of his own children and the crushing knowledge of his own helplessness. His wife keeps his glass filled with gin and tonic and finally the tears come. The next morning something draws him back to the bridge, some memory of something he thinks he may have seen. He walks from the bridge toward the house where the emergency phone call was made and sees it— a bright green garden hose. Back at his own home, he disconnects a garden hose that has lain in his yard all winter. With a pocketknife, he cuts off a length of it, puts it to his mouth, pinches his nostrils and breathes through the tube. "He looked up through a bare maple tree at the sky. Then he walked around the house to the Buick and opened the trunk. His fingers were trembling as he lowered the piece of hose and placed it beside his first-aid kit, in front of a bucket of sand and a small snow shovel he had carried all through the winter." Readers are left to draw their own conclusions regarding the doctor's act. The cut hose could be merely a reminder of his helplessness and inability to think fast during a crisis. However, since he placed it alongside other emergency equipment, he may truly believe that he might be involved in a similar accident someday and is determined to be prepared.

Dubus examines race relations and rape in the pre-segregation South in "In My Life." A black man, Willard "Sonny" Broussard had raped Jill, a young white woman, sixteen months earlier. The day of his execution has arrived and Jill, in this first-person narrative, recounts the event and tries to come to terms with her conflicting emotions. Though she initially wanted him dead, time and her ability to get on with her life in a fairly satisfying way have diminished her desire for revenge. At the time of his death, Jill feels something close to compassion for Broussard. This deceptively simple story contains a subtle condemnation of the justice system and capital punishment.

"If They Knew Yvonne" was chosen by Martha Foley for inclusion in *The Best American Short Stories 1970*. This story of a young man's adolescent angst is dedicated to Dubus' two sons, Andre III and Jeb. As the story opens, Harry is experiencing the warfare of his body against his spirit. He is a student in a Catholic boy's school run by the Christian Brothers in Louisiana. Brother Thomas admonishes the boys that self-abuse is a mortal sin and must be resisted. He recommends that the boys avoid being alone, find some exhausting activity to do, pray to the Virgin Mary, and receive the Holy Eucharist often. Harry, though he tries valiantly, is unable to maintain his purity and slips into a pattern of sin, confession, and absolution. This repetitious cycle torments Harry to the point of considering self-mutilation. Just as quickly as that possible remedy occurs to him, he rejects it—unlike Hemingway's similarly tormented character in "God Rest You Merry, Gentlemen."

In college, Harry finds what he feels is a less sinful release, a willing coed, Yvonne Millet. For a few months they satisfy each other's needs but eventually Harry realizes that he has merely traded self-abuse for other-abuse; he does not love Yvonne. Confession, however, has become much easier. "I only had to confess sexual intercourse, and there was nothing shameful about that, nothing unnatural. It was a man's sin." After breaking with Yvonne, Harry soon returns to his old habit, but his definition of sin has changed. In the confessional, he confronts Father Broussard, "I mean no, Father, I'm not really sorry. I don't even think it's a sin." Father Broussard refuses to give Harry absolution. In a conversation with his sister, Janet, whose husband has left her with five-year-old twin boys, Harry's enlightenment begins. She tells him,

> "I know this much: too many of those celibates teach sex the way it is for them. They make it introverted, so you come out of their schools believing sex is something between you and yourself or between you and God. Instead of between you and other people. Like my affair. It wasn't wrong because I was married. Hell, Bob didn't care, in fact he was glad because it gave him more freedom. It was wrong because I hurt the guy."

Harry, however, still desires absolution and meets with Father Grassi, who leads him to a clearer understanding of what his true sin has been. Father Grassi repeats to Harry a line from the Gospel according to Saint John in which Jesus prays for the well-being and care of his disciples after He is gone, saying, "I do not pray that You take them out of the world, but that You keep them from evil." The meaning is clear to Harry; his self-abuse is "of the world" but his loveless lovemaking with Yvonne was evil. What God loves is the goodness of our hearts. Harry is absolved, his only penance being to say a triumphant "Alleluia" three times.

"Miranda Over the Valley" is the story of an eighteen-year-old girl who lives with her indulgent, protective parents. The story opens on her last day at home before leaving southern California to attend her first year at Boston University. All day she has been daydreaming about her boyfriend, Michaelis, a twenty-two-year-old law student. She imagines in great detail what will be their last evening together before she leaves for school: where they will eat, what she will order, but beyond that her mind is too frightened to venture.

Michaelis picks her up at her parents' home in his old, dented Plymouth (Miranda drives a new Corvette) and, after dinner, drives her to Mulholland Drive. Parked there, overlooking the San Fernando Valley, Miranda passionately overcomes her fears and is soon no longer a virgin.

Two months later, in Boston, a new fear arises. She confides to her roommate Holly that she may be pregnant. A visit to a gynecologist confirms this. Back at her apartment, she calls Michaelis and an oddly passive-aggressive conversation ensues that is reminiscent of a similar conversation in Hemingway's "Hills Like White Elephants." Michaelis asks,

> "It's about two months, is that right?"
> "It was September second."
> "I know. Do you want to get married?"
> "Do you?"
> "Of course I do. If that is what you are thinking about."
> "I'm not thinking about anything. I saw the doctor this afternoon and I haven't thought about anything."
> "Look: do you want to do it at Thanksgiving? That'll give me time to arrange things, I have to find out about blood tests and stuff, and your folks'll need some time—you want me to talk to them?"
> "No, I will."
> "Okay, and then after Thanksgiving you can go back and finish the semester. At least you'll have that done. I can be looking for another apartment. This is all right for me, maybe all right for two, but with a—"
> He stopped.
> "Are you sure you want to?"
> "Of course I am. It just sounded so strange, saying it."
> "You didn't say it."
> "Oh. Anyway, we'll need more room."

Her parents, while not overjoyed by Miranda's news, understand her situation. Her father says, "You're not the first good kids to get into a little trouble." She flies home the next day. On the flight, she is too distracted to read the magazines and play she has brought with her. *Time* and *Holiday* are certainly symbolic of two things she wishes for. *Antigone* seems an odd choice until one remembers that the play is about a young girl's refusal to accept what is "practical." Miranda is clearly preparing for the battle she knows will take place. Both sides present their arguments strongly. Miranda's romantic notion of being a good mother and supportive wife is met head on by her parents' harsh worldview. They foresee nothing but hardships and unhappiness for Miranda and Michaelis if they marry and have the baby. The best course, they feel, is for Miranda and her mother to go to New York, secure the services of an abortionist, get Miranda on the pill, and then continue on with their lives as if this minor bump in the road had never happened. Miranda feels as if she has been sentenced to death. As an additional inducement to see things their way, the parents offer a post-Christmas trip to Acapulco. Miranda stands firm in her belief that marriage and birth, no matter what the cost to her, is what she wants.

In the end, she is defeated. Not by her parents, but by Michaelis, whom she has observed silently nodding in agreement with her parents' arguments.

> She looked at Michaelis. He looked at her, guilty, ashamed; then he looked at her parents as though to draw from them some rational poise; but it didn't work, and he lowered his eyes to his beer can. 'Michaelis? Do you want to go to Acapulco?'
> Still he looked down. He had won and lost, and his unhappy face struggled to endure both. He shrugged his shoulders, but only slightly, little more than a twitch, as if in mid-shrug he had realized what a cowardly gesture the night had brought him to.

Dubus gives a good clue to the man's character by giving him the name "Michaelis." Readers of

D. H. Lawrence's masterpiece, *Lady Chatterley's Lover*, will remember her Ladyship's early lover, the Irish playwright Michaelis. Lawrence's Michaelis was a cad and a bounder whose worst social sin, of many, was his determination to climb higher. Dubus touches very lightly on the social and economic differences between Miranda and her lover by describing the car each drives. Perhaps Miranda's parents see Michaelis as an opportunistic young man and, in front of their daughter, make him an offer he can't refuse. When she sees Michaelis for what they think he is, Miranda will hate him, and they will have rescued her from harm just as surely as her father had when he shot a snake that threatened her when she was a little girl. Whatever her parents' intention, Miranda has the abortion, returns to Boston where she seduces her roommate's boyfriend, and in one final romantic encounter with Michaelis, ends their relationship. The Miranda who existed at the beginning of this story has been destroyed. Dubus said in a 1987 interview with Thomas Kennedy, "That ending surprised me more than most of my endings do. I wrote it over two times, hoping she would do something different, but she didn't. I saw her as defeated. As a friend and poet, Kenneth Rosen, said, 'She was defeated by reason over instinct.' "

Miranda appears in another story in *Separate Flights*, "Going Under." She is three years older and sexually involved with Peter Jackman, a recently divorced, older man. The hardening effects of the events told in "Miranda Over the Valley" are still in control of her heart and she is unable or unwilling to give Jackman more than her body. He takes her to bed like a child who is lonely and frightened and takes comfort with a favorite teddy bear. Jackman, whose downward spiral will continue in "At St. Croix" and "The Winter Father," uses Miranda to fill the spaces left empty by his divorce, but Miranda is too insubstantial. "He looks at her green eyes: they are glazed and she is smiling, but it is a smile someone else hung there; Miranda is someplace else." His wife,

Norma, and his children, David and Kathi, have moved across the country, and though all are damaged by this to some extent, Dubus focuses on the agony of Jackman's isolation and lack of a clear purpose in his new circumstances.

"Separate Flights" is another story of isolation and spiraling descent. Beth Harrison, a forty-nine-year-old grandmother, is suffering from impending "empty nest syndrome." Her youngest daughter, Peggy, is leaving their Iowa home to attend college in New England. Beth dreads life alone with a husband she despises; a man who insists on separate flights when he and Beth travel to ensure that, in case of an airline accident, Peggy will have one parent left to care for her. On one such flight, Beth imagines the possibility of a brief affair with a fellow passenger, Robert Carini, but lacks the nerve to follow through. For weeks after, she dwells on the lost opportunity and slides deeper into alcoholic despair. Dubus uses an effective narrative technique of blending past and present events to tell Beth's story.

One of Dubus' earliest admirers, Joyce Carol Oates, reviewed his first collection in the *Ontario Review*. She wrote, "Dubus' attentiveness of his craft and his deep commitment to his characters make the experience of reading these tales— which are almost without exception about lonely, pitiful people—a highly rewarding pleasure." Other reviewers and the reading public were quick to echo Oates's estimation. In addition, *Separate Flights* was selected to receive *The Boston Globe*'s first Laurence L. Winship Award for the best book of New England origin.

ADULTERY AND OTHER CHOICES

In 1975, Dubus married Tommie Gail Cotter. Writing in *The New York Times Sunday Magazine*, Bruce Weber reported, "After four children, his first marriage collapsed, more or less amicably, in 1970. 'We had a very good divorce,' he says. 'We just stayed in the same town.' The second, to an old college flame, was begun after a one-day reunion and ended shortly thereafter. 'I think the sexual revolution has been damaging to a lot of people,' he says. 'I took part, but finally I just said the next time I make love to a woman I'm going to know her middle name and her hometown.' "

Dubus received his first Guggenheim Award in 1976. In this same year his short story "Cadence" was selected for inclusion in *Best American Short Stories 1976* and he began a series of monthly columns for *Boston Magazine.* Godine published Dubus' next short-story collection, *Adultery and Other Choices,* in 1977. Once again, critics and readers welcomed his new work. Even though these stories replayed all the basic themes of his previous collection, Dubus' craftsmanship drew favorable responses from Frances Taliaferro in *Harper's* and Edith Milton in *The New Republic.*

A poignant story of father and son, "An Afternoon With the Old Man" introduces young Paul Clement. Like Hemingway's Nick Adams, a character who appears in several of Hemingway's short stories, and whose fictional life closely resembles his creator's experiences, Paul is clearly an autobiographical representation of Dubus' childhood. This story presents a young son's anguish at being unable to express his love for his father after spending an afternoon together at the golf course. In "Contrition" Paul and his best friend, Eddie Kirkpatrick, decide to take music lessons at their school. They want to play the trumpet but the band needs French horns. As with most ten-year-olds, the interest soon fades. Paul's father, who has borrowed a hundred dollars to buy the instrument, explodes in a torrent of verbal abuse when he learns that his son wants to quit. Another story, "The Bully," is a dark tale of Paul's torment at the hands of Larry Guidry, an older boy who has been held back in school. Paul's betrayal of his friend and his pitiful imitation of Larry's cruelty are troubling. One wonders what self-betrayals Paul will commit on his journey to manhood.

The next two stories are told from the point of view of young women. "Graduation" is the story of Bobbie, who lost her virginity at the age of fifteen and proceeded to maintain a reputation as "one of those girls." After a vicious cycle of meaningless sex and morning-after regrets, Bobbie comes up with a brilliant idea—she will recreate herself. Her parents agree with her wish to enroll in Louisiana State University immediately after graduating from high school in Port Arthur, Texas. No one knows her or her reputation at the university, and she presents herself as, and remains, "untouched." When the moment of truth comes, with a young man she is determined to marry, she concocts a story of childhood rape by a visiting uncle. Her intended accepts her story and she accepts his proposal of marriage. She is twenty-one and lives in San Diego, California, far from anyone who may know the facts about her first eighteen years in Port Arthur. Although she strongly desires to tell her husband the truth, she understands that her future happiness depends on her ability to keep the truth of the past separate from the truth of the present. Like Bobbie, Louise in "The Fat Girl" is determined to create her own identity. Louise, the daughter of slim, well-meaning parents, must fight the battle of the bulge to find acceptance and love in a world that insists that how one looks is who one is. After enduring humiliation and hurt from family, friends, and an abusive husband (who is enraged that she is gaining weight and obliterating the gorgeous "trophy wife" he thought he had married), she gives up the struggle of maintaining mannequin perfection. She has found that severe dieting has dulled her appetite for life itself. If love comes her way, Louise knows it can see through any number of layers of fat and find her true heart and soul.

"Cadence," "Corporal of Artillery," "The Shooting," and "Andromache," are all drawn from Dubus' life in the Marine Corps. "Cadence" brings back Paul Clement as an officer candidate at the marine training camp in Quantico, Virginia. His need to prove his manhood to his father and to himself is still unresolved. A few months earlier, his girlfriend, Tommie, had broken up with him over the requirements of his church. He finds some comfort in the isolation and mind-numbing enforced conformity of the Corps. His friend, Hugh Munson, however, finds life in the Corps unbearable. Munson, who does not have a father to impress but who does have a girlfriend he longs for, soon leaves the officer training camp. Paul stays on, but one does not sense that this is out of dedication and loyalty. Rather, he stays because he has nowhere else to go except home to face his father. Like Clement, Fitzgerald, the corporal in "Corporal of Artillery," stays on in the service. Unlike Clement, Fitzgerald stays for all the right reasons. Married, a father of three children, and up to his ears in debt, he accepts and even embraces his fate and reenlists for six years to collect the much-needed bonus money. His responsible behavior stands in marked contrast to Paul's lack of character. Another story, "The Shooting" presents a much darker side of military life, that of adultery, madness, and violence.

The archetypal military wife has her literary origins in Homer's story of Andromache told in *The Iliad.* As the wife of the Greek military hero, Hector, Andromache followed her husband to Troy where he met his brutal death and she was left to find a life for herself and their son. Dubus' modern Andromache, Ellen, has followed her Hector, Ed, from wartime Korea to peacetime in the Pacific Northwest. Ed is killed in a plane crash and Ellen reflects on their life together. She hopes to provide a different life for her children, especially Posy, her nine-year-old daughter, who is beginning to show the self-denying characteristics demanded by the Corps—stoicism, repression, and silence.

"Adultery" is the second part of the trilogy that chronicles the lives of the two couples first presented in "We Don't Live Here Anymore." Edith has grown even more cynical; she endures her husband's affairs and pursues her own. She falls in love with a former priest, Joe Ritchie. Ritchie

has left the priesthood to seek the love of a woman before his cancer consumes him. What he brings to Edith is the reality that all people are terminally ill from the moment of birth; that everything matters and there is no time for meaningless behavior. Edith finally develops the strength of character to leave her false and adulterated marriage.

On several occasions, Dubus named "Adultery" as one of his favorite stories. In an interview for *Glimmer Train,* he was asked which of his stories gave him the greatest sense of accomplishment. He replied, "They are mostly gone when I finish them. I remember the ones that were hardest to write. 'Adultery' was hard, and I almost quit writing it a few times." The story went through seven drafts, nearly four hundred pages compressed into sixty, before it was published in the Winter 1977 issue of the *Sewanee Review.*

Adultery and Other Choices was well received by critics and widened Dubus' audience. In 1978 his marriage to Tommie Gail Cotter ended in divorce. They had no children. Also in that year Dubus received his first National Endowment for the Arts grant and "The Fat Girl" was included in the *Pushcart* anthology.

FINDING A GIRL IN AMERICA

The following year, 1979, Dubus met the writer Peggy Rambach (*When the Animals Leave*), who was working for his publisher, David R. Godine. Dubus and Rambach, who was twenty-one years his junior, were married soon after they first met. In 1980, Dubus' mother died at the age of seventy-eight and, in 1982, Cadence Dubus, his first child with Rambach was born.

The dedication page of Dubus' next collection, *Finding a Girl in America* (1980), reads "To Peggy." In the story "Killings," Dubus investigates the intensity of marital and paternal love and the violence that is often committed because of it. Matt and Ruth Fowler's son, Frank, is involved with a young woman, Mary Ann Strout. Mary Ann, who has two children, is in the first month of her separation from her husband, Richard. Unable to accept that his marriage is over and another man has taken his place with his wife and children, Richard beats up Frank. Frank is undeterred and continues to see Mary Ann until the day Richard kills him with two shots to the chest and one to the face.

Richard, out on bail and awaiting trial, seems to be everywhere Frank's devastated parents go. They see him enjoying a life he stole from their son. The certainty that Richard will eventually be convicted and serve a long prison term is not enough for Matt. He enlists the aid of his friend, Willis, and abducts Richard, takes him to a wooded area outside of town, and shoots him to death. Matt and Willis bury the body and it seems unlikely it will ever be discovered. Richard will be considered a bail jumper and eventually forgotten. The questions Dubus leaves unanswered are: does this second murder alleviate the pain and sorrow of Matt and Ruth or increase it, and what purpose does revenge ultimately serve?

In another story, "The Dark Men" of the title are Foster and Todd. They are from the Office of Naval Intelligence and wear dark, civilian clothes. They have come aboard Captain Ray Devereaux's ship in search of Commander Joe Saldi. Devereaux stalls the men until Saldi is ashore. He later meets Saldi at the Officer's Club and tells him of the men's quest. They have evidence of some unnamed crime committed by Saldi. Someone gave them a confession in San Francisco and mentioned Saldi's name. They have come to present Saldi with their evidence and give him the opportunity to resign from the service. Devereaux assures Saldi, who has been his friend for thirteen years, that whatever it is the "dark men" have on him, it doesn't matter. "They brought paperwork and it was sealed and it still is and it'll stay that way. I don't give a good Goddamn and I never *did*. You hear me, Joe?" Devereaux leaves

Saldi with an unstated option—the equivalent of leaving him alone in a room with a pistol and one bullet. Saldi knows what the dark men know. He knows that his military life, the only life he has ever known, is over. He takes a plane from the airfield and crashes it into the sea. Dubus has said that the story is based on an incident he heard of while serving aboard the USS *Ranger* in the Pacific and that the unnamed crime was homosexuality.

"His Lover" and "Townies" are stories about the sometimes violent battles the "have-nots" wage against the "haves." Leo Moissant, a blind man living in a trailer, allows two girls and a boy from New Mexico to park their van nearby. They claim that they are traveling the country and want to see the Atlantic Ocean. One of the girls, Linda, begins to cook for Leo then quickly works her way into his bed and becomes his lover. During the nights she spends with him, however, she leaves the trailer for a period of time and drives off with the others in the van. One night, the group does not return and Moissant learns from the police that these nightly forays involved burglaries and vicious murders. In his memories of his time with Linda, Moissant's physical blindness is matched by his moral blindness. He forgets Linda's psychotic behavior and remembers only the pleasure she brought to him. "Townies" is the story of a college girl, a "have," and two "have-nots," one who ends her life and the other who discovers her dead body but does not report it right away.

In the 1987 interview with Thomas Kennedy, Dubus said that Richard Yates once told him that "The Misogamist" was the ugliest story he had ever read. In this story, Roy Hodges, a young marine in 1944, is loved by chaste Sheila Russell. Hodges, however, loves the Corps and is unable to imagine Sheila having any part in it. As a postsex afterthought, he had proposed to her eight years before and has kept her waiting ever since. The ugliness Yates found presents itself in the form of a burly first sergeant who gives Hodges a misogynistic speech about women and marriage. His long-winded advice is perhaps the most obscene rejection of women as human beings in all of literature.

"At St. Croix" follows immediately after "The Misogamist" in the collection and suffers because of that placement. After such vitriolic misogyny, Peter Jackman's sorrow over the loss of his wife and children through divorce seems ludicrous. However, Dubus may have placed this story where it is to evoke that very reaction in the reader. "The Pitcher" is the story of a young couple that slowly becomes aware of their inability to recognize or understand each other's needs. Billy Wells is minor league pitcher in southern Louisiana, but he could just as easily have been portrayed as a landscape painter in northern Italy or a poet living on the moors of Scotland. The demands on each are similar. Dedication and discipline to each art form leaves little time and energy for anything else. Billy's wife, Leslie, knows this all too well and explains to him the reason she is leaving him for a dentist, "It wasn't the road trips. It was when you were home. You weren't here, for me." Dubus, an avid Boston Red Sox fan, displays a remarkable ability to re-create the smallest details of a baseball game, the players, and their followers.

Juanita Creehan is a thirty-eight-year-old cocktail waitress in "Waiting." Her husband was killed in the Korean War and she has been a widow for twelve years. Although she keeps her sex life alive with occasional one-night stands with servicemen, she remains faithful to her husband's memory by not remarrying or forming lengthy liaisons. Her cleansing visits to the beach perhaps imply that she is waiting for the courage to allow the sea to tenderly carry her away on its dark waves.

In "Delivering" and "The Winter Father," Dubus presents the devastation wrought by the breakup of families from two perspectives. In the first story, two young brothers come to terms with the reality that their mother is gone for good after her one last drunken fight with their father. Dubus had always written brilliantly about children but "Delivering" is truly a triumph of insight into what these boys feel, fear, and need. In "The Winter Father," Peter Jackman appears to finally be aware of the feelings and fears and needs of his own children and there is hope that he will turn the focus away from himself and help them endure their new life of separation and scheduled visitation.

The final installment in the Linhart/Allison trilogy, "Finding a Girl in America," finds Hank suffering from the very freedom he craved in the two previous stories. Jack and Terry have settled into a marriage of friendship if not passion and Edith appears to be happy in her new life as a divorcée. Hank, on the other hand, has only moved through one sexual encounter after another with his young female students. This suits him just fine until he learns from his current coed, Lori, that his previous playmate, Monica, has aborted what would have been his child. In his rage at her action he realizes that the sexual revolution, birth control, abortion on demand, and loveless sex have exacted an enormous price. He vows to cease his irresponsible behavior and adopts what can only be called an "old-fashioned" attitude toward love and marriage. Fortunately, Lori agrees and their future together looks bright.

The stories in Dubus' next two collections, *The Times Are Never So Bad* (1983), and *The Last Worthless Evening* (1986), have all the same ingredients found in his previous work. They reveal his continued dedication to his craft and his profound sympathy for and understanding of the human condition. A quotation from Saint Thomas More provides the title of the 1983 collection, "The times are never so bad but that a good man can live in them." Two stories are of special interest, "The Pretty Girl" for its experimentation in the use of many voices and points of view, and

"A Father's Story" for its stunning dialogue with God. *The Last Worthless Evening* contains the remarkable "Rose." The narrator, a fifty-one-year-old former marine and observer of human nature, begins his story of Rose with a memory from his service days. He begins by recalling a slight young man who was constantly harassed and pushed to his limit by his sergeants. The young man cannot chin himself or manage more than a couple of pushups and is hated by those who will be under his command if they cannot drive him out of officer training. One night during a sleepwalking episode, the young man performs an impossible feat of strength—lifting a fully packed locker six inches off the floor from a squatting position. Awake, he is unaware of his ability to endure the physical demands of training, fails miserably at every test of endurance, believes himself to be a failure, and quits the program.

Like the young marine's, Rose's story is one of abuse and untapped strengths. Her husband's physical and verbal abuse of their three children has slowly intensified over the years. Rose feels helpless since she is completely dependent on Jim and his paycheck. She is frightened to discover a growing lack of patience with the children herself.

Jim finally goes too far. He hurls their boy against a wall, breaking his arm. He then fights Rose's attempts to come to the boy's rescue. Rose finally quits thinking about what she can or cannot do and acts on a mother's natural instinct to protect her young. In an amazing scene of determined violence, she gets her boy into her car, overcomes Jim, rushes through the apartment fire he has set, and brings her two daughters to safety. Jim attempts to block the path of her car. Rose not only runs him down but also, very calmly, backs over his body again and again until the police and fire department arrive.

At the trial, the jury finds Rose's actions to be justifiable homicide but her years of inaction cost her the custody of her children. They are placed in a foster home. She does not challenge this nor does she try to regain custody later. Indeed, at the story's opening, many years have passed and the last time she ever saw her children was in the car as she crushed their father's body beneath the tires. Isolated in a lifelong image of herself as weak and undeserving of any happiness, she is as unaware of her true strengths, a mere thirty minutes of which saved the lives of her children, as the marine sleepwalker was of his.

VOICES FROM THE MOON

In between these two collections of short stories and novellas, there was a curiosity published in 1984: an Andre Dubus novel. Although Dubus had always preferred to call his longer stories "novellas," Godine insisted on marketing *Voices from the Moon* as a novel. Interestingly enough, Godine included it in their edition of Dubus' *Selected Stories* two years later. In this novel, Dubus shows himself to be an accomplished juggler; managing to keep six perspectives in the air for the narrative's twenty-four-hour period. The central perspective belongs to twelve-year-old Richie, a decent boy, mature beyond his years, who aspires to the priesthood. The straight path he imagines his future will take makes two sharp curves. One is his first kiss and the other is the news that his adored divorced father, Greg, has plans to marry Richie's brother's former wife, Brenda. Greg and his first wife, Joan, Richie's mother, had been married for twenty-seven years when Joan left to live alone in town and work as a waitress. It was not a loss of love for Greg that drove her away, but a feeling that she had outlived love for anyone. Richie, in his anger and confusion, turns to the structure and comfort of the Catholic Church, as represented by Father Oberti. He learns that forgiveness must precede love and love, which is God's freely given grace, is essential to an understanding and acceptance of life's mysteries. This brilliant little novel received glowing reviews from John Updike in *The New Yorker* and Richard Eder in *The Los Angeles Times Book Review.*

After eighteen years of teaching four courses every semester, five days a week, exhaustion forced Dubus to retire from Bradford College in 1984 at the age of forty-eight. He devoted himself to his writing but kept in touch with students by making occasional visits to colleges as a lecturer and reader. His feelings about teaching were expressed in the Weber article. "I loved it," he says. "I never would have retired if my body hadn't quit."

THE ACCIDENT

Between midnight and one in the morning on July 23, 1986, Dubus was driving back to Haverhill from Boston, where he had been doing some research for a short story he was writing about a prostitute. Nearing his home, he saw ahead of him a stalled car in the third lane of I-93 North. His first thought was to go around and continue home, but he saw a woman standing beside the car, crying and bleeding. Dubus pulled his car over near the center guardrail and went to see what aid he could give. The woman's name was Luz Santiago and she and her brother, Luis, were from Puerto Rico and spoke little English. They had hit a motorcycle and thought the rider was trapped beneath their car. Dubus saw a dark liquid pooling at their feet and was sure it was blood. Another car, a silver Honda Prelude, was approaching and Dubus attempted to flag it down. Before the car slammed into them, Dubus was able to push Luz out of the way. She escaped with relatively minor injuries but her brother was killed and Dubus' legs were crushed and three vertebrae were broken. Two women had arrived at the accident scene before Dubus and had used a roadside call box to request assistance. Dubus met one of the women ten years later, a meeting he wrote about in his essay "Witness." He expressed his gratitude for her unselfish action. Had a trooper not already been en route before Dubus was hit, he very likely would have bled to death on that quiet stretch of highway. Dubus was rushed to a nearby hospital in Wilmington where Dr. Wayne Sharaf performed emergency surgery to stop the bleeding. Afterward, he was sent to Massachusetts General Hospital in Boston.

Dubus found out later that the motorcycle the Santiagos' car had hit had been abandoned in the road. Its rider was drunk and had fallen off and was found later by the highway patrol confused and wandering farther up the highway. In the Weber article, Dubus recalled the man:

> He never tried to deny it. He made a videotape for the police, and he never changed his story. He was a stand-up guy. His wife had fallen in love with another guy and left him, left his kids. He got drunk. I met him. I said, "Your kids think you're some kind of outlaw or something?" He said, "No." He said, "I explained it to them."

At the trial, Dubus spoke on the motorcyclist's behalf and asked that the court be lenient. The woman who hit Dubus and Santiago was not under the influence of alcohol or drugs and avoided prosecution. The motorcyclist was sentenced to one year in jail.

Dubus was hospitalized for nearly two months. The injury to his back was easily repaired but his left leg had to be amputated just above the knee by surgeon Dr. Fulton Kornack. His right leg was saved but the damage to its nerves and muscles was severe and rendered the leg useless. He learned how to maneuver a wheelchair and received physical therapy at home until he could transfer himself from the chair to the passenger seat of a car. Judith Tranberg provided further therapy at Hale Hospital in Haverhill. Tranberg, who had worked at Walter Reed Hospital caring for amputees from the Korean War, helped Dubus in another way as well. During a particularly difficult session, Dubus broke down in tears. In his essay

"Broken Vessels," he wrote that Tranberg then reminded him of a passage in the Old Testament. "It's in Jeremiah," she said. "The potter is making a pot and it cracks. So he smashes it, and makes a new vessel. You can't make a new vessel out of a broken one. It's time to find the real you."

Peggy visited the hospital daily and cared for Dubus' needs when he was released. Although friends and Dubus' grown children helped during the ordeal, the stress of caring for Cadence, who was then four years old, and the newborn, Madeleine, in addition to her husband, who was severely depressed, proved to be more than Peggy could bear. She left the house on November 8, 1987, and returned five days later with a police officer and a court order allowing her to take custody of the two children.

Faced with loneliness, depression, and enormous medical bills Dubus slid deeper into despair and was unable to write. Friends and fellow writers were quick to come to his aid. Jack Herlihy, manager of a local bookshop, the Phoenix Bookstore, moved into Dubus' basement in December 1987. Herlihy's rent certainly helped Dubus with the mortgage payment but his companionship and help in the day-to-day running of a household proved even more important in Dubus' recovery. Friends built ramps and work surfaces that made maneuvering his wheelchair throughout the house less troublesome. As a gesture of love and respect, the writers E. L. Doctorow, John Irving, John Updike, Stephen King, Gail Godwin, Kurt Vonnegut, Ann Beattie, Tim O'Brien, Jayne Ann Phillips, and Richard Yates held a series of readings from their own works in the ballroom of the Charles Hotel in Cambridge, Massachusetts, in the winter of 1987. The readings not only created a wider audience for Dubus' work but also raised close to $100,000 to help him and his family through a very difficult time. Dubus was astonished by this and by the number of checks that were mailed to him by people he had never met. His financial worries were further alleviated when he won the Jean Stein Award from the American Academy and Institute of Arts and Letters in May of 1988, followed by a MacArthur Foundation "genius" award of $310,000. In addition, he had been awarded a second Guggenheim Fellowship in 1986.

As for helping himself, Dubus knew instinctively that the best thing he could do would be to help others. On Monday nights, he counseled troubled and abused teens who came to him from a neighborhood group home and, on Thursday nights, he held writing seminars in his living room. In return for the kindness and generosity that had been given to him, he did not charge fees for his counseling or seminars, even when he was in need of money. Perhaps the most important and effective action he took to aid in his recovery was to begin to write again. Dubus struggled to write fiction but found it impossible. Confined to the enforced stillness of his wheelchair, he took a deep look inside himself and began to produce essays. Dubus said in an online interview hosted by Barnes and Noble that he received some good advice from his daughter Nicole, who called him from her home in Santa Cruz, California. Knowing of his difficulty she said, "You have been through so much, I don't think you can imagine an imaginary world yet. Keep writing nonfiction about people in wheelchairs, and someday someone will show up in a story in a wheelchair, and then show up in bipeds." Dubus preferred to call himself a cripple, referring to all others as bipeds. In recalling the accident and its aftermath, Dubus consistently maintained that it deepened and made palpable the nature of his Catholic belief in the transforming power of suffering, forgiveness, and love.

THE ESSAYS AND
ANOTHER COLLECTION OF STORIES

The essay collection *Broken Vessels* (1991) was welcomed by readers and critics alike who had not seen anything new from Dubus for nearly five years. The essays present a wide range of subject matter. "Out Like a Lamb" recalls a remarkable insight into the nature of Jesus Christ that was gained while Dubus and his family house-sat for a man who raised sheep. There is a memoir of his old mentor and friend Richard Yates; a disturbing encounter with the injustice often found in the American justice system and several concerning the accident, his hospitalization, and his recovery. Tobias Wolff wrote in his introduction to the collection, "Andre has made of his wheelchair a place to see the world more clearly than ever. I was struck again and again by the range of his vision, by its depth and compassion, and by the music in which he gives it voice." *Broken Vessels* was a runner-up for the Pulitzer Prize in nonfiction.

Meditations from a Movable Chair (1998) contains twenty-five essays that continue Dubus' explorations into the human condition. "About Kathryn" tells of his oldest sister's rape and her eventual ability to forgive and pray for her attacker. "A Hemingway Story" recounts Dubus' discovery of new meanings in a favorite story he thought he knew. Other favorite authors are presented: a sighting of Norman Mailer at the Algonquin Hotel; a poignant farewell to Richard Yates, who died in 1992. Several reveal Dubus' devotion to the Catholic Church: "Grace," "Sacraments," "Communion," and "Love in the Morning." Essays describe a meeting with the actress Liv Ullmann, and an Opening Day outing to a Red Sox baseball game with his agent and friends. All reveal Dubus' profound and broad love of life and all its components.

Dancing After Hours (1996) won the $30,000 Rea Award for Excellence in Short Fiction and was runner-up for the National Book Critics Circle Award. The fourteen stories in this collection include his first published effort in that form, "The Intruder." In addition, Dubus presents a variety of situations that revolve around his central themes of love, fear, and determination to survive. In three of the stories, the reader follows the love story of LuAnn Arceneaux and Ted Briggs. "All the Time in the World" tells of LuAnn's rejection of the pointless promiscuity made possible by the sexual revolution. Despite her lifestyle, LuAnn remains in the Catholic Church. Believing that passion is an essential element of the soul, she receives communion with a clear conscience. One Sunday, after Mass, the heel of her left shoe breaks off and she stumbles. Ted Briggs has seen her plight and offers his assistance. Over brunch she discovers that Briggs is a man she thought no longer existed. A man who holds doors open for her, believes in the slow development of relationships and longs for love, marriage, and children, in that order. LuAnn is happier than she ever believed possible and attributes it to a clear gift from God. "In her apartment she went to her closet and picked up the white shoe with the broken heel. She did not believe in fate, but she believed in gifts that came; they moved with angels and spirits in the air, were perhaps delivered by them."

LuAnn and Ted are married and have three children in "The Timing of Sin" and "Out of the Snow." In both stories LuAnn faces threats to her marriage. In both, she is rescued by God's grace and the strength to survive that He gives her.

A SWIFT AND UNTIMELY DEPARTURE

On Wednesday, February 24, 1999, Dubus planned to have a friend over to watch the Bruce Willis video *Die Hard* on his new, state-of-the-art stereo television. According to an article in *Salon* by a member of his weekly writing seminars, Richard Ravin, Dubus was like a kid with a new toy. "Now we got Sensurroouund," he had been saying all day. The friend, identified by Ravin as "Bob," found Dubus slumped over in his shower chair, the showerhead spraying cold water over his lifeless body. The cause of death was listed as a heart attack.

A wake was held at the H. L. Farmer and Sons Funeral Home in Haverhill on Sunday, February 28. The funeral was held there the next day, March 1, at 10:00 a.m., and a funeral Mass was said in St. John the Baptist Church, where Dubus was privately buried. At the funeral, Dubus' oldest son, Andre III, remembered his father's enormous appetite for life, his enormous ability to create fiction, and his enormous love of God, in four words he shouted from the pulpit: "My Daddy was *big!*"

Selected Bibliography

WORKS OF ANDRE DUBUS

NOVELS

The Lieutenant. New York: Dial Press, 1967.
Voices from the Moon. Boston: David R. Godine, 1984.

SHORT STORIES

Separate Flights. Boston: David R. Godine, 1975. (Contains "We Don't Live Here Anymore," "Over the Hill," "The Doctor," "In My Life," "If They Knew Yvonne," "Going Under," "Miranda over the Valley," and "Separate Flights.")
Adultery and Other Choices. Boston: David R. Godine, 1977. (Contains "An Afternoon with the Old Man," "Contrition," "The Bully," "Graduation," "The Fat Girl," "Cadence," "Corporal of Artillery," "The Shooting," "Andromache," and "Adultery.")
Finding a Girl in America. Boston: David R. Godine, 1980. (Contains "Killings," "The Dark Men," "His Lover," "Townies," "The Misogamist," "At St. Croix," "The Pitcher," "Waiting," "Delivering," "The Winter Father," and "Finding a Girl in America.")
The Times Are Never So Bad. Boston: David R. Godine, 1983. (Contains "The Pretty Girl," "Bless Me, Father," "Goodbye," "Leslie in California," "The New Boy," "The Captain," "Sorrowful Mysteries," "Anna," and "A Father's Story.")
We Don't Live Here Anymore: The Novellas of Andre Dubus. New York: Crown Publishers, 1984. (Contains "The Pretty Girl," "We Don't Live Here Anymore," "Adultery," and "Finding a Girl in America.")
The Last Worthless Evening. Boston: David R. Godine, 1986. (Contains "Deaths at Sea," "After the Game," "Dressed Like Summer Leaves," "Land Where My Fathers Died," "Molly," and "Rose.")
Selected Stories. Boston: David R. Godine, 1988. (Contains "Miranda over the Valley," "The Winter Father," "Waiting," "Killings," "The Pretty Girl," "Graduation," "The Pitcher," "After the Game," "Cadence," "If They Knew Yvonne," "Rose," "The Fat Girl," "The Captain," "Anna," "They Now Live in Texas," "Voices from the Moon," "Townies," "Leslie in California," "The Curse," "Sorrowful Mysteries," "Delivering," "Adultery," and "A Father's Story.")
Dancing After Hours. New York: Knopf, 1996. (Contains "The Intruder," "A Love Song," "Falling in Love," "Blessings," "Sunday Morning," "All the Time in the World," "Woman on a Plane," "The Colonel's Wife," "The Lover," "The Last Moon," "The Timing of Sin," "At Night," "Out of the Snow," and "Dancing After Hours.")
"Sisters." *Book,* May–June 1999, pp. 53–60.

ESSAYS

Broken Vessels. Boston: David R. Godine, 1991. (Contains "Out Like a Lamb," "Running," "Under the Lights," "The End of a Season," "Railroad Sketches," "Of Robin Hood and Womanhood," "The Judge and Other Snakes," "On Charon's Wharf," "After Twenty Years," "Into the Silence," "A Salute to Mister Yates," "Selling Stories," "Marketing," "Two Ghosts," "Intensive Care," "Lights of the Long Night," "Sketches at Home," "A Woman in April," "Bastille Day," "Husbands," "Breathing," and "Broken Vessels.")
Meditations from a Movable Chair. New York: Knopf, 1998. (Contains "About Kathryn," "Letter to a Writer's Workshop," "Digging," "Imperiled Men," "A Hemingway Story," "Grace," "Mailer at the Algonquin," "Brothers," "Good-bye to Richard Yates," "Sacraments," "Bodily Mysteries," "A Coun-

try Road Song," "Carrying," "Girls," "Liv Ullmann in Spring," "Love in the Morning," "Song of Pity," "Communion," "First Books," "Letter to Amtrak," "Autumn Legs," "Giving Up the Gun," "Messages," and "Witness.")

BIBLIOGRAPHY

Kennedy, Thomas E. *Andre Dubus: A Study of the Short Fiction.* Boston: Twayne, 1988. (The bibliography at the back of this book is the best available for literary critical purposes at this time.)

CRITICAL AND BIOGRAPHICAL STUDIES

Breslin, John B. "Playing Out the Patterns of Sin and Grace: The Catholic Imagination of Andre Dubus." *Commonweal* 115:652–656 (December 2, 1988).

Eder, Richard. "Stories from Scratch at Triple Strength." *Los Angeles Times Book Review,* November 20, 1988, p. 3.

Feeney, Joseph J. "Poised for Fame: Andre Dubus at Fifty." *America,* November 15, 1986, pp. 296–299.

Kennedy, Thomas E. "The Existential Christian Vision in the Fiction of Andre Dubus." *Delta* 24:91–102 (February 1987).

———. "A Fiction of People and Events." *Sewanee Review* 95, no. 2:xxxix–xli (Spring 1987).

———. *Andre Dubus: A Study of the Short Fiction.* Boston: Twayne, 1988.

Kramer, Jerome V. "Double Dubus." *Book,* March–April 1999, pp. 43–46.

Milton, Edith. "Adultery and Other Choices." *New Republic,* February 4, 1978, pp. 33–35.

Oates, Joyce Carol. "People to Whom Things Happen." *New York Times Book Review,* June 26, 1983, pp. 12, 18.

———. "Separate Flights." *Ontario Review* (Fall–Winter 1976–1977). Reprinted in Kennedy's *Andre Dubus: A Study of the Short Fiction,* p. 134.

Pritchard, William H. "Some August Fiction." *The Hudson Review* 36, no. 4:742–754 (Winter 1983–1984).

Ravin, Richard. "Remembering Andre Dubus." *Salon Magazine.* http://www.salon.com/books/feature/1999/03/18feature.html (March 3, 1999).

Taliaferro, Frances. "Adultery and Other Choices." *Harper's,* January 1978, p. 87.

Tyler, Anne. "Master of Moments." *New Republic,* February 6, 1989, pp. 41–42.

Updike, John. "Ungreat Lives." *The New Yorker,* February 4, 1985, pp. 94, 97–98.

Weber, Bruce. "Andres Dubus' Hard-Luck Stories." *The New York Times Magazine,* November 20, 1988, pp. 48–56.

Wolff, Tobias. Introduction to Dubus' *Broken Vessels.* Boston: David R. Godine, 1991.

INTERVIEWS

Barnes and Noble Author Chats. http://www.bn.com/community/archive/transcript.asp?userid=3m5L4W7FHF⟨&srefer=⟩⟨&eventId=⟩1270 (July 12, 1998).

Dahlin, Robert. "Interview with Andre Dubus." *Publishers Weekly,* October 12, 1984, pp. 56–57.

"Interview with Andre Dubus." *Excerpt,* the online journal of Southwest Texas State University. http://www.english.swt.edu/excerpt1.dir/ dubus.htm.

Kennedy, Thomas E. "Interview, 1987." In his *Andre Dubus: A Study of the Short Fiction.* Boston: Twayne, 1988. Pp. 89–123.

Levassuer, Jennifer, and Kevin Rabalias. *Glimmer Train* 31:39–59 (Summer 1999).

Samway, Patrick J. "An Interview with Andre Dubus." *America,* November 15, 1987, pp. 300–301.

—CHARLES R. BAKER

George Garrett

1929—

"*I,* MYSELF, AM the books I've written," George Garrett declares in *Whistling in the Dark: True Stories and Other Fables* (1992), "the work, large or small, into which I have poured my life, my self, as carefully and awkwardly as pouring from one bottle to another. In that sense, I am to be found, the life of me, in my work." "This is true of all writers," Garrett goes on to say. But the equation varies from book to book as well as from writer to writer. The life of a writer usually enters the work first, as it does in Garrett's fiction and poetry, as fragments of autobiography, recollections of people and places, incidents, sequences of action remembered, and concrete details of sight and sound and feeling. All of these are refined in the act of writing, and reformed to fit the job at hand. For Garrett, in his first novels and early poems in the late 1950s and early 1960s, the places are towns of Central Florida, which was then a part of the American South as it no longer is. The people are, first of all, his own inventions, and are endowed, as all created characters are, by shards of reality, faces and voices, and gestures and habits randomly observed. These may come from anywhere and doubtless did in Garrett's case: the face of a neighbor, the sound of a politician's or a preacher's voice, the delineations of a house or a landscape finding their way into his work. But more important to his life and to his canon are his relatives who lived by moral imperatives that helped shape the world of Garrett's youth.

There were Garrett's father and mother, his grandparents and aunts and uncles, his sisters and his cousins, and even, as time went on, the spirit of his dead brother whom he never saw. There was an aunt, Helen Garrett, who wrote children's books, and an uncle, Oliver H. P. Garrett, who wrote film scripts, including the shooting script for *Gone With the Wind.* There were among his mother's brothers a dancer, a musician and a pair of athletes, but none of these engaged Garrett's imagination as fully as his father and his grandfather who were lawyers. The grandfather had, before George's time, been sufficiently rich to own trotting horses and a ninety-foot ocean-worthy yacht, but he conducted business with the spirit of a gambler, and his luck did not last. He had, family tradition held, "made two fortunes and spent three," Garrett said in *Whistling in the Dark,* and toward the end of his life he lived in a single room behind the post office and slept on an army cot. He did so, insofar as Garrett ever knew, without complaint or dejection.

Garrett's father, son-in-law of the quondam millionaire, had dropped out of the Massachusetts Institute of Technology, and had gone west to mine copper and lead and to help found the mine workers union. He might have remained there except for being moderately crippled in an accident.

He too became a lawyer and could have been rich as well had he done less work *pro bono* and chosen his clients more carefully. Those whom he represented were often unable to pay and those against whom he contended were well endowed; his victories were many, but frequently, his rewards were scant. His example as a seeker after justice and as a political activist informs Garrett's early work; his spirit, and that of Garrett's grandfather, became increasingly present in Garrett's poetry and fiction as his career advanced. As Garrett, onetime acolyte and continuing believer, makes clear in a moving essay about his father's funeral, his work, though never tendentious, is predicated on his Episcopalian faith, a religion that is at once relaxed and incredibly serious.

BACKGROUND

George Palmer Garrett was born June 11, 1929, in Orlando, Florida, the son of George Palmer and Rosalie (Toomer) Garrett. After graduating from the Sewanee Military Academy (1946) and the Hill School (1947), he spent a year at Columbia University, then graduated magna cum laude from Princeton University in 1952. He served two years on active duty with the field artillery corps of the United States Army in Europe, and returned to Princeton where he earned a master of arts in English in 1956 and a Ph.D. in 1985. He taught at Wesleyan University from 1957 to 1960; at the University of Virginia, from 1962 to 1967; at Hollins College, from 1967 to 1971; at the University of South Carolina, from 1971 to 1974; at Princeton University, from 1974 to 1977; and once more at the University of Virginia, where he has been Hoyns Professor of Creative Writing since 1984.

Garrett has received fellowships from the *Sewanee Review,* the Ford Foundation, the American Academy in Rome, the National Endowment for the Arts, and the Guggenheim Foundation. Among prizes Garrett has won are the *Contempora* writing award, the American Academy and Institute of Arts and Letters award in literature, the New York Public Library Literary Lion award, the T. S. Eliot award for creative writing from the Ingersoll foundation, the PEN/Malamud award for short fiction, the Hollins College Medal, the Aiken-Taylor award for poetry, and a Doctor of Letters degree from the University of the South. From 1993 to 1997, he served as chancellor of the Fellowship of Southern Writers of which he is a founding member. He married Susan Parrish Jackson in 1952. They are the parents of William Palmer, George Gorham, and Alice.

EARLY WORKS

Garrett's first three books were, fittingly for a writer whose future work would include almost every literary genre, a volume of poetry, *The Sleeping Gypsy and Other Poems* (1958); a collection of short stories, *King of the Mountain* (1958); and a novel, *The Finished Man* (1959). It would be easy to dismiss these as the first fruits of Garrett's apprenticeship, which they are in the sense that they exhibit neither the technical skill nor the thematic complexity that inhere in his later verse and fiction. But although they are early efforts, they engage subjects and themes that Garrett later pursued in his major phase as a writer, and they are worth considering for their own literary virtues. Garrett's interest in classical literature and in the Bible, which he has maintained throughout his career, begins in *The Sleeping Gypsy* with poems such as "Caedmon," "Tiresias," and "Old Saws" in which the rock of Sisyphus gathers no moss. There are also poems about King David and Suzanna and about Eve and Adam in the Garden of Eden.

The Sleeping Gypsy's "The Magi," one of Garrett's best early poems, begins with images of personal remembrance: the poet as a boy, recalling figures in a creche—wooden men bowing in reverence over the Christ child. Later, he remembers his own indifferent performance as a Wise Man in a church nativity play, successfully delivering the gold, but muffing his lines. The poet knows, in his maturity, that the glittering costume he wore on that long ago evening was not quite right. Given their time and place, the original wise men were surely dirty, their bodies unbathed and stinking, and their clothes soiled. The gifts they brought were "shabby." They were more superstitious than wise. "Still," the poet says, "I would dream them back." This longing to revisit these gilded details of the Christmas story is at once a recognition of reality and an act of faith. Let the original Magi be what they were, in some respects more imperfect in their roles than the clumsy and forgetful poet was in his youth. But the imperfection of the actors is not in itself a refutation. Soiled and uncertain though they were, their journey continues to resonate in the mind of the poet and in the world.

Although both books are flawed, Garrett's early stories in *King of the Mountain* and his first novel *The Finished Man* contain kernels of the technical skill that Garrett went on to develop in his mature work. Paul Engle, then director of the prestigious writers workshop at the University of Iowa, warmly praised the stories in *King of the Mountain* when it first appeared, discovering in them the techniques that he was attempting to instill in his own students. Engle rightly admired Garrett's talent for structure, his ability, first of all, to put a story together and to give it conflict and development and resolution. Other reviewers admired Garrett's ability to capture the boredom and brutality of army life, and to probe the inevitable separations that plague the relationships of one generation with another. He was praised

for his sensitive portrayal of his female characters, but no one was able then to discern the extent to which Garrett would develop these conventional values into the stunning virtues of his later work.

The source of *A Finished Man,* the Jamesian "germ" of the story, is the 1950 Florida senatorial campaign. During that campaign Claude Pepper, the liberal—for his time perhaps ultra-liberal—incumbent, was opposed by George Smathers who once had been Pepper's protégé. In 1938, Smathers, then president of the student body at the University of Florida, volunteered to manage Pepper's campus campaign. Later, at Smathers' request, Pepper arranged for Smathers to be discharged from the Marine Corps to take a job, also secured by Pepper, as a United States attorney for the southern district of Florida. Five years later, Smathers ran for Pepper's senate seat. Backed by major business interests in Florida, he conducted a well-financed and vicious campaign, and Pepper lost. Here, for an author, was a classic case of good against evil, waiting to be reshaped into a modern fable.

As is necessary in any work of fiction, Garrett significantly alters the facts of Pepper's campaign as he works it into the larger delineations of *A Finished Man.* In his novel, the character based on Claude Pepper is called Senator Allan Parker, and George Smathers' counterpart is John Batten. However, the main character is neither Senator Parker, the liberal, nor Parker's one-time friend and assistant, John Batten, who has betrayed his liberal principles to gain conservative support. The central figure of the novel is Mike Royle, who becomes active in Senator Parker's campaign. The major thrust of the story is Mike's growing disillusionment, not with the political process, but with the way that those who are involved in it seem, sooner or later, to subvert it for their own private ends. At the conclusion of the novel, Mike decides to defend a black man who has tried to kill Senator Parker because Parker has betrayed his own values by posing for a photograph with the leader of the Ku Klux Klan. Clearly there is movement here, within the story and within the character of Mike Royle. But for most reviewers, Garrett failed to integrate the philosophical elements of the story into the dramatic action. The result is a diminution of narrative intensity and a quality of tendentiousness, both of which damage the work.

DEVELOPMENT AS A NOVELIST

Based partially on Garrett's experience as a field artilleryman with United States Army in Trieste, Italy, and in Linz, Austria, during the middle 1950s, the central characters of his second novel, *Which Ones Are the Enemy?* (1961), are John Riche, an American private stationed in Italy, and Angela, a nightclub entertainer. Because both Riche and Angela are characters without moral focus, their relationship, based originally on lust and a search for material fulfillment, is doomed. But the sad ending is somewhat ameliorated by the affection that, before Angela's death, they begin to feel for each other. *Which Ones Are the Enemy?* was widely praised for its narrative voice—Riche tells the story—and for its authentic rendering of army life. But despite its favorable reviews, it failed to gain the critical acclaim that was given to *Do, Lord, Remember Me,* Garrett's third novel, which appeared in 1965.

Do, Lord, Remember Me has a curious publishing history. The novel as seen by the reader is significantly different from the manuscript that the editors at Scribners, publisher of Garrett's first two novels, declined to publish. It was brought out in England by Chapman and Hall in a version considerably shorter than the original, and a few months later, it was published in the United States by Doubleday with even further cuts. The British version was made available in

the United States by the Louisiana State University Press. Garrett has said that the long title story in his *Cold Ground Was My Bed Last Night* (1964), his third collection of short fiction, was originally the first segment of *Do, Lord, Remember Me.* However the book may originally have read, the version now in print is, in the judgment of most critics, sufficiently complete to be considered Garrett's first major novel.

The protagonist of *Do, Lord, Remember Me* is Big Red Smalley, an evangelist, faith healer, hard-drinking womanizer, and an organizer of the sort of itinerant tent meetings that were common in the South when Garrett was growing up. Like all traveling showmen, Smalley is preceded into the small Florida town by his advance men, E. J. Cartwright, whose two concerns in life are sex and money, and Moses, who is burdened with metaphysical longings. Their job is to post signs advertising the meeting, to give tickets to influential citizens, to bribe the sheriff, and to do whatever else is necessary to try to pique public interest and to raise a crowd. Smalley is accompanied by Miami, his mistress who loves him and whom he loves, but without fidelity. Judith, whom Smalley has healed earlier of an unnamed debility, has apparently been following Smalley and she appears on the afternoon of the meeting driving a sports car and wearing nothing but a raincoat.

All of this looks like, and in the hands of a novelist less gifted than Garrett would be, the raw material for an ordinary satirical narrative of dishonest preachers. Smalley is a sinner, and like most evangelists, he is an eager and effective raiser of money. But he is also blessed or cursed—even he does not know which—with a faith in God that he cannot escape and with a genuine gift for healing.

He made me a preacher when I didn't want to be one and when I knew better. He even took all the joy out of it. Because I knew, I always knew I was just as good and just as successful . . . when I was faking it . . . being the pure con man pure and simple, as when He grabbed hold to me . . . and shook and rattled my ribs and timbers until I thought every bone would snap like a match-stick and all my innards would pop out. . . . And I never could enjoy even the relief of being free of Him. . . . He would be back to claim me again and use me again. And nothing I could do would ever set me free of Him.

The ambiguity of Smalley's spiritual life is reflected in the lives of those around him. The concupiscent Cartwright is without conscience, but he lacks the strength to contend successfully with Smalley or even to rob him. Judith has been healed, but not in spirit. Miami is saved from the amorality of Cartwright because she recognizes the holiness in Smalley. Nothing about *Do, Lord, Remember Me* lends itself to clear and uncomplicated interpretation. At the end of the story, Smalley, who has spent his professional life collecting money from his congregations, gives handfuls of silver and currency to those who have come to hear him preach.

In a simpler book, this gesture would be symbolic of Smalley's complete conversion and of the doubts that plague his divided soul, but neither conversion nor deliverance is complete. He makes love to Judith. Then, apparently unable longer to endure the vocation that God has imposed upon him, he kills himself. The thematic strength of this novel resides in its dualities. Good and evil exist not merely in opposition to each other, but as forces that are organically related, joined within individuals such as Smalley and Miami, and in the fabric of life as it is represented by the roles that characters such as Cartwright and Moses play.

The form of *Do, Lord, Remember Me* is both complicated and enhanced by Garrett's including among the narrators—who take turns telling the story—even the most minor characters, the sheriff, for example, and the proprietor of the local department store. Although at the time of the publication of *Do, Lord, Remember Me* some critics suggested that Garrett's method had been borrowed from William Faulkner's *As I Lay Dying,* this technique was not new to either author. In using this technique, the author risks sacrificing precision and even unity because no two observers see the events of the story from the same psychological point of view. The advantages of the method accrue for the same reason. The variety of attitudes toward the events of the narrative and their significance enrich the story by attaching different meanings to the different sequences of the action. In the case of *Do, Lord, Remember Me,* the integrity of the narrative is maintained by Smalley, who is the central and controlling image of the story. He is one of Garrett's best creations at this stage of his career. The contradictions, moral and physical, of Smalley's temperament are the foundations for the theme of the novel—the dislocations and dilemmas of the modern world, both sacred and profane.

A QUIETER PERIOD

Between the appearance of *Do, Lord, Remember Me* and the publication of his novel *Death of the Fox* (1971), Garrett released two books: a collection of poems and a collection of stories, *For a Bitter Season: New and Selected Poems* (1967) and *A Wreath for Garibaldi and Other Stories* (1969). That Garrett, one of the most prolific writers of his age, published only two books in seven years, each of which contained some work that had been written earlier, is indicative of the energy and effort that he was then spending on his novel about Sir Walter Ralegh, *Death of the Fox.* But the two books, coming after *Do, Lord, Remember Me,* contain material that is important both for its own sake and for its foreshadowing of work that is to come: they show Garrett's concern with love and death and with the ironies of individual life juxtaposed with the ironies of humanity's shared history.

In "Excursion," a poem in *For A Bitter Season,* the narrator and his companions explore an Italian tomb where, alongside the chambers that house the ancient dead, there is a room filled with erotic drawings. This is an old poetic device, the coupling of death with love and lovemaking, but Garrett makes it new by the brilliance of his language and by the great separation in time between the ancient artists and their models and the modern tourists who are both embarrassed and aroused. The descent of Garrett's tourists into the underworld is both necessary and sadly flawed.

> Does it seem strange to go to the dead
> for the facts of life?
> Orpheus, Virgil, Dante, Christ
> descended in the dark and stirred
> the troubled bones. And we,
> with all hell in our heads,
> must follow or go mad.

In this same volume, there are poems about the biblical Salome, whose dream of purity recapitulates and enhances the division of good and evil. There is a long and moving tribute to the poet Hyam Plutzik, "Rugby Road," that is not only an elegy for another poet, but a meditation on art, on history, and on life and death. These are serious verses, written, often, in serious language, but Garrett's touch can be light. There are poems written to celebrities such as Ann-Margret and Twiggy, and poems about cheerleaders and country girls, about girls who read books, and about a girl who wears a black raincoat. In both conception and execution, these poems display the development of Garrett's skill.

A Wreath for Garibaldi was published only in England by Rupert Hart-Davis, although some of the work therein—most significantly "Cold Ground Was My Bed Last Night"—had been published earlier in the United States. "Cold Ground" is a complicated story that brings together several disparate themes. It begins with the death of a criminal at the hands of a deputy sheriff who is quick on the draw and apparently indifferent to the life he has taken. The callousness of the deputy is played against the humane instincts of the sheriff who presides with relative kindness over his office and the jail, and is the first administrator of local justice. He releases the town drunk to go home to take care of his goats, and he comes close to releasing the boy who was riding with the man who was shot by the sheriff. The boy is the mysterious center of the story. By his own admission, he is a drifter who has been in trouble with the law, but he denies having participated in the crimes of which the dead man is guilty. That the boy is a musician compounds the mystery in a way that the sheriff cannot fathom. He is a balladeer, a roving artist whose only concern is his art. His presence, disgraceful though it is in many ways, is nonetheless a rebuke to the callous deputy and to the ordinary concerns of the sheriff's world. At the end, the sheriff destroys the boy's guitar and has him incarcerated.

"The Old Army Game," which also appears in *A Wreath for Garibaldi,* is an early manifestation of Garrett's translating his army experience into fiction and memoir. The broad delineations of this story will resonate with anyone who has served in the military: there are the rigid rules, the abusive sergeant, the senselessness of much of what is called training. Up to a point, the story line is equally familiar. Helpless recruits suffer pain and indignities at the hands of a seemingly sadistic sergeant. But when they are asked to give money to help send the sergeant to the bedside of his injured wife, the soldiers have their revenge by contributing ten cents each to the sergeant's expenses. Garrett writes, "That is where it ought to end. It would be a swell place to end, with the picture of [Sergeant] Quince *furioso* throwing fountains of dimes in the air." But the ironic turn that gives weight to the story comes later. In the final scene, the narrator and his friend Sachs, both now sergeants themselves, come upon Quince who, for reasons that are not disclosed, has been reduced in rank to corporal. Sachs tells Quince that the army is "a stupid . . . simple minded game," and delights in calling the former sergeant "corporal." But, as Sachs confesses later, Quince and the army have won; they have elicited from Sachs the sort of behavior that he finds most reprehensible. People are, the story tells the reader, more profoundly affected by experience than they know. In a way, they become what is visited on them.

DEATH OF THE FOX:
THE ELIZABETHAN TRILOGY BEGINS

The subject of Garrett's novel *Death of the Fox* is Sir Walter Ralegh—courtier and statesman, sailor and explorer, writer of prose and poetry, and a man who was famous, in legend if not in provable fact, for having put down his cloak for Queen Elizabeth I to walk on. Ralegh was born in Devonshire, probably in 1552. A favorite of Elizabeth until he impregnated and then married Elizabeth (Bess) Throgmorton, one of the Queen's ladies-in-waiting, Ralegh colonized Virginia, fought against the Spanish and the Irish, made an expedition to Guiana in 1595, and published an account of this journey in 1596. His loyalty to Queen Elizabeth, particularly in her declining years, earned him the enmity of King James I who, shortly after his ascent to the throne, falsely charged Ralegh with treason. He was convicted and sentenced to death. Ralegh was confined in the Tower of London, but James delayed Ralegh's execution for fourteen years. During his imprisonment, Ralegh continued his career as a poet and wrote his longest prose work, *The History of the World*. He was released to make another excursion to South America but the adventure failed and, at the end of it, Ralegh was once more imprisoned in the Tower. He was executed by decapitation in 1618.

Garrett became interested in Ralegh, on whom he planned to write his Ph.D. dissertation, while he was a graduate student at Princeton University. He compiled a file on Ralegh's life and career but in 1957 he accepted a teaching job at Wesleyan University, and left Princeton without taking his degree. Although his work on the subject was temporarily abandoned, Garrett's interest in Ralegh continued undiminished, and in the mid-1960s, at the suggestion of an editor, he began to write *Death of the Fox*. Garrett's stunning portrait of Ralegh as complicated—at once arrogant and humble, courageous and tender of heart, and, above all, mysterious—is enhanced and, in some ways, made possible by the time and place that Garrett has reproduced and by the other actors in the drama. The story begins with Ralegh's trial and ends with Ralegh at the scaffold, waiting for the ax to fall. The more than seven hundred pages between the beginning of the narrative and its conclusion tell Ralegh's story, to be sure, but they also relate, in less detail, the stories of Elizabeth and James, of courtiers and politicians. They are the history of England and the social history of London. They recreate not merely a world but the only world in which the Ralegh whom Garrett brings to life could have lived.

Early in the novel, Ralegh remembers his first visit to London, crossing the bridge near dusk, and finding lodging from which he listens to the sounds of the city, such as church bells, the call of the watch, singing and laughter, and "one wretch puking in the night." Guided by his cousin, Ralegh goes sightseeing, visiting monuments that remain dear to tourists: Westminster Abbey, St. Paul's Cathedral, the Temple Inns. But Ralegh's London is the London of more than four hundred years ago from which much has been lost. Most of the taverns, the playhouses, and even the bridge over which Ralegh crosses the Thames to reach the city for the first time, are gone. To recreate the city as it was in Ralegh's time, Garrett works carefully with small details, such as clothes and weapons, and food and drink. His London is filled with energy engendered by gamblers and prostitutes, cutpurses and cloth merchants, felons brought forth for execution, and prisoners shouting from their windows at passers-by. The city generates a sense of freedom and adventure, of constant danger from thieves, cutthroats, and bearers of fatal diseases, and of lives lived at the queen's pleasure that, at any moment, can be brought suddenly to an end. In a basic way, Garrett's London, with its vagabonds and heroes, its filthy streets, and its crime and its churches, is an image of life in England during Ralegh's life.

Later in the novel, a mature Ralegh travels the Thames and sees buildings that are not obvious from the shore, many of which are ancient because of their proximity to the water. He sees Oxford, where Ralegh studied and "swam when the river was all thinly frozen," Dorchester where "the first West Saxon Christian king was baptized," Wallingford "where the cock crows and the hens lay eggs in the ruins of the abbey. . . ." and Greenwich where "it pleased the late Queen to permit her godson, Sir John Harrington, to build and install his wondrous new invention, the Ajax, a machine designed to replace the privy and the Jordan pot of the chamber." There are Windsor Castle and Hampton Court, Richmond and Whitehall Palaces, the "[l]argest of palaces in Christendom," where during his days at court, Ralegh celebrated the Christmas season, feasting and watching plays in the company of the Queen. Both in the boisterous streets of London and in the more formal precincts of the court, the characters speak, not the speech that in Ralegh's time was actually spoken, but dialogue that is better, tighter, stripped of meaningless social platitudes. It is made convincing, not by the archaisms that were employed by Elizabethans, but by an elevated diction, and a formality of vocabulary and tone.

In the fullness of his personality, Ralegh, more than most men of his or any other age, was a combination of public image and private temperament, of the character he created for the world to see and of his loves and animosities, and his victories and disappointments. When, in the novel, he appears before judge and jury to answer the charge of treason, he wears the colorful, but outmoded, costume that was fashionable in Queen Elizabeth's time, and his quiet speech makes the bombast of his adversaries appear to be "somehow foolish." As Garrett describes him, Ralegh's great height and his features complement his demeanor. He enters the courtroom

> with his high smooth forehead, his hair neatly combed; a wonderfully pointed beard which turned up naturally, to the envy of those who had to use hot curling irons on theirs; above all the eyes, small bright cold eyes, heavy-lidded, now veiled with sleepy languor, now opening as if from a sudden excess of light and fire. A countenance easy to hate, but still easier to remember.

Most of what Ralegh does and says in these proceedings seems calculated to offend not only members of the court but also the king who alone has the power to save Ralegh's life or to end it.

Ralegh is, as the reader sees him in his public moments, almost always the Fox of the book's title. Whether he is careless of his own fate or arrogant even on the brink of death, or simply playing the role that he thinks proper to his circumstances, he remains aloof and mysterious.

Ralegh's private life is less inscrutable. Awaiting his own death near the end of the story, he remembers his son, Wat (short for Walter), whom he had meant to be his heir and his successor. In his wildness and his overblown courage and tendency to mischief, Wat failed to understand the rules by which his father lived, either those that governed the court or those that governed Ralegh's personal behavior. Wat enjoyed pomp and circumstance, but Ralegh could never instruct him in the responsibilities that rank required. Posing with his father for a joint portrait, Wat mimicked Ralegh's posture, but he also made tasteless jokes about his father. Wat died, either a fool or a hero or a combination of both, fighting as a member of one of his father's expeditions to Guiana. Ralegh felt himself, on the eve of his death, to be a stranger not only to Wat while he lived, but to Carew, the child of his old age with whom he had never become fully acquainted, as well. Waiting for the moment of his execution, Ralegh writes his younger son a letter. He speaks to Carew of his own youth, of the England of more than half a century before, of old customs, of people he has known, and of his own education. And, as is proper to such a case as his, Ralegh waxes metaphysical.

We have been given beauty, and the power to make beautiful things from what we have been given, not that we should love these things alone, but that we should love them as the signs and figures of imperishable Beauty.

God has given us the sensual music of this world, not to enchant us, but that we may imagine the celestial harmony which is beyond the limits of mortal hearing.

He has given us dancing that we may feel in our flesh a likeness to the dancing in heaven.

What Ralegh writes here is not a denial of the early part of his life, nor a condemnation of his career, but an extension of it. He comprehends more fully now than he did previously the motives behind his explorations, the good purposes that survived the frivolity of courtly life, and the self-serving machinations of those who lived it.

The same humane impulses inform Ralegh's last meeting with his wife, Bess. "A dying man," Ralegh thinks, "should leave no one saddled with his memory," a difficult—in Ralegh's case, an impossible—rubric to keep, but insofar as she can, Bess helps him. She comes accompanied by her cousin who, unlike a servant, cannot be sent away. The cousin's presence in the tower room where Ralegh waits the hour of his death does not ease the pain of parting, but allows it to transpire with some dignity. Ralegh and Bess talk

hopefully of a future that they know does not lie in front of them, and of a pardon that they know will never come. A supper is laid, but they hardly touch it. The time comes for Bess to leave, and now the almost unutterable words must be spoken.

"There is something that I did not tell you, Wat. I have received a note from Council saying I have permission to bury your body."

The smile does not waver as he bends down close to kiss her.

"It is well, dear Bess, that you may dispose of it dead," he says. "You did not always have the disposing of it alive."

She starts as if to answer something, but as always, there is no answer to his irony, even when it is gentle and loving. So she smiles and shakes her head. Then turns away quickly so that he will not see her eyes fill up with tears.

But the end is not yet. With Bess gone, Ralegh is left with Thomas Hariot, who was his one-time servant, but has also been his teacher, his companion in adventures past, and his friend. Hariot receives the letter Ralegh has written that he will give to Carew. Then he is gone, having said his own goodbyes, but the novel continues for another hundred pages. This last segment of the story shows Garrett at his technical and philosophical best. Without relinquishing his focus on Ralegh, he takes his readers into the larger world of workers and merchants, and of aristocracy and royalty. The life of the world goes on, even though Ralegh is doomed soon to leave it. One of the appeals of this novel to its contemporary audience is that, like much of the literature of the twentieth century, it is, in part at least, existential. For the Fox, particularly in the final sequence of the narrative, his concern is not with his fate but with the form of his life, not with what his end will be but with how he will meet it. He prays that the fever which has recently possessed him will not return to make him tremble on the scaffold or appear to be hesitant when he mounts it.

This sense of himself, of his deportment in a dangerous world, is one of the keys to understanding Ralegh as Garrett presents him. But he differs from, say, the typical Ernest Hemingway hero because he is a Christian. For him the end of his present life is not the end of his existence; and although the manner in which he lives and dies is of great importance, life also has purpose for him and for those he loves. In one of the final ironies of the novel, Ralegh is questioned by the Dean of Westminster concerning his faith. For the dean, this interview is of the utmost importance. He longs to become Bishop of Salisbury, and his appointment hinges on how he is judged to have dealt with the Fox. Now, as the moment of his death approaches, Ralegh, who has lived a life composed of both form and substance, has no need to dissemble. He confesses his faith, receives communion, eats heartily, but then, in a gesture that he knows will not please the tobacco-hating King, he lights his pipe and stands by the window smoking.

THE SUCCESSION: THE ELIZABETHAN TRILOGY CONTINUES

Even to a greater extent than *Death of the Fox, The Succession: A Novel of Elizabeth and James* (1983), the second volume of Garrett's trilogy, depends for its success on Garrett's vast knowledge of the Elizabethan world and his ability to recreate that world convincingly. This is true because in one sense, *The Succession* has no main character. There is Queen Elizabeth, childless, growing old, and seeing in her reflection in her bathroom mirrors harbingers of her own death. And there is James, King of Scotland, who wants to be Elizabeth's successor and King of England. Because Elizabeth must concur for James's ambition to be fulfilled, the plot of the novel, as the title suggests, is built on this royal relationship. Garrett shows James in his rough Scottish castle

and Elizabeth in her more refined court. The reader sees letters that pass between them. In scattered passages and, particularly, in the last chapter, Garrett writes of what the two monarchs think. But because they are who they are, because to maintain their royal presence requires that the author keep them at a distance from the reader, and because in literature as well as in life, familiarity breeds contempt, they are never shown with the intimacy that characterizes Garrett's portrayal of Ralegh.

In *The Succession,* much of the narrative is conveyed by characters who play limited roles in the action. There is an old courtier who appears in the novel once to recount for a young man the story of Elizabeth and Robert Dudley, first Earl of Leicester. There is a player who becomes a spy in the household of Robert Devereux, the second Earl of Essex in the weeks before Essex mounts a futile revolt against the Queen. There is a Catholic priest, an Englishman by birth, whose story conveys the depth and violence of religious animosities during Elizabeth's reign.

The courtier is a baron and an earl, a cousin to the Queen and to the less fortunate Lady Jane Grey and Mary, Queen of Scots, both of whom were executed. The story that he tells is not as much about the people involved as it is a description of the pomp and extravagance which accompanied the Queen's visit, in 1575, to Leicester at Kenilworth castle where the old courtier of this chapter of the book lived then and still does. The courtier's story contains a few anecdotes: of Elizabeth feigning anger when she was offered as a gift a lake that she claimed already to own; and of the Queen's kindness in making a pleasant joke about the name of a singer who had forgotten his lines. But mostly this passage is remarkable for its description of newly created waterways, of fanfares and fireworks, and of noble men and women dressed as divinities from the time of King Arthur and that of the ancient Greeks. The courtier, and the society in which he lived, are as strange to the young man who listens to him as stories he has heard about the New World. "I find myself imagining," he writes to a college friend, "that time of Queen Elizabeth . . . as another country, a place on the far edge of some ragged map. Inhabited by people as different from us as Blackamoors and Chinamen."

Whereas the courtier sets the Elizabethan scene in its sometimes frivolous grandeur the player shows the darker side of Elizabethan life. At the beginning of the player's section which is conveyed in a dialogue between the actor, who has himself been a spy, and a visitor who is an unnamed spymaster, the action takes place in a theater where the company is finishing *Troilus and Cressida,* one of Shakespeare's most enigmatic and least successful plays. Whether or not the play, in its depiction of the fecklessness of both Greeks and Trojans, is meant to suggest the ineptness of the Earl of Essex's attempt to revolt against the Queen, it provides the proper atmosphere for the introduction of the player. The player was born in the country, raised in poverty, and forced, partially by his own character, partially by his profession, to live by his wits. He is, as he tells his visitor, always an actor. He practices his art in the conduct of his life, playing roles, counterfeiting emotions, and dissembling when necessary. One of the roles he has played in the past is as hanger-on at the palace of the Earl of Essex. In pursuit of a recurring theme in Garrett's work, one that is central to *Entered From the Sun* (1990), the third volume of the Elizabethan trilogy, the visiting spymaster seeks to discover what the player knows concerning others, besides the now-dead Essex, who might have been involved in the Earl's plot against the Queen.

The player and his visitor move from pub to pub while the player tells of his past trials and triumphs, of reciting, when he was a boy, for a drunken old knight, and of being whipped at the tail of a cart through the streets of Bristol. In the case of Essex, the player's luck holds. In perusing the player's papers, the visitor finds nothing to incriminate his own masters in Essex's aborted plot; thus the player escapes death as he had on the day of Essex's rebellion. On that day, dressed in the finery that his employers had provided for him, well mounted from the same source, and well armed, the player rode out with Essex's company, but not far. He deserted, exchanged clothes with a ragged drunk, and made his way home without being detained by the Queen's men or even suspected. The reader learns that Essex was also an actor, one whose motives were never fully known, and one who was so skillful at the actor's craft that, like the player, he may never have fully understood himself. Even as he went to the scaffold, he appeared not quite to believe that he was really going to die. But as an image of his time, a man beloved of the Queen who later ordered his execution, and as the Queen's good servant who moved too soon to ingratiate himself with her successor, Essex, like the player, is an image of the moral and political uncertainty of the time and of the general anxiety that increased as the Queen approached death.

The extravagance of Essex's life has a surreal quality, a sense of exaggeration and unreality, which Garrett exploits by using the player, a man of many roles, to tell his story. The confluence of art and reality, as disclosed in the life of Essex, the impingement of one on the other, extends the image of the Elizabethan age as a time alien to those who, like the young man in the courtier's chapter, did not experience it. But the religious animosities which inform the priest's story are, in their basic details, all too real. They are rooted in politics, in King Henry VIII's desire for a divorce from his first wife, in Elizabeth's desire for the throne, and in her relations with Catholic Spain and the Roman Pontiff. In the ensuing struggle, both sides committed atrocities. Elizabeth's half-sister, the Catholic Queen Mary, in her brief reign had Protestant heretics burnt at the stake—among them, Thomas Cranmer, who was the Archbishop of Caterbury and the architect of the Anglican *Book of Common Prayer*. Although Elizabeth tried to treat both Protestants and Catholics fairly when she came to the throne, she was excommunicated by Pope Pius V. in 1570, thus putting his imprimatur on a breach that had long been beyond healing. The situation was only made worse when Elizabeth's cousin, the Catholic Mary Queen of Scots, who had abdicated her throne and fled to England, was convicted for treason against Elizabeth and beheaded in 1587. But along with the political turmoil, for many of the English on both sides, there remained the question of faith.

The story of the unnamed priest is told in his diary entries and in his letters which have been taken from him at the time of his arrest. He is in England, secretly, he thinks, but like his fellow priests, he is under the observation of Elizabeth's chief spy Sir Francis Walsingham's intelligencers. His vocation requires that he make a progress through town and country, hearing confessions and saying mass for recusant Catholics. He is always on the move, hoping to escape arrest, and putting at risk the lives of those he visits. He is frightened. He is afraid of death, afraid of torture, afraid most of all of his own weakness, and of his inability during the suffering that will follow his capture to avoid disclosing information that will condemn his friends. Garrett's intention as a novelist here is not to take sides, but to reveal the human dimension of this sad interval of English history. In a letter to his mother which is never sent, the priest tells of coming near to the home where he was raised, where his family still lives, of the pain his memories cause him, and of his desire to see those he loves once again. He is aware that, in a mundane sense at least, he has betrayed them. They live under suspicion. Opportunities for education and advancement that

normally would have been available to his brother have been revoked. Still, the priest longs, "to turn off the road. To come home, perhaps for good, after all this time. To stand with my back to the fire in the Hall. With a cup of wine in my hands. To see how waves of firelight fall like a lazy surf across the cool, polished silver."

The imagery of the writing here is sharp, yet understated so that it does not call attention to itself. The short and grammatically incomplete sentences that reflect the priest's state of mind are typical of Garrett's prose throughout the trilogy. With its sharp detail, the rhythm of its sentences, its authenticity of thought and dialogue, the prose could make convincing weaker and less dramatic stories than those Garrett tells. It brings the priest to life in time for the reader to learn of his capture and his death. He dies at the beginning of his interrogation and therefore has been delivered from revealing information about his friends. This turn in the story invites the reader, and must have invited the author, to wonder whether the end of the priest is a fortuitous accident or the answer to a prayer. Wisely, Garrett does not turn aside from his story, in which he has created a sympathetic and wholly believable character who pays with his life.

The final chapter of *The Succession* unifies what may otherwise appear to some readers to be a story constructed of disparate sequences. It begins in November, 1602, with Queen Elizabeth's return from her palace at Richmond to that at Whitehall where she will arrive in time for Advent and where she will spend the Christmas season. The focus of this segment is on the Queen, on her laws, and on her people who live by them, which is to say on England. Times are hard, but this will not dampen the spirits of the celebrations of the Queen and her courtiers. There will be plays, games, pageants, and gift giving. Cords of firewood, which has become so dear that honest workmen can no longer afford to burn it, will be consumed. Hundreds of candles will burn. Courtiers will dress in clothes for which they have paid—or owe—fortunes. But neither gaiety nor extravagance can hide the impending end of the era.

> This land of England now in the new century becoming as old and as tired and as frail as [the Queen] is. These shows being contrived in the (foolish) hope of denying that the Queen's natural lifetime. . . . *Her time, therefore also their brief sweet time for power and vainglory; I mean her silly and vicious courtiers, the apes of her Privy Council, her goatish bishops and arrogant, ignorant priests, and her wily and subtle Archbishop Whitgift, cruel as a serpent . . .* has almost ended.

A year previously, in 1601, the Queen made her farewell to Parliament, assured the members of her love, and, significantly, relinquished to them some of her monopolies and patents. Now, at Whitehall, in her private chamber with her ladies-in-waiting, she asks that lists of presents given to her on Christmases past be read. They are, in kind at least, what she has always received: scarves, doublets, gloves, and girdles, most of which are trimmed with gold and jewels. There was jewelry also—precious stones cleverly mounted, pins, and pendants made of gold. The history of her reign is in her recollection of the givers.

At other Christmases, her gifts had come from Essex, once her favorite, whom she had sent to the scaffold. Other gifts came from Leicester whom she had loved, from Sir Christopher Hatton who had loved her, from William Cecil who had served her well, and from Walsingham, "whose knowledge proved to be of more value than armies and armadas." There are gifts from Sir Francis Drake, from Philip Sidney, from the cook, the laundress, and the servant of the cellar. The list of those who gave to the Queen is a list of the dead, and their names serve as mementoes of her own mortality. For her there is only moderate comfort in the knowledge that she had been able to appoint her own successor.

All parts of this book that have gone before, the stories that perhaps seemed to have scant connection with each other, combine in the Queen's memories to make a tapestry of a time and the life thereof that will die when she dies and never come again. She knows that her successor is not worthy of the throne from which she ruled, and this knowledge is an important element of the story. Important, also, is her sense of her own increasing inability, if not impotence. Those around her endure her fractiousness, her harsh words and often harsher actions, in the certainty that they will not have to endure them long. The Queen is soon to die. The succession will not be as much a new beginning as it will be an end to an age. Garrett's skill is such that he makes the meaning of this royal transition not only clear, but deeply moving.

ENTERED FROM THE SUN: THE ELIZABETHAN TRILOGY CONCLUDES

Christopher Marlowe, a contemporary of Shakespeare, playwright—he wrote *Tamburlaine the Great, The Tragical History of Dr. Faustus,* and *The Jew of Malta*—was reputed variously to be an atheist or a Catholic, thought to be a homosexual, and known to have a quick and violent temper. He died under mysterious circumstances at Deptford, near London, in 1593. That he was stabbed in the eye by Ingram Frizer while drinking in a private room at an inn was not doubted. But the question of whether Frizer had struck in self-defense, as he claimed, or whether Frizer, with two companions, had gone to Deptford for the purpose of killing Marlowe, was compounded by the irregularities of Marlowe's life, his strained relations with fellow playwright Thomas Kyd, and his long absences from England that seemed to confirm rumors that Marlowe was a spy in the service of Sir Francis Walsingham. In brief, this was the material Garrett had on which to build *Entered From the Sun,* the third volume of his Elizabethan trilogy.

Garrett met a new challenge in *Entered From the Sun.* The prime motivation of the narrative is Marlowe's death, not his life. Consequently, Marlowe can function neither as the point of view of the novel, as Ralegh does in *Death of the Fox,* nor as the presence, removed by rank but made more important thereby, as Elizabeth is in *The Succession.* Garrett's solution is to employ two investigators who, independently, will seek to discover the truth concerning Marlowe's death. These are Joseph Hunnyman, a player who is employed as a spy as was the actor in *The Succession,* and Captain Barfoot—pronounced "barefoot" by Garrett—the scarred veteran of many campaigns, a Papist, and a loyal servant of the Protestant Queen Elizabeth. The reader sees Hunnyman first. He is detained on the street by two bearlike ruffians whose recurring presence in the shadowy precincts of London becomes a grim leitmotif of the novel. They escort Hunnyman to the room of a young gentleman who offers the player both stick and carrot: if he faithfully investigates Marlowe's death, he will be well paid; should he betray the secrecy of his mission, he will suffer.

Barfoot is induced to search for the facts of Marlowe's death by a man who claims to be another old soldier but who is clearly some kind of spy. Unlike Hunnyman, who, although poor and ill paid, would likely abandon his investigation of Marlowe's death except for fear, Barfoot undertakes his mission partly out of interest, not so much in Marlowe, but in the motives of those who want to know the circumstances of Marlowe's death. For Barfoot, as his scarred face and battered body testify, suffering and the threat of death are no strangers. His battles have left him with an appearance so fierce that "a frown on his face has been known to silence a whole tavern." It is soon apparent, more from Hunnyman's nervous demeanor than from Barfoot's initial investigations, that the employers of Hunnyman and of Barfoot are not friendly competitors. The conflict between them is augmented by the uneasy relationship between Hunnyman and his employers and between Barfoot and his.

The opposing principals in the novel are Thomas Walsingham, who has succeeded his now-dead father, Francis Walsingham, as spymaster and who is Hunnyman's patron; and Garrett's old favorite, Sir Walter Ralegh, who has hired Barfoot and who makes an affectionately drawn cameo appearance in the novel. Barfoot tells Ralegh that he is not suspected of being implicated in the death of Marlowe—the murder was arranged by Walsingham for reasons that Barfoot has not fully uncovered. At the time of his death, Marlowe was under indictment for suspicion of atheism. Whether Walsingham wanted Marlowe to remain in England until the charges against him were settled or to leave England before his case could be tried, Barfoot does not know. In either case, Marlowe was killed because he refused to accede to Walsingham's wishes. Walsingham feared Marlowe, Barfoot believes, because Marlowe knew too much about the activities of both Walsinghams, father and son.

But neither Ralegh, Walsingham, Marlowe, nor Frizer, the murderer, occupies much space in the story. The dramatic force of the novel is generated, as it is in the other volumes of the trilogy, by Garrett's writing, his genius for building scenes, and his ability to make his fictional characters bear the weight of the narrative. Hunnyman, whose wife and children died from the plague, is having an affair with Alysoun, a beautiful widow and astute proprietess of a printing business. Hunnyman wants to marry her, but Alysoun, who has used her beauty to become prosperous and who is acutely aware of the difference between being poor and being comfortably fixed, replics, "Not now. And perhaps not ever." Like Barfoot, whose child she later bears, she is one of Garrett's most complex and compelling characters. In the same way that Garrett makes Barfoot's very ugliness attractive, he renders Alysoun's self-centeredness as a kind of virtue. In her bedroom conversations with Hunnyman, who is likable but like most of Garrett's players feckless, her honest dialogue endows even her most self-serving assertions with a kind of generosity. She is at once totally open and profoundly shrewd.

Garrett makes her coupling with Barfoot seem inevitable. They are both adventurers. She has come to affluence out of deep poverty, her only weapons are her good looks and her wits. Barfoot's scars testify to more than the wounds he has suffered. He has inflicted similar scars; he has raped and pillaged; he has contended with death not only on the field but in bed. In a brilliant sequence that includes a crone endowed with supernatural powers, Barfoot survives the plague. Taken together, these two show, better than any others of Garrett's universally well-drawn characters, the dimensions of Elizabethan life as it was lived away from the court.

Barfoot's dual loyalties to Queen and Pope are individual manifestations of one of the most profound of Elizabethan ambiguities: the competing claims, legitimate and sometimes deadly, of faith and the crown. That he is able fully to maintain his allegiance to both helps to authenticate Garrett's rendition of the Elizabethan world. Alysoun's freedom as a woman to use her talents for business, that talent, itself, and her superstitious nature—she seeks magic potions and the interpretation of dreams from "the notorious Dr. Simon Forman"—augment Garrett's created world.

"Well, now," Garrett writes in the final chapter of *Entered From the Sun*, "We are at the end of it." He has, he says, enjoyed living with the Elizabethans for the experience itself and as a respite from our tawdry modern time. The 1726 pages of the trilogy allow Garrett's readers the same privilege. Judged individually, the separate volumes of the trilogy are the best of Garrett's novels. Viewed together, they are a major literary achievement: the characters are fully realized; the story lines are tight; the prose is clean and often poetic; and the setting, which novelist Andrew Lytle called the "enveloping action" of the story, is utterly convincing. Perhaps most important of all, the trilogy is fiction on a heroic scale: the people, the plots, and the supporting details are all bigger than life, larger than anything available to writers caught in what Garrett calls our "bitter shiny century." These books are destined to endure.

POEMS

In the nineteen years between the publication of *Death of the Fox* and the appearance of *Entered From the Sun*, Garrett published, in addition to the trilogy, ten books. Many of these, *Collected Poems of George Garrett* (1984); and *An Evening Performance: New and Selected Short Stories* (1985), for example, contained work that had previously been published; two were on fellow writers James Jones and Mary Lee Settle; and four, again consisting of old material, were limited editions from Stuart Wright's Palaemon Press. Even so, for Garrett to publish ten books while his attention was focused on the trilogy was indicative of the force of his creative energy. During this time, he sharpened and developed his skill as a poet as the verses in *Days of Our Lives Lie in Fragments: New and Old Poems 1957–1997* (1998) demonstrate. Garrett's major poetic themes remained constant even as his talent matured. *Days of Our Lives Lie in Fragments* includes religious poems: "Judith," "Ash Wednesday," "Jacob," and "David"; poems inspired by the work of previous writers, such as Shakespeare, Thomas More, and Salvatore Quasimodo; and elegiac poems that are particularly memorable. In the title poem of the collection, written in memory of the poet and scholar O. B. Hardison Jr., Garrett recalls sailing with Hardison on the York River on which, on the morning of the poem's present, he has sailed alone. "There is no plot here, no narrative to follow," he writes, but this is itself the plot: death is our universal human fate, but when and how, who dies young and who endures, form no pattern. Still, the imagery here—a gull, some geese, the clarity of light, and the river itself—argues against a universe that is random and meaningless.

> And I think I can see you there among the
>   dancers
> And I suddenly guess the music is the laughter
> Of angels, citizens of incredible ever after.
> Something wakes me, makes me step to the
>   window:
> Tide running out, the river on fire with the sunset
> And gulls overhead, white wings riding the wind.

Part of the splendor of this and much of Garrett's other poetry resides in the metaphysical dimensions of his work. It would be wrong to understand his poems—particularly those written in the 1900s—simply as acts of faith. His verse begins with and is firmly anchored in what he sees, in what he hears and feels and knows, and in the here and now of language and observation. But in his poems earthly images become transcendent and the reality of the mundane is enhanced.

THE KING OF BABYLON
SHALL NOT COME AGAINST YOU

In some ways, *The King of Babylon Shall Not Come Against You* (1996) is a new version of *Do, Lord, Remember Me*. Both novels are set in small towns in central Florida, and some of the characters are similar. Dan Lee Smithers, known professionally as "Little David," is not a copy of Red Smalley, but both are traveling evangelists who

are not totally without faith. Both have mistresses, both are good at collecting money from their congregations, and both are murdered as their stories end. But *The King of Babylon* is a more complicated and profound book than *Do, Lord, Remember Me*. In *The King of Babylon*, Garrett juxtaposes the shooting murder of Little David and of Alpha Weatherby, who dies with him, and the dubious suicide of Father Claxton, an Episcopalian priest, to the assassination of Martin Luther King Jr., all of which occur on the same day in 1968. Twenty-five years later, journalist Billy Tone returns to Paradise Springs where he lived as a boy to gather material for a book that will augment what is known about the Paradise Springs murders and relate them to the climate of violence that marred the late 1960s and to the death of King. By including King and the aberrations of his time—the riots that followed his death, the brutality of the war in Vietnam—Garrett endows *The King of Babylon* with a public dimension that *Do, Lord, Remember Me* does not achieve.

The King of Babylon is constructed around Billy Tone, whose interviews of townspeople establish the local ambiance in the same way—but on a reduced model—that the different chapters in Garrett's trilogy convey the Elizabethan world. Separately, the citizens of Paradise Springs embrace every philosophy. There are, among others, a newspaper editor, a retired professor, a land developer, a lawyer, and a crusty veteran who lost his leg in the Korean War. Another character, a lady of loose morals in 1968, has become a medium who delivers messages of love from the dead that help make more gentle the tone of this violent, bawdy, and very funny novel that never loses its focus on its serious theme.

LITERARY CRITICISM

In addition to *The King of Babylon* and *Days of Our Lives,* Garrett published, in the last decade of the twentieth century, two collections of literary criticism, *The Sorrows of Fat City: A Selection of Literary Essays and Reviews* (1992) and *My Silk Purse and Yours: The Publishing Scene and American Literary Art* (1992) and a volume of personal essays, *Whistling in the Dark*. *Bad Man Blues: A Portable George Garrett* (1998), introduced by Allen Weir and Richard Bausch, is a selection of Garrett's criticism, academic anecdotes, and short stories, most of which appeared in earlier books. The pieces in *My Silk Purse and Yours* are lectures, essays, and book reviews that were originally printed in such publications as the *New York Times, The Michigan Quarterly Review, The Sewanee Review,* and other literary magazines. In some of the essays, Garrett, who has himself been the victim of the vagaries of publishers, describes and deplores what he considers to be the sins of editors and the boards of directors who control them, what he calls "The Literary Star System": the selection of a few writers by a few influential critics whose work receives critical attention beyond its desserts. He defends his novel, *Poison Pen,* or *Live Now and Pay Later* (1986), which was published in a limited edition by Stuart Wright, and condemned by some critics for the vulgarity of its language and the severity of its attacks on other writers. *My Silk Purse and Yours* also contains some splendid reviews of books by Shelby Foote, Madison Smartt Bell, and others.

The title of *The Sorrows of Fat City* comes from Garrett's misreading of "The Sorrows of Facticity," a lecture given at the University of Michigan by Harold Bloom. Besides Garrett's discussion of modern literary theory, this book also contains reviews and essays previously available in magazines. *Whistling in the Dark,* a collection of family stories and reminiscences, is deeply personal and deeply touching. Much serious material appears here: Garrett's father's work for social justice, the careers of his uncles and aunt, the adventures of his grandfather, and even a story about his great-great grandfather who fought in the Civil War. Too young to be in World War II, Garrett served in the army in Europe during two of the most threatening years of the Cold War that followed. In family stories and in his accounts of his tenure as a sergeant on the boundary of the Russian sector of Austria, his gift for discerning the humor and irony that overlie the serious purposes of life is always present. Present also are the gentleness, the wisdom, the skill, and the charity that inform all his writing, early and late.

Selected Bibliography

WORKS OF GEORGE GARRETT

NOVELS AND SHORT STORIES

King of the Mountain. New York: Scribners, 1958. (Short stories.)

The Finished Man. New York: Scribners, 1959.

In the Briar Patch. Austin: University of Texas Press, 1961. (Short stories.)

Which Ones Are the Enemy? Boston: Little Brown, 1961.

Cold Ground Was My Bed Last Night. Columbia: University of Missouri Press, 1964. (Short stories.)

Do, Lord, Remember Me. New York: Doubleday, 1965.

A Wreath for Garibaldi and Other Stories. London: Rupert Hart-Davis, 1969. (Short stories.)

Death of the Fox. New York: Doubleday, 1971.

The Magic Striptease. New York: Doubleday, 1973. (Short stories.)

The Succession: A Novel of Elizabeth and James. New York: Doubleday, 1983.

An Evening Performance. New York: Doubleday, 1985. (Short stories.)

Poison Pen. Winston-Salem, N.C.: Stuart Wright, 1986.

Entered From the Sun. New York: Doubleday, 1990.

The King of Babylon Shall Not Come Against You. New York: Harcourt Brace, 1996.

POETRY

The Reverend Ghost. In *Poets of Today IV.* Edited by John Hall Wheelock. New York: Scribners, 1957.

Abraham's Knife and Other Poems. Chapel Hill: University of North Carolina Press, 1961.

For a Bitter Season: New and Selected Poems. Columbia: University of Missouri Press, 1967.

Welcome to the Medicine Show. Winston-Salem, N.C.: Palaemon Press, 1978.

Luck's Shining Child. Winston-Salem, N.C.: Palaemon Press, 1981.

The Collected Poems of George Garrett. Fayetteville: University of Arkansas Press, 1984.

Days of Our Lives Lie in Fragments: New and Old Poems 1957–1997. Baton Rouge: Louisiana State University Press, 1998.

PLAYS

Garden Spot. Produced by Alley Theater. Houston, 1961.

Sir Slob and the Princess: A Play for Children. New York: French, 1962.

Enchanted Ground. York, Maine: Old Gaol Museum Press, 1981.

SCREEN PLAYS

The Young Lovers. Metro-Goldwyn-Mayer, 1964.

The Playground. Jerand Film Distributors, Inc., 1965.

Frankenstein Meets the Space Monster. With R. H. W. Dillard and John Rodenbeck. Allied Artists, 1966.

Suspense. 1958. (Television series.)

CRITICISM

My Silk Purse and Yours. Columbia, Mo.: University of Missouri Press, 1992.

The Sorrows of Fat City. Columbia, S.C.: University of South Carolina Press, 1992.

Understanding Mary Lee Settle. Columbia, S.C.: University of South Carolina Press, 1992.

OTHER BOOKS

James Jones. San Diego: Harcourt Brace, 1984. (Biography.)

Whistling In the Dark. New York: Harcourt Brace Jovanovich, 1992. (Personal essays.)

Bad Man Blues: A Portable George Garrett. Dallas: Southern Methodist University Press, 1998.

WORKS EDITED BY GEORGE GARRETT

New Writing From Virginia. Charlottesville, Va.: New Writing Associates, 1963.

The Girl in the Black Raincoat. New York: Duel, Sloan and Pearce, 1966.

Man and the Movies. With W. R. Robinson. Baton Rouge: Louisiana State University Press, 1967.

New Writing in South Carolina. With William Peden. Columbia, S.C.: University of South Carolina Press, 1971.

Film Scripts One. With Jane Gelfman and O. B. Hardison, Jr. New York: Appleton-Century-Crofts, 1972.

Film Scripts Two. With Jane Gelfman and O. B. Hardison, Jr. New York: Appleton-Century-Crofts, 1972.

Craft So Hard To Learn: Conversations with Poets and Novelists About the Teaching of Writing. With John Graham. New York: William Morrow, 1973.

The Writer's Voice: Conversations with Contemporary Writers. With John Graham. New York: William Morrow, 1973.

Boetteghe Oscure Reader. With Katherine Garrison Biddle. Middletown, Conn.: Wesleyan University Press, 1974.

Film Scripts Three. With Jane Gelfman and O. B. Hardison, Jr. New York: Appleton-Century-Crofts, 1974.

Film Scripts Four. With Jane Gelfman and O. B. Hardison, Jr. New York: Appleton-Century-Crofts, 1974.

Intro 5. With Walton Beacham. Charlottesville: University Press of Virginia, 1974.

Intro 6: Life as We Know It. New York: Doubleday, 1974.

Intro 7: All of Us and None of You. With James Whitehead and Miller Williams. New York: Doubleday, 1975.

Intro 8: Close to Home. With Michael Mewshaw. Austin: Hendel & Reinke, 1978.

Eric Clapton's Lover and Other Stories from the Virginia Quarterly Review. With Sheila McMillen. Charlottesville: University Press of Virginia, 1990.

Contemporary Southern Short Fiction: A Sampler. With Paul Ruffin. Huntsville: Texas Review Press, 1991.

The Wedding Cake in the Middle of the Road. With Susan Stamberg. New York: Norton, 1992.

Elvis and Oz: New Stories & Poems from the Hollins Creative Writing Program. With Mary Flinn. Charlottesville: University Press of Virginia, 1992.

That's What I Like (About the South): And Other New Southern Stories for the 90's. With Paul Ruffin. Columbia, S.C.: University of South Carolina Press, 1992–1993.

Dictionary of Literary Biography Yearbook: 1997. With Matthew J. Bruccoli. Detroit: Gale, 1998.

Dictionary of Literary Biography Yearbook: 1998. With Matthew J. Bruccoli. Detroit: Gale, 1999.

The Yellow Shoe Poets. Baton Rouge: Louisiana State University Press, 1999.

BIBLIOGRAPHIES

Dillard, R. H. W. "George Garrett: A Checklist of His Writings." *Mill Mountain Review* 1:221–234 (1971).

Meriwether, James B. "George Palmer Garrett." In *Seven Princeton Poets.* Edited by Sherman Hawkes. Princeton: Princeton University Library, 1963. Pp. 26–39.

———. "George Garrett." In *First Printings of American Authors.* Detroit: Gale, 1976. Pp. 167–173.

Stuart Wright, "George Garrett: A Bibliographical Chronicle." In *Bulletin of Bibliography* 38:6–19, 25 (1980).

———. *George Garrett: A Bibliography.* Huntsville: Texas Review, 1989.

CRITICAL STUDIES

Betts, Richard A. " 'To Dream of Kings': George Garrett's *The Succession.*" *Mississipi Quarterly* 45:53–67 (Winter 1991–1992).

Broughton, Irv, and R. H. W. Dillard, eds. *Mill Mountain Review* 1 (1971). (Special issue on Garrett.)

Chappell, Fred. "Fictional Characterization as Infinite Regressive Series: George Garrett's 'Strangers in the Mirror.' " In *Southern Literature and Literary Theory.* Edited by Jefferson Humphries. Athens: University of Georgia Press, 1990. Pp 66–74.

Dillard, R. H. W. *Understanding George Garrett.* Columbia: University of South Carolina Press, 1988.

Peden, William. "The Short Fiction of George Garrett." *Ploughshares* 4:83–90 (1978).

———. " 'Swift Had Marbles in His Head': Some Rambling Comments about George Garrett's More Recent Work." *Southern Literary Journal* 17:101–106 (Fall 1984).

Robinson, W. R. "The Ficion of George Garrett." *Red Clay Reader* 2:15–16 (1965).

———. "Imagining the Individual: George Garrett's *Death of the Fox.*" *Hollins Critic* 8:1–12 (August 1971).

Ruffin, Paul, and Stuart Wright, eds. *To Come Up Grinning: A Tribute to George Garrett.* Huntsville: The Texas Review, 1989.

Slavitt, David R. "George Garrett, Professional." *Michigan Quarterly Review* 25:771–778 (Fall 1986).

Spears, Monroe K. "George Garrett and the Historical Novel." In *American Ambitions: Selected Essays on Literary and Cultural Things.* Baltimore: Johns Hopkins University Press, 1987. Pp. 200–210.

Taylor, Henry. "George Garrett: The Brutal Rush of Grace." In *Compulsory Figures: Essays on Recent American Poets.* Baton Rouge: Louisiana State University Press, 1992. Pp. 152–170.

Tillinghast, Richard. "The Fox, Gloriana, Kit Marlowe, and Sundry." *South Carolina Review* 25:91–96 (Fall 1992).

—WALTER SULLIVAN

Donald Justice

1925—

WINNER OF the Pulitzer Prize for his *Selected Poems* (1979) in 1980 when he was fifty-five years old, Donald Justice has supported a steadily growing reputation since his *The Summer Anniversaries* (1960) was the Lamont Poetry Selection. Compared to the work of slightly older poets—Robert Lowell and John Berryman, for example, who taught Justice in the Iowa Writers' Workshop—Justice's body of poetry appears somewhat slim, but unlike that of many others, Justice's work contains nothing to omit. A title to one of his critical works is *Platonic Scripts* (1984), and it is with a Platonist's eye for what is essential that Justice has proceeded. Over time the unadorned completeness of his poetry has become a benchmark for poets, especially younger ones on whom Justice has exercised a substantial influence.

BACKGROUND AND WRITING STYLE

In its spareness and precision, Justice's writing resembles that of John Crowe Ransom and Yvor Winters, his seniors by several decades. With Ransom, early Justice shares an affinity of tone, whereas with Winters the affinity is found, early and late, in the meters. Justice has clearly identified the limitations of using analogies made between poetry and music, yet given the emotional tone and rhythmical balance of his poems, many critics of his work have favored this very comparison. Melody has the power to stand on the ground of immediate conviction, and Justice's poems enjoy the same strength, deriving from the way the impersonal restraint of meter balances the emotional charge created by tone.

Donald Justice was born the son of Vascoe J. and Mary Ethel Cook Justice on August 12, 1925, and grew up in Miami, Florida, where he later studied composition with Carl Ruggles at the University of Miami. From Miami, Justice moved to the University of North Carolina, turning his talent to literature and receiving an Master's degree before he moved to the University of Iowa to do his doctoral work. Along with a brief stint at Stanford University in Palo Alto, California, where he encountered Winters, these universities not only provided Justice places to develop as an artist, but also served as his introduction to the world in which he would live until his retirement from the University of Florida in 1992.

During the post–World War II educational boom, no poet teaching in master of fine arts programs has been more influential than Justice. Throughout his many years teaching at Syracuse University (1965–1969), the University of Iowa (1952–1953, 1957–1965) and (1970–1982), and at the University of Florida (1982–1992), Justice advised a long list of younger poets whose talents sometimes led to free verse and other times to form. Moving with equal grace under both free and formal poetic arrangements, Justice has been a resourceful guide for developing writers, whichever route their abilities have favored.

The fact that poets on both sides of the free-formal divide in American poetry have benefited from Justice's example matches Justice's own avoidance of the arbitrary either/or of form versus free verse. Justice has drawn the best traits from both sides in ways that reveal the influence not only of the formalists Ransom and Winters, but of freer elders as well, especially Wallace Stevens and William Carlos Williams.

Among poets writing since 1950, few have balanced their work between formal and free rules of play as well as Justice has. But Justice has not been alone. Lowell, Berryman, and others have enjoyed similar successes pitting free verse immediacy against rhythmical control, and the amount of success in this vein suggests that the strongest contemporary American poetry may occupy a middle ground where immediacy of voice joins rhythm's elevation of utterance. Certainly this is true of Justice.

Responding to the double stance by which he joins the two main strains of twentieth-century American poetry, critics have noted the way, on the one hand, Justice's poems are intimate and, on the other, they are impersonal. Of this, in an article by Philip L. Gerber and Robert J. Gemmet, Justice has said his use of form "is connected . . . with the desire . . . to displace the self from the poem." This characteristic of Justice's poetry results from the way he assembles personal details into objectified structures. "Psalm and Lament," from *The Sunset Maker: Poems, Stories, a Memoir* (1987), for example, recounts the death of Justice's mother but then ends more generally with the "black oblivion of a neighborhood and a world / Without billboards or yesterdays." Or

there are Justice's poems about learning to play the piano, which move from the particulars of childhood experience to a more general picture of social and economic ambitions and constraints during the 1930s. In the same sentence a critic can praise Justice for his treatment of "nostalgia" and his "purity of style." Justice is a master at objectifying a subjective experience without losing the original sense of urgency.

The poet and critic Baron Wormser has described Justice's poetry as "a model of non-ideological decorum." Wormser says Justice, "a master of plain English," is too honest to confuse art and epiphany, even as he fixes on "the pain and beauty of memory and loss," which in his hands may sometimes feel like epiphany. As Douglas Dunn has put it, Justice is "tunefully elegiac." Another critic, David Hartnett, says Justice's poetry "shows the act of memory turning into an act of composition." This is what David St. John calls "memory as melody" and Ben Howard terms "lyricism chastened by realism."

Stephen Yenser characterizes Justice's images as "crisply visual, seemingly static, and accompanied by a minimum of interpretation." Yenser adds, "If the object itself says more than anything we can say about it, then Justice has most of his contemporaries beaten." Justice's work is "scrupulously executed and subtly shaded." But Justice operates equally effectively auditorially.

Handling syntax and diction with utmost skill, by the structure of the one and the particularity of the other, Justice achieves a level of understatement that sustains itself like a long note held at the end of a song. Of this characteristic one critic has said, "The emotion is so closely tied to the movement of the poem that its formal intentions are invisible." Frequently movement, the development of some central action, is at the quiet center of a Justice poem, but that movement is not so much linear as periodic. The situation described does not resolve through narrative so much as it curves and repeats, shaping time the way melody does.

Memory is authority in Justice's poetry, and related to this is his plain style, which in its self-control achieves another kind of authority. The plain style, in fact, defines Justice's poetry as much as memory and nostalgia. And the plain style has provided fertile ground for Justice's many students, whether writing free or formal poetry. Not the bulk of his output but the centrality of Donald Justice's aesthetic has made his work influential on younger poets. And this aesthetic is the plain style.

Reviewers have consistently noted the quietness of Justice's poetry. Michael Sheridan sees Justice as descending more from "the elegant hush of Emily Dickinson than the 'barbaric yawp' of Walt Whitman." Thomas Swiss argues that for Justice "poetry is the discovery of what is necessary," and along the way this entails the "conscious effacement of self." Paul Ramsey describes a poem like *The Summer Anniversaries'* "Counting the Mad" as "plainspoken." Alan Young spots "a hard-won new simplicity of diction in [Justice's] improvisations." Charles Molesworth identifies "an indomitable trust that is earned both through and with a clear-eyed humility," while David McClatchy finds Justice a "rarity—an artist at once deeply traditional and resolutely newfashioned." Doug Lang says Justice "is as American as Edward Hopper," and this notion is repeated by Ben Howard's likening Justice's "Manhattan Dawn" (1945) to Hopper. Hopper's and Justice's versions of the plain style are also evident elsewhere, in some of Justice's own paintings, *Black Street, Boston, Georgia,* for example, which was exhibited in the Yager Museum at Hartwick College in Oneonta, New York in the late 1990s. Calvin Bedient finds Justice "plain and poignant" and compares his early poetry to "Auden's portentous flatness" and Ransom's "painful verve," while Michael Rewa notes the

way Justice's "In Bertram's Garden" from *The Summer Anniversaries* echoes the conventions of plain-style master Ben Jonson's poem "Queen and Huntress."

THE PLAIN STYLE

Donald Justice's use of the plain style fits his perennial concerns with memory and loss. "But the years are gone. There are no more years," Justice says at the end of "Psalm and Lament," acknowledging that eventually the exchange rate comes down to zero. The frequent appearance of a word like "perhaps" in his poetry reveals the guardedness with which Justice qualifies almost any assertion, but this is done not so much out of skepticism as out of honesty, a reluctance to be the "epiphany mongerer" Baron Wormser warns against. But the sense of memory and loss in Justice is not passive either. There is a stubbornness in his revisiting the past that refuses to accept the very loss he describes. For Justice, it seems, memory is the place where loss itself loses. Memory is not only the basis of authority, it is the means for repetition.

Memory-as-repetition-and-authority works well with the plain style. The argument Justice makes in the title piece of his 1998 collection of essays, *Oblivion,* is consistent with Justice's use of the plain style in his poetry. Early in the essay Justice says, "There is a mysterious and hidden consciousness within the artist of being other; there is an awareness of some reality-beyond-the-reality that lures and charges the spirit." It is unclear whether Justice considers this "reality beyond" the source of or the resolution to an artist's "oblivion." It seems he may find both there. Still, no epiphany occurs in this, merely the sober assessment of just how little lasts, while even that recognition can be understood only through memory. On the other hand, in Justice's poetry there is the "love that masquerades as pure technique," as Justice tells his audience in *The Sunset Maker*'s "Nostalgia of the Lakefronts." And in this the reader catches a glimpse of another source for Donald Justice's art.

The various ways Justice has devised for torsioning old facts into new perspectives grows out of the struggle he feels between what he remembers so fondly and what he understands to be so permanently missing. This is the subjective watershed that no amount of objectivity has removed from Justice's poetry. For him the past "rains on the other side of the heart," and this is nostalgia, but the causes for nostalgia—the people and places one has loved—remain stubbornly lodged in memory's figurative (that is, objectified) landscape. In Justice the "reality-beyond-the-reality" and his sense of nostalgia (or homesickness) share not only in their physical remoteness but in their longing, even as Justice is someone who will not be ruled by longing, or at least will not admit to being ruled by it. Better to focus on "technique," his example tells his audience. And while one is at it, better to employ the plain style.

Reading Justice's poetry and his commentary on poetry, Oblivion in particular, reminds the reader of the plain style's economies, its brevity of statement and reliance on reason to convey muted but sometimes implosive realizations. For Justice the plain style seems to be a way of retaining some part of the "reality-beyond-reality," or to quote from "Nostalgia of the Lakefronts" again, it is a way to retain "the world we run to from the world." For Justice, *nostos* (home) is distanced by time if not by thought. The virtues of home and the "love that masquerades as pure technique" are never far apart, and each, it seems, calls for the plain style. Highly crafted, Justice's poetry applies technique to the formative past, clarifying and transforming the ordinary into permanent fixtures for the imagination. But if the style is plain, the figurative thought is not. Here

are the first two stanzas of "Nostalgia of the Lakefronts":

> Cities burn behind us; the lake glitters.
> A tall loudspeaker is announcing prizes;
> Another, by the lake, the times of cruises.
> Childhood, once vast with terrors and surprises,
> Is fading to a landscape deep with distance—
> And always the sad piano in the distance,
>
> Faintly in the distance, a ghostly tinkling
> (O indecipherable blurred harmonies)
> Or some far horn repeating over water
> Its high lost note, cut loose from all harmonies.
> At such times, wakeful, a child will dream the
> world,
> And this is the world we run to from the world.

"Nostalgia of the Lakefronts" exemplifies especially well the visual crispness Stephen Yenser praises, but it also models Justice's artfulness with rhetorical patterning, syntax, and diction. In this poem Justice uses apostrophe, anaphora, anacoluthon, homoeoteleuton, and chiasmus to explore the boundaries between the things people experience and what these boundaries mean as they try to locate themselves. He has considered Sherwood Anderson's use of contiguity, and found the above devices resources for contiguity's simile-like play. The repetition of "distance" in the last two lines of the first stanza, for example, gives the reader first spatial then temporal "distance" as a scene described becomes a situation lived. Childhood's "landscape deep with distance" shadows adulthood's backward glance grown deeper with age. The same word is repeated with two different meanings the way the same life is viewed from two different perspectives. And for Justice, it is this double sightedness that counts most.

NOSTALGIA

The nostalgia Justice explores is not just the longing for the past that is commonly associated with that word; it is the double view of someone caught between then and now, which argues that the self doing this is somehow groundless. Thus the last two lines of the second stanza introduce the reader to "the world we run to from the world," finding that like the "child," the one who does not control, people are at once in two worlds and thus never fully in either. What one thinks is boundary; where one stands is edge. The "indecipherable blurred harmonies" of line two, stanza two, are like the two kinds of "distance" named in stanza one, the mutually qualifying and mutually exclusive discoveries of someone who is homesick not just for the past but for that once orderly and harmonic spot called home. Justice renders this person something like the passenger who sits facing backward on a train, finding, as Justice says in *The Sunset Maker*'s "Villanelle at Sundown," that "One can like anything diminishment has sharpened." The passing of time obscures the rough-edged and awkward details of a former situation, and as one locates oneself in relation to what is being left behind, longing declines into the cool tones of long vistas or, in Justice's case, perhaps long notes, the little reclamations available as much to memory through art as to art through memory. The cool tones the reader finds in "Nostalgia of the Lakefronts" also derive from diction. "A mad wet dash to the local movie palace," for example, recaptures the innocence of a time before television and videocassette players when a movie theater really could seem like a palace and when going there was important enough to turn simply running through the rain into "a mad wet dash."

A POET APART

Attending Stanford University, Justice had the opportunity (probably the duty) to absorb the aesthetic principles of Yvor Winters, which included the plain style. However, Justice proceeded rather quickly to separate himself from the more rigid elements Winters represented, and it seems that freedom for the imagination necessitated this, Winters being such a fixed and resolute critical presence. But distant or close to the then-prevailing aesthetic at Stanford, Justice—either by affinity or influence—has retained, indeed perfected, a version of the plain style that Winters championed with such intensity, though Justice has adapted his style to today's idiom in a way Winters would not. And in his generation Justice has not been completely alone in this. Edgar Bowers also perfected a version of the plain style, and the lean virtue of the unadorned is powerfully represented elsewhere by the poetry of Elizabeth Bishop, Howard Nemerov, Mark Strand, Mona Van Duyn, and Richard Wilbur, as well as that of younger poets such as Charles Martin and Timothy Steele. But no one has done more for the cool distances and balanced closures of this mode than Justice, least of all contemporary critics.

The disappearance of practical criticism has been one reason Justice has so importantly influenced younger poets. Justice the practitioner has taught people how to write poetry rather than comment on it, though he is a fine critic when he wishes to be. In contrast to Justice's practical view, many academic theorists seem to have diced their readings into convoluted responses with limited half-lives. But theorists are not the only ones who have missed the boat where the plain style is concerned.

Searching the *Princeton Encyclopedia of Poetry and Poetics, A Handbook to Literature,* and *The Longman Dictionary of Literary Terms* turns up little to nothing about the plain style. The Princeton Encyclopedia has no entry; Holman and Harmon's Handbook makes passing reference to the three classical styles (high, middle, and plain) along with the plain prose that Puritan preachers employed for sermons; and The Longman Dictionary makes the leaping statement that

Gerard Manley Hopkins' and Wallace Stevens' poetry do not equal the plain style while that of Larry Levis does.

"PSALM AND LAMENT"

Donald Justice's poetry being a prime example, today's plain style is succinct, clear, and direct and represents one important way that many poets writing after World War II have proceeded. In the *Norton Anthology of Modern Poetry,* the plain style floats just fine without footnotes. Allusion is not necessary for structural integrity. Absent are the appeals of Ezra Pound and T. S. Eliot to the hierarchies of received tradition; absent the pontoon-like bulk of fine-print footnotes floating the cultural baggage piled above. What is at work is the dramatic core of a situation or event rendered in a way that clarifies rather than obscures. Justice's "Psalm and Lament" provides an example of this:

> The clocks are sorry, the clocks are very sad.
> One stops, one goes on striking the wrong hours.
>
> And the grass burns terribly in the sun,
> The grass turns yellow secretly at the roots.
>
> Now suddenly the yard chairs look empty, the sky
>   looks empty,
> The sky looks vast and empty.
>
> Out on Red Road the traffic continues; everything
>   continues.
> Nor does memory sleep; it goes on.
>
> Out spring the butterflies of recollection,
> And I think that for the first time I understand
>
> The beautiful ordinary light of this patio
> And even perhaps the dark rich earth of a heart.
>
> (The bedclothes, they say, had been pulled down.
> I will not describe it. I do not want to describe it.

> No, but the sheets were drenched and twisted.
> They were the very handkerchiefs of grief.)
>
> Let summer come now with its schoolboy
>   trumpets and fountains.
> But the years are gone, the years are finally over.
>
> And there is only
> This long desolation of flower-bordered sidewalks
>
> That runs to the corner, turns, and goes on,
> That disappears and goes on
>
> Into the black oblivion of a neighborhood and a
>   world
> Without billboards or yesterdays.
>
> Sometimes a sad moon comes and waters the roof
>   tiles.
> But the years are gone. There are no more years.

The poem opens with loss embodied in two "clocks," one keeping the wrong time and the other stopping as a life has stopped. Death is both the wrong time and absolute time. As with the "sidewalks" mentioned in the tenth stanza, the "clocks" are not part of nature, which John Ruskin's notion of the pathetic fallacy requires, but are manmade objects through which there is less chance for extended emotion. The clocks tick temporally as the sidewalks extend spatially, much as distance operates two ways in "Nostalgia of the Lakefronts" where "the sad piano in the distance" winds up being more then than there.

Even when Justice's objects are from nature and not manmade, the "empty sky," for example, torsion is still applied. The sky is not desolate, but the sidewalks are; and the sidewalks are not empty, but the sky is. Conventional description would mention "empty sidewalks" and a "desolate sky." Not Justice. He creates his tone by transposing and muting the emotional qualities of what he describes, subtracting the expected: the sky is merely empty, and it is the sidewalks that are desolate, "desolation" being more believable when it is brought down from the potentially valorized sky to the pedestrian rounds of "sidewalks." Transposing his modifiers this way, Justice creates an understated yet resonant tone. Just what are the larger boundaries of the speaker's world now that the parent is dead? They are the minimums of a vacant sky and sidewalks that lead to nowhere other than what Justice calls "a black oblivion."

The transposed chord, or perhaps muted note, that Justice strikes is found again in the "sad moon" that "waters the roof tiles." The verb "waters" retrieves the "moon" from the tears that "sad" makes the reader expect, and this leaves the scene balanced between the emotional and the mechanical—the sadness of tears and the geared cycles of a sprinkler.

Again here is Justice's impersonal personalism. The sprinkler that does the watering not only avoids the excess of tears that one associates with too much emotion, it suggests the character of a world beyond individual loss, perhaps even the "reality-beyond-the-reality" Justice mentions in "Oblivion." Meteorological conditions, one gathers, occasionally result in wet roof tiles, but they are no more personal than a mechanical sprinkler. There is no pathos in the wet tiles, other than that of the speaker who by stating this bald fact dramatizes the absence of human meaning in the surrounding world.

"Psalm and Lament" also demonstrates two other virtues. First, the poem's imagery well befits its logic: "Out spring the butterflies of recollection," for example. The entire poem is an elegist's recollection and lament, and in this particular line the project is represented by butterflies, which vividly stalling and gliding appear suspended over the landscape like the many small, acute memories triggered by that landscape. Second, the increased pace of information delivery that starts with stanza nine's "Let summer come now" simultaneously lists and dramatizes the predicament the poem unfolds. After the

reader has encountered the preceding figure of the "sheets . . . drenched and twisted" until they "were the very handkerchiefs of grief," a race begins for the absolute end.

The fourteen-syllable line that lists "summer," "schoolboy trumpets," and "fountains" stretches only to tip the reader into what at the end will become the poem's refrain, "But the years are gone." Immediately the pace accelerates with the short line, "And there is only," which causes the reader to speed ahead through a "desolation of . . . sidewalks" that run on, "turn," and "disappear" without "billboards or yesterdays"—that is, without expectation of a future or a memory of the past, two conditions that are necessary for any release from grief. This world is what in another line Justice calls "oblivion." Again, the stark word he chose for the title and title piece of his second collection of prose.

But the accelerated pace that follows stanza nine's "Let summer come now" also needs to be considered simply in terms of the poem's timing and its release of information. Suggestive of a speaker about to lose control, the faster delivery of information dramatizes its own emotional heft; thus Justice finds a subtle response to what has happened and, doing so, creates a response in the reader.

In "Psalm and Lament" the plain style allows an understated fusion of abstract and dramatic meaning to be put to the task of objectifying that which nevertheless remains a subjective experience. A principle of reserve controls the entire poem. "I will not describe it," Justice says. But this restraint vies with the headlong movement that begins in stanza nine, only to be reigned in by the poem's last two lines. Dramatically, this change in the rate of delivery equals the speaker's beginning to lose emotional control. This continues until the poem's last two lines where, regained again, control leaves the described death implosively stuck and threatening somewhere in the back of the reader's memory.

"VILLANELLE AT SUNDOWN"

Abjuring the high modernists' allusions to tradition (and comparison to the tradition), "Psalm and Lament" stands on its own objective feet. It is the core experience the poem records that makes it quietly and overwhelmingly compelling. The success of Justice's aesthetic here provides a good example of how at its best the plain style in late modern poetry, following a century of unprecedented violence, has dealt with our increased skepticism about history, language, the intelligibility of experience, and human reason. The hierarchies of tradition championed by the modernists of the first half of the century have been deemed much less reliable by poets writing in the aftermath of World War II's Holocaust and nuclear bombing of civilian targets, to name only two failures of human reason. But this does not mean that allusion to the tradition is totally absent in Justice's poetry, only that the dramatic core of a poem comes before outside evidence that corroborates and contextualizes. Before anything else, the truth-claims for Justice's work are grounded in firsthand rather than secondhand understanding, though understanding of course comes from both sources. Here is "Villanelle at Sundown":

> Turn your head. Look. The light is turning
>   yellow.
> The river seems enriched thereby, not to say
>   deepened.
>   Why this is, I'll never be able to tell you.
>
> Or are Americans half in love with failure?
> One used to say so, reading Fitzgerald, as it
>   happened.
>   (That Viking Portable, all water-spotted and
>   yellow—
>
> Remember?) Or does mere distance lend a
>   value
> To things?—false it may be, but the view is hardly
>   cheapened.
>   Why this is, I'll never be able to tell you.

> The smoke, those tiny cars, the whole urban
>   milieu—
> One can like anything diminishment has
>   sharpened.
>   Our painter friend, Lang, might show the
>   whole thing yellow
>
> And not be much off. It's nuance that counts,
>   not color—
> As in some late James novel, saved up for the
>   long weekend
>   And vivid with all the Master simply won't
>   tell you.
>
>   How frail our generation has got, how
>   sallow
> And pinched with just surviving! We all go off the
>   deep end
>   Finally, gold beaten thinly out to yellow.
>   And why this is, I'll never be able to tell you.

Traditional material abounds from the fact that the poem is a villanelle to the allusions it makes to F. Scott Fitzgerald, Malcolm Cowley's Viking Portables, the painter Lang, Henry James, and finally John Donne. What nineteen-line poem needs to be more allusion packed? But the drama of the poem rests in the cryptic first and third lines of the first stanza, which tell readers to "Look. The light is turning yellow" and "Why this is," the poet will "never be able to tell" them. Justice has stated in prose that yellow is suggestive of decay. He demonstrated this in the second stanza of "Psalm and Lament." At the heart of what the reader is told is that the poet's world refuses to lend itself to the way the metaphysical poets understood it (long with the modernists who championed the work of the seventeenth-century metaphysical poets). The separation of two souls is not "gold to airy thinness beat," as Donne would have it, but merely "gold beaten thinly out to yellow." Appearance, yellow, has replaced essence, gold. This is the restricted assertion of the skeptic who hastens to add, "And why this is, I'll never be able to tell you."

What that skeptic does know is what has happened since the late 1940s when Viking Portables made masters like James and Faulkner readily accessible. A generation has grown "frail," "sallow," and "pinched with just surviving!" "We all," the audience is told, "go off the deep end / Finally." And here the deep end is a loss of composure owing to a fall of not more than six feet. Surviving has been at a premium following the Holocaust of World War II, and skepticism has been a key part of the rational response to that fact. Donne's metaphysical view of existence diametrically opposes the truth of existence as the speaker sees it. But one thing is even worse.

Not only does the speaker find no spiritual world preexisting and essential to the order of the physical one, neither can he explain the loss he describes. That is, the doubt here goes beyond religious skepticism to the point of challenging language, reason, and the very history people customarily consult to explain why things have happened. The events described in the poem move from an understanding supported by religious faith to a seemingly undifferentiated catalog of plain facts. And for the speaker they lose the tradition's ability to categorize and explain them by matching them with foregoing events. So while "Villanelle at Sundown" uses allusion in a way similar to how the early modernists used it, the results are mostly opposite to what occurred before: the match between today and yesterday does not edify but doubly frustrates, as the speaker remains unable to tell the reader why "We all go off the deep end / Finally," since for him no evidence indicates that anything exists beyond that point. Here "deep" is the physical and the metaphysical abyss of death that no "gold to airy thinness beat" can span.

"THE SUNSET MAKER"

In "The Sunset Maker," the title poem to Justice's 1987 volume, *The Sunset Maker: Poems, Stories, a Memoir,* the speaker describes "The Bestor papers," which he has received on his friend Eugene

Bestor's death. The entire poem is a meditation on the efficacy of art, which boils down to art's ability to liken, not equate, one thing to another. Symbols no longer work; they create false equations. Here again Justice is at odds with a key part of high modernism, the aspiration for symbolic meaning. What does work for Justice is the mind's ability to compare one thing to another. Similes are reliable; symbols are not. Thus the speaker says, "As if . . . but everything there is is that." Meaning comes from likening one thing to another. Here one loss is like another; the loss of a friend, a great talent, a body of work—all this dramatized by the survival of "just this fragment, this tone-row / A hundred people halfway heard one Sunday. . . ." With Justice this kind of reserve seems to go hand in hand with the plain style. Claiming more would be false.

By meter Justice most clearly charts his independent way between the dictates of free verse and formal verse. Nowhere is this independence clearer than in "Thinking about the Past" from *Selected Poems* (1979):

> Certain moments will never change nor stop
>   being—
> My mother's face all smiles, all wrinkles soon;
> The rock wall building, built, collapsed then,
>   fallen;
> Our upright loosening downward slowly out of
>   tune—
> All fixed into place now, all rhyming with each
>   other.
> That red-haired girl with wide mouth—Eleanor—
> Forgotten thirty years—her freckled shoulders,
>   hands.
> The breast of Mary Something, freed from a white
>   swimsuit,
> Damp, sandy, warm; or Margery's, a small,
>   caught bird—
> Darkness they rise from, darkness they sink back
>   toward.
> O marvellous early cigarettes! O bitter smoke,
>   Benton.
> And Kenny in wartime whites, crisp, cocky,
> Time a bow bent with his certain failure.
> Dusks, dawns; waves; the ends of songs . . .

An unrhymed fourteen-line poem of varied line length and substantial metrical substitution, is this a sonnet or something else? The majority of the feet are iambic, and at least half the lines have five stresses, the rest running to six stresses except one that has seven. Much of the poem plays back and forth between iambic pentameter and iambic hexameter, but the first six lines qualify as pentameter, with the first line full of substitutions. This is enough to establish in the reader's mind that the norm is iambic pentameter. All of the above leads to the question of whether or not this is a sonnet. That is as far as Justice needs the reader to go. The rest of the work is carried out by balancing the poem between being an unrhymed sonnet and something that has broken entirely free of sonnet form.

The last line is the poem's ultimate moment in this balancing strategy. It is iambic pentameter with three-fifths substitution, punctuation taking the place of unstressed syllables in terms of duration. The varied timing found throughout the entire poem is recapitulated by the use of three trochaic substitutions opening the line, then two iambic feet closing it. The comma after "Dusks" and the semicolons following "dawns" and "waves" consume the amount of time an unstressed syllable would require; thus in terms of duration the line works as iambic pentameter. Justice, a master of the musical rest, knows that sometimes silence takes up time more effectively than syllables can manage. There are various places where Justice speeds or slows the movement by cataloging items, by caesura, or anacoluthon; this makes the reader's experience of the poem's progress a matter of contingency. In this way "Thinking about the Past" relies on what in "Psalm and Lament" Justice has called "the butterflies of recollection," the authority of memory dramatized by a poem's rhythmical movement.

As Justice says in the penultimate line, people are confronted with "Time a bow bent," time curving back, as in the redundancy of bow and bend. To bow is "to bend," as the noun bow used here goes back to the Old English bugan, "to bend." Bow's first definition is something bent into a curve. Justice's verb "to bend" means to constrain to tension (as is done when a bow is made) or to turn, press, or force something so it is curved. In effect, therefore, when Justice says "Time a bow bent" he is saying, "Time a curve curved," and this is much the way "the ends of songs" curve back to their beginnings, or the way "thinking about the past" causes people's thinking now to round back to their thinking before. The effect of all this rounding is reclamation.

THE THEME OF OBLIVION

"The Telephone Number of the Muse" from *Departures* (1973) provides a good example of Justice's quiet yet shadowy wit, itself another means for reclamation:

> I call her up sometimes, long distance now.
> And she still knows my voice, but I can hear,
> Beyond the music of her phonograph,
> The laughter of the young men with their keys.
> I have the number written down somewhere.

There is the growing sense of oblivion felt on the part of the speaker, who, prior to the above, has recounted in boudoir-joke fashion the details that go with no longer being able to arouse the muse, she now wishing only to be "friends." The speaker says of himself when he learned of the muse's cooled passion, "I smiled, darkly. And that was how I came / To sleep beside, not with her; without dreams." Something as small as the semicolon that precedes "without dreams" reveals the understated way Justice goes about the business of dramatizing what is missing now, with the muse no longer interested in this poet. But there are other tannic details woven into the situation.

The poet's relationship with the muse has devolved into "long distance," though his "voice" is still recognized by her. More disturbing than "long distance," however, is replacement, "the young men with their keys." The implication is that while the younger poets who have replaced the speaker have access to the muse, how long will that last? They may enter by keys, but the locks can be changed. Or if the keys are for the quick rush of automobiles, how sustainable is that? The muse enjoys the passions of younger men, but youth is never anything more than a temporary advantage, as the older poet's dislodged situation demonstrates.

"The Telephone Number of the Muse" depicts a scaled-down vision of what inspiration is to begin with, the muse being the girl whose number men request. But a number is highly reductive: it is not a name, not an address, certainly not someone present; instead it is the abbreviated access afforded by the seven digits one dials. Having someone's number suggests the impermanence and anonymity of the self, a great theme with Justice, who repeatedly tells his readers that most of what they do, think, feel, and say really is impersonal because it is unimportant finally. The muse is indifferent to the speaker, and now, late in the game, the speaker has become indifferent to himself: carelessly, he has "the number written down somewhere." The poem plays its theme of oblivion in the quiet tones of a minor key by which the speaker articulates his lost standing now and that of everyone over time. Oblivion takes a humorous turn and reaches the reader in *Departures'* "Poem." This time it is the audience rather than the poet who is anonymous, the ultimate point to Justice's mordant wit being the impersonal standards of art as it goes about getting things right. Who prevails in this regard? No one, Justice assures the audience. But here is the poem:

This poem is not addressed to you.
You may come into it briefly,

But no one will find you here, no one.
You will have changed before the poem will.

Even while you sit there, unmovable,
You have begun to vanish. And it does not matter.
The poem will go on without you.
It has the spurious glamor of certain voids.

It is not sad, really, only empty.
Once perhaps it was sad, no one knows why.
It prefers to remember nothing.
Nostalgias were peeled from it long ago.

Your type of beauty has no place here.
Night is the sky over this poem.
It is too black for stars.
And do not look for any illumination.

You neither can nor should understand what it
     means.
Listen, it comes without guitar,
Neither in rags nor any purple fashion.
And there is nothing in it to comfort you.

Close your eyes, yawn. It will be over soon.
You will forget the poem, but not before
It has forgotten you. And it does not matter.
It has been most beautiful in its erasures.

O bleached mirrors! Oceans of the drowned!
Nor is one silence equal to another.
And it does not matter what you think.
This poem is not addressed to you.

Here Justice dramatizes the impersonal for its comic potential: everyone feels that their lives are dear but knows otherwise. The incongruity between how people feel about themselves and what they know about themselves is the stuff of Justice's quiet laughter. The high regard for objectivity and impersonalism that dominated the poetics of the first half of the century has been taken to its ultimate conclusion: "This poem is not addressed to you." The trust formerly placed in reason and the tradition has been replaced with an aesthetic that "has the spurious glamor of certain voids," where the mirrors are "bleached" and

"Oceans" are full "of the drowned!" This is the playfulness of Stevens and the hopefulness of Eliot treated to a later set of "beautiful erasures."

What might be called Justice's attitude of oblivion, in the sense that *Departures'* existentialism is considered more an attitude than a systematic philosophy, is perhaps best seen in the poem "Homage to the Memory of Wallace Stevens," which begins,

> Hartford is cold today but no colder for your
>   absence.
> The rain is green over Avon and, since your
>   death, the sky
> Has been blue many times with a blue you did not
>   imagine.
>
> The judges of Key West sit soberly in black
> But only because it is their accustomed garb,
> And the sea sings with the same voice still,
>   neither serious nor sorry.

Justice appears at the end of the first section, as "The poet practicing his scales" who "Thinks" of Stevens "as his thumbs slip clumsily under and under, / Avoiding the darker notes." Here suddenly the reader is close to the blackbirds and peacocks that populated Stevens' world. By the end of Justice's poem the reader has moved through concerns registered by Stevens' "The Comedian as the Letter C," "The Idea of Order at Key West," and "Final Soliloquy of the Interior Paramour," as the sad actuary of Hartford Stevens has been treated to "new flutterings, new adieux." This is the late lost faith of Stevens in "Sunday Morning," the pigeons descending ambiguously to darkness, or in Justice's treatment somewhat less importantly, "the singers" who join "the picnic . . . minus their golden costumes." Justice is not the fabulist that Stevens is, but he uses the embroidery of a Stevens poem to capture the isolation both he and Stevens recognize, what in "Final Soliloquy" Stevens summarizes by saying, "How high that highest candle lights the dark." Justice, in fact, seems to find the inventiveness in

Stevens a dramatization of just how little material there is to spread over the void.

Where Stevens appears almost giddy with invention, Justice is, by comparison, tersely plainspoken. And it is here, in the plain style, that Justice's rewrite of the modernists' objectivity and impersonalism reads most naturally. He sometimes pulls the brocade of a Stevens poem out of the drawer and shows it around, but he always puts it back, and usually does so with some sobering concluding observation. "What has been good? What has been beautiful?" Justice asks. It has been that which in conclusion Justice calls "this almost human cry." A bit less invention on Stevens' part, Justice suggests, would result in a bit more humanity. Nothing is plainer than the "cry," and it is perhaps most human and convincing when lowered or even silenced. In "Men at Forty," from *Night Light* (1967) one of Justice's best known earlier poems, isolation and loss are depicted in a deceptively muted way:

> Men at forty
> Learn to close softly
> The doors to rooms they will not be
> Coming back to.
>
> At rest on a stair landing,
> They feel it moving
> Beneath them now like the deck of a ship,
> Though the swell is gentle.

These men "are more fathers than sons . . . now," as at "twilight" the sound of "crickets" grows immense, "Filling the woods at the foot of the slope / Behind their mortgaged houses." The scale of the world both indoors and out has grown huge in inverse proportion to the diminishment of the middle-aged men Justice describes. Part of the predicament here is dramatized by the details Justice chooses—stair landings one reaches out of breath, boys practicing tying ties discovered suddenly in the faces of fathers, and the peaceful but enveloping immensity of an uneventful twilight surrounding a neighborhood that is not paid for so much as merely mortgaged, the pun here suggesting that ownership and mortality are never separated. Rather than raising his voice or dazzling his reader with bright flourishes, Justice restricts what he has to say to the muted tones of understatement. The effect of understatement in Justice's plain style, with its rhythmical control and economical precision of imagery, is to increase the duration of the poem in the reader's mind. The poet's restraint makes the reader's participation such that he completes some of the poem's business. The effect of this is the reader's strong conviction that the poem is true. Truth is the most durable aesthetic of all.

The guiding principle behind the plain style and the musical balance of Justice's poetry is, finally, honesty found in a clarity of mind that refuses to make anything more or less of our lives than what they are. Precise with every detail, Justice sees things in both their fullest and plainest implications, holding them up to the unadorned light of imagination and technique. Time curves as Justice's poems consistently return to what matters most—those places where the past and present meet as we live our daily lives. In its directness the plain style is open to a variety of talents, and this has made Donald Justice's poetry a safe haven for many younger poets. In its subtleties, however, its modulations of tone and rhythmical movement as well as its nuanced meanings, Justice's poetry offers a wide expanse for anyone to navigate.

Selected Bibliography

WORKS OF DONALD JUSTICE

POETRY

The Old Bachelor and Other Poems. Miami: Pandanus Press, 1951.

The Summer Anniversaries. Middletown, Conn.: Wesleyan University Press, 1960.

A Local Storm. Iowa City: The Stone Wall Press and The Finial Press, 1963.

Three Poems. Iowa City: Virginia Piersol, 1966.

Night Light. Middletown, Conn.: Wesleyan University Press, 1967.

Sixteen Poems. Iowa City: The Stone Wall Press, 1970.

The Seven Last Days: for SATB Chorus, Percussion, 2 Stereo Tape Playback Systems, and 16mm Silent Film. Lyrics for music by Edward Miller. E. C. S. Mixed Media Series, no. 2906. Boston: E. C. Schirmer, 1971.

From a Notebook. Iowa City: The Seamark Press, 1972.

Departures. New York: Atheneum, 1973.

L'Homme qui se ferme: A Poem by Guillevic: A Translation and an Improvisation by Donald Justice. Iowa City: The Stone Wall Press, 1973.

Selected Poems. New York: Atheneum, 1979.

In the Attic. West Branch, Iowa: Toothpaste Press, 1980.

Tremayne: Four Poems. Iowa City: Windhover Press, 1984.

Men at Forty. Colorado Springs: The Press at Colorado College, 1985.

The Death of Lincoln. Libretto for an opera by Edwin London. Austin: W. Thomas Taylor, 1988.

Young Girls Growing Up. Minneapolis: Minnesota Center for the Book Arts, 1988.

Banjo Dog: Poems and Linocut Illustrations. Riverside, Calif.: Thaumatrope Press, 1995.

New and Selected Poems. New York: Alfred A. Knopf, 1995.

The Ballad of Charles Starkweather. With Robert Mezey. West Chester, Pa.: Aralia Press, 1997.

Orpheus Hesitated beside the Black River: Poems 1952–1997. London: Anvil Press, 1998.

PROSE

Platonic Scripts. Poets on Poetry. Ann Arbor: University of Michigan Press, 1984.

Oblivion: On Writers and Writing. Ashland, Oreg.: Story Line Press, 1998.

INTERVIEWS

Walsh, William. "An Interview with Donald Justice." *Chattahoochee Review* 9:77–96 (Summer 1989).

OTHER WORKS

The Sunset Maker: Poems, Stories, a Memoir. New York: Atheneum, 1987.

A Donald Justice Reader: Selected Poetry and Prose. The Breadloaf Series of Contemporary Writers. Middlebury, Vt.: Middlebury College Press, 1991.

BOOKS EDITED BY DONALD JUSTICE

Kees, Weldon. *The Collected Poems of Weldon Kees.* Iowa City: The Stone Wall Press, 1960.

Contemporary French Poetry: Fourteen Witnesses of Man's Fate. With Alexander Aspel. Ann Arbor: University of Michigan Press, 1965.

Syracuse Poems, 1968. Syracuse, N.Y.: Department of English, Syracuse University, 1968.

Coulette, Henri. *The Collected Poems of Henri Coulette.* With Robert Mezey. Fayetteville: University of Arkansas Press, 1990.

Miller, Raeburn. *The Comma after Love: Selected Poems of Raeburn Miller.* Akron: University of Akron Press, 1994.

Bolton, Joe. *The Last Nostalgia: Poems, 1982–1990.* Fayetteville: University of Arkansas Press, 1999.

MANUSCRIPT PAPERS

University of Delaware Library. Dover, Delaware.

BIBLIOGRAPHY

Peich, Michael, and Jeffrey Cobb. "Donald Justice: A Bibliographical Checklist." In *Certain Solitudes: On the Poetry of Donald Justice.* Edited by Dana Gioia and William Logan. Fayetteville: University of Arkansas Press, 1997.

CRITICAL AND BIOGRAPHICAL STUDIES

Baro, Gene. Review of *The Summer Anniversaries. New York Herald Tribune Books,* September 4, 1960, p. 6.

Bawer, Bruce. "The Poetry of Things Past and Passing." *Washington Post Book World,* January 3, 1988, pp. 4, 6. (Includes a review of *The Sunset Maker: Poems, Stories, a Memoir.*)

Bedient, Calvin. "New Confessions." *Sewanee Review* 88:474–488 (Summer 1980). (Includes a review of *Selected Poems.*)

Brainard, Dulcy. Review of *New and Selected Poems. Publishers Weekly,* August 28, 1995, p. 108.

Bruns, Gerald. "Duration Is Destination—Verse in the Eighties." *Southwest Review* 65:218–220 (Spring 1980). (Includes a review of *Selected Poems.*)

———. "Anapostrophe: Rhetorical Meditations upon Donald Justice's 'Poem.' " *Missouri Review* 4:70–76 (Fall 1980).

Burke, Herbert C. "Leaps and Plunges." *Times Literary Supplement,* May 18, 1967, p. 420. (Includes a review of *Night Light.*)

———. Review of *Night Light. Library Journal,* February 1, 1967, pp. 586–587.

Collier, Michael. Review of *The Sunset Maker: Poems, Stories, a Memoir. Partisan Review* 55:490–492 (Summer 1988).

Conarroe, Joel O. "Five Poets." *Shenandoah* 18:84–91 (Summer 1967). (Includes a review of *Night Light.*)

Cook, Eleanor. "He That of Repetition Is Most Master." *Partisan Review* 64:671–673 (Fall 1997). (Includes a review of *New and Selected Poems.*)

De Jong, Mary Gosselink. " 'Musical Possibilities': Music, Memory, and Composition in the Poetry of Donald Justice." *Concerning Poetry* 18:57–67 (1985).

Dunn, Douglas. "Paging the Oracle: Douglas Dunn Reviews Recent Poetry." *Punch,* January 15, 1988, pp. 44–45. (Includes a review of *The Sunset Maker: Poems, Stories, a Memoir.*)

Ehrenpreis, Irvin. "Boysenberry Sherbet." *New York Review of Books,* October 16, 1975, pp. 3–4. (Includes a review of *Departures.*)

Elliott, George P. "Donald Justice." *Perspective* 12:173–179 (Spring 1962).

Fitts, Dudley. "Separate Voices." *New York Times Book Review,* February 19, 1961, p. 36. (Includes a review of *The Summer Anniversaries.*)

Foy, John. "The Marriage of Logic and Desire: Some Reflections on Form." *Parnassus: Poetry in Review* 23:287–308 (1998). (Includes a review of *New and Selected Poems.*)

Gioia, Dana. "Three Poets in Mid-Career." *Southern Review* 17:667–674 (July 1981). (Includes a review of *Selected Poems.*)

Gioia, Dana, and William Logan, eds. *Certain Solitudes: On the Poetry of Donald Justice.* Fayetteville: University of Arkansas Press, 1997.

Gunn, Thom. "Voices of Their Own." *The Yale Review* 49:589–598 (Summer 1960). (Includes a review of *The Summer Anniversaries.*)

Haines, John. "Poetry Chronicle." *The Hudson Review* 50:317–324 (Summer 1997). (Includes a review of *New and Selected Poems.*)

Hartnett, David. "Mythical Childhoods." *Times Literary Supplement*, April 15–21, 1988, p. 420. (Review of *The Sunset Maker: Poems, Stories, a Memoir.*)

Hirsch, Edward. Review of *The Sunset Maker: Poems, Stories, a Memoir. New York Times Book Review*, August 23, 1987, p. 20.

Hofmann, Michael. "Gestures of Intricate Refusal." *New York Times Book Review*, December 10 1995, pp. 13–14. (Review of *New and Selected Poems.*)

Hollinghurst, Alan. "Good for Nothing?" *New Statesman*, August 23, 1980, pp. 17–18. (Includes a review of *Selected Poems.*)

Howard, Ben. "Places and Losses." *Poetry* 154:340–351 (September 1989). (Includes a review of *The Sunset Maker: Poems, Stories, a Memoir.*)

Howard, Richard. "As the Butterfly Longs for the Cocoon or Looping Net." In *Alone with America: Essays on the Art of Poetry in the United States Since 1950.* New York: Atheneum, 1969. Pp. 247–257.

———. "Poetry by the Yard?" *Times Literary Supplement*, March 29, 1974, p. 340. (Includes a review of *Departures.*)

———. "New Work from Three Poets." *North American Review* 259:78–80 (Spring 1974). (Includes a review of *Departures.*)

Irving, John. Review of *The Sunset Maker: Poems, Stories, a Memoir.* In "Summer Reading," edited by Dianne Donovan. *Chicago Tribune Books,* June 21, 1987, p. 3.

Jarman, Mark. "Ironic Elegies: The Poetry of Donald Justice." *Pequod: A Journal of Contemporary Literature and Contemporary Criticism* 16–17:104–109 (1984).

Kirby, David. "Refined Craftsman." *American Book Review* 15:26 (April–May 1993). (Review of *A Donald Justice Reader: Selected Poetry and Prose.*)

Kitchen, Judith. "The Ladybug and the Universe." *The Georgia Review* 50:386–403 (Summer 1996). (Review of *New and Selected Poems.*)

Kniffel, Leonard. Review of *The Sunset Maker: Poems, Stories, a Memoir. Library Journal* 112:71 (May 1987).

Lang, Doug. "The Pleasures of Poetic Justice." *Washington Post Book World,* February 10, 1980, p. 11. (Includes a review of *Selected Poems.*)

Leithauser, Brad. "Getting Things Right." *New York Review of Books,* September 19, 1996, pp. 49–52. (Includes a review of *New and Selected Poems.*)

Lynch, Doris. Review of *A Donald Justice Reader: Selected Poetry and Prose. Library Journal* 116:144, 146 (December 1991).

McClatchy, David. "Summaries and Evidence." *Partisan Review* 47:639–644 (Fall 1980). (Includes a review of *Selected Poems.*)

McConnel, Frances Ruhlen. "Poetic Justice in Haunting Elegies of America's Past." *Los Angeles Times Books,* August 12, 1987, p. 10. (Review of *The Sunset Maker: Poems, Stories, a Memoir.*)

McCorkle, James. "Donald Justice: The Artist Orpheus." *The Kenyon Review* 19:180–188 (Summer–Fall 1997). (Review of *New and Selected Poems.*)

McCoy, James A. " 'Black Flowers, Black Flowers': Meta-Criticism of Donald Justice's 'Bus Stop.' " *Notes on Contemporary Literature* 26:9–10 (November 1996).

McGann, Jerome J. "The Importance of Being Ordinary." *Poetry* 125:44–52 (October 1974). (Includes a review of *Departures.*)

Miller, Jane. "Working Time." *American Poetry Review* 17:9–21 (May 1988). (Includes a review of *The Sunset Maker: Poems, Stories, a Memoir.*)

Molesworth, Charles. "Anniversary Portraits." *New York Times Book Review,* March 9, 1980, pp. 8, 16. (Includes a review of *Selected Poems.*)

Monaghan, Pat. Review of *A Donald Justice Reader: Selected Poetry and Prose. Booklist,* January 1, 1992, p. 805.

Morris, John N. "Making More Sense Than Omaha." *The Hudson Review* 27:106–118 (Spring 1974). (Includes a review of *Departures.*)

Murphy, Bruce. Review of *New and Selected Poems. Poetry* 168:168–171 (June 1996).

Ostroff, Anthony. "A Gathering of Poets: The Jamesian Midwest." *Western Humanities Review* 29:292–307 (Summer 1974). (Review of *Departures.*)

Peters, Robert. "A Child in the House." *American Book Review* 4:15 (January–February 1982). (Review of *Selected Poems.*)

Peterson, M. Review of *Platonic Scripts. Choice* 22:815 (February 1985).

Ramsey, Paul. "American Poetry in 1973." *Sewanee Review,* 82:393–406 (Spring 1974). (Includes a review of *Departures.*)

———. "In Praise of Makers: American Poetry in 1979." *Sewanee Review* 88:665–671 (Fall 1980). (Includes a review of *Selected Poems.*)

Rewa, Michael. " 'Rich Echoes Reverberating': The Power of Poetic Convention." *Modern Language Studies* 9:25–32 (Winter 1978–1979).

Richman, Robert. "Intimations of Inadequacy." *Poetry* 162:160–166 (June 1993). (Review of *A Donald Justice Reader: Selected Poetry and Prose.*)

Ryan, Michael. "Flaubert in Florida." *New England Review and Bread Loaf Quarterly* 7:218–232 (Winter 1984).

Schulman, Grace. Review of *The Sunset Maker: Poems, Stories, a Memoir. Nation,* December 26, 1987–January 2, 1988, p. 803.

Sheridan, Michael. "The Poetry of Donald Justice, Gentleman." *New Letters* 48:114–116 (Fall 1981). (Review of *Selected Poems.*)

Simon, Greg. " 'My Still to be Escaped From': The Intentions of Invisible Forms." *American Poetry Review,* March–April 1976, pp. 30–31. (Review of *Departures.*)

Spiegelman, Willard. "Inflections and Inuendos." *The Yale Review* 84:160–183 (Spring 1996). (Includes a review of *New and Selected Poems.*)

St. John, David. "Memory as Melody." *The Antioch Review* 46:102–109 (Winter 1988). (Review of *The Sunset Maker: Poems, Stories, a Memoir.*)

———. "Scripts and Water, Rules and Riches." *The Antioch Review* 43:309–319 (1985). (Includes a review of *Platonic Scripts.*)

Stefanile, Felix. Review of *A Donald Justice Reader: Selected Poetry and Prose. The Christian Science Monitor,* April 20, 1992, p. 13.

Strand, Mark. "Poetic Justice: Poems of Rapture and Restraint." *New Yorker,* November 13, 1995, pp. 124–126. (Review of *New and Selected Poems.*)

Swiss, Thomas. "The Principle of Apprenticeship: Donald Justice's Poetry." *Modern Poetry Studies* 10:44–58 (Spring 1980).

Turco, Lewis. "Of Laureates and Lovers." *Saturday Review,* October 14, 1967, pp. 31–33, 99. (Includes a review of *Night Light.*)

———. "The Progress of Donald Justice." *The Hollins Critic* 29:1–7 (1992).

Watkins, Clive. "Some Reflections on Donald Justice's Poem 'After a Phrase Abandoned by Wallace Stevens.' " *The Wallace Stevens Journal. A Publication of the Wallace Stevens Society* 17:236–244 (Fall 1993).

Wertime, Richard. "Poets Prose." *The Yale Review* 74:602–609 (Summer 1985). (Includes a review of *Platonic Scripts.*)

Wormser, Baron. Review of *The Sunset Maker: Poems, Stories, a Memoir. Boston Review,* June 1987, p. 27.

Wright, Charles. "Homage to the Thin Man." *Southern Review* 30:741–744 (Autumn 1994).

Yenser, Stephen. "Bright Sources." *The Yale Review* 77:115–147 (Autumn 1987). (Includes a review of *The Sunset Maker: Poems, Stories, a Memoir.*)

Young, Alan. "Identifying Marks." *Times Literary Supplement,* May 30, 1980, p. 620. (Includes a review of *Selected Poems.*)

Young, Vernon. "Two Hedgehogs and a Fox." *Parnassus: Poetry in Review* 8:227–237 (Fall–Winter 1979). (Includes a review of *Selected Poems.*)

—WYATT PRUNTY

William Kennedy

1928—

In the year 2000, William Kennedy turned seventy-two years of age. Although an obscure writer into his fifties, Kennedy more than came into his own in the 1980s and 1990s. The ex-journalist's minimal vision, to which he admitted in an interview with Penny Maldonado in 1969—"All my life I've wanted to live as a writer, where you give your own assignments"—has become maximal reality. He is undeniably one of the elder statesmen of American letters, but he is a rarity even among literary notables: his life's work—a cycle of historical novels grounded with dogged idiosyncrasy in the history and neighborhoods of Albany, New York—continues to expand and knit together like nerve tissue, character by character, dynastic sub-sub-plot by sub-sub-plot, dendrite by dendrite, and word by word. It would hardly be exaggerating to say that each new novel Kennedy publishes raises the already high IQ of those that preceded it.

For this productive focus, this clarity of purpose and literary vision, Kennedy is universally regarded as a Serious writer, a man of intellectual heft and imaginative candlepower. Yet it is his verbal razzmatazz, the rakish play of the sentences, that make up his often comedic Serious fiction, for which he is most admired. It is the medium by which Kennedy's gangsters and pimps and low-life bums achieve momentary no-

bility, a signature creole of street argot and high-flown eloquence.

When Martin Daugherty, a luckless 1930s column writer in *Billy Phelan's Greatest Game* (1978), approaches Albany's political boss Patsy McCall to find out if a younger McCall has been kidnapped, Martin speaks in the accent of Kennedy's mythical Albany: " 'It's what's right,' Martin said, standing up, thinking: I've still got the gift of tongues. For it was as true as love that by talking a bit of gibberish he had verified, beyond doubt, that Charlie Boy McCall had, indeed, been grabbed."

William Kennedy was born in North Albany on January 16, 1928, to William Joseph Sr. and Mary Elizabeth McDonald Kennedy. He received his bachelor's degree from Siena College in Loudonville, New York, in 1949. In 1950 he was drafted into the military where he worked as an editor on the Fourth Division's newspaper. In 1956, he moved to Puerto Rico and worked as a columnist and editor for various publications. He continued his newspaper career after moving back to Albany in 1963, when he also began to write fiction.

William Kennedy is where he has always wanted to be, headquartered both in Albany, New York, and in the forefront of American novelists. The story of his rise to success and the birth story of the Albany Cycle itself have a great deal to tell his audience not only about Kennedy the writer but also about the popular and literary cultures that validated and influenced him. And yet, if one sets the novels of William Kennedy beside the career-story of the novelist William Kennedy, one can't help but notice something strange and seemingly unaccountable: as the Albany Cycle itself has grown larger, more ambitious, and less susceptible to casual analysis, Kennedy's own career-story has been methodically simplified, truncated, and converted into digestible myth. The one seems to have expanded exponentially at the expense of the other.

Nearly all of the interviews and articles on Kennedy published after 1983—and there have been more than a few—begin with some thumbnail variation on what one critic has called the Parable of the Good American Novelist. The story, as it is usually told, is that Kennedy, a working journalist laboring in obscurity over highly literary books about highly uncommercial topics, burst into fame and fortune in 1983, winning a $264,000 MacArthur Foundation Fellowship (also known as the "genius" award), as well as the National Book Critics Circle Award in 1983 and the Pulitzer Prize in 1984 for his fourth novel, *Ironweed* (1983). These events are sometimes cast in explicitly moralistic terms: Kennedy's diligence and refusal to sell out commercially were justly rewarded, as if by magic, with instant recognition of his genius, as well as matching wealth, popular fame, and connections in Hollywood.

While there is, in fact, much truth to this popular sketch, clearly much has been elided in the tale of Kennedy's rise to prominence and the slow evolution of his work. No one has thought more about this phenomenon than Kennedy himself, and he has suggested several crucial reasons for his apparent windfall: a "sudden concentration of books about a single place with interconnected characters," Viking's decision to package

Ironweed with *Billy Phelan's Greatest Game* and *Legs* (1975) and market it as a cycle, and the fact that by 1983, William Kennedy was no longer an apprentice but, as he told Kay Bonetti, "a journeyman now," who knew how to write and structure an excellent novel.

What I will suggest throughout the course of this overview of Kennedy's work is that part of what has made Kennedy a writer of the first note is his penchant not only for writing, but for listening, for acting in dialogue with the writing culture around him. Much of this dialogue has been explicitly, energetically, and evidently joyously conducted: early in his career, Kennedy made a specialty of interviewing writers of note, including among many others Gabriel García Márquez, Saul Bellow, and Norman Mailer, and since coming to prominence himself he has been unstintingly generous in providing interviews to others.

Two facets of this ongoing dialogue bear mentioning here. First, I'll address a running critical disagreement over the size, scope, and what might be called the narrative physics of Kennedy's books of fiction, neatly labeled the Albany Cycle—a classification that can be applied only confusingly to Kennedy's first and most aggressively experimental novel, *The Ink Truck* (1969). In this instance, Kennedy has both profited by—and been the ongoing victim of—preconceptions about the *shape* of the story he tells. While the MacArthur Foundation recognized the rare genius in Kennedy's first tentative attempts to tell outsized stories with the sprawl and the occasional cul-de-sac feel of history itself, later critics have found fault (particularly with the later novels) for what they see as their disjointed or uneven quality. It will be my contention that Kennedy's novels' relationships are simply too complex to be contained by the generic term; each winds up becoming something more and different than a linear, self-contained narrative.

Second, I will drop in and out of a debate—some of it fascinating, some of it arguably overblown—concerning the nature and the role of women in the Albany Cycle. Criticism on this score has not been pervasive by any means, but it has been persistent, and it is perhaps the one area where Kennedy has proven maladroit in the many cultural conversations I'll reference. A writer who associated himself early and often with progressive and liberatory political movements, from the Civil Rights movement of the 1960s to the early Puerto Rican Social Democrats, he has clearly been stung by the insinuation that his own work might be seen as unconsciously complicit in oppression of any sort, patriarchal or otherwise.

Although, as he told the interviewer Neila C. Seshachari, Kennedy often makes a point of maintaining "I've never answered a critic in my life that I can remember," he has answered his feminist critics on a number of occasions, usually in language less than good-humored. He has occasionally counterattacked in somewhat personal terms, as in a 1996 interview with Kay Bonetti when he maintained that "not all critics are serious. Some are not even critics. . . . The idea that I either make them [women] Madonnas or prostitutes, or projections of the male protagonists is literary slander. It often comes from male critics who wish they were feminists."

More frequently Kennedy has answered this critical line with the argument that his historical subject is a sexist society, thus necessitating a central place for male institutions and male objectification of women, but he has made the argument both dismissively and repetitively. In 1984, he suggested to Kay Bonetti that "That's a ridiculous criticism because that was a book about men, about a society of males. You didn't see women in that society. . . . You can't satisfy partisan critics, advocacy critics, in every book and I think generally it's unfair to attack a writer on these grounds until you look at the body of the work and see if he's truly what you say he is."

To the careful student of Kennedy's work and thought, these responses can have an uncharac-

teristically touchy, even illogical feel. The counterattack on "advocacy critics," to take one instance, seems at odds with the Kennedy otherwise so dedicated to politically potent fiction, and to critiquing the work of other writers in explicitly political terms.

The paradox is a small one in the wealth of Kennedy's literary contribution, but it is worth examining as a window onto Kennedy's growth as an author. For while his interview responses on the subject have been occasionally defensive and arguably static, Kennedy's novels have deepened and gained complexity on this score. His point above is well taken: a writer should be judged on the qualities of more than one piece of work, in particular where that judgment has direct political ramifications, and indirect ramifications for the author's literary character. That is what I intend to do as part of an overall examination of his novels and their changing character over time.

THE EARLY NOVELS:
THE INK TRUCK AND *LEGS*

I've suggested only half jokingly above that each Kennedy novel, operating within an expansive and interconnective framework, manages to raise the already high IQ of those that preceded it. By that I mean that *Billy Phelan's Greatest Game, Ironweed, Quinn's Book, Very Old Bones,* and *The Flaming Corsage* draw provocatively on fragments of backstory from earlier books in the sequence. Seemingly throwaway bits of character history in one book bloom into entire novels— complex, only seemingly self-contained works which drop their own narrative seeds for later novels. The eponymous hero of *Legs,* for example, makes a cameo appearance in *Billy Phelan;* Francis Phelan, Billy's absent father, moves from the background of Kennedy's third novel to the foreground of *Ironweed,* his fourth, and so on.

In a roundabout way, then, the earlier novels—when reconsidered after a reading of the later novels—seem to resonate with added meaning, drama, and historical import. It is an effect that Kennedy and his publishers have attempted to extend to the earliest novels over the years, with mixed success.

But the Albany Cycle, as malleable a construct as it may be, is not infinitely flexible. Kennedy's first novel, a brash and strange book called *The Ink Truck,* remains an orphaned work in this regard, in spite of Kennedy's attempt in a 1984 author's note to insist that the nameless, somewhat featureless city in his first novel was and is Albany, an implicit argument that his first effort belongs in the Cycle as well. Many critics, in fact, simply pass over *The Ink Truck* in their reckoning of Kennedy's novels, mistakenly referring to *Legs* as his first, and so on.

To be frank, Kennedy's first novel is in many ways forgettable. Kennedy invariably describes it as a story "six inches off the ground"—a reference to the various unreal and surreal elements, but the phrase inadvertently captures the book's alienating qualities as well. Still, there are moments of imagistic brilliance, and its structure and themes are not far removed from those of *Billy Phelan* or *Ironweed,* for instance. Moreover, in its disregard for much of the factual world of the sixties, Kennedy's first novel was an early indication that given the choice between a carefully revivified past and an unpredictably unfolding present, Kennedy would almost always instinctively choose the former.

THE INFLUENCE OF DAMON RUNYON

A strange effect dominates the first half of *The Ink Truck.* In spite of the occasional mention of a late 1960s detail—acoustical-tile, polyunsaturated margarine—the novel immediately develops a dated feel, the sense that it is taking place not amid moon shots and the flowering of hippie culture, but instead in the 1930s world of Damon Runyon, Raymond Chandler, and true labor militancy. While Kennedy himself prefers to see the work developing out of the Civil Rights movement, that connection is much harder to trace than his "residual affection for the Wobblies and the other labor organizations of the thirties and forties."

Before long, *The Ink Truck* shrugs off even the superficial connections to the writer's contemporary scene and becomes, for all practical purposes, a novel set in the 1930s. In part, the effect stems from Kennedy's diction, inflected as it always is with outdated argot, slang that sounds ironically fresh because it is clearly from a bygone era. The tone gently verges, now and again, on the archaic: "Bailey, never bored with this condition, always mystified by it, took comfort from the emptiness, the fixed quality, preferred it to that formless clot of old."

The connection to Runyon, mentioned above, is not incidental—Kennedy invokes Runyon's popular 1930s fiction and journalism faithfully in nearly every interview he gives. Runyon's Broadway and Kennedy's, though cutting through ostensibly different New York cities, share a great deal in terms of character and linguistic style. The similarities occasionally extend to plot as well, though Kennedy's acknowledgment of the debt is not only clear, but typically rendered in the form of homage.

Damon Runyon's fictional world, composed as it is of lovable tough guys and gold-digging dolls, provides an especially crucial context for Kennedy's first three novels. *The Ink Truck, Legs,* and *Billy Phelan* draw heavily from a Runyonesque vision of life on the margins of society, and if that vision is essentially sentimental beneath its grit, it is also an avowedly and raucously male environment. "Dolls," in Runyon's lexicon, are exotic dancers and B-girls, with the addition of the occasional society woman slumming with the better-looking gangsters on Broadway. In Runyon's hands the men and women of Broadway maintain the sort of rough parity suggested by the title of his most famous work, *Guys and Dolls:* if the guys come first, they are more or less in balance with the dolls, neither better nor braver, usually equally quickly drawn, two comic stereotypes tripped up again and again by the unexpected presence of Love.

Kennedy's early work not only bypasses Runyon's trademark farce for the semiserious (*Billy Phelan*), even the authentically tragic (*Ironweed*), it passes more completely into the all-male realm, and in so doing Kennedy accomplishes what Runyon never could: probing, often searing portraits of lone Broadway characters, and powerful denunciations of the herd mentality that underlies the seeming individualism of Albany's night world. But in so doing, early Kennedy also occasionally grades into a jarringly simplistic approach to the female characters. These two poles—serious, soul-searching prose offset by clumsy or whimsically sexualized interludes—particularly define both *The Ink Truck* and its central character, Bailey.

THE INK TRUCK: A FIRST NOVEL
"SIX INCHES OFF THE GROUND"

Bailey, the striking Guildsman hero of *The Ink Truck,* moves in and out of consciousness on a regular basis throughout the novel. His dreams, visions, prolonged bouts of semiconsciousness, and hunger-induced (mis)perceptions all contribute to a cumulative sense of uncertainty as to the essential facts of the novel—Bailey often does not know, for instance, exactly where he is, a rarity in a Kennedy novel.

And Bailey, while a newspaperman, is a writer of columns without reference points for his readers, absurd parodies of the columnist's art. One of these reads, in part, like the pleasantly inscru-

table flights associated with Richard Brautigan: "Thank you for your pooka. . . . If you ever get out this way stop in for a pooka. Yours truly, Joe the dog." Like "Trout Fishing in America," Brautigan's seemingly simple but finally impenetrable metaphor for 1960s America, the word "pooka" becomes Bailey's own neologistic refuge from a world he no longer trusts.

Bailey has embraced the lack of relevance, the lack of meaning, of the absurdist world that confronts him; in his case a world in which his newspapermen's Guild has been striking against their employers unsuccessfully for one full year, over issues not much grander than seating in the lunchroom and a minimal pay increase. Of the four Guild members remaining, only Bailey, his friend Rosenthal, and their female counterpart Irma have remained true to the principles of the strike.

Quickly Bailey learns that Irma, too, is quitting the Guild to marry a respectable undertaker, and that the Guild's official leader, a buffoon named Jarvis, has ordered them to stage a one-car motorcade in front of the newspaper building. Bailey's perception that he's hit bottom is suddenly exposed as a fantasy; he learns that, outside the protective dictatorship of the Company (the newspaper), there is always farther to fall.

A chance barroom meeting with a truck driver offers Bailey the opportunity to strike back in an unexpected and highly symbolic way. The driver confides to Bailey that he used to drive an ink truck, and that he knows how to pull the pin beneath the main tank. It is an image that immediately entrances Bailey, but the reader gets ample warning that the rules of Bailey's world will not allow a perfectly straightforward counterattack. His meeting with the truck driver dives quickly into absurdity. Kennedy's dialogue, meticulously crafted and second to no other writer's, is as sharp in his first book as in any that follow:

> "You drove an ink truck," Bailey said.
> "I heard you talkin' about one."

"You heard us talking."

"This is too deep for me," Rosenthal said. "See you at lunch," and he went out.

"Now," Bailey said to the driver.

"No. Not now. I used to."

"I'm afraid I don't understand."

"I say I used to drive an ink truck."

"An ink truck," Bailey said.

The words "ink truck" become a senseless mantra, like Bailey's use of "pooka," suggesting that the meaninglessness of language, and the things it describes, is spreading progressively throughout the world of the novel. And when he meets the driver later to learn precisely how to pull the truck's pin, Bailey's tutorial grows absurdly complex until Bailey's sense of understanding is extinguished. Yet at the end of it, he nods.

Still, flushed with new confidence, Bailey's dreams of the ink spill provide the novel's spiritual and symbolic center. In the black void of ink, forced onto white snow, Bailey finds an image that matches his desire for sustenance and salvation outside the confines of social institutions. The vision unfolds completely only when he has crawled under the truck, his friends' diversion holding the guards' attention for a fleeting moment, only to discover that there is no pin visible at all. A square of padlocked sheet metal covers all.

> From an unseen source inside the steel sheet, ink dripped, only one drip since this instant began, but it caught his eye. It had soaked outward into the snow in concentric circles, black into gray into white. At the center, where it fell, where it had fallen for all the time that the ink truck was parked, the ebony blackness shone up like the eye of the devil. Transfixed by the spot, he stared into the timelessness and the futility of his deeds. Why did he rely on others? Why did he yield to the seduction of impossible dreams? He knew he was better than his failures, but in the center of himself a seed burst and a black flower bloomed. Did only the seeds of new abomination lurk beneath the crust?
>
> Another drop.

Kennedy's symbolic play—coupled with the almost effortless distension of time here—suddenly takes the examination of Bailey's character to a bracing new level. It is a trademark Kennedy moment: a deep, almost meditative focus on a seemingly pedestrian object, a focus that suddenly and mystically touches the soul of a character. And the novel surges forward once Kennedy has found access, through image, to the depths of his character. It becomes, qualitatively, an entirely different work.

It is in this mode that Bailey, and Kennedy, punch through to something strange and wonderful, something that would later become the Albany Cycle itself. After having been temporarily beaten by the Company, Bailey goes to work in the subterranean levels of the city library. It is a narrative move that both Kennedy and a number of critics have linked to the epic model, in which the classical hero visits the underworld and reemerges with a renewed sense of purpose. While there he becomes literally immersed in ancient newspapers and this, in conjunction with his growing alienation and physical weakness, leads to a narrative leap into historical surrealism:

> He moved toward it, touched the wall, then a door, pushed it and stepped into what he took, because of the overcast, to be the waning light of day. But he had lost track of time and could not be sure. The overcast was almost a fog, and the air had an acrid smell when he swallowed it. He had left his coat in the library, but he did not need it . . . he walked down a slight hill, and when he looked back he could no longer see the library, so shrouded in the pall of fog was the hill. He walked on a planked sidewalk and was swept backward by a stream of people coming at him from the city gate.

Again, as with the vision of spilling ink, this passage shows Kennedy at his surest, his most visionary, even in the midst of his earliest and arguably his worst novel. He manages to move Bailey and the reader out of the nominal 1960s framework of the book and directly into a stunning re-creation of an actual nineteenth-century Albany cholera outbreak. It is the high moment of the novel, without doubt, one that shows Bailey as a serious character, one with uncharted depths.

But throughout the book, this deeper Bailey—as well as the central narrative line that seeks to illuminate him—competes with a ribald, undeniably juvenile Bailey, and in various ways the novel proves unable to isolate itself from this Bailey's failings. Here Kennedy seems to be working with a fictional strain closer to Chandler or Ian Fleming, creating an effortless sexual hero, a man perfectly constructed to expose the weakness of women. Typically, and oddly, a childish verbal play characterizes Bailey's sexual thoughts, and the same holds true for his best friend Rosenthal, a fact that seems to point more to the omniscient narrator than anything else. This fact has led even some of Kennedy's most sympathetic critics to balance their defenses of *The Ink Truck* with puzzled attempts to explain the novel's fetishistic attention to breasts (one critic has gone so far as to portray Bailey's desperate attempts to milk the ink truck itself as a crude exaggeration of this tendency).

Kennedy has made clear his distaste for critics who act as "literary cops," as he called them in an interview with Neila Seshachari, and I should clarify that my point here is neither that breasts in novels are taboo, nor that portraying a sexist character or society is taboo. What seems worthy of note, rather, is that the sexual vulgarity of *The Ink Truck* often seems to exceed any individual character or indeed any particle of the society at issue. Instead, the narrative itself occasionally assumes the unenlightened status assigned within it to Bailey.

When Bailey and Rosenthal meet and discuss Irma's defection, they immediately reduce her to a set of erogenous zones, and they do so again with a narrative wink. When Bailey criticizes Rosenthal's attempts to sexualize Irma, he does so only in such a way as to make a mockery of such criticism:

> "I hate to see her go. She's our last contact with sex."
> "You circumcised pig. Just because Irma has mountains like the Alps, a valley like the Rhine and the lips of a queen bee, you forget she has a mind. Curb your Semitic dangle, Rosenthal. Remember there's more to life than humpybumps."

The warning from Bailey couldn't be more undercut, not that the reader could take it seriously coming from him in the first place. He has, after all, bedded and dropped Irma somewhere in the not too distant past. Even as he's making a pose of treating Irma with some respect, Bailey is engaging in more lascivious play with her image, finishing as per usual with another naughty nursery rhyme-like reference to her breasts.

And this is the direction that the novel as a whole pursues: even as it occasionally offers a (mock) admonition against blatant sexism, it seems unable or unwilling to prevent itself from more or less blithely pursuing blatantly sexist exposition throughout. Almost any woman in *The Ink Truck* provides a case in point. The worst of these caricatures is Miss Blue, the big-chested, nymphomaniacal secretary to the head of the Company. Miss Blue exists only to service her boss sexually; in the narrative, she is clearly meant to provide comic relief, but the passages featuring her have an inadvertently painful feel to them. At one point, Bailey has been beaten and handcuffed and dropped off at her apartment. She agrees to free him if he will participate in an incredibly elaborate sexual ritual, in which, with the help of a gear-driven framework and two cow hides, she will play a demure cow to Bailey's bull.

What began with the intriguing character of Irma reduced again and again to her breasts ends here with a two-dimensional character literally nothing more than a set of udders: "Bailey . . . ran his fingers tenderly over her hair. She smiled, bovine eyes blinking, magnificent milk pods trembling like new Jell-o. . . . 'Don't move,' he told her. While she held the pose he fled into the morning." Bailey's tenderness strikes a false note; the truer note is his flight from the female.

The re-publication of *The Ink Truck* in 1984 (following Kennedy's surge to prominence) prompted a good deal of criticism on these related scores, some of the harshest criticism ever directed at Kennedy. Joel Conarroe, writing in the *New York Times,* noted that:

> The sexual attitudes expressed by the voluble Bailey are mostly of the locker-room variety, with women seen as either nurturing goddesses or insatiable shrews. What is especially disturbing is not just that the female characters lack credibility but that they are consistently linked with decay and bestiality . . . the book leaves an unpleasant impression and raises questions about the level of the author's social consciousness at this early stage of his career.

It is worth noting that Kennedy chose to republish his first novel intact, as opposed to either rewriting it or leaving it in out-of-print obscurity, and as I've noted earlier, none of Kennedy's numerous interviews suggest that he sees *The Ink Truck* as anything other than an early, if small, success. It is one of the few points on which his critics have not eventually joined him.

LEGS: MYTHS, LEGENDS, AND STEREOTYPES

There is a nice irony in Kennedy's current status as literary myth as simplified literary commodity: Kennedy's second novel, *Legs,* while ostensibly a gangster/bootlegger story full of smoking guns and fast Packard roadsters, provides an insightful and extended meditation on the compulsive myth-making aspects of American culture.

It is with this particular theme, and with the overtly historical template of Legs Diamond's life and times, that Kennedy managed to clarify and focus his talents, producing a second novel infinitely superior to his first. The mainstream and literary recognition Kennedy had craved for most of his life came his way, in other words, only once he had set himself the task of examining the craving itself. "I have a favorite quote from Kafka," Kennedy said on this score, " 'You are the problem, no solution far and wide.' You have to figure yourself out. . . . I figured myself out reasonably early, and stayed with it."

And too, the earlier, more tentative identification with Runyon's 1930s world of gangsters and B-girls becomes in *Legs* a wholehearted embrace. Kennedy's novel begins, like a Runyon short story, in a wash of beautifully evocative nicknames and ethnic handles. Names are as much a currency as booze, as cash, and making a name is as crucial as making a fortune:

> "Sit down, Jack, don't mind him. Have a drink. Meet Teddy Carson from Philly. We been tellin' him about you, how you come a long way from Philly."
>
> "How you makin' out, Jack?" Teddy Carson said, another big fist. He shook Jack's hand, cracking knuckles. "Some boys I know in Philly talk about you a lot. Duke Gleason, Wiggles Mason. Wiggles said he knew you as a kid."

Jack, known as Legs Diamond, is a two-bit hood with the capacity to reach the greatness of true infamy. To Marcus Gorman, the unassuming lawyer who narrates Jack's story, there is something Gargantuan in Diamond that is missing in Gorman's own sedate life and practice.

Legs traces the slow growth and the fast decline of Legs Diamond's power, and along the way it showcases many of Kennedy's burgeoning talents and trademark effects. As with Bailey's sudden emergence into historical time, Jack's occasional brush with the uncanny and the mystical lends the novel an unexpected imagistic lushness. At one point, Jack returns on an ocean liner from an unsuccessful attempt to buy heroin abroad. The ship's cargo is forty-five hundred canaries, an authentic historical detail that Kennedy expands into an impromptu vision of great impact: "The Hartz Mountain birds, yellow and green, stopped singing when Jack entered their prison, and he thought: *They've smelled me*." A few scenes later Kennedy returns Jack to the canaries' hold, only to take the vision to an even higher level. This higher flight is revealed, as is much of Kennedy's sharpest material, in the play of dialogue:

> "How's all the birdies," Jack asked the sailor.
> "Very sad," said the sailor. "They sing to overcome their sadness."
> "That's not why birds sing," Jack said.
> "Sure it is."
> "Are you positive?"
> "I live with birds. I'm part bird myself. You should see my skin up close. Just like feathers."
> "That's very unusual," Jack said.
> The sailor rolled up his sleeve to show Jack his biceps, which were covered with brown feathers.

It is the best of Kennedy—crisp dialogue, set in an impromptu narrative detour into intriguing historical detail, and all of this suddenly rendered unforgettable by the single stroke of the surreal, or what would in the mid-1980s come to be known as the magically real. And all of these elements lend themselves directly to the concerns of this strand of the narrative, tracing the rise of the legend of Legs Diamond, and the corresponding distance between that legend and the sad bird of a man caged inside it.

Like Bailey and many of Kennedy's male heroes, Jack has a super sex appeal that women find impossible to resist, but in the case of the mythical Jack Diamond this quality is taken to mythically extreme lengths. Women write begging him to "dominate me thrice . . . on my husband's side of the bed"; men write to him requesting that he "shoot several small-caliber bullets into my anus at no quicker than thirty-second intervals until I am dead"; a librarian he beds during an ocean crossing tells him, "You turn women into swine," and Jack thinks about it, then nods. Jack's world is not merely controlled by men and male institutions and alliances, but infused with an extremely aggressive male sexuality, a sexuality almost constantly at play, metaphorically, allusively, and literally.

The civilized Marcus Gorman's first introduction to Jack's world involves the firing of a machine gun, which, he admits excitedly, "even jogged my scrotum," and that introduction finally takes Marcus to a point, later in the narrative, where he will attempt to emulate Jack during their ocean crossing by having painfully aggressive sex with a woman he picks up at the ship's bar, "ripping her and myself . . . so that we both bled." He does so, he tells us, "because I was now addicted to entering the world of Jack Diamond as fully as possible . . . I was condoning the worst sort of behavior. Absolute worst. I know, I know." It is a world where men go to prison and invite certain death so other men will think they have "big balls," an arguably homoerotic and violent world not far removed from the picture of the Mafia offered only a few years earlier in Mario Puzo's *The Godfather*, a runaway best-seller that may have paved the way for Kennedy's own mob boss. *Legs*, for all its insightful ruminations on the American soul, was then and remains today Kennedy's most commercial production, and its treatment of sex, which is to say its treatment of women, was a distinct element of that appeal.

The Warner Books paperback of *Legs*, released in 1976, demonstrates the straightforward marketing of the sexual aspects of the novel by a mass-market publisher. The cover shows an androgynously beautiful young man, dressed in the three-piece suit associated with mid-1970s disco, holding a huge tommy gun erect and flanked by a lanky blonde in a short pink negligee, twirling a long white string of pearls. The jacket copy promises "a thief, a murderer, a man subject to insane rages, the darling of the ladies. . . ." The disco feel to the cover is strengthened by a stylized glint of light—standing in for the inevitable mirror-ball—over Diamond's head.

Kennedy no doubt cringed when he saw the way his book was packaged, but Warner's lurid view of the text was not entirely the product of a commercial artist's imagination. As with *The Ink Truck,* the intellectual energy, the imaginative power, and the verbal artistry of *Legs* are dulled by an often highly conventional approach to women. The text itself, like the biddable Marcus, seems almost against its own better judgment to savor Jack's attempts to control and dominate the women in his life.

Like most of Kennedy's novels, *Legs* makes use of an elongated, meandering, and branching historical narrative, and in this way any discussion of plot as such has to be carefully qualified. But it is fair to say that the novel has a generally twofold plot structure, and it is pure Runyon: guys and dolls. On the one hand, there are Jack Diamond's rise to celebrity status, and his transformation into "Legs," a creature spawned by the media as much as by his own deeds and misdeeds; on the other hand are Jack's efforts to "balance" the two women in his life, his loyal gangster wife, Alice, and his mistress, Kiki.

I expected him to emphasize one or the other woman when he arrived, depending on his mood: horny or homey. But he balanced them neatly, emphasizing neither, impatient to see them both, moving neither away from one nor toward the other but rather toting one on each shoulder into some imagined triad of love, a sweet roundelay which would obviate any choice of either/or and would offer instead the more bountiful alternative of both. More power to you, old boy.

The criticism of his work that Kennedy labeled "literary slander" in 1996—"that I either make them [women] Madonnas or prostitutes"—would seem to have its roots in the bipolar portraits of Alice and Kiki. "Horny or homey," as Marcus puts it, and this is a synopsis offered by a man with intimate knowledge of *Legs.* Admittedly, Kennedy is acutely aware throughout that he is working with matched stereotypes. And clearly, he means not merely to invoke the stereotypes but to analyze and complicate them, in much the same way he complicates Jack. Kiki, the reader is told,

personified her calling in her walk, in her breathing, in the toss of her head . . . in her willingness to conform to the hallowed twentieth-century chorus-girl stereotype that Ziegfeld, George White . . . and so many more men, whose business was flesh, had incarnated, and which Walter Winchell, Ed Sullivan, Odd McIntyre, Damon Runyon, Louis Sobol, and so many others, whose business was to muse and gossip on the ways of this incarnated flesh, had mythicized.

The debt to Runyon is explicitly acknowledged here, as in so many other instances, but there is an odd disconnection between Kennedy's sociological analysis of the business of flesh and his inability to move beyond his own character's flesh and face. Like Grace Bailey and Miss Blue in *The Ink Truck,* Kiki's impoverished intellect is matched only by the insatiability of her sexual desire. She is capable of asking Jack in all earnestness, "Am I your real lay?" The thoughts attributed to her have none of the searching quality of Kennedy's other characters, but instead smack of authorial condescension: "She knew she wasn't smart enough to understand the reasons behind that sort of thing." Kiki's internal monologues are mostly extended remembrances of sexual marathons with Jack, or pathetic attempts to convince herself that another sexual marathon with Jack can't be far away.

Alice, on the other hand, is an early demonstration that Kennedy could, and would, create more complex and multifaceted women beneath the stereotypes suggested by his 1930s setting. While skilled in playing the role of the faithful wife, Alice demonstrates throughout her understanding of and control over that role. Kennedy puts it best when he introduces her as a "modified spitfire." She is a spitfire in her ability to fire a machine gun, strangle a pet bird in a fit of rage, and occasionally lay down the law to her Gargantuan gangster husband; she is modified by the disturbing streak of subservience that more generally surfaces in her relations with Jack. Alice, while presented as a thinking woman of strong religious convictions, finally betrays the same masochistic impulses demonstrated by all of Jack's other women, a state of affairs that allows him finally to accomplish his goal of "balancing" the two women in his life.

In a late section titled "Jack Among the Maids," Jack recuperates very publicly at the Kenmore, an Albany hotel in the grand old tradition. He has been riddled with bullets and left for dead, but Jack refuses to die, instead slowly gaining strength and putative insight into the essential dilemmas of his life. This time his foremost desire is to think his way out of an age-old paradox: he loves his wife, in his way, but he wants his mistress as well, wants her not only occasionally but placed somewhere in his daily life. Finally, he moves Kiki into the six-room suite he shares with his wife, Alice.

It is admittedly a startling and original turn in the narrative—none of the story's stereotypical templates prepare us for a man who will insist on both stereotypes at once. And Kennedy builds with undeniable skill upon this turn. "Jack Among the Maids," after solving the first, develops a higher order of unsolvable dilemma. Having moved his mistress into his apartment, having forced his wife to accept this arrangement, Jack takes his lawyer and his "twin receptacles," as Marcus unflinchingly calls them, to the Kenmore's ballroom for dinner and dancing. But there, of course, he must choose one of them as his partner for the first dance. He must prefer one to the other.

The scene is stretched skillfully, with the main narrative intercut by newspaper interviews with Jack and meditations on the rise of "Legs," Jack's media image. But the entire foundation of this section of *Legs* is Jack's need to demonstrate, sadistically, publicly, his power over the two women in his life. Jack turns women into animals, and the Kenmore scene in which he ponders the problem of the first dance seems designed to drive the point home. As Jack is deciding who to hurt and how much, a random "doll" from the crowd takes the situation to a by now almost predictable extreme:

> A voluptuous woman in a silver sheath with shoulder straps of silver cord paused at the table with her escort. . . . She looked at Alice and Kiki, then rolled down the right strap of her gown and revealed a firm, substantial, well-rounded unsupported breast.
> "How do you like it?" she said to Jack.
> "It seems adequate, but I'm not interested" . . . .
> "I can also get milk out of it if you ever feel the need," she said, squeezing her nipple forward between two fingers and squirting a fine stream into Jack's empty coffee cup.
> "I'll save that till later," Jack said.

As with *The Ink Truck,* in which Miss Blue becomes finally and almost literally a pathetic bovine creature pining after Bailey, here the anonymous woman literalizes the role that women are increasingly assigned in Jack's world, the only world of the narrative: she is not merely an animal, a beautified cow, but desperate to be treated as a cow.

Kiki and Alice never offer their real thoughts or emotions about their enforced domestic arrangement, other than the isolated line here or there. Instead, they become improbably docile, exchanging domestic details about the dry-cleaning and the cooking, welcoming Marcus as dual hostesses. And as Jack moves forward to decision, they recede further, each into her own narrow stereotype. The loss is more pronounced for Alice, of course, in that Kiki has no complexity, really, to lose.

Jack's legend is built both implicitly and explicitly on the killing of men and the desperate domination of women. These things are associated with gangsters and outlaws, of course. But there is no denying that Kennedy's second novel aspires to more than a journalistic depiction of brutality. It seeks, as does the best of Kennedy's writing, to illuminate the deep reaches of the unconscious, if not the soul itself. In the case of Legs Diamond, Kennedy succeeds, and often fabulously. Legs's memory of his first killing compresses more character revelation than the entire cumulative space devoted to Kiki, the Ziegfeld beauty. It is with the female characters that *Legs* stumbles, not only in its portrayal of them but in its heavy-handed use of them to establish and define the central male hero.

Each of Kennedy's post-1984 paperbacks carries a quote from Ward Just, hailing the Albany Cycle as "one of the few imperishable products of American literature since the Second World War." I think Just is absolutely correct—there are few comparable bodies of work in the last fifty years—but I would amend his praise to predict that if any of Kennedy's work fades over the decades, it will be the two early novels, fading almost certainly in order of their appearance and in proportion to their lack of attention to the lives and minds of the women who inhabit them. This is not a function of "advocacy" politics, as Kennedy has suggested, but a marked distinction in quality. It is no accident that Kennedy's major

successes came after he had evolved well beyond the sexual supermen and the painfully limited B-girls of his first efforts.

THE ALBANY CYCLE PROPER: *BILLY PHELAN'S GREATEST GAME* AND *IRONWEED*

If the Albany Cycle began anywhere, it began with *Billy Phelan's Greatest Game,* first published in 1978. *Legs,* while partially set in Albany, bore no relation to Kennedy's first book, and it suggested no relation to books to come. It was in the writing of the third novel that Kennedy began the twofold self-referential process that would make his fortune: that of tying his current book to his last, both through actual history and created narrative, and of generating in the current book an outsized subplot that would become the central storyline of the next. The beautifully stylized death scene from *Legs* surfaces early in *Billy Phelan,* connecting Martin Daugherty, newspaperman, to the media legend of the previous Albany generation.

Billy Phelan also looks forward, of course, to *Ironweed,* and it does so by introducing a wealth of history for a minor character, Francis Phelan, an amount of backstory that might seem puzzlingly complete if one looked at *Billy Phelan* in isolation. But none of the books in the Albany Cycle can be read properly in and of themselves. To do so is like watching a 3–D movie with no special glasses, possible but impossibly limiting.

BILLY PHELAN'S GREATEST GAME: UNDERRATED, OVERLOOKED

Billy Phelan's Greatest Game, as I've asserted earlier, seems the product of a writer at the apex of his own game, a writer who, in Kennedy's own terms, has inarguably "figured himself out." Kennedy here manages to isolate and enhance the elements that drove the successful sections of his earlier fiction. In addition to establishing connections to previous and future books, Kennedy's third novel is set entirely in Albany, and it is populated almost entirely by Irish families struggling for survival and respectability in their corners of the city, families of Kennedy's own creation. It is *Billy Phelan* that truly signaled Kennedy's desire to excavate, revivify, and preserve the history and the legacy of the Irish in America.

Martin Daugherty, the moderately successful newspaper columnist who observes Billy in the novel's opening line, remains throughout a more thoughtful observer of the action than Billy, the hero at the center of it. It is a narrative pairing that worked well enough in *Legs,* but Martin Daugherty is a much more compelling and principled character than Marcus Gorman, and as a result his perceptions lend the small-timer Billy Phelan a unique glamour, as well as a peculiar sort of honor. Martin, as a habitué of Albany's nighttown himself, makes superbly clear the quality of Billy's seemingly insignificant triumphs.

> Billy's native arrogance might well have been a gift of miffed genes, then come to splendid definition through the tests to which a street like Broadway puts a young man on the make: tests designed to refine a breed, enforce a code, exclude all simps and gumps, and deliver into the city's life a man worthy of functioning in this age of nocturnal supremacy.

Martin's philosophizing, at once profound and half-serious, strikes the tone for the novel as a whole. *Billy Phelan* is mere verbal play, on one hand, a pulp-fiction story of kidnapping and small-time political intrigues, but on another it presents very serious meditations on the place and the worth of the individual, what he or she is capable of alone, and what must be accomplished by and within the community.

These latter issues come almost immediately into focus when Charlie Boy McCall, the only heir to the city's political bosses, Patsy and Bindy McCall, is kidnapped. Through a chance connection, Billy Phelan is tied to another man, Morrie Berman, who is suspected of being one of the kidnappers. Martin is asked to sound Billy out, to find out what he may know—or what he can find out—about Berman. Martin, the student of character and particularly of Billy, senses the problem immediately: to Billy this will be no different from informing. "I'm not one of the McCalls' political whores," Billy tells Martin.

As Billy moves through his nighttime world, trying to get a firmer grip on the rumors that have suddenly come to dominate his life, Kennedy takes the reader smoothly through all of the homes away from home that the fatherless Billy has acquired over the years—the card games, the diners, the bowling alleys, and the brothels. Each locale is specific and magical in its own right: "When Billy walked into Louie's pool room on Broadway across from Union Station, Daddy Big, wearing his change apron and eyeshade, was leaning on a cue watching Doc Fay, the band leader, run a rack." This extended narrative tour shows in detail the world that Billy has stripped from him by the McCalls when they later decide that he has not been quick or complete enough in his help with Morrie Berman.

Matched against Billy's dilemma with the McCalls is Martin's own struggle to come to terms with a fitful gift for prophecy. For shadowy reasons, Martin's precognitive ability is tied to his father, a renowned playwright, and to Martin's inability to escape his father's reputation. Martin understands this connection only after a tryst some years earlier with Melissa, his father's lover, caused the gift of prophecy to vanish. In a triumph of associative thematics, Kennedy links Billy's troubles with his own absent father, and the kidnapping of the McCall's only son, to Martin's returning second sight. And Martin's second sight, to complete the mystic circle, leads him back to greater understanding and greater peace in his relations with his own father.

Martin Daugherty's second sight represents Kennedy's first full-scale movement into magic realism. Visions begin to rise in Martin's consciousness—some biblical, some more overtly Freudian—as well as hunches directing him to particular places and people on the map of the city. The intuitions are Martin's answer to his more politically radical father's "concrete visions of the Irish in the New World, struggling to throw off the filth of poverty, oppression, and degradation." Martin grows up a passive receiver, tuned magically into the tragedies and troubles of the actual Irish-Americans around him.

It is in this way that Martin runs across Francis Phelan sitting in a bar, gnarled and seemingly near death. This meeting eventually leads to a reunion between Francis and his son Billy: Martin's gift throughout the novel remains attuned to healing breaches and separations between fathers and sons, a motif that will be reprised in *Ironweed,* when the ghost of the infant Gerald commands Francis to expiate his sins against his family.

Billy, on the other hand, remains something of a prisoner of the codes that earlier represented his salvation. In deciding not to "rat," he breaks ties with the Broadway world as he knows it. He does a potentially destructive thing for very honorable reasons, and Martin remonstrates with him to no avail. Yet the novel allows the moral ambivalence of the dilemma to persist, never finally resolving it. Billy returns to the nighttime world he's known all his life to find it subtly changed. Not only has Broadway seen that Billy will prefer his own moral code to the needs of Broadway, but Billy has seen that Broadway will follow the word of the McCalls whether the word is just or unjust.

In contradiction to his own remark, quoted earlier, that Billy's was a world where you "didn't see women," this Kennedy novel does manage to examine the narrow but complicated roles occupied by 1930s women. In so doing, it creates not stereotypes but originals who rise from seeming stereotypes. It shows the lengths to which women in particular were sometimes driven. In one of the novel's finest scenes, Billy meets his on-again off-again lover Angie in a hotel. Just as he has placed her in his own mind—"Too goddamn smart. A college dame. Thinks like a man"—Billy is brought up short by Angie's news that she's just had an abortion. Billy quickly grows angry:

> "Goddamn it, I had a right to know."
> "You had a *right?*"
> "You bet your ass. What the hell, I don't have a say in my own son?"
> "Of course it was a boy. You're really classic, Billy."

After another moment, Angie tells Billy that she hasn't had an abortion—in fact, she's pregnant right now with his child, and she pretended to have an abortion to see if he really wanted to be a father to it. Billy, in blind response, does an about-face: "Hell no, I don't want no baby." After Angie runs through their options—marriage, running away together, abortion—Billy sits stunned, the picture of immaturity. The reader has a chance to understand that the process of evolution that has rendered Billy "worthy of functioning" in Broadway's world of "nocturnal supremacy" has also rendered him unfit for the variety of life, an impressive boy at thirty-one but well shy of actual manhood.

> "Then you want me to get rid of it?"
> "No, I don't want that. I think you oughta have it."
> "But you don't want anything to do with it?"
> "I'll do something."
> "What?"
> "I'll go see it."
> "Like a cocker spaniel? Why shouldn't I get rid of it?"

Once again, it is Kennedy's dialogue, its careful rhythms and pacing, that perfect the scene. It turns out, of course, that Angie is not really pregnant after all—she's made up even the pregnancy as a way to force Billy to confront the realities of their relationship. The journeyman gambler is stunned. "You conned me right out of my jock," he says in wonder.

Angie is a character who begins in stereotype—Runyon's well-educated and wealthy woman slumming with gangsters—but immediately resolves on the page into a thinking, complicated character, one capable of taking the novel in surprising directions. In this way, too, *Billy Phelan* anticipates *Ironweed*. There Kennedy would pair an even more substantially flawed hero, Francis Phelan, with the even more indomitable Helen, and in so doing he would find literary success almost exactly in line with his wildest imaginings.

IRONWEED:
EVERYTHING COMING TOGETHER

In many ways *Billy Phelan's Greatest Game* and *Ironweed* are matched halves of the same novel. The action of *Ironweed* begins roughly at the moment *Billy Phelan* ends. Martin's assistance in *Billy Phelan* keeps Francis alive, and among other things provides Francis with a lawyer to keep him out of jail for voting fraud. After Marcus has gotten Franny's case thrown out on a technicality, he finds that Franny has no money to pay him, and sets up a day job for Franny digging graves as a way to pay off the debt. Also, in his short *Billy Phelan* reunion with his son, Francis has promised offhandedly to visit the family he abandoned years before after dropping and killing his son, Gerald, while drinking. The two novels' connections, then, involve narrative lines, familial lines, and historical lines, as well as the peculiar lines of magical force that precipitated Martin's healing visions and which now, in *Ironweed,* lay hold of the aimless Francis Phelan.

"Riding up the winding road of Saint Agnes Cemetery in the back of the rattling old truck, Francis Phelan became aware that the dead, even more than the living, settled down in neighborhoods." The truck passes the splendid monuments of the rich, the captains of industry and the privileged, before entering the simpler ward occupied by dead Phelans. We enter Francis Phelan's consciousness, and the novel begins, at the precise moment that Francis becomes aware of the historical lot of his people, the Irish; the reader has the sense that this history of tragedy and hard times has infused the cemetery with both a shapeless bitterness and a very focused sense of morality, a morality driven by justice if not vengeance.

In a direct manifestation of this watchful justice, the dead observe Franny from their strange homes beneath the earth. Here Kennedy's earlier play with magic realism reaches full bloom, and this startling segment of the novel reads much like something out of Márquez or Isabel Allende. Francis's dead father, for example, packs his pipe with dried, pulverized grass roots; his dead mother "wove crosses from the dead dandelions and other deep-rooted weeds." The grass and dandelion roots provide the dead with a physical connection to the living, a symbolic inversion of the rootedness of the living in the ancestors laid out in graves. Every single part of the world is rooted in or bound together with every single other part, the opening of the novel argues, setting Francis on the road to far greater awareness than that reached by his son in *Billy Phelan*.

Half-consciously, Francis moves to the grave of his infant son, Gerald. The moment is perhaps the high point of Kennedy's art.

> In his grave, a cruciformed circle, Gerald watched the advent of his father and considered what action might be appropriate to their meeting. . . . His web was woven of strands of vivid silver, an enveloping hammock of intricate, near-transparent weave. His body had not only been absolved of the need to decay, but in some respects—a full head of hair, for

instance—it had grown to a completeness that was both natural and miraculous. . . . Swaddled in his grave, he was beyond capture by visual or verbal artistry.

The moment stretches out much longer than can be conveyed properly here, and in so doing, Kennedy allows himself to stretch in a different artistic direction than the tragic-comic, half-serious musings of *Billy Phelan*. Here he reaches for, and attains, the eloquence of high tragedy. The unspeakable horror of accidentally killing an infant is translated into a speaking presence, which has evolved spiritually from that tiny corpse into a force powerful enough to drive the narrative as a whole:

Gerald, through an act of silent will, imposed on his father the pressing obligation to perform his final acts of expiation for abandoning the family. You will not know, the child silently said, what these acts are until you have performed them all. And after you have performed them you will not understand that they were expiatory any more than you have understood all the other expiation that has kept you in such prolonged humiliation. Then, when these final acts are complete, you will stop trying to die because of me.

It is as close as Kennedy comes, in the Albany Cycle as a whole, to describing God or the influence of God—Gerald functions as an unabashedly divine force, acting from divine wisdom, exacting just punishment and expiation even as he puts a period to Francis's long years of suffering. More than a Catholic mythos, from which Kennedy continues to distance himself, the scene seems to draw on preceding traditions, Greek myth in particular. A number of recent articles have linked *Ironweed* with various Greek storylines, pointing out, for instance, similarities between the acts required of Francis and the twelve labors of Heracles, not to mention the central presence of Helen as the woman who spurs Francis to live and to fight.

Francis's suffering serves a larger purpose than merely reinforcing his own failings. The narrative's focus on a "lowlife bum," as Kennedy has called him, disturbs classic rules of storytelling in order to question the health of society itself. If Francis Phelan is to blame for dropping Gerald, then Francis's uprootedness, his alcoholism, and his tortured family history do not occur in a vacuum. The captains of industry who occupy the best parts of the cemetery share in Francis's guilt, as do his parents. Everyone in the novel is beset by, yet judged and perhaps protected by, forces beyond their own immediate control.

Francis's personal torments come in the form of hauntings by the walking dead. Men Francis killed and men Francis helped but not enough follow him silently as he unknowingly sets about his acts of expiation. These acts take Francis and his friend Rudy all over Albany, creating a haunted geography, a cursed map from which Francis uncertainly works. His only sense of actual rootedness comes from the presence of Helen Archer, one of the most memorable characters in all of Kennedy's work.

Helen is, to use Kennedy's word, a bum, as Francis is a bum, and as Rudy is a bum. Like Francis, she has seen better days, and in fact she comes from a social class above the Phelans, although how far above is never made clear. But she is no Runyon society doll, slumming with the guys from Broadway. Nor is she one of the "balanced" halves of Legs Diamond's imagined domestic tranquility. Helen demonstrates that the tramp's world occupied by Francis is not one necessarily sectioned according to sex or gender; in her desperation, she achieves a strange and painful equality.

When Francis finds Helen at the Methodist shelter and brags that he has worked all day without taking a drink or a smoke, Helen clucks over him: "Oh that's so lovely. I'm very proud of my good boy." Yet Helen has no more control over the domestic world than Francis; she too is in panicked, lifelong flight from responsibility and obligation, from home, in a word. She is as streetwise as Francis, if not more so—she holds their only property, a suitcase with their few worn possessions.

Helen and Francis share an intimacy that has ceased to include sex, and there are hints that Francis's sexual potency, like his tremendous baseball skills, has withered. In this, Francis is much the opposite of Legs, or of Bailey. Far from being a sexual superman, he has been effectively neutered by alcohol. Francis watches with real loathing as other men act the role of sexual aggressor: Rosskam the ragman, servicing lonely housewives, and Finny the bum who charges sexual favors for the privilege of sleeping in his derelict automobile. With Francis and Helen, Kennedy manages to create a minimal world in which man and woman are rendered equal through possessing nothing, not even sexual desire.

The final chapters of *Ironweed* have a pronounced elegiac feel, moving soberly between the death of Helen, seemingly from cancer, to Francis's reunion with the rest of his family, projected in the final chapters of *Billy Phelan's Greatest Game.* Bearing a turkey as a peace offering to his long-abandoned family, Francis does have the air of a tragic Greek hero returning from a decades-long war. But Kennedy's story does not end neatly; Francis is too deeply troubled a character to achieve peace so quickly and so completely. Although his wife Annie has made it clear that the family will accept him back, Francis ultimately hops another freight train.

In a bold move, with Francis's departure Kennedy shifts into the conditional tense, creating and maintaining a palpable tension between what is happening and what may happen: "By dawn he would be on a Delaware & Hudson freight heading south toward the lemonade springs." But his thoughts are also dwelling on "setting up the cot down in Danny's room," and it is possible to read the novel's finish in several ways, some

more hopeful than others. Most critics, however, view this decidedly purposeful ambiguity as a stylistic triumph.

Whatever the ultimate fate of Francis Phelan, he attains a grandeur in direct opposition to his social status. The lowest of all of Kennedy's underworld characters, he achieves the highest artistic status, that of the authentic tragic hero, whose greatness is inseparable from his deep and ineradicable flaws. The novel's finish reinforces the central theme of its opening: no one, however seemingly isolated, exists in true isolation. Martin Daugherty's cynical refrain from *Billy Phelan*—"We are all in conspiracy against the next man"—is stood upon its head. We are all in league with the next man, Gerald shows his father from the grave, Gerald's own grave being linked to the graves of other Phelans and other families by vast networks of flowering weeds.

THE POST-PULITZER NOVELS

By the end of 1984 Kennedy had won most of the largest honors available to American writers, as well as some of the most lucrative cash grants. And nearly all of these various ratifications of his vision had come within a single two-year period. If any single message emerged from the critical and popular wings of the literary world, it was that Kennedy's method—the linking of historically based narratives, a method compressed into the single word "cycle"—evinced sheer literary genius. When *Ironweed* won the Pulitzer Prize, nearly every report noted the book's cyclical connection to the other Kennedy books. In the case of the National Book Critics Circle Award, the message was driven home explicitly by the committee's ultimate elevation of *Ironweed* (and Kennedy's maximalist cycle) over Raymond Carver's minimalist masterpiece, *Cathedral.* Kennedy, the committee ultimately argued, was simply working from a "larger canvas."

Anyone who reads the first three novels in the Albany Cycle, and then in succession reads the fourth and fifth, *Quinn's Book* (1988) and *Very Old Bones* (1992), will almost immediately perceive a dramatic difference: rather than focused studies of single characters or isolated climactic events, the post-1984 books function as compilations of stories and histories, moving rapidly across decades, even centuries, and employing a sweep of characters loosely linked by fortune or genealogy. It is very much as though *Quinn's Book* and *Very Old Bones* were each designed as an Albany Cycle within itself.

QUINN'S BOOK:
FIRST OF THE MOSAIC NOVELS

If it's true that the world had ratified Kennedy's vision of a historical cycle of interlocking novels, a cycle spanning centuries but mostly comprising the branches of three Irish-American family trees, then *Quinn's Book* must be seen as a bold, sweeping effort to make good on that exceptional promise. Having spent his last two novels in the Runyonesque world of 1930s Albany, Kennedy drops back in time by two generations, nearly another century, to the Albany of the mid-nineteenth century. His central characters are full-fledged literary ancestors of his *Billy Phelan/Ironweed* cast: the protagonist, Daniel Quinn, is the direct ancestor of Billy Phelan's nephew, Danny Quinn, and *Quinn's Book*'s Emmett Daugherty is the grandfather of Billy and Francis' friend, Martin Daugherty.

Kennedy sets out in this fifth novel to revivify history with a vengeance. Young Daniel Quinn, a fortunate orphan in the tradition of both eighteenth- and nineteenth-century novels, moves restlessly across the landscape of upstate New York, and later the whole of America, a journeyman journalist and writer, always coincidentally provided not only with money and status but a

bird's-eye view of the most sensational events of the pre- and post-Civil War eras. In a 1969 interview with Penny Maldonado, Kennedy calmly insisted, "I have no interest in the sprawling journalistic novel incorporating everything," but twenty years later he produced precisely that, a novel narrated by a traveling rogue journalist who witnesses and records, among other things, as it says on the jacket of *Quinn's Book,* "the rise and fall of great dynasties in upstate New York, epochal prize fights, exotic life in the theater, visitations from spirits beyond the grave, horrific battles between Irish immigrants and the 'Know-Nothings,' vicious New York draft riots, heroic passages through the Underground Railroad, and the bloody despair of the Civil War."

Daniel Quinn's style as a writer, and as a narrator, makes a virtue of rhetorical excess. Kennedy has fashioned it in part from the narrative voices that power early popular British novels, novels like *David Copperfield,* but he has inflected Quinn's voice with the peculiar journalistic bombast associated with nineteenth-century journalism. While Quinn is capable of more straightforward narration, his first paragraph is good-sized, and all one sentence.

> I, Daniel Quinn, neither the first nor the last of a line of such Quinns, set eyes on Maud the wondrous on a late December day in 1849 on the banks of the river of aristocrats and paupers, just as the great courtesan, Magdalena Colón, also known as La Última, a woman whose presence turned men into spittling, masturbating pigs, boarded a skiff to carry her across the river's icy water from Albany to Greenbush. . . .

The sentence runs on for another full moment, allowing Daniel Quinn to introduce—as a good journalist would—his subjects, their whereabouts, the time frame, and not incidentally, his own penchant for elaborate phrasing. This is the first of the magics Kennedy brings to bear on the potentially scattered materials of *Quinn's Book:*

Quinn's own verbal artistry, simulating for the reader the strong pull of nineteenth-century narrative.

The second magic is more actual, and it springs (as do Martin Daugherty's visions) from Quinn's complex human connections: to the fake spiritualist Magdalena Colón, and to her young charge, the actual spiritualist and Quinn's first and only love, Maud Fallon. In *Billy Phelan,* the visions remain unexplained, and that lack of explanation serves in part as proof of their mystical validity. In Quinn's case, his love for Maud produces what a wealthy fan of Magdalena's fittingly calls "an adventure of the heart." The visions and the touch of magic Quinn experiences at key moments in his life are all wrought up in his love for Maud, whom he rescues from an icy river in the novel's opening scene. The same boating accident that nearly kills Maud succeeds in killing Magdalena Colón, and as Quinn, his master John the Brawn, and Maud bear the corpse to the estate of Hillegond Staats, a wealthy and eccentric widow, Quinn looks into the corpse's open eye. He sees:

> the maroon iris, the deep-brown pupil, the soft white transparency of the conjuctival membrane striped with the faintest of frigid purple rivers and tributaries. And then in the center of the suddenly luminous pupil I saw a procession of solemn pilgrims moving through a coppice: night it was, but snowing, and as fully bright as this true night that surrounded us. And there was Maud, her hand held by an old woman.

Quinn sees several scenes that will eventually come to pass, and in this way the narrative, capricious as it often is, maintains what might be called an overall precognitive structure, the sense (a very happy sense, for the author) that wherever characters and readers find themselves in the novel's wash of history, that place is precisely where they were meant to be. It is a clever formula for encouraging reader enjoyment: a roving journalist passes on his account of a variety of enjoyable, but seemingly disjointed events, yet the reader is periodically assured that these events are part of a larger pattern, falling unknowably but precisely into place.

In this way, a variety of kinds of scenes pass before the reader's eyes. Madame Colón, it turns out, is not really dead, but locked in some sort of hypothermic near-death state. John the Brawn, Quinn's riverbank employer and a comic nineteenth-century caricature not unlike those created by Herman Melville or Mark Twain, is tending to the corpse when suddenly the narrative veers sharply and enters the mock-heroic, mock-pornographic realm of John Cleland's *Fanny Hill:*

> John the Brawn climbed aboard Magdalena Colón and began doing to her gelid blossom what I had heard him boast of doing to many dozens of other more warm-blooded specimens. The sight of his gyrations aroused Hillegond to such a degree that she began certain gyrations of her own, uttering soft, guttural noises I associate solely with rut, and which grew louder as her passion intensified. Magdalena looked vapidly toward us as John gave her the fullness of his weight, her one eye still open and staring. . . .

Like Cleland's infamous eighteenth-century fiction, Kennedy's scene partakes of various pornographic elements, ribald and overblown description, and overblown metaphor, all presented from the reluctantly voyeuristic viewpoint of Quinn, who watches from just outside the door with Maud. Like Francis Phelan watching the ragman, Quinn looks on from a distance, with a journalist's detachment. The scene is a shock to the reader, but one that leaves none of the unpleasant sensations evoked by *The Ink Truck*—here the effect is a momentary and thought-provoking one, as though the narrative were a train that had made a brief, allusive stop in one particular sub-genre of pre-twentieth-century discourse.

The narrative pulls quickly away from this scene, leaving its style and raw qualities behind and carrying forward only the aftereffects: John the Brawn's "roostering" brings Madame Colón out of her near-death state, returns her to life, and brings Maud and Daniel to consider, in higher nineteenth-century style, their own passions. The young lovers make a vow that will drive the remaining pages forward. "When I'm ready to do it," Maud tells Quinn as they work their way punctiliously through the logic of their desire, "I shall seek you out." Quinn replies politely, "I look forward to it."

In the same way that Quinn spies John raising the dead, he spies other signal events of the age, and he presents them unfailingly to the reader in the language appropriate to each. When John the Brawn goes on to become a famous boxer, Quinn faithfully passes on a description of one of his fights from the *Albany Telescope*. The description, rather than a line or two run into the flow of the book, is set off typographically, a long paragraph or two or three devoted to each round of the fight. Such impromptu generic diversions fill the text.

Rather than a plot as such, the late Kennedy novels, what I've called the "mosaic novels," tend to be reverse-engineered from a single concluding event strongly forecast in the opening pages. As these novels near their conclusions, the looming presence of these long-projected events begins to create a more orderly, tightly wound narrative. With *Quinn's Book,* the consummation of Quinn and Maud's love is projected almost from the moment of Maud's rescue, with the frustration and eventual satisfaction of this desire ultimately taking over the narrative from the wealth of other plotlines.

When Quinn returns to Albany from the battles of the Civil War, which he has covered as a roving correspondent, he and Maud pick up where they left off, almost heedless of her engagement to another man. The novel ends with the fulfillment of the lovers' matched vows: Quinn steals Maud away, as she asked him to do in childhood, and

they consummate their love in a house on the eastern shore of Saratoga Lake. It is a delicate scene, langorously written, and the novel closes with Kennedy's final commentary on his own new style, a sprawling novel including everything and anything, but all of it somehow also rightly selected and leading up to a single intimate moment between two people: "And then Maud and Quinn were at last ready for love."

Kennedy's new sort of novel garnered mixed reviews, but as I've suggested earlier, he again seems simply to have been one artistic step ahead of his critics. The interior sweep of *Quinn's Book* prompted some immediate doomsaying, with more than one critic suggesting that he had lost his voice. But by the time *Very Old Bones* was released, only four years later, critics had accustomed themselves to the new style and remarked upon it with real relish.

VERY OLD BONES: THE MAGIC OF METAFICTION

Very Old Bones begins with a Phelan-Quinn-Purcell family tree entitled "The Family 1813–1958." It is a relatively uncomplicated genealogy, and it allows the reader of Kennedy's work to place the earlier events of the Albany Cycle mentally, before moving on to this new installment. The lower rungs of the Phelan line show the Francis-to-Billy connection laid out in *Billy Phelan* and *Ironweed;* Billy's sister Margaret's marriage to George Quinn suggests another branch of the tree stretching generations back to the protagonist of *Quinn's Book.*

The family tree is a highly self-conscious device, a means of reinforcing for the reader the superstructures of the Albany Cycle, or at least the majority of it made up by an interlocking Irish-American family history. This self-consciousness swells into full-scale metafiction in the opening pages of *Very Old Bones,* cueing the reader that in large part, this will be a novel about the dynastic structure of Kennedy's created families, or more simply put, a novel about Kennedy's novels.

The reader learns quickly, for instance, that the narrator is Orson Purcell, listed in the family tree as the son of Peter Phelan. Yet the relationship is unexpectedly in question: Orson's mother, Claire Purcell, was an assistant to a stage magician, Manfredo the Magnificent, and may well have had an affair with him near the time of Orson's conception. Peter Phelan has steadfastly refused throughout Orson's life to acknowledge him publicly as a son. It is classic Kennedy, the suffusion of an odd legerdemain into the opening pages of his novel. It is as though a curse of opacity prevents Orson from knowing himself, and the reader from knowing the true ties between the novel's central characters. In the metafictional sense, this ambiguity directs the movements of the novel toward an explicit and in-depth examination of who in Kennedy's Cycle begets whom, an almost biblical task.

Greatly enhancing this self-referential element is the fact that Peter Purcell—the only truly successful Phelan—is a renowned painter, who found success only after realizing that his own family was his key to inspiration. When his career was foundering, "Peter returned to figurative drawing, sketches of the people closest to him, and felt instant strength." As a result, the Phelan house on Albany's Colonie Street, which Orson shares with Peter at the novel's outset in 1958, has become a veritable museum of scenes from earlier Phelan life, which is to say earlier Kennedy novels. This profusion of family-based art is linked directly, from the very opening moments of *Very Old Bones,* to Kennedy's own ever-expanding fictional project. It is not pushing the point too far, I don't think, to read Peter's career as a self-conscious allegory for Kennedy's own. As Marcus Gorman did in *Legs,* Orson Purcell exists in part to comment upon the celebrity in

whose shadow he stands. Orson's intimate view of his father and his father's tortured artwork dominates much of *Very Old Bones*. And even when Orson is not explicitly analyzing the qualities of Peter's work and life, his own disturbed life shows the constant influence of his father and the enigma of his true parentage. Much of the early novel centers on Orson's stint in Germany while serving in the Army. There he meets Giselle, a French translator and photographer with a taste for expensive pleasures, and immediately Orson is caught up in a cycle of ecstasy and despair, depending on whether he has enough money on a given day to wine and dine Giselle. In order to take care of his financial problems, Orson begins a descent into petty crime—black-marketing American dollars, cheating at cards—that eventually leads to a nervous breakdown in a German dive called Fritz's Garden of Eden.

During his breakdown Orson gives a madman's sermon, during which he bites into his own flesh and rants about his "wonderful, lascivious mother, my saintly, incestuous father." He is eventually examined by a psychotherapist who reports that "He believes he is a bastard. . . . He is so insecure he requires a facade to reduce his anxieties to manageable size; and so every waking moment is an exercise in mendacity, including self-delusion." Orson's zombie-like breakdowns recur throughout the novel, returning the reader to the understanding that all of Peter's art springs from the real pain of his real family, and his own artful evasions of responsibility as a father are in turn productive of their own new pain. Orson is simply the latest manifestation of the Phelan's generational cycle of injury, but he is somehow aware of this cycle in motion. He is a metafictional commentator who is also alive to his own real psychological pain, like a surgeon who is himself undergoing surgery without the benefit of anesthesia.

Peter also realizes the dimensions and causes of this cycle of pain, and the major thrust of the novel involves his attempts to dispel the hurt by dispelling the ignorance that characterizes much of the Phelan world. With the death of Kathryn Phelan, the matriarch whose bitterness and narrow-mindedness led in part to the breakup of the family, Peter returns for the funeral bearing light—literal light. He has decided to do what his mother would never allow, electrify the Phelans' Colonie Street house. It is clear to the reader that again Kennedy has self-consciously set his characters about the task of further illuminating the Albany Cycle.

> Peter, squatting, his right hand still in the box's mysterious interior, suddenly lifted the chandelier into freedom (like a magician, I could say), and with his other hand pulled away the tissue paper that surrounded it, then held it aloft. Presto!
> . . . "We don't want it," said Sarah.
> "How well I know *that*, dear sister. But we *shall* have light on the corpse of our mother, light unlike any that ever found its way into this arcane cave of gloom. . . ."

The chandelier incident, made possible by the death of the mother Kathryn, prefigures Peter's reconciliation dinner in 1958, made possible by the death of his sister Sarah. The two events are matched as well in that Peter's brother, Francis Phelan, estranged from Colonie Street for years, returns for the funeral of Kathryn; Francis's son Billy finally returns to the Phelan household for Peter's dinner. There is an orderliness to these movements on Peter's part, which is to say on Kennedy's part, a sense of generational rifts being healed in order of occurrence. Of course, true healing can only take place with the understanding of the original injury, and for this reason Peter's *Malachi Suite*—a series of paintings telling the mythical history of Peter's own father and mother—takes center stage at the reunion.

Kennedy's movement from 1958 to the Staatskill/Hudson River region of 1887 for the story of Malachi and his unfortunate wife Lizzie recalls Bailey's sudden movement backward in time in

Kennedy's first effort, *The Ink Truck*. Kennedy's (which is to say Peter's) story of Malachi provides a mythical point of origin for the Phelans' tragedies; at once it is clearly the stuff of legend, and historically grounded in newspaper accounts, place names, dates, and so forth. The gist of the story is that Malachi, whether insane or himself the victim of some malevolent supernatural force, becomes convinced that his wife Lizzie has been replaced by a demon who has magically stripped Malachi of his genitals, and in retaliation, Malachi and his friend Crip Devlin burn Lizzie to death in an attempt to exorcise the demon. This gruesome narrative is stretched over the panels of Peter's masterwork, an explicitly mythic insertion into the Albany Cycle. It is a creation myth to be precise, and it points up the irony of Orson's first breakdown in Fritz's Garden of Eden.

After having moved from Germany to New York to Albany, from 1958 as far back as 1887 and back again, *Very Old Bones* finally brings off the reconciliation dinner set out in the opening scenes. The dinner is an explicitly patriarchal resolution to a number of the conflicts in the Albany Cycle. Orson, formally acknowledged as Peter's son during the dinner, notes with satisfaction that "we sat where Peter placed us . . . the first formal resumption of the patriarchal seating arrangement since Michael Phelan died in 1895." And Orson quickly reiterates the theme, calling Peter "Paterfamilias," then explaining to Billy that the term "just means 'father of the family.' " The pregnant Giselle, for her part, has returned to Orson and Colonie Street for a number of reasons, but one of which is "her weariness with being a pioneer feminist in a man's world."

Yet Kennedy goes equally far out of his way to argue explicitly that it is the male Phelans who have fled traditionally, leaving misery in their wake, a misery to be endured by strong Phelan women:

> I think of Peter's creative act . . . as independent of his art, a form of atonement after contemplating

what wreckage was left in the wake of the behavior of the males in the family . . . in sum, a pattern of abdication, or flight, or exile, with the women left behind to pick up the pieces of fractured life: a historic woman like Kathryn, an avant-garde virgin renegade like Molly, a working girl like Peg, and, to confirm this theory with an anomaly, there is the case of Giselle.

Again, if Peter's and Kennedy's work exhibit close, almost allegorical connections, and they certainly seem to, then Orson's final analysis of *Malachi Suite* represents something of a meditation on the place of women in the Albany Cycle generally. Without doubt the passage reads like a piece of literary criticism, albeit a piece written by the author in question. Kennedy seems aware of the criticism generated by the Cycle's early treatment of women, and he counters it with an argument of his own: that the Albany Cycle has itself always implicitly recognized such male-induced pain, and implicitly celebrated the "historic" and "working" women who have borne up under it.

Very Old Bones is metafiction pursued to the highest level, and is precisely what one might expect from a playful intellect of Kennedy's rank— it is not merely a novel that comments on itself as a novel, as well as the other fictions in the Cycle, but is a novel that also manages to comment on the *criticism* engendered by this and the other novels making up the Cycle. Orson may refer disparagingly to "The disease of self-contemplation," but Kennedy's unrelenting self-referential focus in *Very Old Bones* produces one of the sharpest and most challenging novels of his career.

THE FLAMING CORSAGE: THE FINAL, LOGICAL CONSTRAINTS OF THE CYCLE

As with a number of Kennedy's novels, *The Flaming Corsage* (1996) originated as a bit of seemingly peripheral backstory conceived and laid out in the course of an earlier book. *The Flaming Corsage,* like *Ironweed,* has its roots in *Billy Phelan's Greatest Game.* Martin Daugherty's own affair with his father's mistress, the actress Melissa, is the family scandal that affects Martin and his gift of foresight most directly, but during the course of *Billy Phelan* he also recalls an earlier, more explosive scandal: his father's involvement, along with the young Melissa, in a hotel shooting with strange sexual overtones, commonly known as the Love Nest shootings.

More than a decade after the publication of *Billy Phelan,* Kennedy decided to expand this small kernel of backstory into a component novel in its own right. It's likely that this decision was based in part on a desire to explore the remaining family tree from *Billy Phelan*'s—the Daughertys—inasmuch as *Quinn's Book* had already taken up the Quinn line, and the examination of the Phelans was ongoing. But in all of Kennedy's post-Pulitzer work there is an element of self-conscious expansion of the Cycle, a straightforward attempt to do so from multiple viewpoints and social situations. As Kennedy has said of his approach to each new book, "It's always different because the attack is always from a different angle." And so it seems as likely that *The Flaming Corsage* represented an attempt to chronicle a social stratum of Albany that none of Kennedy's earlier novels had approached: the "lofty perch in America's high culture."

Yet having decided to dramatize this particle of an earlier novel, Kennedy unexpectedly hit a wall. He created books from notes, but he has spoken often since of the over-intellectualized feel of those early attempts: "You have great characters, you have this column of time, and the conflict and so on. But something is missing." Kennedy's response here is illuminating. Not only is he constrained, in a sense, by his earlier plot sketch of the Love Nest killings, but he is working within "this column of time," as well as within the actual boundaries of Albany itself. Like a veteran Scrabble player confronting an already packed board, Kennedy's composition process necessarily grows more complex, more daunting, as he nears the completion of the game.

In the case of *The Flaming Corsage,* Kennedy had decided to dramatize the lives of the uppermost reaches of Albany high society, and yet none of his other books had quite prepared him to do so. Half of the ultimate solution to the problem lay in the pleasantly Dickensian character of Edward Daugherty himself. Raised by a fantastically rich Protestant robber baron-diplomat-inventor named Lyman Fitzgibbon—whom Edward's father had once rescued from a mob—Edward is a fantastic hybrid. He is the son of a laboring Irish-Catholic; he is also the handsome and favored godson of one of Albany's ruling Protestant elites, with easy access to the favored haunts of Elk Street, the Albany Country Club, the Fort Orange Club, and Columbia College.

The other half of the solution Kennedy found, not unpredictably, in Shakespeare's *Romeo and Juliet,* and no allusive model could signal more clearly his desire to re-create and heighten the class and religious tensions at work in Albany of the early twentieth century. Katrina Taylor, the granddaughter of Edward's patron, Lyman Fitzgibbon, is young, beautiful, wealthy, and—although she and Edward move in the same social circles—off limits. Not only is Edward Irish and Catholic, he has chosen to become a writer, and his income seems uncertain at best.

On Edward's side, there is the strong opposition of his father, Emmett: at some time in the past, Emmett's brother was employed by Taylor's father, and was savagely beaten and crippled for daring to initiate a strike. It is a fairly stagey setup, one that continues in matched chapters dedicated to parental meetings. Edward's meeting with the Taylors, for example, occurs in the Taylor library, stocked with books, some of these histories of the bloody Cromwellian conquest of Ireland. In the course of asking for Katrina's hand, Edward delivers what he comes to call his "Manifesto of Love," but what is actually an uncon-

cealed broadside at the Taylors, their wealth, their arrogance, and their history. For all of its artificial qualities, the scene is eloquent, and the irony on which it rests satisfying:

> I'm vividly aware also that your ancestors . . . in the name of God, tried to eliminate the entire population of Ireland and almost succeeded. Then I sit here and all that self-glorifying butchery leaps out at me from the pages of books in this room . . . and you, Jake, and you, Geraldine, have the strength and courage to keep—*in your own library* the record of these unspeakable crimes. Hurrah, I say to this. . . . hurrah for facing the worst history has to offer, and moving forward. . . .

Katrina's visit to the poorer section of North Albany is also fraught with tension, and is moving for the reader in spite of its choreographed social problematics. Kennedy seems more than willing to acknowledge the heavy debt to Shakespeare, another sign that self-consciousness in the later novels obviates a host of problems. When Edward's mother remarks that Katrina is still quite young for a bride, the response is both prophetic and allusively to the point: "I'm almost twenty. Juliet, had she lived, would've been married six years at my age. Perhaps I'm older than I seem."

Katrina, like most female characters to whom Kennedy gives his full attention, is captivating: undeniably and oddly morbid, sharply defined and carefully nuanced. She is possessed of an intuition bordering on, but not quite equal to, second-sight. In this Kennedy sets the stage for her son Martin, with his clearer visions, but Katrina's intuition is directed primarily at her own spiritual development. In the most impossible circumstances, she knows instantly which of two difficult choices is the necessary choice—that is, necessary for her to remain true to herself. When Edward's parents point out to her, for instance, that marrying in a Protestant church will lead to Edward's excommunication, she immediately solves the unsolvable by agreeing to become a

Catholic: "I do what I think I should do, so I can become what I feel I must be."

Similarly, when Emmett is on his deathbed and wishes for a last glass of ale, Katrina offers to fetch it from the saloon herself, knowing it to be an all-male establishment. The all-male rule is a "silly one," Katrina announces to the stunned bartender, because "My father-in-law is dying, and the ale is for him, and for Father Loonan when he comes to perform the last rites, ten minutes from now." Katrina understands intuitively that this errand requires her doing, as a way finally to heal the rift with her father-in-law, and to seal her connection to the Church, as well as, not coincidentally, to make a stand for women in a bastion of male privilege. Yet it is a deceptively complex scene, one that carefully recasts an icon of early twentieth-century gender politics. Kennedy shows a woman forcing her way into a male pub—but not to rail against drink, nor to militate for women's rights. Instead, Katrina is primarily demonstrating fidelity to the Father. Katrina is a pioneer, but a pioneer within Kennedy's particular zone of comfort.

Unfortunately for Kennedy, the heart of *The Flaming Corsage* is Katrina Daugherty, and when he leaves her to begin the dramatic elaboration behind the Love Nest shootings, he is forced to leave her behind. The novel suffers from that point forward. In her place, Kennedy erects a machinery of characters and motives—actresses, best friend's wives, hoods with small grudges, love, jealousy, rape, false rape, lesbianism, false lesbianism, practical jokes, and severed animal heads—to explain the shootings sketched so long before in *Billy Phelan*. But almost all of these narrative threads have a strained feel, and the author picks them up and puts them down so quickly that after a while they cease to have any real impact. Kennedy seems to come to them reluctantly, or haphazardly.

The actress Melissa Spencer, to take one example, so captivating, raw, and quirky in *Billy Phelan*, is reduced in the last half of *The Flaming Corsage* to a breathy ingenue not unlike Jack Diamond's mistress, Kiki. Like Kiki, Melissa is portrayed not as a woman, but as a creature of the footlights and the early movie camera, gorgeous but nearly nonexistent beneath the skin-deep masterpiece of beauty. "If a headbirth by Aphrodite and The Prince were possible she could have been the progeny: born with passion's mouth and sacred swath, and wisdom from below." Like Kiki, and in a way reminiscent of the early Kennedy, she is a concept and a body, with most of her first appearance—at a dinner party thrown by Edward—devoted to Edward's sudden leering (and out-of-character) enchantment with her breasts. "Her gown became the object of silent speculation: would it offer the table, before dinner's end, an unobstructed chest-scape?" The complex father-son sexual competition for Melissa—a deft series of suggestions in *Billy Phelan*—here becomes a game of who-controls-the-breasts, with Edward at one minute fuming that Martin now has "an unobstructed view of the chest-scape," but then exultant a moment later when Melissa leaves his son to lean again toward Edward, "offering him her beautiful moonlit breasts."

The Flaming Corsage's most resonant and moving images remain those of Katrina, sifting through the ruins of a hotel fire that killed her mother, sitting for a photograph in her own frankly exhibitionistic way, and dying in Edward's arms as a second fire finishes the work of the first. Where the novel succeeds it succeeds, in the force of the original portraits of Edward and Katrina, framed in Shakespeare's time-honored plot of warring families. And there Kennedy accomplishes the almost sociological exploration he set out to provide—the reader sees the upper and the lower classes of Albany in protracted struggle.

It is when Kennedy is forced, finally, into the constraints of his own Love Nest shootings outline, done many years before, that his story falters. There is a very particular brittle quality to fiction written in the service of someone else's ideas and wishes. In Kennedy's case, at least once late in the composition of the vastly impressive Albany Cycle, that someone else proved to be his own younger self.

Note: I interviewed William Kennedy for an article published in the *New England Review* in 1998. Excerpts from this interview appear in this article. All other interviews mentioned in this article appear in Neila Seshachari's *Conversations with William Kennedy,* which is listed in the Bibliography.

Selected Bibliography

WORKS OF WILLIAM KENNEDY

FICTION

The Ink Truck. New York: Dial Press, 1969.
Legs. New York: Coward, McMann, 1975.
Billy Phelan's Greatest Game. New York: Viking, 1978.
Ironweed. New York: Viking, 1983.
Quinn's Book. New York: Penguin, 1988.
Very Old Bones. New York: Penguin, 1992.
The Flaming Corsage. New York: Viking, 1996.

NONFICTION

O Albany! Improbable City of Political Wizards, Fearless Ethnics, Spectacular Aristocrats, Splendid Nobodies and Underrated Scoundrels. New York: Viking, 1983.
Riding the Yellow Trolley Car: Selected Non-Fiction. New York: Penguin, 1993.

SCREENPLAYS

The Cotton Club. With Francis Ford Coppola. New York: St. Martin's Press, 1986.
Ironweed. For Taft-Barish Productions, 1987.

CRITICAL STUDIES

Adamson, W. D. "Very Old Themes: The Legacy of William Kennedy's Humanism." *Classical and Modern Literature* 15, no. 1:67–75 (1994).
Black, David. "The Fusion of Past and Present in William Kennedy's *Ironweed.*" *Critique* 7, no. 3:177–184 (1986).
Clarke, Brock. " 'A Hostile Decade': The 60's and Self-Criticism in William Kennedy's Early Prose." *Twentieth-Century Literature* 45, no. 1:1–17 (1999).
Clarke, Peter P. "Classical Myth in William Kennedy's *Ironweed.*" *Critique* 7, no. 3:167–176 (1986).
Estess, Ted L. "Angels in the Primum Mobile: Dimensions of the Sacred in William Kennedy's *Ironweed,* Novel and Film." In *Screening The Sacred: Religion, Myth and Ideology in Popular American Film.* Edited by Joel Martin and Conrad Ostwalt. Boulder: Westview Press, 1995. Pp. 30–43.
Giamo, Benedict. *The Homeless of Ironweed: Blossoms on the Crag.* Iowa City: University of Iowa Press, 1996.
Griffin, Paul F. "Susan Sontag, Franny Phelan, and the Moral Implications of Photographs." *The Midwest Quarterly* 29, no. 2:194–203 (1988).
———. "The Moral Implications of Annie Phelan's Jell-O." *San Jose Studies* 14, no. 3:85–95 (1988).
Kennedy, Liam. "Memory and Hearsay: Ethnic History and Identity in *Billy Phelan's Greatest Game* and *Ironweed.*" *MELUS* 18, no. 1:71–82 (1993).
Michener, Christian. "Martin Daugherty's Victories in *Billy Phelan's Greatest Game.*" *Papers on Language and Literature* 31, no. 4:406–429 (1995).
Novelli, Cornelius. "Francis Phelan and the Hands of Heracles: Hero and City in William Kennedy's *Ironweed.*" *Classical and Modern Literature* 12, no. 2:119–126 (1993).
Reilly, Edward C. *William Kennedy.* Boston: Twayne, 1991.
Taylor, Anya. "Ironweed, Alcohol, and Celtic Heroism." *Critique: Studies in Contemporary Fiction* 33, no. 2:107–120 (1992).
Tierce, Michael. "William Kennedy's Odyssey: The Travels of Francis Phelan." *Classical and Modern Literature* 8, no. 4:247–263 (1988).
Van Dover, J. K. *Understanding William Kennedy.* Columbia: University of South Carolina Press, 1991.
Whittaker, Stephen. "The Lawyer as Narrator in William Kennedy's *Legs.*" *Legal Studies Forum* 9, no. 2:157–164 (1985).

Yetman, Michael G. "*Ironweed:* The Perils and Purgatories of Male Romanticism." *Papers on Language and Literature* 27, no. 1:84–103 (1991).

INTERVIEWS

Baruth, Philip. "Beyond Realism: William Kennedy on the Surreal and the Unconscious, the Religious, the Sublime, and the Gonzo." *New England Review* 19, no. 1:116–126 (1998).

Seshachari, Neila. *Conversations with William Kennedy.* Jackson: University Press of Mississippi, 1997. (Collects twenty-four interviews, dating from 1969 to 1996.)

—PHILIP E. BARUTH

Jane Kenyon

1947–1995

AT A GRAVESITE in the cemetery in Proctor, New Hampshire, stands a gravestone with the lines "I BELIEVE IN THE MIRACLES OF ART BUT WHAT / PRODIGY WILL KEEP YOU SAFE BESIDE ME." These lines are from Jane Kenyon's poem "Afternoon at MacDowell" and were written by Kenyon with her husband, poet Donald Hall, in mind. At the time Kenyon wrote the poem, Hall had cancer and was "supposed to die." The sad irony here is that Jane Kenyon died first of leukemia on April 22, 1995. The lines now stand in testimony to Kenyon, and they look, mistakenly, like the words were written for her. Consequently, both the "I" and the "you" in the epitaph refer to Kenyon herself and provide an odd, but telling, testament to her identity as a poet. Throughout her life Kenyon's work explored the difficulty of locating herself in the world, in a sense, "inhabiting a home." Her poems and prose repeatedly articulated the region of her senses: what she saw, what she heard, what she touched, what she smelled, and what she tasted. Her evocatively descriptive language attempted to map her relationship to her surroundings. In her poem "From Room To Room" she writes:

I move from room to room,

a little dazed, like a fly. I watch it
bump against each window.

I am clumsy here. . . .

Critics have described Kenyon's work as exploring the inner psyche, especially in relation to her own battles with depression. Essayist Gary Roberts noted in *Contemporary Women Poets* that her poetry was "acutely faithful to the familiarities and mysteries of home life, and it is distinguished by intense calmness in the face of routine disappointments and tragedies." Although accurate, these characterizations only partially encompass Kenyon's work, which should be remembered as much more courageous, passionate, and unblinking in the belief that people can find comfort and understanding in their immediate world.

KENYON'S BACKGROUND

Jane Kenyon was born on May 23, 1947, in Ann Arbor, Michigan. The second of two children, her family lived in an area that is now within the city of Ann Arbor, but then was merely part of the township and was primarily populated by small farms and orchards not far from the Huron River. Her father was a musician who also taught music while her mother stayed home to raise the children. Her father suffered throughout his life from clinical depression, and her mother suffered from manic depression which made home life difficult.

The family was staunchly Methodist and had several Methodist ministers on both sides. This doctrinal influence had a powerful effect on forming Kenyon's sense of herself in the world. Her brother Reuel and she stayed often at her fraternal grandmother's big house on State Street in Ann Arbor where her grandmother took in University of Michigan students as boarders. Her grandmother, Dora Baldwin Kenyon, had a strong influence on Kenyon as a child because of her dark obsessions with Christ's Second Coming and the end of the world as we know it. In an unfinished essay titled "Childhood, When You Are in It . . . ," collected with all of her prose in *A Hundred White Daffodils: Essays, The Akhmatova Translations, Newspaper Columns, Notes, Interviews, and One Poem* (1999), Kenyon described a defining experience: "I might have been seven or eight when my grandmother first said to me, opening her eyes wide, and then wider. 'The body is the temple of the Holy Ghost.' We were sitting in the dark living room, dark because the shades were kept half-drawn, and the sheer curtains were never pulled back. . . . I know that grandmother had said something solemn, and I knew that somehow *my* body was under discussion."

It was hard for Kenyon to fall asleep at the house on State Street because there was always a lingering sense that "Jesus would come in the night to judge [her] life." Like her grandmother's favorite hymn, "Onward Christian Soldiers, Marching As To War," Dora Baldwin Kenyon instilled in Kenyon a sense that life was indeed a battle for salvation in the eyes of the Lord. These doctrinal conditions helped underscore a deep sense of discomfort in both her body and her environment. Objects contained an aura or power beyond their material manifestations. These feelings of presence in things would come to influence her belief in the evocative nature of images.

By the age of nine or ten, Kenyon began to resent the dominance that her religious fear held over her. Out of this resentment grew a germ of distrust for the overwhelming responsibility of being judged by Christ. Concurrently, she became aware of the surprising absence of moral authority in the natural world. In her 1993 interview with David Bradt, collected in *A Hundred White Daffodils,* Kenyon described this time: "I spent long hours playing at the stream that ran through my family's property. We lived on a dirt road near the Huron River, across from a working farm. I fell in love with the natural world." She wrote about this time years later in the poem "In the Grove: The Poet at Ten," collected in *Let Evening Come* (1990), describing how "She lay on her back in the timothy" and "Nothing would rouse her then / from that joy so violent." These newfound feelings of comfort led her to denounce her Methodist heritage that promoted the notion that she was sinful by nature and to embrace a belief system akin to Jean Jacques Rousseau's noble savage. In her essay "Childhood, When You Are in It . . ." she wrote, "I announced to my parents that one could not be a Christian and an intellectual, and that I would no longer attend church. . . . Nature will be my god, and I'll be a good person simply because it is the right thing to do." Her grandmother's notions of a world threatening her salvation were transformed into a belief that it was exactly her grandmother's dangerous world that eventually would redeem her.

While she nurtured this safe haven in nature, other areas of her life underscored what little affinity she experienced elsewhere. In addition to her discomfort at home and at her grandmother's, she never fit in at school. At her one-room elementary school, Foster School No.16 Fractional, it was obvious to Kenyon that her teacher, Mrs. Irwin, did not like her, and Kenyon returned the favor. This mutual disregard made it difficult for Kenyon to enjoy school. Instead, much like her home and her grandmother's house, it became is place of dread. In her essay "Dreams of Math," collected in *A Hundred White Daffodils,* she writes, "I had math anxiety, as it's come to be called. Letters, reading, spelling made sense to me, but numbers had such strange proclivities.

That zero times four was zero, canceling out the existence of the four, seemed dubious at best." She no longer accepted authority's interpretation. No one could ever say, "because that's the way it is." She learned that she must come to the knowledge on her own through an examination of the evidence before her. From her previous experiences she had learned to rely on her senses to lead her to truth. It was this almost doctrinaire reliance on the inductive process that seemed to open her to the power of metaphor and poetry. To support these feelings about self-reliance, nothing in her junior high and high school years that followed fostered a sense of belonging to a community. Instead, she felt even more lost among the nine hundred students.

Several thematic concerns that appear in Kenyon's later work seem to have evolved from the conflict of childhood experiences. In *A Hundred White Daffodils* Kenyon has characterized this time as one in which she discovered that she "had neither the courage to rebel, nor an obedient heart." This skepticism and mistrust played a significant role in the poetic project of attempting to articulate a physical, emotional, and spiritual relation to the world that is uniquely authentic. In her early poems she had almost a rigid adherence to the transcendent power of the image, so that her poems were more like observations absent of a discriminating eye. In her notes for a lecture given at a literary conference in Enfield, New Hampshire, and collected in *A Hundred White Daffodils,* she said, "We celebrate the world by writing about it, we observe it more closely, with more love. We are more fully alive and aware because of our efforts."

YEARS AT THE UNIVERSITY OF MICHIGAN

On graduation from high school, Kenyon attended the University of Michigan at Ann Arbor where she received a bachelor's degree in 1970 and a master's degree in 1972. It was there that she met her husband, the poet Donald Hall. In the spring of 1969 Hall led a class of more than 100 students. Jane Kenyon was among those students, but it was not until the following fall semester that they finally met when she was admitted to his poetry workshop. In an interview with Jeffrey Cramer published by *The Massachusetts Review* Hall describes how they met, "I remember one particular poem . . . . 'The Needle' . . . . I think maybe that poem got her in the class. Thank God." Along with ten or eleven other students, Kenyon met with Hall once a week for several hours in his living room. Nineteen years her senior, Hall led this workshop for two and a half years. Over this time Kenyon and Hall developed a friendship. Even though the relationship was initially a student-to-teacher one, over time there grew a deeper, more intense connection that led to marriage in April, 1972.

Clearly, this relationship defined Kenyon's development as a poet. A tenured professor at the University of Michigan, recently divorced, and father of two when they met, Donald Hall was a mature poet in his forties. In contrast, Kenyon was a graduate student who was not altogether clear that poetry would be her life's work. As the two describe the development of their relationship, it was an attraction that both resisted at first, but somehow the inevitability of it was impossible to avoid. In the beginning, the imbalance of power with Hall having been her teacher was difficult. In an interview with Marian Blue, collected in *A Hundred White Daffodils,* Hall described the difficulty of their change in relationship from student and teacher to lovers, "When we were first married, we had to cope with that earlier relationship. I couldn't criticize her poems, because then I became her teacher. It was physically confusing: her husband suddenly turns into Professor Hall." To resolve this dilemma, Hall and Kenyon invited a third person, their friend and poet Gregory Orr, to their home. This made all the difference. "When Gregory Orr would join us, then I could say anything about Jane's poems and she could say everything about mine. Greg's presence made it a workshop in which we were equals," Hall said. They adhered to this formula for the first two and a half years of their marriage. Orr then moved to Virginia and Kenyon and Hall relocated to New Hampshire.

Kenyon described the differences between Hall and herself in the same interview with Marion Blue, "I think our visions are very different. Don has been writing a long time, and he has passed through many shapes and sizes, if you will, for his poems. He is writing large, ambitious, loose-limbed poems these days, poems in which all his wisdom appears. I am working at one thing—the short lyric. It is all I want, at this point: to write short, intense, musical cries of the spirit. I am a miniaturist and he is painting Diego Rivera murals. I'm not being modest about trying to write short lyrics in the tradition of Sappho, Keats, and Akhmatova." Kenyon's comparison of Hall to the famous Mexican painter Diego Rivera seems an unconscious acknowledgment of Hall's towering aesthetic presence in her life. To complete this allusion by then comparing Kenyon to the artist Frida Kahlo, Rivera's wife, might be considered a stretch, but the effort does hold a grain of truth in that Kahlo's canvases were much more contained and psychically pained than Rivera's, just as Kenyon's poems map a difficult psychic landscape that is much more personal and inward-looking than Hall's.

EAGLE POND

This towering presence did not diminish, however, when they moved in 1975 from Ann Arbor to Eagle Pond, Hall's family farm in Wilmot, New Hampshire, for Hall's year-long sabbatical from the University of Michigan. The farm had been settled by Hall's great-grandfather in 1865. In the *Life at Eagle Pond: The Poetry of Jane Kenyon and Donald Hall* website, Hall, who spent his childhood summers and wrote his first poems there, described this return as both a coming home and a "coming home to the place of language." For Kenyon, the farm was an environment that was similar to the rural landscape of her childhood where she first discovered herself. This return to nature was essential to her beginning to write seriously for the first time. Within the woods and rolling hills populated with small farms, she rediscovered the subject that nurtured her own inner journey toward self-discovery. As Charles Simic observed on the website, "Kenyon's country is both our rural New Hampshire and her inwardness in which we all recognize ourselves."

Before her arrival at Eagle Pond, Kenyon's commitment to writing was haphazard and undisciplined. In her interview with Bill Moyers, collected in *A Hundred White Daffodils,* she described this time, "I really didn't get going in my work until we came here (Eagle Pond). I have all the time in the world here. I had to do something to fill those hours, so I began to work more. I used to work only when the spirit moved, but when we came here I began to write every day . . . [and was] getting serious about this poetry business." The shape of her and Hall's days centered around a morning of writing in their own offices.

At the end of Hall's sabbatical year, they decided that Eagle Pond was where they would make their home. Hall resigned his professorship at the University of Michigan and embarked on a career as a freelance writer. By the late 1990s he was the author of thirteen volumes of verse, and author or editor of nineteen anthologies and books of prose. Over the years, it was primarily his work that provided the income that sustained him and Kenyon on the farm. While Hall continued mining the aesthetic veins that he had been working for years, Kenyon embarked upon a two-year immersion into the poetry of John Keats. Although she wrote very little about other poets, it is clear that Keats' sense of the lyric as meditation on one's relationship to the physical world influenced Kenyon's work. In her first book *From Room to Room,* published in 1978, most of the poems are anchored in observation, rather than engagement, of the world.

FROM ROOM TO ROOM

All but two of the forty-three poems, "The Needle" and another unnamed poem, from her first book *From Room to Room* were written at Eagle Pond. Though beautiful, the strategies of "The Needle" are not quite consistent with the rest of the poems from the collection and do not bear the stamp of Keats' influence. Instead, the poem seems more consistent with her later work. The poem begins with a comparision: "Grandmother, you are as pale / as Christ's hands on the wall above you." Kenyon's early poems are typically absent of such figures of speech, particularly in the first few lines, as well as direct Christian references. Instead her poems arrive at the connotative much more timidly. She relies on her eye to describe and allows the image to evoke its own aura. The first poem in the collection is "For the Night." It is on the surface a series of descriptions:

> The mare kicks
> In her darkening stall, knocks
> Over a bucket.
>
> The goose . . .
>
> The cow keeps a peaceful brain . . .

Reminiscent of early twentieth century Imagism, the inflection in the poem arises ever so quietly in line five with the adjective "peaceful." Surprisingly, the entire poem rests on this adjective while what follows describes rather neutrally the way light moves and a bat flies. Its delicacy and spare lines appear anachronistic and somewhat derivative of William Carlos Williams' poems like "The Red Wheel Barrel" or "This Is Just To Say" in the way that Williams sometimes placed inordinate emotional weight on isolated parts of speech. The odd thing in "For the Night," however, is the speaker's absence. It is almost as if such a serene environment can only be observed from the outside, not from within. This void of presence leaves the reader wondering if the speaker's location, in contrast to this peace, is some kind of discomfort. As a first poem in a collection, "For the Night" is a strong statement of Kenyon's aesthetic and spiritual principles that nature holds the key to finding acceptance.

It is ironic that *From Room to Room* begins with such a strong description of a safe haven because much of the book examines moving from one place to another and the difficulty of giving up one home to find another. The second poem in the book is even titled as such, "Leaving Town." It again is primarily a description except for one simile at the end. "I felt like a hand without an arm." In the poem the speaker tracks the giving away of plants, the loading of the truck, the journey out of town, and the increasingly fainter radio signal of a Tiger's game. The images play on the reader's sympathy for the painful experience of separation. "Friends handed us the cats through the half-closed windows." The last separation with the past is made through a window that is already "half-closed," not half-open, as if leaving can only be seen in the pessimistic terms of closure. This gesture of faithfulness to the past and to established relationships stands as a beacon for the difficulty she has discovering her place in her new home. The poems that follow in the book explore this conflict of making a context in a place where she had no context before and where there existed a rich context already without her.

Kenyon first catalogs experiences that set her apart from her new home. There's a strange absence and powerlessness in these poems in which the world that surrounds her has much more weight and presence than she has herself. One poem is titled "Here," but the lines describe a place in which the speaker is struggling to find a "here" for herself. Even though there is an epigraph from *The Book of Common Prayer,* which is supposed to emphasize her acceptance of her new place in New Hampshire, the actual poem contradicts this quotation by underscoring a sense of frailty, impermanence, and vulnerability because the speaker compares her connection to her home to a cutting just rooting in a glass of water.

> I feel my life start up again,
> like a cutting when it grows
> the first pale and tentative
> root hair in a glass of water.

Other poems, such as "From Room to Room," "The Presence of Others," and "The Cold," seem to highlight the permanence of what is already there in contrast to her own unrootedness. On the whole these poems are in creating a vivid sensory experience of this conflict, except in a poem such as "This Morning," in which the speaker's presence is so absent that the reader has no voice or identity on which to anchor himself or herself. The pronoun "I" appears subordinated and located in the past.

> A nuthatch drops
> To the ground, feeding
> On sunflower seed and bits of bread
> I scattered on the snow.

In contrast, everything else in the poem is so present that even the noise of the plow passing on the road draws the attention of the cats and makes "the house / tremble as it passes." This attendance by the world, however, does not add up to much, and this reflects so poorly on the "I" of the poem that the speaker has no real value and, thus, is not

worth listening to. At times the humility in Kenyon's poems can devolve too dangerously into an expression of no self-worth. These tendencies seem like a foreshadowing of the clinical depression that she wrote about later on.

Nevertheless, the tenuousness of the speaker's presence provides some of the most lyrical moments in the collection. In "The Thimble," her discovery of this object leads her not only to feelings of connection to the past, but also to her community and, ultimately, to God. Not surprisingly, the connection to her new home is found through objects left behind by women who once lived there—the gray hair, the thimble. She finds a kinship with these women that culminates in "Hanging Pictures in Nanny's Room," in which Kenyon imagines the mentality and daily rituals of an ancestor in a parlor photograph. This finally leads to a sequence in the second part of the book where she finds a link to her past and to her mother and grandmother. From this axis that connects her legacy to her future, Kenyon is able to construct an environment in which she belongs. In this book it becomes clear how important women are to her sense of place. As a child her grandmother and teacher were key to her dislocation within her community. Now, it is the artifacts of long-dead women who help her find a home, and later in *From Room to Room,* it is the poetry of the Russian poet Anna Akhmatova that informs her poetry.

In the next to last section of *From Room to Room,* the speaker tentatively discovers happiness, but the journey is strange in that the speaker seems not to have an active role in the arrival of this emotion. Instead, she is merely a recipient. Critics have commented on Kenyon's work as being eerily calm and egoless, but this absence of self has deeper implications in its relation to how she defines herself. In "The Suitor" the speaker personifies happiness as someone who pursues her. This is further explicated in the next poem

"American Triptych" where her only sense of being an active force in her happiness is as a member of a community.

> The store is a bandstand. All our voices
> sound from it, making the same motley
> American music Ives heard . . .

The poem's three parts feature the country store where "Cousins arrive like themes and variations;" kids playing baseball in a hayfield, beyond "deaths or separations;" and a potluck supper at the Baptist church whose wholesomeness restores a sense of personal and national innocence:

> On the way home we pass the white clapboard faces
> of the library and town hall, luminous in the moonlight, and I remember the first time I ever voted—
> in a township hall in Michigan.

> That same wonderful smell of coffee was in the air,
> and I found myself among people trying to live ordered lives. . . . And again I am struck with love
> for the Republic.

From here, Kenyon is able to arrive at the final poem of the section, "Now That We Live." This poem celebrates the natural world around her with playful descriptions of a "Fat spider" and a "Brow of hayfield." Her use of adjectives has changed from the ponderous inflections of the poems early in the volume to an expressiveness that underscores a feeling that she is at last at home: "I belong to the Queen of Heaven!"

TRANSLATING ANNA AKHMATOVA

The journey explored in *From Room to Room* is not limited, however, to the author's efforts at finding a place of comfort, but also is a expedition into Kenyon's identity as a poet. Kenyon in a sense moves "from room to room" trying on styles like prose-poems and compressed imagist poems to find a poetic structure that she can inhabit. This journey concludes with translations of six early poems by Akhmatova, whose imagist techniques provide a model for the poetic sensibility that coalesces in *From Room to Room* and matures in Kenyon's later work. In his introductory essay to *A Hundred White Daffodils,* Hall described how crucial Akhmatova was to Kenyon's development: "[A]s she worked with Akhmatova's early lyrics, condensations of strong feeling into compact images both visual and aural, she practiced making the kind of poetry she admired most—an art that embodied powerful emotion by means of the luminous particular."

It was poet and translator Robert Bly who first suggested Kenyon study Akhmatova, and who, along with poet Louis Simpson, directed her to Vera Sandomirsky Dunham, a professor of Russian literature at the State University of New York at Stonybrook, in 1977. For the next eight years Kenyon immersed herself in Akhmatova's pre-revolutionary poems. In 1985, she published *Twenty Poems of Anna Akhmatova,* a small book of translations that is now collected in *A Hundred White Daffodils*. While Kenyon was working on the translations, Dunham apparently pressed her to render the poems in meter and rhyme to reflect the formal aspects of the Russian originals. Kenyon resisted however. In her introduction, which was her only essay in literary criticism, Kenyon wrote, "Because it is impossible to translate with fidelity to form and to image, I have sacrificed form for image. Image embodies feeling, and this embodiment is perhaps the greatest treasure of lyric poetry. In translating, I mean to place the integrity of the image over all other considerations." This adherence to the primacy of image not only fit neatly into Kenyon's own poetics, but was also based in the poetics of the group of poets Akhmatova belonged to before the 1917 revolution. Kenyon wrote, "Acmeism held that a rose is beautiful in itself, not because it stands for something . . . . clarity, concision, and perfection of form. They summed up their goals in two words: 'beautiful clarity.' " These words could function as Kenyon's own aesthetic principles, just as the poems she selected to translate speak directly to her own poems.

In the first translation in the collection "The memory of sun weakens my heart," the lines evoke an elegance that Kenyon aspired to in *From Room to Room*. Readers can hear echoes of Akhmatova's lines, such as "Against the empty sky the willow opens / a transparent fan. / Maybe it's a good thing I'm not / your wife," in "Now That We Live" and other poems in Kenyon's first book. The difference, however, is that Akhmatova's voice has the confidence and power that is lacking in *From Room to Room*. Even though Kenyon's efforts to master the pre-revolutionary poetic concerns of Akhmatova was her way of constructing a poetics of her own, there is a troubling thought that arises when considering what she ignored: Akhmatova's later more epic and political work, including "Requiem" and "Song Without a Hero," two poems considered her greatest and most ambitious achievements. Nevertheless, this choice is typical of Kenyon who seemed to refuse to look where others have already gazed.

RELIGIOUS AWAKENING

While immersed in the translations, Kenyon was clearly aware of the irony that both she and Akhmatova considered their marriages to be the beginning of their lives. For Kenyon, this was not simply because her adult life began at the same time as her marriage to Hall. The life at Eagle Pond and the surrounding community that she discovered through Hall's roots gave Kenyon a surge of power and clarity that led to the resolution of the spiritual emptiness she experienced as

a child. Her spiritual journey began as simply and prosaically as an image in one of her poems. One Sunday, Hall suggested they go to church. At first it was more of a social act than a spiritual one, but soon the experience became "luminous." She started to take comfort from prayer and the assurance of pardon for sins. The sense of relief that came from this acceptance coincided with her realization that she couldn't avoid those human qualities, like selfishness and irritability, which she had hoped she would transcend. Prayer offered her a chance to acknowledge her own failings and start over.

At the suggestion of her pastor at South Danbury Church Kenyon began to read the New Testament. She started with Mark's Gospel with Barclay's commentary, and went on to read the other gospels as well as the Acts of the Apostles, the Epistles, the Prophets, and the Psalms. In her essay "Gabriel's Truth," collected in *A Hundred White Daffodils,* she wrote, "Mary teaches us to trust God always, to live in hope, to respond with love to whatever happens, to give and not count the cost, to be faithful in the worst circumstances. She teaches us, men and women, not to insist on ourselves, on our own comforts and satisfactions. And she shows us, finally, that her strenuous love was able to defeat death." Not surprisingly, this passage encompasses many of the concerns Kenyon had had since childhood. It also accentuated another connection of hers. Once again, Kenyon finds truth and meaning through the words, actions, and legacy of a woman.

In most of her prose and interviews Kenyon refers to a turning point in her life. In 1980 she had a vision that deepened her faith and clarified her understanding of her place in the world. "It was like a waking dream. My eyes were open and I saw these rooms, this house, but in my mind's eye, or whatever language you can find to say these things, I also saw a great ribbon of light and every human life was suspended. There was no struggle. There was only this buoyant shimmering, undulating stream of light. I took my place in the stream and after that my life changed fundamentally. I relaxed into existence in a way that I never had before," Kenyon described in an interview with Bill Moyers, collected in *A Hundred White Daffodils*. After this experience, her poetry changed profoundly. It became more assertive and more clearly spiritual, which particularly becomes clear in her last book, *Otherwise: New and Selected Poems* (1996). In her short essay "Thoughts on the Gifts of Art" from *A Hundred White Daffodils,* Kenyon described her belief that every poem is "a state-of-the-soul address" and expanded on this with the statement, "Artists report on the inner life, and the inner life distinguishes us from centipedes, although I may underestimate centipedes."

THE BOAT OF QUIET HOURS

Kenyon's next collection of poems, *The Boat of Quiet Hours,* published the year following her translations and contains sixty-two poems. In this collection, a New England stoicism arises that cannot help, with its reference to John Keats' *Endymion, Book I* in the title, to be perceived as a contemporary permutation of Kenyon's beloved poet Keats' concept of negative capability. In these portraits of domestic and rural life in northern New England there exists a selfless receptivity to the subject. In a review of *The Boat of Quiet Hours* poet and critic Carol Muske wrote in the *New York Times,* "These poems surprise beauty at every turn and capture truth at its familiar New England slant. Here, in Keats' terms, is a capable poet" (June 21, 1987). The book opens with "Evening at a Country Inn" where the dramatic situation is the speaker empathizing with her companion's mourning. The poem is striking for its active energy, which is expressed in lines such as that describing a red cloud as "impaled on the Town Hall weathervane." This kind of verb

signals a definite change for Kenyon from the tentativeness of the speaker in *From Room to Room.* A few lines later she writes, "Red-faced skiers stamp past you; their hunger is Homeric." The hyperbolic looseness reminds the reader that the process of dying happens in the midst of living. The wrenching tenderness of the last lines of the poem are particularly Keatsian in their attempt to redeem her lingering on death with a kind of gusto for life. The lines look for comfort in the quiet reduction of self's presence through its identification with the inanimate:

> I know you are thinking of the accident—
> of picking the slivered glass from his hair.
> Just now a truck loaded with hay
> stopped at the village store to get gas.
> I wish you would look at the hay—
> the beautiful sane and solid bales of hay.

These last lines of the first poem in the book could easily be taken as a statement of her poetics: what you see will redeem you. In this vein, the collection is then arranged into four seasons as if to track how life follows the cycles of nature, but there is a difference. Kenyon subtracts autumn and inserts what all New Englanders consider the fifth season, mud season. The first section, "Walking Along in Winter," contains poems about death and loss. "At the Town Dump" echoes Theodore Roethke's poem "Root Cellar" in the belief in the value of even the most useless trash. "I offer it to oblivion / with the rest of what was mine." Not only what you see, but also what you leave behind, will redeem you. In "Killing the Plants" she takes this position a step too far by comparing her neglect of her plants to Hamlet's rehearsal of murdering Claudius. Clearly, the plants cannot be as guilty or deserving of revenge as Claudius. The extremely tenuous connection of this hyperbole to the scene described in the poem cannot sustain the exaggeration.

Section Two, "Mud Season," has a kind of Frostean edge in that the poems examine transitional spaces. Just as spring is a season that has the characteristics of both winter and summer, the poems in this section exhibit an occlusion that explores the difficulty of making clear distinctions in life. "The Pond at Dusk" looks at that time of day that is neither day nor night, when it is most difficult to see: ". . . what looks like smoke / floating over the neighbor's barn / is only apple blossoms." The speaker's descriptions seem contradictory because nothing can be made out in this light: "A fly wounds the water but the wound / soon heals" and "The green haze on the trees changes / into leaves." The titles of poems like "Evening Sun," "Sun and Moon," and "Frost Flowers," embody these confusions, while the poem "Photograph of a Child on a Vermont Hillside" explores how a photograph, which is a representation of someone, cannot really know that person. The photograph, like a poem, can contain an image but its meaning will always be elusive.

The third section, "The Boat of Quiet Hours," takes its inspiration from the lines in Keats' poem *Endymion, Book I:*, "And, as the year / Grows lush in juicy stalks, I'll smoothly steer / My little boat, for many quiet hours. . . ." Consequently, the poems offer images that are finely observed.

> Now all the doors and windows
> are open, and we move so easily
> through the rooms. Cats roll
> on the sunny rugs, and a clumsy wasp
> climbs the pane, pausing
> to rub a leg over her head.

This first stanza of "Philosophy in Warm Weather" celebrates how in spring "all around physical life reconvenes." Kenyon explains her premise a few lines down: "Heat, Horatio, *heat* makes them / put this antic disposition on!" And again she references Shakespeare's *Hamlet*. This time, however, it works because she is not only taking on Hamlet's identity, but is also explaining what makes the world seem so crazy. There is no stretch in the playfulness of her reference the way

the hyperbole failed in "Killing the Plants." Her feelings about being as alive as everything is in spring are brought into focus in "Camp Evergreen." The optimistic slant of the title cues the audience even before they encounter the mischievous images of "boats like huge bright birds" and "a fish astonishes the air, falls back / into its element." All she really does in this poem is luxuriate in the sunlight, but still she knows that this ecstasy cannot be sustained.

> Now it is high summer: the solstice:
> longed-for, possessed, luxurious, and sad.

This quiet turn toward darkness resonates in this section because Kenyon can never seem to fully release herself into rapture. She tries, however, in poems such as "The Bat," which describes a moment when the speaker is suddenly confronted with a bat in her room. The poem explores how inspiration occurs without explanation and uses a startling comparison to illustrate this violence of the experience.

> At every turn [the bat] evaded us
> like the identity of the third person
> in the Trinity: the one
> who spoke through the prophets,
> the one who astonished Mary
> by suddenly coming near.

In her interview with Bill Moyers, Kenyon explained "The Bat": "What I had in mind was being broken in upon, the way Mary was broken in upon by Gabriel. You think you're alone and suddenly there's this thing coming near you, so near that you can feel the wind from the brushing of the wings." At least there is the possibility of exultation in the notion that a bat's sudden appearance can be similar to the experience of the Holy Ghost. Just this kind of contingency represents how Kenyon's poems move toward a resolution, but never quite arrive. In an interview with David Bradt, Kenyon had talked about the importance of Anton Chekhov to her work. This resistance on her part to closure, as well as her absence of moral judgment, in her poems seems directly influenced by Chekhov and stories like "Misery" and "Lady with the Pet Dog." In a letter to Aleksey S. Suvorin in *Letters on the Short Story, the Drama, and Other Literary Topics by Anton Chekhov,* Chekhov insisted on the importance of "objectivity. . . . The artist is not meant to be a judge . . . his only job is to be an impartial witness." Because of her own history of coming in conflict with others' truths, Kenyon would never insist on a particular way.

The Boat of Quiet Hours ends on an optimistic note in the season of summer. Section Four, "Things," starts with a song that reaches past Kenyon's strict adherence to T. S. Eliot's notion of the objective correlative. Instead, the speaker of "Song" attempts to say that there are times when even an external equivalent cannot stand for the internal state of mind that she feels right now.

> . . . But even this
> is not the joy that trembles
> under every leaf and tongue.

The statement is remarkable for its implications of an abundance that extends beyond the limits of summer's verdant tangle. In Kenyon's attempt to map out this unmarked territory in some of the poems that follow, the reader discovers that this outer region actually is the beyond. First, "The Visit" acts like a familiar landmark by occupying that transition space of dusk between life and death, while suggesting a presence of what is beyond the known.

> . . . but now I am aware
> of the silence, and your affection,
> and the delicate sadness of dusk.

This anchor in the darkness leads the reader through a series of poems that follow the dying of Kenyon's father. The series begins with "Par-

ents' Weekend: Camp Kenwood," which contrasts the parents visiting across the pond to the freedom that she has in her own world. This is followed by several poems that directly address her father dying, "Reading Late of the Death of Keats," "Inpatient," "Campers Leaving: Summer 1981," "Travel: After a Death," and "Yard Sale." The pages end with the title poem of the section "Things." This is a poem of acceptance.

> Things: simply lasting, then
> failing to last: water, a blue heron's
> eye, and the light passing
> between them: into light all things
> must fall, glad at last to have fallen.

These last lines in the poem offer comfort by reminding the reader that things change. After summer, autumn arrives. The leaves fall. This ending is the beginning.

LET EVENING COME

Like *The Boat of Quiet Hours,* Kenyon's third volume of poetry, *Let Evening Come* (1990), explores nature's cycles, but these five-dozen first-person lyrics take "a darker turn." Published four years after her previous collection, this book picks up where *The Boat* left off by leaving that in-between space of dusk and entering evening, as well as by beginning with a poem that marks the end of summer. "Three Songs at the End of Summer" offers a shift in tone from one of rapture and hopefulness to sadness. The first song speaks of campers no longer having the time to learn to water ski, while the second song pushes beyond simply time running out to a sadness that is unhinged outside any seemingly causal chain.

> Then why did I cry today
> for an hour, with my whole
> body, the way babies cry?

The last song in the series suggests a deep change in Kenyon's countenance by discarding her faith in the redeeming potential of the image with the line "A white, indifferent morning sky." The song goes on to describe a state in which she "did not / comprehend" and closes with words of deep hopelessness: "It was the only life I had."

The surprise about this change in demeanor is that *Let Evening Come* is clearly a work of a mature poet and exhibits this maturity in the cohesiveness of the collection. Unlike those in Kenyon's earlier books, the poems here are not divided into sections. Poet and critic Alfred Corn observed this harmony in his March 24, 1991, *New York Times* review, "This 'sunset' collection is unified around themes of nightfall, the sense of endings, the death of family and friends and, implicitly, the maturing of a poetic talent." Kenyon locates herself in and around the countryside near her home, but in this territory she is plainly at loose ends as the last lines of "After Working Long" express.

The sky won't darken in the west
until ten. Where shall I turn
this light and tired mind?

As in this poem, the lines turn from certainty to uncertainty. The use of questions and ellipses multiplies in relation to earlier collections. It is as if she has found the place, both emotionally and aesthetically, she so desperately searched for, and has discovered that the arrival did not supply the answer. Consequently, she wanders with her dog in a landscape that cannot console her.

In "Catching Frogs" the speaker waits for the right moment to scoop up the creature that never seems to come. Instead, "It grew dark." The poem ends with a meditation about the sense of absence after her father's death.

I came into the warm, bright room
where father held aloft the evening
paper, and there was talk, and maybe
laughter, though I don't remember laughter.

For Kenyon in these times, the evening can no longer be held "aloft" or at bay. She must "let evening come" just as she says in her title poem, and have courage in the face of its darkness.

Let the cricket take up chafing
as a woman takes up her needles
and her yarn. Let evening come.

In this poem, a series of details are presented in a declining light in order to offer a prayer at the end of day: "God does not leave us / comfortless, so let evening come." At this moment of impending darkness and desolation the speaker turns to prayer, because as Kenyon had discovered a decade earlier and had written about in "Childhood, When You Are in It . . . ," people can take "comfort from the prayer of confession and the assurance of pardon." From this point of expectancy Kenyon makes it possible for the reader to turn to the last poem in the book, "With the Dog at Sunrise." Like the setting's time of day this poem offers rejuvenation of a kind. The drama of the lyric is situated around a meditation on what to say to a friend who is widowed at the age of thirty-one. This thematic dilemma is reflective of the struggles explored in the previous poems in the book, but suddenly there is a change in energy. Her eye notices "that the poplars / growing along the ravine / shine pink in the light of winter dawn." With the first lines the redemptive power of the image has returned. Kenyon has restored her faith in the "luminous image." Consequently, as she ranges the countryside she affirms that "Searching for God is the first thing and the last, / but in between such trouble, and such pain." This collection represents a turning toward the trouble and pain, and then finally a gazing toward God.

From this anchor Kenyon was able to examine a thematic concern that has lurked in all her poems but which until *Constance* (1993) was not directly addressed. Kenyon's work has been compared to Sylvia Plath in this respect, but there are, however, important differences in their treatments of depression as a theme. While Plath's poems can be overwrought, self-absorbed, and self-dramatizing, Kenyon's work contains a New England reserve that makes her poems much quieter and absent of histrionics. Also, Plath was obviously consumed by her depression. In contrast, Kenyon never gives up the fight. When discussing her depression with Bill Moyers, she explained why she would never commit suicide: "My belief in God, such as it is, especially the idea that the believer is part of the body of Christ, has kept me from harming myself. . . . I've thought to myself, 'If you injure yourself you're injuring the body of Christ, and Christ has been injured enough."

CONSTANCE

No matter how emotionally exhausted Kenyon became, her faith pulled her through. This is evident in *Constance,* in which she dips to the depths but then finds a way to break through the melancholy. This "was lost, but now found" theme is apparent in earlier poems in *The Boat of Quiet Hours.* In "February: Thinking of Flowers" Kenyon writes, "A single green sprouting thing / would restore me." In *Constance* she has learned to call out more vigorously. The poem "Peonies at Dusk" focuses on the glory of the lifting, rather than the pale hope of a sprout.

> White peonies blooming along the porch
> send out light
> while the rest of the yard grows dim.
> . . . .
> I draw a blossom near, and bending close
> search it as a woman searches
> a loved one's face.

Her lover is joy, not depression. This is perhaps why *Constance* begins with a long portion of Psalm 139 as an epigraph. This psalm describes the presence of God everywhere, even in darkness: "Yea, the darkness hideth not from thee: / but night shineth as day." Without this faith, it is clear Kenyon would not have been able to battle depression to a draw most times, and sometimes win. "Having It Out With Melancholy" is her longest poem and rightfully so since it is here that she illustrates that confrontation. The poem begins with an epigraph from Chekhov that sounds a note of hopelessness: "If many remedies are prescribed for an illness, you may be certain that the illness has no cure." The poem itself is divided into nine parts and covers one hundred lines. For a poet who describes herself as dedicated to the lyric, this poem extends to the outer boundaries of its possibility, but because of the divisions, the poem reads more as a series of nine lyric poems. Part One, "From the Nursery," is an indictment of melancholy's persistence. Framed in a series of second person accusations, the speaker catalogs how melancholy wronged her and concludes with an apostrophe calling the disease "the mutilator of souls."

As a counterpoint, Part Two, "Bottles," describes medications used to cope with depression.

> Elavil, Ludiomil, Doxepin,
> Norpramin, Prozac, Lithium, Xanax,
> Wellbutrin, Parnate, Nardil, Zoloft.

Part Three, "Suggestion from a Friend," records the pain of others not understanding, while Part Four, "Often," chronicles how she copes with depression by going "to bed as soon after dinner / as seems adult." Until this point the poem is more like a report than a poem, as if the world of melancholy was prosaic, not poetic. The next section, "Once There Was Light," gives an account of the transforming vision she had in her early thirties, but this reprieve is not long lasting.

> Like a crow who smells hot blood
> you came flying to pull me out
> of the glowing stream.

The unrelenting presence of depression becomes a battle that has only small victories, such as the comfort of her dog's companionship and the sudden effectiveness of "monoamine / oxidase inhibitors."

> I come back to marriage and friends,
> to pink fringed hollyhocks; come back
> to my desk, books, and chair.

Surprisingly, Kenyon calls her personified depression the "Unholy ghost." This characterization seems to represent the depths that it can take her, since repeatedly in the past Kenyon has spoken about the redemptive power of the Holy Ghost. Fortunately, the poem turns optimistic in Part Nine, "Wood Thrush." This section echoes Frost's poem "Come In," in which the song of a thrush draws his attention away from the coming darkness and from thoughts of suicide. The speaker in Part Nine finds peace of mind while "waiting greedily for the first / note of the wood thrush." At this moment, her anticipation leads her to a feeling of being "overcome / by ordinary contentment." The word "overcome" emphasizes the degree of melancholy she has reached because it implies a depression so deep that achieving ordinariness is an extraordinary feat. There is an underlying sadness that reverberates in her final celebration of the thrush.

> How I love the small, swiftly
> beating heart of the bird
> singing in the great maples;
> its bright, unequivocal eye.

The superlatives in these lines feel desperate in their over-reaching descriptiveness.

Melancholy, however, is not the only kind of suffering *Constance* records. In "The Pharaoh" the reader learns that the speaker's husband, like her father a number of years before, has been diagnosed with cancer. The poem first delves into how life changes after the news.

> Things are off: Touch rankles, food
> Is not good. Even the kindness of friends
> Turns burdensome. . . .

But the last stanza reminds the reader that her husband's potential death is what the speaker really must confront. To do so, she attempts to ennoble him and his life by comparing him to an Egyptian pharaoh, saying:

> The things you might need in the next
> life surround you—your comb and glasses,
> water, a book and a pen.

One of the powers of this book lies in the ability of the speaker to transcend self-pity. This trait manifests itself most sharply in poems like "Coats," "Sleepers in Jaipur," and "Gettysburg: July 1, 1863" in which the speaker can separate from herself and appreciate the grief and emotional pain of others. Nevertheless, this unsparing eye can be directed at herself as well. The poem "Otherwise" deals with the troubles she had to overcome, not just her depression and her husband's cancer, but her own bout with a cancerous salivary gland in the late 1980s. The poem is structured in a kind of call-and-response arrangement where the speaker makes a rather mundane statement about the day and follows it with response of "It might have been otherwise." The poem's last lines contain what can be considered the final call-and-response.

> I slept in a bed
> in a room with paintings
> on the walls, and
> planned another day
> just like this day.
> But one day, I know,
> it will be otherwise.

OTHERWISE: NEW AND SELECTED POEMS

In *Constance* Kenyon draws on her deep belief that there is a regenerative force operating in the world. This belief was what sustained her as more tragedy entered her life. Though her husband Donald Hall survived two bouts with cancer, Kenyon contracted fatal leukemia. Her last book, *Otherwise: New and Selected Poems* (1996), was published posthumously and provides a remarkable document of her life's work. One hundred and fifty-five poems came from her first four books, while twenty poems were previously unpublished; the last poem in the collection, "The Sick Wife," was the last poem that she worked on. The lack of a thematic cohesiveness to the new poems gives them an unfinished feeling in comparison to the polished and considered arrangement of her poems in previous books. In this vein the lead poem seems appropriate. "Happiness" observes how the emotion arrives suddenly "like a prodigal / who comes back" and visits so randomly that,

> It even comes to the boulder
> in the perpetual shade of pine barrens,
> to the rain falling on the open sea,
> to the wineglass, weary of holding wine.

In the end, the poem appears sadly ironic because the apparent subject of happiness is undermined by an undercurrent of helplessness and lack of control. Happiness comes without reason, and by extension everything else arrives by similar means. This submerged desperation breaks out in the next poem, "Mosaic of the Nativity: Serbia, Winter 1993," where God bemoans His inability to control what He has created.

> On the domes ceiling God
> is thinking:
> I made them my joy. . . .
> But see what they do!

"Mosaic" is perhaps Kenyon's most non-Kenyonian poem. Located far from her home in New Hampshire, the poem contains an explicit political message framed in religious terms.

The poems that follow exhibit a quiet withdrawal by the speaker to a stance of observation, but this position is different from earlier work in that her eye reveals a world predicated on suffering. In "Man Eating" the speaker focuses on what the food is not ("caused no animal / to suffer") and ends with an inorganic image that is clearly not life affirming ("he is eating / with a pearl-white plastic spoon"). The speaker asks what has happened to her gardens and the countryside she has spent her life ranging.

This dislocation manifests more plainly in "Cesarean," a poem in which the speaker imagines herself at birth being delivered by C-section. Aside from the unnatural violence of the procedure, the poem is equally disturbing in its improbability. The baby, the speaker of the poem, observes, "The clatter, / the white light, the vast freedom / were terrible." Kenyon is no longer simply facing the darkness; she is being consumed by it. The poem "Surprise" exhibits a similar turn. The speaker finds betrayal, rather than the delight she has expressed in so many earlier poems, when her husband throws her a surprise party,

> . . . . The gathering
> itself is not what astounds her, but the casual
> accomplishment with which he has lied.

Other poems journey far from home into the past, the funeral home, the doctor's office, the nursing home, the New Hampshire MacDowell artists' colony and the town of Franklin, Dutch design, and finally her father's bedside. What is striking is how displaced from the cycles of nature these poems are. The only poem really inhabiting the natural world is a spare seven-line, thirty-five-word poem called "Spring Evening." The poem is remarkable in its utter absence of a self. It is as if the speaker does not exist within this province where images of abundance are observed.

Again the thrush affirms
both dusk and dawn. . . .

Frost's thrush returns, but its song is not special. The bird merely sings as it has seemingly done a hundred times before, the "again" underscoring the notion that the image cannot resonate.

The final poem in *Otherwise,* perhaps unfinished, is "The Sick Wife." This poem aches with just the kind of self-pity that Kenyon was able to avoid in the face of her depression, but cannot do so when confronting her mortality. She has earned this self-indulgence, however, because she is dealing with a fatal illness. She should be bitter and angry as well, but she is not. Instead she is simply overwhelmed with a sense of sadness.

The windows began to steam up.
The cars on either side of her
pulled away so briskly
that it made her sick at heart.

The occlusion and abandonment described in these lines offers enough of a glimpse at her suffering for the reader to understand the magnitude of knowing you are about to die. This is intensified by Kenyon's understatement. She does not list all the people she loves whom she will leave behind. Instead, she merely hints at the immensity of that loss by describing the sense of separation she feels sitting alone in a car. This lack of explicitness makes these lines all the more powerful and attest to Kenyon's enormous poetic gifts.

OTHER POSTHUMOUS WORKS

Just before her death, Pulitzer Prize-winning composer William Bolcom contacted Kenyon to put a selection of her poems to music. In her last months she and Bolcom worked together to select the texts. The result was a carefully planned sequence called *Briefly It Enters: A Cycle of Songs from Poems of Jane Kenyon: For Voice and Piano 1994–1996.* This work takes a listener progressively deeper into a sense of Kenyon's life, beginning with "Who," which imagines Kenyon's poetry emerging from some source beyond herself, "The Clearing," "Otherwise," "The Sick Wife," and concluding with "Briefly It Enters, and Briefly Speaks." This delicate, nuanced composition with discreetly melodic turns flirts with sentimentality, but just as Kenyon's poems resist melodrama so does Bolcom's piece. A year after her death composer J. Mark Scearce put three of Kenyon's poems to music in a piece called *American Tryptich: For Soprano, Flute, Clarinet/Bass Clarinet, Violin, Cello, Piano, and Percussion: On Three Poems by Jane Kenyon.*

The last book of Kenyon's work, published in 1999, was *A Hundred White Daffodils.* This book essentially assembles in one volume everything but her poetry. Though Kenyon did not write much prose, in the early 1990s she did write a column for her local newspaper, *The Concord Monitor.* These pieces celebrate in prose the world she loved so deeply—her garden, friends, and activities. Each of these columns could stand in some sense as a statement on her art. In the column "The Five-and-Dime" she writes "half the fun of real dime stores, aside from their dedicated *thinginess,* is that the stuff is really cheap." Kenyon appreciation for dime stores seems so appropriate since in her own way she was dedicated to *thinginess.*

The only poem collected in *A Hundred White Daffodils,* "Woman, Why Are You Weeping?" is one that Kenyon did not want included in her selected poems. It is a poem she did not feel was finished and so was reluctant to publish. Hall, rightfully so, includes this powerful and ambitious work. "Woman, Why Are You Weeping?" points to a complexity and depth that Kenyon might have turned to if she had lived. Deeply and explicitly religious, it compares her loss of faith to the disappearance of Christ from his grave after his crucifixion. Dying and alone, the speaker feels forsaken by all gods.

> The fire cares nothing for my illness
> nor does Brahma, the creator, nor Shiva who sees
> evil with his terrible third eye; Vishnu,
> the protector, does not protect me.

The utter despair in this poem is unrelenting. The only response for the reader is to mourn. The speaker asks " 'What shall we do about this?' " but offers no answer other than pain and indifference.

> . . . . The reply
> was scorching wind, lapping of water, pull
> of the black oarsmen on the oars . . . .

The weather, trees, animals, tender companionship, home, and work where she found joy, healing, and answers to significant questions are now absent. A terrible truth about the world has descended upon her, and the tools Kenyon had spent a lifetime honing fail her. A reader cannot help but be deeply saddened by the loss of this profound talent.

Selected Bibliography

WORKS OF JANE KENYON

POETRY

From Room to Room. Farmington, Maine: Alice James Books, 1978.

The Boat of Quiet Hours. St. Paul, Minn.: Graywolf Press, 1986.

Let Evening Come. St. Paul, Minn. Graywolf Press, 1990.

Constance. St. Paul, Minn: Graywolf Press, 1993.

Otherwise: New & Selected Poems. Afterword by Donald Hall. St. Paul, Minn.: Graywolf Press, 1996.

UNCOLLECTED POEMS

"What It's Like." *Ploughshares* 5, no 2:58 (1979).

"Indolence in Early Winter." *New Letters* 47, no. 1:23 (Fall 1980). Reprinted in *New Letters* 49, nos. 3–4: 33 (Spring–Summer 1983).

"At the IGA: Franklin, New Hampshire." *Ontario Review* 31:87 (Fall–Winter 1989).

TRANSLATIONS

Twenty Poems of Anna Akhmatova. Translated by Jane Kenyon and Vera Sandomirsky Dunham and with an introduction by Jane Kenyon. St. Paul, Minn.: Eighties Press and Ally Press, 1985; St. Paul, Minn.: Nineties Press and Ally Press, 1994.

OTHER WORKS

Green House. Coedited with Joyce Peseroff. Danbury, N.H.: Vol. 1, No. 1 (Spring 1976); Vol. 1, No. 2 (Winter 1977); Vol. 1, No. 3 (Summer 1977); Vol. 2, No. 1 (Winter 1978); Vol. 2, No. 2 (Summer 1978); Vol. 3, No. 1 (Winter 1980).

"Cages," "The Circle on the Grass," "The Suitor," "At a Motel near O'Hare Airport." In *The Third Coast: Contemporary Michigan Poetry.* Edited by Conrad Hilberry et al. Detroit: Wayne State University Press, 1976.

"From Room to Room." In *Good Company: Poets at Michigan.* Edited and with photographs by Jeanne Rockwell. Ann Arbor, Mich.: Noon Rock, 1977.

"Three Songs at the End of Summer." In *The Best American Poetry 1989.* Edited by Donald Hall. New York: Scribners, 1989.

"Let Evening Come." In *The Best American Poetry 1991.* Edited by Mark Strand. New York: Scribners, 1991.

"Kicking the Eggs." In *Walking Swiftly: Writings in Honor of Robert Bly.* Edited by Thomas R. Smith. St. Paul, Minn.: Ally Press, 1992.

"Having It Out With Melancholy." In *The Best American Poetry 1993.* Edited by Louise Gluck. New York: Macmillan/Collier Books, 1993.

"Reading Aloud to My Father." In *The Best American Poetry 1996.* Edited by Adrienne Rich. New York: Scribners, 1996.

"Three Songs at the End of Summer." In *The Best of the Best American Poetry, 1988–1997.* Edited by Harold Bloom. New York: Scribners, 1998.

A Hundred White Daffodils: Essays, Newspaper Columns, Notes, Interviews, and One Poem. St. Paul, Minn.: Graywolf Press, 1999.

PHOTOGRAPHY

Hall, Donald, with Dock Ellis. *Dock Ellis in the Country of Baseball.* With thirteen photographs by Jane Kenyon. New York: Coward, McCann & Geoghegan, 1976.

VIDEO RECORDINGS

Poets Read Their Work, Donald Hall and Jane Kenyon. Stony Brook, N.Y.: Educational Communications Center, State University of New York at Stony Brook,1977.

The Poetry of Jane Kenyon, Ai, Lawrence Kearney and Kathleen Spivak. Stony Brook, N.Y.: Poetry Center Production, State University of New York at Stony Brook, 1978.

A Life Together: Donald Hall and Jane Kenyon. Princeton, N.J.: Films for the Humanities, Inc., 1994. (First broadcast on PBS on December 17, 1993, as *Bill Moyers' Journal.*)

Jane Kenyon: A Celebration of Her Life and Works. Durham, N. H.: University of New Hampshire Library, 1995

Donald Hall and Jane Kenyon: "Keeping You Safe Beside Me." Indiana, Pa.: The Indiana University of Pennsylvania, 1999.

SOUND RECORDINGS

Jane Kenyon I. Kansas City, Mo: University of Missouri, 1987.

Jane Kenyon II: Memorial. Kansas City, Mo.: University of Missouri, 1995.

MUSICAL SCORES

Bolcom, William. *Let Evening Come: A Cantata.* (Text based on poems by Jane Kenyon, Emily Dickinson and Maya Angelou. Premiere, New York City in 1994. Soprano, Benita Valente; piano, Cynthia Raim.)

———. *Briefly It Enters: A Song Cycle.* (Sets nine Jane Kenyon poems to music. World premiere, University of Michigan, Ann Arbor, on September 27, 1996. Soprano, Benita Valente; piano, Cynthia Raim. Commissioned by Benita Valente.)

———. *Briefly It Enters: A Cycle of Songs From Poems of Jane Kenyon: For Voice and Piano 1994–1996.* Milwaukee, Wisc.: E. B. Marks. Exclusively distributed by H. Leonard, 1997.

Scearce, J. Mark. *American Triptych: For Soprano, Flute, Clarinet/Bass Clarinet, Violin, Cello, Piano, and Percussion: On Three Poems by Jane Kenyon.* N.p., August 1997.

ADDITIONAL WORKS BY OR ABOUT JANE KENYON

Blue, Marian. "A Conversation with Poets Donald Hall & Jane Kenyon." *AWP Chronicle* 27, no. 6:1–8 (May–Summer 1995).

Bly, Robert. "The Yellow Dot." In *The Morning Poems.* New York: HarperCollins, 1997.

Bradt, David. "Jane Kenyon Interview." *The Plum Review* 10:115–128 (September 1996).

Corn, Alfred. "Plural Perspectives, Heightened Perceptions." *The New York Times,* Late Edition, section 7, March 24, 1991, p. 26.

Cramer, Jeffrey. "With Jane and Without: An Interview with Donald Hall." *The Massachusetts Review* 39, no. 4:493–511 (Winter 1998–1999).

Farrow, Anne. "Into Light All Things Must Fall." In *Northeast: The Hartford Courant Sunday Magazine.* August 27, 1995, p. 9.

The First Jane Kenyon Conference: April 16–18, 1998. Louisville, Ky.: Bellarmine College, 1998. (Sound recording.)

Germain, Edward. "Jane Kenyon." In *Contemporary Poets,* 6th ed. Edited by Thomas Riggs. New York: St. James Press, 1996.

Hall, Donald. "Life After Jane: An Essay." *Northeast: The Hartford Courant Sunday Magazine.* August 27, 1995, pp. 6–8.

Hornback, Bert, ed. *Bright Unequivocal Eye: Poems, Papers, and Remembrances from the First Jane Kenyon Conference.* New York: Peter Lang Press, 2000.

"Jane Kenyon Portfolio." *Meridian: The Semi-Annual from the University of Virginia.* 4:37–80 (Fall 1999).

Life at Eagle Pond: The Poetry of Jane Kenyon and Donald Hall. Special Collections Library website, University of New Hampshire, Durham, N.H. wwwsc.library.unh.edu/specoll/exhibits/kenhall .htm (1996).

Moyers, Bill. "Jane Kenyon." In *The Language of Life: A Festival of Poets.* New York: Doubleday, 1995. (Includes an interview with Jane Kenyon and eleven poems: "Here," "From Room to Room," "Finding a Long Gray Hair," "February: Thinking of Flowers," "Depression in Winter," "Having It Out With Melancholy," "Peonies at Dusk," "The Bat," "Pharaoh," "Otherwise," "Let Evening Come." This book is based upon the PBS television series of the same name.)

Muske, Carol. "Reading Their Signals." *The New York Times,* Late Edition, section 7, June 21, 1987, p. 13.

"Special Section Dedicated to the Memory of Jane Kenyon." *Xylem: The University of Michigan Undergraduate Literary Journal* XII:54–64 (Winter 1996).

"A Tribute to Jane Kenyon 1947–1995." *Columbia: A Journal of Literature and Art.* 26:154–181 (1996).

—LABAN HILL

Jamaica Kincaid

1949–

JAMAICA KINCAID ACKNOWLEDGES that she blurs the line between fact and fabrication in her writing. A persistently autobiographical writer whether she is writing about family, colonialism, or gardening, she finds traditional genre distinctions confining and prefers to use literary forms—the short story, novel, memoir, and essay—as though they were colors on a palette to be mixed at will within any one composition. In an interview with Moira Ferguson, she said, "I am so happy to write that I don't care what you call it," and, indeed, her self-referential fiction and nonfiction alike are charged with the same sense of urgency and the same need to come to terms with her past and with her place in the world. For Kincaid, writing is a cathartic act, and not only does she find genre categories irrelevant to her quest for understanding and clarity, she willfully embraces ambiguity and contradiction: In an interview with Kay Bonetti, she said, "Everything I say is true, and everything I say is not true."

Kincaid's name, for instance, is true because she bestowed Jamaica Kincaid on herself when she became a writer, but she was born Elaine Potter Richardson on May 25, 1949, in St. John's, the capital of the small Caribbean island of Antigua. Precocious and outspoken as a schoolgirl, she loved to read and consumed British novels by the shelfful, lingering most intently over the works of Charlotte Brontë, whose influence on her work is enormous. But Kincaid also became highly sensitive to the racial prejudice and deep-rooted chauvinism inherent in her British-oriented education, refusing, at age nine, to stand up for the refrain "God Save Our King" in "Rule, Britannia." She has written often about her intuitive opposition to colonial culture, and her recognition, which was triggered in part by the packaging for household products imported from England—drawings of pale-skinned, flaxen-haired, blue-eyed girls, spring flowers, and snowy Christmases—of just how alien the English sensibility was to her, a brown-skinned, dark-eyed, black-haired resident of a mountainous, drought-afflicted tropical island saddled with a relatively unexamined history of conquest, genocide, slavery, and five centuries of imperialism. Long-simmering anger over this legacy is integral to Kincaid's work, but it is her impassioned, not to say obsessive, scrutiny of her relationship with her mother that imbues her writings with their searing vehemence, arresting clarity, and harsh beauty.

KINCAID'S CHILDHOOD

Kincaid has described her childhood relationship with her mother, Annie Richardson Drew, as a "love affair," and her childhood as a paradise. An only child, Kincaid was made to feel that she was the center of a benign universe ruled by her mother, who she revered. Drew was politically active in her youth, and is by all accounts an extremely intelligent, well-read, strict, and commanding woman. She doted on her young daughter, taught her to read well before she entered school, and fostered her love of books by bringing her to the library every week. Kincaid also adored her father, David Drew, a skilled carpenter who was much older than his wife. But her reign as the only child came to a crushing end when she was nine years old (the same year she refused to honor England's sovereignty), when her mother had the first of her three sons. Joseph was followed quickly by Dalma, and then Devon, in spite of Annie's efforts to terminate that pregnancy, an experience that Kincaid has never forgotten, and that appears repeatedly in her books with all the disquiet of a recurring nightmare.

Tall like her mother, skinny, and smart, Kincaid was the best student in her grade each year in spite of her resistance to the British point of view. At first her mother was proud of her scholastic achievements, but she soon began to criticize her daughter for her bookish ways. In an interview with Selwin Cudjoe, Kincaid said that "it grew to be a bone of contention between us because I liked to do nothing but read and would neglect my household duties. She could see that it gave me ideas, and that it took me away from her influence." Sure enough, the idyll of her early years gave way to persistent, bewildering, and painful adversity.

During Kincaid's thirteenth year, her father became ill and couldn't work, and she was taken out of school against her will to help her mother care for the boys, for whom she felt no affection. Furious at having her education terminated, and at the shocking realization of how little her parents valued her abilities or respected her desires, she left Antigua for the United States when she was seventeen in 1966 to work as an au pair for a family living in Scarsdale, New York; a momentous event that became the catalyst for her

writing. Kincaid has said that she never would have become a writer if she had not gone to America. In fact, she did not even know that writers still existed. Her schooling, and the public library collection she depended on to feed her unquenchable hunger for books, brought her no further than 1900, so it never occurred to her that great literature could be written in her lifetime.

LIFE IN AMERICA

Kincaid's parents expected her to study nursing in the United States and then return to Antigua to work, but Kincaid, who could not stand the sight of blood and had no interest whatsoever in either becoming a nurse or in returning home, went her own way. New York City drew her like a magnet, and she soon found a position in the Manhattan home of Michael Arlen, a writer for the *New Yorker* magazine, his first wife, and their four daughters. Her life with the Arlens surfaced, years later, in her second novel, *Lucy* (1990), an angry tale about a West Indian au pair in the employ of a family that closely resembles the Arlens. So thinly veiled and acerbic is her portrayal (which was perceived as an act of biting the hand that feeds), it sparked the first of many controversies ignited by her frank and uncompromising vision.

In spite of her fictionalized critique of their world, Kincaid would be the first to admit that her time with the Arlens was a crucial interlude. She transformed herself from a proper and modest Antiguan into a fashionable, hip, and fearless American, secured a high school equivalency diploma, and took photography courses at the New School for Social Research. She won a full scholarship to Franconia College in New Hampshire, but, unhappy and uninspired, she left after less than two years. She returned to New York City, held a series of low-level jobs at art galleries and magazines, and began to write. Meeting with success as a freelance journalist, she changed her name in 1973 to keep her work secret from her family, whom she knew would disapprove. She chose Jamaica to affirm her Caribbean roots, and Kincaid just for the way it sounded.

EARLY WRITINGS

Kincaid's earliest journalistic coups included an interview series she created for *Ingenue* magazine in 1973 titled "When I Was Seventeen," which got off to a good start with a conversation with Gloria Steinem. Reveling in the freedom of living on her own in a city open to every form of expression (she has said that she is American in spirit), Kincaid—cash-poor, bold, creative, and resourceful—concocted a new look to go with her new name. Already conspicuous by virtue of her height (5 feet 11 inches) and extreme thinness (107 pounds), she cut off her long black hair and dyed it blond; favored three-alarm red lipstick, and dressed in an extraordinary array of eccentric vintage clothing.

Kincaid's look was so provocative that she attracted the attention of Michael O'Donoghue, who worked for the *National Lampoon* and was one of the original writers for "Saturday Night Live." He introduced her to George W. S. Trow, a contributor to the *New Yorker*. Trow, suitably impressed, began writing about his flashy, outspoken, and smart black friend in "Talk of the Town" articles, and in 1974, he introduced her to the magazine's now legendary editor, William Shawn. Recognizing her unusual talent, Shawn invited Kincaid to write her own "Talk of the Town" pieces, and she wrote eighty-five pithy, unsigned essays for the magazine's front section over the course of her twenty years with the *New Yorker*. She became a staff writer in 1976, and much of her work appeared first in the *New Yorker*'s venerable pages, with two notable exceptions, the first of which was her first full-length essay, a veritable manifesto announcing her presence on the literary scene.

In October 1977, *Rolling Stone* devoted an entire issue to New York City. Andy Warhol's postage-stamp-like portraits of Bella Abzug graced the cover and within were articles by John Cage, Michael Herr, and Kincaid's former employer, Michael Arlen, as well as her own gutsy, self-revealing piece, "Jamaica Kincaid's New York." The article was accompanied by a full-page photograph of, as Kincaid slyly explains, the clothes she would have worn had she agreed to give the editors a photograph of herself. Kincaid actually is present albeit in the form of a silhouette. A shadow of her hatted profile is visible, as is one long, muscular arm clad only in a wristwatch, the hand holding a pen. The clothes—a jaunty outfit of striped shorts, with a pack of Lucky Strikes in the waist band, pink blouse, ribboned ballet shoes and purple anklets—are displayed, according to the arch and unsettling caption, in the manner in which authorities in South America display the clothes of the guerrillas they've murdered.

In her article, Kincaid chronicles her first impressions of New York, her surprise at the weather—"the sun is shining and you can still freeze to death"—and her "almost childish" delight at finding herself walking along Fifth Avenue. She then moves on to more piquant observations, articulating her perceptions of white and black Americans and their perception of her—whites love her fluty West Indian accent, blacks find her "ridiculous"—her ire at sophisticated people who unintentionally espouse racism at cocktail parties, and her preference for "bad" girls. Then she broaches the subject dearest to her heart, her devastating rift with her mother. In a startling admission, Kincaid confesses that in spite of how much anguish this causes her, she does not want to see a psychiatrist because she does not want to be cured of her feeling that her "mother's love is like a poison." Already she senses that her anger is the wellspring of her art.

This uncollected essay stands as a strikingly candid self-portrait of the artist as a young woman. Already on her way to becoming a master of narrative compression, Kincaid was working in a prose style as incantatory and multilayered as Gertrude Stein's, and as selective, concentrated, rhythmic, and repetitive as poetry, a voice that seems to have been forming inside her long before she put pen to paper. Kincaid comes across as self-possessed and tough, but there are unmistakable intimations of the little girl inside her, still longing for her mother's approval. She is cool and taunting, and she wants desperately to be loved.

The story of Kincaid's life is one of disenfranchisement, transformation, and self-expression. She has felt compelled to revisit her experiences as a girl in Antigua, as a newcomer in the United States, as a reluctant au pair, and as a struggling young woman trusting to fate, her muse, and her gift for survival over and over again, so much so that her work essentially forms a series of self-portraits. Traditionally, self-portraits serve as microcosms. The close study of the self is conducted first in an effort to divine the source and nature of one's own deepest feelings. The artist then applies this hard-earned self-knowledge to the study of others, beginning with family and then moving out into the community, society, and the world at large. This extrapolation from the personal to the universal has occupied Kincaid for more than two decades.

In her earliest writings, Kincaid stands close to the mirror and examines herself as her mother's darling. Then she steps back to include her mother within the frame, where she has remained. Annie Drew grew up on the island of Dominica, the daughter of one of the very few surviving Carib Indians and a part-Scot, part-African policeman, both of whom make their way into Kincaid's fiction, most prominently in her novel, *The Autobiography of My Mother* (1996). Kincaid's field of vision also includes her mother's husband, the man Kincaid loved as a father, and who raised her as his own. But David Drew is her stepfather. Kincaid did not meet her biological father, Frederick Potter, an illiterate taxi driver, until she was an adult and a published writer. Her feelings about him can be divined by how often criticism of irresponsible men who sire children and never evince any interest in them appears in her writings.

Father figures are important in Kincaid's literary universe, but it is her mother, an entity as awesome and mercurial as Mother Nature herself, who breathes life into her work. In speaking with Selwyn R. Cudjoe, Kincaid said, "the fertile soil of my creative life is my mother," and, indeed, it was her oft-stoked anguish over their estrangement that drove her to write "Girl," her first short story, in one epiphanic afternoon in 1978. Kincaid has said that after reading a poem by Elizabeth Bishop titled "In the Waiting Room," an unforgettable rendering of a child's sudden recognition of the self and its connection to all of humanity, she simply knew how to write, and "Girl," the first of many stories to be published in the *New Yorker*, became the first story in Kincaid's first book, *At the Bottom of the River* (1983), a short story collection which earned her instant critical success.

AT THE BOTTOM OF THE RIVER

A breathtaking, diabolically witty, and thoroughly unnerving performance, "Girl" is a three-page, one-sentence-long duet between a mother (who takes the lion's share) and a daughter (who speaks only twice), in which an entire lifetime is condensed. The mother begins by instructing her daughter in household chores, telling her methodically how to do the laundry, how to cook certain dishes, how to sweep, and then suddenly her instructions turn venomous: ". . . always eat your food in such a way that it won't turn someone else's stomach; on Sundays try to walk like a lady and not like the slut you are so bent on becoming . . ." Her ferocity and bitterness increase as she goes on matter-of-factly to instruct her daughter in the art of deceit and to explain how to make medicine "to throw away a child before it even becomes a child." Then she cautions her nearly speechless daughter not to "throw stones at blackbirds, because it might not be a blackbird at all." By the end of this perfectly orchestrated rant, Kincaid has touched on every aspect of womanhood and identified every dark force that shadowed her childhood. "Girl" is a spontaneous blooming, a flower of the subconscious, and it has seeded all her subsequent writings.

The mother's references to medicinal plants and to animals being other than what their shape suggests, allude to the obeah beliefs held by Kincaid's mother, maternal grandmother, and so many others in the West Indies. Obeah, like voodoo, is a spiritual practice based on a recognition of and communion with the supernatural, and it involves sorcery, witchcraft, spells, charms, and healing practices. Throughout the Caribbean, European values—the Christian church, Eurocentric education, and European goods—form a facade behind which the majority of the population holds firm to the metaphysical and spiritual perceptions they inherited from their African ancestors. And so Kincaid attended government schools and the Methodist church, but at home she was given special baths at the direction of an obeah woman, and wore protective sachets beneath her clothes to ward off the evil eye. In talking about obeah in Diane Simmons' work *Jamaica Kincaid,* Kincaid has said she "hated the whole thing," which she describes as "a world of nervous breakdowns," but, highly attuned to the workings of the subconscious and fully aware that life is lived on many levels, she also expresses respect for the profound psychological power of obeah, and it is, in fact, an essential ingredient in her fiction's volatile chemistry.

In "In the Night," one of the stories in *At the Bottom of the River,* the young narrator lies awake listening to all the night sounds, which include the benign—the house creaking, a cricket, the night-soil men at work—and the terrifying: the sound of a woman's "spirit back from the dead." Then, when the narrator asks her mother about the light she sees in the mountains at night, her mother explains that it is a *jablesse,* "a person who can turn into anything." You can tell a *jablesse* by its eyes, she says, because they "shine like lamps, so bright you can't look." And its favorite shape is that of a beautiful woman, just like the narrator's all-powerful mother.

Kincaid's prose itself works magic. *At the Bottom of the River* is her most dreamlike, enigmatic, and surreal book. Nonlinear and impressionistic, each story is a flickering montage of images and feelings, a fast-moving stream of consciousness much like those evoked by Virginia Woolf, a writer Kincaid greatly admires. Kincaid's modernist sensibility was also influenced by an avant-garde film titled *La Jetée,* which consists of a series of black-and-white photographs, until, as she explains in the Cudjoe interview, "somewhere in the middle of this film there is actual movement, and then it goes back to still photographs. I used to watch it over and over—I was incredibly moved by it."

With their oblique mode of storytelling, abrupt turnarounds and revelations, the stories in *At the Bottom of the River* echo the improvisational lifestyle Kincaid was pursuing at that time she wrote them. Like her funky getups, these stories are flamboyant, puzzling, and alluring. Kincaid is trying out various modes of expression as she scrutinizes the boundary between girlhood and womanhood and seeks to understand the nature of female power. At first, her unnamed heroine basks in her mother's love, but after she goes through puberty, thus becoming a threat to her mother's dominance, they become enemies on a truly cosmic scale. Kincaid renders them as mythical, shape-shifting, and world-transforming beings, especially the larger-than-life mother, who, like a jablesse, is cunning, monstrous, and cruel. Their battles are epic until, in the title story, a masterful interpretation of psychological crisis and resolution, the narrator discovers a perfect world at the bottom of the river. She falls into a basin, a hole, and her old self dissolves. She feels no fear; her mind is "conscious of nothing;" she is cleansed and liberated. Kincaid writes,

emerging from this pit, I step into a room and I see that the lamp is lit. In the light of the lamp, I see some books, I see a chair, I see a table, I see a pen; I see a bowl of ripe fruit, a bottle of milk, a flute made of wood, the clothes that I will wear. And as I see these things in the light of the lamp, all perishable and transient, how bound up I know I am to all that is human endeavor, to all that is past and to all that shall be, to all that shall be lost and leave no trace. I claim these things then—mine—and now feel myself grow solid and complete, my name filling up my mouth.

This passage resonates throughout Kincaid's entire corpus. It marks her heroine's narrow escape from her dangerous, unloving mother, and from the underground, a dark and ambiguous Hades, an obeah universe where things are not what they appear to be. Kincaid's heroine is reborn, and finds herself transported to a safe, well-lighted place where she finds sustenance for the body and the soul. She knows that this realm of "human endeavor," more specifically, the realm of the artist, is fragile and fleeting, but it is the best, she suggests, that one can hope for.

At the Bottom of the River elicited mixed critical response. In a review for the *New York Times,* critic Edith Milton described Kincaid's stories as "eccentric, visionary pieces" featuring "apocalyptic imagery" and "gospel-like seriousness, reverberating with biblical echoes." Others were harsher in their criticism, including Anne Tyler, who, writing for the *New Republic,* characterized the stories as "insultingly obscure." But Kincaid was enthusiastically praised by Susan Sontag and

Nobel Laureate and fellow Caribbean Derek Walcott, and was awarded the Morton Dauwen Zabel Award of the American Academy and Institute of Arts and Letters. She was well on her way to literary renown.

ANNIE JOHN

Kincaid's first novel, *Annie John* (1985), a coming-of-age story rich in cultural and political undertones, is written in an entirely different narrative style than *At the Bottom of the River.* Direct and linear, it reflects the skills Kincaid acquired at the *New Yorker:* the gift for concrete and exacting yet seemingly effortless description, and the confidence and authority that exemplify the magazine's standard-setting prose. Kincaid flourished at the *New Yorker,* an artistic paradise, where editor William Shawn was not only a father in terms of his literary mentorship but literally so when Kincaid married his son, Allen, a composer in 1979. Their first child, Annie, was born in 1985, followed less than four years later by a son, Harold. In 1985, Allen had accepted a teaching position at Bennington College, and the family had moved to Vermont. All these auspicious events helped give Kincaid the security she needed for writing about her childhood and her homeland in a more incisive manner than before.

Annie John is a classic *bildungsroman,* a novel about the moral and psychological growth of a young protagonist, which, as Lizabeth Paravisini-Gebert writes in her book *Jamaica Kincaid: A Critical Companion,* "has been a favorite genre of Caribbean writers, who have used its focus on the central character's growth and formation to establish parallels between their experiences and those of the small West Indian colonies in which their characters' lives unfold." While *At the Bottom of the River* was almost entirely internalized, in *Annie John* Kincaid achieves what has become her signature style, the deft weaving of the inner realm with the outer world. Hence obeah, a sphere of ambiguity separate from and in opposition to the British order imposed on Antigua, becomes aligned with Annie John's emerging sexuality and opposition to her mother's sovereignty.

At the outset, Annie John adores her mother, watching everything she does with great attention, and her mother returns her love and attentiveness. "It was in such a paradise that I lived," she muses, but like all paradises, it is destined to be lost. As long as Annie John is a cute, worshipful, and obedient little girl, her mother coddles her, but as Annie John's body begins to change, her mother turns stern and judgmental. Now the mother is aligned with mother country, and the "young-lady business" her daughter so deeply resents is associated with British values. Annie John's natural state is no longer considered good enough, but rather than conform to imposed codes of behavior, Kincaid's headstrong heroine behaves like a colony ripe for revolution and independence, and defies her mother on all fronts.

Confounded by her mother's sudden hostility, Annie John seeks approval not from her prissy and prejudiced teachers, standard-bearers for the British empire, but in the shining eyes of her classmates, and her relationships with these mischievous girls is frankly sexual. Kincaid has said that she "grew up with a great acceptance of female bonding," and that she was interested in dramatizing the intense passion young girls feel for one another, but these ardent attachments also function as covert forms of rebellion against the sexism implicit in the rules of ladylike subservience, which attempt to repress not only feminine sexuality, but intelligence and creativity.

Annie John's resistance also takes place in the classroom. Bored and impatient, she opens her history textbook to her favorite portrait of Columbus, one in which the explorer sits in chains "quite dejected and miserable," and carefully inks in a caption, quoting a phrase she heard her mother use in reference to her once domineering, but now ailing father: "The Great Man Can No Longer Just Get Up and Go." Caught in the act, Annie John is punished for this brazen defacement, and, as part of her penance, is made to memorize the first two books of *Paradise Lost* by John Milton, a punishment actually meted out to the young Kincaid, who was meant to understand that she was being compared to Satan. The punishment backfired: the epic has had a profound influence on decisively anti-colonial writings. In Kincaid's 1991 interview with Kay Bonetti, Kincaid explains, "I was brought up to understand that English traditions were right and mine were wrong . . . I was forced to memorize John Milton and that was a very painful thing. But I'm not going to make myself forget John Milton . . . I find John Milton very beautiful." Kincaid refers to the Milton episode again in her second novel, *Lucy,* in which her protagonist is named after Lucifer.

As she enters full-blown adolescence, the once vibrant and defiant Annie John grows despondent and takes to her bed. Weeks go by and she is lost in a twilight of dreams, memories, and delusions. Feverish and confused, she scrubs a set of family photographs with soap and water, thus eradicating her past. Finally, after three and a half months, her mysterious illness recedes, and she finds herself utterly alienated from her surroundings. She has outgrown her bed and all her clothes, and she towers over her mother. Annie John has survived nothing less than a terrifying visit to the underworld, just like the heroine in *At the Bottom of the River,* and she, too, returns transformed, strong, and invincible. She now has the power to leave her mother, her confining little house, and her small gossipy island, and so she sets sail for England ready to start a new life.

At the Bottom of the River ends with the heroine thinking, I "feel myself grow solid and complete, my name filling up my mouth." The last chapter of *Annie John* begins: "My name is Annie

John." She, too, fills her mouth with her name; she, too, affirms an identity separate from that envisioned by her mother, and declares the autonomy of the self. Kincaid then maintains this narrative continuity in her second novel, *Lucy,* another self-portrait, in which a young West Indian woman arrives in a strange, cold land. This scenario seems to pick up exactly where *Annie John* left off, but Kincaid wrote another book, her first work of sustained nonfiction, in between the composition of these two novels, and its influence on the texture and timbre of her later fiction is prodigious. Small in size but immense in impact, as are all her books, *A Small Place* (1988) caused a furor.

A SMALL PLACE

Kincaid had not been back to her homeland in almost twenty years when she received a Guggenheim Fellowship in 1986. Antigua had achieved full independence in 1981 and the time seemed right for a visit, but Kincaid was appalled at what she found there, and the anger that had surfaced in her earlier work now and then, like a fish rising to snatch an insect, surges across the pages of *A Small Place* like a tidal wave. At every turn, Kincaid contrasts the carefree attitude of tourists with the islanders' hardships, beginning with how Anglo vacationers feel blessed by the island's dependably sunny weather, oblivious to the persistent drought that plagues the lives of dark-skinned Antiguans. Page by page, she exposes all that is wrong, perverse, corrupt, and brutal about island life, and then audaciously confronts her readers (many of whom, thanks to her *New Yorker* affiliation, are white and affluent): "An ugly thing, that is what you are when you become a tourist, an ugly, empty thing, a stupid thing, a piece of rubbish pausing here and there to gaze at this and taste that, and it will never occur to

you that the people who inhabit the place in which you have just paused cannot stand you."

Kincaid wrote *A Small Place* for the *New Yorker* while William Shawn was still at the helm, but after his retirement, Robert Gottlieb, the new editor, refused to publish it, telling Kincaid that it was just too angry. Shawn encouraged Kincaid to submit it as a book manuscript and Farrar, Straus and Giroux, the house that had published all of Kincaid's other books released it in all its fury in 1988. In a conversation with Donna Perry, Kincaid agreed that *A Small Place* was a turning point in her writing. "I wrote with a kind of recklessness in that book. I didn't know what I would say ahead of time. Once I wrote it I felt very radicalized by it." Kincaid also came to "love anger." Citing a *New York Times* book review by Susan Kenney that praised *Annie John* for its charm, Kincaid remarked, ". . . when people say you're charming you are in deep trouble. I realized in writing that book that the first step to claiming yourself is anger."

It must be stated that Antiguans are not spared the sting of Kincaid's invective in *A Small Place.* If anything, their failure to run a compassionate and rational society inflames Kincaid even more than the self-centeredness of tourists. Kincaid is outraged by how Antiguans continue to accept the colonialist point of view, by how mired everything is in greed, by how illiterate young people are, and how small-minded the adults are. "The people in a small place cannot see themselves in a larger picture . . . No action in the present is an action planned with a view of the future. When the future, bearing its own events, arrives, . . . their mouths and eyes wide with their astonishment, the people in a small place reveal themselves to be like children being shown the secrets of a magic trick."

A Small Place enraged many readers. The government of Antigua attempted briefly and ineffectually to ban the book. Critics both lambasted it and sang its praises. Not surprisingly, British reviewers took particular offense. Isabel Fonseca, in the *Times Literary Supplement,* found it "shrill," "subjective," "dogmatic," and "shapeless." But Salman Rushdie declared it in a statement published on the jacket "a jeremiad of great clarity and a force that one might have called torrential were the language not so finely controlled." And Michiko Kakutani wrote in the *New York Times,* "Ms. Kincaid writes with passion and conviction, and she also writes with a musical sense of language, a poet's understanding of how politics and history, private and public events, overlap and blur."

But where did her indictment of Antigua leave Kincaid? Not only had she grown apart from Antiguan society over the course of her self-imposed exile, she never felt integrated into that confining world in the first place. Indignant over the bitter ironies and injustices of colonial life since girlhood, she always felt like an outsider. As she explained to Donna Perry, "I noticed things that no one else seemed to notice. And I think only people who are outsiders do this. I must have felt very different from everybody. When I tell people there now how I felt then, they look at me with pity." Her passion for reading and the life of the mind, considered so useless for an Antiguan girl, also set her apart. Even in the United States, where she was free to pursue her calling, she could not ignore society's inequities and the myriad hypocrisies inherent in a life of privilege. And so when Kincaid sat down to continue her fictionalized autobiography in *Lucy,* all her feelings of ambiguity, conflict, and guilt erupted, and not even the most fawning or inaccurate critic would call the results charming.

LUCY

Annie John made the passage from childhood to teenager; Lucy's tale of awakening intellectually, sexually, morally, and aesthetically tracks her crossing the threshold into adulthood. Unlike Annie John, who was England-bound, Lucy leaves her West Indian home for America, where she works as an au pair for a wealthy New York family. Kincaid's subtle description of Lucy's entry into her new world perfectly expresses her shrewd heroine's immediate attunement to the paradoxes inherent in her new home: "I could not see anything clearly on the way in from the airport, even though there were lights everywhere." Named after the devil, she has indeed been cast out by a god, her mother, who persists in making her disapproval felt across the miles. Lucy's employers, the blond, blue-eyed, well-meaning Mariah, and her careless husband, Lewis, try to act as surrogate parents to their nineteen-year-old employee (they have four young daughters, after all), but Lucy, tough and uncompromising, and drained dry by her mother's demands and the unforeseen onslaught of homesickness, angrily resists.

Lucy resents her role as servant, her mother's cautionary letters, which she soon stops reading, and Mariah's relentless cheerfulness and naiveté. "How does a person get to be that way?" Lucy asks herself, a question that becomes a refrain throughout the novel as Lucy and Mariah's personal differences become emblematic of their being on different sides of the social equation. When Mariah, the employer, tells Lucy, the servant, that she'll take her to see daffodils bloom as soon as spring arrives, Lucy responds by telling her about how she was made to learn and recite "an old poem" about daffodils by William Wordsworth and how much she loathes the very idea of those flowers of evil. What Mariah sees as beauty and promise, Lucy sees as a symbol of oppression and a trope of colonialism.

Although Lucy is grateful to Mariah for introducing her to art and culture, she cannot help but feel contempt. In one clarion scene, she admires Mariah's beauty, even describing her as glowing with an "almost celestial light." But Lucy notices that Mariah smells pleasant, and her admiration abruptly turns to scorn. "Just that—pleasant. And I thought, but that's the trouble with Mariah—she smells pleasant. By then I already knew that I wanted to have a powerful odor and would not care if it gave offense."

Kincaid herself, who deliberately embraces whatever qualities she is criticized for, is more than willing to offend her readers. She said in her interview with Donna Perry that she had come to realize that "people couldn't stand a certain sort of frankness. But I knew that what I wanted to be, more and more as a writer, was frank about what the lives I wrote about were really like . . . I wanted to be very frank and to be unlikeable within the story. To be even unpopular."

Lucy consistently interprets Mariah's complacency as evidence of a form of ignorance almost as disgraceful as the obviousness of the tourists Kincaid lambasted in *A Small Place*. When they summer on the Great Lakes in the house in which Mariah grew up, for instance, Mariah tells Lucy, the granddaughter of a Carib Indian, that she has Indian blood. Indignant and skeptical, Lucy thinks, "To me my grandmother is my grandmother, not an Indian." Her insistence on recognizing the uniqueness of an individual as opposed to identifying someone by race is indicative of Kincaid's own resistance to being categorized as a writer of color or a feminist writer. She has said in her interview with Cudjoe that she finds the idea of belonging to a group "deeply disturbing." After all, that's what conquest and prejudice are all about, stereotyping and the denial of individuality. To drive her point home, Kincaid has Lucy sneer at her employer's pride in her alleged Indian heritage: "I could swear she says it as if she were announcing her possession of a trophy. How do you get to be the sort of victor who can claim to be the vanquished also?"

Thanks to Mariah's generosity, however, Lucy embarks on a study of photography, Kincaid's own first artistic medium. She then moves out and embarks on just the sort of bohemian life her mother feared she would choose, indulging in lust but staying resolutely closed to love. At the very end of the novel, she and Mariah meet for dinner. Still acting as a guide along the path to creativity, in spite of Lucy's hostility, Mariah gives her a prescient gift, an elegant notebook. Later that night, feeling more alone than she had ever felt before, Lucy opens it, prints out her full name, Lucy Josephine Potter (Kincaid frequently uses her family's names in her fiction), and then writes the following shattering declaration: "I wish I could love someone so much that I would die from it."

Kincaid ends her third book of fiction as she ended the first and second, with her heroine asserting her identity by stating her name and taking control of her story. She closes the curtain on Lucy just as she is about to find her writer's voice and open herself to love. She has now brought her alter-ego up to the point in her real life at which she changed her name from Elaine Potter Richardson to Jamaica Kincaid and took up her pen. As an autobiographical writer, she had two choices at this conjuncture. She could either return to her past, or continue her series of self-portraits by stepping into the present, but a tempestuous visit from her mother inadvertently gave rise to a third option. The two women quarreled violently in Kincaid's Vermont home, and, after Annie Drew returned to Antigua, Kincaid suffered a nervous breakdown and a freak case of chicken pox, which she'd already had as a child.

THE AUTOBIOGRAPHY OF MY MOTHER

Just as her fictional heroines are laid low by mysterious maladies at the turning points in their lives, and then recover transformed and empowered, Kincaid emerged from her breakdown contemplating not herself but her mother. She began to imagine what Annie Drew's life might have been like if she hadn't had children, and soon found herself conjuring stories that illuminated more than familial traumas. And so, three years after the publication of *Lucy,* the *New Yorker* published the first installment of what became *The Autobiography of My Mother* (1990), Kincaid's most complex, virtuosic, and harrowing novel. It is a memorial to the lost tribes of the Caribbean, and a protest against the oppression of women, and the entire horrific tragedy of conquest and colonialism.

In speaking with Moira Ferguson, author of *Jamaica Kincaid: Where the Land Meets the Body,* Kincaid said that for her, writing "was really an act of saving my life, so it had to be autobiographical. I am someone who had to make sense out of my past. It is turning out that it is much more complicated than that when I say my past, because for me I have to make sense of my ancestral past . . . I used to think I was writing about my mother and me. Later I began to see that I was writing about the relationship between the powerful and the powerless."

The opening scene of *The Autobiography of My Mother* is gothic in tone. The unnamed narrator could almost be a Brontë heroine writing by candlelight, and with nineteenth-century British correctness, the story of her disinheritance, intent on leaving some trace of her lonely struggle. But this Caribbean island is a very different place than the British Isles, a small place where mysteries abound and cultural collisions spawn a confusion of legacies in the mixed blood of the survivors. The novel begins:

> My mother died at the moment I was born, and so for my whole life there was nothing standing between myself and eternity; at my back was always a bleak, black wind.

The very ink itself seems to turn into venom as this taut and tragic voice describes how her father brought her, a newborn, and a bundle of his soiled clothes, to a woman he paid to take care of both, and her tone implies that the clothes were his primary concern. Ma Eunice, still nursing her sixth child when this motherless babe is added to her brood, treats the newcomer with routine indifference and frequent cruelty, and the quiet girl's childhood is stark and lonely. At least her absentee father sees to it that she attends school, an uncommon choice for girls at the time. Pleased to be taught how to write letters, she intuitively writes to her father, complaining of her misery. Unable to actually mail these pleas for help, she places them beneath a rock where, almost magically, they are discovered and eventually delivered. Having remarried, her father appears and takes her to his new home. Kincaid's narrator marvels, "I had, through the use of some words, changed my situation; I had perhaps even saved my life," potent testimony to the power of the pen.

The narrator's stepmother, who is of African and French descent, is as malevolent as a figure in a fairy tale, and she attempts to vanquish her husband's daughter with obeah sorcery, but the girl possesses an innate knowledge of such dangers and is able to protect herself. She is also on guard against her father, who, as a policeman, is "part of a whole way of life on the island which perpetuated pain." Not only is he an archetypal tyrant, he is one of the conquered who eagerly takes up the cudgel of the conqueror and wields it against his own people. Kincaid also uses him as a catalyst for her most sustained inquiry into the war between the sexes.

As a teenager, Kincaid's still nameless protagonist is sent by her controlling father to board with Jack LaBatte, a friend just as greedy and unscrupulous as he is. Once again, Kincaid creates a fairy tale-like ambiance, as LaBatte counts his money like a miser, and his childless wife fusses over their boarder, dressing her up and encouraging her to sleep with her husband so as to deliver them a child. It is at this exigency that

Kincaid's heroine assumes her full powers, declares her pride and independence in spite of her claustrophobic and potentially degrading circumstances, and, in keeping with Kincaid's penchant for ritualized self-actualization, finally reveals her name: Xuela Claudette Richardson.

Xuela does have sex with LaBatte, because she wants to, and she does indeed conceive, but she drinks a potion to abort the fetus and endures days of agony. After her recovery, she states: "I was a new person then, I knew things I had not known before, I knew things that you can know only if you have been through what I had just been through. I had carried my life in my own hands."

Xuela slips away in the night, walks many miles past the next village, rents a tiny house, takes a job sifting sand for a road construction project, and works ten grueling hours a day. She realizes that her refusal to bear one child is actually a refusal to mother any, and she has an electrifying vision in which she pictures herself as some terrible goddess who bears an "abundance" of children ("they would hang from me like fruit from a vine"), only to dispassionately watch them die. Her vision is cataclysmic and a horrific reversal of maternal instinct. To accentuate her unnaturalness, her rage, and her adamant refusal to nurture others, Xuela cuts off her long braids, dresses in the clothes of a dead man, and gives herself over to a penitent's life of isolation, deprivation, and contemplation. This is her descent to the underworld, a journey into profound self-reliance. "I began to worship myself," she explains. "My own face was a comfort to me, my own body was a comfort to me, and no matter how swept away I would become by anyone or anything, in the end I allowed nothing to replace my own being in my own mind."

After yet another of her father's godlike interventions, Xuela ends up marrying a white doctor named Philip, a man she does not love. Their liaison prompts one of the most arresting passages in the book, a towering diatribe against slavery and the colonialism left in its wake. Stoic and pitiless, Xuela, like a warrior infused with the strength of the righteous, throws back the covers of everyday life and reveals the tentacles of the European monster that continues to strangle island life. She declares: "I am of the vanquished, I am of the defeated. The past is a fixed point, the future is open-ended; for me the future must remain capable of casting a light on the past such that in my defeat lies the seed of my great victory, in my defeat lies the beginning of my great revenge." Over decades of marriage, she denies Philip, whom history has decreed the victor, her love, and so presides ruthlessly over his slow but inexorable diminishment and demise.

Kincaid takes her reader deep into the soul of the conquered, and far beyond the comforts of romance, religion, and even simple decency. She descends to the very bedrock of the human soul, where her anger is a lamp and the language of the captor the tool with which to keep the past alive, and where a woman's absolute control over her body and mind serves as the only defense against annihilation. *The Autobiography of My Mother,* stunning both in its beauty and in its pain, shouts a resounding "No!" to the conqueror's version of history. But there is a theatricality to Xuela's rage, and an artificiality to the plot that subtly undermine the bleak, nihilistic vision Kincaid so brilliantly proffers, and this contradiction, almost a betrayal, of her own creation is rooted in her obsession with her mother, which is both the boon and bane of her work. Driven to castigate her mother, Kincaid inadvertently stifles her heroine's humanity by using her as a symbol for what she believes her own mother is capable of in terms of emotional withholding, cruelty, and self-love.

RECOGNITION AND CHANGES

As before, Kincaid had her champions and her detractors, although no one could honestly deny the rigor, might, and fire and brimstone of her prose. Cathleen Schine, writing for the *New York Times,* articulated the reservations of many readers by describing *The Autobiography of My Mother* as "pure and overwhelming," but writing, too, that "there is also something dull and unconvincing about Xuela's anguish." Other critics expressed more positive opinions, and Kincaid's powerful novel was nominated for the National Book Critics Circle award and chosen as a finalist for the PEN/Faulkner award, ultimately garnering the Cleveland Foundation's Anisfield-Wolf Award and the *Boston Book Review's* Fisk Fiction Award.

The writing and publication of this demanding book was bracketed by professional upheaval and family trauma for Kincaid. Just before *The Autobiography of My Mother* was published, Kincaid, long critical of the *New Yorker*'s British editor, Tina Brown, left the magazine that had made her a writer and provided her with a literary home. Her departure was precipitated by her anger over Brown's decision to invite sitcom star Roseanne Barr to guest-edit a special women's issue. Kincaid publicly accused Brown of sacrificing literary quality for crass commercialism and celebrity worship. Then, in a telling remark made to Sally Jacobs of the *Boston Globe* over the course of an astonishingly antagonistic interview, she compared the *New Yorker* to Antigua: "it was beautiful, an ideal of some kind, but it had been made vulgar and ugly by the incredibly stupid people who had become attracted to it."

What Kincaid did not tell Jacobs was that she was distraught about far more than her break with the *New Yorker:* earlier that same day she had learned that her youngest brother, Devon, had died. Because Kincaid writes to make sense of her life, Devon and his battle with AIDS became the subject of her next book, an unsparing and profoundly resonant memoir titled *My Brother* (1997). Devon was only three years old when Kincaid left Antigua and he remained a virtual stranger, yet when she heard that he was ill, she took immediate action, much to her own surprise,

and did everything she could to help him. As she chronicles Devon's life and death, she mulls over her relationship with her family from a new vantage point, acutely aware that what befell her brother could have happened to her, a humbling realization that instills her meticulously observed memoir with a sense of there-but-for-the-grace-of-God-go-I.

MY BROTHER

Kincaid's gift for distillation is more finely honed than ever: within the first few pages of *My Brother,* she announces Devon's illness, remembers his birth—he was born at home in 1962 when she was thirteen (she was sent to fetch the midwife)—recalls that he almost died the next day when "an army of red ants came in through the window and attacked him," and reports on the still-active animosity between her and her mother. The crisis of Devon's illness brings them into close proximity but not into accord, and the friction between them is as much (and as inevitably) the theme of the book as is her brother's fate.

Kincaid knew enough about her brother's life to know that he used drugs, was promiscuous, and would most likely not bother to use condoms. That he contracted the virus, then, is not a shock, but the state of medical care in Antigua, and the lack of understanding of the disease, is an outrage. All that she found to condemn about her homeland in *A Small Place* comes back into focus with a vengeance as Kincaid reports on her discovery that AIDS sufferers are essentially condemned to die in Antigua: the hospital is filthy and under-staffed, and no treatments are available. Undaunted, she finds the best doctor on the island and brings her brother the drug AZT from the United States. For the first time in their lives they say the words "I love you" to each other.

In spite of all that Kincaid, her mother, and the doctor do for him, Devon does not change his ways, and that is what kills him. In her grief and frustration, Kincaid composes what is essentially a koan: "I love the people I am from and I do not love the people I am from." Devon's death sends her spiraling back down into the past yet again, and she returns from her submersion with new evidence to submit in the proceedings against her mother, fresh insights about how to face the presence of death in life, and a keen awareness of her own maternal fears, especially regarding her son. Kincaid says, "If I should fail him—and I very well might, the prime example I have is not a good one—he will experience something everlastingly bitter and awful; I know this, the taste of this awfulness, this bitterness, is in my mouth every day."

Kincaid's sorrow over her brother's wasted life and premature death unlock long-sealed doors to her psyche, and Kincaid suddenly reclaims the repressed memory of a day on which she was supposed to be taking care of Devon. As unflinchingly honest about her own selfishness and renegade ways as she is about the flaws of others, she writes, "I did not like my mother's other children, I did not even like my mother then; I liked books, I liked reading books." So she read that fateful day, ignoring her baby brother and neglecting to change his diaper. Her mother was livid. "In a fit of anger that I can remember so well, as if it had been a natural disaster, as if it had been a hurricane or an erupting volcano, or just simply the end of the world, my mother found my books, all the books that I had read, some of them books I had bought, though with money I had stolen, some of them books I had simply stolen . . ." Her mother not only confiscated her daughter's talismans against despair, in a scene as devastating and extreme as anything found in *The Autobiography of My Mother,* she piled them all on the stone heap on which she ordinarily bleached the stains out of white clothes and set them on fire. This is a scene no book lover can contemplate without some degree of horror, and Kincaid wonders if she became a writer in a

subconscious attempt to bring those lost books back to life.

Kincaid makes it clear that she speculated endlessly about how Devon contracted the virus. Something bothers her, but she cannot quite put her finger on it. Then, in a strange twist of fate, she learns the truth at a bookstore in Chicago. She has traveled there as part of her tour for *The Autobiography of My Mother,* and after her reading, a familiar-looking woman introduces herself. It turns out that she and Kincaid had participated in the same AIDS support group in Antigua, and that she knew Devon well—well enough to know that he had relations with men as well as with women. Kincaid understands instantly not only that her brother had to keep his bisexuality secret in that small, judgmental place, but that such secrecy caused him much unhappiness. Nearly overwhelmed with despair and empathy, she sees that her brother could not be himself in Antigua, just as she never would have been able to be herself, to be a writer, had she stayed.

My Brother marks a deepening and maturing of Kincaid's work. A multifaceted narrative, it addresses one of the great forces of human nature: the inescapable gravity of family. No matter how much distance, geographical or emotional, is created between family members, each remains inextricably attracted to the other, caught in the push and pull of resentment and love. Kincaid's memoir is also an unusually lucid meditation on death, and a near perfect depiction of memory itself, as Anna Quindlen observes in her *New York Times* review. She describes *My Brother* as resembling "the meandering of human memory, which ebbs and flows and runs white with the rapids of rage and loss and then sags and stalls."

Kincaid's penchant for obsessive rumination over her past, her overly obvious attempts to exorcise her demons, and her undisguised vindictiveness have very nearly soured and encumbered her otherwise brilliant, lyrical, and profoundly moving novels. But in her nonfiction, where she is free of the demands of invention, her portrayals of herself in the act of unearthing the roots, studying the blooms, and tasting the bittersweet fruits of her past are compelling and clarifying for both writer and reader. The memories and experiences articulated so sharply in *My Brother* also explicate Kincaid's need to mythologize her life, which is key to understanding the cohesion of her corpus.

TENDING ONE'S GARDEN: WRITING ABOUT PLANTS

Any close reader of Kincaid's will notice how often she writes about plants, a passion she's harbored since her school days when botany was a favorite subject, and one that has translated into a devotion to gardening, the subject of her seventh book. Gardening may sound innocuous enough, but nothing is simple or genial for Kincaid, and she cannot help but filter her interest in plants through the lens of imperialism. Plants, Kincaid declares, have, like people, been conquered, renamed, and even enslaved. She alludes to her unusual perspective on plants in *The Autobiography of My Mother,* when Xuela ponders Philip's obsession with "the growing of flowering plants for no other reason than the pleasure of it," a hobby that she condemns as "an act of conquest, benign though it may be." Kincaid expounds at length on this theme in what became her final essays for the *New Yorker,* a piquant series about colonialism, plants, and her own gardening adventures. Not only did she come to love working in the garden, she fell in love with garden literature, and she celebrates her literary horticultural ardor in a beautifully produced anthology titled *My Favorite Plant: Writers and Gardeners on the Plants They Love* (1998).

Katherine S. White, one of the anthology's illustrious contributors, must be an inspiration to Kincaid. A renowned editor at the *New Yorker* for thirty-four years, White also wrote a series of gardening essays for the magazine that were later assembled into a book titled *Onward and Upward in the Garden.* Kincaid, too, has also made a book out of her *New Yorker* gardening essays, a peppery collection titled, *My Garden [Book]:* (1999). A review by James Fenmore in the *New York Review of Books* compares it favorably to White's and accurately describes it as taking "its place in an agreeable tradition of garden literature, in which the personality and general concerns of the author are of just as much interest as what is actually being said about gardening."

Like *My Favorite Plant, My Garden [Book]:* is lavishly designed and produced. The green border framing each page lends it the look of a notebook, and a smattering of cheerful line drawings imbues it with a cheerfulness previously absent from Kincaid's writings. Obviously, the writer who so adamantly erased any hint of the charm readers found so pleasing in *Annie John* in her subsequent fiction enters a new phase in her self-portraiture. After the elegiac and cathartic intensity of *My Brother,* Kincaid, who, in spite of her frequent harshness on the page and notoriety for abrasive behavior, seems, still, like a girl longing for approval but willing to accept mere attention, allows evidence of her more winsome side to creep in and blossom like an unexpected vine of morning glories on a chain-link fence. Not that her contrariness has abated. It has not. In fact, cheeriness serves as camouflage for the true nature of Kincaid's garden writings.

Although some of Kincaid's essays, such as one about reading her favorite gardening catalogue in a hot bath on a cold day, do match the contented mood of the illustrations, others stand in jarring contrast. For Kincaid, a rose is not a rose is not a rose; it's a thorn, and a thorn is an emblem of pain and the ongoing anguish of conquest, and a thorn is a symbol of her anger, and a weapon she employs in her literary assault against the evils of tyranny. But Kincaid has a credibility problem: she is writing about oppression not from her home ground in ravaged Antigua—once cordoned off into slave-worked plantations, now turned into a theme park for marauding tourists—but from her own private sanctuary, from the bounty of her position of privilege in one of North America's most pleasant communities, Bennington, Vermont. Just as her heroine did in *Lucy,* Kincaid both relishes the good life, and rails against the injustices that make it possible for a lucky few. But if anyone can thrive in this zone of ambiguity and contradiction, Kincaid can.

At the start of *My Garden [Book]:,* Kincaid confides that she began her life as a gardener in Vermont when her husband gave her some seeds and a set of garden tools for her first Mother's Day. The connection between motherhood and gardening is felicitous, but she immediately curdles the tone by writing about a pair of missing earrings: "they were never seen again, by me, nor anyone else, not the lady who cleaned the house, not the women who helped me take care of my child." The only discernible point to this catty complaint, it seems, is to make it clear that the lady of the house (once a servant herself) has servants. Kincaid then proceeds to complain nastily about her neighbors, portraying herself, however unintentionally, as a woman much like her much maligned mother—the snake in her own paradise.

The next bit of personal information Kincaid shares is that while she was planning her garden, she was reading about the conquest of Mexico and the appropriation of native plants by European botanists. She then realizes that the strange shapes and seemingly arbitrary layout of her flower beds "resembled a map of the Caribbean and the sea that surrounds it," and she "marvels at the way the garden is for me an exercise in memory . . . a way of getting to a past." Kincaid has planted the flag of her epic rage over the crimes of colonialism in the stony soil of the small, feisty northern state of Vermont.

The most robust and memorable essays in *My Garden [Book]:* are those which examine the legacy of conquest through a gardener's eyes, such as "To Name is to Possess." Kincaid reminds readers that the First World is not the only world, and that plants indigenous to the so-called New World, such as the cocoxochitl of Mexico, were flourishing and much valued long before they were brought to Europe and renamed—in this case as the dahlia, after the Swedish botanist Andreas Dahl. The tacit assumption, she remarks, is that nothing has any value until the white man stumbles upon it and imposes his nomenclature. This acute perspective yields many more sobering and provocative insights into botanical and cultural history, but not even Kincaid can remain grim in the presence of nature's vigor. She cannot help but express a perverse but giddy delight in the inevitable vexations of the garden, and recounts skirmishes with rabbits, bugs, and woodpeckers, relishing, all the while, the frenetic energy of life and the futility of our stubborn efforts to control it.

Kincaid herself sprouts and flowers in the rows of words planted on these fertile pages. She is irascible, smart, knowledgeable, sly, poetic, needy, mischievous, and proud. And she wraps things up with a wily meditation on paradise, the setting of all her works, whether lost or regained. She writes that her personal Eden is "so rich in comfort, it tempts me to cause discomfort; I am in a state of constant discomfort and I like this state so much I would like to share it."

CONCLUSION

Kincaid seems proud of her contrariness as she divulges her chronic uneasiness, not in an effort to exorcise it but rather to plant it in the minds of her readers. This is classic Kincaid. In all of her work, she draws people in with her candor only to push them away with her anger, a combination of intimacy and distancing which feels both manipulative and inevitable given the facts of her life and the compulsive nature of her writing. A series of hard-edged self-portraits, her books closely follow the course of her experiences. But they also link her autobiography to the greater world past and present, and Kincaid's artistic singularity is rooted in her profound identification with her homeland, the conquered and colonialized Caribbean, and her irrevocable decision to exile herself from it. Kincaid is a champion of autonomy, a prose poet of individuality, yet for all the clarity of her perceptions, she writes out of frustration, sorrow, and emotional need. For her, the act of writing is nothing less than a bid for survival. She writes not out of ambition, but, as she has often claimed, to literally save her life. That is the source of her consistency of vision and subject matter, and no one is more aware of this than she. In an interview with Dwight Grarner, she said "If I had consciously designed my career, perversely enough, I might have worried about what people would say and done something different. I am not troubled, however, to be seen to be of one whole cloth—that all that I write is a further development of something." Then Kincaid says it all: "I couldn't help but write these books."

Selected Bibliography

WORKS OF JAMAICA KINCAID

FICTION

At the Bottom of the River. New York: Farrar, Straus & Giroux, 1983.

Annie John. New York: Farrar, Straus & Giroux, 1985.

Annie, Gwen, Lilly, Pam and Tulip. Illustrations by Eric Fischl. Limited edition. New York: Library Fellows of the Whitney Museum of American Art, 1986. Trade edition, New York: Alfred A. Knopf, 1989.

Lucy. New York: Farrar, Straus & Giroux, 1990.

The Autobiography of My Mother. New York: Farrar, Straus & Giroux, 1996.

NONFICTION

A Small Place. New York: Farrar, Straus & Giroux, 1988.

My Brother. New York: Farrar, Straus & Giroux, 1997.

My Garden [Book]:. New York: Farrar, Straus & Giroux, 1999.

EDITED WORK

The Best American Essays 1995. Boston and New York: Houghton Mifflin Co., 1995.

My Favorite Plant: Writers and Gardeners on the Plants They Love. New York: Farrar, Straus & Giroux, 1998.

AUDIO RECORDINGS

Annie John/At the Bottom of the River/Lucy. Read by Jamaica Kincaid. Columbia, Mo.: American Audio Prose Library, 1991.

The Autobiography of My Mother. Read by Jamaica Kincaid. New York: Airplay Audiobooks, 1996.

My Brother. Read by Jamaica Kincaid. New York: Penguin Audiobooks, 1998.

UNCOLLECTED STORIES

"Antigua Crossing." *Rolling Stone,* June 29, 1978, pp. 48–50.

"Ovando." *Conjunctions* 14:75–83 (1989).

UNCOLLECTED ESSAYS

"Jamaica Kincaid's New York." *Rolling Stone,* October 6, 1977, pp. 71–73.

"On Seeing England for the First Time." *Transition* 51:32–40 (1991); *Harper's Magazine,* August 1991, pp. 13–17.

"Biography of a Dress." *Grand Street* 43:93–100 (1992).

"Putting Myself Together." *New Yorker,* February 20, 1995, pp. 93–101. Reprinted in *Leaving New York: Writers Look Back.* Edited by Kathleen Norris. St. Paul, Minn.: Hungry Mind Press, 1995.

CRITICAL AND BIOGRAPHICAL STUDIES

Bloom, Harold, ed. *Jamaica Kincaid: Modern Critical Views.* New York: Chelsea House, 1998.

Covi, Giovanna. "Jamaica Kincaid and the Resistance to Canons." In *Out of the Kumbla: Caribbean Women and Literature.* Edited by Carol Boyce Davis and Elaine Savory Fido. Trenton, N.J.: Africa World Press, 1990. Pp. 345–354.

Donnell, Alison. "When Daughters Defy: Jamaica Kincaid's Fiction." *Women: A Cultural Review* 4, no. 1:18–26 (1993).

Ferguson, Moira. *Jamaica Kincaid: Where the Land Meets the Body.* Charlottesville and London: University Press of Virginia, 1994.

Mangum, Bryant. "Jamaica Kincaid." In *Fifty Caribbean Writers.* Edited by Daryl Cumber Dance. Westport, Conn.: Greenwood Press, 1986. Pp. 255–263.

Morris, Ann R., and Margaret M. Dunn. " 'The Bloodstream of Our Inheritance': Female Identity and the Caribbean Mothers'-Land." In *Motherlands: Black Women's Writing from Africa, the Caribbean, and South Asia.* Edited by Susheila Nasta. London: The Women's Press, 1991. Pp. 219–237.

Murdoch, H. Adlai. "The Novels of Jamaica Kincaid: Figures of Exile, Narratives of Dreams." *Clockwatch Review* 9, no. 1–2:141–154 (1994–1995).

Paravisini-Gebert, Lizabeth. *Jamaica Kincaid: A Critical Companion.* Westport, Conn. and London: Greenwood Press, 1999.

Simmons, Diana Ellis. "The Rhythm of Reality in the Work of Jamaica Kincaid." *World Literature Today* 63, no. 3:466–472 (1994).

Simmons, Diane. *Jamaica Kincaid.* New York: Twayne, 1994.

Timothy, Helen Pyne. "Adolescent Rebellion and Gender Relations in *At the Bottom of the River* and *Annie John.*" In *Caribbean Women Writers: Essays from the First International Conference.* Edited by Selwyn Cudjoe. Wellesley: Calaloux Publications; distributed by the University of Massachusetts Press, 1990. Pp. 233–242.

BOOK REVIEWS

Fenmore, James. Review of *My Garden.* January 20, 2000, pp. 31–32, 37.

Fonseca, Isabel. Review of *A Small Place. Times Literary Supplement,* January 16, 1988, p. 30.

Kakutani, Michiko. "Portrait of Antigua, Warts and All." Review of *A Small Place. New York Times,* July 16, 1988, p. 19.

Kenney, Susan. Review of *Annie John. New York Times Book Review,* April 7, 1985, p. 6.

Milton, Edith. "Making a Virtue of Diversity." Review of *At the Bottom of the River. New York Times,* January 15, 1984, p. 22.

Quindlen, Anna. "The Past is Another Country." Review of *My Brother. New York Times,* October 19, 1997, p.7.

Schine, Cathleen. "A World as Cruel as Job's" *Review of The Autobiography of My Mother. New York Times,* February 4, 1996, p. 5.

Tyler, Anne. Review of *At the Bottom of the River. New Republic* 189:32 (December 31, 1983).

INTERVIEWS

Bonetti, Kay. "An Interview with Jamaica Kincaid." *The Missouri Review* 20, nos. 1–2:7–26 (1991).

Cudjoe, Selwyn. "Jamaica Kincaid and the Modernist Project: An Interview." *Callaloo* 12, no. 2:396–411 (Spring 1989). Reprinted in *Caribbean Women Writers: Essays from the First International Conference.* Edited by Selwyn Cudjoe. Wellesley: Calaloux Publications; distributed by the University of Massachusetts Press, 1990.

Ferguson, Moira. "A Lot of Memory: An Interview with Jamaica Kincaid." *The Kenyon Review* 16, no. 1:163–188 (Winter 1994).

Garner, Dwight. "Jamaica Kincaid: The Salon Interview." *Salon Magazine.* www.salon.com/05/features/kincaid.html (December 8, 1999).

Jacobs, Sally. "Don't Mess with Jamaica Kincaid." *Boston Globe,* June 20, 1996, p 57.

Perry, Donna. "An Interview with Jamaica Kincaid." In *Reading Black/Reading Feminist.* Edited by Henry Louis Gates. New York: Penguin, 1990. Pp. 492–509.

Snell, Marilyn. "Jamaica Kincaid Hates Happy Endings." *Mother Jones,* September–October 1997, pp. 28–32.

—DONNA SEAMAN

Barbara Kingsolver

1955—

THE EPIGRAPH TO Barbara Kingsolver's book *Holding the Line: Women in the Great Arizona Mine Strike of 1983* (1989) is by Mother Jones: "No nation is greater than its women." This quotation succinctly points to themes prevalent in Kingsolver's work: feminism, motherhood and family, human interdependence on a local and global level, and individual empowerment—both personal and political. These multiple themes are related in their balancing of necessary self-sufficiency and the complex interdependence of everything on earth. In contrast to this intricate web of ideas, Kingsolver's literary values are fairly straightforward. In an interview with Sarah Kerr, Kingsolver stated that "complex ideas can be put across in simple language," "a good plot never hurt anybody," and novels need to be written to promote "social change." In an interview with L. Elisabeth Beattie, Kingsolver said stories should "have a be-ginning and an end and a moral and a theme."

Kingsolver's feminism leads her to create char-acters who are either slaves to standard gender constructions (such as Barbie in *Pigs in Heaven* [1993]), refreshingly free of some of the traps of womanhood (such as Taylor in *Pigs in Heaven,* who loves her body to the point of kissing her own knees), or in the process of developing from a resigned woman with a circumscribed life and imagination to one who dreams and acts (such as Lou Ann in *The Bean Trees* [1988] and Alice in

Pigs in Heaven). Drawn on a spectrum of self-actualization, Kingsolver's characters highlight the pitfalls of conventional modern womanhood, and both the advantages in and possibility of psy-chological and situational makeovers. Kingsol-ver's characters live both within the real world and in the doorway to a better one.

One way Kingsolver points to female empow-erment is by celebrating motherhood and family. Critics such as Maureen Ryan may take issue with Kingsolver's "deceptive insistence that if we love our children and our mothers, and hang in there with hearth and home, the big bad world will simply go away," but Kingsolver's value of mothers involves more than sending Mother's Day cards. *Holding the Line* almost makes the essentialist argument of proletarian feminists such as Meridel Le Sueur that mothers are natural-born social activists; women watching out for the best interests of their children and families will natu-rally want the world to become a better place. Kingsolver says in her interview with Kerr, "Ev-erything I do, from writing to raising my kids, is about preparing for the future." The "big bad world" will not automatically disappear, but thoughtful, loving mothers can make it better, es-pecially once they understand relationships be-tween their individual plights and those of the wider community. While Orleanna, the mother in *The Poisonwood Bible* (1998), cannot find the strength to improve her personal situation for her own sake, she finally acts on behalf of her daughters.

People can understand the potential of mothers only if they accept the interdependence of all living things on earth, and Kingsolver is also an environmentalist. Although Krista Comer argues that Kingsolver's beautiful descriptions of the Southwest encourage people to move there, and she calls Kingsolver "a real estate developer in the cultural realm," Kingsolver's depictions of the beauties of nature seem intended to help people value it and recognize themselves as part of it. Kingsolver's background in the biological sciences results in her using organic metaphors for the human condition. These metaphors are based in an understanding of the way organisms within ecosystems are mutually dependent. By way of these metaphors of the organic community, Kingsolver presents her most likely reader—an American who values individualism—with the importance of shared work and responsibility within the human community.

This wide-ranging interdependence would be overwhelming if people felt that it were completely out of their control, but Kingsolver's novels represent the ways in which people can empower themselves, both personally and politically. Her characters can change their behavior, and this change can turn their lives around. Moving, divorcing, landing a new job, making a new friend, and changing one's mind are all effective ways to change one's life. Kingsolver's world is not deterministic. People can decide to act, and their actions make a difference. As she says in her interview with Beattie, "A lot of this stuff [such as environmental problems] can only be fixed through massive individual action."

KINGSOLVER'S BACKGROUND

Barbara Ellen Kingsolver is the daughter of a homemaker—Virginia Lee Henry Kingsolver— and a country doctor—Wendell Roy Kingsolver. Her parents' lives affected her writing career, as her writing focuses on people building homes and communities, and making the moral decision to help others. Born in Annapolis, Maryland, on April 8, 1955, Kingsolver and her two siblings were raised in "the middle of an alfalfa field" in Nicholas County, eastern Kentucky, except for the year her family spent in the Congo when she was seven. Switching her major from instrumental music (classical piano) to zoology, Kingsolver graduated magna cum laude from DePauw University in Greencastle, Indiana, in 1977. After a couple of years of traveling and working in Europe, Kingsolver visited Tucson, Arizona, decided to stay, and began graduate work in ecology and evolutionary biology at the University of Arizona in Tucson, where she wrote a master's thesis on the social life of termites and earned her Master of Science in 1981. Kingsolver was married to Joe Hoffman, a chemist, from 1985 to 1993, and she married Steven Hopp, an ornithologist, in 1995. She has a daughter with each. As she writes in *High Tide in Tucson: Essays from Now or Never* (1995), "I've spent my life hiding a closetful of other lives," but in the same essay she argues for "parti-colored days and renaissance lives." She is now "a writer who does other things," including playing keyboard for "an all-author band," The Rock Bottom Remainders.

Having written all her life—she began a journal when she was eight years old, and she wrote poetry and short stories throughout high school— Kingsolver started work as a technical writer for the Office of Arid Land Studies at the University of Arizona in 1981. In 1982 she decided to become an independent writer, boldly stating her decision in her journal. She took on freelance writing assignments as well as writing her own fiction and nonfiction, some of it on behalf of causes about which she feels strongly, including human rights abuses, American influence in Latin America, environmentalism, and the madness of war—nuclear and otherwise.

Her books repeatedly nominated by independent booksellers for the American Booksellers Book of the Year (ABBY), Kingsolver has been the recipient of many other prizes. In 1986 she received a feature-writing award from the Arizona Press Club. In 1989 she was lauded by the United Nations Council of Women. *The Bean Trees,* which has been published in over twelve languages in at least sixty-five countries, received an award from The American Library Association (1988), an Enoch Pratt Library Youth-to-Youth Books award, and was a New York Times Notable Book in 1988. In 1990, the American Library Association cited the short story collection *Homeland* as a notable book. In 1991, the Edward Abbey Ecofiction Award and the PEN/USA West Fiction Award went to *Animal Dreams* (1990). *Animal Dreams* was also the Arizona Library Association Book of the Year and a *New York Times* Notable Book. *Pigs in Heaven* won the *Los Angeles Times* Fiction Prize (1993), the Mountains and Plains Fiction Award (1993), and the the Cowboy Hall of Fame Western Fiction Award (1993). *Pigs in Heaven* was on the *New York Times* best-seller list for many weeks, and *The Poisonwood Bible* was also on the list. To encourage the writing and publication of literature that promotes social change, Kingsolver has endowed the Bellweather Prize, to be awarded every May Day.

THE BEAN TREES

In *The Bean Trees,* Kingsolver's main character moves from rural Kentucky through the outlying areas of the Cherokee Nation, and then farther west to Tucson, Arizona. Along the way she takes in a Cherokee child, and the novel relates the story of her first five months as a mother. In Tucson, Taylor meets and moves in with the defeatist Lou Ann, whose husband has just left her, and her newborn son. Ultimately working for a used-tire store which doubles as a sanctuary for Gua-temalan refugees, Taylor meets a couple whose daughter has been kidnaped by members of the oppressive regime in their home country. In spite of all this pain, the novel emphasizes the positive: the way hope grows from hopeless terrain, like wisteria from dry desert dirt or a resilient person from a scarred childhood. *The Bean Trees* is a surprisingly uplifting story about the stubborn—even joyful—survival of the downtrodden.

Kingsolver's characters are surprisingly good at making what they can from a bad situation, which can be uplifting or annoying, depending on the reader. While often praised for her ability to deliver novels rich with imagery and linguistic play as well as advice and inspiration, some critics, such as Maureen Ryan, argue that "the big subjects, the looming dangers, are always dismissed" and that Kingsolver's characters are too good to be true. Kingsolver's characters are usually good-hearted, but they are not heroes. She mainly offers encouragement for survival or amelioration. As one character says, "in a world as wrong as this one, all we can do is to make things as right as we can." Writing while pregnant with her own first child, Kingsolver has Taylor gradually realize that a mother has "no business just assuming [she can] take the responsibility for a child's life," and that "Nobody can protect a child from the world." But trying—with the help of other women—is good enough.

Although it is a job that can never be done perfectly, motherhood is depicted as an empowering role. During Taylor's high school years, her mother has said, "practically every other day," "I don't know how the good Lord packed so much guts into one little person," and her praise encourages Taylor's smart-alecky confidence. Taylor explains, "There were two things about Mama. One is she always expected the best out of me. And the other is that then no matter what I did, whatever I came home with, she acted like it was the moon I had just hung up in the sky and plugged in all the stars. Like I was that good." Taylor supports her daughter in the same way.

When she discovers that the child, whom she calls Turtle because of her stubborn grip, has been sexually abused, Taylor puts her to bed in a T-shirt that says "DAMN I'M GOOD." Mothers can instill in their daughters self-esteem and confident self-sufficiency.

Kingsolver argues for autonomy and self-determination, and she is perfectly willing to reconfigure the family unit in support of those goals. Taylor's mother taught her "how to handle anything that might come along," but she also taught her to let a child live its own life. Before Taylor leaves home, "Mama" makes sure she knows how to deal with two simultaneously flat tires. Later, when her car breaks down again, Taylor blames nobody but herself for her sudden financial crisis, saying, "I should have been able to fix it myself." Taylor does not expect three-year-old Turtle to be self-sufficient, but she notices and respects the resiliency she has already demonstrated in resuming growth after a developmentally static period of abuse. And Taylor allows Turtle to develop at her own pace, in her own directions, telling one young man that Turtle "makes up her own mind about what she's into." One apt landmark on Taylor's drive across the country is the Pioneer Woman Museum.

Kingsolver's recipe for female empowerment includes female community, female traditions, and female empathy. Kingsolver's women help one another, while many of her misguided (but often sympathetic) male characters strike out for themselves or strike out at their loved ones. Taylor feels "lucky" she "didn't have a daddy" when she is face-to-face with a young woman who is bleeding because her husband tried to kill her, alone because her husband has succeeded in killing himself, and scared because she will now have to live alone with her abusive father-in-law. Making a transition between violent alienation and loving community, Lou Ann's mother Ivy has transformed her husband's belt, the one that Lou Ann "had been whipped with years ago,

when her father was alive" into a suitcase strap she uses to go visiting. Lou Ann and her mother and grandmother are one female community, but they cannot speak openly—or at all—with one another. Improving on this female group, two mothers and their small children form a cooperative and supportive household, and they purposefully avoid falling into the traditional breadwinner and homemaker roles. The shape of a family is less important than the love.

While rejecting or sometimes reversing traditional gender roles, Kingsolver embraces others. For example, eating and talking are "good solid female traditions," and they allow these women to reveal eccentric fears and personal experiences so that they can understand each other better. Lou Ann is drawn to Taylor because, she says, "You talk just like me." After living together, and after many evenings of raiding the kitchen and staying up late talking, Taylor realizes "that nobody else on earth could have understood what Lou Ann had just said" in a certain cryptic telephone conversation.

This feminine empathy seems to be at least the local and interim solution for many of the world's ills. After meeting a man who steps on a bug for no reason, Taylor meets a woman who can not bear to: the woman says, "I can't see my way clear to squashing them. A bug's just got one life to live, after all. Like us." This same man wanted to scare Taylor; the woman invites her in to feed her later saying, "I wasn't trying to make a sale. I just thought you two needed some cheering up."

At moments such as these—and there are many—Kingsolver seems to be slipping into inadvertent self-parody. The alignments are predictably earnest and left-liberal: liberated women and little children and poor immigrants and nonhuman nature are all good, and good to each other, while white men (with some exceptions) are insensitive and have little self-understanding. The women persevere amid suffering and injustice with simple truth on their side. Though she argues for nuance and multiplicity, Kingsolver's early fiction works from binary distinctions that resist those qualities, pairing up opposites (women/men, poor/rich, Latino/Anglo, natural/technological) and assigning them opposite moral valences.

Coming out in favor of good mothers may not be as courageous a stand as it sometimes pretends to be either, although Kingsolver is convincing when she contrasts cultural attitudes towards children and child caring. She makes American readers rethink their "nation's creed of every family for itself" as she says in *Tucson,* but "it takes a village" is not a radical stance, either.

But perhaps Kingsolver argues that it takes a village for anyone to flourish; what is good for kids may be good for grown-ups too. Kingsolver's characters flourish in one another's empathy. While Lou Ann is self-defeating when it comes to her own abilities, she has complete confidence in Taylor. Once Taylor has helped Lou Ann stop worrying about her hair and her weight, Lou Ann's job gives her a sense of accomplishment—she is quickly promoted and her feeling that she's "got responsibilities now" keeps her from relocating every time her husband suggests she join him. When Taylor becomes depressed about the evil in the world, and her feeling of powerlessness makes her less spunky than usual, Lou Ann's faith in Taylor helps her recover. Similarly, two elderly neighbors, Virgie Mae Parsons and Edna Poppy form a symbiotic relationship: Edna is Virgie Mae's "public-relations department," and Virgie Mae is so helpful to Edna that Taylor does not realize that Edna is blind until the first time she sees her alone.

Birds and plants are important symbols in *The Bean Trees,* as they continue to be in Kingsolver's later work, and they often point to hope, symbiosis, and resiliency. The birdsong that comes from "Dead Grass Park" suggests hope, adaptation, and triumphant survival. In this same dirt lot are wisteria vines which "looked dead" but eventually "sprouted a fine, shivery coat of pale leaves . . . You just couldn't imagine where all this life was coming from. . . . flowers out of bare dirt. The Miracle of Dog Doo Park." Later in the summer, silent Turtle looks up at the green pods and says "Bean trees." Turtle becomes "April" later in the novel, suggesting her development from a child desperately hanging on for survival to a child who has moved past dormancy to flourish. Reading a reference book on plants in the library, Taylor and Turtle learn that "Rhizobia" are "microscopic bugs" which form the "whole invisible system for helping out the [wisteria] plant." Kingsolver makes an explicit connection: Taylor says, "It's just the same as with people . . . The wisteria vines on their own would just barely get by . . . but put them together with rhizobia and they make miracles."

Kingsolver connects but does not exactly equate female oppression to the political situation in Guatemala. These different forms of "ugliness" are comparable in Taylor's mind, who in a depressed state sees that "the whole way of the world is to pick on people that can't fight back." Unlike the life and death situation in Guatemala, however, which is treated with great seriousness, Kingsolver treats the female condition with humor, depicting the many silly ways women enforce their own oppression, but also pointing to the much less humorous origins of that self-immolation.

HOLDING THE LINE: WOMEN IN THE GREAT ARIZONA MINE STRIKE OF 1983

Kingsolver's account of a miner's strike in *Holding the Line* affords her much of the material for her later fiction, as well as being at least a partial catalyst for her woman-centered themes of cooperation. The sense of community in these small mining towns contributed to their ability to survive "one of the longest strikes there has ever been, anywhere," and this narrative of the strike asserts that women have always been strong, and that they become even stronger when they begin to recognize, practice, and pool their powers. The labor struggle with the mining company Phelps Dodge first showed women their powerlessness: "It gave them a new perspective on a power structure in which they were lodged like gravel in a tire." But when jobs are withheld and homes are threatened, women discover their importance: Anna O'Leary, homemaker turned strike organizer, says, "You know how when you're cooking, you put in an egg and it holds the rice and everything together. That's what we are. We're the egg of the family. Just trying to hold together all these falling-apart things." Establishing women's strength outside the home as well, Kingsolver interviews an old-timer, Mike Baray, born in 1921 and a miner since before 1939 who says: "During the war . . . there weren't hardly any men, so they brought in a bunch of Jamaicans, and a lot of women started working there too . . . After, I think, about eight months, the Jamaicans left. They said the work was too hard. But the women stayed." Women became a necessary force in the strike, largely because a court injunction barred striking miners from congregating outside the mine. Kingsolver writes, " A little bit of success is a powerful thing. For the first time in their lives, the women of Clifton began to see themselves as a force to be reckoned with. Before they knew it, they were keeping the whole town running."

This sense of power was a big change in the lives of these mainly Mexican-American women. Kingsolver reports that, "the strike had begun to unravel some of the deepest threads in the fabric of Hispanic family life." Anna O'Leary says, "Many of us have started seeing a connection between the company abusing authority over strikers and men abusing authority over women." In emphasizing this connection between the individual experience of patriarchy and the group experience of injustice, Kingsolver starts to build

the foundation of a relationship between individual responsibility and worldwide change. In *The Bean Trees,* then, Taylor and Lou Ann's development of a sense of self-empowerment is not a separate topic from the way that the Guatemalans are treated by their violent and hateful government. This sense of personal agency carries over to her later work: in *The Poisonwood Bible,* Leah believes she can make "something right in at least one tiny corner of the vast house of wrongs." Each of us can only do what we can, but we must do it.

Anna O'Leary, who has moved from a grass-roots strike organizer to a confident public speaker, makes the relationship between local and global issues more specifically when she says, "I've grown as a person, just by uniting all these issues I was only vaguely aware of before . . . We mothers are having pathetic little bake sales to buy our kids books, while the government squanders billions and billions of *our* money over there" in Nicaragua. Here O'Leary brings up an issue close to Kingsolver's heart: Kingsolver says in a 1990 interview with Joseph Cincotti, "I can't sit by and think about my tax dollars buying phosphorus bombs for El Salvador. . . . I have to do something—scream and yell—and write novels." Kingsolver makes the reader aware of the relationship between people's individual choices and the global environment—the political as well as physical environment. She reveals the absurd state of affairs people put up with, and the even worse situations they cause by putting up with them.

HOMELAND AND OTHER STORIES (1989)

In this collection, Kingsolver writes female-centered short stories, which augment and fortify her themes of resilience and empowerment. Because of the concentration of twelve stories in one book, a reader might get the sense that Kingsolver is repeating herself. In an interview about her work,

Kingsolver admits to Cincotti, "I have the disturbing idea that I'm writing the same book again and again." But she adds, "I think that writers try to write the truth, as they see it, and the truth remains the same."

In the title story, Kingsolver's peaceful representation of the long-term view—geologic time instead of human time—allows her to argue that human aggression will not win present or future arguments. The narrator says that her great-grandmother's "true name was Green Leaf, although there is no earthly record of this," and Great Mam's burial returns her to the earth the way flowers die on the stem "fall where they are, and make a seed for next year." The narrator's mother disrespects most of Great Mam's beliefs, but Green Leaf wins out because she will ultimately become what is undeniably a green leaf, and her stories will be remembered by her great-granddaughter. Great Mam says, "In the old days . . . whoever spoke the quietist would win the argument." This "long view" is a theme that repeats in other works as well, and in her essay "The Forest in the Seeds" from *Tucson* Kingsolver praises the patience of Charles Darwin and Henry David Thoreau who allow nature to get "around to the revelations."

In "Blueprints" and "Stone Dreams" female characters recognize and then overcome their apathetic responses to their own lives. In "Blueprints" Kingsolver contrasts New Age living with real and drastic internal change. Alluding to the way animals imprint on their parents, her characters struggle with the difficulty of radically changing the nature of couplehood. In "Stone Dreams" Kingsolver contrasts truly appreciating and loving something with collecting or photographing it, and she uses the characters' love of rocks and passion for cabinetry to contrast their death-in-life and life-in-life lives. The main character recognizes herself as a petrified forest; she must destroy the forest in order to live again.

"Covered Bridges" and "Quality Time" focus on the decision to have a child, and how to raise it in the busy, modern world. "Covered Bridge" has a male narrator, an appealing botanist, who leaves the decision to have a child up to his wife at the same time that he knows that he will be expected to (and is willing to) change his own life to care for the child. Put in this somewhat feminized position, he watches how his wife determines that her bee sting allergy gives her too fragile a hold on life to commit to raising a child. She decides to love what she has. The world is dangerous enough for "normal" parents. The single mother in "Quality Time" recognizes the fragility of life (a relative dies in a car crash, she hears sirens several times, and she envisions car crashes) but also sees her five-year-old's strength: "the resilience of . . . children's lives. They will barrel forward like engines, armored by their own momentum, more indestructible than love." Although she would like to have more time with her child and would like to be a better parent, she realizes that "Parenting is something that happens mostly while you're thinking of something else," that "parenting was three percent conscious effort and ninety-seven percent automatic pilot."

Kingsolver's stories often show the transformation of a person who has been predatory or just self-absorbed into someone observant and empathetic. In "Bereaved Apartments" a thief observes the results of another person's thievery, and although she does not act in this instance to prevent what happens, she learns enough about pain and betrayal to move on with new understanding. In "Jump-Up Day" a motherless child whose father is sick and thousands of miles away learns that "Nothing is all good or all bad," that sometimes someone else will appear out of nowhere to protect and heal (and offer a "soft arm" and "a lap"). She realizes that she too can "jump up" and intervene for the benefit of another person or animal. In "Rose-Johnny" an eleven-year-old girl learns to identify with every sort of outcast: black children, a woman who is ostracized as a lesbian, people who have stories told about them, and even her own older (and, of course, sometimes mean) sister who is molested. At the same time that she learns just how badly people can behave in this world, she learns to treat people with dignity.

"Why I Am a Danger to the Public" is a conglomeration of incidents from the strike that Kingsolver describes in *Holding the Line,* emphasizing the trickery involved in entrapping the strikers into appearing to be on the wrong side of the law. Kingsolver, however, suggests that the company and the police have outsmarted themselves, since the union leader they have jailed—Vicki Morales—is one of the strongest voices against violent action. Although readers might rightly surmise that this impending violence will make the union look even worse in the public eye, Vicki's children "would rather have a jailbird than a scab mom" and Kingsolver asserts the persistence and strength of this individual when Vicki concludes that she's still "all in one piece."

ANIMAL DREAMS

While the points of contention in *Animal Dreams* are varied—the mining company versus the town it is killing with chemicals, the struggling people's revolution in Nicaragua, a man's attempt to perfect himself and his family, and a woman's search for purposeful confidence and riskless love—the novel consistently celebrates personal strength while arguing against self-sufficiency and heroics. People do what they need to do to lead a full life, and doing what they need to do often involves working hard for little or no guaranteed rewards. The novel advocates keeping one's ideals and finding one's way almost blindly towards making a useful minor contribution to the world—a suggestion at once deflating and inspiring. As Kingsolver says in her interview with Beattie, "The most important thing is what you can do for people that will make the world better in some way," and "the meaning of life is con-

tained in that old Girl Scout axiom of leaving the campsite better than you found it."

Alternately narrated by Doc Homer and his eldest daughter Cosima, *Animal Dreams* shows how Cosima's high expectations of herself, her pursuit of perfection and avoidance of partial failure prevents her achievement and action. Kingsolver describes her in the Beattie interview as "the sort of walking wounded who has never quite found the engagement with life that her sister has." Cosima's good-hearted if sometimes misplaced or unsuccessful efforts to help others inspire her younger sister Hallie to follow her heart and act on her beliefs. Cosima's father and childhood neighbors remember Cosima trying to rescue a litter of coyotes whose den was about to be flooded by a rising river. The two sisters can carry all but one of the babies to safety, but Cosima sits crying in the den because she cannot take every one of them with her. Homer remembers, "after crouching for a half a day in the small shelter of that gravel bank, waiting for the mother coyote to come back and save her children, [the girls] had to leave them." Cosima has forgotten this incident, erasing her good intentions as well as her indecision and inaction, but Hallie sees her as a moral mentor.

In their sadness, the girls ask "if the baby coyotes died" and "If animals go to heaven," and Homer "has no answers." He wonders, "why does a mortal man have children? It is senseless to love anything this much." These thoughts point to the imperfect nature of life, the lack of guarantees, and the wide chasm of unknowningness that surrounds every enterprise, even (or especially) the most important and meaningful. Homer has lost his beloved wife, and he recognizes the loss that is the inevitable result of the love his daughters have for each other: he wants to weep "For how close these two are, and how much they have to lose. How much they've already lost in their lives to come." Instead of dreamily depicting perfect, endless love, Kingsolver suggests that humans can only make the best of their real lives, which involves loving in spite of the fear of eventual pain. Cosima and her beau Loyd speculate about animal dreams, and decide that animals, including human animals, can dream only about what they do when they are awake. While Cosima, who is wary of love because of the pain it can cause, is disappointed at this idea of dreams, Loyd says, "If you want sweet dreams, you've got to live a sweet life." He seems to teach her to take the risk of accepting a "sweet life" instead of running away from the prospect of losing it.

Kingsolver repeatedly and effectively compares humans to other living things—both plants and animals—and she thus shows both human vulnerability and empowerment. The novel opens with the two young sisters "curled together like animals whose habit is to sleep underground, in the smallest space possible." Cosima is frightened by a truck honking at her, and she "froze up, like one of those ridiculous squirrels that darts one way and then the other and is doomed to end up a road kill." At a Labor Day "fiesta," the kids "ran underfoot like rebel cockroaches." Loyd compares himself to his "mongrel" dog, and Cosima compares a tortured refugee woman from San Salvador to a "zoo animal" whose "eyes offered out . . . flatness" Loyd gives up cock fighting because of the similarity he suddenly sees between the death of the birds and the death of his twin brother. The dead and acidic water discovered by the students in Cosima's biology class, water empty of protozoans, signals the future of all other living things in the valley. Some of these metaphors suggest human weakness: people are as vulnerable as confused squirrels when we run from the unknown, and we are susceptible to the same physical or emotional death as the protozoa and zoo animals. On the other hand, some of the comparisons emphasize human strength. For example, we retain certain survival instincts—love, memory, empowerment through either biological or mental mongrelization, and

even powers we cannot know in ourselves (as cockroaches no doubt are unaware of their rumored singular power to live through a nuclear blast). These metaphors should give us hope; perhaps some of their animal instincts can help us out of our troubles as a species. As Cosima concludes, "We're animals. We're born like every other mammal and we live our whole lives around disguised animal thoughts."

While Cosima becomes a biologist, her sister Hallie gravitates to the plant kingdom. Hallie says, "plants do everything animals do—give birth, grow, travel around . . . have sex, etc. They just do it a lot slower." Thus it is not surprising perhaps that Kingsolver compares humans to plants, too. For Dioecious carob trees, for example, "it takes two to tango" just like humans, and Cosima sympathetically pats the bark of a lone female tree. The geraniums near Cosima's front door wilt in the heat, but recover perfectly when watered, and Cosima thinks, "I could only wish for such resilience." It turns out that she is that resilient: by changing his name, speaking only English, and telling his daughters they are outsiders in Grace, Arizona, Cosima's father has purposefully attempted to uproot and destroy her family tree, but this family tree—like the trees in the valley being destroyed by acids—is maintained by the cooperative matriarchy of the town.

Kingsolver alludes to a worldview in which humans not only learn about themselves through metaphors with the living natural world, but see themselves as united with even the inanimate world of dirt and rock—and comport themselves based on this perception. Loyd takes Cosima to Kinishba, "prehistoric condos" built by the Pueblo—his "mama's folks"—eight hundred years ago. Cosima exclaims, "It doesn't even look like it was built . . . It's too beautiful. It looks like something alive that just *grew* here." The "walls are thick" in this "maze" of "two hundred rooms" because they are "graveyards." Loyd explains, "When a baby died, they'd mortar its bones right into the wall. Or under the floor . . . So it would still be near the family." While the architects envision and design an organic structure, the children's bones make it literally organic, and they nourish the home in the only way they can once they haveve died. Relatedly, Kingsolver alludes to the battlefields of northern France, where the "fields were blessed . . . by the bones. The soil was rich in calcium." Dead or alive, it seems, humans can do good works. Awful wars in Europe or Central America can still result in something good, if only rich soil. Instead of a world in which living people are objectified, Kingsolver depicts a world in which living people are empowered and dead people can still be useful.

Cosima becomes aware of other subtle powers as well, such as the powerful matriarchy of the town in which she grew up. Motherless from toddlerhood on, it is not until she is in her thirties that she realizes how she and her sister were cared for by a close-knit but somehow invisible network of women. This realization is even more surprising to her than the way in which the women of Grace work together to save the town's water supply. While the men think lawyers can save them, the women resort to less conventional—and faster-acting—methods of resistance. Learning as they go, they succeed in drawing attention to the town's plight by selling piñatas made with peacock feathers and enclosing a one-page "written history of Grace and its heroic struggle against the Black Mountain Mining Company." The women are just oppressed enough to recognize how oppressive and unfair the system can be, and they know how to work outside of it. When the town complains that the water is acidic, the EPA decides that it is acceptable for the company to build a dam and reroute the river away from the human population—saving them from acid but leaving them with no water. Cosima "couldn't believe it" but Viola, a knowing grandmother who has seen a lot in her time, is not surprised. To Cosima's morally enraged question, "How could they do that?" Viola responds with a physical, materialist answer: "With bulldozers." After learning her away around the "matriarchy of Grace," Cosima realizes that "The Stitch and Bitch Club wasn't banking on the good old boys."

While Hallie goes to Nicaragua to aid the people's agricultural revolution, Cosima has another farmer's revolution brewing at home. While the copper company has stopped employing the town's population, it has started ruining their crops. While Hallie has driven out of North America in order "To give [her]self over to utility, with no waste," the women in Grace have always found multiple ways to make themselves useful: caring for orphaned children, feeding an increasingly senile old doctor, raising their own children, and retaining family and community traditions. Hallie writes, "it's what you *do* that makes you who you are" and "Wars and elections are both too big and too small to matter in the long run. The daily work—that goes on, it adds up. It goes into the ground, into crops, into children's bellies and their bright eyes. Good things don't get lost."

But while Kingsolver offers an encomium to the everyday love, patience, resistance, and accomplishments of mothers, she also makes a political statement about American "amnesia" and ignorance, the budding hopes of a developing agricultural nation, and the blindness of most Americans to our own complicity in the destruction of those hopes. The news media is chastised for misrepresenting the conflicts in Nicaragua. Reminding the reader that one person can make a difference, Kingsolver also reminds the reader that one casualty of war is both as important and as unremarkable as any other of the multiple casualties: as the man on the telephone from a Managua church says in Spanish, "You understand that this occurs every day. We're a nation of bereaved families." When Cosima sips a margarita with salt on the rim, "the crystals felt like sand in [her] mouth, or broken glass." Instead of succumbing to the pleasant, opiatic effect of a Mexican cocktail, she thinks "of walls I'd seen in Mexico—high brick *hacienda* walls topped with a crest of broken bottles imbedded in cement, to keep people on their correct sides of the fence." Claiming that Americans are willfully blind to the pain of others, Kingsolver infuses hard memories into one of the favorite acts of American recreational forgetting, thus invoking the readers' memories when they least expect or desire it. She gets under her readers' skin, or at least pulls them away from the bar.

What is most surprising is that Kingsolver can nonetheless succeed as a storyteller, offering works of consistent political advocacy that still reach a wide popular audience, to which they must provide a considerable burden of guilt along with the pleasure of entertainment. Reviewer Lynette Lamb writes of *Animal Dreams,* "Any novel that can bring multiple political themes into a love story and still remain a good read must be doing something right." But reviewer Wendy Brandmark writes of *Homeland and Other Stories,* "The power of these stories rests as much with their moral awareness, their righteousness, as it does with their charm and the ease of her story-telling."

ANOTHER AMERICA/OTRA AMERICA

That Kingsolver's poetry has been less warmly received than the novels, however, may reflect the loss of narrative compensation, and the fact that poetry is more easily flattened by advocacy than fiction—though a few poets such as Carolyn Forche have managed to write successfully with a political agenda similar to Kingsolver's. Lorraine Elena Roses divides Kingsolver's poems into two types: "highly political poems by a committed human rights activist who seeks to stir our consciences and enlist us in the cause of social justice and pacifism" and more successful "poems about the female condition and our spiritual connection to animal life, either wild or free."

Another America/Otra America immediately calls attention to its embrace of two languages. Written by Kingsolver in English, each left-hand page is a Spanish translation of Kingsolver's poems by the Chilean writer Rebeca Cartes. In an interview with Donna Perry, Kingsolver explains that she wanted her poems to "be accessible to the citizens of that other America. In Tucson about a third of the people speak Spanish at home." Kingsolver also explains that during a book tour in Spain, readers of *The Bean Trees* said they were surprised to read about poverty in the United States. She depicts a different America than that seen on "Dallas" or in Danielle Steele novels, saying in her interview with Beattie that "All of us have lives that are worthy of literature, not just here in Nicholas County [Kentucky], but everywhere that the paint on the fences is peeling, and life keeps going behind them." These people do not just offer new material for a fiction-writer, but rather Kingsolver argues that it is "imperative . . . to record . . . the voices of those who've had their voices taken away from them."

The first section of this collection is titled "The House Divided/La Casa Divida," and the poems record and analyze several divisions: between Spanish and English speakers within the United States, between North and South America, a rift in female solidarity, women divided from themselves, and—less strongly—the divide between male and female. One epigraph is the last two lines of Adrienne Rich's poem "Storm Warnings": "These are the things that we have learned to do / Who live in troubled regions." Kingsolver's first poem, "Deadline," describes one of these "things": a candlelight vigil in front of a missile base. These protesters are mainly powerless—"wondering what it is—[they] can hold a candle to"—but the very fact that the female narrator has spent so much effort keeping her child "undamaged to this moment" makes protest necessary. All that love and work would be useless if she did not also try save her from becoming collateral damage to a "bomb that flings gasoline in a liquid sheet." Hopeless, standing on "the carcass of hope," this narrator still hopes that "somewhere" there is "a way out."

Kingsolver's poetry also depicts the way that women are divided against themselves, partly by alienating themselves from their own natural bodies, and she argues for women's powerful potential if that energy were only turned to other purposes. In "Reveille," a "bloodless" woman does "not smell like any living thing," and she is "engaged in war with her mammalian origins." Kingsolver's narrator asks, "If I should abandon this battle / . . . if I were to become / the animal that I am, then / what? In *Animal Dreams*, Kingsolver points out the "slavish attention" girls pay to their appearance, the pain they are willing to undergo for their multiple earrings, and the surprising corollary that they "can't be bothered with prophylactics," but in "Reveille" there is the sense that this redirected energy could give birth to a new society, not just prevent conception.

The second section, "The Visitors/Los Visitantes," discusses the plights of immigrants and refugees to the United States. In "Refuge," Kingsolver writes about betrayal by a person or nation who says, "*Give me your hand*" in assistance, and then—noticing that the hand "offers nothing"—cuts it off, only saving it to prove "*the great / desirability / of my country.*" Kingsolver suggests a parallel between these victims and female victims of rape, and the poem is dedicated to "Juana, raped by immigration officers and deported." This section includes "For Sacco and Vanzetti" and allusions to other historical immigrants and exiles, as well as poems contrasting the experience of refugees with someone who has been born and raised in the United States.

If "The Visitors" make her see her world differently, the people described in "The Lost/Los Perdidos"—the title of Section III—have been completely transformed by their own experiences. Refugees can sometimes leave the place in which they have experienced or witnessed horrors, and in "This House I Cannot Leave" a woman can sell her house and move after it has been burglarized. But the "me" in "This House" cannot leave herself. She is "thinking / of the man who broke and entered / me. / Of the years it took to be home again / in this house I cannot leave." The narrator in "Ten Forty-Four" also describes the emotional effects of a rape, the result of which is that it "peeled off what there was / of faith" in her. As her kindness was used against her, so was her paring knife, and now she keeps all these things "in a locked drawer." The very fact that these poems exist, however, attests to human resiliency, since Kingsolver was raped at age nineteen. These are poems of betrayal ("Family Secrets"), human fragility ("For Richard After All"), and the necessary risks we take in empathizing with others ("The Loss of My Arms and Legs"). Kingsolver simultaneously yearns for people's ease, and their pain: she writes, "I looked into the round bird eyes / of my children, and prayed they were feeling nothing, / prayed they would feel forever." Let them live happily, yes, but if not that, then at least let them live, and live with empathy.

Section IV, "The Believers/Los Creyentes," annotates belief and celebrates the hope of a "way out" via "Bridges" between nations, family history, and self-invention ("Naming Myself"), "everyday incarnation" in the face of daily robbery ("Apotheosis"), and dreams that might tell "some truth / that could save us" ("Watershed"). "Elections, Nicaragua, 1984" describes "the vote" that is so important: "The sun has never shone in exactly this way / on my children's hair." While in the United States "Pierre Cardin is showing / a feminine look for winter," Kingsolver's narrator writes that "in another country of my heart / I've known homelands I would die for." In "Our Father Who Drowns the Birds" Kingsolver describes the "season when all wars end: / when the rains come." In the rain, "every ancient anger / settles," "all of the old grudges / fall" and the airplanes have to give up the sky. Nature, faith, and the human imagination may be keys to the "way out." The first step may be believing there is one.

Section V, "The Patriots/Los Patriotas," describes people who are not nationalistic but rather globally concerned for human rights and human love. One narrator is "not repentant" even when she discovers her phones have been tapped. "The Middle Daughter" would "float upstream" if she were thrown in the water, and has a "problem" with her "vision": she sees everything differently and "believes / she will make history." In the poem "In the City Ringed with Giants" Kingsolver berates the "talismans" that have allowed people to accept the uncontrollable dangers they have created and allowed to proliferate in the world; now "bereft of talismans" she says we have the responsibility to "live as if our lives belonged to us." In "The Blood Returns," Kingsolver depicts several characters who see things for themselves and make hard decisions: a soldier "who can't forgive himself," other soldiers who learn to kill but whose hearts "fill again" and they desert, and a woman who refuses to give in to torture out of love for her children. The collection ends with a poem about survival ("Remember the Moon Survives") and a poem that describes love, hope, and beauty being spawned from hatred and forgiveness ("Your Mother's Eyes"). Kingsolver makes her reader angry, but not cynical.

PIGS IN HEAVEN

Pigs in Heaven is—and is not—a sequel to *The Bean Trees*. A complete work in itself, and treating several additional themes, *Pigs in Heaven* deals with the legal and moral issue of Taylor's illegally adopting Turtle and taking her from her Cherokee tribe. While *The Bean Trees* depicts lonely individuals building a supportive community, *Pigs in Heaven* discusses the way that the Cherokee community has been dismantled and the efforts to rebuild it. In *The Bean Trees* anyone can form a family; here families are a given, extended family members have commitments to each other, and Taylor comes to believe that she would like to make her own family more official (by stating her commitment to her boyfriend) so that it too is more likely to weather hard times and can offer more stable support to Turtle.

Kingsolver does not believe in the romance of poverty, as shown by Taylor's awful struggles "on the lam," but she does spotlight (and idealize) how a loving community can overcome poverty. Taylor's mother Alice remembers that during the Depression people formed special bond. Although the town on the reservation is surprisingly impoverished from Taylor's mother's point of view, Kingsolver shows the way that communal poverty is so much richer and more pleasant than Taylor's when she is alone: she is robbed by someone she helped, people ridicule her child's poverty, keeping up appearances is expensive, there is little sympathy or understanding, and people do not think to share.

Kingsolver writes about the Cherokee people as alive and vital, emphasizing that Native Americans are part of the present. In her essay "The Spaces Between" from *High Tide in Tucson,* Kingsolver expresses frustration that her daughter understands Native Americans to be "People that lived a long time ago." In *Pigs in Heaven* Kingsolver reminds the reader that the woman posing in the Trading Post window and doing beadwork is the mother of teenagers, and that young men go to Stomp Dances to meet girls. In spite of the presence of living, working Native Americans, one scholar, A. LaVonne Brown Ruoff (cited in an article by Sarah Kerr), asserts the position that Kingsolver's Native Americans are "objects," "backdrop," and "local color," but not real people.

In *Pigs in Heaven* Kingsolver praises women as the fortification of families and attacks television as one of the things that disintegrate human relationships. Somebody says that television "promises whatever you want, before you know what you want," thus contributing to a constant state of desire and competition. Alice leaves her husband because he spends more time with the Home Shopping Channel than with her, and because he thinks that seeing something on television is better than experiencing it in person. Alice theorizes that television encourages people to behave passively in interpersonal relationships—it does all the talking, and people forget that they have to "hold up [their] end" of the deal. Alice discovers that being there in person is the difference between being dead and being alive. At the end of the novel, her new romantic interest, Cash Stillwater, makes a public display of destroying his television in order to persuade Alice to marry him.

Kingsolver does not completely idealize interpersonal relationships either, recognizing their complexity and even seeming impossibility. Her characters recognize "how entirely inside themselves they are" and how difficult it therefore is to read them and understand other people. Love is hard—hard to maintain and hard to define—but Kingsolver defines love as "stay[ing] in the same room." A readership raised on the idea of self-sufficiency may find the idea of caring for the poor and insane less than appealing, but Kingsolver even suggests that loving and caring for local lunatics can bring people together, and thus these lunatics are the truest of citizens.

The biggest struggle is between the individual (Taylor) and the community (the Cherokee tribe), which, Kingsolver told Beattie, is "the thing [she] always write[s] about . . . How to balance community and autonomy." Both are valued, and Kingsolver represents a situation in which as Ly-nette Lamb wrote in 1993 "there are no good guys or bad guys—only well-meaning people overwhelmed by history, racial issues, and love." Should a child be raised by its loved and loving individual parent or by the heretofore unknown but also loving extended family and tribe? Which is better for the individual child? And does that matter? Which is better for the tribe? In an interview with Lynn Karpen, Kingsolver says, "The media view the basic unit of good as what is best for the child; the tribe sees it as what is best for the group. These are two very different value systems with no point of intersection." The novel offers a friendly compromise, which is probably the best answer, although some readers will find the outcome disappointingly contrived. Not only do the Cherokee benefit from their knowledge of their ancestry and cultural heritage, Taylor, too, is helped along by knowing her family's history with men, and her mother finds great happiness not only in her new romance but also in joining the tribe to which she never knew she belonged.

THE POISONWOOD BIBLE

Kingsolver's novel, *The Poisonwood Bible,* which was on the *New York Times* best-seller list, expands on—and outdoes—her earlier themes and strengths as a writer. As the Price family moves from Bethlehem, Georgia to the rural village of Kilanga in the Congo, Kingsolver leaves her usual setting—the South and Southwestern United States—for Africa, where she lived for a year as a child. While in previous texts Kingsolver explored issues relating to women and Native Americans or Mexican Americans, here Kingsolver explores the similarities and differences between women's oppression and the oppression of the Africans, both victims of white Bible-wielding—or otherwise self-righteously self-appointed—male messengers of what can only be called a single, limited, and uninclusive idea of civilization. Kingsolver's earlier novels are marked by conversational and distinctly drawn female narrators, and *The Poisonwood Bible* is narrated by the voices of five different females who mature thirty years between the beginning and end of the novel.

Orleanna Price and her four daughters—Rachel, Leah, Adah, and Ruth May—move to the Congo because the man of the house feels called to be a Baptist missionary. From their varying perspectives, Nathan Price is both impressively terrifying and ridiculously blind to the realities around him. As Adah writes, "It is a special kind of person who will draw together a congregation, stand up before them with a proud, clear voice, and say words wrong, week after week." Her twin Leah writes, "Watching my father, I've seen how you can't learn anything when you're trying to look like the smartest person in the room." After a couple of years of missionary work—or, rather, working to survive in difficult and threatening conditions with no money and little food, responsibility for which falls on the women and girls—the family unit disintegrates. In a single day, after the death of her youngest daughter, Orleanna gives away all their possessions and walks out of town toward Leopoldville, her remaining daughters trailing behind. How they each leave the Congo, or do not, is the rest of the narrative, which lets the reader see the perspectives of these women shift over the next few decades.

Kingsolver treats her reader to a brief version of the long history of the Congo, offering a historical and geographical perspective, as well as a microscopic one. For example, if one takes a longer historical view, and is open-minded enough to accept different shapes of social organization, one can appreciate the impressive civilization present in the Congo before European enslavement and imperialism. Leah writes, "The kingdom was held together by thousands of miles of footpaths crossing the forest, with suspension bridges of woven vines swinging quietly over the rivers." If one takes into account the geography of the Congo—the extreme climate changes, the soil, and so on—one might even recognize that this previous civilization was the best ordered for this area of the world. But without "commodity agriculture—no cities, no giant plantations, and no roads necessary for transporting produce from the one to the other"—the Europeans could not recognize an advanced culture. While she may be as Aamer Hussein has claimed, "idealizing and mythologizing Africa's precolonial past," Kingsolver argues that in a place where mud makes vehicle travel impossible, where one cannot count on crops coming to fruition, where the jungle can provide food enough for a local group of people, and where anything saved up can disappear the next day because of an attack of ants or just bad luck, commodity agriculture and the large cities that are dependent on that agriculture cannot be the best system. Population density is as dangerous as trying to baptize people in a river full of crocodiles—and both of these are impositions from blind outsiders who think they know best, but do not.

A unifying characteristic of these two very different cultures, though, is their dependence on women's work and disregard for women. Reverend Price has four intelligent daughters, none of whom he expects to send to college, and even his least thoughtful daughter realizes, "It's just lucky for Father he never had any sons. He might have been forced to respect them." In the Congo, women carry "the world on their heads" and "While the little boys ran around pretending to shoot each other and fall dead in the road, it appeared that little girls were running the country." Ruth May teaches her friends to play "Mother May I," and they chant this refrain as Nathan Price overlooks the ironies and baptizes them "In the name of the Father, the Son, and the Holy Ghost." While struggling to understand her own complicity in the pain of others—the Africans, her daughters—at the hands of patriarchs like her husband, Orleanna Price also sees that she and the Congo were similarly occupied and had similar means of resistance. She writes, "Nathan was in full possession of the country once known as Orleanna Wharton, asks "What is the conqueror's wife, if not a conquest herself?" and adds "To resist occupation, whether you're a nation or merely a woman, you must understand the language of your enemy." White women are in the same position, and in a different position, from the blacks that their husbands enslave, conquer, instruct, or just disrespectfully depend on.

The easiest point to make about *The Poisonwood Bible* is that it is complex. As Leah writes, "There are more words in the world than yes and no." The novel contains Kingsolver's best representation of complexity and nuance, how life comes from death, and good can come from evil. But it is not that easy: the life that comes from death will soon be dead, and the present good that comes from now-clear evil may be bad in hindsight. In short, everything is a struggle, and nothing is as simple as it looks from a single perspective. A few of Kingsolver's morals might be share whatever you have (you don't know if you'll have it tomorrow anyway), people do not need much to survive, civilizations can take more than one kind of shape, the United States government was absolutely wrong to assassinate Patrice Lumumba, the premier of the newly independent Congo from June through September 1960, closing one's eyes to problems does not make one less guilty, "democracy" is not the only fair way to make decisions, and Americans should recognize the contradictions in their nation's combination of political, economic, and religious values.

Coming across more clearly than all these morals is the importance of nuance and tone, translation and context. One character—a minister who "consort[ed] with the natives too much"—not only highlights the possible translation mistakes of the Bible into English, but also points out that some biblical rites are probably irrelevant outside the context of Jesus' Middle Eastern culture and climate. He believes that "whole chapters" of the Bible must be "throw[n] away" because "God's word [is] brought to you by a crew of romantic idealists in a harsh desert climate eons ago, followed by a chain of translators two thousand years long." He asks, for example, if "All that foot washing" was "really for God's glory, or just to keep the sand out of the house?"

Nathan Price has "never been troubled by any such difficulties with interpreting God's word," but he should be. Unable to notice the tonal differences between one Kikongo word and another, he shouts "Jesus is Poisonwood"—"the plant that bites"—instead of saying—"The word of Christ is Beloved." *Nzolo* means "most dearly beloved," "a type of tiny potato" and "a thick yellow grub highly prized for fish bait," and Adah asks, "And so we sing at the top of our lungs in church: '*Tata Nzolo!*' To whom are we calling?" She then answers, "I think it must be the god of small potatoes." These confusions do not occur only in foreign languages: Rachel and Ruth May, the oldest and youngest Price daughters, both make telling mistakes in English. When she hears a doctor remind her father of the actual or practical enslavement of the Africans by Belgians and Americans, she thinks her father is "stuck with the job of trying to make amens"—which he certainly is, and which will not end up being an effective way of making amends. Self-involved Rachel says her chances of getting a boyfriend are "dull and void," she "prefer[s] to remain anomalous," that "it's a woman's provocative to change her mind," and that she is "determined to use [her] feminine wilds." In each case, and there are many others, the doubling or tripling of the semantic codes enrich and complicate the speakers' meanings, as Adah's allusions to Emily Dickinson ("no snickcidy lime") should remind us. Adah's hemiplegia and subsequent aphasia—her tendency to read things backwards and forwards—and her interest in palindromes also multiplies meaning: "star pupil" becomes "*lipup rats.*"

Adah says that Kikongo is "a language even more cynical than [her] own," but she may also mean more cyclical. For example, "*syebo* is a horrible, destructive rain, that just exactly does not do what it says backward." This cyclical nature of the languages intimates the cyclical nature of life itself—life that includes rather than excludes death, and there is a word for this, *muntu.* In redeeming himself from his guilt at living when all his company marched to their deaths on the Bataan Peninsula in the Philippines, Nathan Price eventually wanders through African jungles until he is killed. Physical injuries caused him to escape this fate in World War II, but the moral injuries from that war cause him to repeat himself by abandoning his family to the Congo. Trying to "make amens" and spread Christianity in this heathen land, Nathan Price dies in a "boss tower" and is called a "witch doctor." His personal cycle is just one part of a larger cycle: he dies in a tower "where in the old days the Belgian foreman would stand watching all the coffee pickers so he could single out which ones to whip at the end of the day." What goes around comes around.

Not just a psychic or historical tendency, nature too works in cycles: "sucking life out of death[,] [t]his forest eats itself and lives forever." Instead of seeing their father in heaven, Adah and Leah use non-biblical verse (lines from William Shakespeare's *The Tempest*) to express his return to nature: "*Full fathom five thy father lies; / Of his bones are coral made: / Those are the pearls that were his eyes: / Nothing of him that doth fade, / But doth suffer a sea-change / Into something rich and strange.*" Participating in a hunt, all the girls realize that "all animals kill to survive, and we are animals"; they see themselves as part of a natural cycle in which sometimes they

hunt and sometimes they are the hunted (as when an army of Congolese ants attacks the village one night). The one daughter buried in the Congo concludes the novel (from death), "Think of the vine that curls from the small square plot that was once my heart. That is the only marker you need. Move on. Walk forward into the light."

The Poisonwood Bible finds ways to complicate binary polemical alignments without surrendering its moral energy and its provision of hope. The Congo provides a larger canvas, but Kingsolver is also working with more delicate strokes. Right and wrong are still important, but they are not so obvious, and the personal beliefs of the author are variously refracted by multiple narrators. Language itself has become a topic of interest, not just a supplier of pleasant and vernacular speech or a transparent means of a sociopolitical end. While many writers are drawn toward self-caricature by great popularity—and Kingsolver is widely regarded as a likable person true to her beliefs—*The Poisonwood Bible* shows this writer challenging herself and her readership to rethink their complacencies without forfeiting their obligations.

Selected Bibliography

WORKS OF BARBARA KINGSOLVER

NOVELS
The Bean Trees. New York: Harper & Row, 1988.
Animal Dreams. New York: HarperCollins, 1990.
Pigs in Heaven. New York: HarperCollins, 1993.
Poisonwood Bible. New York: HarperPerennial, 1998

NONFICTION AND ESSAYS
Holding the Line: Women in the Great Arizona Mine Strike of 1983. Ithaca, N.Y.: Industrial & Labor Relations Press, 1989.

High Tide in Tucson: Essays from Now or Never. New York: HarperCollins, 1995.

OTHER WORKS

Homeland and Other Stories. New York: Harper & Row, 1989.

Another America/Otra America. Seattle, Wash.: Seal Press, 1992.

CRITICAL AND BIOGRAPHICAL STUDIES

Aamer, Hussein. "Daughters of Africa." *Times Literary Supplement,* February 5, 1991, p. 21.

Aay, Henry. "Environmental Themes in Ecofiction: In the Center of the Nation and Animal Dreams." *Journal of Cultural Geography* 14, no. 2:65–85 (Spring–Summer 1994).

Brandmark, Wendy. "Kinship with the Earth." *Times Literary Supplement,* January 24, 1997, p. 22.

Comer, Krista. "Sidestepping Environmental Justice: 'Natural' Landscapes and the Wilderness Plot." In *Breaking Boundaries: New Perspectives on Women's Regional Writing.* Iowa City: University of Iowa Press, 1997. Pp. 216–236.

DeMarr, Mary Jean. *Barbara Kingsolver: A Critical Companion.* Westport, Conn.: Greenwood Press, 1999.

Lamb, Lynette. "Books Bound for Glory." *Utne Reader,* March–April 1991, p. 152. (Review of *Animal Dreams.*)

———. Review of *Pigs in Heaven. Utne Reader,* July–August 1993, p. 122.

Murrey, Loretta Martin. "The Loner and the Matriarchal Community in Barbara Kingsolver's *The Bean Trees* and *Pigs in Heaven.*" *Southern Studies* 5, nos. 1–2:155–164 (Spring–Summer 1994).

Roses, Lorraine Elena. "Language and Other Barriers." *The Women's Review of Books* 9, nos. 10–11: 42 (July 1992).

Ryan, Maureen. "Barbara Kingsolver's Lowfat Fiction." *Journal of American Culture: Studies of a Civilization* 18, no. 4:77–82 (Winter 1995).

Smith, Ruth L. "Negotiating Homes: Morality as a Scarce Good." *Cultural Critique* 38:177–195 (Winter 1997–1998).

INTERVIEWS

Beattie, L. Elisabeth. "Barbara Kingsolver." *Conversations with Kentucky Writers.* Lexington: University of Kentucky Press, 1996.

Cincotti, Joseph A. "Intimate Revelations." *New York Times Book Review,* September 2, 1990, p. 2.

Karpen, Lynn. "The Role of Poverty." *New York Times Book Review,* June 27, 1993, p. 9.

Kerr, Sarah. "The Novel as Endictment." *New York Times Magazine,* October 11, 1998, pp. 53–55.

Lyall, Sarah. "Termites Are Interesting, But Books Sell Better." *New York Times,* September 1, 1993, pp. C1, C8.

Neill, Michael, and Michael Haederle. "La Pasionaria." *People,* October 11, 1993, pp. 109–110.

Perry, Donna. *Backtalk: Women Writers Speak Out.* New Brunswick, N.J.: Rutgers University Press, 1993.

Ross, Jean W. "Barbara Kingsolver: Contemporary Authors Interview." In *Contemporary Authors,* Vol. 134. Detroit: Gale Research, 1992. Pp. 286–289.

—DANA CAIRNS WATSON

Jerzy Kosinski

1933–1991

JERZY KOSINSKI WAS one of the most puzzling and controversial writers of the last half of the twentieth century. Kosinski was a Polish citizen who immigrated to the United States in 1957 to study sociology at Columbia University. He was the author of two nonfiction books, *The Future is Ours, Comrade: Conversations with the Russians* (1960) and *No Third Path* (1962) which were sociological studies of life in the Soviet Union. He was also a prolific writer of fiction who won a National Book Award and wrote the screenplay for the popular movie *Being There* (1979).

WORKS AND AWARDS

Kosinski wrote nine novels: *The Painted Bird* (1965), *Steps* (1968), *Being There* (1971), *The Devil Tree* (1973), *Cockpit: A Novel* (1975), *Blind Date* (1977), *Passion Play* (1979), *Pinball* (1982), and *The Hermit of 69th Street: The Working Papers of Norbert Kosky* (1988). He skyrocketed to fame with the phenomenal success of his first novel, *The Painted Bird*. The book was originally conceived as a nonfiction autobiography, but was eventually published as a novel. It generated a whirlwind of generally favorable reactions from literary critics and the public and it received the

French *Prix du Meilleur Livre Etranger* (Best Foreign Book Award) in 1966.

Steps won the prestigious National Book Award. Kosinski's screenplay for his novel *Being There* won a British screenplay award from the British Academy of Film and Television Arts (BAFTA) in 1981. The movie, which starred Peter Sellers and Shirley MacLaine, was a huge critical success. Kosinski also wrote long self-published essays attempting to explain his writing methods and philosophy.

Kosinski was a winner of a Ford Foundation fellowship to study at Columbia University and a Guggenheim Award for his writing. He served as president of the national writer's organization PEN for two years. He also taught at Princeton, Yale, and Wesleyan Universities.

Kosinski married the widow Mary Weir in 1962. Weir was heir to a steel magnate's fortune, and when he married her, Kosinski entered into a celebrity lifestyle, traveling the world and getting to know many famous politicians and writers such as Henry Kissinger and Arthur Miller. The couple later divorced. He also appeared on television many times and in the movie *Reds,* which starred and was directed by Warren Beatty. He was a friend of the Polish director Roman Polanski, whose actress-wife Sharon Tate was killed by the Charles Manson "family" in 1969 and at whose house Kosinski was supposed to be on the night of the murders.

BACKGROUND

Born in Lodz, Poland, in 1933 to well-to-do Jewish parents, Kosinski's youth coincided with Hitler's rise to power in Germany. Jerzy Kosinski, his parents, and younger brother were survivors of the German occupation and narrowly avoided the Holocaust. For many years after his arrival in the United States, Kosinski maintained the fiction that he had been abandoned by his parents as a six-year-old child in Eastern Poland. His personal narrative about fleeing hostile peasants and Nazi capture was eventually exposed as a fabricated story, but nonetheless it was a tale that had garnered him sympathy in many circles.

After World War II, the Kosinski family was liberated by the Russians and Jerzy returned to school in Lodz under the new Soviet government. He earned two advanced degrees and traveled to the Soviet Union to study the Soviet collective system.

In 1957, Kosinski left Poland for the United States. He enrolled at Columbia University, where he studied to get a Ph.D. in political sociology. Later, at the request of his wife and friends he began writing an autobiographical manuscript that he later turned into the novel *The Painted Bird.*

Kosinski's life started in dangerous circumstances and his fondness for risk-taking was a confirmed habit by his late teens. He often tested himself through extreme challenges as an aggressive skier and polo player. In his later years he wandered the streets of New York alone at night.

A barrage of negative criticism of Kosinski's work erupted in 1982. In an article entitled "Jerzy Kosinski's Tainted Words" two writers for the *Village Voice* questioned the truthfulness of Ko-

sinski's account of himself and his writing methods, and accused him of plagiarism in *The Painted Bird* and *Being There.* What followed was a damaging critical review of Kosinski's whole oeuvre which precipitated a major crisis in his life.

In fact, much of Jerzy Kosinski's life was shrouded in mystery. He denied his Jewish heritage until 1977 when he publicly acknowledged his identity at the opening ceremony of the Holocaust Memorial in New Haven, Connecticut. It is only with the publication of the excellent and exact *Jerzy Kosinski: A Biography* (1996) by James Park Sloan that the true facts of Kosinski's complicated life became known.

During the late 1980s Kosinski wrote his last novel, *Hermit on 69th Street,* in a partial attempt to explain his writing methods and personal history. He also became involved in business projects in Poland, including plans to open an American bank. He created the Jewish Presence Foundation, an organization devoted to promoting the positive achievements of Jews. He married his long-time partner Katherina von Fraunhofer, known as Kiki, in 1987. He continued to travel extensively, including trips to Israel and Poland.

In the early morning hours of May 3, 1991, after an apparently normal day, Jerzy Kosinski committed suicide in his New York City apartment with a combination of drugs and alcohol. He was 57 years old.

THE EARLY YEARS: FACT AND FICTION

Kosinski would draw upon his early experience as a child in Poland during the German occupation for his most famous novel, *The Painted Bird.* However, the stories that Kosinski told of his early life as a deserted child fleeing the Nazis are untrue. Kosinski's well-maintained fiction asserted that he was abandoned by his parents in 1939 in rural Eastern Poland. There he was tortured and persecuted by a series of sadistic peasants because of his dark Gypsy or Jewish looks. He escaped death at the hands of the Gestapo more than once and hid in the forest on his own. Because of a trauma caused by being thrown into a pit of manure, he lost his speech. Supposedly, he was found mute and half-crazed by his parents in an orphanage in 1945. His parents took him to the mountains for therapy where he was taught to ski. At fourteen he had a serious skiing accident and regained his speech in the hospital.

Much of this story was related in Kosinski's first novel, *The Painted Bird*. The real story is much different. Kosinski's confusion over his own identity began early. The war had destroyed the normal pattern of a child's upbringing and threw him into incredible danger. Kosinski's exaggerated tales of his personal history were ways to deal with this secretive past. Kosinski had to learn lessons about absolute secrecy at a very early age.

Kosinski was born Jerzy Lewinkopf to a Jewish father and mother living in Lodz, near the German border. Kosinski's father, Moses Lewinkopf, was a successful businessman dealing in textiles, and a lover of music with an interest in chess. His mother, Elzbieta Weinrich, was a concert pianist who came from a well-to-do Jewish family. Jerzy was their only child, but they would later adopt another young Jewish boy, Henryk, who became Jerzy's brother. The family lived in comfortable circumstances in the Jewish section of Lodz.

On September 1, 1939, Germany invaded Poland. Kosinski's father decided to remove his family to a rural district of Poland near the Russian border. He obtained papers that officially changed the family's name to Kosinski, a common Gentile name in Poland. For the rest of the war, they lived in precarious circumstances in a farmer's house in the remote town of Dabrowa near the Russian border. The section of Lodz where the Lewinkopfs had lived became the second largest Jewish ghetto in Poland. Eventually all 165,000 Jewish citizens from that ghetto were sent to Auschwitz to be exterminated.

In Dabrowa, Jerzy Kosinski grew up as a mystery to himself. His own name could no longer be used. His past and his heritage had to be denied. The family joined the Catholic Church and Jerzy received communion and became an altar boy. For almost six years the Kosinskis lived under these dangerous circumstances coming close to being discovered several times.

In 1945, the Russians liberated Poland and the Kosinskis came out of hiding. The Kosinski family returned to Lodz and Jerzy went to the University of Lodz, receiving a master's degree in History in 1953 and a degree in Political Science in 1955. He enrolled as a Ph.D. candidate in Sociology at the Polish Academy of Sciences in Warsaw. While a student there, he visited what was then the Soviet Union several times to pursue research for his doctoral studies on the relationship between the individual and the collective. This material would eventually provide the content for his two books on the collective life in Russia.

During this period, Kosinski developed a strong individualist streak that ran up against the collective socialist ideal. He was involved in minor scrapes at the university, was kicked out of a Polish communist youth organization, and was considered suspicious because of his outlandish style. Around this time, he enrolled in night school for photography, achieved some success, and was invited to join the Royal Photographic Society of Great Britain. Throughout his life he took pictures and had an affinity for the darkroom. During these years Kosinski developed an interest in the United States, listened to jazz music, and studied English assiduously.

IMMIGRATION TO THE UNITED STATES

The story that Kosinski told about how he got to the United States might be looked at as his first piece of creative fiction. For years afterward Kosinski wove a tale of imaginary grants and inverted academicians to write his recommendations. The fullest version of this tale can be found in his fifth novel, *Cockpit.*

The real story is that Kosinski cleverly but legitimately manipulated the system in his favor. Using the influence of his professors in Lodz, he obtained a student visa to become a graduate student at the University of Alabama in Tuscaloosa for the term beginning January 31, 1958. At the same time, he applied and was accepted into the doctoral program in sociology at Columbia University.

On December 20, 1957, the 24-year-old Jerzy Kosinski arrived in New York. He maintained that he only had $2.80 in his pocket—he neglected to mention the $500 deposited in a bank account by his uncle in New York who had immigrated to the United States before the war. He also quickly applied for a Ford Foundation fellowship for Polish exchange students and was granted financial support for his studies.

Kosinski worked at a variety of menial jobs to survive during his first year in New York City. Soon he was studying for a doctorate in political sociology at Columbia's New School for Social Research. He never completed his degree program, but to pursue his work at Columbia he had to have more than a basic understanding of English. He set out to complete his English education by watching television and, according to one of his famous stories, calling telephone operators to ask them the meaning of words. In less than a year he had gained a fair proficiency in the spoken language but his written English was not as accomplished.

After his second semester at Columbia, Kosinski signed a contract with Doubleday to produce a book on life in the Soviet Union. In fact, he published two nonfiction books under the nom de plume Joseph Novak. How a foreign graduate student obtained a book contract for an as-yet unwritten book is somewhat of a mystery. James Park Sloan suggests that the CIA by way of the USIA (United States Information Agency) may have interceded in promoting the book, recognizing its value as Cold War propaganda. Furthermore, Kosinski recorded a number of broadcasts in Polish for Radio Free Europe, a CIA-supported news program.

The Future is Ours, Comrade took the form of a series of interviews by an unnamed narrator, presumably the Joseph Novak of the title page. The book presents a dim view of Soviet collective society at a time when the United States needed fuel for its ideological war with the Soviet Union. The book's depiction of collective life in the Soviet Union is highly critical and suggests that there is little space for individual rights. *The Future is Ours, Comrade* was serialized in *Reader's Digest* and excerpted in *The Saturday Evening Post.* The book had limited success in certain circles but did not earn the author substantial money. For those who wondered how Kosinski had written such a book in English with his flawed language skills, it was later discovered that he used a translator who turned his Polish text into perfect English.

In 1960, Kosinski worked on his second book about the Soviet Union and attended classes at Columbia. *No Third Path* was published in 1962. It contains a number of debates with a party official by the name of Gavrila. The system of Soviet justice as represented by the figure of Gavrila is all-powerful and infallible. The author increasingly finds the Soviet collective way of life distasteful and dehumanizing. The book also contains a story about a sparrow painted purple that was killed because of its difference. This story would eventually provide the central metaphor for Kosinski's most famous novel, *The Painted*

Bird. Although the two books Kosinski published on Russian life are nonfiction they demonstrate techniques Kosinski would later use in his fiction. They were both written with an episodic structure in simple prose. Also, the anecdotes are strung together by an almost faceless narrator who manages to manipulate the people in the books to his own ends.

The Novak books provided Kosinski with academic credentials and an entrance into American society. They achieved some measure of notice, particularly among conservative Cold War politicians. Soon after the publication of the second book, the Novak alias was unmasked. Kosinski saw an advantage in taking credit for the books under his own name. It also offered legitimacy to his life as the husband of the very rich widow Mary Weir, who he had married in January, 1962.

After marrying Weir, Kosinski lived a life of relative luxury. There were trips to Europe and vacations in villas and on yachts. During this period he failed to finish his qualifying exams for a Ph.D. at Columbia. With the encouragement of friends and his wife, Kosinski began to write out the story of his experiences during the Nazi occupation of Poland. This book, which began as work of autobiographical sketches, soon developed into a major novel that would cement Kosinski's reputation in the literary world.

THE PAINTED BIRD

The Painted Bird enjoyed immediate success on its publication in 1965. Kosinski's novel of imaginative brilliance is based on his experiences in Poland during the war. Many reviewers at the time took the novel as thinly disguised autobiography. But the public knows now that Kosinski had creatively exaggerated his past. *The Painted Bird* is a written tale similar to the oral narrative of the fictionalized incidents he was so fond of telling his friends about his experiences during World War II.

In the beginning stages of writing the book, Kosinski had let it be understood that he was writing an autobiographical account of his early life in Poland hiding from the Gestapo. Yet by the time his manuscript was reviewed by the committee of editors at Houghton Mifflin, there were serious reservations voiced about both the content and style of the manuscript.

While most editors found the book a harrowing tale of survival, some questioned the veracity of many of the incidents. Furthermore, the graphic violence, brutal sex, and despicable human behavior alienated at least one important editor. Kosinski entered into serious negotiations with the company and submitted to heavy editing of the manuscript.

The Painted Bird was finally published as a work of fiction with a 21-page essay attached entitled "The Art of Jerzy Kosinski," in which Kosinski attempted to explain his writing methods. The essay would later be self-published by Kosinski's own imprint, Scientia-Factum. In this essay, Kosinski argues against reading *The Painted Bird* as pure autobiography. He talks about the artifice of an author using natural subplots paralleling human behavior and theorizes about the autobiographical quality of his book.

With recent revelations about Kosinski's past it has been proven that *The Painted Bird* is almost completely the product of the author's imagination. However, at the time of its publication the book engendered a critical discussion about autobiographical fiction. Eight novels later, Kosinski's work still continued to puzzle readers and reviewers who strained to identify real facts in the welter of bizarre scenes Kosinski was fond of portraying. Kosinski maintained that his writing was a creative refashioning of personal stories that shared elements of autobiography enhanced by imagination and crafted to an allegorical timelessness.

The Painted Bird stands on its own as a great literary achievement. Written in simple but evocative prose it relates the trials and tribulations of a nameless and deserted six-year-old boy running fearfully from the Nazis. The essential core of the book is based on Kosinski's own experiences in the rural Polish village of Dabrowa.

The central character manages to survive tremendous persecution by a combination of good luck and sharp wits. He is persecuted as either a Gypsy or a Jew because of his dark looks. But the story is highly stylized and exaggerated for dramatic effect, blending fairy tales and myth with harsh episodes of alienation and brutality. In some ways, it reflects a universal childhood state of wonder, mystification, and fear. But in others it depicts a pastoral world that can suddenly turn into a personal nightmare of horrible human behavior such as murder, bestiality, and incest.

The style of *The Painted Bird* might be described as magical realism where the bizarre episodes unfold like something out of a dream. A key episode describes the boy being beaten and flung into a pit of manure for dropping a missal during Mass, resulting in the muteness of the boy. Kosinski stuck to the story of his own muteness at this early age throughout his life. Perhaps the muteness stands as a powerful analogy representing Kosinski's problems in recovering and giving coherent articulation to the terrors of his childhood experience.

The main metaphor of the painted bird, which gives title to the book, is another revelatory episode. The demented peasant Lekh paints birds with bright colors for his enjoyment and then releases them to the wild where they are attacked and destroyed. In this way Kosinski shows how the alien individual, set apart by beauty or difference, can be destroyed by its own kind.

The last section of the book, in which the boy is liberated by the Soviets, focuses more on the psychological change brought out in the boy. He has journeyed through pain and suffering and he now manifests an appetite for revenge. He aspires to throw off the role of victim and become a victimizer. He even begins to envy the uniform and power of the Nazis who had hunted him. The boy is desperate to reverse his status through revenge on his enemies. The theme of revenge became a constant in Kosinski's later writings.

LIFE AFTER *THE PAINTED BIRD*

Later re-examination of Kosinski's first novel shows that he relied on background information about peasants from published anthropological sources such as Henryk Biegeleisen's *At the Cradle, In Front of the Altar, Over the Grave* (1929). Literary antecedents for the book include Wladyslaw Reymont's *The Peasants* (1942) and Henryk Sienkiewicz's *Pan Wolodyjowski* (1955) as well as the international tradition of the picaresque or episodic novel.

Another problem that surfaced over *The Painted Bird* was Kosinski's extensive use of translators and line editors in his writing process. He was known to write many drafts of his work and often revised extensively up until the publishing deadline and sometimes even after the book had been published. *The Painted Bird* was a good example of this method. Initially, Kosinski wrote it in Polish and hired a number of translators to help him put it into English.

The Painted Bird was translated into most languages. It became a best-seller in Europe and an instant cult classic on American college campuses. It was nominated for a National Book Award and it won the French *Prix du Meilleur Livre Etranger* book award. With this one book, Kosinski established himself as a major literary figure.

The Painted Bird changed Kosinski's life. The book's success made him an independent person.

His circle of friends and acquaintances grew to include some of the most influential people of the day. In March of 1966 Kosinski was notified that he had won a Guggenheim Award in writing. Indeed, the support came at a critical time of hesitation and doubt in his writing life. *The Painted Bird* was being questioned in Poland for its negative views of Polish citizens and its truthfulness. Also, Kosinski was in the process of getting divorced from his wife Mary Weir and could no longer count on her financial support.

At the same time, doubts about his ability to write in English and worries that the stories he had told would be revealed as lies upset his life. The Guggenheim Award gave Kosinski legitimacy as a writer and the financial support to be one. During the next few years Kosinski worked on a new manuscript and also took temporary teaching jobs at Wesleyan, Princeton, and Yale Universities.

Kosinski moved to a sparsely furnished Manhattan apartment, which he soon began sharing with Katerina Von Fraunhofer who he married in 1987 and who was his companion for the rest of his life.

STEPS

Kosinski's second novel, *Steps,* extends his experimentation with modern fiction techniques. There is an underlying tension and an aura of alienation about the book. *Steps* seems in tune with the tensions of the late 1960s when Martin Luther King Jr. and Robert Kennedy were assassinated and student revolts disrupted American college campuses. The book reflects a consciousness that has no continuity. It is a series of fragments maintained by no overriding moral order.

Steps is written in the first person. It is composed of thirty-five episodes or dramatic incidents separated by thirteen italicized dialogues between a man and woman. Seventeen of the incidents are in some respects autobiographical and derive from the years just before and after Kosinski came to the United States.

A few of the jobs Kosinski took on first arriving in the United States are dramatized in the book, among them parking cars, driving a truck, cleaning apartments, and scraping paint and rust from ships. Of the remaining episodes, six deal with revenge and fifteen involve sex.

The nameless narrator's consciousness seems to be the only connection between the episodes. There is no plot. Kosinski maintained that plot was a falsification of reality. The narrator's relationships with others in *Steps* is manipulative, aggressive, and destructive. The increasing domination of the nameless male protagonist through episodes of personal power and revenge structure the narrative; no overall purpose is revealed. The vague hallucinatory tone of the book adds a chilling aspect to the narrator's noncommittal presentation. His ruthless behavior toward women makes him unattractive. The complexities of the narrator's identity are puzzling and the burden of moral decision is placed on the reader.

For example, there is a scene in a sanatorium in which the protagonist makes fantasy love with a tubercular inmate as she touches his image in a mirror. The protagonist is not fully invested in his own actions while he manipulates the other characters to his own ends. The solitary nature of the narrator suggests his inability to participate in a social environment.

Such a fragmented story presents an unclear picture of its characters. Life becomes a series of broken episodes that seem to have no logical connection. The separate events are related only in their having happened to a single central consciousness. This lack of continuity and plot places all emphasis on the individual incident. This existential approach to life suggests that the moment is the essence of meaning in life.

The dissociative behavior of the protagonist might reflect a common symptom of survivors of the Holocaust. Many survivors feel emotionally disconnected from life and are unable to justify their existence. Individuals such as this who are wounded by deep trauma feel guilt at their own survival.

The ambiguous ending of the book is very puzzling. Without warning the point of view of the final episode shifts to the woman, who declares herself free of the past while mysteriously watching a leaf floating in the water.

Steps was again followed by an essay that was eventually self-published. *The Art of the Self: Essays apropos 'Steps'* contains part of Kosinski's correspondence with his Dutch publishers. It consists mainly of a long statement of personal philosophy and aesthetics. Kosinski connects his writing style with film montage and action painting. He also likens the self to an image that undergoes constant metamorphosis.

Steps won the National Book Award in 1969, only twelve years after Kosinski had moved to the United States. Some critics speculated that the award was given to *Steps* to make up for the far more popular *The Painted Bird*'s rejection. The years following the National Book Award were busy ones for Kosinski. He and Kiki traveled for several months of every year throughout Europe and America skiing and playing polo.

During this same period, Kosinski taught at Princeton University, where he became disillusioned with the student activists of the period. He wrote about this in the *New York Times* in an article entitled "Dead Souls on Campus" (Oct. 12, 1970). Some of his criticism would eventually be included in Kosinski's book *The Devil Tree*. The following year, he taught at Yale University, where he lived next to Svetlana Stalin, the daughter of the former dictator of the Soviet Republic. During this period, Kosinski began collecting statistics on every aspect of American television, and this research inspired the writing of the manuscript of what was to become the novel *Being There*.

BEING THERE

Kosinski enjoyed a substantial literary success with the publication of *Being There*. This novel, written in stripped-down prose, might be read as a satire or an allegory. It is a novel with a peculiar premise that struck a nerve in America at the time. The protagonist, Chance, lives in total isolation and only knows the world outside his walled-in garden through his constant television watching.

Chance bears less biographical resemblance to Kosinski than the protagonists in his first two novels, but there are some similarities. The book reworks Kosinski's own life story and at the same time it draws heavily in structure and theme upon one of Kosinski's favorite Polish books, Dolega Mostowicz's 1932 novel *The Career of N. Kodem Dyzma*.

Chauncey Gardiner, or Chance, is a mystery man, an idiot savant with no recognizable past and whose connection to real life is artificial and removed. Chance lives in the walled garden of the Old Man. He has no idea who his parents were or virtually anything of his past. Perhaps he has suffered brain damage. He has no education and doesn't read or write. He watches television constantly.

When the Old Man dies, Chance is turned out into the street where he is struck by a chauffeured limousine. The woman in the car takes him to a mansion to recover. It is there that Chance's random comments are taken for brilliant statements by the rich and powerful people who visit the woman's immensely wealthy disabled husband. One of these visitors is the president of the United States who ends up quoting Chance in a major policy speech.

Chance's ambiguous comments about gardening entertain this company but they also seem to contain a moral allegory applicable to their lives.

Chance, the solitary gardener, is courted by people in powerful positions. Chance's bland statements and impenetrable personality allow for all manner of interpretation.

Chance also looks good on television. He has learned everything from watching television so that he has a perfect projected style. His off-the-cuff remarks amuse the television audience and seem to possess great profundity at the same time.

In a great satirical moment, it is realized that Chance makes a perfect politician. No one can distinguish between his actual substance and his empty image. The lessons behind the book suggest that television is the enemy of experience and that popular culture dulls a culture's awareness of the importance of the moment.

Being There is a parable of a simpleton who becomes a respected advisor to the rich and powerful. Kosinski presents his bleak view of the universe in which all meaning is suspect. In some ways, the story may reflect Kosinski's own rise over the previous ten years as an outsider into the upper levels of society.

Being There cemented Kosinski's literary reputation. After the outstanding success of his first three novels, Kosinski had reached the pinnacle of literary success and parlayed that success into a more general celebrity. He appeared frequently on Johnny Carson's *Tonight Show*. When he acted in *Reds,* he received higher billing than Jack Nicholson.

Although he continued to publish on a regular basis, Kosinski's later novels were not as well received as his first three. The books appeared at regular intervals but their audience was limited and critical. Kosinski's last novel, *The Hermit of 69th Street,* took almost a decade to write and appeared just before his death.

THE DEVIL TREE

The Devil Tree is saturated with the background of Kosinski's own life with Mary Weir living among other wealthy people. The main protagonist, Whalen, is a young man modeled after Mary Weir's son David from her first marriage. Whalen is the wayward scion of an enormously wealthy family.

When his father dies Whalen's inheritance includes $25,000 a month on interest alone. Yet Whalen is a wanderer who has drifted through India, Burma, and Africa. Among other bizarre episodes, Whalen kills old friends of his family who try to wean him from his hippie ways. He has used drugs and has been treated for serious addiction while confined in a clinical sanatorium.

The novel takes its title from a common name for the baobab tree, which the devil punished by reversing it so the roots are the branches and the branches roots. The novel seems to reflect this upside-down world as Whalen, the rich man's son, loses contact with reality.

The novel has 137 brief vignettes and dozens of these depict cruel and violent behavior. There are also numerous episodes centering on sexual relationships as Whalen pushes his behavior to extremes. Finally, Whalen beats a woman and finds himself in a clinic recovering from a mental breakdown. The book ends with him standing by a lake where forms become empty figures and he seems ready to commit suicide by drowning.

Kosinski later rewrote this novel to make it more straightforward in plot and narration and to make it more autobiographical and less pessimistic. But even in its initial form the book is obviously a reworking of his complicated relationship with David, who was almost Kosinski's age.

COCKPIT: A NOVEL

Cockpit is more confessional and accessible than Kosinski's earlier novels. Its episodes are longer and fewer. There are only 19 compared to the 137 in *The Devil Tree.* However, the book is virtually plotless. It is written from the viewpoint of Tarden, the mysterious male protagonist. It uses autobiography in a different way than Kosinski's previous books. Recognizable bits of his own biography are directly inserted into the text.

Human beings are more clearly identifiable. The book starts with an open letter to a woman in which loneliness and transience are the themes. But it all seems a shadowy contrivance of Tarden's. The book goes on to depict Tarden's brutal quest for power. Tarden was formerly a secret agent in some type of unspecified "Service." He hunts down defectors from this service and kills them mercilessly.

Tarden's sole pleasure derives from control over other lives. His methods are unscrupulous. He uses disguises and manipulations in his revenge dramas. He seems at war with a vague unspecified totalitarian state. But at no place does the reader learn what this state is or who the people are who pursue Tarden. Tarden is constantly on the run, escaping from one veiled plot after another. Tarden's crime, his position, and his status in the real world are a mess of contrary images. Tarden has apartments with combination locks, multiple exits, and hiding places. He is menaced by vague and unexpected dangers. For example, he is attacked by a friend who tries to cut his head off but the reader never finds out why.

In his own view of things, Tarden sees himself as the self-appointed reformer of an unjust world. But his elaborate revenges are mostly personal actions directed against people who have crossed him. In his worst behavior he does things like punish a girl by raping and abusing her for not giving in to his demands. The book is about power and omnipotent wish fulfillment.

A fleeting positive human contact for Tarden has produced a son with a Lebanese woman named Theodora. But then the child is given away. Tarden loses contact and is left by himself. In the end he is a lone, aging survivor trapped in an elevator endlessly going up and down in a building with no name.

BLIND DATE

Blind Date takes the now-familiar form of a series of incidents involving a central male character. In this case the protagonist is named Levanter, another lone-wolf hero who intermingles flashbacks with descriptions of his violent activities in various countries.

Levanter is an older man who, as a studied adventurer, is capable of capitalizing on the chance events of the moment. At times he is the butt of comic episodes but more often he is ruthless when agitated. His heroes are Israelis who hunt down German war criminals. In one episode he kills the Internal Affairs head of an unspecified totalitarian government but never informs the reader as to why. Levanter, like other disturbing Kosinski protagonists, is a rapist who abuses what are called "blind dates" or random forced sexual encounters.

Some rationalization for Levanter's behavior may be derived from Kosinski's use of the philosophy of Jacques Monod. Monod is a French biologist who won a Nobel Prize and wrote a book called *Chance and Necessity*. One of Monod's premises is that there is no predictable direction for life to take. If there is no preordained destiny and everything in life is based on chance or coincidence, then human beings create their own moral universe. The text is also influenced by the German philosopher Martin Heidegger and his book *Being and Time*. Heidegger's quest for being or selfhood depends on an existential act of making the world one's own through individual acts of will. In a world of one's own making, the individual is all-powerful. Fear and the awareness of death help push aside the daily routine so one can live and experience fully the present moment.

Blind Date has many fragments of autobiography. Real people such as Svetlana Stalin and Charles Lindbergh enter the narrative as characters. Perhaps most disturbingly the night of the Manson murders is graphically re-created in the novel. This blend of reality and fiction challenges the reader's response and further supports Kosinski's experiments in plotless narratives.

Like Tarden in *Cockpit,* Levanter swings back and forth from seeing himself as a noble righter of wrongs to a conflicted man obsessed with revenge. Levanter is constantly aware of his own mortality and he uses some of the standard ways other Kosinski protagonists have used to make his life more meaningful. These include dangerous skiing challenges and plunging himself into wayward adventures with strange people in strange places.

In some ways Levanter is a more humane and more compassionate protagonist than those of Kosinski's earlier novels. He seems more sympathetic to other people's problems and personal pain but he is still a disturbing presence who struggles with his own definition of life and finds no solace in the bleak atmosphere around him.

The novel concludes with Levanter's own death by choice. High on a dangerous mountain, Levanter figuratively tosses himself into the abyss. "A descent was like life: to love it was to love each moment, to rejoice in the skill and speed of every moment." Levanter eventually wanders on the mountain until he gets lost in the fog and the cold claims him.

PASSION PLAY

Passion Play, Kosinski's seventh novel, was massively rewritten after it was sent to the publishers. The novel is about Fabian, a wandering philosopher who travels around America and the Caribbean living out of his motor home. Fabian is a curious individual who makes a living from intense, one-on-one polo matches. He is also a teacher and writer who publishes books on horses and horsemanship. His book titles are sendups of Kosinski's own books including a hidden reference to *Steps* winning the National Book Award.

Passion Play has more plot structure and forward movement than Kosinski's other books but the overall effect of the book is once again a detached reality. The depictions of Fabian's sexual interests, including visits to sex clubs, provide a disturbing insight into a man obsessed by sexual perversions. The book includes some cleverly written pieces on the art of seduction but Fabian's overly clever manipulations suggest psychosis rather than romance.

The book goes back and forth in time, moving associatively among unrelated anecdotes. The sum total suggests weakness and confusion. Fabian, the protagonist, is older, more vulnerable, and less vengeful. The tone of the book is tired and depleted. The protagonist and the author behind him seem to be struggling to find a way to rekindle hope and desire.

The reader eventually learns that Fabian has been blackballed from the sport of polo for killing his millionaire friend Stanhope in a revenge match. The murder is a direct result of a betrayal by Fabian's girlfriend Alexandra with Stanhope. Personal retribution is a major theme in this work.

Fabian has the characteristics of a lone warrior, a quixotic figure battling demons of his own design. But underlying this romantic conception is the revealing story of an older man who devotes most of his energy to the pursuit of teenage girls. He solicits young girls by paging through a magazine called the *Saddle Bride.* In Fabian's mind the girls are equated with horses and described in horselike terms. In one episode he even puts a bridle and saddle on a woman.

Fabian conceives of himself as a mentor and guide to these young woman. He teaches beautiful high school girls riding and horsemanship, but his main intent is to initiate them sexually. He claims that his power frees them to their full potential as individuals.

At the core of the narrative is an unrealistic romantic tale involving Vanessa, the niece of Stanhope, the man Fabian killed in a polo match. When she was young, Fabian trained her in horsemanship skills and then they lost touch with each other. Years pass, and when Fabian finds Vanessa again, she is still a virgin who has been waiting for him. But by now Fabian is old, gaunt, and penniless. The rich Vanessa offers him a million dollars but Fabian refuses, choosing instead the independence and solitude of a nomadic life.

The epigraphs to *Passion Play* are from *Don Quixote* and *Moby Dick*. Fabian is associated with doomed madmen on hopeless quests. There is some quiet comedy of language in the novel and a sentimental lush tone creeps into the text more often than in earlier novels. Kosinski has called Fabian his most perfect autobiographical character. It is interesting then to speculate on how exactly Kosinski saw himself in relation to this novel which reveals such a contorted male personality. The burden of being Jerzy Kosinski has become a difficult weight to bear. Perhaps this impression is not inadvertent. The "passion play" of the title refers to Christian religious pieces that dramatize the sufferings of Christ.

PINBALL

Pinball is a mock thriller set in the world of music. It uses many of the constructions of the suspense genre in an imaginative way. It offers some acute insights into the situation and methods of the artist. For the first time, a Kosinski novel has two protagonists. One is Domostroy, an older classical composer who has reached an impasse in his work. The other is Goddard, a young rock star whose concealed identity is the pivotal plot motif. The thriller aspect of the plot is driven by attempts to unmask Goddard that culminate in a shootout.

Pinball is at one level an artist-novel, examining the creative personality and its methods, and in particular the incorporation of personal history into works of art. Once again the book is filled with teasing allusions to Kosinski's own life. Also, Kosinski's awareness of his own work-

ing methods of constructing fiction are examined here. The novel is about divided personality and disclosure.

Both sides of Kosinski's personality are represented in *Pinball* through the two protagonists. The rock star figure suggests the public side of Kosinski as actor, screenwriter, and celebrity. Domostroy is the inner Kosinski suffering from a sense of hollowness and inauthenticity. The inability to pull these two identities together represents the core problem of Kosinski's own life.

THE HERMIT OF 69TH STREET: THE WORKING PAPERS OF NORBERT KOSKY

The Hermit of 69th Street is Kosinski's last novel. It took more than a decade to write, and in some ways it is an attempt to rectify misunderstandings about his past. In a series of evocative episodes he describes a family much like his own. The protagonist, Norbert Kosky, looks back on his youth and redefines it with the wisdom of age. Although the book attempts to reconsider what is obviously Kosinski's own past in relation to his fabrications, the book creates new mythical scenarios.

As he purports to represent his experience as fragments of memory, Norbert Kosky reflects on other great writers of the past, particularly Honoré de Balzac. He tries to defend his own use of line editors and translators by paralleling them with Balzac's methods. Balzac was also an incorrigible liar, a fact from which Kosinski obviously draws some consolation.

With its preoccupation in reexamining the past, *Hermit* in some ways seems to revolve around the year 1982 when the negative attack on Kosinski began. It is almost as if time stopped for Kosinski then and his own sense of reality was badly shaken. Some of this anguish is reflected in the book where Kosinski consistently has his character Kosky interrogate himself in a morbid fictive theater of retribution. One of the most important issues Kosky examines is the historical relationship between Poles and Jews and his place in that duality.

Hermit is long and rambling, and it is footnoted as if it were a research project. All of the author's life, both factual and fictional, is projected on the page for review. There is a strange interplay of the sacred and profane throughout the text. Both spirituality and sexuality are cleverly intertwined. In Kosinski's hands, the past almost seems like a living entity that can be molded, stretched, and manipulated to suit the desires of the artist.

CONCLUSION

Jerzy Kosinski achieved remarkable success with his first three novels. Later in his career controversy developed over his writing methods, suspicion of plagiarism and his public misrepresentations of his past. The public learned that translators were secretly used for drafts of his work and that Kosinski actually wrote his first three books in Polish before having them translated into English.

The Painted Bird established Kosinski's literary reputation. It was a unique novel about surviving the Holocaust told from a child's point of view. The book will remain a lasting achievement. There is an undeniable connection between Kosinski's life and the stories he wrote. Yet from the very beginning both critics and admirers were puzzled by their inability to distinguish fact from fiction in Kosinski's work. The blend of current news events and real people in the novels complicated the issue.

The later novels certainly reflected the secretive nature of Kosinski's life. Fame and celebrity came to Kosinski but his personal life seems to have been as manipulative and sexually bizarre as those depicted in his books. His life, as reflected in his fiction, appeared predominantly constructed around fragmented short episodes, accentuated by extreme violence, sexual encounters, and bizarre and threatening images.

Kosinski's novels are difficult testaments of a unique personality. His main theme seemed to be the fallibility of memory, which makes every life a fiction created by its own author. Memory is both a help and a hindrance to living our lives fully and richly.

Selected Bibliography

WORKS OF JERZY KOSINSKI

NOVELS

The Painted Bird. Boston: Houghton Mifflin, 1965; New York: Pocket Books, 1966 (paperback; author's original text restored); New York: Modern Library, 1970; New York: Bantam, 1972.

Steps. New York: Random House, 1968; New York: Bantam, 1969 (paperback).

Being There. New York: Harcourt Brace Jovanovich, 1971; New York: Bantam, 1974.

The Devil Tree. New York: Harcourt Brace Jovanovich, 1973; New York: Bantam, 1974; New York: St. Martin's Press, 1981 (revised and expanded edition); New York: Bantam, 1981.

Cockpit. Boston: Houghton Mifflin, 1975; New York: Bantam, 1976.

Blind Date. Boston: Houghton Mifflin, 1977; New York: Bantam, 1978.

Passion Play. New York: St. Martin's Press, 1979; New York: Bantam, 1969.

Pinball. New York: Bantam, 1982; New York: Bantam, 1983 (paperback).

The Hermit of 69th Street. New York: Seaver, 1988; New York: Zebra, 1991 (paperback).

SELECTED NONFICTION AND PAMPHLETS

The Future is Ours, Comrade. Garden City, N.Y.: Doubleday, 1960. (Under the pseudonym Joseph Novak.)

No Third Path. Garden City, N.Y.: Doubleday, 1962. (Under the pseudonym Joseph Novak.)

Notes of the Author on "The Painted Bird." New York: Scientia-Factum, 1965.

The Art of the Self: Essays a Propos "Steps." New York: Scientia-Factum, 1968.

Passing By: Selected Essays, 1962–1991. New York: Random House, 1992.

SELECTED OTHER WORKS

"Dead Souls on Campus." *New York Times,* October 12, 1970, p. 45.

"The Reality Behind Words." *New York Times,* October 3, 1971, p. 3.

"Our 'Predigested, Prepackaged Popular Culture.' " *U.S. News and World Report,* January 8, 1979, pp. 52–53.

"How I learned to Levitate on Water." *Life,* April 1984, pp. 129–132.

"Death in Cannes." *Esquire,* March 1986, pp. 82–89

"Restoring a Polish-Jewish Soul," *New York Times,* October 22, 1988, pp. 1, 27.

SELECTED CRITICAL AND BIOGRAPHICAL STUDIES

Aldridge, John W. "The Fabrication of a Culture Hero." *Saturday Review* 54:25–27 (April 24, 1971).

Anderson, Don. "The End of Humanism: A Study of Kosinski." *Quadrant* 113:73–77 (1976).

Baker, Russ W. "Painted Words." *Village Voice,* March 15, 1994, pp. 58–59.

Brown, Earl B., Jr. "Kosinski's Modern Proposal: The Problem of Satire in the Mid-Twentieth Century." *Critque Studies in Modern Fiction* 22:83–87 (1980).

Corry, John. "A Case History: Seventeen Years of Ideological Attack on a Cultural Target." *New York Times,* Arts and Leisure section, November 7, 1982, pp. 1, 28–29.

Everman, Welch D. *Jerzy Kosinski: The Literature of Violation.* Vol. 47, *The Milford Series, Popular Writers of Today.* San Bernardino, Calif.: Borgo Press, 1991.

Klinkowitz, Jerome. "Betrayed by Jerzy Kosinski." *The Missouri Review* 6:157–171 (Summer 1983).

Lavers, Norman. *Jerzy Kosinski.* Boston: Twayne, 1982.

Lupack, Tepa, ed. *Critical Essays on Jerzy Kosinski.* New York: G. K. Hall & Co., 1998.

Schiff, Stephen. "The Kosinski Conundrum." *Vanity Fair,* June 1988, pp. 114–119, 166–170.

Sloan, James Park. *Jerzy Kosinski: A Biography.* New York: Dutton, 1996.

Stokes, Geoffrey, and Eliot Fremont-Smith. "Jerzy Kosinski's Tainted Words." *Village Voice,* June 22, 1982, pp. 1, 41–43.

SELECTED INTERVIEWS

Abrams, Garry. "Jerzy Kosinski Leaves 'Em Amused, Bemused, and Confused." *Los Angeles Times,* View section, November 14, 1984, pp. 1, 12.

Gefen, Pearl Sheffy. "Jerzy Kosinski, the Last Interview." *Lifestyles,* Winter 1991, pp. 18–24.

Grunwald, Lisa. "Jerzy Kosinski: Tapping into His Vision of Truth." *Vineyard Gazette,* July 29, 1977, pp. A1–2.

Klinkowitz, Jerome. "Jerzy Kosinski: An Interview." *Fiction International* 1:30–48 (Fall 1971).

Plimpton, George, and Rocco Landesman. "The Art of Fiction." *Paris Review* 54:183–207 (Summer 1972).

—STEPHEN SOITOS

Mary Oliver

1935–

"I LIKE TO say that I write poems for a stranger who will be born in some distant country hundreds of years from now." So writes Mary Oliver in *A Poetry Handbook* (1994), addressing both poets and casual readers. It is a simple comment but also a controversial one, for it assumes that poetry is the most universal and timeless of the arts. As she says in another manual, *Rules For the Dance: A Handbook for Reading and Writing Metrical Verse* (1998): "[t]ime is meaningless to a poem; if it is about something that pertains to the human condition, then it is about something of interest to the most modern man, if he is a thoughtful man." Such simple, seemingly obvious definitions fly in the face of current ideas about American poetry. For such comments diminish, even disregard, the importance of a poet's biography or even of the specific social and political moment of the poem. As Oliver puts it in her *A Poetry Handbook:* "everything necessary must be on the page. I must make a complete poem—a river-swimming poem, a mountain-climbing poem. Not *my* poem, if it's well done, but a deeply breathing, bounding, self-sufficient poem. Like a traveler in an uncertain land, it needs to carry with it all that it must have to sustain its own life—and not a lot of extra weight either." If poetry is about things, particularly natural things, then its subject, she believes, must be transhistorical—true and necessary in all times.

To best understand Oliver's poems, then, one must look away from the poet, and even from the social and political context of their origin.

CHILDHOOD AND THE
EARLY YEARS OF THE POET

Although she has written many poems to friends, loved ones, and family Mary Oliver is, for all that, a remarkably reticent poet: she does not, in her work, record her life in minute, confessional detail. Given her views of poetry's transhistorical character, it would, one suspects, arouse her ire to speak of her biography at all. As she declares in a book of essays, *Blue Pastures* (1995), "I would not be a biographer for all the tea in China." And, in an interview in *The Bloomsbury Review,* she explained her authorial role as a literary vanishing act: "if I've done my work well, I vanish completely from the scene. . . . I am trying in my poems to vanish and have the reader be the experiencer. I do not want to be there."

Whatever Oliver's own feelings may be about the importance of an author's biography, however, readers of her work will want to know that she was born on September 10, 1935, in Maple Heights, Ohio. Her father, Edward William Oliver, was a teacher in Cleveland, Ohio. Her mother, Helen M. Vlasak, came from a family that immigrated from Bohemia to the farms of Ohio in the nineteenth century. Throughout Mary Oliver's childhood, adolescence, and early adulthood, she lived in Ohio. In *Blue Pastures,* she reports that she knew she wanted to be a poet by the time she was thirteen but that, in terms of her poetry, the most exciting and important experience occurred in 1953: "the morning after I graduated from the local high school—I left Ohio" in order to visit the poet Edna St. Vincent Millay's sister, Norma, in Austerlitz, New York. By then, Norma and her husband were living on the Millay estate: Steepletop. Oliver had been corresponding with Millay's sister since she was fifteen and, eventually, as Oliver says, "I moved in," becoming—in terms she admitted do not really give "substance" to her role in that home— "secretary, amanuesis, companion." The first original and decidedly eccentric literary personality Oliver had ever met, Norma would have a lasting impact. So, too, would the stories she heard about Millay and about the circle of poets and artists Millay had known, particularly in her Greenwich Village years of the late 1910s and 1920s.

Throughout this period, Oliver also went to college, first at Ohio State in Columbus, and then, as if to follow in Edna St. Vincent Millay's footsteps, to Vassar College in Poughkeepsie, New York, where she stayed only one year. By 1963, three other major influential events occurred. First, continuing to follow in Millay's footsteps, she had settled in the artistic and poetic bohemia of Provincetown, Massachusetts, on the far end of Cape Cod. Second, she had traveled to England and published her first book *No Voyage and Other Poems* (1963). Third, and certainly, for her, most importantly, she had, as she says in *Winter Hours: Prose, Prose Poems, and Poems* (1999), "met someone, fallen in love." That someone, Molly Malone Cook, has since been the dedicatee of almost every book Oliver has published; she

is, however, largely absent (at least explicitly) in most of the poems. Indeed, only in the late 1990s, in *Winter Hours,* has Oliver spoken of this relationship, which has lasted more than forty years in duration, at all. She writes: "M. and I met in the late fifties. For myself it was all adolescence again—shivers and whistles. Certainty." She adds: "Privacy, no longer cherished in the world, is all the same still a natural and sensible attribute of paradise. We are happy, and we are lucky."

OLIVER'S APPROACH TO POETRY

Oliver's approach to poetry, manifested from her first published book, *No Voyage, and Other Poems,* set her on a distinctly different course than the one followed by most of her famous peers. When Oliver began to publish, nothing short of a revolution had occurred in American poetry. Not only had poets broken once and for all from meter and traditional poetic forms, but they had also turned, en masse, to a far more private, intimate subject: their own lives and families. In 1959, when Robert Lowell—perhaps the most important poet of his generation—published his collection, *Life Studies,* American poets everywhere began to change their style. For when Lowell, the most traditionally metrical and "difficult" poet of his generation, turned to free verse and subjects based on his family life, he, as it were, gave permission to his peers to follow suit. By 1960 W. D. Snodgrass in *Heart's Needle* (1959) had described his divorce and the custody battle for his daughter, while Anne Sexton, in *To Bedlam and Part Way Back* (1960) depicted her own breakdown, and the pyschodrama of her feelings as a mother and daughter. And, in 1965, when *No Voyage, and Other Poems* was published in the United States, the literary event in that year's poetry world was the posthumous publication of Sylvia Plath's *Ariel.* The whole poetic universe had changed, according to the critic, M. L. Rosenthal, who had, in a famous review of Lowell, dubbed such poetry, "Confessional." Into such a soul-baring world did Mary Oliver, committed to a poetry at once personal and intensely private, local, and transhistorical, launch what would become, as of 2000, eleven collections of poetry, two collections of prose, and two poetry handbooks, among other writings.

No Voyage, and Other Poems announces what will become Oliver's grand, career-long theme: the relationship between the human and natural worlds. This theme, which suggests Oliver's connection to Romantic poetry, inspires in her a set of questions that have a distinctively modern, fresh, and ever-present urgency. In her first book, she wonders if nature really does refuse to "betray the heart that loves her," as the great Romantic poet, William Wordsworth, claimed. In that first book, an alienated Oliver looks to nature for comfort and finds instead only more disconnection, more alienation. In her second book, *The River Styx, Ohio and Other Poems* (1972), Oliver focuses on people, her family, and the characters from her Ohio youth in equal proportion to her attention to nature. She seems to hope that if nature will not offer the kind of comfort she seeks then at least people will. But this, too, proves more difficult than comforting. Beginning with her third book, *Twelve Moons* (1979), Oliver decides to cast her lot with nature, insisting on its ability to soothe, relieve, and comfort. Refusing to give up on the possibility that the human and the natural can find solace in one another, that there is a deep fundamental connection between the two, Oliver's books since 1979 have returned again and again to the felt experiential union between the human and the natural worlds. Like a Cubist painting, her books approach the same site, the same image of Mary Oliver (or some person) in nature. Each time she returns to this image, this scene, she means to present, describe,

and communicate what the American poet Walt Whitman called, "the merge."

FIRST BOOKS: DISCOVERING HER THEME

In the Confessional environment of the early- and mid-1960s, Mary Oliver's first book certainly did stand out. Its poems did not depend on free verse but returned again and again to fixed patterns of meter and rhyme. Less knotted or opaque than the allusive poetry of John Berryman, Lowell, Plath, Randall Jarrell and others of that era, her poems favor the plain speech and vernacular language of Robert Frost. Also, while plenty of the poems refer to events in her life and to people she knows, they are not soul-baring revelations about her inner psychological state of being. In the title poem, "No Voyage," which won first prize from the Poetry Society of America, Oliver alludes to Frost's "Mowing" and to that poem's famous line, "the fact is the sweetest dream that labor knows." In that line, Frost—with whom Oliver was to continue to be compared—tells the reader that if labor, one's action in the world, were able to dream and imagine things, it would imagine only facts, tangible realities. But facts, here, are always more than just functional or pragmatic. There is in every fact a spiritual aura as well, a soulful utility. In "No Voyage," Oliver, after looking out of her window, thinks of the wide world and realizes that for her it is best to:

> [t]urn back
> To sort the weeping ruins of my house:
> Here or nowhere I will make peace with the fact.

"Facts" from this poem forward will be the very stuff of Oliver's poetry. From her first book on, one meets, again and again, the specific items of the natural world. While the reader witnesses Oliver in her encounters with such natural facts, her poetry's emphasis is not on her individual self so much as any human self's relation to the natural world: as the great American essayist and poet, Ralph Waldo Emerson put it, "in speaking for myself, I speak for all."

When it first hit the stores in its American edition in 1965, *No Voyage* received an unusual amount of attention from the literary community. It was reviewed in a number of prominent magazines of intellectual discussion (*Commonweal, The Christian Science Monitor, New Statesman,* and the *New York Times Book Review*), often by important American poets such as Philip Booth and James Dickey. Booth, in *The Christian Science Monitor,* wrote that "[h]er inclination toward what's 'poetic' becomes openly embarrassing." Dickey in the *New York Times Book Review* echoed these sentiments and added that too much was "conventional and ordinary." Referring in each case to "Miss Oliver," the reviewers of the American edition expected from American poetry a decidedly masculine aggression in both rhythm, tone, and imagery. In their reviews, each man complains of the too "feminine" quality of Oliver's book, and holds the connection to Millay—noted by almost all of the reviews—as a mark against rather than a compliment to the poet. One suspects that had Oliver been more revealing, more set on opening her own life to the scrutiny of readers such comments would not have been made. As it was, this book's attention to nature in such strict forms set the critics of what would be soon called a "naked poetry"—a poetry of personal anecdote in free verse—on edge.

Whether stung by those criticisms or not, it would be seven years before Oliver published another collection, *The River Styx, Ohio, and Other Poems* in 1972. Dedicated both to her mother and father, "and for Molly Malone Cook," this collection maintains her interest in traditional forms. But whereas the first book returned again and again to nature hoping to find some kind of sol-

ace, this book concentrates far more on the human, social world of family, friends, and neighbors. Ultimately, this second collection is what Robert Frost called *his* second collection: "a book of people." In it one meets, all titles of poems, "Tom," "Hattie Bloom," "Alex," "Anne," "Aunt Mary," "Isabel Sparrow," among many others not named in the titles. While the Confessional impulse in American poetry during the late 1960s may in part explain this turn to the social and personal—the first poem "Stark Boughs on the Family Tree" is about her family—it might just as well be due to the impact of James Wright, another Ohio poet, who had, in the late 1960s, become a powerfully original poet and who, like Oliver, attempted to join the world of nature to the social world of people. In two books from the 1960s, and in such powerful poems as "A Blessing," and "Lying in a Hammock at William Duffy's Farm in Pine Island, Minnesota," Wright had, with his friend Robert Bly, brought into American poetry a new method of image-making: "The Deep Image." By invoking surreal imagery, focusing on obviously spiritual themes set in nature, and using a new, pared-down diction—what Oliver called, "a heightened vernacular"—Wright, Bly, and others hoped to turn American poetry away from what they felt were Confessional poetry's too limited concerns.

Even before Wright and Bly, however, one might find in Frost's poetry a precedent for Oliver's turn to the local, social, and vernacular in her second book. In two of its poems, "The Fence," and "Mr. Frost's Chickens" Oliver even refers to Frost. In the latter, which refers to a time when Frost was a chicken farmer in the hard soil of northern New England, Oliver writes:

When things go wrong, I think of Mr. Frost
And his flock of chickens,
And the poems that were lost, maybe
While he shoveled coops,
Picked eggs,
Threw grain.

She thinks of these facts and, in so doing, concludes, in the poem's final lines:

> Thank you, Mr. Frost, for the chilly interval
> Of chicken farming.

Oliver, in this collection, invokes those who, like Frost, live off of the hard-scrabble land of rural America, scraping out their existence in what she refers to in the title poem as, "Farms . . . bankrupt, in the wind." The poems in this collection often reveal a bleak, haunted land where even the River Styx is less myth than local fact. In the end, this second book leaves Oliver exactly where her first book had: without any felt comfort for the all-too-real feelings of alienation she continued to record. Even the social world, in other words, had failed her.

"ENTERING THE KINGDOM": MYTHS, ARCHETYPES, AND DEEP IMAGES IN THE 1970s

Another seven years passed before Oliver published a full-length collection of poems, *Twelve Moons* in 1979. Just before that book was published, however, she released two limited edition books, *The Night Traveler* (1978) and *Sleeping in the Forest* (1979), both from small Ohio presses. While all three of these collections reveal Oliver's continued debt both to Millay and to Frost, one can also see in them a new willingness to invoke the rhetoric of the Deep Image. This turn to such Deep Images as "bone," "blood," "darkness," and "dreams" enables her to reconcile the human and the natural worlds using a new set of poetic techniques. Because the Deep Image demands, as its premise, faith in a fundamental spirituality coursing through the universe, its image system, by definition, ought to reconcile human experience with natural phenomena. Specifically, the Deep Image movement offered certain kinds of metaphors—Deep Images—designed to bridge the gap between the uncontainable, unrepresentable world of the spirit and the world of natural, material facts. By 1979 such major American poets as Galway Kinnell, Louis Simpson, W. S. Merwin, Mark Strand, and William Stafford had all been inspired by Bly's and Wright's Deep Image. In her own work from this decade, Mary Oliver joins this male company not only by using the Deep Images mentioned above, but by creating her own set of resolutely sensual, female, and sexualized Deep Images.

In *Twelve Moons,* the two Deep Images that stand out are "moon," and "bear," both of which, invoked again and again, allow Oliver to reconcile what neither of her first two books could. *Twelve Moons* represents the realization of Oliver's unique vision. It begins her voyage into the terrain of what Whitman had called "the merge." In this collection, "the merge" is charted by resorting not only to the rhetoric of the Deep Image but also to a fully developed mythology similar in scope to that of William Butler Yeats or to Oliver's more near contemporary, the American poet Theodore Roethke.

Specifically, *Twelve Moons* reprinted many of the poems from Oliver's two chapbooks, setting them in what was, for her, a new, mythic, archetypal structure based on the ever-changing but never-different facts of the passing seasons: nature's cyclical calendar. The book begins in spring (April) and ends in spring (March). Its fifty-one poems follow the course of a year, each month of which is marked by one of twelve moon poems. These twelve moon poems, in turn, each present a moment of connection, an intersection between nature and the human—a moment presented in explicitly gendered terms. In the very first poem, "Sleeping in the Forest," Oliver announces her project of connecting nature and the human through the use of her imagination. Describing a night spent in the forest, she tells the reader: "By morning / I had vanished at least a dozen times / into something better." Imagining herself as part and parcel of nature becomes the book's visionary purpose. In the first moon poem, "Pink Moon—The Pond," Oliver describes an evening when she immerses herself in a night-enshrouded pond. She becomes, as it were, one with the frogs:

> you see everything
> through their eyes,
> their joy, their necessity;
> you wear their webbed fingers;
> your throat swells.

This transformation signals Oliver's willingness to welcome her own explicitly female body into her poetry.

> So you relax, you don't fight it anymore,
> the darkness coming down
> called water,
> called spring,
> called the green leaf, called
> a woman's body
> . . . .
> in the moonlight, as it says
> yes.

Having given into the "darkness coming down" that is her body, beginning with "The Truro Bear," Oliver attempts to recover nature's body, introducing into her work the bear as a Deep Image for the spiritual basis of the animal world. In this poem, the "things of the wood" are, like Oliver, given a body. Having admitted to her own animal nature, her own body, and having accepted the physical presence of the things of the wood, Oliver then attempts to reconnect the two. In "Entering the Kingdom," she claims: "They know me for what I am. / No dreamer, / No eater of leaves." But in "Hunter's Moon—Eating the Bear," the seventh moon poem in the cycle, Oliver invokes the act of eating: adopting the persona of a hunter, she literally kills and eats the

things of the forest. In so doing, she enters into the sacrament of communion: "And I will put you into my mouth, yes. / And I will swallow, yes." In this way, Oliver welcomes the material, physical kingdom into her body, into her poetry, and into her psyche as well. In the last line of the last poem of *Twelve Moons,* "Worm Moon," she tells the reader, "everything / is possible."

Despite Oliver's new mythological, archetypal direction, the seriousness of the book's structure, and the importance of the theme it explored, the most important review of the book was highly critical. Writing in the *New York Times Book Review* in 1979, the poet Hugh Seidman found the structure and the forms too artificial, complaining of " 'purple' adjectives and clumsy alliteration . . . inflated rhetoric" and what he felt to be a strained "heaviness" of theme. Fortunately, poets reviewing the book in the literary press had far better things to say. In an article in *The Hudson Review* the poet Emily Grosholz, for example, found the abundant, rich detail of the animals, woods, plants, and terrain of Oliver's Provincetown to be particularly impressive: "surely one function of a poet / naturalist is to tell the reader to go out and look."

THE WORK OF PRIMITIVE DREAMS: THE 1980s

Not long after publishing *Twelve Moons,* Oliver also began her long association with academia. In 1980 she became Mather Visiting Professor of Creative Writing at Case Western Reserve University in Cleveland. It was a welcome home-coming for Oliver. This return to her native state as an accomplished poet may in part explain the joy that informs her next two books, *American Primitive: Poems* (1983) and *Dream Work* (1986). These collections are, by far, her most popular; more than ten years later, they both remained in print and there is no doubt that they are the books on which her reputation is built and on which it will continue to rest.

In *American Primitive: Poems* and *Dream Work,* Oliver leaves the mythological structure and the reliance on archetypal Deep Images behind. Instead, each of these books attends to the material, specific, and literal fact. Description, not myth, becomes the single stylistic and thematic feature of Oliver's poetry. Insight into the fundamental poetics of these two books can be found in a small essay Oliver contributed to a symposium held by *The Georgia Review* (1981). The symposium, to which many poets contributed, concerned a powerful book-length attack on contemporary poetry's failure to connect with everyday life. In her response to that book, Christopher Clausen's *The Place of Poetry: Two Centuries of an Art in Crisis* (1981), Oliver wrote, "For the Man Cutting the Grass." When teaching some students at a poetry workshop, she was asked who she imagined her audience to be. She looked out the window and said, " 'For that man, out there on the lawn, cutting the grass.' " By that she meant to insist on the transhistorical, interpersonal, timeless character of poetry: its eternal presence and presentness. Admitting that, "At no time in history . . . has this separation between literature and life been so foolishly deep," Oliver insists on her desire to bridge that gap:

> There is . . . discontent and fever everywhere. Under every rationale we live according to our differences rather than our sameness. Poetry, an art form boiling up from the archetypal inner world, is one of the medicines for that fever. We need it. We need those orderings of thought, those flare-ups of imagination . . . proclaiming our sameness, calling the tribal soul together. The man out there, cutting the grass, is more astute than we give him credit for.

Turning first to *American Primitive,* one finds fifty poems not divided into any sections. Instead, the poems weave a cyclical tale charting Oliver's own engagement with the natural world as precisely, directly, and descriptively as possible. Ranging from the landscape of Cape Cod to that of Ohio, she also includes a number of history poems, discussing such figures as Johnny Appleseed and Tecumseh. Significantly, too, this book is dedicated not to Molly Malone Cook but rather to the poet James Wright, who had died tragically in 1980 of cancer. In his later poems from the 1970s, Wright, too, had left the rhetoric of the Deep Image behind, becoming more and more descriptive, precise, and focused on his own interactions with the natural world. In Oliver's *American Primitive,* she offers fifteen poems that, like Wright's later poetry, chart an easy, often ecstatic communion with nature. Here, woman and nature converse; here, Oliver celebrates nature's body: "There is this happy tongue" ("August"). She delights in its power: "how sensual / the lightning's / poured stroke!" ("Lightning"). She declares, in "Moles," that the earth is "delicious." After these first poems' opening blast of enthusiasm, however, there follow ten poems of grief, where pain, the nature of terror, and unreconcilable cruelty are described. Such poems as "Vultures," "An Old Whorehouse" (this is an allusion to James Wright's famous "In Response to a Rumor that the Oldest Whorehouse in Wheeling, West Virginia, Has Been Condemned"), "University Hospital, Boston," and "Skunk Cabbage" all point to the reality of pain and death. Instinct and the primitive here are not tempered.

Of all the poems, the harshest is "A Poem for the Blue Heron." It seems to follow directly from the assertion that "everything is possible," the last words of the last poem in *Twelve Moons.* Now, in "A Poem for the Blue Heron," Oliver writes, in italics for emphasis:

> *Not everything is possible;*
> *some things are impossible*

In other words, just when the book achieves its most ecstatic communion with nature, it backs away and asserts what Oliver discovered in her very first book: nature is not just unforgiving but, even worse, it is fundamentally indifferent to the human. Sometimes, it appears, communion *is* impossible. Sometimes, the primitive is horrifying in its meaninglessness.

This is particularly the case in "Web"—"So this is fear." It is also holds for "Skunk Cabbage"—"What blazes the trail is not necessarily pretty." But the cycle of joy and despair, as a cycle, cannot end and so, the next poems in the book offer a set of sensual, earthly delights. In these poems, a renewed sexual imagery asserts itself, particularly in "Something," "White Night," "Music," "The Gardens," and "The Fish." In the latter, Oliver again eats an animal but there is no archetypal or mythic gesture to some otherworldly system as there had been in *Twelve Moons*. When she eats the fish in this poem she merely means to describe a genuine organic fact: "Now the sea / is in me: I am the fish, the fish / glitters in me." The fact, however, offers her an experiential jolt of happiness. And, in "Happiness," she returns to her bear image. This time, a she-bear looking for honey becomes the very image of female, natural, embodied bliss. And, towards the end of the book, in "The Honey Tree," Oliver becomes this same bear: "And so at last I climbed / the honey tree, ate / chunks of pure light." This allows her to say, "how I love myself at last! / how I love the world!"

American Primitive, then, tells a cyclical story of wild happiness and profound anxiety and alienation. It revels in the experience of communion in nature as well as laments the seemingly impossible rift between nature and people. In one collection, it foreshadows what will become the future project of each of Oliver's subsequent poetry collections. By charting the range of her emotions when in nature, she means to address, through close analysis and description,

the truth of her sense that the human and the natural are linked together; that they are far more similar than different. Each of her subsequent books, then, will examine this problem from a slightly different perspective, but, fundamentally, the cyclical structure, and descriptive style of *American Primitive* will become the paradigm for each of Oliver's future poetry books.

The book itself was by far her most widely reviewed. Daily papers in Los Angeles, San Francisco, Louisville, and New York all praised it, as did the literary press. In 1984, *American Primitive* won the Pulitzer Prize for poetry. What accounts for this overdue acknowledgment of Oliver's talents was the intervening success of feminism in American literary circles. By 1983, Oliver's obviously sexual and sensual themes, her association of the feminine with the natural world, and her willingness to risk an exploration of often devalued sentimental themes met with a far more receptive audience. Feminism, by then, had made the literary community's ongoing, unchecked sexism—its disdain for so-called "women's poetry"—unacceptable. By the 1980s, one would no longer expect a woman to be condemned for writing about nature, the sentiments, or even the more traditionally "feminine" domestic themes. Quite the contrary! Bruce Bennett, in the *New York Times Book Review,* for example, praised the "Luscious objects and substances—blackberries, honey" that were "devoured" in Oliver's book. The poet Linda Gregorson, discussing the book in *Poetry,* reveals another possible reason for Oliver's success: "Oliver appears to be almost wholly uninterested in the strategies of artifice." Her decision to forgo both the Deep Image, and her predecessors' (Millay's and Frost's) commitment to metered, fixed-form poetry met with almost universal critical approval. Here was a mostly free verse poetry of stunning clarity.

Oliver published her fifth major collection *Dream Work* when she was appointed poet-in-residence at Bucknell University in Lewisburg,

Pennsylvania. (From this point onward, she would enjoy the roving life of the contemporary American poet as academic. Eventually, she would move, in 1991 to Sweet Briar College in Sweet Briar, Virginia, and then, in 1996, to Bennington College in Bennington, Vermont.) Like *American Primitive, Dream Work* continues to explore the connection between the spiritual and material without any extra apparatus, without resorting to myth, archetype, literary allusions to her predecessors, and the like. But unlike *American Primitive,* it is divided into two sections. In the first section, the poems move from despair and profound alienation to an almost pure sense of absolute joy. Additionally, they return their focus to the human world—even concluding in a homage, "Stanley Kunitz," to her friend, Cape Cod neighbor, and poetic guide. In the book's second section, the poems follow a wave-like pattern, a rise-and-fall tension between joy in the human connection to nature and doubt that such a connection is possible—doubt, in other words, that such a connection is more than a merely human dream.

In the book's first section, the poem, "Wild Geese," succinctly states Oliver's newfound sense of her poetic task:

> You do not have to be good.
> You do not have to walk on your knees
> for a hundred miles through the desert, repenting.
> You only have to let the soft animal of your body
> love what it loves.

Gone is any need to invoke grand explanations, systems, religions, or myths. Instead, she demands only an absolute attention to "the soft animal of your body."

Intriguingly, in this book Stanley Kunitz is the one person who seems to have found just such a home in the world, in nature, and in his body. Looking at him in his garden she tells us: "Oh, what good it does the heart / to know it isn't magic!" The hard work of dreams—the real and earnest digging into the soil: that is what Oliver wishes for herself and admires in Kunitz. As he is a man at home in his world, so she longs to be a woman at home in hers.

Oliver's newfound cyclical, wave-like method of organizing her books means that every upbeat will, inevitably, be followed by a downbeat. To her credit, Oliver pushes the questions she raises about the truth and value of the human connection to nature to their twentieth century extreme in her most moving and justly celebrated poem from *Dream Work:* "1945–1985: Poem for the Anniversary." There, Oliver addresses the question of evil raised by the Shoah (the Holocaust). In this poem, she juxtaposes her recollection of a stroll in the woods with meditations on images from the German war against the Jews. One section of the poem describes, for example, a beautiful garden, and a decidedly cultivated gentleman enjoying its luxuriant scent with a glass of wine only to conclude: "It is the face of Mengele." Such scenes are juxtaposed with a description of a time when she was, essentially, a hunter in the woods; when she and her dog confronted a fawn but did nothing. When the doe returns and smells Oliver's human scent: "she knew everything." Here, through this juxtaposition, Oliver meditates on her own unwillingness to kill, and, in so doing, wonders what "animal" and "human" really mean when the cultivated man is a doctor committed to torturing children, and the wild beast is a protective mother. The final section of the poem, describing the doe's return reads:

> The forest grew dark.

> She nuzzled her child wildly.

More than just ethical questions are raised here. For in this poem, Oliver's ongoing attempt to bridge the human and the natural has met, for the first time, a profound problem. What, in the end, do people mean by the terms "human" and "nature"? Given their potential meanings, ought they to be brought together at all?

No doubt as a result of her increasing reputation and prominence, a number of major literary critics reviewed *Dream Work*. The poet-critic Alicia Ostriker, whose *Stealing the Language: The Emergence of Women's Poetry in America* was one of the first examinations of a specifically female American poetic tradition, declared Oliver to be "as visionary as Emerson." She also praised the book for its obvious "advance on her earlier writings." She particularly admired the "meditation on the Holocaust" because it, and the other poems in the collection, put Oliver "further into the world of historical and personal suffering." Sandra M. Gilbert, poet, scholar, and future president of the Modern Language Association, writing in *Poetry,* also singled out the book's turn to history. Gilbert, however, noted that Oliver "finds a way to escape the rigors of human chronicles through attention to natural history." Seeing in Oliver a continuation of the work of D. H. Lawrence, Marianne Moore, and Elizabeth Bishop, Gilbert becomes the first critic to see that Oliver's poetics moralize "on the other history we can learn from natural history." Also notable is that, for the first time in Oliver's career, no critic lambasted her for her style. In the *Michigan Quarterly Review,* the literary critic Lisa M. Steinman declared: "One might distrust such epiphanic moments . . . Yet the poetry, in the iambs, in the careful mixture of statement and image, avoids sentimentality and is, in the final analysis, deeply moving."

Following the publication of *Dream Work,* Oliver herself contributed an important aesthetic statement, "Some Thoughts on the Line," for a symposium on poetics published in *The Ohio Review* (1987). There, she implicitly revealed the impact that James Wright's poetry had on her work. Speaking of Wright's ability to use vernacular language, plain speech, and "the conversational tone" in his poetry, she writes: "What is forceful and gives pleasure is not just the use of

the vernacular but its transformation. The unassuming phrase, as familiar to us as our own name, is worked into the mechanical structure and literary body of the poem, it is resurrected; it is changed utterly." These are words one might apply just as well to *American Primitive* and *Dream Work*.

TURNING TO A NEW LIGHT: OLIVER IN THE 1990s

Beginning with *House of Light* (1990), Oliver's poetry moved into a decidedly spiritual realm. It is as if, once she admitted the ethical and moral problems of pain, suffering, and evil into her ongoing project of reconciling the natural and the human worlds, she had no choice but to turn to the various world religions, and to her own Christian heritage for tropes, images, and even usable myths and frames. At the same time, this invocation of Christianity, Buddhism, and even the myths and archetypes of the Deep Image movement do not mean that Oliver was returning to the poetry of *Twelve Moons*. Instead, she now finds herself wondering what the great philosophers, religions, and poets have had to say about the very meaning of the words "human" and "nature," words whose meaning were thrown into such serious doubt in *Dream Work*.

In the book's very first poem, "Some Questions You Might Ask," these questions return, and, as is now standard for Oliver, they return as direct, simple, unencumbered questions. More and more, hers is a poetry of assertion, of a "heightened vernacular":

> Is the soul solid, like iron?
> Or is it tender and breakable, like
> the wings of a moth in the beak of the owl?
> Who has it, and who doesn't?

The last question is perhaps the most serious, for if nature does not have a soul, then what would, she wonders, be the point of joining one's self to it. And in her poem about the Nazi period, she even finds herself wondering if humans, as a species, really have a soul.

In "The Buddha's Last Instruction," she describes one answer to this last question. That poem's title refers to the Buddha's last words " 'Make of yourself a light.' " After quoting this last instruction, the poem then describes a time when Oliver became a literal house of light. She went outside in the sunrise. The sun shines on her body; she begins to glow with the dawn:

And then I feel the sun itself
as it blazes over the hills,
like a million flowers on fire—
clearly I'm not needed,
yet I feel myself turning
into something of inexplicable value.

Here, the Buddhist view of the interconnectedness of all things releases Oliver from the human specificity of her questions. She is transformed into "something" else, joined, as it were, to nature—itself a "house of light" as well. At the same time, in "Spring," she describes her familiar animal, a black she-bear:

coming
    down the mountain,
        breathing and tasting . . .

Unlike the word-loving Oliver, this bear is "wordless" and has a "perfect love." In this poem, Oliver is apparently still too alienated to join in such "breathing and tasting."

In *House of Light,* not only is the desire to connect met with the reality of disconnection between animal and human, but also between humans themselves. In "Singapore," which David Baker, a reviewer for *The Kenyon Review* (1991), called, "one of her most important and powerful poems," Oliver tells the story of a woman who cleans the airport bathroom. The poem stands out in Oliver's work, both in its setting (in an airport,

far from the United States, among people), and in its use of long, breathy lines. Thinking of the cleaning woman, Oliver asks, "If the world were only pain and logic, who would want it?" This desire to transcend "pain and logic" constitutes the ethical and spiritual quest behind Oliver's poetic project. For her need to connect to nature is a need to accept, discover, and realize beauty, Being, and even kindness. Are such things of this world? Are they only human and if so, as human, are they merely artifice? Dreams? Illusions? In "Singapore," she affirms her faith: the woman represents, for her, "the light that can shine out of a life." In *House of Light,* the world of light, the spiritual fire shining from within, is not only Buddhist but Christian as well. In "Maybe" she describes "Sweet Jesus, talking / his melancholy madness." In "Some Questions You Might Ask," a moose is "as sad / as the face of Jesus" and an owl in "Little Owl Who Lives in the Orchard" is imagined reading the Book of Revelation. But, in the end, neither Christianity nor Buddhism provides Oliver with answers—as she admits in "The Summer Day," "I don't know exactly what a prayer is."

Although many of the reviews of this book were glowing (Robert Richman, in the *New York Times Book Review,* praised it as "genuine, moving, and implausible as the first caressing breeze of spring"), Oliver as perceived by at least one reviewer was said to be lacking in any struggle or spiritual quest. David Baker, in *The Kenyon Review,* found that the poems in *House of Light* had "the same, perhaps too-easy solution—politically and aesthetically—merely to rise and float away from a troubling world, to erase it or to erase the self within that world." He praised "Singapore" precisely because it acknowledged Oliver's own guilt, her role in what she observed. In effect, Baker was unable to see the ethical and spiritual turn of these poems. Fortunately, Oliver herself made a case for such a reading in the first major interview of her career with Eleanor Swanson, which was published in 1990 in *The Blooms-*

bury Review. There, she reports that *House of Light* concludes a long poetic journey: "The books . . . beginning with *Twelve Moons* and concluding with *House of Light,* I think of as a unit." Pressed for more detail, she replied, "I won't say much about them except that they all employ the natural world in an emblematic way, and yet they are all—so was my intent!—about the human condition." She added: "What I write next will be quite different."

Despite this claim, Oliver did not really change direction. Instead, her next substantial publication, *New and Selected Poems* (1992), spanned her entire publishing career and included poems from each of her books. Arranged in reverse chronological order, it demanded that readers account for her current work not her past work. In fact, its very first section, simply titled "New Poems," included 30 new poems. This book, then, by breaking with a chronological narrative, told readers that development and change was less important to her work than it might be to other poets. In the "New Poems" section, for example, one finds far more consistency than difference. Like *House of Light,* they too probe deeply into the world of nature. The only detectable thematic difference is that, in these new poems, Oliver removes herself even more completely from the poem than before. As if to emphasize and endorse her presence and importance to contemporary American poetry, the literary establishment gave this volume the National Book Award for 1992. In her acceptance speech, she paid her first public homage to her companion, "my first reader, and the light of my life, Molly Malone Cook," to whom *New and Selected Poems* is dedicated.

The new poems included in this collection exhibit a wide variety of prosodic technique. Here are the familiar short lines of two, three, or four beats, and the progressively indented left-hand margins in three- and four-line stanzas. Here are longer, breathy, almost prose-like lines that stretch across the page, and poems printed in double col-

umns on a single page, a technique to which she will return often. Despite this prosodic variety, and despite Oliver's claims for a "new direction," one can locate in these poems—and between them and their predecessors—significant thematic continuity. Returning to the ethical and spiritual questions she had begun to raise overtly in *Dream Work* and *House of Light* the new poems manifest a willingness to accept that which is inscrutable and strange in nature. In, "This Morning Again It Was in the Dusty Pines," Oliver tells the reader "the owl / turns its face from me." She admits that even if people could talk to the animals they would nonetheless still find themselves strangers to nature; she appears to agree with the philosopher Ludwig Wittgenstein, who famously wrote: "If a lion could speak we would not be able to understand him." But Oliver's poem actually makes the problem far more severe:

> even if we came by some miracle
> upon a language which we both knew,
>   what is it I might say
> there in the orange light of early morning

Whereas the earlier Mary Oliver might have found pessimism in such a conclusion, here she finds instead a new acceptance: "So. I cannot improve upon the scene."

These new poems from *New and Selected Poems* fundamentally depend on such acceptance of nature's self-containment. The alienation that Oliver had been recording in her previous books is not, in these poems, resolved. But in the new poems it is now met with a new, even joyous acceptance. As she says in "Poppies":

>   light
> is an invitation
> to happiness,
> and that happiness,
>
> when it's done right,
> is a kind of holiness,
> palpable and redemptive.

In the last stanza of the last new poem, "October," Oliver states:

so this is the world.
I'm not in it.
It is beautiful.

That Oliver can find beauty in nature's separateness does mark a new approach, another angle of vision by which to measure her central theme: the relationship between the natural and human worlds. The new approach may explain why "When Death Comes" became the new poem most often singled out for praise. In it, Oliver writes:

When it's over, I want to say: all my life
I was a bride married to amazement.
I was the bridegroom, taking the world into my
    arms.

Because *New and Selected Poems* spanned Oliver's career, the National Book Award testifies to an important and in some respects new recognition of Oliver's contribution to American poetry. In 1992, the poet Stephen Dobyns, in the *New York Times Book Review,* declared her to be the best living practitioner of the free verse line, asserting that only the late James Wright "controlled the free verse line as well as she does." Beyond the praise for her prosody, reviewers were also single-minded in their praise of her exactitude of description. Using such words as "simplicity," "clarity," "directness" over and over again in their reviews, they also noted the consistent quality of her craft from her first book to the new poems.

But while Oliver had finally shed much of the criticism that had dogged her since her first book had appeared almost thirty years earlier, some reviewers continued to find Oliver's insistent epiphanies and ecstasies hard to believe. Although praising Oliver's newfound refusal to be "indifferent to a nature indifferent to her," one reviewer, Judith Kitchen, writing in *The Georgia Review,* also complained that "Oliver's failure to be adequate to her own epistemological questions makes many of these poems both interesting and irritating." In fact, this had, by 1992, become a persistent criticism of Oliver's work. As the reviewer for *Poetry,* David Barber put it: the new poems had become "all too predictable . . . the epiphanies come thick and fast, and the exaltations are strictly routine." He added that "Oliver skates perilously close to the overweening rhetoric of the self-help aisle and the recovery seminar." By contrast, the poet Maxine Kumin, writing in the *Women's Review of Books* in 1993, felt that the poems were not only perfectly believable but contained a subject all too rare in contemporary American poetry: "the frail links between the human and the natural world." Similarly, Paul Oppenheimer, writing in the *American Book Review* in 1993, disagreed that the ecstasy and joy was false or mannered: "freshness of perception . . . together with an admirable coolness of diction . . . is totally engaging," he wrote.

CRITICS ON OLIVER

Given Oliver's ability to galvanize and spark debate among reviewers, it is all the more remarkable that, by 1992, few literary scholars had paid attention to her work. Perhaps most significantly, the few critics who did critique her work took up and debated, from the beginning, the meanings and implications of Oliver's engagement with the natural world.

In 1988, Jean B. Alford, writing for *Pembroke Magazine,* argued that the lack of attention to Oliver resulted from her unwillingness to be like other poets of her generation. Oliver's poems, Alford claimed, "engross the reader in a fully sensual union with nature." Such positive affirmation, she added, is not acceptable to a current literary and scholarly establishment more inclined than she to find despair and hopelessness in both the human and natural worlds. Maintaining this reading of Oliver's "outsider" status, Patricia Yaeger, also in 1988, claimed that to reject such affirmation was to reject the role of women in nature. It was, in effect, to keep women in their silent place as muse or subject of the poem, but not as speaking voice. Oliver, says Yaeger, protests against such an idea and develops her own countertradition."

While critics were beginning to draw attention to Oliver's erasure in a male-dominated tradition of nature poetry, it was not until Janet McNew's 1989 essay in *Contemporary Literature* that Oliver's place in a "countertradition" began to gain serious and controversial attention. In her article, the first theoretical, academic consideration of Oliver's work, McNew placed Oliver's poetry in an ongoing tradition of "visionary nature poetry." She did so by emphasizing the gender issues at stake when a woman addresses nature, or attempts to understand it. According to McNew, the "nature poetry" tradition that most critics and poets know—"the Romantic nature tradition"—assumes "a speaking male subject who explores his relation to a mute and female nature." As a result, says McNew, women poets come to nature as a terrain already figured by male poetry as female. In other words, the woman coming to nature through the established poetic tradition sees in nature another woman; from this perspective, nature is not a threatening, or mute "other." McNew argues that the epiphanies, ecstasies, and "visionary dissolutions" that occur so frequently in Oliver's poetry are possible because she can identity without "fear or loss of consciousness" with nature: "With all the strength of mythic association to body and to nature intact, Oliver and other 'bad' daughters create mythic patterns unmarred by the shame of denied origins." Simply stated, Oliver's is a female tradition where epiphany is the rule, not the exception.

For McNew, this life-affirming female alternative to the male tradition becomes nothing less than a feminist myth for Romantic nature poetry in general, and American nature poetry in particular. In creating such a myth, says McNew, Oliver is among the few contemporary poets to remain faithful to "the original romantic project" of linking the human to the natural.

McNew's argument sparked a lively and ongoing debate about Oliver's poetry; the debate, once begun, initiated more and more academic attention to her work. In a 1992 article in *Women's Studies,* Diane Bonds argued that McNew's position had one flaw. To say that nature was itself feminine was to assume that the male tradition, which had for so long read nature in feminine terms, was correct. Bonds noted that many feminists dismissed Oliver's work precisely because the counter-myth that McNew traced smacked of a capitulation to male ideas of nature. According to Bonds, Oliver's poetry is far more complex even than McNew's countertradition and feminist mythology would suggest, for it "reshapes assumptions about language and poetry that attend [both feminist and masculine] myths." Oliver, said Bonds, insists on the literal and precise image of nature's things because she means to get beyond the very idea of mythic readings; such readings, said Bonds, inevitably imprison women in a proscribed and gendered rhetoric. Through the anti-mythic attention to the literal, Oliver claims for herself, and for women, a language of nature poetry that does not "give up the identification with nature that clearly empowers Oliver's work." Also, by refusing the language of myth, Oliver is able to make a "powerful and critical rereading of theological and ethical assertions associated with the Judeo-Christian tradition." Specifically, says Bonds, Oliver's poetry "employs the terms of patriarchal Christianity to repudiate a dualistic and sometimes otherworldly ideology which splits or separates human and nonhuman nature, spirit and matter . . ." For Bonds, Oliver's poetry does not assume a lost unity that some myth must rebuild; it accepts no Fall, asserting that "connectivity" has always been there between nature and people. Nature, in other words, is not, for Oliver, an allegory, not mere language, and not mere symbol. The things of nature are themselves: and nothing more, and people, as humans, are part of these things too.

Following up on Bonds' reading in *Papers,* Vicki Graham asks what it might mean to insist on the material fact of nature in the highly artificial and symbolic world of poetry. Agreeing with Bonds that Oliver is no mythmaking, allegorical, or traditionally Romantic poet, she asks a probing question that even Bonds ignored: how can one avoid mythmaking language in poetry? Is that not the very nature of poetry? Graham answers this question by asserting that, for Oliver, language is not artificial, but is a natural, bodily, and material thing. Oliver's sense of poetry is, therefore, fundamentally physical: it embodies the reader through its rhythms. Poetry expresses the physical and sensual self. As such, it is the only medium for direct apprehension of the natural world. In the actual physical space of the poem, Oliver and nature greet one another: "once mind and body stop fighting, direct, sensuous contact with the other becomes possible, allowing an exchange of energy which leads to identification and then merging."

In making this argument, Graham becomes the first scholar to single out the bear poems as a particular sequence. She singles these poems out in order to prove that, "Miming and becoming another is a willed artistic act that carries her across boundaries that she nonetheless remains conscious of." In other words, Oliver, on the one hand, is not making allegories and symbols, but, on the other hand, she is writing a poem which might lead one to expect symbols, emblems, and the like. Oliver never lets her readers forget that

they are actually reading a poem, or even that she is writing one. She does not pretend that the fact of her poem is somehow transparent or not there. But Oliver's self-conscious awareness of the poem, of the very act of writing, the very act of reading, is, nonetheless, part and parcel of the natural world. If language is natural, then, so too, are poems.

EMPHASIZING THE WORDS: PROSE, PROSE POETRY, AND THE LATER POEMS

One can never be sure how poets will accept critical and theoretical responses to their work. Even when they discuss such responses they tend to hedge and hide. What is certain, however, is that in the work Oliver has published since the academic discussion outlined above began, she has been far more self-conscious about the act of poetry, the writing process itself. Not only has she written specific handbooks for poets, but she has also written two books of essays, many of which discuss her ideas about poetry, and, in two more collections of poems, *White Pine: Poems and Prose Poems* (1994) and *West Wind: Poems and Prose Poems* (1997), she has begun not only to depict the art of poetry in her poems, but to write in a genre new to her work—the prose poem.

White Pine contains forty poems of which sixteen, including the title poem, are prose poems. In the very first poem, "Work," Oliver describes herself writing: "All day I work / with the linen of words." Following this work, she comes out of her house and makes sure to "walk back through the pinewoods / to Pasture Pond." Words here are compared to linen, but linen is itself a natural fabric: words, in other words, are crafted aspects of the natural universe she inhabits. In the prose poem "Yes! No!" she concludes, "To pay attention, this is our endless and proper work." This line seems to allude to the French writer,

Gustave Flaubert, one of the greatest craftsmen and most careful artificers in any language. In her 1990 interview with Eleanor Swanson, well before this poem was published, Oliver herself could not resist quoting from Flaubert: " 'Talent is long patience, and originality an effort of will and of intense observation.' I lived for years with that, trying for intense observation, believing in it. Well, I still do!"

In *White Pine*, Oliver includes her instrument of observation—language crafted into poetry—in a far more self-conscious way than ever before. Many of the poems are exquisite observational set-pieces. Also, each poem—either because it is in prose or because of its wildly variant lineation—demands that the reader notice the poetic style, the material fact of the poem itself. One of her most deliberate and skillful poems, "At the Lake" observes a fish leap out of the water and vanish. In the final stanza, Oliver tells the reader:

> but the words are in place—
> and the fish leaps, and leaps again
> from the black plush of the poem,
> that breathless space.

Literally, the fish *will* always leap again and again in these words, in this description. Poetry, as observation, is a kind of "breathless space"—a space without a body, mere words, but also a place where real bodies, women, fish, and water coexist.

The major poem of this collection is certainly "In Blackwater Woods." In a series of fourteen lyrics ranging across many poetic styles including the prose poem, Oliver confronts both her major theme and her main medium, poetry. In the untitled poem "9," she offers these lines:

> Still, listen, I swear, I have not set one word down
> on top of another without breathing into it!

Here, Oliver embodies her own poetry; its rhythm, she implies, is quite literally her body's rhythm,

her breath. By the end of this complex and important poetic sequence, in "14: In a Dark Wood: Wood Thrushes," she reminds the reader that nature too breathes with its own language: all creatures communicate and, make noise. Listening to sounds in the woods, she says: "This is not song, this is not singing, this is not thoughtful . . ." She does away with any anthropomorphizing. Instead, she tells her readers that what they hear is: "no idea, simply noise, call it noise . . ." To say, "call it noise," denies that even the word "noise" is an accurate indicator of the sound she hears. Asking the reader to recall nothing but unmediated sound, Oliver concludes: "Each voice shimmers; yet it is one voice: the damp and sonorous exaltation of the dead, or the not-yet-born, who still know everything." Nature consists of voice, language, be it snakes in the leaves, birds in the trees, or the poet at her desk. The last stanza of the last and title poem, "White Pine," says:

> And now I have finished my walk. And I am just
> standing,
> quietly, in the darkness, under the tree.

The book itself moves as if its poems, too, were taking a walk. By the time the book's walk is over, Oliver has learned to stand quietly and listen. This time, though, she explains how what she hears is itself always filtered through these natural, yet crafted poems.

Despite the turn of attention in *White Pine* to the fact of poetry itself, reviewers continued to emphasize Oliver's status as a nature poet whose approach to nature was meant to be unmediated. In *The Bloomsbury Review,* the reviewer, Thomas R. Smith, declared: "As a practitioner of the 'nature' poem, she is currently without rival; no poet in recent times has honored deer, pine trees, hummingbirds, spiders, and owls with the intense sustained, and loving scrutiny she brings to even the least of her poems." In a 1996 article in *Poetry* the poet Richard Tillinghast praised the volume precisely because it refused to anthropomophize nature: "its otherness is acknowledged." Finally, writing in *Provincetown Arts* in 1995, Mark Doty, one of the more important young poets to come to prominence in the 1990s, singled out Oliver's spirituality: "nature is viewed in light of a spiritual crisis."

Oliver continued to insist, however, on the importance of the art of poetry writing not just in her poems but in general publishing, *A Poetry Handbook,* in 1994. There, Oliver provides a map to the inner workings and elements of poetry: *"A Poetry Handbook* was written with writers of poetry most vividly in my mind; their needs and problems and increase have most directly been my concerns." The fact that, off and on for close to fourteen years, Oliver had been teaching poetry writing in colleges and universities across the country certainly played a role in her decision to set forth her ideas in a specific manual. There, speaking out of more than thirty years of struggling with the very idea of poetry, Oliver announces that *everything* is, fundamentally, poetic, if, poetry means the recognition of a deep spirituality in things, in nature, and in ourselves:

> If it is *all* poetry, and not just one's own accomplishment, that carries one from this green and mortal world—that lifts the latch and gives a glimpse into a greater paradise—then perhaps one has the sensibility: a gratitude apart from authorship, a fervor and desire beyond the margins of the self.

In the prose poem, "December," from *White Pine,* Oliver had used remarkably similar language. There, she describes a deer coming out of the woods and then vanishing. She tells the reader that: "The great door opens a crack, a hint of the truth is given—so bright it is almost a death, a joy we can't bear—and then it is gone." This fleeting glimpse of what she here calls "truth" is what she believes the best poetry provides and what, in her handbook, she means to convey to the next generation of poets.

This turn to the act of poetry writing itself perhaps made it inevitable that Oliver would collect her essays and publish them in her first prose collection, *Blue Pastures* in 1995. There, in fifteen essays, Oliver offers her first autobiographical pieces to a general public, as well as an extended appreciation of Walt Whitman's poetry in "My Friend, Walt Whitman." Particularly interesting to those who wish to know more about her work are two essays, "Pen and Paper and a Breath of Air," and "The Poet's Voice." In the first, she explains how and where she writes: "For at least thirty years, and at almost all times, I have carried a notebook with me, in my back pocket." She says that she literally writes much of her work in its initial drafts in the woods, or on the beach, or wherever in nature she happens to be. In the second essay, she describes the poets who first affected her deeply. Then, she complains about a contemporary American poetic culture that is obsessed only with autobiography and free verse. She proceeds to defend metered poetry even though she herself had, in her most recent collections, left not only meter but also the free verse line behind, favoring instead the prose poem's unlineated blocks of text. Also in this collection one finds the beginnings of an interconnected series of prose poems called "Sand Dabs"—gnomic aphorisms in the spirit of Emerson and Thoreau.

As with *White Pine,* the reviews of this prose collection were generally enthusiastic. But in the leading journal devoted to the review of poetry, *Parnassus,* Gyorgyi Voros offered what can only be called a stinging critique of Oliver's work. In so doing, he resurrected the controversy over the rapturous, epiphanic poetry that had asserted itself throughout her career. Taking her *New and Selected Poems, White Pine,* and *Blue Pastures* as his subject, Voros began his essay with the flat assertion that "Mary Oliver exhibits a peculiar lack of genuine engagement with the natural world." He reserved his harshest comment for her spirituality, labeling it an "addiction to spiritual thrill-seeking" and finding in it a "complacency of thought" and a spirit of "self-congratulation." Dismayed by, if not outright disgusted with, Oliver's depiction of what he called "a transcendent vision of wholeness," Voros concluded that her entire vision is "ecologically unsound. The last thing we need to do in the current urgency of reconsidering our relationship to the natural world is to 'cast aside the weight of facts' and 'float . . . / above this difficult world.' " For Voros, Oliver "does not answer to the needs of our own historical moment, or to the particulars of the late twentieth century's conflicts with Nature." He even goes so far as to gender his attack, labeling her "schoolmarmish." Perhaps, not surprisingly, Voros reserves his enthusiasm for a very "manly" poet, Gary Snyder, two of whose books he then reviews with vigorous praise in order to point, through the contrast, to Oliver's failings. Unwittingly, Voros proves the point of such feminist scholars as McNew, Yaeger, Bonds, and Graham: there does seem to be a gendered inflection to the critical response to Oliver's work.

As if to counter both Voros and his feminist predecessors, Douglas Burton-Christie, in 1996, contributed the first article to consider Oliver's "transcendence" from a specifically Christian point of view. Writing in *Cross Currents,* Burton-Christie argues that the command to pay attention and observe, which Oliver attributes to Flaubert, refers to a far older Christian tradition of attending to the particular. Writing in a journal for religious scholars, Burton-Christie means to make Oliver's work accessible to that community, arguing that Oliver's complexity of vision consists of both what McNew discovered—a new set of symbols, a new myth–and what Graham discovered—the refusal to read nature through mythological symbols. According to Burton-Christie, the tension between these two methods of reading nature inform Oliver's poetry.

Reading this tension in Oliver's poetry, Burton-Christie sees the work as a deliberate refusal to allegorize to "impose upon nature an alien symbolic structure of meaning." By implication, then, Burton-Christie defends her work from charges leveled against it by readers like Voros. According to Burton-Christie, if one is not reading carefully, one will inevitably think, as does Voros, that one is reading merely a poetry of flat statement: unoriginal, and banal. In fact, argues Burton-Christie, Oliver's careful, precise language and description "appears to have less an aesthetic than an ethical connotation." Such a desire, after all, is deeply respectful of all life: it says that Oliver refuses to fossilize the things she describes, to forever trap them in her own prison house of meaning. Burton-Christie, in this article, establishes a new direction for the continued scholarly study of Oliver's work, probing what he calls her "spirituality of the ordinary."

In *West Wind,* Oliver continues to engage such spirituality. In 1997, a year after she was appointed to the Catharine Osgood Foster Chair for Distinguished Teaching at Bennington College in Vermont, she published this book, her ninth full collection of poetry. In it, Oliver continues her exploration of the connections between nature and the human by finally entering the Romantic tradition reviewers and critics have for so long said she inhabited. Divided into three sections, *West Wind* contains some of her longest poems. The second section, the title poem, "West Wind," is, itself, a series of thirteen poems. Deliberately echoing Shelley's famous "Ode to the West Wind," it joins with her previous long poem, "In Blackwater Woods," as a lyric in the manner of the great Romantic odes. If, in *White Pine,* she finally wrote about the act of writing poetry, then in *West Wind* she finally writes directly out of a specific literary tradition invoking through her literary allusions, and addresses to past poets—Percy Shelley, William Blake, John Clare—the world of poetry that precedes her own and in which hers will finally come to rest. As important as this literary "home" is to Oliver, *West Wind* also signals in a singular way Oliver's true home.

In the last stanza of the poem comprising the book's final section, Oliver writes:

I climb. I backtrack.
I float.
I ramble my way home.

After years of climbing, backtracking, and floating through nature, Mary Oliver, in this book, returns to the human world as part and parcel of the natural world. In this poem, "Have You Ever Tried to Enter the Long Black Branches," written to her companion, Molly Malone Cook, the ever-personally-reticent Oliver finds in human love her home.

After *West Wind,* Oliver published *Rules for the Dance* and a mixed genre collection of prose, poems, and prose poems, *Winter Hours.* These books continue her ongoing goal of reconciling nature and the human by accounting for, and examining the art of poetry as the instrument used to achieve that goal. In *Rules for the Dance,* for example, Oliver hopes to teach the metrical tradition to a new generation of poets. As a result, it is as much a book of practical poetic history as it is a manual; she even includes an anthology of her favorite metered poems at the end of the book. Throughout the book, however, one finds that Oliver returns again and again to the spiritual urgency of poetry in order to impress that central fact of the art on the present and future poets who will be her readers. *Winter Hours,* meanwhile, is equally "literary," in that it contains a number of essays devoted to specific poets who have long had an impact on her: Gerard Manley Hopkins, Robert Frost, Edgar Allan Poe, and Walt Whitman. And in the lovely poem/essay, "The Boat," Oliver meditates on Shelley, reflecting on his death by drowning. The hardback edition of the book includes a cover picture of his boat, as if to underline the Romantic heritage behind Oliver's own poetic career.

But it is perhaps the final section of *Winter Hours,* consisting of the title essay, that is, for readers of Oliver, both the most surprising and the most welcome. In the poet Maxine Kumin's 1993 review, she lamented that "It is our misfortune that she has never shined the bright light of her introspection on human love." Having turned this bright light onto her *own* "human love" in *West Wind,* Oliver in the title essay to *Winter Hours* invites her readers, at last, into the home she has shared with her companion for so long. For the first time she describes publicly her life with Molly Malone Cook, her domestic routine, the daily events she has spent a career excluding from her poetry. Like Mary Oliver, her readers have rambled home with her as well.

What might one expect of Oliver in the future? Only the poet can know but her recent literary turn, joined as it is to her return home, indicates that Oliver's search for connections, and for a home in the world, for what Whitman called "the merge," is far from over. In her future poetry, her readers can expect her to tell them where next to look.

Selected Bibliography

WORKS OF MARY OLIVER

POETRY AND PROSE
No Voyage, and Other Poems. London: Dent, 1963; Boston: Houghton Mifflin, 1965.
The River Styx Ohio, and Other Poems. New York: Harcourt Brace Jovanovich, 1972.
The Night Traveler. Cleveland: Bits Press, 1978.
Sleeping in the Forest. Athens: Ohio Review Chapbook, 1979.
Twelve Moons. Boston: Little Brown, 1979.
American Primitive: Poems. Boston: Little Brown, 1983.
Dream Work. Boston: Atlantic Monthly Press, 1986.
Provincetown. Lewisburg, Penn.: Appletree Alley, 1987.
House of Light. Boston: Beacon, 1990.

New and Selected Poems. Boston: Beacon, 1992.

A Poetry Handbook. San Diego: Harcourt Brace, 1994.

White Pine. San Diego: Harcourt Brace, 1994.

Blue Pastures. San Diego: Harcourt Brace, 1995.

West Wind: Poems and Prose Poems. Boston: Houghton Mifflin, 1997.

Rules for the Dance: A Handbook for Writing and Reading Metrical Verse. Boston: Houghton Mifflin, 1998.

Winter Hours: Prose, Prose Poems, and Poems. Boston: Houghton Mifflin, 1999.

UNCOLLECTED ESSAYS

"For the Man Cutting the Grass." *Georgia Review* 35, no. 4:7–11 (1981).

"Some Thoughts on the Line," *The Ohio Review* 38: 41–46 (1987).

Introduction to *Holyoke,* by Frank Gaspar. Boston: Northeastern University Press, 1988.

CRITICAL AND BIOGRAPHICAL STUDIES

Alford, Jean B. "The Poetry of Mary Oliver: Modern Renewal Through Moral Acceptance" *Pembroke Magazine* 20:283–288 (1988).

Baker, David. Review of *House of Light. Kenyon Review* 13, no. 1:192–202 (1991).

Barber, David. Review of *New and Selected Poems. Poetry* 162, no. 4:233–242 (1993)

Bennett, Bruce. Review of *American Primitive. New York Times Book Review,* July 17, 1983, p. 10.

Booth, Philip. Review of *No Voyage and Other Poems. The Christian Science Monitor,* April 15, 1965, p. 9.

Bonds, Diane "The Language of Nature in the Poetry of Mary Oliver." *Women's Studies* 21:1–15 (1992).

Burton-Christie, Douglas. "Nature, Spirit, and Imagination in the Poetry of Mary Oliver." *Cross Currents* 46, no. 1:77–87 (1996).

Dickey, James. Review. *The New York Times Book Review,* November 21, 1965, pp. 61–62.

Dobyns, Stephen. "How Does One Live?" *New York Times Book Review,* December 13, 1992, p. 12.

Doty, Mark "Natural Science: In Praise of Mary Oliver." *Provincetown Arts* 11:26–27, 29 (1995).

Gilbert, Sandra. "Six Poets in Search of a History." *Poetry* 150, no. 2:113–116 (1987).

Graham, Vicki. "Into the Body of Another: Mary Oliver and the Poetics of Becoming Other." *Papers on Language and Literature* 30, no. 4:352–372 (1994).

Gregorson, Linda. Review of *American Primitive. Poetry.* 145:38–39 (October 1984).

Grosholz, Emily. "Poetry Chronicle." *Hudson Review* 33, no. 2:303 (1980).

Kitchen, Judith. Review of *New and Selected Poems. The Georgia Review* 47, no. 1:145–159 (1993).

Kumin, Maxine. "Intimations of Mortality." *Womens Review of Books* 10, no. 7:19 (1993).

McNew, Janet. "Mary Oliver and the Tradition of Romantic Nature Poetry." *Contemporary Literature* 30, no. 1:59–77 (1989).

Oppenheimer, Paul. "The Innocence of a Mirror." *American Book Review* 15, no. 4:11 (1993).

Ostriker, Alicia. "Review of Dream Work." *The Nation* 243, no. 5:148–150 (1986).

Richman, Robert. "Polished Surfaces and Difficult Pastorals." *New York Times Book Review,* November 25, 1990, p. 24.

Seidman, Hugh. "Natural Universe." *New York Times Book Review,* October 21, 1979, p. 24.

Smith, Thomas R. Review of *A Poetry Handbook* and *White Pine. Bloomsbury Review* 15, no. 4:28 (1995).

Steinman, Lisa. "Dialogues Between History and Dream." *Michigan Quarterly Review* 36, no. 2:428–438 (1987).

Voros, Gyorgyi. "Exquisite Environments." *Parnassus* 21, nos. 1–2:231–250 (1996).

Tillinghast, Richard. "Stars and Departures, Hummingbirds and Statues." *Poetry* 166, no. 5:288–290 (1996).

Yaeger, Patricia. *Honey Mad Women: Emancipatory Strategies in Women's Writing.* New York: Columbia University Press, 1988.

INTERVIEWS

"An Interview with Poet Mary Oliver." *AWP Chronicle* 27:1–6, 8 (1994).

Swanson, Eleanor. "The Language of Dreams: In Interview with Mary Oliver." *The Bloomsbury Review* 10, no. 3:1, 6 (1990).

—*JONATHAN N. BARRON*

Annie Proulx

1935–

WITH THE PUBLICATION of her first two novels—*Postcards* (1992) and *The Shipping News* (1993)—Annie Proulx (Proo) emerged from obscurity to become one of America's most celebrated writers. Both books garnered glowing reviews and a number of prestigious awards. In April 1993 *Postcards* bested 284 other works to win the PEN/Faulkner Award for Fiction, making Proulx the first woman writer to win the $15,000 prize since it was established in 1980. *The Shipping News* was an even greater triumph. In August 1993 it won the *Chicago Tribune*'s Heartland Prize for fiction; in September it won the *Irish Times* International Fiction Prize; in November it won the National Book Award for fiction and was nominated for a National Book Critics Circle Award. In April 1994 *The Shipping News* was awarded the Pulitzer Prize for fiction. After the Pulitzer was announced Proulx told an interviewer, Sybil Steinberg, that she had "run out of being stunned. Except I am stunned. Each time this happens, I can't believe it."

As is true of many an "overnight sensation," Annie Proulx's phenomenal success was the culmination of a long apprenticeship in her craft and an even longer period of struggle and frustration. She began her life as a professional fiction writer in her mid-fifties, a fact that makes her achievement all the more remarkable.

BACKGROUND

Edna Annie Proulx was born on August 22, 1935, in Norwich, Connecticut, the first of five girls. Her father, George Napoleon Proulx, quit school at the age of fourteen to work as a bobbin boy in a textile mill. He eventually worked his way up to vice-president of another textile firm. Annie Proulx recalls with some sorrow that, as her father rose in the world, he "deliberately cut himself off from his childhood [that is, Franco-American] culture and reinvented himself as a New England Yankee." Annie Proulx's maternal ancestors, the Gills, had lived in Connecticut since 1635 and had made their livings as farmers, inventors, artisans, or mill hands. Proulx characterizes her maternal grandmother, Sarah Geer, as "a wonderful storyteller" and a bit of an eccentric (who washed and ironed all her paper money). Proulx's mother, Lois Nellie (Gill) Proulx, was a painter and an amateur naturalist. In a 1994 interview with Sara Rimer for a *New York Times* profile, Proulx credited her mother with teaching her how to observe life with focused attentiveness: "From the time I was extremely small, I was told, 'Look at that.' Most often it was anthills. My mother would say, 'Look at that one carrying a stick.' All these guys had characters. She would give them voices. We'd be watching them, and pointing out the various ones. There was Charlie. There was Mr. Jones. She had an animistic universe in her mind." From an early age, Proulx learned to see "Everything—from the wale of the corduroy to the broken button to the loose thread to the disheveled mustache to the clouded eye."

What Proulx got from her father's side of the family was a ferocious work ethic and a tendency to move around. Her father's ancestor, Jean Prou, came from Anjou to Montmagny (on the St. Lawrence River, just north of Quebec City) in 1666 and worked for some years as a servant in the house of the Seigneur of Montmagny. The maternal branch of Proulx's family, LaBarge, arrived in Canada around the same time and settled northwest of Montreal. Joseph LaBarge left the province of Quebec on his twenty-first birthday, paddled to St. Louis, and there joined up with General Ashley to trap beaver in the Rockies. The town of LaBarge, Wyoming is named after him. Proulx's father's more immediate ancestors came to New England in the 1860s to work in the woolen mills.

During her youth, Proulx's family moved frequently as her father transferred from one mill job to another. She lived in numerous towns all over New England and North Carolina. For a while Proulx attended a one-room schoolhouse in Brookfield, Vermont. She and her family later moved to the mountainous Appalachian country of western North Carolina. There she attended Black Mountain High School, not far geographically from Black Mountain College, the legendary artists and writers' community. A couple of years later the Proulx family relocated again to the coastal city of Portland, Maine, where Proulx finished high school at Deering High School.

Proulx's interest in fiction writing started early. Confined to bed with chicken pox at the age of ten, Proulx wrote her first short story (she no longer remembers what it was about). After graduating from Deering High School in 1953, Proulx enrolled at Colby College in Waterville,

Maine. She dropped out without graduating in 1955 to marry H. Ridgely Bullock, a fellow student. Bullock and Proulx moved to New York City where Bullock pursued a career as a theatrical producer. In 1958 Proulx gave birth to her first child, a daughter named Sylvia "Muffy" Marion Bullock (Clarkson). An ROTC candidate in college, Ridgely Bullock was called to active duty in the air force and subsequently stationed in Japan. The Bullock family lived outside of Tokyo for a couple of years. When Proulx's marriage to Bullock ended soon thereafter, her young daughter, Sylvia, went to live with her father. Proulx soon remarried but her second marriage was, in her words, singularly "stupid." She says "It was the thing to do in the 50s—marriage."

Proulx moved to Vermont in the 1960s. She enrolled at the University of Vermont in Burlington in 1966 and graduated cum laude and Phi Beta Kappa with a degree in history in 1969. That same year Proulx married for a third time to James Hamilton Lang. Their three sons are: Jonathan Lang, Gillis Crowell Lang, and Morgan Hamilton Lang. After graduating from the University of Vermont, Proulx enrolled as a doctoral student in history at Sir George Williams University (now known as Concordia University), Montreal, some seventy miles north of her home in St. Albans, Vermont. She earned her master's degree in 1973 and passed her Ph.D. oral examinations in 1975. Her areas of concentration were in Renaissance economic history, the Canadian North, and traditional China. According to an unpublished autobiographical essay sent to me by Proulx, the "disparate subjects suited my interests as did the department's leaning toward the *Annales* school of history associated with [Fernand] Braudel, [Marc] Bloch, and [Lucien] Febvre; at the time the great scholar George Rudé of *The Crowd in History* was in residence. It was invaluable training for novel writing and set my approach to fiction forever—the examination of the lives of individuals against the geography and *longue duree* of events, that is, that *time and place are major determining factors in a human life*" (emphasis added).

As interested as she was in history, Proulx became "increasingly restless with the idea of an academic career." She abandoned her thesis "in mid-stroke" and quit the program. As she put it in a brief autobiographical piece to *Contemporary Authors* in 1994: "In 1975, facing the lack of teaching jobs in my field, I abandoned my doctoral thesis and jumped head-first into freelance journalism. A classic example of shifting from the frying pan into the fire. I lived, at this time, with a friend in a rural shack in Canaan, Vermont, up on the Canadian border [at the extreme northeastern corner of the state] in brutally poor circumstances. Compensations were silence and decent fishing, both vanished now."

So began another distinct phase in Proulx's life that lasted the next thirteen years. In Vermont's desolate Northeast Kingdom for the first year or so, Proulx fished, canoed, hunted, chopped wood, and generally became adept at all of the arts and crafts of rural survival on a subsistence budget— all while raising three young boys alone after she and James Lang separated. As she told the journalist Katie Bolick in a 1997 interview, "What interested me at this time was the back-to-the-land movement—communes, gardening, architecture, the difficulty of maintaining a long, dirt-road driveway. Not only could I solve some of those problems in real life and observe what people were doing to make things work in rural situations, I could write about them and make some money." To pay the bills she wrote what she has since described as "tedious nonfiction": articles on weather, snow removal equipment, winter clothes, gardening, wild berries, home repair, and so forth, for many different magazines. By the early 1980s Proulx was also writing magazine articles and "how to" books on similar subjects, such as landscaping, bartering, making cider, preparing dairy foods, and making insulated window

shutters. In 1983, after living in a dozen different towns all over Vermont, Proulx moved to Vershire (twenty miles southeast of Montpelier), a town of 400 residents. Once she was settled in, Proulx founded a newspaper with some friends (ironically titled the *Vershire Behind the Times*) and built a house.

HEART SONGS AND OTHER STORIES (1988)

All of her adult life Proulx's real passion was to write fiction but circumstances conspired against her. As she told David Streitfeld for the *Washington Post,* "Everything was in a logjam for many years. I did magazine journalism for 19 years, keeping bread and butter on the table. I yearned to write fiction, but there wasn't any money in it. I could only write one or two stories a year. It was my pleasure, my indulgence, when I wanted to do something that wasn't fishing or canoeing." During her university stint—from the mid-sixties to the mid-seventies—Proulx published, on average, a story a year in *Seventeen* magazine. She wrote "Stone City" and a few other stories during her stint in the Northeast Kingdom. She placed "Stone City" with *Gray's Sporting Journal* in 1979. Proulx fondly remembers *Gray's* as "a handsome new magazine" which "concerned itself with wildlife art and the blood sports through a serious literary approach— nothing like it had been since the famous *Field and Stream* of the late nineteenth century." Thereafter, Proulx again averaged several stories a year in various journals throughout the 1980s.

A milestone in Proulx's career as a fiction writer occurred in 1982 when she published a story in *Esquire* (and another in 1985). The *Esquire* connection also led to her big break. When Tom Jenks, assistant to *Esquire*'s esteemed fiction editor Rust Hills, took an editorial job at Scribners in 1987, he suggested his new employer publish a collection of Proulx's short stories. Soon thereafter Proulx's literary agent, Liz Darhansoff, negotiated a contract for her with Scribners that called for a short story collection and a novel. Proulx selected some stories she had written over the last decade and added several more to create *Heart Songs and Other Stories*. Tom Jenks had already left Scribners to become fiction editor at *GQ,* so John Glusman, a new senior editor, edited *Heart Songs*. Proulx credits Glusman with turning her into a professional fiction writer. She says in her autobiographical piece, "In a very real sense I learned to write from John Glusman. He encouraged me to try a novel as one of my failings was cramming too much into a short story."

Not surprisingly, all of the stories in *Heart Songs* are set in rural New England and focus on the lives of country people. The leadoff story, "On the Antler," introduces all the key elements that characterize Proulx's fiction. First there is the sardonic narrative voice and a detailed, taut, and exacting style that is both highly realistic and intensely lyrical. Proulx's vivid prose, full of nature imagery, compliments her thematic concerns. As she herself noted, Proulx's narrative method is based on the conviction that "time and place are the major determining factors in a human life." Accordingly, she is keen to contradict the *Yankee* magazine version of the New England countryside as serene, even idyllic, where a strong sense of community still prevails. Contemporary country life in Proulx's New England has a desperate tinge to it, its denizens painfully aware that the old ways are being overwhelmed by the brutal imperatives of a new and alien economic order that has little patience for nature, tradition, and independence. Proulx is equally avid to demolish smug popular stereotypes of rural folk as amiable bumpkins living lives that lack inwardness and intensity. For the nonaffluent country life is, and always has been, hard; it tends to produce people who are troubled, combative, and suspicious of outsiders.

"On the Antler" focuses on Bill Stong, a dishonest, mean-spirited loner who has made an avocation of playing nasty practical jokes on his neighbor, Leverd Hawkheel, a bibliophile and an avid hunter, who plots revenge against Stong. The feud escalates when Hawkheel cheats Stong by paying him a pittance for valuable rare books on country lore and Stong retaliates by making Hawkheel sick with spiked brandy so that he and a "flatlander" (an émigré from out-of-state) named Mr. Rose can usurp Hawkheel's private deer stand on Antler Mountain. After the two interlopers bag a record-breaking buck, an enraged and sobbing Hawkheel takes the valuable books he bought from Stong, rips out pages and breaks spines, and throws the ruined books at the deer carcass hanging from a tree near Stong's house, thus spiting Stong and himself.

Proulx's depiction of Hawkheel and Stong is unflattering, even grotesque. Yet the story is also marked by a countervailing concern to show that traditional rural culture, as petty and mean as it often is, is fast disappearing due to the encroachments of moneyed outsiders. Bill Stong seems to win his private war but the reader's sympathies are set against him because he is so obviously the hateful instigator of trouble. Equally reprehensible are Stong's greed and opportunism. When the bourgeois refugees from the megalopolis start "coming into the country, buying up the old farmhouses and fields and making the sugarhouses into guest cottages," Stong sets "his tattered sails to catch this changing wind." He caters to the flatlanders' yearning for authenticity by striking the pose of a local "character" and selling them the old junk from his house as authentic Americana. Because he was never really connected to his neighbors, Stong has no compunction about breaking ranks with them in order to curry favor with the new dominant class. Ironically, but perhaps typically, the worst of the natives proves to be the most adaptable. Conversely, Hawkheel's inability to prevent Stong and Rose from invading his turf figures for the larger failure of an impoverished and disorganized rural populace to fight the takeover of the countryside by affluent urbanites bent on transforming the boondocks into their own yuppie paradise. Stong sells off tradition but Hawkheel, in a fit of impotent rage, willfully destroys it. Implicitly, Proulx asks, who is worse?

Neighbors in conflict is more centrally the subject of the collection's second offering, "Stone City." Proulx's unnamed first person narrator has moved to the fictional Chopping County, Vermont, to retreat "from other people in other places." He soon enters into an affair with Noreen, his cleaning lady, and tries to befriend a local named Bill Banger, in hopes that Banger will take him grouse hunting. With no such invitation forthcoming, the narrator goes hunting alone until he accidentally meets Banger, also hunting, in a clearing in the woods that contains a number of cellar holes. The crumbling foundations are all that is left of "Stone City," a settlement that once housed the locally infamous Stone family, a lawless, predatory clan that was eventually tarred and feathered and driven out of the area at gun point after young Floyd Stone shot a man for no reason. Apparently Banger led the angry mob against the Stones. They later exacted vengeance on him by burning his house down, thus killing his wife and son.

In the story's present Banger has only his trusted hunting dog, Lady, but she too dies when she steps into an animal trap set by Raymie Pineaud Jr., Noreen's half-brother but also of Stone descent. Convinced that the long-vanished Stones are still taking revenge on him, a shaken Bill Banger sells his hardware store and moves away. Raymie also moves away, as does the narrator, who sells his house to a retired couple from New Jersey who are "innocently enthusiastic about the country." Apparently the evil that men do not only lives after them but is sometimes capable of haunting the place where it occurred like a brood-

ing and malevolent force. In the story's rather chilling denouement, the narrator asks the town clerk who owns Stone City. She consults her records and replies "William F. Banger. He bought it years ago for back taxes. He still owns it." "She was wrong," replies Proulx's narrator, "The Stones owned it and they always would."

The meanness of country life is examined from a different angle in "Bedrock," a story about Perley, a 69-year-old widower who has been tricked into marriage by a devious and secretly incestuous brother-and-sister team, Maureen and Bobhot Mackey, for the sole purpose of stealing his farm. Perley begins to discover the truth about his marriage to Maureen (who is two years younger than his youngest daughter) when she savagely beats him over a trivial matter. Bobhot intrudes with increasing frequency and Perley realizes that he can no longer delude himself as to the Mackeys' real intentions. In the end, Perley strikes down a drunken Bobhot and retreats to the barn for the night. It is not clear, in the end, if Perley will be able to escape his predicament, but that is not the point of the story. Proulx's real interest is in Perley's downfall, from prosperous farmer, to a desperately lonely widower at the mercy of people he had once looked down on as country trash. Time and decay can effect extraordinary reversals of fortune. In Perley's case they have worn away the topsoil of his life to reveal the cold, hard bedrock of mortal need that lies beneath. True to her naturalist creed, Proulx also takes pains to illustrate that the desperate and conniving Mackeys are only products of the worst sort of rural poverty.

"A Run of Bad Luck" can be considered something of a companion piece to "Bedrock"; it, too, is about love and marriage (and just about everything else) gone wrong. The main character, a logger named Amando, believes that he has been cursed with a run of bad luck. As he tells his mother, "All this year I had bad luck with everything I touch. My wife quits me. I got this goddamn toothache keeps comin' back. The heater in the truck don't work good, and now this thing with the road on top of the rest of it." The "thing with the road" is a $1,200 invoice from the selectmen for the repair of a town highway that Amando severely damaged by dragging logs on it after a heavy rain. Amando's father, Haylett, sees what his son fails to grasp: that all of Amando's misfortunes are the result of his own neglect and impatience: "*He* thinks it's bad luck . . . It's his life. It's the way his life is turnin' out, and he don't know it yet." Amando is guilty of bad faith; he willfully misreads his own situation in order to evade accountability. His family is guilty of a different kind of bad faith; they try to shield Amando from the truth of his life. A hunting trip takes Haylett and his two other sons, Clover and Phil, past the house trailer Amando used to share with his soon-to-be ex-wife, Julia. Parked in the driveway is a pick-up truck belonging to Ray, the family's hired hand. It is clear from the amount of snow on the truck that it had been there all night. Haylett and his other sons try to prevent Amando from driving up the same road but he persists and his father and brothers fear that he will shoot his wife and her lover in a fit of jealous rage. True to life, though, the story ends with a whimper rather than a bang; Amando comes back down the road and tells his kin that he already knew.

Amando's self-delusions pale in comparison to Snipe, the protagonist of "Heart Songs," Proulx's darkly comic title story (*Webster's Dictionary* defines snipe as the whole genus of limicoline birds but a second definition is more applicable here: "a contemptible person, a fool, skunk, etc.") Not unlike the first-person narrator in "Stone City," Snipe has come to Vermont to escape the city, his wife, and the bourgeois clothing shop they ran together. Indeed Snipe represents a distinct type: the affluent, aging ex-hippie with romantic fantasies about the rugged authenticity of life in the heartland. As Proulx wryly notes, Snipe "has rec-ognized in himself a secret wish to step off into some abyss of bad taste and moral sloth, and Chopping County seemed as good a place as any to find it." Set up in a rented country house by the wealthy parents of his girlfriend, Catherine, he lets her support him while he attempts to develop an appropriately romantic career as a guitarist working in country roadhouses. Snipe soon receives an invitation to sit in with a country group at their secluded farmhouse. Much to his delight, the musicians—Eno, Nell, Shirletta, and Ruby Twilight—are superb and the tunes they play are "good, authentic rural songs" that are entirely unfamiliar to him. Though largely ignored by the Twilight family as "a foreign tourist who did not know the language," Snipe thrives on the Wednesday night music sessions.

As his absorption in the music of the Twilights increases, Snipe's relationship with Catherine deteriorates. And though he has never spoken to her, Snipe becomes infatuated with Nell, the fat vocalist of the group who is, presumably, Eno's daughter. Snipe seduces Nell in the kitchen while Shirletta is in town and the men are out back cutting wood. Immediately thereafter, Eno and Ruby come in, the latter with an arm torn up by a chain saw. After Eno dresses Ruby's wound, he realizes why Snipe is there. Snipe, panicking, vows his love for Eno's daughter even though he knows he does not love her; what he loves is "the truck in the weeds," that is, the ineluctable realness of rural poverty. Ruby corrects Snipe on one vital point: Nell is Eno's *wife,* not his daughter. Barely escaping Eno's wrath, a shaken Snipe returns home, wins Catherine back with a feast paid for with bad checks, and plots a new daydream that involves their moving out West where Snipe will affect the dress and manners of a cowboy.

"The Unclouded Day" artfully skewers another "flatlander" who rivals Snipe in his quixotic delusions about country life. Earl is a yuppie stock analyst who works at home in his "enormous Swiss chalet," drives a late model Saab, has the requisite perky young child and a trophy wife "as thin as a folded dollar bill." None of this is enough. In order to complete his self-image as a bona fide country squire, Earl feels the need to become proficient in the fine art of hunting partridge. Smug in his assurance that *everything* is a commodity that can be purchased, Earl hires Santee, a grizzled old Vermonter, to teach him how to shoot. Santee does not want the job but is too polite to say no. The two men (and Santee's dog, Noah) spend an entire season hunting but Earl, with "the reflexes of a snowman," is unable to bring down a single bird. At $100 an outing Santee becomes increasingly guilty about taking Earl's money and is finding that "all the fun is goin' out" of hunting for him. Next fall, Earl shows up at Santee's door, much to the old man's chagrin. A sudden electrical storm curtails their hunting day together but not before Earl fires at a grouse. Mistakenly thinking he has hit the bird, Earl orders Santee's dog, Noah, to retrieve it. Noah rightfully refuses since there is nothing to retrieve. When Earl yells at Noah, Santee reaches the end of his patience with the affluent dilettante who is driving him crazy. He picks up three grouse just killed by a lightning strike and convinces Earl that they were felled by his shotgun blast. He also tells Earl that he will not have his dog "called down" and that their association is at an end. Flushed with deluded triumph, Earl runs to his car with his prize grouse, foolishly thinking that Santee is only jealous of his newfound shooting prowess. Santee, of course, has the last laugh, "wondering what Earl had said when he plucked three partridges that were already cooked."

Having contrasted native Vermonters with interlopers, Proulx offers something of a hybrid case with "In the Pit," a story that features Blue, a longtime exile returning to Vermont from Las Cruces, New Mexico to visit his mother. Notified that the family's vacation camp in the back woods has been broken into and vandalized, Blue decides to go up there to make repairs. Visiting Mr. Fitzroy, a camp neighbor (who has taken to the bottle after the death of his wife), Blue sees what he thinks is the family's old toaster. The sight of the toaster touches off a painful childhood memory. Blue once started a small fire when he tried to make a cheese sandwich in the toaster: a blunder that brought his father's wrath upon him and precipitated a nasty fight between his parents. Assuming that Fitzroy's lodger, Gilbert, an ex-con, removed it from the camp after trashing the place, Blue confronts the two men and confiscates "his" toaster. He later discovers the family toaster in the trash pit behind the camp and has to deal with the fact that he has displaced his lingering anger at his father, seven years deceased, on to his hapless neighbors. The appearance of the genuine article at story's end is quite literally a return of the repressed from the pit of Blue's unconscious and an ironic emblem of the distance he has traveled from the world of his origins.

"The Wer-Trout" is a character portrait of Rivers, a self-deceiving, unhappily married middle-aged alcoholic who runs The March Brown, a country angler's shop that is steadily losing money. Another exile from the city and his own past, Rivers "cures himself of all suffering and worry by memorizing ancient Chinese poems and casting artificial flies in moving water." His tenuous grasp on emotional stability begins to dissolve when his wife, "who has had enough for a long time," leaves him. Coincidentally his closest neighbor, a trailer-dwelling native named Sauvage, has to have his mentally ill wife hospitalized after he discovers her eating a mouse. Normally separated by class differences, Rivers and Sauvage find themselves suddenly bonded by the fates of their wives. They seek mutual consolation by going on a fishing trip together. Or such is the plan. As it turns out, Rivers, who thinks of himself as "the Great Fisherman," catches nothing while Sauvage hauls in trout after trout. Filled with smug condescension toward Sauvage, Rivers cannot stand being bested at his favorite pastime. Succumbing to puerile egotism, Rivers starts drinking again, insults his superstitious companion with ridiculous ravings about a "wer-trout" (half-man, half-trout) that haunts the forest, accidentally breaks his prize fishing rod, but still manages to convince himself that he is untouchable, that "there is no mouse on *his* plate" (emphasis added). In the end, Rivers *becomes* the wer-trout, a creature of stupid need and no self-awareness.

With "Electric Arrows" Proulx returns to one of her primary interests: that crucial historical moment when a region undergoes profound change, in this case, the disappearance of an older way of life in the New England countryside. The Moon-Azures, an affluent couple from Maryland, buy the Clew homestead in Ironworks County, New Hampshire, as a summer vacation home. They come up every June and go back to Maryland every August. Hungry for the rustic authenticity that country living seems to offer, the Moon-Azures cheerfully expropriate their rural neighbors' land, labor, time, and folk culture with a serene sense of entitlement and absolutely no hint of irony or guilt. As the laconic first-person narrator, Mason Clew notes, "The Moon-Azures are after us . . . for help with things, getting their car going, clearing out the clogged spring, finding their red-haired dog. They need to know how things happened, what things happened." After Dr. Moon-Azure retires, he and his wife stay at the former Clew place from mud season to the onset of winter: a sign of the further encroachment and growing power of moneyed outsiders. Mrs. Moon-Azure is even interested in old Clew family photographs, as if she could take ownership of the family's past. Mason's aunt wisely refuses to relinquish any pictures. She knows that the Moon-Azures "will pass [them] around among their weekend guests . . . and we will someday see our grandfather's corpse in his homemade coffin resting on two sawhorses, flattened out

on the pages of some magazine and labeled with a cruel caption." The absurdity of the Moon-Azures' hunger for things old and authentic is pointed up when they think they have discovered "complex [Indian] petroglyphs" carved in stone on their property. Mason laughingly notes that what they have found is a self-portrait chiseled by his father, a former stone mason turned lineman, in the 1930s.

POSTCARDS

Contracted by Scribners to write a novel after her short story collection, Proulx applied for residency at the Ucross Foundation in Wyoming to work on the book there. As she later told interviewer Sybil Steinberg in *Publishers Weekly,* the locale proved salutary: "What an enormous help the sight lines were, and the room to walk. There's something about being able to shoot your eyes very far ahead. In Northern New England the trees got in the way." Proulx used some postcards she had from the 1930s and 1940s that featured mug shots of escaped Vermont convicts as a springboard for the story. She recalls that there "was one really handsome guy. I can't remember what he did, but he had this incredibly wavy hair, the kind you just don't see anymore." Proulx conjured a character out of the haunting photo and he became Loyal Blood, a 30-year-old dairy farmer who kills his girlfriend, Billy, at the outset of the novel and is doomed to live the rest of his life as a fugitive and an outcast. The "price of getting away" is to have "no wife, no children, no human comfort in the quotidian unfolding of his life . . . restless shifting from one town to another, the narrow fences of solitary thought, the pitiful easement of masturbation, lopsided ideas and soliloquies so easily transmuted to crazy mouthings."

After Loyal disappears in the spring of 1945, his enraged father, Minkton Blood, shoots Loyal's two Holstein cows in revenge. Without Loyal's help, the "weight of the work" falls on aging Mink and his remaining son, one-armed Marvin ("Dub"). The Blood farm, which has no electricity, languishes in the post-war economy. By the winter of 1951 the Bloods have fallen so far behind in mortgage and tax payments that the situation has become hopeless. Yet Mink refuses to sell the farm, knowing that he will not break even after paying off the mortgage. Instead, he and Dub resort to the desperate expedient of burning the barn (and the remaining cows) for the insurance money. Hard pressed by insurance investigators, Dub confesses to first-degree arson, implicates his father, and both men are sentenced to one-to-four-year terms in the State Prison at Windsor. Minkton Blood hangs himself in his prison cell shortly after his incarceration. Mink's suicide signals the end of the farm, which, in a small way, figures for the overall decline and fall of an agricultural era in New England that lasted some three hundred years. If Loyal is exiled from home and the life he knew, the other surviving family members—his mother, Jewell Blood, his brother, Dub, and his sister, Mernelle—find themselves exiled as well. The attempts of all four Bloods to adapt to radically changed circumstances comprise the bulk of the narrative as Proulx chronicles how the exploding post-war economy buried the settled traditions of community and family forever and turned America into a lonely nation of rootless drifters, social climbers, and petty individualists.

Mink's death brings challenges and opportunities for his widow, Jewell Blood. Ronnie Nipple, a longtime neighbor turned real estate agent, convinces Jewell to sell off the farm in parcels in order to retain the house and a bit of land. She follows Nipple's advice but is soon outraged to discover that she has been betrayed. Nipple never told her that one of the parcels would be turned into a 40-lot trailer park. Yet, in many ways, Jewell's life is transformed for the better by her husband's death. Alone "for the first time in her adult life" and "cast free of Mink's furious anger," Jewell Blood revels in her freedom. She is able to wake when she wants, eats what she wants, and having never learned how to drive, begins to take driving lessons in the late 1960s. When Jewell drives, "her stifled youth unfurl[s] like ribbon pulled from a spool." Ironically, her newfound mobility is also the cause of her doom. In mid-November of 1969 she decides to drive her '66 Volkswagen beetle up Mount Washington in New Hampshire. After taking an ill-advised short cut on a logging road at the start of a snowstorm, Jewell gets stuck and has a fatal aneurysm while attempting to dislodge her car. Like her late husband's demise, Jewell Blood's is a lonely death in a desolate place, also the result of poor judgment. But unlike Mink, who dies in despair and defeat, Jewell at least dies free and in pursuit of adventure.

Jewell's daughter, Mernelle, fares somewhat better. Though "she took what happened hard" and dropped out of school when her father was arrested, Mernelle Blood decides she wants a better life for herself and begins to seek a husband. When Robert "Ray" MacWay, a 19-year-old lumber worker, advertises for a wife in the local paper, Mernelle answers the ad and the two marry amidst much condescending "human interest story" publicity. Ray MacWay is a good man and the marriage is a long and happy one but ends tragically when Ray succumbs to cancer—industrialism's plague—and dies a slow and agonizing death that almost drives Mernelle to distraction.

Amoral, reckless, and possessed of a piratical temperament Dub, of all the Bloods, predictably adapts best to the casino capitalism of contemporary America. Some years after his release from prison Dub drifts down to Miami, just then experiencing a massive influx of Cubans that have escaped Castro's revolution. Initially involved in petty scams, Dub works his way into the burgeoning Miami real estate market, becomes rich, marries a smart, ambitious Cuban émigré, and achieves his own version of the American Dream. Though he stays in touch with his mother and sister, he has, in classic American fashion, reinvented himself and sloughed off his past. The true price of such an irrevocable transformation becomes apparent when Dub runs into tax problems and formerly halcyon Miami degenerates into a cesspool of decadence, violence, and class warfare in the 1980s, especially after the Mariel boatlift. Writing a consolatory postcard to Mernelle after Ray's death, Dub reports that "things down here are bad. Killings, riots, drugs, bankrupts, crime, hurricanes. It used to be beautiful." In a larger sense, Dub's words form an epitaph for the American Dream and for the country as a whole.

While Dub represents the new breed of post-War World II America come to an ambiguous end, Loyal Blood embodies the forsaken spirit of pre-corporate, working class America. Like Hamlet's father, he is a ghost "doomed for a certain time to walk the earth." After leaving the farm, Loyal crisscrosses the country in search of work and perhaps a place to start over. The ensuing decades are marked by intense isolation, constant movement, and all manner of misfortune and hardship. Loyal is robbed by hitchhikers, almost killed in a mine cave-in, injures his eye in a freak accident, is barricaded by tumbleweed, buys a farm in North Dakota but soon loses it to fire, has his trailer stolen, contracts bronchitis, and ends up destitute after a lifetime of backbreaking labor. The reader last sees a terminally ill and exhausted Loyal Blood "hoofing it" along a dusty road out West, his worldly possessions reduced to a "bedroll, a few utensils, a change of ragged clothes, wad of paper, pencil stubs, jar of instant coffee, plastic razor with dull blade." In the final analysis the tragic history of the Bloods comprises a devastating portrait of the United States in the second half of the twentieth century: a country that lost its soul by abrogating its connection to the land and to its own past.

THE SHIPPING NEWS

Although she wrote most of the novel in Wyoming, Proulx considers *Postcards* (1993) her "road book." While researching it, she visited the places Loyal Blood lives and works in order to capture the look and feel of them. Her next novel, *The Shipping News,* involved the same kind of on-site research. A fishing trip first brought Proulx to Newfoundland, a remote island province in eastern Canada, in 1987. She later told John Blades of the *Chicago Tribune,* she "just fell quite madly in love" with the "rugged" and "immensely interesting" island and its people, whom she experienced as the "warmest, kindest, most interesting anywhere." She went back more than a dozen times. Quite naturally, Newfoundland became the principal setting and to a large extent, the subject of *The Shipping News.* To supplement her explorations of the island, Proulx read omnivorously on the history of the island and absorbed the Newfoundland dialect by going to bed every night with *The Dictionary of Newfoundland English.* Another key book for Proulx, which she obtained for a quarter at a yard sale, was Clifford W. Ashley's *The Ashley Book of Knots,* quotations from which supply the symbolically resonant epigraphs at the head of most chapters.

The protagonist of *The Shipping News* is R. G. Quoyle, "a third-rate newspaperman" living in Mockingburg, a small town in upstate New York. An ineffectual bear of a man, Quoyle is possessed of "a great damp loaf of a body" on which sits a "head shaped like a Crenshaw, no neck" and "a monstrous chin, a freakish shelf jutting from the lower face." Desperately in love with his unfaithful and verbally abusive wife, Petal Bear, Quoyle suffers her humiliating infidelities with a cringing meekness bordering on outright masochism. Then, quite suddenly, Quoyle's sorry life is transformed by catastrophe. First, both his parents commit suicide after each is diagnosed with cancer. Next, Quoyle is fired from his newspaper job. Then the coup de grace: Quoyle's wife, Petal Bear, is killed in a car accident after having sold their two young daughters, Sunshine and Bunny, to a child pornographer. Luckily, the girls are rescued before evil befalls them. Quoyle is nonetheless grief-stricken by the death of his wife and parents. With $50,000 in insurance money and no ties left to hold him in Mockingburg, Quoyle is persuaded by Agnis Hamm, his somewhat eccentric lesbian aunt, to take his daughters with him to ancestral digs at Quoyle's Point, Newfoundland, to "start a new life in a fresh place."

More than one commentator has noted that *The Shipping News* is structured like a fairy tale. Not surprisingly the book treats the quintessential theme of all fairy tales: healing psychic wounds in order to grow up. Emotionally a stunted child, Quoyle begins his long-delayed maturation when he arrives in Newfoundland. A stark version of J. M. Barrie's Neverland—that mythical place safely bracketed from the protagonist's painful past and modernity's crushing decadence—"The Rock" is as remote, wild and close to Nature as it possibly can be. Despite its harsh climate and quirky folkways, Newfoundland proves to be Quoyle's salvation. He gets a job at a small, comically disreputable newspaper, *The Gammy Bird,* reporting on the arrival and departure of ships (hence the novel's title). Wise, solicitous Jack Buggit, Quoyle's boss, becomes his surrogate father, Quoyle's own father having been a heartless, abusive tyrant. Learning to "read" his world with newfound acuity, Quoyle eventually transforms *The Shipping News* into a respected column and, with the help of his aunt Agnis (a tough but benevolent mother figure), he also restores the "half ruined, isolated" ancestral home at Quoyle's Point. By meeting these daunting challenges, Quoyle recovers himself and also restores his connection to his familial past. Quoyle's unlikely transformation—from emotional cripple to responsible adult—allows him to become a nurturing father to his daughters, especially Bunny, who has developed a morbid fear of death in the wake of her mother's sudden demise. The only thing missing from Quoyle's life is the love of a good woman and Proulx supplies that in the figure of Wavey Prowse, a widow who is the perfect mother to her retarded son. Both gun-shy from traumatic experiences of love and loss, the two court slowly and cautiously but eventually wed in what constitutes the novel's triumphal moment.

Despite some dark elements, *The Shipping News* remains the most optimistic and enchanting of Proulx's books. It was both a resounding *succès d'estime* and a wildly popular bestseller, selling an astonishing million copies, cloth and paperback editions combined. The book's tremendous appeal is easy to explain: it is thoroughly researched and superbly written, has dashing narrative drive, interesting characters, the romance of Newfoundland, and something like a happy ending. (For Proulx "happiness" is defined "as the absence of pain.") In the final analysis, though, the novel probably struck a chord with the public because it champions the underdog and affirms the notion that even the most damaged and demoralized people have the innate potential to redeem themselves and reclaim their lives. Furthermore, the novel celebrates the virtues of genuine—as opposed to abusive—love, home, family (however constituted), and a rooted sense of community as the true underpinnings of a viable self. Commenting on the book, Proulx notes that Quoyle "is a man in the wrong place who finds the right place. This is a novel about the power of home territory on us all." In an oblique way it is Proulx's most autobiographical work.

ACCORDION CRIMES

For her third novel *Accordion Crimes* (1996), Annie Proulx decided to focus on the American immigrant experience, a topic that had intrigued her for some time. Proulx told interviewer Sybil Steinberg she wanted to write "about the cost of coming from one culture to another. I wanted to get a sense of that looming overculture that demands of newcomers that they give up their language, their music, their food, their names. I began to wonder: where did our taste for changing identity come from? Was it the immigrant experience where the rite of passage was to redefine yourself as an American?"

A topic so large calls for a James Michener-like historical epic but Proulx did not want to write that sort of book. Instead she devised a complex narrative mosaic consisting of four interlinking parts, vaguely reminiscent of John Dos Passos' Depression-era *USA* Trilogy (but without Dos Passos' carefully demarcated shifts in narrative style). Proulx's primary narrative follows the travels of her protagonist, a green enamel nineteen-button accordion, as it is passed from one owner to another over a century (from 1890 to the 1990s). Within that overarching narrative are nine shorter stories, each one focusing on a different immigrant group. Within that, there is, in Proulx's words, "an increasing multiplicity of shorter stories of intersecting lives." And within that there are even smaller narrative units that Proulx calls "tiny flashforwards, fiction bites," that is, vignettes, some tragic, some amusing, that sum up marginal characters' lives in a few deft strokes. "Instead of the river of time," Proulx notes, "you get a lawn sprinkler effect, a kind of jittery, jammed, off-balanced feeling." Proulx also informs the reader in a short preface that she peppers her book with "real newspaper advertisements, radio spiels, posters, song titles, scraps of verse, labels on common objects and lists of organizations; mixed in with them are [many that are] fictional and invented." In sum, *Accordion Crimes* is a densely textured, polyphonic rendering of the myriad voices that comprise the immigrants' America.

As critic Mark Shechner noted, the accordion at the center of the narrative is rich in symbolism, "an archetypal folk instrument . . . a talisman of immigrant dynamism and desire, a condensation of all the spiritual, physical, and creative powers that post-Plymouth arrivals set loose on our shores." The instrument is brought to New Orleans by its Sicilian maker, who aspires to own a music shop, but is murdered in an anti-Italian riot (an incident inspired by March 1891 articles in the *Daily Picayune* that reported the lynchings of eleven Italians in New Orleans). Terrified of American xenophobia, the accordion maker's son, Silvano, changes his name to Bob Joe and sets out to discard all vestiges of his Sicilian heritage. The accordion subsequently becomes the possession of Hans Beutle, a hearty German immigrant farming in Iowa who plays it to feel connected to his homeland. After Beutle's death from, ironically, gangrene after an operation to restore virility, Abelardo Relámpago Salazar, a Mexican-American living in Texas, acquires the accordion. His daughter, Félida, wants to play the instrument but when her chauvinist father forbids it she runs away and is never seen by him again. After Salazar dies of a spider bite, the accordion turns up in Maine, owned by a French-Canadian orphan named Dolor Gagnon. After Gagnon's suicide, the accordion goes to Buddy Malefoot, a Louisiana Cajun, and then on to Octave, a black zydeco musician, who takes it to Chicago. Following stints with Harry Newcomer (a.k.a. Hieronim Pryzbysz), a Polish musician, and Fay McGettigan, a ranch hand in Montana, the accordion ends up on a trash pile in Mississippi. In existence for more than one hundred years, the accordion is finally smashed to bits when some children throw it into the path of an eighteen-wheeler to savor its destruction.

One of the epigraphs Proulx chose for the novel was a quote from Cornel West's book, *Race Matters*. "Without the presence of black people in America, European-Americans would not be 'white'—they would be only Irish, Italians, Poles, Welsh, and others engaged in class, ethnic, and gender struggles over resources and identity."

Proulx's vision of the immigrant experience is not the apologist notion of the melting pot where the various nationalities, tribes, and races assimilate without too much trouble. Though obviously in accord with Howard Zinn's brand of historical revisionism in her refusal to whitewash America's execrable treatment of its immigrant poor, Proulx does not rest her case there. Though rife with violent death and misfortune, *Accordion Crimes* is far too exuberant to qualify as a screed about victimization. As Mark Shechner astutely observes, the novel is "a brawling, cacophonous, inharmonious, dense, tangy, overpopulated, overwritten book that makes few concessions to the reader," a book that "does for accordions what *Moby Dick* did for whaling."

CLOSE RANGE: WYOMING STORIES

After her mother, Lois Nellie Gill, died in 1995 Proulx was no longer tied to New England. In love with the rugged beauty of Wyoming since her first stint at the Ucross Foundation in the late 1980s, Proulx moved to a log cabin in a tiny town on the eastern edge of Medicine Bow Routt National Forest, thirty miles west of Laramie. Having demolished idyllic notions of New England country life, Proulx cast an observer's eye on the stock-raising culture of the West, a region shrouded in romantic mythology as no other. Asked by the Nature Conservancy to contribute something to a proposed collection of short fiction (*Off the Beaten Path,* [1998]), Proulx wrote "The Half-Skinned Steer." She says in the preface for the following book that she found "working again in the short story form so interesting and challenging . . . that the idea of a collection of short fiction set in Wyoming seized me entirely." What resulted was *Close Range: Wyoming Stories* (1999), a book that does for the West what *Heart Songs* did for the Northeast. In marked contrast to the smug clichés recycled by tourist brochures and popular culture, Proulx offers a vast, starkly beautiful, but lonely country that breeds bluntly forceful and sometimes horrifically violent people. Indeed, the stories in *Close Range* are so real they frequently shade into the *surreal*. Proulx notes in the book's acknowledgments section that the "elements of unreality, the fantastic and improbable, color all these stories as they color real life. In Wyoming not the least fantastic situation is the determination to make a living in this tough and unforgiving place."

For her opening story, "The Half-Skinned Steer," Proulx borrowed her central image from an Icelandic folk-tale called "Porgeir's Bull." She also borrowed from herself, taking her protagonist and basic plot from "In the Pit" (*Heart Songs*). In that story Blue returns to his childhood home after a long absence and confronts lingering demons. In "The Half-Skinned Steer" Mero Corn, "an octogenarian vegetarian widower" residing in "a colonial house in Woolfoot, Massachusetts," is called back to his family's ranch in Wyoming to attend the funeral of his brother, Rollo (killed by an emu of all things). Physically fit for his age, Mero decides to drive instead of fly. The rather ordinary story of Mero's journey West is crosscut with a lurid "tall tale" Mero heard in his youth, some sixty years before, from his father's girlfriend. It seems that a lackadaisical rancher named Tin Head bled, cut out the tongue, and began to skin a steer but left off in the middle of the operation to have dinner. When he returned Tin Head was shocked to find that the steer was not dead but had gotten up and begun to wander away, "the raw meat of the head and the shoulder muscles" exposed and the suffering animal "glaring at him" with "pure teetotal hate." Having sinned against Nature, Tin Head feels cursed ever after.

On an emotional level, Mero is himself a "half-skinned steer," a soul ravaged and silenced by the routine cruelties of ranch life in his youth but one who managed to escape to the relatively civilized

East—and denounce meat—before he could be destroyed. And like the wounded steer, Mero is largely uncomprehending of the damage that has been done to him. His lack of self-awareness impairs his usual competence; as he journeys "home" he has a rare and uncharacteristic car accident en route. Later, when he reaches the area of the ranch, he takes the wrong road and gets his car stuck in a gathering snowstorm (much like Jewell Blood in *Postcards*). In the end, Mero has no choice but to try to walk to safety, eerily followed by a lone steer on the other side of the fence. Only then does Mero have an epiphany about the inexorable pull of the past he thought he had avoided when he realizes "that the half-skinned steer's red eye had been watching for him all this time." The haunting power of "The Half-Skinned Steer" can, in part, be gauged by the accolades it received. Garrison Keillor selected the story for inclusion in *The Best American Short Stories, 1998* and John Updike went Keillor one better by including it in *The Best American Short Stories of the Century*.

Diamond Felts, the protagonist of "The Mud Below," is also in unconscious flight from early emotional trauma. Small of stature, Felts "heard himself called Half-Pint, Baby Boy, Shorty, Kid, Tiny, Little Guy, Sawed-Off" all his life. Worse yet, when he was thirteen, his angry father said the cruelest thing imaginable to a son: "Don't call me [father] again. Not your father and never was." Insufficiently imposing in physique and filled with corrosive doubt about his real paternity, Diamond Felts enters the rodeo world as a bull rider—perhaps to prove his manhood. Bull riding provides Felts with an adrenaline rush and a vivid sense of being alive that he usually does not have: "In the arena everything was real because none of it was real except the chance to get dead. The charged bolt came, he thought, because he wasn't." After a particularly harrowing ride, though, Felts realizes that the "euphoric charge had never kicked in this time." Having narrowly

escaped with his life, Felts is at least temporarily unable to use bull riding as an escape from self-doubt. He calls his mother, long distance, and asks her who his father was. Her reassurances do not satisfy him. Driving all night with a badly injured arm to his next rodeo, Felts feels "as though some bearing had seized up inside him and burned out." Stripped of his usual evasions, he begins to realize that his frantic chase after glory "was all a hard, fast ride that ended in the mud."

In contrast to men governed by submerged emotions, Proulx emphasizes economic factors that determine lives in the tersely written "Job History." Leeland Lee, born in 1947, is the youngest child of a Wyoming hog farmer. Leeland impregnates his high school girlfriend, Lori, and they both drop out of school to marry and start a family. What follows for them is a succession of failed small business ventures and dead-end jobs. Lee and Lori will never "make it"; the area is too barren and the Lees do not have the education or business acumen to rise above subsistence wages. For such people, jobs are not vehicles for self-expression or creative fulfillment; the dogged, unending pursuit of any sort of paid work dictates the warp and woof of their lives. Much like the Bloods of Vermont, the Lees slowly disintegrate as a family. Leeland's father dies in bankruptcy and his hog farm has to be sold to cover debts. Lori Lee eventually succumbs to cancer. The children marry and move away. There is no flourishing, only a kind of grim endurance until death and desertion make all struggles moot.

To leaven the mood, Proulx presents "The Blood Bay," a comic "tall tale" that she characterizes as "a Wyoming twist on the folk-tale 'The Calf That Ate the Traveler,' known in many stock-raising cultures." A young Montana cowboy freezes to death "on Powder River's bitter west bank" in the "terrible" winter of 1886–1887. Three "savvy and salty" cowpunchers discover the corpse in the snow the next day. One of the men, Dirt Sheets, covets the dead man's boots but cannot remove them so he saws off the man's legs "just above the boot tops" with his Bowie knife and puts the booted feet in his saddlebag for thawing later. The three men stay the night at Old Man Grice's shack, which also houses his two horses. Just before dawn Sheets gets up, removes the boots and socks from the now thawed feet, puts them on, throws the feet in a corner with his old boots, and leaves. Old Man Grice soon awakens and discovers the grisly objects. He thinks that one of his horses, the blood bay, ate one of his guests and sends the "hell-bound fiend" to "sleep out with the blizzards and wolves" though he is secretly "pleased to own a horse with the sand to eat a raw cowboy."

Equally grotesque but much darker in tone is "People in Hell Just Want a Drink of Water." In the late 1920s a young man named Rasmussen (Ras) Tinsley suffers severe disfigurement and brain damage in a car accident in Schenectady, New York, and is subsequently shipped back to Wyoming to recover at his parents' farm. Things go from bad to worse when demented Ras begins to expose himself to neighborhood women. His father, Horm, warns him that the Dunmires, arrogant local cattle ranchers, have threatened to "cut" Ras if "he doesn't stop pestering the girls." But it is already too late; Ras comes home ill and Horm soon discovers that he has already been castrated with "a dirty knife" and is dying of gangrene. In a brief coda to the story Proulx's narrator notes that the crime happened "sixty years ago and more . . . We are in a new millennium and such desperate things no longer happen." Just as the reader is warmed by the comforting notion of social progress, Proulx retracts the illusion with a final, chilling line: "If you believe that you'll believe anything."

The somber effect of "People in Hell" is mitigated by "The Bunchgrass Edge of the World," a more diffuse, loosely focused story that chronicles the zany lives of the Touheys, an isolated ranching family. After introducing the family patriarch, "old Red, ninety-six years young," his marijuana-smoking son Aladdin, Aladdin's wife, Wauneta, "their boy, Tyler, object of Aladdin's hopes," and daughter Shan (who lives in Las Vegas), Proulx's narrator focuses on the youngest child, Ottaline "the family embarrassment." Lonely, corpulent, prone to "minstrel troubles," Ottaline is a hopeless young woman stuck on a ranch in the middle of nowhere, her identity "dissolving" in sexual frustration and boredom. One day she hears a derelict tractor speak to her of its neglect and isolation and decides to undertake its repair. Unless Proulx is telling a fairy tale, the voice surely emanates from Ottaline's own unconscious. Attempting to fix what her father deems "ain't fixable" (both tractor and self), Ottaline pulls out of her torpor and wins her father's respect. Consequently he delegates her to handle the family's annual cattle sale when he takes ill— a duty that allows her to meet her future husband. As Old Red notes, "The main thing in life was staying power. That was it: stand around long enough you'd get to sit down."

Given enough patience, life on the range may change for the better but it is more likely to change for the worse. With "Pair a Spurs" Proulx adapts a much more fanciful version of the plot device she employed for *Accordion Crimes,* that is, examining lives by tracing the ownership of an enchanted object: in this case, an expensive pair of handmade spurs. Sutton Muddyman buys a $300 pair of spurs for his wife, Inez, as a birthday present. When she is killed in a riding accident, Sutton moves to Oregon and Mrs. Freeze, a ranch hand, buys them for a pittance at auction. She later gives the spurs to rancher Haul Smith as part of an employment deal. Smith loses his spurs while foolishly trying to cross the swollen Bad Girl Creek on horseback. Still, Proulx's ultimate focus is on Car Scrope, a rancher in the aftermath of a divorce gradually going insane from loneliness that he misinterprets as sexual need. The enchanted spurs lock onto him and he is forced to "love" whoever wears the spurs. After unsuccessfully propositioning Inez and even his hired hand, the manly Mrs. Freeze, Scrope takes to sitting "down by the creek all day eatin tater chips," increasingly immersed in catatonic reverie as the lost spurs, rusting in water, still call to him.

Loneliness misinterpreted as sexual need is also the theme of the aptly titled "A Lonely Coast." Proulx generally favors third-person omniscient narrators with distinctly masculine voices. In keeping with her focus on women's loneliness, she has a woman bartender narrate "A Lonely Coast" in the first person. The protagonist, an acquaintance of the narrator's named Josanna Skyles, is a middle-aged divorcee who spends her nights and weekends trolling for male companionship. She has two women friends, Palma Gratt and Ruth Wolfe, also divorcees, "both of them burning at a slower rate than Josanna, but in their own desperate ways also disintegrating into drifts of ash." Mistaking sexual attention for love, all three women frequent bars, drink to excess, do drugs, and compete with each other for the few eligible men they meet. Josanna, "bone tired of being alone," seals her own fate when she succumbs to the dubious charms of Elk Nelson, a handsome "restless drifter" with absolutely no respect for women. Nelson, the archetypal cowboy, cheats on Josanna and generally humiliates her. He also causes her death, and his own, by indulging in armed road rage with two other angry cowboys. Once a spirited and beautiful woman, Josanna coasts downhill toward the abyss, driven by the emotional poverty of her circumstances. As the narrator notes in closing, "Friend, it's easier than you think to yield up to the dark impulse."

The dark impulse can also be expressed through politics, the ostensible subject of "The Governors of Wyoming." The raged filled son of a slaughterhouse worker who died of a job-related infection at the age of forty-two, Wade Walls is a radical anti-meat activist dedicated to sabotaging ranching operations by poisoning cows and cutting fences. Much of Walls' economic and political analysis of the cattle industry is undoubtedly accurate but his ideological rigidity, hateful rhetoric, and violent ways brand him as a mean-spirited egotist who will accomplish nothing useful. Walls's partner in crime is Shyland Hamp, a dimwitted rancher's son, who joins Walls's personal crusade as a means to assuage his own conscience for marital infidelities involving child prostitutes. When the two are caught in the act of cutting fences and fired upon by an outraged rancher, Shy Hamp is wounded by a ricochet. Wade Walls shows his true colors by running off and leaving his comrade to face the music alone.

Perhaps inspired by the saga of Ed Gein, the isolated Wisconsin farmer turned serial murderer and cannibal in the 1950s, "55 Miles to the Gas Pump" rates as Proulx's most macabre story. After Rancher Croom commits suicide by jumping into a canyon, his wife cuts a hole in the roof to find out why she had been forbidden, "by padlocks and warnings," to go into the attic. She discovers what she expected to find: "the corpses of Mr. Croom's paramours . . . some desiccated as jerky and much the same color, some moldy from lying beneath roof leaks." The sardonic coda of the story: "When you live a long way out you make your own fun." Commenting on the story, Proulx notes that "55 Miles" is a quick look at how imagination flourishes in isolated circumstances. The leap off the cliff is *imagined;* the corpses in the attic are *imagined.*"

Close Range concludes with "Brokeback Mountain," a moving story of love denied by societal prejudice. Ennis Del Mar meets Jack Twist in 1963 when both men are hired to tend sheep on Brokeback Mountain. Del Mar and Twist have a lot in common: "both [are] high school drop out country boys with no prospects, brought up to hard work and privation, both rough mannered, rough-spoken, inured to the stoic life." Sleeping out together to guard the sheep against coyotes, they end up in the same bedroll on a cold night. Twist propositions Del Mar, commencing a torrid homosexual affair that lasts the entire summer. Remaining in stolid, absurd denial about their true sexual orientation, the two go their separate ways, marry and have children. After a four-year interval without any contact, Twist visits Del Mar, and the intense erotic attraction between the two men is instantly rekindled. After a night together in a motel, Twist pleads with Del Mar to leave his family and start a new life with him. Remembering a gay neighbor who was savagely murdered years before, Del Mar refuses to take the extreme risk of an openly committed relationship; homophobia in the hyper-masculine culture of the West is no laughing matter. Instead, the two lovers meet a couple of times a year for ersatz fishing trips for the next twenty years—until Jack Twist is found dead, perhaps the victim of a freak accident, perhaps murdered. Grief stricken, Del Mar visits Twist's parents and offers to take Jack's ashes to Brokeback Mountain, as their son had requested, but the offer is refused and the two men are kept apart in death as they had been in life.

Part of what makes "Brokeback Mountain" so powerful and instructive is that it demolishes popular stereotypes of gay men as self-indulgent, bourgeois fops. In most ways Del Mar and Twist are typical working class men; their homosexuality contains no traces of effeminacy or narcissism and in no way compromises their essential masculinity. Nonetheless, a rigid heterosexual ideology rules their world, oppressing and sometimes destroying those who would dare to transgress normative definitions of sexuality. "Brokeback Mountain" won a 1998 O. Henry Short Story Award, and through its publication in *The New Yorker,* a National Magazine Award for Fiction.

"GETTING IT RIGHT"

In a 1997 interview with Katie Bolick for *Atlantic Unbound,* Proulx was asked what advice she would give to aspiring writers. She answered: "Spend some time living before you start writing. What I find to be very bad advice is the snappy little sentence, 'Write what you know.' It is the most tiresome and stupid advice that could possibly be given. If we write simply about what we know we never grow. We don't develop any facility with languages, or an interest in others, or a desire to travel and explore and face experience head-on. We just coil tighter and tighter into our boring little selves. What one should write about is what *interests* one." In another interview (with Sarah Rimer in 1994), Proulx said that the point in work is to get it right. "You get it right, or you don't do it. Everything depends on your getting it right."

Note: I would like to thank Annie Proulx for her cooperation in the writing of this essay. Several of her comments and responses have been incorporated as quotes in this essay.

Selected Bibliography

WORKS OF ANNIE PROULX

NOVELS AND SHORT STORIES
Heart Songs & Other Stories. New York: Scribners, 1988.
Postcards. New York: Scribners, 1992.

The Shipping News. New York: Touchstone, 1993.
Accordion Crimes. New York: Scribners, 1996.
Close Range: Wyoming Stories. Watercolors by William Matthews. New York: Scribners, 1999.

UNCOLLECTED SHORT STORIES
"All the Pretty Little Horses." *Seventeen,* June 1964, pp. 142–143.
"Thief." *Seventeen,* October 1966, pp. 128–129.
"Lost Friend." *Seventeen,* February 1970, pp. 142–143.
"Treachery." *Seventeen,* February 1971, pp. 128–129.
"Miss Loudmouth." *Seventeen,* February 1972, pp. 156–157.
"Ugly Room." *Seventeen,* August 1972, pp. 242–243.
"Perfect Specimen." *Seventeen,* August 1973, pp. 198–199.
"Yellowleaves." *Seventeen,* April 1974, pp. 148–149.
"Yellow Box." *Seventeen,* December 1974, pp. 102–103.

EDITED WORKS
The Best American Short Stories of 1997. Edited by Annie Proulx, John Edgar Wideman, and Katrina Kension. Boston: Houghton Mifflin, 1997.

OTHER WORKS
"Country Journal Guide to Snow Removal Equipment." *Blair & Ketchum's Country Journal,* January 1978, pp. 88–93.
"Mend Your Own Home." *Blair & Ketchum's Country Journal,* August 1978, pp. 51–55.
"How to Make Damn Good Hard Cider." *Blair & Ketchum's Country Journal,* September 1978, p. 24.
"North Woods Provender." *Gourmet,* November 1979, p. 46.
"Flying Mouths." *Blair & Ketchum's Country Journal,* June 1980, pp. 84–89.
"Cedar-oil Man." *Blair & Ketchum's Country Journal,* October 1980, pp. 76–79.
"Clothes For the Cold." *Blair & Ketchum's Country Journal,* December 1980, pp. 45–49.
Great Grapes! Grow the Best Ever. Charlotte, Vt.: Garden Way, 1980.
Making the Best Apple Cider. Charlotte, Vt.: Garden Way, 1980.
"Tame Wild Apples & Berries." *Mother Earth News,* March/April 1981, pp. 110–111.

Make Your Own Insulated Window Shutters. Pownal, Vt.: Storey Communications, 1981.
What'll You Take For It?: Back to Barter. Charlotte, Vt.: Garden Way, 1981.
"The Juice of the Apple." *Blair & Ketchum's Country Journal,* October 1982, pp. 56–61.
The Complete Dairy Foods Cookbook: How to Make Everything From Cheese to Custard in Your Own Kitchen. With Lew Nichols. Emmaus, Penn.: Rodale Press, 1982.
"Poplars." *National Wildlife,* October/November 1983, pp. 54–59.
The Gardener's Journal and Record Book. Emmaus, Penn.: Rodale Press, 1983.
Plan and Make Your Own Fences and Gates, Walkways, Walls and Drives. Emmaus, Penn.: Rodale Press, 1983.
"A Case for the Cloche." *Organic Gardening,* January 1984, p. 78.
The Fine Art of Salad Gardening. Emmaus, Penn.: Rodale Press, 1985.
"Sharing the Bounty." *Organic Gardening,* August 1988, pp. 24–27.
"Greens Through Winter." *Organic Gardening,* September 1988, pp. 52–54.
"Warm Winter Coats." *Organic Gardening,* December 1988, pp. 23–27.
"Our Vanishing Forests." *Organic Gardening,* March 1989, p. 60.
"Dimming the Night Sky." *Utne Reader,* July/August 1991, pp. 120–121.
"Books on Top." *The Writer,* November 1994, pp. 7–8.
Cider: Making, Using & Enjoying Sweet & Hard Cider. With Lew Nichols. 2nd edition. Pownal, Vt.: Storey Communications, 1997.
"House Leaning on Wind." *Architectural Digest,* October 1997, p. 48.

CRITICAL AND BIOGRAPHICAL STUDIES

"Annie Proulx." In *Contemporary Authors.* Vol. 145. New York: Gale Research, 1994.
"Annie Proulx." In *Current Biography Yearbook.* New York: H. W. Wilson, 1995. Pp. 481–483.
Baker, Suzanne. "A Very Bad Marriage." *Metroactive Books.* http:www.metroactive.com/papers/cruz/11.21.96./lq-crimes-9647.html (November 21, 1996).

Bradley, D. Review of *Postcards. New York Times Book Review,* March 22, 1992, p. 7.

Blades, John. "Out in the Cold." *Chicago Tribune,* March 29, 1993, section 5, p. 3.

Cumming, L. Review of *Heart Songs & Other Stories. Times Literary Supplement,* 1990, p. 148.

DeMont, John. "An Epiphany on the Rock." *Maclean's,* April 25, 1994, p. 57.

Flavin, Louise. "Quoyle's Quest: Knots and Fragments as Tools of Narration in *The Shipping News.*" *Critique* 40, no. 3:239–247 (Spring 1999).

Garner, Dwight. "Northeastern Exposure." *VLS* 114: 29 (April 1993).

Gerard, Nicci. "A Gale Force Winner." *The Observer,* November 14, 1993, p. 18.

Graeber, Laurel. Review of *Accordion Crimes. The New York Times Book Review,* June 15, 1997, p. 36.

Kaveney, Roz. "Local Hero." *New Statesman & Society* 6:39 (December 3, 1993).

Kendrick, Walter. "*The Shipping News.*" *The Yale Review* 81:133–135 (October 1993).

McDermott, Philip. "*The Shipping News.*" In *Magill's Literary Annual 1994.* Pasadena, Calif.: Salem Press, 1994. Pp. 733–737.

Norman, Howard. Review of *The Shipping News. The New York Times Book Review,* April 4, 1993, p. 13.

Pierson, Stuart. "E. Annie Proulx's *The Shipping News:* A Newfoundland Perspective." *Newfoundland Studies* 11.1 (Spring 1995).

Rackstraw, L. "*Heart Songs & Other Stories.*" *North American Review* 274:67–69 (1989).

Reisman, Rosemary M. Canfield. "*Accordion Crimes.*" In *Magill's Literary Annual 1997.* Pasadena, Calif.: Salem Press, 1997. Pp. 5–8.

Rimer, Sara. "At Midlife, A Novelist is Born." *The New York Times Biographical Service,* June 1994, pp. 934–935.

Shechner, Mark. "Until the Music Stops: Women Novelists in a Post-Feminist Age." *Salmagundi* 113: 220–238 (Winter 1997).

Skorupa, Susan. "*Shipping News* Author Lures Book-Fair Fans." *Reno Gazette-Journal,* September 25, 1999.

Skow, John. "True (as in Proulx) Grit Wins." *Time,* November 29, 1993, p. 83.

Streitfeld, David. "For the First Time, PEN Picks a Woman." *Washington Post,* April 21, 1993, pp. B1, B9.

Weaver, Thomas. "E. Annie Proulx '69: Extraordinary Talent, An Eye for the Ordinary." *Vermont Quarterly* 10:12–13 (Summer 1994).

INTERVIEWS

Bolick, Katie. "Imagination is Everything: A Conversation with E. Annie Proulx." *Atlantic Unbound.* www.theatlantic.com/unbound/factfict/eapint.htm (November 12, 1997).

Kanner, Ellen. "Interview with Annie Proulx." *BookPage Fiction Review.* http://www.bookpage.com/9606bp/fiction/accordiancrimes.html (1996).

Steinberg, Sybil. "E. Annie Proulx: An American Odyssey." *Publishers Weekly,* June 3, 1996, pp. 57–58.

—ROBERT NIEMI

James Purdy

1923—

"I am a man, nothing human is alien to me."
—Terence

THE SMALL TOWN of Fremont, Ohio, lies along the old interstate highway, U.S. 20, not far from Lake Erie's Sandusky Bay, in the northernmost part of the state. Fremont is hometown to writer James Purdy, who was born on July 17, 1923, only two generations after the birth of another well-known Ohio writer, Sherwood Anderson, who spent his childhood in nearby Clyde, Ohio. Within the perspective of American literature, Purdy's birth was timed as if he were in a relay race, taking the baton from Anderson at the time of his (Purdy's) first published story in 1939. Anderson died shortly thereafter in 1941, just as Purdy was beginning his long and distinguished literary career that continues to captivate readers.

Like Anderson, Purdy saw Ohio as a place to escape from as soon as possible. Though the people and places of his childhood left an indelible impression on him, forever marking his writing, he was not able to leave until he completed high school when he would attend the University of Chicago. Being the middle child of five boys, Purdy grew up in a family that had more children than income. Purdy spent his early years moving from school to school as his family tried to keep the bills paid and food on the table. Purdy, how-

ever, recalls some bright moments. He received encouragement from his high school English teacher who encouraged him to write. Later, while attending the University of Chicago, he obtained distance from his family and began to read many of the great writers such as Miguel de Cervantes, Xenophon, Jean Genet and others that he still reads today. Transferring from the University of Chicago to the University of Puebla in Mexico, Purdy learned to write and speak Spanish, an experience that became useful to him when writing his later novels and stories such as "How I Became A Shadow," the story of Pablo Rangel and how his cousin betrayed his trust by stealing his pet cock to use in a local cock fight. In this story, Pablo's beloved animal dies in the fight and Pablo kills his cousin in vengeance before vanishing into the mountains to live out his life as a "shadow."

The time Purdy spent in Mexico also helped him obtain a position teaching English at a private boys' school in Havana, Cuba. He later returned to the United States to take a few graduate courses at the University of Chicago before traveling once again, this time to the University of Madrid in Spain. When asked in a January 2000 telephone conversation why he made the traveling choices that he did, Purdy responded simply, "I was young, I wanted to go! It didn't really matter too much where I went as long as it was interesting. The dollar was much stronger back then, you can't travel like that any more for as little cost."

Still in his early 20s, Purdy used his skills as a linguist to help him find temporary jobs interpreting and teaching in Latin America, Spain, and France, experiences that would inspire his writing for years to come. It was not until 1949 when at the age of twenty-six, Purdy attempted to settle down, becoming a faculty member at Lawrence College in Wisconsin. He was able to endure "the dead air of the suburbs" for four years before he quit and finally pursued his writing full-time.

EARLY WRITINGS

The transition from faculty member to writer was not easy. Purdy had to overcome great disappointment with his early attempts at writing. Many magazines rejected his stories.

As so many of Purdy's fictional characters such as Malcolm in *Malcolm* and Fenton Riddleway in *63: Dream Palace* come from the same circumstances of broken homes and poverty, the reader can not help reading these early works as though they were autobiography. One of Purdy's hopeful dispatches to *The New Yorker* in the early 1950s, a collection of his then-latest short stories, was rejected. Purdy had "no talent at all," said the editors of the magazine. Still, like a hero in one of his own novels, he carried on, eventually placing stories such as "Sound of Talking" and "Eventide" in *Mademoiselle, The Black Mountain Review, Creative Writing,* and other publications where he found a more sympathetic audience.

Purdy felt that women's magazines in particular were also the first to be open to his writing. "Women liked my writing," said Purdy, "magazines like *Mademoiselle* published quite a few of my early stories. In fact, after Marilyn Monroe died and they auctioned her personal affects, it

seems she owned many of my early novels like *Malcolm* and *63: Dream Palace.*" However, he made no attempt to hide his contempt for the publishing establishment as a whole. Purdy told *Contemporary Authors* that "reviewing in America is in a very bad state owing to the fact that there are no serious book reviews, and reputations are made in America by political groups backed by money and power brokers who care nothing for original and distinguished writing, but are bent on forwarding the names of writers who are politically respectable." Despite all the recognition that has come to Purdy in later years, such as the nomination for the PEN/Faulkner and Morton Dauwen Zabel Fiction awards, he still finds it a battle to gain a proper readership. In 1999, Purdy was unable to find an American publisher for his manuscript, *Moe's Villa and Other Stories.* Rejected by William Morrow and others, *Moe's Villa* was finally placed with a publisher in England, the country that was first to champion Purdy's early work.

In 1955, Osborn Andreas, an American businessman who was to become a friend of Purdy's, had the chance to read some of his rejected works. Andreas, who was working on a study of Henry James at the time, believed, as did another early admirer, the chemist Dr. J. J. Sjoblom, that Purdy's stories deserved immediate printing, even if they were published privately. Thus, the two men borrowed a large sum of money and one of Purdy's early, major works, the novella *63: Dream Palace* was published in a small edition of one thousand copies. Purdy was now able to send copies of his work to writers he admired such as John Cowper Powys and Dame Edith Sitwell, hoping for some sort of encouragement.

Purdy was not disappointed. Both Powys and Dame Edith responded with praise. Dame Edith's enthusiasm in particular helped Purdy find a publisher in England for *63: Dream Palace.* The following year, 1956, New Directions became Purdy's first American publisher, releasing *63:*

Dream Palace and several other stories under the title *Color of Darkness* after rejecting Purdy's work for ten years. Dame Edith it appears, had enough of a reputation to sway the opinions of the editors at New Directions.

In many of these early stories, Purdy pursues a theme that appears in many of his later books, that of the abandoned child overcoming isolation, poverty, and depression. Purdy is often reluctant to discuss his early life, believing that his work is his biography. Purdy also has trouble recalling the pain of his early years.

PURDY'S CHARACTERS

The autobiographical elements in Purdy's early novels are easily recognized. An oft-repeated theme is the struggle for the main characters to find their identities. His protagonists are isolated from family, friends, and their own emotions, struggling to find serenity of some sort. Many of his heroes, such as Malcolm in *Malcolm* (1959), come from the same circumstances of broken homes and poverty. They are often-times naive, the victims of a love destined for disaster. Malcolm's whirlwind marriage to Melba, a woman he hardly knows, is a disaster and ends when he dies from alcoholism. In these characters, Purdy may be describing how the he felt while growing up in a religious and conservative community in Ohio. Characters such as Cliff in *The Nephew* (1960), who grow up in families that are financially and emotionally secure, are either nonexistent or severely fractured in many of these early works.

Purdy's main characters in his early works search for a mentor or parent figure, someone to love, in a variety of ways in many of these episodes. In his novel *Malcolm,* which continues to be one of his most popular books, the young hero is Malcolm, who "could not have been more than fifteen" and "seemed to belong nowhere and to

nobody . . ." Indeed, it turns out that Malcolm's father has "disappeared," leaving the poor boy to sit on a public bench, waiting for fate to unfold the next episode. Through a series of surreal events such as his strange meeting with the astrologer Mr. Cox, Malcolm is introduced to the mysterious and eccentric Estel Blanc, the first of a long line of Purdy's dubious fictional mentors. In his novel *The Nephew,* young Cliff is raised by his aunt and uncle from the age of fourteen after his parents die in a plane crash. After Cliff's death in the Korean War, his aunt and uncle learn that he had once turned to Willard Baker and Vernon Miller for companionship and perhaps direction in life. These two men were suspected by some members of the community of being homosexual and thus, of dubious moral rectitude. Purdy's characters repeatedly escape from disaster, survive dead or vanished parents, and shake off the dust as they rise like some literary phoenix from a doomed or nonexistent home life.

After establishing such wrecked or disadvantaged beginnings, Purdy will have his protagonist draw the reader into the story to see how well the hero will cope, and try to overcome such difficult beginnings. The writer Guy Davenport summed up this situation very well when he wrote in the *New York Times Book Review:* "All the characters . . . are trying to wake up and live, they tell themselves; their tragedy is that they do not know what this means, and remain as bewildered as children on a dull afternoon who want something but do not know what they want." This may be most true of Malcolm, who exercises little will in his own life. He literally waits, as he does in the beginning of the book, sitting on a bus stop bench, for someone to tell him what to do next. Purdy believes that one of the reasons *Malcolm* is such a popular book (it has been translated into languages such as Turkish, Korean, and Chinese) is because of his character's ambiguity. Readers apparently identify with the indecisiveness of Malcolm's character. Malcolm could be the abused child, the youth struggling with sexual identity or even a Buddhist or existential philosopher!

Another of Purdy's central characters, Garnet Montrose in the novel *In A Shallow Grave* (1975), is a Vietnam veteran whose parents died while he was in the army. Injures from the war have left Montrose a veritable monster at best in outward appearance. At the book's opening, Montrose has just returned home from the war. A doctor assures him that his "bone structure is wonderful, fine and strong," a diagnosis which is of little consolation to Montose.

Just as Malcolm's father has "disappeared" and Cliff is driven to an early death in the war perhaps accelerated by the death his parents, Garnet Montrose becomes another walking casualty. One of the questions that Purdy's characters raise is, do they redeem themselves in the end; that is, do they change or rise above their suffering, or do they simply live wounded and broken lives?

Reflecting back on Purdy's phrase that his "work is his biography," the reader might begin to wonder if the challenges and obstacles of Purdy's characters are merely that, biographical details drawn from life, or is there a larger plan at work? Is Purdy really commenting on the larger problem of morality (or lack thereof) in current times, targeting perhaps the increase in divorce, child abuse, and rape? In an interview conducted in 1964, Purdy stated that "our moral life is pestiferous: we live in an immoral atmosphere."

Certainly, it is difficult to pick up any news magazine or watch any program without encountering society's ills. Children are abandoned, like garbage in a trash can. News reports tell of children who grow old enough to seek vengeance on those who tormented them as children. However, Purdy writes not simply for shock value, for readers can pick cheaper pulp mystery books that luridly portray these same problems much more graphically with not much more than an in-your-face attitude. Purdy's work is so finely crafted,

his prose so subtle and tightly controlled, as if to say to the reader, "Wake Up! This is what's going in our world, it's not somebody else's problem, it's yours and mine too."

In the United States, a country that arguably is the wealthiest in the world and supposedly offers open arms to the tired and poor from all walks of life, Purdy shows how it is at times amazingly difficult to find real love being expressed. Just as Martin Luther King Jr. tried to bring his message of love to the world only to be assassinated by those who were threatened by this idea, many of the characters in Purdy's stories are laid to waste in various metaphorical ways. Purdy suggests that only by being conscious of their actions and how they affect fellow beings can people begin to mend their ways.

In *Malcolm,* the title character, for example, is feted with superficial love and attention because of his youth and good looks. Yet Malcolm, who only wants to find his father in whom he might find his one chance at real love, fails, and begins to die amidst the hangers-on who think they have found in Malcolm some ideal of their own lost or unfound love. Meanwhile, Malcolm offers his own real affection to those he comes to know. A strange black comedy is at work in this story, as Purdy's characters, who are so desperate to find happiness, actually end up feeling nothing at all. For example, Malcolm's wife, Melba, to whom he was paired in an arranged, whirlwind marriage, takes a drug that would "not allow her to feel extreme grief or unpleasantness of any kind . . ."

Malcolm's proverbial fifteen minutes of fame are over. As he begins to die, so does his physical beauty and the attention of his "friends." A year after his death, a rumor suddenly surfaces that he is actually still alive. The rumor dies quickly, however, when everyone begins to realize that "Malcolm, in the interim, had been almost entirely forgotten, and was no longer a subject of conversation anywhere." Finally, Malcolm's grave, "which has no marker beyond a stone bearing his name, has been poorly cared for and fallen into complete neglect . . ."

Malcolm's fate, while not as dramatic or tragic as being assassinated by a sniper, has the same result. Beginning his life by waiting on a bench for his father from whom he only wanted the paternal love to which he felt he was entitled, Malcolm is used by a long line of shallow misfits until he has nothing left to give. Indeed, with Purdy's cast of orphans, strays, and eccentrics, the reader can begin to see why nothing human is alien to this writer. Not to mention inhuman.

GAY THEMES

It is only with the beginning of what may be called Purdy's middle years, those covering the late 1960s and early 1970s, that his books begin to leave the cast-offs of his earlier novels. It is almost as if he is saying to his readers, "You know from what stock my characters come, now see how they cope with middle age!" Another major turning point in these middle works is the release from secrecy for many characters from their gay relationships, characters whose homosexual liaisons were strongly hinted at in his earlier works but who are, starting with the novel *Eustace Chisholm and the Works* (1967), openly gay.

In the above book, the title character Eustace Chisholm lives with his male companion, Clayton Harms, who rents electric signs for a living and is one of the few people who are impressed by the poems Eustace has been writing. Eustace writes his epic poems on old scraps of newspaper with the ends of burnt matchsticks. Eustace has just been left by his wife Carla, but this seems to cause him little dismay. However, she suddenly returns, only to find herself playing second fiddle to Harms. She decides to stay regardless. Thus begins the entry of various characters who revolve around Eustace's world. Only a brief men-

tion is made of Eustace's father, who shot himself in the head when his business began to fail—just enough of a reminder to readers that, yes, things are about the same as with the earlier books in the area of difficult family histories. Eustace Chisholm continues as a sample piece for tangled relationships, the majority of which are homosexual. Many of the gay men orbit the building in which Eustace lives before spinning off into their own strange scenarios. Such is the case with Daniel Hawes, a disgruntled man who is the landlord of another of the book's characters, Amos Ratcliffe, a boy of just seventeen years. Unable to achieve satisfaction in his relationship with Amos and others, Hawes sets a new course, joining the army and becoming "Private Hawes." He forges a new relationship with an army cohort, Captain Stadger, a relationship that becomes deadly to them both. Their erotic relationship entails bizarre rituals of body mutilation until finally, Captain Stadger brings about a terrible ending.

The middle novels set quite a different course from Purdy's earlier works. The reader finds no hinting or whispering here about who is and who is not gay. This openness allows Purdy to develop the theme that he has been nurturing since *Malcolm,* that is, the complexity of relationships between several people, both heterosexual and homosexual, making already complex relationships even more so.

Eustace Chisholm and the Works shows the competition for Amos between Daniel Hawes and Eustace, competition for Eustace between his wife Clara and Clayton Harms, until there are webs within webs of entanglements, a continuation of Purdy's fascination with complicated liaisons. *The Nephew* only suggests the competition between Boyd and Alma for their nephew Cliff's affections. In *Malcolm,* characters engage in a free-for-all for the boy's attention. At this early point in Purdy's career, these competitions for affection are ambiguously based in terms of the character's sexual persuasion. The aunt and uncle have what anyone might deem as a normal and even gentle conflict over who earns the majority of nephew Cliff's affections and respect. In *Malcolm,* the reader begins to sense sexual yearnings for Malcolm from many of the book's characters, both male and female. However, Purdy's writing is ambiguous enough only to suggest what designs on Malcolm these people might have.

In a phone interview I conducted with Purdy, he said that all human beings, regardless of their sexual persuasion, have some physical attraction to their own sex. When asked how he felt about the label critics sometimes attach to him of "gay author" he scoffed: "I'm no more a 'gay author' than I am say, an 'Ohio author.' I write about feelings, the struggle to express who you are, whether it be gay or straight." He then added, "Being a gay author . . . that to me means you are political and I'm not political in that way." Still, several of Purdy's books have been published under the imprint of Guernsey Press' "Gay Modern Classics." These include *Narrow Rooms* (1978), *Eustace Chisholm and the Works,* and *I Am Elijah Thrush* (1972).

When one reads Purdy's books, even those titles that are considered "Gay Modern Classics," the reader comes away with the feeling that sexual persuasion is not a main theme. When compared with books such as Alan Hollinghurst's *Swimming Pool Library* or some of Edmund White's novels, the reader discovers a deeper theme at work in Purdy's stories. Hollinghurst and White do focus on the homosexual experience in some of their books, but with Purdy the reader can see that the struggle of his characters in finding their own identity is what interests him as a writer. It is a struggle that takes precedence over whatever ending the book might have and one of the things that makes Purdy a writer of such originality and scope. One of Purdy's favorite quotes—the ancient Greek playwright Terence's "I am a man, nothing human is alien to me"—further echoes the truth that Purdy is not simply interested in one aspect of human nature.

The main works of Purdy's middle years, beginning roughly at the end of the 1960s and the beginning of the 1970s, include *Jeremy's Version* (1970), *The House of the Solitary Maggot* (1974), and *Mourners Below* (1981). The first two constitute part of a continuing novel, or trilogy that Purdy calls *Sleepers in Moon-Crowned Valleys.* In these works Purdy begins to find a more reflective mode, thinking of stories from his past. He makes use of tales of his ancestors, episodes recounted and set in the backwoods of Ohio, incorporating them into fiction. *Jeremy's Version* begins in an Ohio town called Boutflour and depicts the Fergus family. Wilders and Elvira Fergus raise a family of three boys, who each in their own way battle to find their own place in the world amidst the provincial environment of a small Ohio town. The reader follows the emotional and physical progress of these boys as they are shaped by the misdeeds of their elders and react to the regular, gossiped-about events of small town life.

All the ingredients for small town scandal are in *Jeremy's Version:* rapes, drunkenness, and violence. How do these events shape and change three boys who are growing up amidst this turmoil? Are they trapped, are they damaged for life, do they pass these traits on to the next generation? Do they want to stay or go? Purdy does not tell his readers what to think. He does show them and lets the readers decide for themselves. His are not-so-still-life's of the literary venue.

The next work in the *Sleepers* trilogy is *The House of the Solitary Maggot,* a title that cannot help but give the reader pause (the hero is actually a local "magnate," which the townsfolk pronounce as "maggot"). In this novel, set in the town of Prince's Crossing (not far from Boutflour), a village so small as to not even make it onto a map, the narrator, Eneas Harmond, listens to Lady Bythewait as she speaks into a tape recorder, telling the sordid history of her family.

The tape is meant for her great-great nephew. Harmond, however, confuses his own story of the present with the past of Lady Bythewait. The reader is then introduced to Mr. Skegg, the "maggot," and husband to Lady Bythwait, and sees that the two of them have not turned out to be ideal parents. As they have sown, so do they reap—their crop of three sons has grown into maturity with few of the basic social skills needed to cope with daily living. Purdy ends his book having given the reader a good portrait of the modern dysfunctional family.

Next in the chronology of Purdy's trilogy is *Mourners Below,* a story set in an unnamed location, the residence of Eugene Bledsoe and his son Duane. Duane's two half-brothers were recently killed in a war that Purdy does not name (most likely the Korean War). Duane feels survivor's guilt and has frequent communication with the ghosts of his half-brothers, Justin and Douglas. Justin had started an affair with Estelle Dumont, the town's single, middle-aged, and wealthy figurehead of gossip. Duane, who resembles Justin physically, feels compelled to continue the relationship that his half-brother started. At this point the reader can begin to sense a set-up for a rural fairy tale. What is the right thing to do? Another tangle of emotions snares Duane as he becomes involved with Estelle, for a group of townies attack and rape him, leaving him in the dirt.

What makes these novels distinct from those of other writers of his time who have tried the same or similar story is the fine achievement of Purdy's prose. It sings with a rich poetic style, lightening the sometimes dark and gothic atmosphere of these novels. In a review written for the *Glasgow Herald,* Douglas Dunn states very matter-of-factly that Purdy's prose "elevates the emotional squalor of his story and its characters to a level of effect that is hauntingly beautiful and pure."

Several other writers and critics have noted a "gothic" element in Purdy's work. Purdy, however, balks at any such description of his writing. "My characters are real," he said during our phone interview. "I didn't intend any such caricature."

"Gothic" is a literary term often used loosely by critics and needs further definition. While the reader may not help but recall a slight hint of William Faulkner's southern gothic in Purdy's trilogy, regardless of how he may define such terms, Dunn's phrase "hauntingly beautiful and pure" is one the reader familiar with Purdy's work can understand and appreciate when reading the *Sleepers* trilogy.

ON GLORY'S COURSE

As mentioned earlier, the *Sleepers* trilogy draws on Purdy's "aftermath years." Purdy's characters still come from troubled origins, but they are more concerned with how to live their lives after growing up in disadvantaged circumstances. The events and action in these particular books call attention to how a character who grows up deprived of love and nurturing can suffer in his adult years, not just suddenly, but slowly and painfully.

Though many of his stories are set in Ohio or a Midwest region like Ohio, Purdy, unlike Sherwood Anderson, "never looked back." He has not returned to Ohio for pleasant, nostalgic visits since leaving it in his youth. Anderson, by comparison, returned to Elyria in northern Ohio to run various business ventures. Whatever personal troubles may have plagued Purdy in his early years, he hopefully purged them by writing this trilogy.

In 1984 Purdy finished *On Glory's Course* which, though not really part of the *Sleepers* trilogy, serves as an epitaph to those three books. Set in the Midwestern town of Fonthill during the 1930s, Purdy makes an even stronger attempt to catch the speaking rhythms of not just the place but the time. Though a 1984 *New York Times*

Book Review article cited the novel for its "ponderous idiom," the book was nominated for the PEN/Faulkner Award in 1985. Other reviewers also found the speech appropriate for its depiction of time and place.

In *On Glory's Course,* the reader follows the efforts of a middle-aged and wealthy woman, Adele Bevington (a woman with a "sinful past"), as she tries to locate the whereabouts of her illegitimate son whom she was forced to give up for adoption many years earlier. The time period as well as the place creates another sexually repressed atmosphere that comments on Adele as she consorts with the town's younger men. These young men are the same age her son would be, a fact that escapes the locals. Instead of understanding and compassion for the sorrows of this woman's life, the reader sees the town's jealousy of her wealth and sexual vitality. It is a conflict that allows Purdy to underscore the narrow-minded thinking of small towns and permits him to drive another stake into the heart of such unenlightened thinking.

On Glory's Course gives the reader a kaleidoscopic view of a time and place, thoroughly investigated by an accomplished writer, magnificent not just for its story but also for the explorative style in prose and speech rhythm. Content for the meantime to put the Midwest to rest, Purdy turned his attention to the eastern seaboard.

POETRY

Purdy is a prolific writer. As of the year 2000 he had written eleven novels excluding five volumes of poetry and another five published plays, many of which were already produced. However, it is his poetry that allows a playful outlet for Purdy. In 1970 he published *On the Rebound: A Story and Nine Poems,* which along with the story and poems, contains a few of Purdy's own drawings. The lead untitled poem sets the mood for the book:

Cruel zoo
    release your beasts
        unbar
tiger & jaguar
    to roam the street
& feast on all they meet.

Distilled into Purdy's poetry are pure and streamlined satire and wit, qualities that the reader finds in his short stories and novels. At times, he even reads like a Mother Goose writing for adults, as in the following untitled poem, also in *On the Rebound:*

Bang the kettle
Bang the harp
Bang the inside of your black heart

The rhymes and rhythms are simple, but the content is more complex. After reading the last line of the above poem, the reader might wonder whether Purdy is being bitter or just trying to be funny.

The contrast of the rhythm of the nursery rhyme with the more "adult" content of the piece creates an interesting juxtaposition—a refreshing surprise as the reader considers the entire poem. This is a technique not unknown to Purdy's longer prose works. His careful and exacting style of prose leads his audience to unexpected results. Purdy's readers do not arrive at the expected destinations as they travel the routes of Purdy's sentences. His prose style might lead readers to believe that they will, for instance, be delivered into the living room of a nineteenth-century Henry James story instead of say, the surreal enactments of Malcolm's adventures. Purdy raises deception to a new high in this manner, always surprising the reader with the hidden complexities of what seems on the surface to be a simple story line.

Since writing *On the Rebound,* Purdy has published many volumes of poetry, though they number fewer than his works of prose. Although poetry may not be Purdy's main medium, he gives it the same concentration and effort as he does his prose work. Perhaps he believes, as Matthew Arnold wrote in the nineteenth century, "More and more mankind will discover that we have to turn to poetry to interpret life for us, to console us, to sustain us."

PURDY'S DRAMATIC WORKS

When needing a rest from his poetry and prose, Purdy has turned his focus to drama. Productions of Purdy's theatrical work, though, have met with limited success. Friend and famed playwright Edward Albee attempted to transform *Malcolm* into a stage play in the early 1960s. Purdy thought Albee the only person capable of performing this task. With only a few suggestions in the manuscript, Purdy gave his blessings.

Unfortunately, the project turned into a disaster and received generally poor reviews. First there was trouble with the casting. Unable to find an actor to fit the role of small Malcolm (Michael Dunn was the first choice but was not available), Albee changed the character to the oldest man in the world. Said Purdy, "the play went off course" without a midget or dwarf (Albee's idea for casting) to play the role of Malcolm.

Purdy consequently concentrated on writing for the stage. To do otherwise was to leave too many loopholes for producers, as evidenced by Albee's failed production of *Malcolm*.

Purdy's first major drama was *Children Is All* (1961), a work that contains many of Purdy's classic themes—the broken home, the complex mother-son relationship and the ongoing struggle between characters unable to receive or give love.

Children Is All is the story of Edna Cartwright who, nearing death as the play opens, bitterly recalls her life. She tells of her marriage early in life to a husband who died shortly thereafter and the burdens of raising her son Billy alone. Bitterness turns into resentment and becomes, finally, her rejection of Billy who of course, wants

badly to be loved by his mother as most children do. Billy's clamor for attention serves only to widen the gulf between them. Ultimately, Billy becomes the fall guy in a theft at the bank where he works—the true culprits are his co-workers, but Billy is sentenced to fifteen years in prison. Edna adds to her list of resentments the loss of respectability that is all so important to her and, ironically, the loss of her chance to know her son as a young man (Billy is only twenty years old when he is sentenced to prison).

All these memories come flooding back to Edna as the play begins. Billy, now thirty-five, is soon to be released from prison. He first plans to visit his mother, who is still living in her own house with her friend, Leona Khetchum.

The only bright spot in Billy's life is young Hilda, a parentless girl raised by Uncle Ben, a neighbor of Edna's. Hilda visits Billy often while he is in prison, trying to cheer him up. This relationship makes for a stark contrast to the one Billy has with his mother, who is unable to visit her son in prison, overwhelmed each time she attempts to visit him by the bleakness of the prison walls. Finally, she gives up on any attempt to see him at all.

The approach of Billy's release from prison sends Edna into fits of anxiety, she even faints on his arrival. Billy has gotten a head wound during his escape from prison that further terrifies his mother and prevents her from immediately recognizing her son. "No, no," she wails, "you're not him, Billy was only a boy."

Attempts to hurry Edna's recognition of her son by Hilda and Leona increase as it becomes quickly apparent that Billy's head wound will soon prove fatal. Billy dies unrecognized by his mother who also failed to recognize him in a more symbolic way as he was growing up. It is only after Billy dies (ironically, on Independence Day) that Edna can begin to love him.

Cracks, another of Purdy's early dramatic works, was not very popular in the eyes of the critics. This one-act play was also written in the early 1960s and contains only four characters: Nera, who is eighty years old, the Nurse, who takes care of Nera, the Child, who gives the play its title as he complains of the "cracks" in his upstairs room, and finally the Figure, or "Creator," as this character introduces himself.

Cracks begins with Nera, who has been abandoned by her husband who, in her own words, was a "petty embezzler" and who left her with a large family to support. The Nurse and the Child have no names other than the roles that they play and both go to sleep as the last character, known as the Figure, enters the story. As the Figure and Nera enter into conversation, a muffled noise is heard outside which the Figure later explains was the end of the world. Poor Nera has little left in the world, all of her children are dead and her brother is a "hopeless invalid, and cannot speak or read." Nera's mother, also dead, is still her only comfort as she was the only one who loved her. It is a mystery to all involved, including the Figure (who claims to be the "Creator"), why Nera was excluded from the end of the world.

The Child, according to Nera, was left by a neighbor one summer evening and she did not have the heart to take him to an institution. The Child is indeed unusual and according to Nera, is "not only ill, he's upset within."

Nera informs the reader that "cracks" are the Child's words for ghosts. The reader can then surmise that when the Child (who is upstairs during the entire play) complains about drafts coming through the walls, that it may actually be the arrival of the Figure.

As Nera and the Figure begin to talk, she finally asks a question the answer to which has eluded her for her entire life, "Why should we go through the pain of giving birth if it's all going to come to . . . nothing?" The Figure, or perhaps he should be called the Creator from this point on, gives the only answer he can, "After all the pain of creation, the created will continue, after all the pain, after all the pain . . . no matter what we do or say."

The reader might agree with the statement quoted later in this essay by Henry Chupack, that this play may not be among Purdy's best writing efforts, but nonetheless, it is revealing in that it shows the question that was preoccupying the author's mind during that time.

Nera's question is applicable to many characters in Purdy's early books. The fact that life can be so difficult might make one ask the question, "why go on?" The Creator's answer is not entirely satisfying to the reader, that "the created will continue, after all the pain . . ." seems to offer little comfort to the distraught. Yet it is the question that is more interesting than the answer, as it represents the collective confusion suffered by many of Purdy's early characters. The distilled question that could be asked by Malcolm is simply "why?" So whether they like it or not, many of Purdy's creations choose to go on. Until they can stand it no more.

Though replete with the themes that worked so well for Purdy in his novels, critics felt that *Children Is All,* as well as his other early dramatic works such as *Cracks,* lacked the merits of his prose work. Henry Chupack wrote about Purdy's two early plays that "while the dialogue is excellent and the plots logically worked out, the ominous mood which suffuses his best stories and gives them particular flavor is practically absent from the plays."

Undismayed, Purdy has pursued the dramatic genre intermittently throughout his career. Two of his plays, *Dangerous Moonlight* and *Down the Starry River* played Off-Broadway in the late 1990s. Purdy thanks his long-time friend, playwright Tennessee Williams, for his avid support and enthusiasm for his dramatic works over the years.

In 1986 Purdy continued writing with his usual energy. He wrote two novels and a volume of short stories over a four-year period. *In the Hollow of His Hand* was published in 1986, *The Candles of Your Eyes and Thirteen Other Stories* appeared in 1987, and finally, *Garments the Living*

Wear was published in 1989. Purdy's high rate of production, however, did not mean the sacrifice of the quality of his work. Admired by fellow writers such as Dame Edith Sitwell and John Cowper Powys in his very early years and later, Dorothy Parker, William Carlos Williams and Jonathan Lethem, Purdy still felt excluded by the 'New York Circle.' This stable of writers and publishers were the ones generally show-cased in such publications as *The New Yorker,* such as writers John Updike and Truman Capote among others. Purdy's work continues to win him few literary awards. In 1958 he received a grant from the National Institute of Arts and Letters, was made a Guggenheim Fellow in the same year (as well as in 1962,) and he received another grant from the Ford Foundation in 1961. Purdy also earned a nomination for the PEN/Faulkner Award in 1985 for *On Glory's Course.* Later, he received a much needed grant from the Rockefeller Foundation and an award from the Morton Dauwen Zabel Fiction Committee that was given to Purdy in 1993. Purdy remains a well-kept secret known only to those who are well-rounded readers, his best books being what critics condescendingly call "minor masterpieces." This term may be used because Purdy's books make critics uncomfortable, as Purdy openly writes about sex, self-honesty and personal struggle. Yet his works are far too good to pass over. His name is not spoken in the same breath John Steinbeck's, or William Faulkner's, or John Dos Passos', an oversight that deprives a large reading community of a major writer.

IN THE HOLLOW OF HIS HAND

As the 1980s drew to a close, Purdy finished one more novel, *In the Hollow of His Hand.* This novel tells the story of Chad Coultas, a young boy of Ojibwa Indian background with more interest in daydreaming than his studies. He lives with his parents, Eva and Lewis Coultas in the small town of Yellow Brook. Everything is just fine until Decatur, a hometown boy and also part Ojibwa Indian, returns from his service in the army after fighting in World War I.

When Decatur returns to Yellow Brook, he brings with him his re-arrangement of the Coultas family structure, for Decatur has announced himself as the real father of Chad Coultas. As the shockwaves from his declaration begin to settle down, Decatur is asked for proof of his parenthood.

Yellow Brook at the time is still decades away from DNA testing. However, Decatur suddenly flashes back to a humiliating moment in the army barracks when he is undressing with the rest of the enlisted men. By chance, a fellow soldier happens to look down at Decatur's feet and soon all the soldiers are looking at Decatur's feet, as he has feet like nobody elses—his toes are webbed. The memory sparks an idea for Decatur. He decides to take Chad out to buy him some new clothes, namely some shoes and socks. Sure enough, as Chad is taking off his socks to try on some new ones, Decatur looks down at the young boy's feet. Like father, like son; Chad has webbed feet also. Chad becomes a bit embarrassed when he notices Decatur staring down at his feet, "You are looking at it too. Mama says my feet are a little like a water fowl's there . . ."

That's all the proof Decatur needs as a battle of loyalties begins when Chad is tempted to Decatur's side, interested in spending time with him as his original family feels the loss of their son. The implications of this new revelation about parenthood set the novel into motion.

Once again, Purdy has begun a tale of push and pull as Chad and his family discover that everything is not as it seems. Tensions mount as the struggle for control of Chad and his affections begins. The battle, however, is moved on to family ground in this novel as compared to earlier works, where Purdy used this same conflict in intimate relationships. In *Eustace Chisholm,* for example, the characters are almost falling over each other as they compete for the same person. *In the Hollow of His Hand* is the last of a series in which Purdy reaches back to his Midwestern roots for tales of his ancestors in the tradition of *On Glory's Course* and *Mourners Below.*

In our recent phone interview, Purdy recalled the funeral of his great-grandmother while still a child in Ohio. Suddenly, a strange woman entered, who Purdy remembered as a full-blooded Ojibwa Indian, and walked up to the casket where his great-grandmother lay. The strange woman bent over and kissed the woman on her forehead as she lay in her casket and said, "She was one of us." Then as quickly as she came, the strange woman disappeared. "Nobody knew my great-grandmother had any Indian blood in her," said Purdy. "It was all quite sudden."

With such stories in his past, it is easier for the reader to see how such novels as *In the Hollow of His Hand* came to be written. Purdy knew from first-hand experience that what one takes for granted one day could be completely changed the next.

As the 1990s arrived, Purdy quietly continued with his next ideas for novels and stories. With over thirty books to his name and the praise of many of his fellow writers, Purdy still found it not always easy to publish his next book. Perhaps the fact that James Purdy has not lived the life of a flamboyant, self-destructive alcoholic or drug addict has not given him headlines of more outwardly excessive writers. He is merely a craftsman, a great writer tending quietly to his work. He told the staff of *Contemporary Authors* in 1984 that "this is an age of exhibitionists, not souls. The press and the public primarily recognize only writers who give them 'doctored' current events as truth. For me, the only 'engagement' or cause a 'called' writer can have is his own vision and work. It is an irrevocable decision: he can march only in his own parade."

The reader who appreciates literature likely remembers where he was when he read his first

memorable book and hence looks forward to more writing from that author. It is always a bright note on the calendar when a forthcoming title by Purdy is announced by a publisher or book reviewer. It was disappointing to learn that Purdy's collection in the United States, *Moe's Villa and Other Stories,* was turned down by his regular publishers. After creating so many books of prose and poetry, much to great acclaim, Purdy learned he could not count on the vagaries of the publishing world (*Moe's Villa* was quickly and happily picked up by a publisher in England, the first country to recognize Purdy's promise and ability). It is saddening that this recognition did not come from his own country.

GARMENTS THE LIVING WEAR

Garments the Living Wear is the first novel by Purdy that deals with the issue of AIDS, or "the Pest," as the book's characters call it. The fantastic is mixed with the realistic in this novel as one of the main characters, Edward Hennings makes his appearance. He arrives in time to see the erosion of New York's gay theater, the result of a lack of funding and the loss of many actors to AIDS. Hennings is an aging homosexual who gives the impression of having more money than he does and begins to impact on the lives of the book's two main characters, Jared Wakeman and Peg Sawbridge, in both positive and negative ways. Jared, who is young and good looking, is partly supported by his benefactor, Peg Sawbridge, an aging drag queen. Tensions develop as Hennings begins to seduce Jared. However, the resentment Peg feels from the attention Hennings lavishes upon Jared lessens as it becomes known that Hennings can perform miracles such as healing the sick, especially those with AIDS.

With the discovery of such powers, Hennings becomes a sort of gay messiah, performing his fantastic cures. Alas, as Hennings brings his miracles and salvation to New York City, he disappears, his job done. Shortly thereafter, news arrives that Hennings has died in the Caribbean, devastating those whose lives he had touched.

AIDS has been defined at times by some of the most conservative evangelists as a disease that homosexuals brought upon themselves as their "wages of sin"—they are suffering God's wrath. Purdy could not resist this opportunity to satirize such beliefs by creating a gay messiah who can cure AIDS.

Despite some of this book's morbid elements, Purdy's humor and wit are working at full force. He has written an upbeat book that takes a turn from some of his darker themes of alienation, poking fun at the Christian Right Wing. Purdy carries his fast-paced wit and satire into the next decade with his next book, *Out with the Stars,* right on the tail of the *Garments the Living Wear.*

Two major works by Purdy appeared in the 1990s, *Out With the Stars* in 1992 and *Gertrude of Stony Island Avenue* in 1997. In these works Purdy moves his characters from the woods to the city, taking his cast to Manhattan in *Out with the Stars* and Chicago in *Gertrude of Stony Island Avenue.*

Out with the Stars represents a change of pace for Purdy, offering a mixture of some of his favorite themes, such as the complexity of relationships and the struggle to find self-identity, in a more optimistic mood. This book takes place in the mid-1960s when AIDS is not yet a news item and many of the characters who are gay are still in the closet. Abner Blossom, for example, has recently left retirement to write an opera about an infamous Russian novelist-turned-photographer, Cyril Vane. Vane is married to a once-famous star of the silent screen, Madame Olga Petrovna, who still clings to the glory days of her past. The trouble begins when Olga and others who know Cyril go to amazing lengths to keep quiet some of the more sordid facts of their lives. It seems Cyril has

one especially dark secret that he is determined to take to the grave. Who else has something they wish to hide?

For one thing, many of the book's characters have homosexual liaisons that they are content to keep quiet rather than have aired as common knowledge in the local community. It is sometimes the price one must pay for the cost of fame: complete loss of privacy that feeds the public hunger for gossipy chatter.

What Purdy has created is a vehicle for developing one of his favorite themes, that of the character's struggle to find his own true identity. The twist however, is that some of the characters know their own identity and do not want anyone else to know. This is one of Purdy's most commercial books as the action is much more exterior than interior, the humor richer and more varied, and the characters more diverse. Another central character, a Midwestern bumpkin from Kentucky, Val Sturgis, comes to the big city to make good and eventually becomes the protégé of Abner Blossom. As the story progresses, so does the complexity of the relationships between characters as values are tested as well as loyalties and ties to friendships old and new. *Out with the Stars* is one of Purdy's busiest books in terms of action, satire, and intrigue.

As usual, reviews were mixed though mostly favorable. Irving Malin, writing for the *Review of Contemporary Fiction,* saw the book as a "cruel and comic meditation on the meaning of fame." Firdaus Kanga wrote in the *Times Literary Supplement* that Purdy "had never been funnier" and his writing "never more self-assured." Indeed, *Out with the Stars* is a book that approaches slapstick even if it is close to black humor. The same reviewer in the *Times Literary Supplement,* Firdaus Kanga, had reservations though he thought the book funny, saying that still, the book "comes to one without meaning," and added "he has made his characters into playthings without fitting them into a grand construct."

Responding to such a backhanded compliment, Purdy said with a laugh, "Oh why didn't they just come out and say they didn't like the book!" A reader who sees all the ups and downs of Purdy's career might wonder why he continues to write. When asked that very question in a phone interview, Purdy responded, "I'd still write even if I was never published," adding, "I'd probably be a very different writer if that were the case."

Different or not, Purdy followed up *Out with the Stars* in 1997 with *Gertrude of Stony Island Avenue*. In this book Purdy at last returns to the land of his youth, Chicago, the city he first visited after he left Ohio. In novel, Purdy relates the story of the Chicago family of Carrie and her husband, a man known only as "Daddy."

The story takes place in the near present when Carrie and Daddy are mourning the loss of their talented bohemian daughter, Gertrude, in what seems to be a self-willed death. As a sort of therapy, Daddy suggests to Carrie that she write a book about their daughter. Gertrude was a talented and well-known painter in her time, one who punctuated her career with copious amounts of sex and drink. As Carrie ponders the suggestion of writing their daughter's biography, she becomes obsessed with the need to discover what motivated Gertrude's frantic life.

Thus Carrie, who lives in great fear of disappointing Daddy, begins her investigation that leads her to old friends and haunts that Gertrude favored, all the while reading her daughter's secret journal. Each discovery brings an illumination, such as meeting friends Carrie never knew Gertrude had, and helps pull her out of her confusion while Daddy watches from the sidelines with a mixture of encouragement and resentfulness. As Daddy's health fails, he becomes slightly envious of her revitalized energy.

Carrie is not overjoyed by a visit from her sister-in-law Gwendolyn from London, but eventually they befriend each other somewhat and work together to understand Gertrude's life. They are also helped by the eccentric Evelyn Mae, a scholar of Elizabethan times. Their quest for Gertrude becomes frantic as Carrie is drawn deeper into her daughter's world, places she never dreamed existed. The next character to be introduced is Cy Mellerick, Daddy's lawyer and, unbeknownst to all, a close friend of Gertrude's. With Cy's help, some of the final questions about Gertrude are answered. The frenzy of activity peaks into a happy ending for all. Carrie, who narrates the book, discovers that even though her daughter died an early death, ". . . Gertrude had lived . . . unlike myself . . ." Even though she and Daddy had been such poor parents, their daughter triumphed despite them. When Carrie is at last able to accept the fact that she had failed her daughter, she exclaims "I knew then that I was free . . . forever free." To which Daddy answers, "By George, Carrie, are you telling me we have a happy ending on our hands?" The answer seems to be yes, or as Carrie puts it, quoting Gwendolyn, "The search of Demeter for her Persephine is ended."

A new pattern has emerged in Purdy's writing, that of death as a vehicle for self-discovery. In *Children Is All,* Edna Cartwright discovers her love for her son Billy only after he has died; the aunt and uncle in *The Nephew* learn about their own feelings of love after Cliff dies in the war; and now Carrie and Daddy fill the void in their own lives after discovering who Gertrude really was and how she lived.

The reader might wonder what it is about human nature that makes people want to romanticize their loved ones once they are dead. There seems to be an instinct to gloss over the more sordid aspects of the life in an attempt to alleviate guilt or unfinished business in the lives of those left behind. One could almost say that there seems to be a need to compartmentalize the lives of the deceased so they may fit nicely into the remaining scheme of one's own life. Or perhaps it is simply easier to love an acquaintance or family member once they are dead and cannot talk back. Purdy offers no answers. He does offer a wide variety of works that explore these themes. His work, not the subject of Norman Rockwell pastiche, nevertheless represents a side of humanity everyone knows exists, but may be unwilling to admit.

CONCLUSION

James Purdy began to find his writing voice in the post-war 1950s, a period famous for its conformity and almost religious appreciation for material possessions. It was a time when Mom and Dad made the rules, Communists stalked the land, and homosexuals ("homos") were perverts who roamed dark alleys looking for victims.

In the 1950s, the Beats began to howl and famous obscenity trials were launched over books as varied as Lawrence's *Lady Chatterley's Lover* and Allen Ginsberg's *Howl.* Could there have been a more perfect climate in which to rebel and challenge traditional mores? Experimental writing was beginning to make news, abstract expressionism was already "in," and by 1960 the world was a reflection on shattered glass, or so it seemed.

Yet in a small apartment in Brooklyn, on a quiet street, in a tiny neighborhood, James Purdy picked away at the world, letter by letter, on an old Underwood typewriter. While bombs exploded around the world, Purdy organized his own revolution on blank white bond paper. At first, his writing did not seem so shocking. The writing was straightforward, very precise and yet these were not stories for the family hour. While other writers were creating manifestos by the minute, Purdy was sounding his own alarm. He was quietly showing the world-at-large just what was happening to them.

It is not until people are taken outside of themselves and are forced to look inward that they see what they are doing and have done. That is what great literature can do—how many times have people read a scene that describes something that happened to them while failing to recognize its implications until they saw it described in print? Have you ever said, " 'Hey, I've done that too,' " or " 'That's happened to me!' "? Literature can allow people to be honest with themselves, they know a book will not talk back, condemn or judge them. How many Edna Cartwrights are there out there, denying love to their offspring until they are dead and gone, wishing they had a second chance? How many loveless families, abusive relationships, and exploited children are out there? James Purdy sounds the alarm almost every time he picks up his pen.

Yet Purdy is more than a social worker who likes to spin a yarn. He is a writer, a solid craftsman in the best American tradition. William Carlos Williams said "The pure products of America go crazy," but we are happy to see that a pure product such as Purdy is still sane. As time passes, his readers see that the problems Purdy wrote about in the 1950s and 1960s are still relevant. Purdy's work has grown and changed with the world, depicting the emergence of AIDS and gay rights in his pages as his sometimes dour pessimism transforms into a finely honed voice of satire and humor. Purdy's writing and his themes continue to interest his readers. Hopefully his books will not be lost and forgotten on the shelves of twentieth century literature, but will grow in stature and gain the fine reputation that they deserve.

Purdy will not be the first American writer to reappear from obscurity. Readers have forgotten the limbo that some writers, who have since been taken for granted as immortals in the Literary Hall of Fame, slipped into during and after their lifetimes. William Faulkner was saved from obscurity during his career when Malcolm Cowley created and edited the *Portable William Faulkner* for Viking Press. Even Ernest Hemingway was, in the late 1960s after his death, lodged in a slump that did not really lift until the later half of the 1970s—his work was actually passe and taboo for a number of years. So Purdy's readers hope that this quiet writer of exceptional prose, who has worked consistently at his craft for well over a half century, will someday gain the wider readership he deserves. In the meantime, it is a comfort to know he is still in Brooklyn, baton in hand, typing away. He is not done with his readers yet.

Note: In January 2000, I conducted a series of telephone interviews with James Purdy. Many quotations in this essay are from those interviews.

Selected Bibliography

WORKS OF JAMES PURDY

NOVELS AND SHORT STORIES

63: Dream Palace. London: Victor Gollancz, 1956.
Color of Darkness. New York: New Directions, 1957.
Malcolm. New York: Farrar, Straus & Giroux, 1959.
The Nephew. New York: Farrar, Straus & Cudahy, 1960.
Children Is All. New York: New Directions, 1961.
Cabot Wright Begins. New York: Farrar, Straus & Giroux, 1964.
Eustace Chisholm and the Works. New York: Farrar, Straus & Giroux, 1967.
An Oyster is a Wealthy Beast. San Francisco: Black Sparrow Press, 1967.
Jeremy's Version. New York: Doubleday, 1970.
I Am Elijah Thrush. New York: Doubleday, 1972.
The House of the Solitary Maggot. New York: Doubleday, 1974.
In a Shallow Grave. New York: Arbor House, 1975.
Narrow Rooms. New York: Arbor House, 1978.
Mourners Below. New York: Viking Press, 1981.
On Glory's Course. New York: Viking Press, 1984.
In the Hollow of His Hand. London: Weidenfeld & Nicolson, 1986.

The Candles of Your Eyes and Thirteen Other Stories. New York: Weidenfeld & Nicolson, 1987.
Garments the Living Wear. San Francisco: City Lights Books, 1989.
Out with the Stars. San Francisco: City Lights Books, 1992.
Gertrude of Stony Island Avenue. New York: Morrow, 1997.

POETRY

On the Rebound: A Story and Nine Poems. Los Angeles: Black Sparrow Press, 1970.
The Running Sun. New York: James Purdy, limited edition, 1971.
Sunshine is an Only Child. New York: Aloe Editions, 1973.
Lessons and Complaints. New York: Nadja Editions, 1976.
The Brooklyn Branding Parlors. New York: Contact II Publications, 1986.
Collected Poems. Amsterdam: Athenaeum-Polak & Van Gennep, 1990.

PLAYS

Cracks. Cosmopolitan, August 1962, pp. 64–69.
Wedding Finger. New Directions in Prose and Poetry 28:77–98 (1974).
Proud Flesh. Northridge, Calif.: Lord John Press, 1980.
What Is It, Zach? New Directions in Prose and Poetry 43:171–179 (1981).

BIBLIOGRAPHY

Ladd, Jay L. *James Purdy: A Bibliography.* Columbus, Ohio: Ohio State University Libraries, 1999.

CRITICAL AND BIOGRAPHICAL STUDIES

Adams, Stephen D. *James Purdy.* New York: Barnes & Noble, 1976.
Chupack, Henry. *James Purdy.* Boston: Twayne, 1975.
Contemporary Authors Autobiography Series. Vol. 1. Detroit: Gale Research, 1984.
Davenport, Guy. *"Jeremy's Version." New York Times Book Review,* November 15, 1970, p. 4.

Dunn, Douglas. Review. *Glasgow Herald,* January 18, 1986.

Kanga, Firdaus. "From the High Ceiling." *Times Literary Supplement,* June 26, 1992, p. 21.

Kostelanetz, Richard, ed. *On Contemporary Literature.* New York: Avon, 1964.

Malin, Irving. "Book Review." *Review of Contemporary Fiction* 14:208–209 (Summer 1994).

Schwarzchild, Bettina. *The Not-Right House: Essays on James Purdy.* Columbia: University of Missouri Press, 1968.

Seidman, Robert J. "War Between Mothers and Sons." *New York Times Book Review,* February 26, 1984, p. 25.

Skeen, Anita, "The Importance of Age in the Short Stories of James Purdy." Master's thesis, Bowling Green University, 1970.

RECORDINGS

Eventide and Other Stories. New Rochelle, N.Y.: Spoken Arts, 1970.
James Purdy. New York: Full Track Press, 1979.
Malcolm. Deland, Fla.: Everett/Edwards, 1970.
63: Dream Palace. New York: Spoken Arts, 1968.

—DAVID BREITHAUPT

Anne Rice

1941–

ALTHOUGH SHORTLY AFTER the 1976 publication of her first novel, *Interview with the Vampire,* Anne Rice stated in *Contemporary Authors* (1977), "I doubt that I will deal with the supernatural again in my fiction," she has since become one of the most prominent authors of popular horror fiction. The second of the four daughters of Howard O'Brien and Katherine Allen O'Brien, Howard Allen O'Brien was born on October 4, 1941, in New Orleans, Louisiana. Named after her father and embarrassed because she had a name that traditionally referred to a boy, Rice created and revealed the nickname Anne to a nun who asked for her name on her first day of school.

Rice's mother was a very religious woman who insisted her children adhere to Catholicism and its rituals. However, amidst the sometimes oppressive religious environment, Rice's childhood was filled with frequent storytelling by her mother, who also inspired her children to reach for genius. Additionally, her father read classical literature to his daughters, filled the house with classical music, and encouraged his daughters to sing, to dance, and to play musical instruments. A precocious child, Rice showed interest in the arts from an early age, when she began to play the violin, write novels, and perform in plays with her sisters.

Along with the positive influence of exposure to the arts during her childhood, Rice's early years were spent in an environment troubled by her mother's alcoholism. As Katherine Ramsland points out in her biography of Rice, *Prism of the Night: A Biography of Anne Rice,* Rice's mother frequently drank alone in her room, causing disasters such as setting the mattress on fire. Rice's mother demanded perfection from her children, and her children often played the role of enabler, hiding their mother's drinking and excusing her irrational behavior. Consequently, Rice assumed the role of family caretaker, performing domestic duties such as cleaning house and preparing meals, and taking on nurturing responsibilities such as caring for her sisters. When Rice was fourteen, her mother died of alcoholism. Maintaining fond memories of her mother in spite of her disease, Rice recalls in *Prism* that her mother inspired her to maintain self-confidence and taught her many practical skills: "[my mother] gave me the belief in myself that I could do great things, that I could do anything I wanted to do. When it came to accomplishments in the world, to manner of dress, to intellectual curiosity or achievement, she gave me a sense of limitless power. She put no premium at all on conformity. I never doubted she loved me or was interested in me."

After her mother's death, Rice returned to Redemptorist High School, a Catholic school. It was an institution, ironically, that challenged her to begin to question the teachings of Catholicism.

She disagreed with the rigid doctrines advocated by Catholicism, especially sexist dogmas that place women near the bottom of a clearly established social hierarchy, and outdated ideologies that deny women sexual pleasure. In addition to her rebellion against religious teachings, Rice also began to question broader social norms that promoted sexism by encouraging young women to marry and have children while motivating young men to pursue business opportunities and to seek education. Years later, in an interview with Susan Ferraro, Rice explained her motives for forsaking the Catholic teaching her parents and some of her peers tried so hard to instill in her: "It struck me as really evil—the idea you could go to hell for French-kissing someone. I just didn't believe it was the one true Church established by Christ to give grace. I didn't believe God existed. I didn't believe Jesus Christ was the son. I didn't believe one had to be Catholic in order to go to heaven. I didn't believe heaven existed either." The emotional pressure of resisting social and religious pressures was intensified when Rice's father enrolled her and her younger sisters in St. Joseph's Academy boarding school. The boarding school upheld very strict rules and demanded structured daily routines, sources of confinement that deeply oppressed Rice.

Rice's father remarried in 1957 and the family moved to Richardson, Texas, where Rice completed high school. There, she met her future husband, Stan Rice. She also began to write for the school newspaper, *The Talon.* During high school Rice held numerous service jobs such as waitress and drugstore clerk. After graduating, she attended Texas Woman's University, in Denton, Texas. Exposure to philosophies taught at college challenged Rice to question her religious faith even more seriously than she had in high school. After studying for a semester at Texas Woman's University, Rice transferred to North Texas State (now the University of North Texas), where Stan Rice also enrolled. During her sophomore year of college, she moved to San Francisco, where she worked in an insurance office. After Stan's marriage proposal, Rice returned to Denton to live with him. Shortly afterward, they moved to San Francisco.

While both Anne and Stan took courses at San Francisco State College (which became San Francisco State University), Anne also acted in a few plays and worked in an office, and Stan also painted and worked as an accountant. During this time, the Rices held parties for artists, and they began to drink heavily. Rice began to write short stories and novels. In 1964, both she and Stan received undergraduate degrees from San Francisco State University, where later Stan also received a master's degree. The Rices' daughter, Michele, was born in 1966, while Anne attended graduate school and Stan taught creative writing at San Francisco State University and continued to pursue a poetry writing career.

EARLY WRITING

Shortly after moving to Berkeley in 1969, Rice wrote the short story "Interview with the Vampire," began an erotic novel, *The Tales of Rhoda,* and wrote a novella, *Katherine and Jean,* which became her master's theses. In 1972, Michele Rice died of leukemia; although Rice was able to complete her master's degree during her daughter's terminal illness, shortly afterward she and her husband began to drink more heavily—a habit they continued through the time the novel *Interview with the Vampire* appeared in 1976. During this period, the Rices began to have intense arguments, exacerbated by drinking and complicated by frustration experienced because of their daughter's death. Rice's intense relationship with Stan continues, as she admits in a 1999 interview in *Contemporary Authors:* "I fell completely in love with Stan, and I'm still completely in love with him. . . . It's a passionate, stormy love. The ferocity of our arguments frightens away many people, and our affection for each other inspires them." To escape her troubled relationship and emotional problems, Rice went to stay briefly in Dallas with Stan's parents. When she returned to San Francisco, she took a job as a copy editor for a book publisher.

After a bout with Guillain-Barre Syndrome, a nerve infection that partially paralyzed her for months, Rice began to join writing groups and to pursue her writing career more seriously. Still grieving over her daughter's death, experiencing obsessive–compulsive behavior, and seeking psychiatric help, Rice sold *Interview with the Vampire* to Knopf for $12,000. She subsequently sold the paperback and movie rights for large sums, which provided her with the financial security to travel. The Rices traveled to Europe and Egypt, where Rice gained insights into settings for future novels. In 1978, the Rices' son, Christopher, was born, which prompted both Anne and Stan to quit drinking. Rice continued to write and publish her novels, and experienced immense frustration that her novels were not taken seriously by critics. After residing in several houses in and near San Francisco, the Rices moved in 1988 to New Orleans, where they reside in a Garden District mansion adorned with Gothic memorabilia such as statues, skeletons dressed in vintage attire, and crystal balls.

RICE'S RELATIONSHIP WITH HER FANS

Rice shows remarkable loyalty to her fans, and they return her displays of loyalty. Similar to rock-star groupies, Rice's fans dress in Gothic-like costumes that include black attire, exaggerated decorations of jewelry, Mohawk haircuts, and tattoos to attend book signings and various other social events. Rice often entertains her fans with activities such as riding in limousines and tossing rubber rats to her fans during Mardi Gras

parades, and arriving at public events in horse-drawn coffins. Similarly amusing her fans, Rice celebrated the 1995 publication of *Memnoch the Devil* by staging a pseudo-funeral, in which she appeared wearing a wedding gown and riding in a coffin. No doubt Rice performs such acts to entertain her fans and provide a public image that helps promote her novels.

Rice also engages in public activities that only vaguely relate to her writing career. In 1997, she paid for a full-page newspaper ad that promoted the boycott of the opening of a neon-lighted restaurant on St. Charles Avenue in New Orleans because she thought it disrupted the ambiance of the otherwise charming district. Coincidentally, the restaurant opened at the location where Rice had portrayed Lestat's disappearance in *Memnoch the Devil*, and some viewed Rice's tactics as self-promoting attempts to advertise her novels. Keeping the matter in the news, the restaurant owner countered with his own ad and sued Rice. Such public demonstrations keep Rice in the limelight and provide her fans with notions of Rice as an individual, an image they may add to notions of her as an author.

More important than the colorful adventures outside of writing that Rice provides for her fans, she continues to entertain them through her novels. In addition to those written in the horror, Gothic, and fantasy genres of popular fiction, Rice's novels can be classified as historical or erotic fiction. However, of Rice's many novels, she is most recognized for her vampire novels. In Katherine Ramsland's *Vampire Companion: The Official Guide to Anne Rice's The Vampire Chronicles,* Rice speaks about her inspiration for writing her first vampire novel, *Interview with the Vampire.* She also makes comments relevant to her vampire novels in general, explaining what motivated her interest in depicting vampires: "I was just sitting at the typewriter wondering what it would be like if a vampire told you the truth about what it was like to *be* a vampire. I wanted to know what it really feels like. I wanted to see through the vampire's eyes and ask the questions I thought were inevitable for a vampire, who once had been human to ask. What do you feel when you drink blood? Is it erotic? Is it glorious? Is it spiritual? I followed my imagination and my instinct."

VAMPIRE WORKS

Rice's vampire works consist of two series of novels: The Vampire Chronicles and New Tales of the Vampires. The first series, The Vampire Chronicles, consists of six novels: *Interview with the Vampire, The Vampire Lestat* (1985), *The Queen of the Damned* (1988), *The Tale of the Body Thief* (1992), *Memnoch the Devil,* and *The Vampire Armand* (1998). Written as a series, the same characters appear throughout The Vampire Chronicles, typically with each volume focusing on a specific character's point-of-view. Additionally, some of the same incidents are referred to across the volumes, but readers are offered a different character's perspective on the events. Throughout the series, a complex and elaborate epic history of a coven of vampires, along with details of specific vampires, unravels.

The Vampire Chronicles are structured similarly: they begin with brief introductory chapters that establish why the protagonists tell the stories revealed in the forthcoming chapters. The beginnings of the novels, which provide frameworks for the books, establish that the protagonists are either writing novels or participating in interviews. Typically, the novels end with epilogues, in which the protagonists offer insights about the experiences revealed in the framed narratives. The epilogues bring the novels full-circle, back to the prologues, and together the epilogues and prologues provide interesting frameworks that add layers to the narratives. The framed chapters usually provide histories of the protagonists' ex-

periences, beginning with accounts of how and when they were created. Additionally, the framed narratives contain the action and provide historical accounts of the settings as well as mentioning characters that appear throughout the chronicles.

The Vampire Chronicles series begins with *Interview with the Vampire,* which marks Rice's popular novel debut. *Interview with the Vampire* is set up as an interview between the vampire Louis and a reporter called Daniel that takes place in San Francisco. Organized into four sections, the novel traces Louis' life from 1791 to the present. In the final section, Louis interprets the events and tells how they have impacted his life. After recounting his experiences, the reporter asks to be transformed into a vampire. Although confused as to why the reporter would desire such status after the trials Louis has explained, Louis nevertheless fulfills the reporter's wish.

Louis spends much of the novel fighting humanlike internal conflicts, including feeling empathy for mortals and experiencing guilt. Louis's human traits separate him from other vampires and he becomes a sort of "other" in both human and vampire societies. Whereas Lestat, the vampire who transformed Louis into a vampire, clearly belongs in the vampire world and lacks human emotions, Louis constantly struggles between the desire for blood and the compassion he feels for his victims. The characterization of Lestat provides a foil for that of Louis: Louis is "[t]orn apart by the wish to take no action—to starve, to wither in thought on the one hand; and driven to kill on the other," while Lestat, who tells Louis, "Vampires are killers! They don't want you or your sensibility!" is "masterfully clever and utterly vicious." Repeatedly, Louis expresses remorse for killing people to fulfill his own need for blood. Contrary to Louis' emotional anguish, Lestat frequently celebrates the deaths of his victims and even seems to prolong their suffering to fulfill his own need to kill violently. Lestat is impatient with Louis' internal struggles and tries to teach him to take pleasure in killing his victims, a notion unimaginable to Louis.

After living with Lestat for four years, Louis announces his intention to leave him. Determined to prevent Louis from leaving, Lestat creates Claudia, a five-year-old vampire whom he refers to as their daughter. Louis's attachment to Claudia inspires him to remain with Lestat for another sixty-five years. Claudia serves as a sort of middle ground between the extreme personalities represented by the characterization of Lestat, as evil, and of Louis, as good. The transformation from innocent child to vampire through the characterization of Claudia has been interpreted by some critics as an unconscious means for Rice to cope with her grief over the death of her own daughter, Michele.

The reporter to whom Louis tells his story publishes the interview, an event which provides the beginning for the second novel in the Vampire Chronicles, *The Vampire Lestat.* Here, Lestat learns about the novel *Interview with the Vampire* from a rock band, reads it, and decides to correct misinformation provided by Louis. *The Vampire Lestat* opens with Lestat awakening in the 1980s from fifty-five years of sleep. He is awakened by noises from various media sources, including entertainment programs and news broadcasts. The sound that finally awakens him fully is that of a rock band rehearsing. Motivated to awaken by the urge to join a rock group, Lestat rides a Harley and dresses in leather. His immediate reaction to his contemporary environment is that people have rebelled against the need to conform that beset the era of the industrial revolution, and have learned to express eroticism. He also notices that since he has last been awake, society seems to have adapted an economy in which wealth is more equally distributed.

Lestat approaches the rock band, Satan's Night Out, to inquire if he might join them. Members of the rock band recognize his name and inform him that he is the protagonist of a book they re-

cently read. After the group shows Lestat a copy of *Interview with the Vampire,* he consults his lawyer and demands to be given fame that will transcend continents and time. Lestat changes the rock group's name to The Vampire Lestat to gain the fame he seeks. Lestat realizes that during the interview that appears in print as *Interview with the Vampire,* Louis had committed worse crimes than merely breaking the vampire code that states that mortals must not be told about vampires. Furious about the lies that Louis has told about him in *Interview with the Vampire,* Lestat seeks revenge.

To add to Louis' story, Lestat wants to reveal to the mortal world the events that he has seen and learned before he had met Louis. He is also motivated to write his autobiography because he wants mortals to understand vampires in general, even if they would not believe the tales he plans to tell. Since Louis' story is considered fiction by mortals, Lestat hopes to create a more believable account of vampire life. A further motive for Lestat to write his autobiography concerns his desire to entice the vampires to join forces and fight a lustrous war.

The character of Lestat disguised as a mortal rock star in the framing chapters of *The Vampire Lestat* parallels his character as vampire in the framed chapters. As a rock star who rides a Harley, he represents a social rebel in the earthly realm; similarly, as a vampire who challenges traditional codes, he represents a rebel amongst his coven of vampires. He writes his story on a word processor after the speaker of a cassette of *Death in Venice* claims that evil is necessary. The cassette recording inspires Lestat to consider his own philosophies concerning good and evil. He tries to believe that evil is necessary and that immorality is unavoidable in order to evade the guilt he feels about the acts he commits as a vampire.

After the opening section of *The Vampire Lestat,* Lestat's autobiography, "The Early Education and Adventures of the Vampire Lestat," begins.

It consists of seven chapters that trace Lestat's history, beginning with his birth in France in the eighteenth century. Born the seventh son of a marquis, Lestat desires to live in a monastery but his father forbids it, so he runs away. The story chronicles his adventures after joining a group of traveling actors. Demonstrative of his bravery, Lestat fights a pack of wolves and is befriended by Nicolas, with whom he goes to Paris, where he is transformed into a vampire by Magnus. Lestat goes on to transform his mother, Gabrielle, and his friend Nicolas into vampires. Lestat convinces Armand's coven to forgo their long-held religious rituals. Lestat spends ten years searching for Marius, an old vampire whom he believes will teach him the traits of a vampire. Eventually Marius finds Lestat and explains the origins of vampires.

The Vampire Lestat concludes with an epilogue, "Interview with the Vampire," which is divided into two sections, and a concluding chapter that follows the epilogue. The concluding chapter, entitled "Dionysus in San Francisco, 1985," is further divided into three parts. "Interview with the Vampire" describes Lestat's decision to remain asleep since 1929. Lestat recounts his relationship with Louis and Claudia, and includes information that Louis could not have known in his account of the triangular relationship he describes in *Interview with the Vampire. The Vampire Lestat* ends with Lestat's concert, the music of which awakens Akasha who is the Queen of the Damned and the mother of all vampires. Left open-ended, the final pages announce that "the third book in The Chronicles of the Vampires will follow." True to the serial novel form, the ending of *The Vampire Lestat* leaves readers wondering what will happen next. The concluding page invites readers to consider possibilities for future action, while also promoting the next book.

Continuing the climactic conclusion of *The Vampire Lestat, The Queen of the Damned* is the next volume of the Vampire Chronicles. Unlike the first two novels in the series, *Interview with the Vampire* and *The Vampire Lestat,* each of which focuses on specific character's points of view, traces their histories, and reveals their thoughts, *The Queen of the Damned* illustrates several plots and many equally important characters. The novel begins with a poem "Tragic Rabbit," written by Stan Rice, followed by an untitled section that begins "I'm the vampire Lestat. Remember me? The vampire who became a super rock star, the one who wrote the autobiography?" Lestat's testimony provided in the untitled section serves to reorient readers with the previous book in the series. He reminds readers that he was most recently viewed as "hanging from the proverbial cliff," a situation he says he survived. After informing readers that he now resides in Miami with other vampires, he announces that he will leave the reader but will return when the time is right. Told within a narrative that introduces a framed narrative, Lestat's opening is much like the openings of the earlier novels in the Vampire Chronicles.

Whereas both the poem and Lestat's introductory speech occur before the table of contents in *The Queen of the Damned,* the book's prologue proper "Proem," begins as if it were "found fiction," representing a long section of graffiti found on a bathroom wall; however, later it is implied that someone is reading the prologue's message out loud. The message consists of a formal declaration by Marius seeking Lestat's death for having revealed vampire secrets. Marius refers both to *Interview with the Vampire* and to *The Vampire Lestat.* Like Lestat, who attempts in his autobiography to correct Louis's accounts of vampirism, Marius warns his listeners (and inadvertently readers) to ignore some of Lestat's "gobbledygook" and questions why both Louis and Lestat have not been condemned for revealing secrets to mortals. Marius announces a need to destroy Lestat and all of his friends and invites listeners to attend Lestat's rock concert, scheduled to occur on Halloween, in which Lestat will perform.

As in the opening narrative, the point of view throughout *The Queen of the Damned* is cumbersome. While in the beginning Lestat claims to be writing the novel using various characters' points of view, it is not always clear that these multifarious points of view are filtered through Lestat's fictional authorial stance. Despite point of view complications, the gist of the main plot concerns the conflict between Lestat and Akasha, an Egyptian queen whose ploy to redeem humanity from evil involves destroying almost all of the male population. Akasha abducts Lestat and takes him to France to be her lover, but eventually he refuses her offer to join her as a god because he does not want to forsake his vampire status. Although Akasha claims to teach him goodness, her notion of virtue contrasts with that of Lestat's. Among many others, one minor plot involves Daniel, the reporter who interviewed Louis in *Interview with the Vampire*.

Although several plots intertwine to some degree and the characters mingle to form at least some sort of unity, the action of *The Queen of the Damned* is difficult to follow. It does, however, involve the internal, philosophical struggles of the vampires, especially Lestat's ethical conflicts. For example, after the confrontation with Akasha, in which Lestat denies her perspective of good and evil, he reveals in terms of age-old philosophies why he embraces Marius: "It had to do with the whole struggle of good and evil which he understood exactly the way I did, because he was the one who had told me how we must wrestle forever with those questions, how the simple solution was not what we wanted, but what we must always fear." Similar concerns are explored when Lestat and the other vampires attempt to deny the reasons Akasha provides for why evil exists. As Maharet argues:

I tell you, we would be hard put to determine what is more evil—religion or the pure idea. The intervention of the supernatural or the elegant simple abstract solution! Both have bathed this earth in suffering; both have brought the human race literally and figuratively to its knees.

Don't *you* see? It is not man who is the enemy of the human species. It is the irrational; it is the spiritual when it is divorced from the material; from the lesson in one beating heart or one bleeding vein.

Like previous volumes in the Vampire Chronicles, *The Queen of the Damned* refers to earlier volumes as well as to itself as a text. The conclusion of *The Queen of the Damned* summarizes the various characters' current conditions and says that people will assume that this book is fiction, much as they had considered *Interview with the Vampire* and *The Vampire Lestat*.

The sequel to *The Queen of the Damned, The Tale of the Body Thief* is the fourth volume of the Vampire Chronicles. Referring to itself as a text in a manner commonly featured in the series, the narrator of the prologue to *The Tale of the Body Thief* announces, "This is a contemporary story. It's a volume in the Vampire Chronicles, make no mistake. But it is the first really modern volume, for it accepts the horrifying absurdity of existence from the start. . . ." Whereas the fictional authors of the second two volumes in the Vampire Chronicles write their stories in order to correct information written in previous volumes, Lestat, in *The Tale of the Body Thief*, says that he will elaborate and build on tales told in earlier volumes of the Vampire Chronicles.

The Tale of the Body Thief concerns Lestat's desire to be mortal. After failing a suicide attempt, he exchanges bodies with the mortal Raglan James, a con artist who trades his soul with others so that he can assume their bodies. James manipulates Lestat into exchanging bodies with him so that James may experience vampirism and Lestat may experience being human. However,

James escapes with Lestat's body with no intention of returning it. Lestat and David Talbot search for James, find him, and knock him out of Lestat's body. However, James later appears to Lestat in David's body and asks to be transformed into an immortal. *The Tale of the Body Thief* concerns Lestat's internal conflict over the evil deeds he must perform as a vampire. He sums up his moral dilemma: "My greatest sin has always been that I have a wonderful time being myself. My guilt is always there; my moral abhorrence for myself is always there; but I have a good time . . . you see that's the core of the dilemma for me—how can I enjoy being a vampire so much, how can I enjoy it if it's evil?" Lestat is pleased with his decision to turn David into a vampire and further celebrates his own vampire state, acknowledging that he had the "opportunity for salvation—and had said no."

Adhering to the structural organization of the first four volumes in the Vampire Chronicles, *Memnoch the Devil,* the fifth volume, begins with a prologue. It opens, "Lestat here. You know who I am? Then skip the next few paragraphs. For those whom I have not met before, I want this to be love at first sight." He entices readers to continue reading *Memnoch the Devil* and asks if they are familiar with the previous vampire stories. The first chapter opens with David approaching Lestat a year after the ending of *The Tale of the Body Thief,* when Lestat had turned David into a vampire. Lestat reveals to David his plan to choose Roger, a drug dealer and murderer, as his next victim. Representative of Lestat's goal to satisfy his physical need for blood without disrupting the "good" of the universe, he explains that he plans to wait to kill Roger until after Roger's daughter, Dora Flynn, has had the chance to tell her father goodbye. The central conflict the novel poses, a battle between good and evil, is foreshadowed in this early conversation, in which David questions whether it is morally acceptable to kill a man, even if he is a drug dealer and murderer. Lestat replies, "Think of the suffering in the world tonight. Think of those dying in Eastern Europe, think of the wars in the Holy Land, think of what's happening in this very city. You think God or the Devil gives a damn about one man?"

After Lestat kills Roger, Roger returns as a ghost and asks Lestat to protect Dora because his criminal past has threatened her safety. After a brief narrative digression, in which Roger tells his life story to Lestat, the central plot, which involves a struggle between Lestat and Memnoch the Devil, begins. Memnoch stalks Lestat to persuade him to become his prince and leads him on a tour of heaven, hell, and purgatory. Memnoch tries to convince Lestat to inspire souls in hell to repent so they can go to heaven, but Lestat flees from Memnoch because he is distressed after witnessing the suffering in hell. Along the way, Lestat is given the Veil of Veronica, a relic that he gives to Dora. Dora, who is an evangelist, proclaims the veil a miracle and uses it to teach Christianity. Memnoch sends Lestat a thank you note for helping to revive Christianity, a religion filled with a history of human bloodshed. Ironically, Lestat has unwittingly performed Memnoch's true wish to perpetuate evil. At the end of *Memnoch the Devil,* Lestat says that he has told all the stories he knows and requests that his life story be recast from fiction to legend.

In terms of the titles of the series in which Rice categorizes her novels, the Vampire Chronicles ends with *The Vampire Armand,* the sixth volume in the series. Unlike the earlier volumes, *The Vampire Armand* does not open with a prologue; however, like the earlier chronicles, it begins with an explanation of why it is being written. In the opening chapter, David Talbot persuades Armand to tell him his story so that he can write it down, and Armand agrees so that he may leave a legend for his children, Sybelle and Benjamin. Similar to the opening chapter that acts as a prologue but is not titled as such, the final chapter begins "This is no epilogue" yet serves as one in ways similar to the epilogues in some of Rice's earlier vampire novels. Armand says that he will write this final chapter in his own handwriting because he has left the manuscript with David. The epilogue explains Armand's epiphany, in which he questions Marius' philosophical beliefs. Armand reminds Marius that he once "championed the human soul, saying it had grown in depth and feeling . . ." However, Marius claims no longer to believe the ideals he once taught Armand. He says that he "was ignorant" and refused "to see the very horrors that surrounded me, all the worse in this century, this reasonable century, than ever before in the world." Debating Marius, Armand defines the Lord as "the symbol of all brothers" who advocate "simply love." Armand continues his definition of God: "He was human, whether He was God or not, and He was suffering and He was doing it for things He thought were purely and universally good." As Marius and Armand sit silently after their speeches, Lestat appears and joins Armand. The sudden appearance of Lestat creates a new plot twist that provides the suspense on which the next volume in the series builds.

The framed section of *The Vampire Armand* reveals Armand's story. The story begins with Armand's childhood, in sixteenth-century Italy, where he becomes Marius' protégé after he is kidnapped and sold into slavery. Together Marius and Armand prey only on those they perceive as evil. Their humanistic goals make them the target of a Satanist coven that Armand is forced to join. *The Vampire Armand* explores themes such as good versus evil, familiar subjects in Rice's earlier vampire novels.

After the publication of *The Vampire Armand*, Rice began a new vampire series, New Tales of the Vampire. The two volumes Rice categorizes as New Tales of the Vampire are published in a format that distinguishes them visually from the volumes in the Vampire Chronicles. Volumes in New Tales of the Vampire are slimmer in width and do not contain as many pages as those in the Vampire Chronicles. Although the series is marketed as beginning with *Pandora: New Tales of Vampires* (1998), according to theme and character, the first novel in the series is *Vittorio, the Vampire* (1999). *Pandora* continues the action of *The Vampire Armand,* developing a plot that overlaps with *The Vampire Armand.* As does Armand in *The Vampire Armand,* Pandora, the central character of *Pandora,* tells her story to David. She says that she will explain her mortal life, describe her love for Marius, and reveal how her relationship with him ended. Like the narrators of volumes in the Vampire Chronicles, Pandora directly refers to texts from the Vampire Chronicles and briefly summarizes events that occurred in earlier volumes. At the end of *Pandora,* Pandora announces that she will join Lestat, who lies on a chapel floor, a reunion that connects the book to *The Vampire Armand.*

Unlike *Pandora,* the first volume in the New Tales of the Vampire series, *Vittorio, the Vampire* does not intertwine with the Vampire Chronicles. Marketing strategies aside, thematically *Vittorio, the Vampire* is the first volume in the new series. While narrators of novels in Rice's Vampire Chronicles repeatedly refer to earlier volumes and acknowledge that the current narratives will continue earlier plots, the narrator of *Vittorio, the Vampire* establishes that his narrative will depart from patterns developed in the Vampire Chronicles. After stating outright, "I am a vampire," Vittorio reveals that he has been challenged to write his own story in book form so that it may randomly or through destiny be read by some of those who have read the other vampires' stories. Although he indirectly refers to the Vampire Chronicles, he immediately informs readers that this story will not intertwine with the stories told in that series. He says, "I know nothing of those heroes of macabre fact masquerading as fiction. I know nothing of their enticing paradise on the swamplands of Louisiana. You will find no new knowledge of them in these pages, not even, here-after, a mention." Instead of epilogues such as those that conclude the novels in Vampire Chronicles, *Vittorio, the Vampire* ends with a section entitled "Selected and Annotated Bibliography," in which Anne Rice, as author, claims that she personally received the manuscript from Vittorio while in Florence.

Although the plots of many of Rice's vampire novels may seem a bit contrived, one of the strengths of the novels is the characterization. Rice builds on earlier depictions of vampires such as Bram Stoker's *Dracula,* while also departing from those portrayals. Rice breaks the pattern of the traditional vampire as a beast who has no human characteristics, primarily by telling her stories from a vampire's point of view. The vampires identify with humans when they speak directly to readers in the prologues of many of the novels. Additionally, the vampires tend to persuade readers to support them in the conflict that will be told of in the narrative sections of the books. A good example of one way the vampires relate to readers occurs in the prologue of *Memnoch the Devil,* in which Lestat says, "We have souls, you and I. We want to know things; we share the same earth, rich and verdant and fraught with perils. We don't—either of us—know what it means to die, no matter what we might say to the contrary. It's a cinch that if we did, I wouldn't be writing and you wouldn't be reading this book." Rather than characterizing monstrous, evil creatures who mercilessly kill humans, Rice creates vampires with whom her readers can identify. In Ramsland's *Vampire Companion,* Rice explains her attempt to create vampires with complex human characteristics: "That is what interests me: the idea that these characters are tragic heroes and heroines, that they have a conscience. They have hearts, they have souls, they suffer loneliness, and they know what they're doing. They don't want to be doing it [killing], and yet it's their nature."

Indeed, Rice's vampires suffer human emotions such as grief, sorrow, anger, jealousy, and guilt. Perhaps most importantly, her vampires struggle with serious ethical concerns and seek answers to profound philosophical questions.

Rice's vampires also possess extraordinary, supernatural powers. In *Vampire Companion,* Ramsland divides Rice's portrayals of vampire powers into three categories: physical powers, mental powers, and emotional powers. Physically, the vampires possess magnificent strength, move at incredible speeds, and project their voices to high degrees and speak at levels so low that their voices can only be discerned by other vampires. In addition to their abilities to fly and jump, they can manipulate their bodies to produce extraordinary forms. They cry tears of blood. Although their wounds heal very quickly, they can be destroyed by fire and sunlight.

The mental powers of Rice's vampires include exaggerated perception, heightened degrees of pleasure and pain, mental telepathy, the ability to hear moral voices from long distances, and the capability to read the minds of others. With their acute vision and intense consciousness, they can read quickly, learn other languages easily, recreate sounds, and move objects with their minds.

Emotionally, vampires love members of both sexes and create stronger emotional bonds with other vampires than humans do with other humans. Because Rice's vampires do not consider incest taboo, interpersonal relationships are multifaceted: roles between mothers, sons, siblings, and companions become intertwined. Because, like their mental strengths, their emotional senses are intensified, Rice's vampires feel emotions more intensely than do humans. For example, they feel loneliness more extremely. They recognize and feel that they are "others" among humans and sometimes long to interact more emotionally with humans.

Although Rice's vampires struggle with the same ethical and philosophical questions that humans encounter, they tend to support or oppose either end of polarized arguments. Their sincere desires to seek truth create internal struggles concerning ethical conflicts. They become novice philosophers who question spiritual issues, usually in terms of clearly dichotomized categories such as good versus evil, heaven versus hell, or God versus Satan. Although their internal battles are revealed in terms of extreme polarities, the answers to their dilemmas are not always easily determined. Typical of philosophical pondering of Rice's vampires is the answer Lestat gives in *Memnoch the Devil* when Memnoch asks him why he drinks the blood from his victims: "I don't justify what I do or what I am. If you think I do, if that's why you want me to run Hell with you, or accuse God . . . then you picked the wrong person. I deserve to pay for what I've taken from people. Where are their souls, those I've slain? Were they ready for Heaven? Have they gone to Hell? Did those souls loosen in their identity and are they still in the whirlwind between Hell and Heaven? Souls are there, I know, I saw them, souls who have yet to find either place." A similar philosophical conclusion is drawn by Lestat in *The Queen of the Damned:* "We live in a world of accidents finally, in which only aesthetic principles have a consistency of which we can be sure. Right and wrong we will struggle with forever, striving to create and maintain an ethical balance; but the shimmer of summer rain under the street lamps or the great flashing glare of artillery against a sky—such brutal beauty is beyond dispute." *Interview with the Vampire* is filled with such philosophical musings, as reflected in Louis's comment: "[N]either heaven nor hell seemed more than a tormenting fancy. To know, to believe, in one or the other . . . that was perhaps the only salvation for which I could dream."

In addition both to building on and departing from classic portrayals of vampires, Rice frequently makes allusions to other forms of classical literature in her vampire novels. These allusions are bountiful but examples include: references to the mythological figure of the first woman from whom the vampire Pandora, who is also full of surprises, takes her name; the Dantesque tour of the underworld given to Lestat by Memnoch; overt references to Blake's poem "The Tyger" in *The Tale of the Body Thief;* and the Faustian dilemmas the vampires face throughout the Vampire Chronicles. Additionally, notions of good versus evil and sin versus virtue take on levels of spiritual inquiry posed both by Dante and Milton. References to classical literature add meaning to Rice's texts by allowing readers to build on familiar ideologies and to consider broader contexts for questions Rice raises. When portraying discussions about ethics and religion, Rice challenges traditional Christian beliefs and promotes a form of secular humanism that seeks to alleviate human suffering. Although such complex issues are conveyed in relation to superhuman beings, readers come to identify with the internal struggles of Rice's vampires. When vampires consider moral and philosophical issues and question their own codes of conduct, readers are inspired to do likewise.

CRITICS' REACTIONS

From the appearance of the first book in the Vampire Chronicles, *Interview with the Vampire,* Rice's vampire novels have received mixed reviews. However, all her novels have sold well and continue to achieve popular appeal as horror fiction as first established by *Interview with the Vampire.* Most of her novels have appeared on the *New York Times* best-seller list, where they have remained for long periods of time. Despite the mixed reviews, for the most part, individual reviewers either exclusively praise or condemn specific novels.

Critics who review Rice's vampire works favorably often note the fresh perspectives she offers to the genre. For example, Irma Heldman calls *Interview with the Vampire,* "Spellbinding, eerie, original in conception, and deserving of the popular attention it appears destined to receive;" Edmund Fuller notes, "It is hard to praise sufficiently the originality Miss Rice has brought to the age-old, ever-popular vampire tradition; it is undoubtedly the best thing in that vein since Bram Stoker, commanding peer status with *Dracula.*" Critics also praise Rice for her unique portrayal of the victim as protagonist and narrator, a technique that allows the stories to be told from the vampire's perspective. It also invites readers to view the world from a perspective that allows them to identify with what is traditionally considered a monster. Other critics praise the intellectual capacity and emotional power of Rice's vampires.

Unfavorable reviews of Rice's vampire and other Gothic novels often caustically criticize and sarcastically mock not only the novels but Rice personally, as author. Edith Milton, in her scathing review of *Interview with the Vampire* in *The New Republic,* concludes, "Unfortunately, the catastrophes which come to Anne Rice's mind in *Interview with the Vampire* are none of them quite as awful as the book itself." In her 1999 review of *Vittorio, the Vampire,* Andrea Higbie talks directly to Rice: "I may not have been born five centuries ago, but I wasn't born yesterday, and I know that Vittorio did not hand Rice this manuscript in Florence. . . . Anne, you can believe in the infernal ones all you wish, but here you and I must part ways, forever and always." Daniel Mendelsohn's review of *Servant of the Bones* begins, "Anne Rice's latest supernatural melodrama, *Servant of the Bones,* is dedicated to God, and if God has any commercial savvy whatsoever, He'll dedicate His next book to her."

Ironically, Rice's vampire novels are often praised for some of the same characteristics for which they are faulted. For example, Rice's verbosity is regarded as a strength by some yet a weakness by others. Michiko Kakutani, writing for the *New York Times,* says that *The Vampire Lestat* reveals Rice's use of "cliche ridden sentences" and her "penchant for repeating herself" and faults Rice for heavy-handed philosophizing and wordy prose: Lestat's character is "buried under heaps and heaps of wordy philosophizing about good and evil, heaven and hell, and even more wearisome meditations about the nature of Beauty and Truth." Pearl K. Bell flaws Rice for "all talk and no terror." Phoebe-Lou Adams says that Rice's vampires "could talk an adder to death". Contrary to Kakutani, Bell, and Adams, Jack Sullivan praises Rice's dialogue, noting that "enough of what [Lestat] says is fascinating to make Rice's vampire mythos . . . one of the more memorable horror sagas of recent years." Similarly, Nina Auerbach overlooks the loquaciousness of Rice's vampires because "even when they annoy us or tell us more than we want to know, [*The Vampire Lestat's*] undead characters are utterly alive."

One element of Rice's Vampire Chronicles that remains ignored by critics is the humor Rice often expresses in these works. Generally, the humor is created by characterizing vampires who have human attributes. Sometimes, Rice portrays supernatural beings with intricate details that would seem overly descriptive even for human characters. For example, in *Memnoch the Devil,* Lestat remarks that another vampire has carefully selected clothes for Lestat to wear. Looking at the clothes, he recalls that many times he and David have "been utterly entangled in the adventure of clothes." Realizing that he is wearing only one shoe, he notes that even vampires "have to worry about the latches on sandals." It is amusing for Lestat to be concerned with such unimportant details such as attire because he has recently experienced complex trials and tribulations that trivialize a decision about what outfit to wear. Much of Rice's humor involves the vampires' dialogue when they state in a literal sense clichéd expressions often used in common language. Examples include Lestat recalling in *Memnoch the Devil* that he heard the man he plans as his next victim say, "You know I sold my soul for places just like this." When Armand sensually bites Lestat in *The Vampire Lestat,* Lestat remarks, "He was draining me!" a comment with layered levels of humor because Lestat intends the phrase both literally and in the sense of the cliche, as Armand is both sucking his blood and exhausting him emotionally. In *Queen of the Damned,* Lestat passes an elderly homeless woman sitting on a bench at midnight, and she says, "When you're old you don't need sleep anymore," an axiom Lestat understands better than she does. While in the midst of stalking his next victim in *Memnoch the Devil,* Lestat tells David, "I'm being *stalked,*" never realizing himself the irony of his fear. Rice's vampires are unaware of the double entendres and puns created when their literal statements also assume cliched meanings used in everyday language.

WITCH NOVELS

In addition to a compendium of vampire novels, written as volumes for two series, Rice has written three novels known collectively as the Mayfair Trilogy: *The Witching Hour* (1990), *Lasher* (1993), and *Taltos: Lives of the Mayfair Witches* (1994). The Mayfair Trilogy provides a complex, interweaving story of the Mayfair dynasty, from the origin of the Mayfair family in Scotland to the present generation, who reside in the Garden District of New Orleans. The trilogy also portrays the Taltos clan and the Talamasca, a group of paranormal phenomena scholars with spiritual and religious beliefs who have studied both the Taltos and the Mayfairs for centuries. The Taltos are humanlike creatures who resided on Earth before humans. These creatures possess intense memory capabilities, which enable them to recall centuries of past history. They are also immune to many diseases that infect humans.

Because the Mayfair Trilogy involves thirteen generations of witches, keeping track of the many characters and their relationships to each other is somewhat difficult, but the legacy of the Mayfairs adds unity to the trilogy. As Rice says in Ramsland's *Witches' Companion,* "The Mayfair trilogy works as a whole. It is about the Mayfair family struggling through time to survive. The Mayfairs represent an ideal for me of a clan that stays together. These books contain very heartfelt ideas of mine about how we struggle for survival, how we fear other races, and how the more aggressive tribes wipe out the gentler ones. The question of earthbound souls and ancestor ghosts are central to my drama of birth, death, and rebirth."

The Witching Hour is set in a New Orleans mansion that belongs to the Mayfair family and its generations of witches. Dr. Rowan Mayfair, a thirteenth-generation witch, who was raised away from the Mayfairs, in San Francisco, must defend herself from Lasher, the epitome of evil. Lasher is a spirit who appears to the Mayfairs in the guise of a young man. The human protagonist of *The Witching Hour* is Michael Curry, who resides in San Francisco, where he restores Victorian houses. Although he is a wealthy man, he takes an interest in the lives of those who work for him. When Michael drowns, he is rescued by Rowan, who possesses mystical healing powers. Rowan's rescue of Michael grants him supernatural powers, and his friends abandon him because of his resulting mental delusions. After Michael falls in love with Rowan, she discovers that her family background involves a group of powerful witches. Michael's knowledge of what has enabled him to survive his awareness of horror is revealed in the book's epilogue: "And I suppose I do believe in the final analysis that a peace of mind can be obtained in the face of the worst horrors and the worst losses. It can be obtained by faith in change and in will and in accident; and by faith in ourselves, that we will do the right thing, more often than not, in the face of adversity."

Lasher, who first appears in *The Witching Hour,* is the protagonist of the second volume in the Mayfair Trilogy, *Lasher.* Here, pieces of Lasher's tissue are sent to doctors to test his genetic breakdown, and Lasher and Rowan have a child, Emaleth. Michael Curry's adventures from *The Witching Hour* are continued in *Lasher* as well. In *Lasher,* Michael pines for Rowan, while another sect of Mayfairs appears. Lasher imprisons Rowan so he can look for other Mayfairs to bear his children. Julien Mayfair warns Michael that Lasher poses danger to the clan. Michael eventually kills Lasher and is reunited with Rowan, who shoots Emaleth in order to annihilate the Taltos. After Charlotte's mother, Deborah, is executed for allegedly having sex with Satan, Lasher gives Charlotte an emerald, a gesture that symbolizes that she is Lasher's favorite witch.

The final volume in the Mayfair Trilogy, *Taltos,* centers on the giant Ashlar, who is introduced in *Lasher* as one of few survivors of the Taltos. Named as a partial anagram of Lasher, Ashlar is a doll maker who resides in New York. He goes to London to meet Yuri Stefano and to investigate alleged corruption in the Talamasca. Ashlar soon becomes involved with the Mayfair clan. The plot also continues Rowan's adventures, depicting her quest to avenge the death of Aaron Lightner, who has been killed by members of the Talamasca. After Michael and Rowan meet Yuri, Michael accepts his witch status. The central conflict between the Taltos and the Mayfairs ends when they finally make peace.

Like Rice's vampire novels, the volumes in the Mayfair Trilogy have received mixed reviews. Susan Isaacs says that Rice moves beyond simple plot to create myth, adding that she creates her mythological world with "consummate skill." Elizabeth Hand praises *Lasher* because Rice "makes what should be an unpalatable mess as wickedly irresistible as a Halloween stash of Baby Ruths." Other critics fault the Mayfair Trilogy for flaws similar to those pointed out in Rice's vampire novels. Patrick McGrath, reviewing *The Witching Hour,* says, "despite its tireless narrative energy, despite its relentless inventiveness, the book is bloated, grown to elephantine proportions because more is included than is needed." Dick Adler in a review of *Lasher* says that keeping up with all the Mayfair witches requires a "scorecard." Susan Ferraro says that "Ultimately, what creaks loudest [in *The Witching Hour*] is not the haunted house, but the plot."

HISTORICAL FICTION

Along with her novels that explore the lives of vampires and witches, Rice has written two novels that might be classified as historical fiction: *The Feast of All Saints* (1979) and *Cry to Heaven* (1982). *The Feast of All Saints* explores the plight of mulattoes in nineteenth-century Louisiana. The novel reveals the struggles Marcel and Marie, the children of Cecile, the black mistress of Ferronaire, a plantation owner, experience because of racism. For example, Marcel is denied an education and Marie is raped by white men. Rice uses irony to demonstrate oppression caused by hierarchical status based on color. For example, white men cannot even read the papers they demand to see from Marcel to prove he is not a slave.

Two major themes the novel explores, especially in the characterization of Marcel, are the search for cultural identity and the search for a father. After his travels in search of a sense of community and after his initial goals are not achieved, Marcel concludes, "Everything existed, perhaps, but the act of faith, and we were always in the midst of creating our world, complete with the trappings of tradition that was nothing more than an invention like the rest." He foregoes his pride in belonging to the white Ferronaire family and joins African Americans in New Orleans, where he celebrates his African American heritage.

While illustrating the struggles faced by mulattoes in *The Feast of All Saints,* Rice also addresses the exploitation of women. She challenges traditional roles for women in her characterization of Marie, who is expected to become a "kept woman" because of her beauty. However, Marie resists the role society gives her and instead desires to marry Richard Lermontant, a black man whom she loves. Through her lover's mother, Madame Suzette, Marie comes to realize that "[a] woman could have substance, simplicity, and vigor which all her life she had associated entirely with men." Marie eventually marries Richard and celebrates her black identity.

Like *The Feast of All Saints, Cry to Heaven* reveals social and political issues. *Cry to Heaven* explores the Italian castrati, famous male soprano singers castrated as boys so their voices would stay high. Tonio Treschi, the protagonist, is a Venetian heir whose brother has him abducted, castrated, and exiled from his home. Although he strives to become the best singer in Europe, he eventually concludes, "I am only a man. That is all I am. That is what I was born to be and what I've become no matter what was done to prevent it." However, his realization is a positive epiphany for him, for it shows progress toward his search for masculine identity. Rice alludes to the atrocities of both the physical and psychological cruelties of castrating children in the title of the novel, which illustrates "children mutilated to make a choir of seraphim, their song a cry to heaven that heaven did not hear."

THE ROQUELAURE AND RAMPLING NOVELS

In addition to the many novels Rice has written as Anne Rice, she has also written under the pseudonyms A. N. Roquelaure and Anne Rampling.

These novels are considered erotic novels, some of which have been referred to as sadomasochistic pornography and banned from libraries. Using the pseudonym A. N. Roquelaure, Rice wrote what is referred to as the Sleeping Beauty Trilogy: *The Claiming of Sleeping Beauty* (1983), *Beauty's Punishment* (1984), and *Beauty's Release: The Continued Erotic Adventures of Sleeping Beauty* (1985). As the titles suggest, the novels allude to the Sleeping Beauty fairy tale while graphically illustrating sex. *The Claiming of Sleeping Beauty* opens with Sleeping Beauty's awakening by the Prince, who carries her to his kingdom and presents her as a sex slave to royal men. Initially mortified because she becomes the object of men's pleasure, she eventually becomes sexually aggressive. She is sent to another village for disobeying the Prince, which opens the second novel in the trilogy, *Beauty's Punishment.* In this book, she is sold on an auction block to an innkeeper, where she experiences humiliations similar to those experienced when she first enters the Prince's chambers. *Beauty's Release* portrays Beauty, Tristan, and other slaves at Sultan Palace. Beauty discovers that her protégé, Innana, has been circumcised to prevent sexual pleasure. Nevertheless, Beauty and Inanna experience sexual pleasure together. After her rescue, Beauty returns home and becomes a princess. The novels in the Sleeping Beauty Trilogy defy plot; instead, they provide a series of situations in which people crave sexual gratification.

Similar to the Sleeping Beauty Trilogy, *Exit to Eden* (1985) and *Belinda* (1986), written under the pseudonym Anne Rampling, present erotic situations. These novels also defy plot, instead, unfolding boy-meets-girl situations in which sexual gratification is sought through the acting out of sexual fantasies. Although Rice's erotica has been criticized as portraying women as willing victims who satisfy men sexually at the expense of their own sexual pleasure and of their dignity, Rice states in a *Playboy* interview with Digby

Diehl that she does not portray women as "victims who have to be protected from everything." In a *People Weekly* interview with Joyce Wadler, she says of her erotic works, "I wrote about the fantasy that interested me personally and that I couldn't find in bookstores. I wanted to create a Disneyland of S & M. Most porno is written by hacks. I meant it to be erotic and nothing else—to turn people on. Sex is good. Nothing about sex is evil or to be ashamed of."

Rice's erotic novels appeared before the majority of her vampire novels were written and before any novels in the Mayfair Trilogy appeared. After publishing the first four volumes in the Vampire Chronicles, erotic fiction, historical fiction, and the Gothic novels *Servant of the Bones* (1996) and *Violin* (1997), Rice returned to what she is best known for: her portrayals of vampires. With the completion of the Vampire Chronicles and the beginning of New Tales of the Vampires, no doubt, Rice is continuing a fruitful career. However, recognized primarily as an author who writes popular genre fiction, she has received very little serious critical attention. Although she is grateful to her readers, she admits in a *Rolling Stone* interview with Mikal Gilmore, "If I lack any reader, if there's any audience I've failed to reach in America, it's the elite, literary audience. If there's been a failure to communicate, it's at the top—at the so-called top." Always outspoken, she speaks of having been scorned for writing bestsellers and for writing seriously about vampires. In the same interview, she says that part of the reason she is ignored critically is because current critical trends preferring "pedestrian realism of the 20th-century novel" have turned from those who write in the tradition of canonized American writers such as Hawthorne, Melville, Poe to "books about ordinary people and ordinary lives and ordinary events and little-bitty epiphanies . . ." Rice claims that the sort of books taken seriously by contemporary critics

are "simply garbage" and "not worth reading most of the time."

That the line between commercial fiction and serious fiction is blurred in the case of Rice's writings is demonstrated in Jennifer Smith's *Anne Rice: A Critical Companion,* a volume in Greenwood's Critical Companions to Popular Contemporary Writers. As the series title reveals, volumes chosen for interpretation are considered popular, commercial fiction; however, selection for interpretation also assumes that they are worthy of critical attention, which suggests they have crossed the line from popular to serious fiction. Smith offers overviews of Rice's novels and explicates them in terms of elements of literature such as theme, point of view, and structure. Also, Rice is the subject of a 1994 study in the Twayne United States authors series by Bette B. Roberts. While Roberts acknowledges that Rice is considered primarily a writer of popular fiction, she also observes, "Rice's best novels may also be analyzed on the more traditional assessments that guarantee a lasting reputation for a major writer: philosophical substance, stylistic richness, and most pertinent to Rice, impact on the chosen genre."

Similar to Roberts' assessment, other scholarly approaches to Rice's works examine her vampire books in terms of the impact they have had on the Gothic tradition. A 1996 collection of scholarly essays entitled *The Gothic World of Anne Rice,* edited by Gary Hoppenstand and Ray B. Browne, includes fifteen essays, most of which discuss one or more of Rice's novels in terms of ways they present the Gothic tradition. Kathryn McGinley's essay situates Rice's vampire novels in the literary vampire tradition by comparing Rice's characterization of vampires with those of Byron and Stoker. She addresses portrayals of the vampire myth in terms of philosophical subjects such as death, afterlife, and good versus evil. She also examines the ways various vampires express human emotions such as love and guilt, and looks at sensual experiences such as the sex act of vampires. Similarly, Edward J. Ingebretsen, in "Anne Rice: Raising Holy Hell, Harlequin Style," demonstrates Rice's unique contribution to the vampire tradition by analyzing *Interview with the Vampire* specifically as an "Americanized version" of the Gothic tradition. Although she does not refer to her novels as Gothic, in her interview with Gilmore, Rice reveals her motives for portraying what critics have labeled Gothic elements in her novels: "You can put the most horrible things into a frame, and you can go into that frame safely and talk about those things. You can go into the world of Louis and Lestat and Claudia and be able to talk about grief or loss or survival and then come back safely . . . I would find it much harder to write a realistic novel about my life. I would find it too raw. I just wouldn't be able to get the doors open, I wouldn't be able to go deep enough."

Other critics have examined the erotic element of Rice's Vampire Chronicles. Terri Liberman's "Eroticism as Moral Fulcrum in Rice's *Vampire Chronicles,*" published in *The Gothic World of Anne Rice,* suggests that eroticism in the novels "serves not merely to titillate but as a fulcrum for moral awareness. Through the choice of erotic object, Rice challenges moral taboos, suggesting that morality must be defined anew." Liberman sees the dichotomy between evil and good expressed in the novels as ambiguous, both relished and avoided by the vampires.

The Mayfair Trilogy is also beginning to receive some serious critical attention. For example, Frank A. Salamone, in an essay published in *The Gothic World of Anne Rice,* examines it in terms of anthropology, noting that Rice reveals the temperament of an anthropologist, who assumes that nothing is inherently unnatural. Rice also adheres to the anthropologist's belief that perceptions of "strange" practices, behaviors, or beliefs of another culture are due to our own culturally-biased perspectives. Salamone also argues

that Rice raises the key anthropological questions that concern nature versus nurture and that reveal family habits. Kay Kinsella Rout suggests that throughout the Mayfair Trilogy when situations arise in which ruthless, self-seeking victimizers exploit helpless victims Rice consistently cheers for the victims.

More recently, scholarly essays about Anne Rice's works have appeared in distinguished journals such as *Paradoxa, Journal of the Fantastic, Mosaic, The Kenyon Review, Novel,* and *Feminist Review.* In these journals, scholars examine elements of Rice's works such as Barbara Waxman's "Postexistentialism in the Neo-Gothic Mode: Anne Rice's *Interview with the Vampire,*" Jean Marigny's "The Different Faces of Eros in the Vampire Chronicles of Anne Rice," and George E. Haggerty's "Anne Rice and the Queering of Culture." Rice also is compared with other writers in essays presented in scholarly journals. For example, Maureen King, in "Contemporary Women Writers and the 'New Evil': The Vampires of Anne Rice and Suzy McKee Charnas," argues that both Rice and Charnas characterize vampires that challenge "binary oppositions— such as good/evil, human/alien, and masculine/ feminine—which underlie oppressive patriarchal structures." Even Rice's Sleeping Beauty trilogy, among her works with the least literary merit, has received a smidgen of serious scholarly attention. In "The Pervert's Progress: An Analysis of *Story of O* and the Beauty Trilogy," Amalia Ziv establishes the significance of female authorship in Pauline Réage's *Story of O* and Rice's Beauty Trilogy. Both works, "non-lesbian-identified erotic works," employ fantasy that is not confined by attempts to depict myths and customs that exemplify specific communities.

As the above critics testify, although Anne Rice is recognized primarily as a writer of popular novels, the line between commercial fiction and literary fiction is not always clear. Indeed, Rice continues to build her reputation as a serious writer. She has taken an age-old genre—horror fiction—and made it new. She is as devoted to her fans as they are to her, and she continues to add to the already prolific number of novels she has published. She understands the value of marketing her works as serialized novels as a strategy to entice readers to buy her next book. More importantly, beyond the marketing strategy of inviting loyal fans to buy her next book, her cliff-hanging endings and persuasive narrators might tempt them to read it as well.

Selected Bibliography

WORKS OF ANNE RICE

NOVELS

Interview with the Vampire. New York: Knopf, 1976.
The Feast of All Saints. New York: Simon & Schuster, 1979.
Cry to Heaven. New York: Knopf, 1982.
The Claiming of Sleeping Beauty. New York: Dutton, 1983. (Under the pseudonym A. N. Roquelaure.)
Beauty's Punishment. New York: Dutton, 1984. (Under the pseudonym A. N. Roquelaure.)
Beauty's Release: The Continued Erotic Adventures of Sleeping Beauty. New York: Dutton, 1985. (Under the pseudonym A. N. Roquelaure.)
Exit to Eden. New York: Morrow, 1985. (Under the pseudonym Anne Rampling.)
The Vampire Lestat. New York: Knopf, 1985.
Belinda. New York: Morrow, 1986. (Under the pseudonym Anne Rampling.)
The Queen of the Damned. New York: Knopf, 1988.
The Mummy or Ramses the Damned. New York: Ballantine, 1989.
The Witching Hour. New York: Ballantine, 1990.
The Tale of the Body Thief. New York: Ballantine, 1992.
Lasher. New York: Knopf, 1993.
Taltos. New York: Knopf, 1994.
Memnoch the Devil. New York: Knopf, 1995.
Servant of the Bones. New York: Knopf, 1996.
Violin. New York: Knopf, 1997.
The Vampire Armand. New York: Knopf, 1998.
Pandora: New Tales of the Vampires. New York: Knopf, 1998.
Vittorio, the Vampire. New York: Knopf, 1999.

CRITICAL AND BIOGRAPHICAL STUDIES

"Anne Rice." In *Contemporary Authors.* Vol. 65. Edited by Jane A. Bowden. Detroit: Gale, 1977. P. 486.
"Anne Rice." In *Contemporary Authors.* New Revision Series. Vol. 74. Edited by Scott Peacock. Detroit: Gale, 1999. Pp. 332–338.
Badley, Linda. *Writing Horror and the Body: The Fiction of Stephen King, Clive Barker, and Anne Rice.* Westport, Conn.: Greenwood Press, 1996.
Beahm, George, ed. *The Unauthorized Ann Rice Companion.* Kansas City, Mo.: Andrews and McMeel, 1996.
Cohen-Safir, Claude. "Perspectives Transgeneriques: Joanna Russ, Anne Rice, Ursula Le Guin." *Revue Francaise d Etudes Americaines* 15:33–46 (1990).
Dickinson, Joy. *Haunted City: An Unauthorized Guide to the Magical, Magnificent New Orleans of Anne Rice.* Secaucus, N.J.: Carol Publishing Group, 1995.
Doane, Janice, and Devon Hodges. "Undoing Feminism: From the Preoedipal to Postfeminism in Anne Rice's Vampire Chronicles." *American Literary History* 2:422–442 (1990).
Haas, Lynda, and Robert Hass. "Living with(out) Boundaries: The Novels of Anne Rice." In *A Dark Night's Dreaming: Contemporary American Horror Fiction.* Edited by Tony Magistrale and Michael A. Morrison. Columbia: University of South Carolina Press, 1996. Pp. 55–67.
Haggerty, George E. "Anne Rice and the Queering of Culture." *Novel* 32:5–17 (1998).
Hoppenstand, Gary, and Ray B. Browne, eds. *The Gothic World of Anne Rice.* Bowling Green, Ohio: Bowling Green State University Popular Press, 1996.
Johnson, Judith. "Women and Vampires: Nightmare or Utopia?" *Kenyon Review* 15:72–80 (1993).

King, Maureen. "Contemporary Women Writers and the 'New Evil': The Vampires of Anne Rice and Suzy McKee Charnas." *Journal-of-the-Fantastic-in-the-Arts* 5, no. 3:75–84 (1993).

Marcus, Jana. *In the Shadow of the Vampire: Reflections from the World of Anne Rice.* New York: Thunder's Mouth Press, 1997.

Marigny, Jean. "The Different Faces of Eros in the Vampire Chronicles of Anne Rice." *Para-Doxa* 1, no. 3:352–362 (1995).

Ramsland, Katherine. *Prism of the Night: A Biography of Anne Rice.* New York: Dutton, 1991.

———. *The Vampire Companion: The Official Guide to Anne Rice's The Vampire Chronicles.* New York: Ballantine, 1993.

———. *The Witches Companion: The Official Guide to Anne Rice's Lives of the Mayfair Witches.* New York: Ballantine, 1994.

———. *The Anne Rice Trivia Book.* New York: Ballantine, 1995.

———. *The Roquelaure Reader: A Companion to Anne Rice's Erotica.* New York: Plume, 1996.

Reed, Julia. "Haunted Houses." *Vogue,* November 1993, pp. 280–283.

Roberts, Bette B. *Anne Rice.* New York: Twayne, 1994.

Rout, Kay Kinsella. "The Least of These: Exploitation in Anne Rice's Mayfair Trilogy." *Journal of American Culture* 19, no. 4:87–93 (1996).

Smith, Jennifer. *Anne Rice: A Critical Companion.* Westport, Conn.: Greenwood Press, 1996.

Tsagaris, Ellen M. " 'Men Must Be Manly and Women Womanly': Influences of Woolf's *Orlando* on Anne Rice's *The Witching Hour.*" In *Virginia Woolf: Emerging Perspectives.* Edited by Mark Hussey and Vara Neverow. New York: Pace University Press, 1994. Pp. 178–182.

Waxman, Barbara. "Postexistentialism in the Neo-Gothic Mode: Anne Rice's *Interview with the Vampire.*" *Mosaic* 25, no. 3:79–97 (1992).

Ziv, Amalia. "The Pervert's Progress: An Analysis of *Story of O* and the Beauty Trilogy." *Feminist Review* 46:61–75 (1994).

SELECTED REVIEWS

Adams, Phoebe-Lou. Review of *Interview with the Vampire. Atlantic Monthly,* June 1976, p. 105.

Adler, Dick. "Warlocks, Gore, and Purple Prose: Anne Rice Does It Again." Review of *Lasher. Chicago Tribune,* October 17, 1995, sec. 14, p. 3.

Auerbach, Nina. "No. 2 With a Silver Bullet." Review of *The Vampire Lestat. New York Times Book Review,* October 27, 1985, p. 15.

Bell, Pearl K. "A Gemeinschaft of Vampires." Review of *Interview with the Vampire. New Leader,* June 7, 1976, p. 15.

Fuller, Edmund. Review of *Interview with the Vampire. Wall Street Journal,* June 17, 1976, p. 14.

Hand, Elizabeth. "The Demon Seed." Review of *Lasher. Washington Post Book World,* October 10, 1993, p. 4.

Heldman, Irma. "The Fangs Have It." *Village Voice,* May 10, 1976, p. 50.

Higbie, Andrea. Review of *Vittorio, the Vampire. New York Times Book Review,* March 28, 1999, p. 28.

Isaacs, Susan. "Bewitched and Bewildered." Review of *The Witching Hour. Washington Post Book World,* October 28, 1990, p. 1.

Kakutani, Michiko. "Vampire of Our Times." Review of *The Vampire Lestat. New York Times,* October 19, 1985, p. 15.

McGrath, Patrick. "Ghastly and Unnatural Ambitions." Review of *The Witching Hour. New York Times Book Review,* November 4, 1990, p. 11.

Mendelsohn, Daniel. "All This and Heaven Too." Review of *Servant of the Bones. New York Times Book Review,* August 11, 1996, pp. 5–6.

Milton, Edith. Review of *Interview with the Vampire. New Republic,* May 8, 1976, p. 29.

Sullivan, Jack. "Fangs for the Memories." *The Washington Post Book World,* December 1, 1985, pp. 1, 7.

INTERVIEWS

Diehl, Digby. "Anne Rice Interview." *Playboy,* March 1993, pp. 53–64.

Ferraro, Susan. "Novels You Can Sink Your Teeth Into." *New York Times Magazine,* October 14, 1990, pp. 27–28, 67, 74–77.

Gilmore, Mikal. "The Devil and Anne Rice." *Rolling Stone,* July 13, 1995, pp. 92–103.

Preston, John. "Anne Rice: The Fire from the Heavens . . . That's What Makes Us Different from

Other People." *Interview,* December 1990, pp. 126–129.

Ramsland, Katherine. "Interview with the Vampire Writer." *Psychology Today,* November 1989, p. 34.

Riley, Michael. *Conversations with Anne Rice.* New York: Ballantine, 1996.

Summer, Bob. "*PW* Interviews Anne Rice." *Publisher's Weekly,* October 28, 1988, pp. 59–60.

Virgits, Ronnie. "An Interview with Anne Rice: The New Orleans Experience." *New Orleans Magazine,* June 1991, pp. 48–50.

Wadler, Joyce. "Anne Rice's Imagination May Roam Among Vampires and Erotica, But Her Heart Is Right at Home." *People Weekly,* December 5, 1988, pp. 131–134.

FILMS BASED ON THE WORKS OF ANNE RICE

Exit to Eden. Screenplay by Anne Rice, Deborah Anelon, and Bob Brunner. Directed by Garry Marshall. Savoy Pictures, 1994.

Interview with the Vampire. Screenplay by Anne Rice. Directed by Neil Jordan. Geffen Pictures, 1994.

—LAURIE CHAMPION

Carol Shields

1935–

CAROL SHIELDS, A dual citizen of Canada and the United States, is the first fiction writer to win the top literary awards of both countries: the Canadian Governor General's Award and the American Pulitzer Prize. In an interview with Donna Hollenberg in *Contemporary Literature,* Shields says she feels "fortunate to have a foot on each side of the border." In fact, her two nationalities have shaped her career in ways neither could do alone. Canada, where she has lived all her adult life, gave her the nurturing environment of a small country that celebrates and supports its artists. American citizenship made her eligible for the Pulitzer that gave her access to the most powerful international publicity. The extraordinary string of prizes collected by her 1993 novel *The Stone Diaries* transformed Carol Shields from a respected Canadian writer to an international literary figure.

Shields was born Carol Warner in the Chicago suburb of Oak Park, Illinois, on June 2, 1935. She grew up, with her brother and sister, twins a year and a half older than she, in the kind of environment she depicts in her novels: white, middle class, safe, self-contained. Her father, Robert, she told Eleanor Wachtel in an interview, "disappeared downtown every day to work," where he managed a candy factory. Her mother, Inez, the daughter of Swedish immigrants, was a fourth-grade teacher who stopped teaching, as women

of her generation were required to do, when she had children, but went back after the Second World War when there was a teacher shortage. The family lived in "a big old white stucco house" built in about 1910. They attended the Methodist Church and frequented the public library. Although they lived just fourteen blocks from the Chicago city line, Carol knew no one who lived in the city and almost never went there except on an annual trip to the Art Institute with the Girl Scouts, of which her mother was the leader.

Shields told Wachtel she "was always involved with language" and remembers learning to read, around age four, as "the central mystical experience of my life." She loved fairy tales for a time and enjoyed the Dick and Jane stories, about which she has written a poem. She read the few late nineteenth- and early twentieth-century children's books on her parents' shelves, such as her father's Horatio Alger books and four books from her mother's childhood: Lucy Maud Montgomery's *Anne of Green Gables,* Gene Stratton Porter's *A Girl of the Limberlost,* John Habberton's *Helen's Babies,* and Margaret Marshall Saunders *Beautiful Joe.* In an essay entitled "Thinking Back Through Our Mothers: Traditions in Canadian Women's Writing," Shields asks what her mother and other girls of her generation might have seen in these books and finds that they not only echo established tradition but subtly interrogate it.

In a written interview with Joan Thomas, Shields assesses what Oak Park in the 1940s and 1950s meant.

> Everyone went to church—well there was one family who admitted to being atheists, but I never quite believed this could be; it seemed too preposterous. . . . Before I went away to college I had never spoken to a black or Asian person, never tasted garlic, and had never heard the word 'shit' uttered aloud. On the other hand, I knew how to write a thank-you note, which occasions demanded hat and gloves, and how to conduct polite introductions.

Although "this society . . . appears seamless and banal," however, Shields continues:

> there were hundreds of disruptions in its surface, signs that I seem almost deliberately to have suppressed, persuaded as I was that Oak Parkishness represented a desirable reality, perhaps the only reality. The father of one of my friends was America's leading Lincoln scholar, but I didn't know it then. Another friend lived with her mother on welfare, but this was, somehow, never acknowledged or made clear. A neighbour fell into a depression and jumped in front of a train, but I—ten years old— was told he had a heart attack on his way to work and "fell" off the platform. A local clergyman made inappropriate gestures towards teenage girls in his congregation. All these anomalies, and many more, failed somehow to enter the record I was assembling.

A similar tension between actual and acknowledged experience marks Shields's development as a writer. Even in elementary school, she was writing—"little ditties, class plays." In high school she wrote sonnets. While her parents and teachers encouraged her, she was also absorbing and fulfilling the contradictory assumption that she couldn't be a writer, because as she wrote in the Thomas interview,

> Writers were like movie stars. Writers were men. Hemingway grew up in Oak Park, but aside from

him I suspected that suburbia did not produce writers. My real life, as I saw it, was entirely predictable: I would get married, have children and live in a house much like the one I grew up in. Along the way I would acquire a university education so that I would have 'something to fall back on,' should any part of the plan fail. I have to say I was quite happy with this future; in fact, I was enchanted by it.

In interviews, Shields frequently borrows Annie Dillard's idea that "childhood is a long waking up" and describes herself as taking an exceptionally long time to wake up. One way of looking at Shields's progress toward becoming a writer is as a long period of waking and dozing. Another is as a dance of doing and denying. Although she told Eleanor Wachtel that she concentrated in college, at Hanover, a small Presbyterian-related college in Hanover, Indiana, on "falling in love and going to dances" and that the poems she wrote for a Canadian Broadcasting Corporation (CBC) competition when she was twenty-nine were the first she had written "since those sonnets in high school," her Hanover classmate Kent Thompson, who later became editor of the Canadian literary magazine *The Fiddlehead* and published some of Shields's early work, remembers that she won a prize judged by Randall Jarrell for a poem she had contributed to the college literary magazine and observes that it already revealed her interest in biography, as it was one of a series of poetic portraits of famous people.

The defining experience of Shields's college education was her junior year abroad at Exeter University in England. There she encountered intellectual fervor and personal independence: "We were on our own in England," she told Eleanor Wachtel. "To go to lectures or not. People took their subjects seriously. This was all a revelation to me, I couldn't believe it, that people would sit in the dining hall and talk about Christopher Marlowe, it was wonderful, I loved it once I caught on to it." There she also met Donald Shields, a graduate student in engineering from Saskatchewan. She was so unconscious of herself as a writer that they were engaged before he ever learned, from her mother, that she wrote. She "sort of forgot" about writing while caught up in courtship: "I was just interested in being in love and having a house, the whole *Ladies Home Journal* thing."

Immediately after she graduated from Hanover, in 1957, Shields and Don married and moved to Canada, to Vancouver briefly and then to Toronto. The first of their five children, John, was born the following year. After their second child, Anne, was born, in 1959, her husband suggested she take a magazine writing course at the University of Toronto. The first piece of writing Shields sold was a story that the teacher of the course sent to the CBC without her knowledge.

Shields dates her definitive awakening to the period from 1960 to 1963 that the family spent in England while Don worked on his Ph.D. at Manchester University. There she read, listened to the BBC, started going to films, traveled on the continent, and discovered *The Guardian,* a left-leaning newspaper that "opened the world" to her. She told Eleanor Wachtel, it "had this wonderful women's page, for example. I was reading about what women were really doing and thinking about. It wasn't what we were doing and thinking about in Canada at all." In Manchester, Shields also had a third child, Catherine, born in 1962, and back in Canada, while she was thinking about what she would do next, she had a fourth, Margaret, in 1964. She told Eleanor Wachtel that she continued reading, joined a "Great Books" discussion group, and fell into the circumstances that revealed to her what she wanted to write. (She also wrote some "highly conventional stories" she later told Harvey De Roo, and a never published novel that she mentions in "Giving your literary papers away.") A book review sent her to the poetry of Philip Larkin. "I was amazed. I loved it. I'd read Eliot and Pound and so on in university, and modern poetry had disappointed me, but I thought, 'Good heavens, this man is

being honest . . . I'm going to write some poetry.' " She worked all spring on seven short poems and sent them off the day before the deadline to a CBC Young Writers competition, which she won. She remembers "Robert Weaver phoning and saying: 'We're really pleased because none of us has every heard of you.' " Those seven poems, provoked by accident, set Shields on a five-year period of writing poetry and a lifetime of writing. Yet she was still only dimly aware of the literary world she was entering. She sent all the poems she wrote to *The Canadian Forum,* a politically progressive general magazine she subscribed to, until the poetry editor finally said, "Look, I just can't keep publishing these, can't you send them somewhere else?" She did not know anywhere else, so he gave her a list of little magazines.

Shields's process of coming to consciousness as a writer parallels the process she and other women of her time were going through of coming to consciousness as women. On the way home from England on the boat in 1963, Shields read Betty Friedan's newly published analysis of middle-class white women's lives, *The Feminine Mystique,* which touched off the women's movement of the 1960s and 1970s. *The Feminine Mystique* identified the equation of femininity and domesticity as a myth that kept women from self-fulfillment. It argued that the only way women could find fulfillment was through creative work of their own, which was not, contrary to the myth, incompatible with marriage. Reading Betty Friedan "made an enormous difference" Shields told Eleanor Wachtel; "everything she said seemed right." Throughout her career, Shields has integrated art and domesticity, in the subjects of poems, the lives of fictional characters, and her own practice. She never considered family life an impediment to writing. In fact, she told Joan Thomas, "I do not think I would have become a writer if I hadn't had children. . . . Having children woke me up, in a sense. I knew I had to pay attention. I *wanted* to pay attention." As her children were growing up, her typewriter shared a room with the sewing machine, used more and more by her growing daughters. Now her daughters are among her first readers, and she has collaborated with Anne on a story and with Catherine on a play.

POETRY

The seven poems Shields submitted to the CBC Young Writers competition are included in her first book, *Others,* published in 1972, which was followed by another collection of poems, *Intersect: Poems,* in 1974. These early poems come directly from the experiences of family life. They portray her children ("John," "Anne at the Symphony"), relatives and acquaintances ("Our Old Aunt Who Is Now in a Retirement Home," "A Physicist We Know"), and the seasons of family life ("The New Mothers," "A Wife, Forty-five, Remembers Love"). As the titles of the two collections suggest, they are concerned with the separateness and intersections of individual lives. Many of them look at marriage, the primary or secondary focus of so much of Shields's fiction. Their form is as self-contained as their world. Like Cartier-Bresson's photographs, they snap portraits at telling moments. They are pulled tight by startlingly apt metaphors, unconventional line breaks that call attention to metaphor and rhyme, and suspense held until a final word throws the whole into perspective. "A Physicist We Know" makes "terrier / leaps of speculation / on the quiet." "Our Old Aunt Who Is Now in a Retirement Home" lies "stewed / in authentic age." "Anne at the Symphony" listens "like someone submitting / to surgery." In their brevity, economy, and irony, these poems recall not only Philip Larkin, but Emily Dickinson, who is invoked in a four-line poem in *Intersect.* The voice of these poems is as reticent as that of the traditional wife and mother, who focuses on "others," takes her identity from membership in the family—"our" relative, someone "we" know—and protects the family's privacy.

The domestic subjects and the relentless reaffirmation of a collective experience and perspective define a snug, even smug, familial world. Yet over and over the poems pierce the complacency of the world they seem to create. The speaker of "An Old Lady We Saw" rages on behalf of a woman who has fallen and broken her hip, and whom a world evoked by needlepoint and oatmeal has taught not to rage but to think of others:

> She should have cursed
> the deceitful ice, the murderous cold,
> not to mention our thinly gathered
> concern, our clockwork sympathy.
> Instead her needlepoint mouth moved, blue
> against the oatmeal snow,
> saying the wrong thing, the worst
> thing, thank you, thank you

"John" denies the sufficiency of its own family context:

> My young son
> eating his lunch, heard a plane go
> overhead, and put down his spoon
> remarking: the pilot doesn't know
>
> I'm eating an egg. He seemed shocked,
> just as if he'd never known
> nor suspected he was locked
> in, from the beginning, alone.

The surprise of this deceptively simple poem is not just the child's sudden self-consciousness, but the mother-speaker's assumption of her child's detachment. The formal artistry of these poems, at first veiled by their colloquial rhythms, serves not only to wrap them tight, but also to undermine conventional expectations and reveal the darkness under conventional social relations. The stanza break in mid-sentence in "John" emphasizes the moment of self-consciousness and isolates the progressive rhyme from *know* to *known* to *alone* that links selfhood and isolation. The oddly short first line of the third (first quoted) stanza of "An Old Lady We Saw" underscores the connection between *cursed* and *worst* and the irony that the polite response is worse than the proscribed.

A few autobiographical poems in *Intersect* anticipate *Coming to Canada: Poems,* published nearly twenty years later, in 1992. This sequence of scenes from Shields' childhood—from "Getting Born" to "Coming to Canada—Age Twenty-Two"—develops the theme of coming to consciousness, or adulthood. In "I/Myself," the poet's recreation of a moment of childhood self-consciousness is also a moment of adult self-consciousness:

but there I was, three
years old, swinging on the gate
thinking (theatrical even then)
here I am, three years old
swinging on the gate.

Many of the poems conclude with a revelation of chaos beneath the calm: In a grandfather's otherwise mundane diary of weather and expenditures, the one-word entry "woe." Beneath Aunt Violet's Rinso-lady look, "the pinkness of her rage." In "When Grandma Died—1942," the speaker discovers that chaos in herself:

When no one was looking I touched
her mouth—which had not
turned to dust
It was hard and cold
like pressing in the side
of a rubber ball

Later I would look at my hand
and think: a part
of me has touched dead lips.
I would grow rich with disgust
and a little awed
by my hardness of heart

I tried to pretend
it was a gesture of love but
it wasn't. It was a test,
one of the first, one of the easiest,
something I had to do.

Coming to Canada was reissued in 1995 in an edition in which the title sequence is followed by selections from the first two books and a group of new poems. While the early poems and those dealing with early childhood capture illuminating moments, the last few poems in the "Coming to Canada" sequence and many of the new poems gather experience and perception over time. In "Coming to Canada—Age Twenty-Two," the fading of a postcard marks time backward to "Aunt Violet's Canadian honeymoon / 1932" and forward to the time, unspecified, when the postcard's address to visitors, "COME BACK SOON"

. . . changed to
here and now and home
the place I came to
the place I was from.

Identity develops in Shields's earliest poems through "Coming to Canada" from an attribute of others to an examination of self and from something perceived in a moment of illumination to something accrued over time.

Some of the new poems in *Coming to Canada* record the next stage, as the layers built up over time chip and fade down to the essential core—as the family house is sold ("Now that the house is officially listed / we like it less") and the older generation dies off. The continuity of Shields's vision is illustrated in the poems about Aunt Violet that appear in each sequence and repeatedly expose a life beneath the life. Finally, in "Aunt Violet's Things," a fluttery valentine falling out of a book is a

Niggling parody
of that truer heart

infinitely more fragile
shy, misshapen and spent,
beating in its own rough cage
merely to keep time.

Aunt Violet is a constant reminder of the unknowability of the most ordinary and familiar of human lives. Read in the order presented, the poems in this inclusive edition of *Coming to Canada* trace the stages of human life. Read in the order of composition, they constitute a poetic autobiography and a distillation of the themes and techniques of Shields's writing in all genres.

EARLY NOVELS

Shields's first four novels are domestic comedies about marriage and art, the two anchors of her own life. When she began writing fiction, she repeatedly tells interviewers, she wanted to write the books she and her friends wanted to read, but could not find in the early 1970s, books about women like themselves, who had children, friends, work, and a habit of reflection. The characters in Shields's early novels lead lives devoid of dramatic event. They do not fall in love or betray their spouses; they do not lose their homes or their children; they do not commit or fall victim to or solve crimes. Instead, they have supper with their families and coffee with their friends, go to conferences and parties, get the flu, do their work. Trauma—marital separation, the loss of children—happens to other people. Their own conflicts are those of ordinary people who have been "fairly lucky," as Brenda Bowman of *A Fairly Conventional Woman* (1982) puts it, in their marriages, children, and careers: conflicts between who they think they are and who they want to be. These conflicts take place inside the head and get worked out, for the moment of the narrative, without confrontation or articulation. At one point, Brenda thinks of telling a temporary friend

she has met at a convention about the time when her love for her husband Jack lapsed and months later was suddenly restored. But she decides against it because "it seemed a betrayal to pronounce aloud what had been resolved in silence." Later she does tell him. These novels, like Brenda's disclosure, tell stories that take place in the silences between people.

Three of the four main characters in Shields' first four novels are writers, and they all reflect on writing. The exception, Brenda Bowman, is a quilter; hers is the story of a woman's discovery that she is an artist. Shields works out her principles of fiction most directly in her first novel, *Small Ceremonies* (1976), which makes use of the material "left over" from her master's thesis on the novels of the mid-nineteenth-century Canadian writer Susanna Moodie. The Shields family moved to Ottawa, and their fifth child, Sara, was born, in 1968. In 1969, Shields began a master's degree program in Canadian literature at the University of Ottawa (where her husband's position on the faculty gave her free tuition). At this time, she was working for the New Democratic Party (NDP) during elections, and in 1971 she became a Canadian Citizen in order to vote.

In the period when Shields was working on her M.A., which she completed in 1975, "Canadian literature," as distinguished from "literature that happened to be written in Canada," was just being defined as a discipline (much as African-American literature was being defined in the same period in the United States). Scholars of Canadian literature were caught up in the two quests articulated in the first paragraph of Margaret Atwood's now-classic, and controversial, entry into this discussion, *Survival: A Thematic Guide to Canadian Literature* (1972): to identify Canadian "classics" and to define "what's Canadian about Canadian literature." Shields chose as a thesis subject a writer who had been recognized as a founder of Canadian literature, but resisted the question of her subject's "Canadianness." Instead of the more or less autobiographical miscellanies about life in Canada, *Roughing It in the Bush* and *Life in the Clearings,* that had won Mrs. Moodie a place in the emerging Canadian canon, Shields focused on the pot-boilers with English settings that she wrote to support her family.

In the introduction and conclusion to the published version of her thesis, *Susanna Moodie: Voice and Vision* (1977), Shields takes issue with Margaret Atwood and others who have "reduced" Mrs. Moodie to a type, however mythic, "of the anguished immigrant who embodied the alienation and neuroses of the whole nation;" she represents her instead as an artist struggling to make sense of her position between "two continents, two cultures, two political philosophies." Shields sees in Moodie's novels three themes: "the complexity and variability of human personality"; "the oppositions and interaction of male and female roles"; and "a debate about the nature of society." Despite her personal interest in politics, social issues are notably absent from Shields's fiction. But the first two themes she ascribes to Susanna Moodie also focus her own writing. In fact, Shields identifies Moodie's "overriding concern" in exactly the same terms as she speaks of her own: "the power and mystery of personality."

The mystery of personality ties together the two main concerns of *Small Ceremonies* (1976): family relations and the nature of fiction. Judith Gill, who is writing a biography of Susanna Moodie, has the same problem as a wife and mother that she has as a biographer, understanding character. As a biographer, she keeps looking for, but never finds, definitive evidence of the reason Susanna changed from "a rather priggish, faintly blue-stockinged but ardent young girl into a heavy, conventional, distressed, perpetually disapproving and sorrowing woman." The defining moment "seems to be unrecorded, lodged perhaps in the years between her books, or else—and this seems more likely—wilfully suppressed, deliberately withheld." Judith's difficulty reading Su-

sanna Moodie parallels her difficulty reading the other members of her family. What is behind her sixteen-year-old daughter's exasperated silences? What do her twelve-year-old son, Richard, and Anita Spalding, the daughter of the family whose flat they rented in Birmingham, whom he has never met, write about in the air letters they exchange every week? What is her husband Martin, associate professor of English and Milton specialist, doing with a drawerful of yarn? When she tries to ask him, the question comes out, "Are you happy?" (a question that surfaces again in Shields's subsequent novels). She does not know that either, and he does not answer. Judith completes her manuscript without feeling that she has quite got her subject, and the family tensions are resolved without the fundamental questions getting answered.

Judith's interactions with two other writers develop a discussion of the relation between fiction and "real life." While frustrated at the inability of the real-life evidence she depends on to reveal personality, Judith is also critical of her friend Furlong Eberhardt for writing mythic prairie novels removed from his own or anyone else's real experience. Furlong in turn advises Judith that her subject's self-concealing poses probably "pinpoint her true self" better than "buckets and buckets of personal revelations." Situated between Judith and Furlong is John Spalding, the owner of the flat the Gills rented in Birmingham, who appears at the end of the novel as a novelist. Blocked and bored in Birmingham, Judith read the unpublished novels Spalding left on a bookshelf, in a biographer's effort to figure out the man who wrote them. Now Spalding, having finally had a novel published, comes to Canada and visits his former tenants, partly to warn them that his new novel is about them; it is based on their situation as North Americans abroad, the traces they have left behind in his apartment, and the letters Richard has written to his daughter, who unlike Richard has not kept the letters she received secret but read them aloud to the family. While Judith has attempted to create biography from fiction, Spalding has created fiction from the sort of evidence accepted for biography. As Spalding turns out to be nothing like the man Judith has constructed from the evidence of the apartment and the self-pitying plots of his abandoned novels, she concludes that her family will probably not recognize themselves in Spalding's book: "our family situation seen through the eyes of pre-adolescent Richard and translated into his awkward letter-writing prose, then crossing cultures and read by a child we have never seen, to a family we have never met, then mixed with the neurotic creative juices of John Spalding and filtered through a publisher—surely by the time it reaches print, the least dram of truth will be drained away." It is a measure of Shields's wit that none of these fictional writers fully represents her own practice, which is to invert from observed life, but not from the lives of the people she knows.

Small Ceremonies has little plot. It traces instead the seasons of life and the rhythmic forces that push people apart and pull them back together again. Its chapters follow the nine months of the academic year from September to May, during which time Judith develops her biography of Susanna Moodie from notecards to manuscript; her husband Martin turns the mysterious yarn in his desk drawer into a pictorial analysis of the themes of *Paradise Lost,* which is recognized as both scholarship by his colleagues and art by collectors and museums; and their friends Roger and Ruthie have a baby. Each of these acts of creation contributes to a reconciliation. The baby brings Roger and Ruthie, who have split up in January, back together. Completing her biography, incomplete as she feels her grasp of Susanna Moodie is, heals a rift between Judith and Furlong. Martin's success with a project Judith has not understood removes the barrier of a subject they have avoided since September. These connections between artistic creation and per-

sonal relationships emphasize the continuity between life and art that the ordinariness of the characters and the absence of dramatic incident proclaim. "What I can't understand," Martin says, speaking of John Spalding's novel, "is how you could find material for a novel out of our rather ordinary domestic situation." This is exactly what Shields's novel itself does. The "small ceremonies" of the title are the ways people mark the seasons of ongoing life: the Gills' habit of high tea on Sunday, brought back from their year in England; the annual English Department dinner; Roger and Ruthie's wedding. The ending is rescued from the patness of its simultaneous reconciliations by the sense that they are temporary and contingent. Roger and Ruthie's wedding, in the Gills' suburban backyard, concludes with a reference to the ongoing strains of married life—an exchanged look of resignation, the baby's five o'clock cry. "Everything will be fine," Judith wants to tell them, but nothing is final.

When *Small Ceremonies* was accepted for publication the week Shields turned forty, she knew, she told Eleanor Wachtel, that she was "going to be a novelist all my life." The same week, her supervisors told her they would publish her thesis on Susanna Moodie and the family left for a sabbatical year in France. A day or two after they arrived, she began *The Box Garden* (1977), making use again of bits of her own life and material left over from previous writing, this time Judith Gill's briefly mentioned sister Charleen Forrest in Vancouver. Charleen, divorced mother of fifteen-year-old Seth, lives a shrunken life on the salary from a part-time job editing a botany journal (a job Shields based on her own experience editing *Canadian Slavonic Papers* part time as a graduate student). Although she has published four volumes of poetry, she has written little lately. She feels she was robbed of courage in childhood by her judgmental, penny-pinching, perpetually aggrieved mother. *The Box Garden* picks up the theme implicit in the structure of *Small Ceremonies,* that things and people change. The title image, a box of growing grass that the mysterious author of an article rejected by the journal has sent her, reinforces the idea; what this Whitman-esque anti-scientist likes about grass "is the way it adapts to any condition," its "almost human resilience." In the course of the novel, in which Charleen and Eugene, the nice orthodontist she cannot quite commit to, travel from Vancouver to Scarborough, Ontario, for her mother's wedding, Charleen changes enough to stand up to her mother, Mrs. McNinn, and choose her own happiness with Eugene, and the occasion for the trip shows, even if her behavior does not, that Mrs. McNinn, who has clung to all the English-Canadian Protestant prejudices as to her pennies, has changed enough to marry a man who is not only an asthmatic cancer-victim smoker, but also a French-Canadian ex-priest.

The Box Garden shows where Shields's strengths do and do not lie. She told Eleanor Wachtel she had taken her editor's observation that "there was not much happening" in *Small Ceremonies* as "a set of instructions [to] make something happen" in her next book and put into *The Box Garden* a clumsy kidnaping plot that intrudes on the interior story of Charleen's rebirth as an adult. What brings the novel alive is the satiric yet sympathetic portrait of Charleen's mother, who obsessively redecorated their cramped bungalow throughout Charleen's childhood, and then, inexplicably, stopped. This portrait of a woman whose talent for twisting compliments into insults ("Mrs. Mallory said she admired my new slipcovers. Imagine that, she *admired* them. She couldn't just say she *liked* them, no, she *admired* them. I do not know what gives her the right to be so high and mighty. I've seen *her* slipcovers,") equals her talent for transforming velvet and brocade remnants into tassels and draping—and has the same effect of strangling her family—is comic to the point of caricature. Yet the par-

allels between Charleen, lapsed poet of "minutiae" and "surfaces," and her mother, former obsessive redecorator of the surfaces of her house, help the reader to see Mrs. McNinn as another artist, handicapped by limited resources, trying to make a world through which to define herself. She is the first of Shields's eccentric artists, a group that grows to include Mary Swann from *Swann* and Cuyler Goodwill from *The Stone Diaries,* and an example of her talent for layering together, as Margaret Atwood put it in a tribute to Shields twenty years later, "hilarious surfaces" and "ominous depths."

In 1977 *The Box Garden* was published, *Small Ceremonies* won the Canadian Authors' Award for best novel of 1976, and Shields began a twenty-year part-time career teaching creative writing—the first year, 1977–1978, at the University of Ottawa, the following year at the University of British Columbia, as the family had moved to Vancouver, and from 1980, when they moved to Winnipeg, at the University of Manitoba, where she taught literature as well. The reviews of *Small Ceremonies* had been uniformly good; those of *The Box Garden* were mixed. Shields took to heart the minority of reviews that called her novels "women's books" and was particularly irritated by one reviewer who, she told Marjorie Anderson, "always damned me with faint praise, thinking I would be a fine writer if I ever found a subject worthy of my abilities. . . . meaning he thought I should stop writing about women in domestic situations, I suppose." She responded with *Happenstance,* written in Vancouver and published in 1980, which puts a man in a domestic situation; historian Jack Bowman holds the fort at home in Elm Park in suburban Chicago for five days while his wife Brenda, a quilter, is off in Philadelphia attending a crafts convention. When she finished *Happenstance,* Shields embarked on the novel that later became *Swann,* but got stuck, put it aside, and started a novel to answer readers' questions about what happened to Jack's wife while she was away, which was published as *A Fairly Conventional Woman* in 1982.

When *Happenstance* and *A Fairly Conventional Woman* were published in Britain in 1991 and the United States in 1994, they were bound together, back to back and upside down to each other, as *The Husband's Story* and *The Wife's Story* in a single volume entitled *Happenstance*. This format, which Shields told Linda Burgess "was the way it should have been done in the first place," reveals the formal and thematic play between the two stories. The counterpoint between Jack's story and Brenda's dramatizes the idea with which Shields began Jack's—that men and women are more alike than different though they use different language—and offers a narrative example of the interplay of perspectives that has fascinated Shields since her first published poetry. In these novels, Shields also shifts to a third-person point of view, which emphasizes the limits of each character's perspective and situates the narrator in a position consistent with Shields's own sense of herself a spectator, a posture she feels she shares with Jack. She told Marjorie Anderson: "Jack's basic life posture is one of watching rather than doing; he is someone who always stands slightly outside of events. This is how I have always felt. I had to write that book to know that." With Brenda, Shields shares the experience of discovering herself as an artist. The fact that both husband and wife reflect aspects of Shields herself, and that in the course of the double novel each partner takes a few steps into the other's mental world, underlines what men and women have in common.

The stories reverse common gender roles and bring husband and wife to similar understandings of their work and their marriage that they never express to each other. Jack, who at the beginning of his story is pontificating to his friend and fellow historian Bernie that "History consists of endings," spends the rest of the week coping with domestic crises—from his daughter Laurie's conviction that her Home Ec teacher will kill her if he does not find time to get her the pattern and material Brenda forgot to pick up last week before his ten o'clock meeting with the institute director about Chapter Six of his book, to the collapse of Bernie's marriage, a neighbor's suicide attempt, and his secretary's confession (fortunately on the eve of her departure for Tucson) that she has sexual fantasies about him. Brenda, whose story starts with her preparing breakfast for the family before leaving for the airport, enters the public and professional world of a hotel convention, where she luxuriates in room service, gets drunk, and contemplates an affair—none of which she has ever done before. Back in Elm Park, the personal crises of his friends mirror Jack's loss of faith in the book he has been laboring over for too long. Seeing an ad for a forthcoming book on exactly his topic, by an old grad school flame no less, sinks him into despair, and he spends the week persuading others—Bernie, the director, his parents—to give him permission to abandon it. In Philadelphia, by contrast, recognition for herself and her art—her quilt, *The Second Coming,* wins honorable mention in the exhibit—gives Brenda the confidence to speculate on the meaning of what she does, as Jack continually speculates on history. "What sets quilting apart from other crafts," she hears herself saying in the quilting seminar, "is the built-in shiver of history." Later, when a boozing reporter stuck covering the crafts convention gets her drunk, she goes further: "Art poses a moral question; craft responds to that question and in a sense provides the enabling energy society requires." Although she recognizes "the shiver of history" as Jack's phrase and when sober tries to disown "all that pompous junk about art posing questions," this new-found self-reflexivity represents the culminating step—following on her turning the guestroom into a workroom and deciding she *can* leave the family to go to the convention—in

Brenda's self-recognition as an artist. Her foray into Jack's world, professional and speculative, brings her into her own.

Back in Elm Park, Jack also does new things, the strangest of which is to walk ten miles home from "the Loop" in a snowstorm. "Why?" his daughter accuses. "You never did it before." He cannot tell her that he was walking off a farewell lunch at which both the wine and the departing secretary's declaration of love have gone to his head, so he says, "Maybe that's why I did it. . . . Just because I'd never done it before." Like Brenda's statement about art and her attempt to retract it, both these reasons are true. As Brenda's moment of drunkenness brings her into Jack's world of speculation, Jack's brings him into Brenda's world of practical realities, through "the whole harsh, seedy nexus of city blocks and masonry and traffic." In the course of his story, Jack's view of Brenda's quilting and of history changes. At first he sees her quilting as "bringing hundreds of separate parts together to form a predetermined pattern . . . not so different from his own research on Indian trading practices. (She had smiled at this analogy—what an ass he was at times!)." At the end, he looks into her workroom and is bewildered by her quilt-in-progress. "This was a simple—no, not simple—a strange and complex explosion of light," a "whirlpool . . . laid down in cipher." He recognizes the stitching as what Brenda has told him is called the meander stitch. "But meander seemed the wrong word for it, for this stitching was purposeful and relentless, suggesting something contradictory and ironic that interested him." His view of history has undergone a parallel but less conscious change. "History is not the mere unrolling of a story," he has told Bernie on page one. "It's the end of the story." His own unrolling of the grid of streets from the Loop to Elm Park and a couple of reminders of the unreliability of the written record (his journalist neighbor's suicide attempt is being explained as an accident, the absence of his column as a vacation) bring him closer to accepting that history is as indeterminate as the design of Brenda's unfinished quilt. The night before Brenda comes home Jack discovers that the advertised book is no reason to abandon his own, but we the reader does not learn whether he carries on with his book or not, only that "he had lost faith; but had undergone a gradual and incomprehensible mending of spirit. It could happen again, he saw. And again." The "piercing apprehension" Brenda achieves, as she strides off to her newspaper interview, of what she might have been or might still become" is more optimistic than Jack's mending of spirit, but still uncertain. At the ends of the stories, both Jack and Brenda think of telling the other their inner experiences, but Jack thinks Brenda "wouldn't know what his question meant" and Brenda thinks Jack, like his father, wants reassurance not revelations. They settle for expressions of love that both know are simultaneously insufficient and enough.

Brenda's quilting is a metaphor not only for Shields's narrative theory, as Jack's observation of the unfinished quilt makes clear, but also for her narrative art in this double novel. Shields has spoken of her pleasure in fitting the two stories together, "like a game." They are composed of common elements: a drunken aberration, a defining city walk, a friend's lost child and failed marriage, a rush of love for someone other than the spouse, an unfinished work, and many more. As Isobel Armstrong observes in an acute review, "each story is made to act as figure and ground to the other." Yet they read not as pieced patterns but as domestic realism. The common, even conventional, narrative elements are so individually imagined and so variously combined that their effect is that of a generously told story welling up irrepressibly from family life, as Brenda's quilt designs come from "some interior reservoir." Brenda's situation as a quilter also captures Shields's as a novelist at the moment of composing Brenda's story. The quilt Brenda enters in the exhibit reflects her development from the domestic representation of her early quilts "to something more abstract;" it is "experimental in workmanship" but "less risky for an exhibition" than "the unfinished quilt—that was how she thought of it, *The Unfinished Quilt*"—which is experimental in design as well. *Happenstance* is Shields's *Second Coming,* a narratively complex realization of her established pattern of domestic comedy published while a structurally experimental novel, *Swann,* waits at home unfinished. Brenda's self-representation in the newspaper interview may also be a wry parody of Shields's own interview persona of a writer who got started by accident, with a push from others, and created her first works easily from leftover scraps. "The worst part," Brenda laments when she reads the write-up in the paper, "is that dumb 'presto' stuck in the middle. Did I really say presto? I probably did."

SWANN AND OTHER LITERARY EXPERIMENTS

When she finished *A Fairly Conventional Woman,* Shields returned to *Swann,* but again ran into difficulties. She decided, she told Harvey De Roo, "to rescue myself by spending a year experimenting with different narrative approaches." In fact, the next ten years can be viewed as a period of continual literary experiment. All of Shields's fiction is experimental in the sense that she is always posing herself a new narrative problem. In the 1980s, however, she pushed not only her own narrative experience but also the conventional bounds of literary genre and authorship. She published two collections of highly varied, often odd, short stories; completed *Swann,* whose five chapters consist of four nearly freestanding but interlocked character biographies and a screenplay; began to write short, distinctly theatrical

plays; and collaborated with a friend on an epistolary novel. When Harvey De Roo asked, "What dictates your choice of form?" Shields shot back, "The question of form! I am, to tell you the truth, more indifferent to the boundaries between literary forms than your question indicates."

The stories she wrote during that year off are collected in *Various Miracles,* published in 1985; in them, she tries out memoir, word games, pathos, fantasy, and metafiction. Although some stories are realistic ("Fragility," "Sailors Lost at Sea," the autobiographical "Scenes"), more turn on irony, coincidence, word play, and the surreality of the everyday; and many are about language and writing. A professor proves that metaphor is dead in a lecture composed entirely of metaphor. A man falls in love with the woman he imagines is the subject of the enigmatic sign in the window of an orthopedic shoe store proclaiming "WENDY IS BACK!" A second collection, *The Orange Fish,* published in 1989, is similar in subject matter, but less varied in range. As Shields moved back from the first-person point of view in her first two novels to a third-person limited perspective in *Happenstance,* she moves back again in most of these stories to an omniscient narrative perspective. She wanted to try "the old storyteller's voice," she told Eleanor Wachtel, a voice that calls attention to the fictionality of stories. Two of the more substantial stories in the *Various Miracles* illustrate the range of what she does with it.

The story "Various Miracles," is a series of vignettes that recount increasingly complex and abstract coincidences. Seven women in line at a lingerie sale in Palo Alto, California, are all named Emily. Four strangers on the back seat of the Number 10 bus in Cincinnati, Ohio, are each reading a paperback copy of John Le Carre's *Smiley's People.* A husband and wife in Morocco have the same dream, except that the husband finds it threatening, the wife liberating. "Twin" parrots, sold in Marseilles twenty-two years earlier, die on the same day in Exeter, England, and River Forest, Illinois. A small watercolor of a bridge falls off a wall in Billings, Montana, and at the same moment, a French leather-goods merchant, who painted the picture at age twelve from a postcard sent by his remote father, finds himself on "a small stone bridge not far from Tournus" and feels he has been there before, though he does not connect the feeling with the postcard or his watercolor copy.

Finally, in a Borgesian piece of metafiction, a Cuban-born novelist on the way to her Toronto publisher has the revised manuscript of her new novel torn from her hands by a gust of wind while she waits for a bus at the corner of College and Spadina. All the pages are retrieved but one, the "keystone page," which has "blown around the corner of College Street into the open doorway of a fresh-fruit and vegetable stand where a young woman in a red coat [is] buying a kilo of zucchini." The young woman picks up the page and reads "*A woman in a red coat is standing in a grocery store buying a kilo of zucchini. . . .*" The editor, who has told the novelist that her first draft "relied too heavily on the artifice of coincidence," now asserts that the novel "stands up without the missing page. Sometimes it's better to let things be strange and to represent nothing but themselves." The coincidences in this story illuminate and bridge various physical and conceptual divides—between continents, between male and female perspectives, between representation and reality, between the world in the story and the story in the world. The narration, too, as Simone Vauthier observes in the journal *Prairie Fire,* negotiates between opposites—between discontinuity (each vignette is unrelated to the others) and continuity (each is dated, each depends on coincidence, they progress in development and complexity) and between the common— richly developed in such details as the lingerie sale, the bus number, and the well-known Toronto street corner—and the uncommon, the coinci-

dence. The omniscient perspective also negotiates between the whole truth and the fraction, or distortion, of it that any person grasps. In her interview with Harvey De Roo, Shields explains the idea of "miracle" in these stories as a "transcendental moment . . . in which we are able to glimpse a kind of pattern in the universe." The woman in the red coat buying zucchini who picks up a wind-blown page from a novel describing herself experiences such a moment.

A different kind of miracle is revealed in "Mrs. Turner Cutting the Grass," which won the Canadian National Magazine Award in 1985. This story juxtaposes the life story of Mrs. Turner, a Winnipeg widow who cuts her grass in "an ancient pair of shorts" and "Gord's old golf cap," with the judgments of her eco-conscious neighbors, who wonder why she does not use a grass catcher, since "everyone knows that leaving the clippings like that is bad for the lawn," the high-school girls who walk by her house and wonder why she does not take the trouble to hide her cellulite, and a professor-poet from a Massachusetts college in her tour group of Japan, who makes his reputation with a comic poem that casts her as the apotheosis of the vulgar tourist. The miracle here is Mrs. Turner's self-survival in the face of hard circumstances and the judgment of others. She has not blamed the married farmer for getting her "into hot water" in Boissevain, Manitoba, or her father for driving her away from home, or Kiki, the black man who took her in when she fled to New York, for leaving her a few months after the baby came; and now that she has a house, a modest income, and the memory of a good husband, she enjoys herself and "cannot imagine that anyone would wish her harm." The story uses the language of her judges and of Mrs. Turner herself to put the reader into their perspectives and then, from the omniscient narrator's pinnacle, transcends them. The last line of the story echoes the first, which represents the schoolgirls' and neighbors' point of view—"Oh, what a sight is Mrs. Turner cutting her grass"—and then transforms the meaning of "sight" from "spectacle" to "vision" by adding, "and how, like an ornament, she shines."

While writing the stories in *Various Miracles* and *The Orange Fish* Shields was also experimenting with drama. In 1983, she won first prize in a CBC competition for a radio play entitled "Women Waiting." *Departures and Arrivals* was workshopped in 1983 and produced in 1984, though not published until 1990. A one-act version of *Anniversary,* co-written with Dave Williamson was produced in 1986, although the full-length version was first produced in 1996 and published in 1998. Drama is another way of exercising an omniscient perspective, experimenting with voices, and portraying randomness, shifting perspectives, and the power and failure of language. *Departures and Arrivals,* a series of vignettes that take place in an airport, develops the fly-on-the-wall perspective Shields had already used in party and convention scenes in *Small Ceremonies, The Box Garden,* and Brenda's story in *Happenstance.* Instead of the random remarks overheard in these scenes, the play offers random encounters that slip into absurdity. A couple who have been divorced for eight years run into each other and improvise a way for him to look once again at the backs of her knees. A family keeps retaking its reunion until it satisfies Hollywood expectations. The conversation between two women who meet at the flight insurance booth after seeing their husbands off on business trips slides from mutual reassurance, to contingency plans, to freedom fantasies, to visions of the men they might meet in their new lives. In both narrative fiction and drama, Shields was looking, as she told Harvey De Roo, for "ways of providing . . . tension that avoid the old, artificial rhythms of convergence, catastrophe and reconciliation."

In *Swann,* the novel she put aside twice and finally published in 1987, Shields works the nar-

rative forms she had been trying out and also her longstanding interest in the unreliability of the written record and the erasure of the lives of women into a kind of postmodern literary sampler. The novel centers on the life and work of Mary Swann, an impoverished Ontario farm wife who delivered a bagful of Dickinsonian poems to the editor of a small press (called the Peregrine Press) in Kingston in 1965 and went home to be murdered and dismembered by her husband that same night. Nearly two decades later, having been resurrected by a young feminist critic who found her posthumously published book of poems in a Wisconsin cottage, Mary Swann is about to be the subject of an academic symposium.

The first Canadian edition of *Swann* included the subtitle *A Mystery,* dropped in the American and later editions (and probably responsible for its being considered for the Arthur Ellis Award for Best Canadian Mystery, which it won in 1988). The novel contains three mysteries: First and least, in a parody of the conventional mystery plot, who is stealing the few remaining copies of Swann's book and the scanty documents of her life? (This germ for the story comes from the fact that when Shields was working on her thesis some of the Susanna Moodie materials had been stolen from the University of Western Ontario archives.) Second, is Mary Swann real? Within the terms of the story, she clearly existed and wrote poems, but are these the poems she wrote and are they any good? And third, the related questions that drive all of Shields's novels, "the mystery of personality. How do you know anyone? How does art come out of common clay?" The first four chapters of the novel focus in turn on the four individuals responsible for "creating" Mary Swann: Sarah Maloney, 28, the feminist critic; Morton Jimroy, 50, famous biographer of Ezra Pound, John Starman, and now Mary Swann; Rose Hindmarch, 51, town clerk and librarian of Nadeau, Ontario, curator of the Nadeau Local History Museum, founder of the Mary Swann

Memorial Room therein, and the only person, apart from Swann's daughter, known to have ever spoken to Mary Swann; and Frederic Cruzzi, 80, European intellectual, retired editor of the *Kingston Banner,* and, with his late wife Hildë, publisher of Mary Swann's poems in a stapled pamphlet infelicitously titled *Swann's Songs.*

Sarah's story is a first-person narrative full of self-conscious references to the personae she presents to others, especially through her letters (one-draft and typed to friends, two-draft and handwritten to others). Jimroy's is told in the third person from his own completely self-absorbed point of view. Rose's and Cruzzi's mix perspectives. We see Rose from her own point of view (Rose's loss of faith "caus[ed] her not an ounce of pain and scarcely, for that matter a trace of nostalgia. Only the nuisance of remembering to keep it to herself," as well as from a distance as though pointed out by the voice- over in a juvenile documentary ("Here comes Rose now, a shortish woman with round shoulders and the small swelling roundness of a potbelly, which she is planning to work on this fall,"). Cruzzi is developed through a variety of textual forms, including his correspondence with dear friends and annoying petitioners, "His (Unwritten) One-Sentence Autobiography," and similarly "unwritten" or "untranscribed" accounts of the history of the Peregrine Press and the events of "the fifteenth of December, 1965," the day of Mary Swann's visit and death; these accounts are titled as though from the first person, but written in the third. Each narrative presents multiple personae, through correspondence and other forms of self-representation, and portraits of each character are embedded in the narratives of the others, as they have all met and/or corresponded with each other. The text also includes fragments of Swann's poems, whose various interpretations by the characters serve both to characterize the interpreters and to satirize literary critical discourse. Rose remembers Jimroy explaining to her that the poem that

begins "Blood pronounces my name" is " 'a pretty direct reference to the sacrament of holy communion. Or perhaps, and this is my point, perhaps to a more elemental sort of blood covenant, the eating of the Godhead, that sort of thing.' Rose said nothing. . . . She was unable to utter the word menstruation. She would have died first."

Each character not only interprets but constructs Mary Swann according to his or her own needs and perpetrates some form of theft or fraud to preserve that construction. Sarah, who is struggling with the tension between her professional and female identities, wants to think that Swann invented modern poetry out of her own female experience and thus throws Swann's rhyming dictionary, given to her by Rose (to whom it does not occur to put textual material in the Mary Swann Memorial Room, which she has set up as a domestic environment) in a roadside litter bin. Jimroy, who, abandoned by his wife, takes refuge in his role in literary tradition, can not bear to think of Swann as outside that tradition and so insists, *"It is highly probable that Swann read Jane Austen during this period because . . ."* despite the fact that the only author he has evidence that she read is Edna Ferber. Rose, who thinks her only distinction is her tenuous association with Mary Swann and wants the Mary Swann Memorial Room to reflect well on her, has discarded most of the meager contents of the Swann house and bought pretty antiques to furnish the room supposed to represent Swann's material circumstances. But the greatest deception is Frederic Cruzzi's. Out of their mutual desire to mend injury to the other, he and his wife have reconstructed Swann's poems from the bits that remained legible after Hildë wrapped fish guts in the bag she thought contained scrap paper. "They puzzled and conferred over every blot, then guessed, then invented." The first line of the blood poem Jimroy interprets—was it "Blood pronounces my name," or "renounces"? In each subsequent line they have chosen one verb over another equally possible "because—though they didn't say so—they liked it better." These thefts not only parallel, but outweigh, the theft of Swann's poems, and even her murder, because they call into question what literature is and how it comes to be.

The final chapter brings the four characters together in the screenplay of a film called *The Swann Symposium,* in which the apparent collegiality with which the scholars have prepared for the symposium breaks down into academic posturing and self-interest, the theft of the Swann materials is discovered, and the identity of the thief is revealed. The narratives of the individual characters have balanced on the wire between textual artifice and psychological realism. In this last section, Shields separates out the components of the balance. The symposium is a parody (whether hilarious or obvious, critics disagree) of academic discourse and detective novel conventions. The parody resolves into poignancy in the last scene as, having lost all copies of the poems, the symposium participants draw together, "subtly transformed," to reconstruct the poems from memory, or create them from need, beginning with one called "Lost Things," which speaks personally to each of the four main characters as well as to the life of Mary Swann and the question of the sources of art.

Reviews of *Swann* and Shields's other experimental works respond to a perceived contradiction between the realist and postmodern directions of her work. Positive reviews focus on her wit and narrative innovation; negative ones find the characters thin or ordinary. Maggie Helwig in *The Canadian Forum* disparages Shields's early novels as "really women's-magazine fiction with a bit of extra intelligence" and praises *Swann* as "daring" yet accessible. Josh Rubins in the *New York Times Book Review* finds the *Swann* characters "one-dimensional . . . to the point of caricature." Norman Sigurdson praises *Swann,* where

"the little peculiarities of our daily existence . . . provide a convincing backdrop to a strong narrative instead of being obtrusively front and centre as they were in the other novels." Chris Johnson, director of the first full production of *Departures and Arrivals* for the University of Manitoba's Black Hole Theatre in 1984, concludes an appreciative discussion of the wit and economy of Shields's plays with the reservation that, "I'm not convinced that Shields always comes to terms with the idea that the characters in her plays, as opposed to the characters in her novels, will eventually be inhabited by living, breathing, creative human beings, actors. The result is sometimes awkwardnesses. . . . sometimes stasis. . . . sometimes scenes . . . thinner than they need be."

The farcical elements of the last section of *Swann* and the collective creation of the poem at the very end point to two distinctive aspects of Shields's art: her willingness to play and her impulse to share authorship. Reviewers have frequently invoked television comedy in both positive and negative characterizations of Shields's dramatic works. Her plays are deliberately light; *Anniversary,* the Playwrights' Note says, is "particularly suitable for summer theatre and dinner theatre." Her willingness to entertain is related to her desire to include in her plays people who have been left out of conventional drama, the well-adjusted middle-class that forms the base of the theatre audience, and particularly ordinary women. She wrote *Thirteen Hands: A Play in Two Acts,* she told Val Ross, to valorize the lives of women who are disparaged as "the blue rinse set," but who, in the safety of the bridge club, form communities of women that pass on traditions and transform values. Theatre people said it would not work as a play because it lacked conflict; they "suggested one of the women should quarrel with another. . . . For me, the central conflict was how these women are regarded." According to Chris Johnson, the 1993 premiere attracted a large contingent of bridge-players, and the pleasure of women in the audience seemed to arise from "a recognition of emotions, situations, womanly communication and social custom not commonly seen on stage."

Shields's impulse to inclusiveness in the subjects of her plays and her representation of collective authorship at the end of *Swann* extends to actual collaboration, with her friend Dave Williamson on *Anniversary,* her daughter Anne on the story "Words" in *Various Miracles,* her daughter Catherine on the play *Fashion, Power, Guilt and the Charity of Families,* and her friend Blanche Howard on *A Celibate Season.* Comprised of the letters a husband and wife write to each other while she is away from their North Vancouver home on a one-year job in Ottawa, this playful novel, which Shields was working on throughout the writing of *Swann* and the stories in *Various Miracles* and *The Orange Fish,* extends the premise of *Happenstance* and derives from the actual correspondence of the two authors. It is another example of the integration of Shields's domestic life and her art. Shields has also submitted to the more common and riskier collaboration of having a novel adapted to film. A British and Canadian co-production of *Swann,* with, in Shields's words (in an interview with Linda Rosborough), "major shifts in emphasis," was released in Canada in 1996.

NOVELS OF THE NINETIES

What Shields told Harvey De Roo about how she develops a novel applies to her *oeuvre* as well: "I write it over and over, and each time it gets longer, thicker." Shields's best known novels are longer, thicker tellings of stories she has been working on, and working out, throughout her career. Their characters are more fully realized, their worlds denser, their narrative and symbolic structures more complex, but they are the same

stories, approached from new angles, recombined, and filled up with fresh and fully integrated supplies of personal history and everyday detail.

The Republic of Love (1992), is a romance and, like *Thirteen Hands,* a defiant effort to write a story that does not fit contemporary conventions: "It's possible to speak ironically about romance," Fay McLeod thinks in the flush of her new love for Tom Avery, "but no adult with any sense talks about love's richness and transcendence, that it actually happens, that it's happening right now, in the last years of our long, hard, lean, bitter, and promiscuous century." The novel opens with a hint that it will also be a revision of Jane Austen as Peter Knightly, the decent fellow Fay wakes up realizing she does not love anymore, has the same surname as the man Austen's Emma finally discovers she does love. Like the prospective lovers in any Jane Austen novel, Fay and Tom live in the same village. It is called Winnipeg and it has a population of six hundred thousand, but its networks of family, friends, and alliances through marriage are as tight as, though different from, any in an Austen village. Fay and Tom meet in their roles as godfather and aunt to boys at the same birthday party. They are connected before they meet by the fact that Tom's first wife, Sheila, subsequently married Sammy Sweet, who later married Fritzi, Peter Knightly's ex-wife. As in any Austen novel, these connections provide a colorful and instructive variety of approaches to marriage. Unlike that of Austen characters, however, the difficulty Fay and Tom face is not in recognizing that they are in love—each falls in love at first sight—but in coping with life alone before love and then in adjusting their separate selves to life together. After they have been living together for several months, and shortly before their planned wedding, Fay backs out and Tom makes no move to change her mind.

This separation of an established couple—married in the sense that they love each other, live together, and, by announcing a wedding, have made a public commitment difficult to undo— turns Fay and Tom's romance into a version of a story Shields returns to again and again: the couple who separate, in an endless range of ways and emotional registers, and come back together again. For Fay and Tom do, of course, reunite, marry (their impromptu wedding in the court-house a sign that the real marriage has already taken place), and make the small adjustments that allow them to live happily, for some years any-way, thereafter. Shields's permutations of this story of separation and reunion include *Happen-stance* and *A Celibate Season* and the story of the Moroccan couple in "Various Miracles," whose dream reveals the husband's fear of and the wife's desire for permanent separation, but who wake up and go on. They also include the play *Anniversary,* in which a separating couple who pretend to be together for the benefit of old friends who drop in on their property division end up convincing themselves to stay together; and the stories of Larry and Dorrie in *Larry's Party* and of two other couples in *The Republic of Love*—Fay's parents, Richard and Peggy Mc-Leod, whose separation immediately after their fortieth anniversary is the catalyst for Fay and Tom's, and Peter Knightly and Fritzi Knightly Sweet, who after Sammy Sweet dies and Peter and Fay split up, remarry each other. This "cycle of rupture and reconciliation," as Fay realizes, not transcendent love, is the real character of ro-mance.

In all these stories, Shields probes the bonds and barriers between people through the details with which the stories are so packed. *The Repub-lic of Love* is told in chapters that alternate be-tween Tom's and Fay's viewpoints and build both their relationship and the discussion of love from all the social and material facts of everyday life. The problem of the novel is the perennial prob-lem of love, balance between selfhood and con-nection to others. Their history, routines, and so-cial interactions portray Tom as "a lost soul,

loveless," "attached to no one," and Fay as so enmeshed in a web of connection as "daughter, sister, girlfriend," that her identity "can quickly drain away when brought face to face with some-one else's identity." Fay sees her parents a couple of times a week, meets her sister for dinner on Wednesdays and her father for breakfast at Mr. Donut's on Saturdays, baby-sits her nephews, and is planning her parents' fortieth anniversary party. Tom never had a father; his mother lives up in Duck River; his connections in Winnipeg are three ex-wives; he jogs alone on Saturday mornings; and his regular social event is the Newly Single Club at the Fort Rouge Community Center.

Tom and Fay's work reflects their psychic selves. Tom's job as a late-night talk-show host creating a simulated community among lonely in-somniacs reflects the desire for connection that has led him to marry too hastily three times. Fay's research on the folklore mermaids is a projection of the fear of invasion that makes her flee when the wedding looms: "This, Fay decides . . . is the mer-condition: solitary longing that is always be-ing thwarted. No, not thwarted—denied." When they do find a balance together, Tom gets moved to the driving-home show on the radio, and Fay finally has enough distance on mermaids to finish her book. What makes both the pattern and the particulars of the repeated stories interesting is their relationship. In this, Shields's stories are like Fay's mermaids, which in their common fea-tures and enormous variation embody both com-mon and individual contours of the psyche, and like romance itself, the eternal quest for the union of opposites.

In *The Stone Diaries* (1993), and *Larry's Party* (1997), Shields lengthens and thickens her stories to the scope of a lived life. *The Stone Diaries* confronts the mystery of personality head on. It traces the life of Daisy Goodwill Flett, who is born in Tyndall, Manitoba, in 1905, to a mother who dies in childbirth without having realized she was pregnant; is raised by a neighbor, Clarentine Flett, who takes Daisy with her to Winnipeg when she abandons her husband; is taken to Bloomington, Indiana, at age eleven by her father, Cuyler Goodwill, a stone cutter who metamorphoses into a stone carver and then an American entrepreneur; is married at twenty-two and widowed on her honeymoon when her drunken husband falls out of a hotel window in France; is married again at thirty-one to Barker Flett, Clarentine Flett's son, twenty-three years her senior, in Ottawa; is occupied, when the reader glimpses her in 1947, with mothering three children; is subsequently widowed, and engaged to take on her husband's newspaper gardening column—which she writes from 1955 to 1964, when she is replaced by a staff writer and falls into depression; is next seen in 1977 in Florida, where she enjoys bridge games and a trip to the Orkney Islands with her grand-niece Victoria; declines into illness in the 1980s, and dies sometime in the 1990s. But who is Daisy Goodwill Flett? And who is telling her story?

The mystery of Daisy's identity is contained in the novel's narrative ambiguity. The narrative opens as if it were Daisy's autobiography, "My mother's name was Mercy Stone Goodwill," and its chapter divisions follow life stages from "Birth, 1905," through "Death." Yet it is written in a number of voices and from seemingly incompatible points of view that sometimes share the same passage. At eleven, sick with pneumonia, Daisy "could only stare at [the] absence inside herself for a few minutes at a time. It was like looking at the sun. . . . The long days of isolation, of silence, the torment of boredom—all these pressed down on me, on young Daisy Goodwill and emptied her out. Her autobiography, if such a thing were imaginable, would be, if such a thing were ever to be written, an assemblage of dark voids and unbridgable gaps." As she declines into illness and sheds the personae of Mrs. Flett, Mrs. Green Thumb (the gardening columnist), and her

niece Victoria's Great-Aunt Daisy, Daisy Goodwill—as the mistakenly abridged name on her hospital bracelet identifies her—becomes ironic: "But I can't go on living a lie," protests Reverend Rick who has asked whether he should tell his mother he is gay. "Why not?" replies Daisy. "Most people do." At this point it becomes possible to imagine all the voices as Daisy's, peeling the layers of self-deception from the selves with which she has gotten through a long life of being what others expect her to be, and the narrative as a deathbed review, both survey and critique of her own life.

The narrative is indeed "an assemblage of dark voids and unbridgable gaps" that reflect the absence Daisy feels inside herself. Decades gape between chapters. Critical points in Daisy's life are represented by the perspectives of others: her first marriage by the society page notices of parties in honor thereof; her marriage to Barker Flett by the "the things people had to say about the Flett-Goodwill liaison"; her work—that critical center of all Shields's characters lives—not by the columns Mrs. Green Thumb writes but by the letters she receives. The photograph album at the center of the book contains pictures of Daisy's parents, children, grandchildren, and college friends, but none of Daisy. The chapter entitled "Love, 1936," defines love as "mostly the avoidance of hurt." Like the stone tower her father has built over her mother's grave, Daisy's life, which the novel's epigraph also identifies as a "monument," has a hollow core.

And yet, if the narrative is Daisy's own ironic autobiography, it is a work of self-reflection, and thus of a self. In old age, Daisy thinks about her two fathers, Cuyler Goodwill and her father-in-law, Magnus Flett. She feels closer to Magnus Flett, whom she has never met, because he, unlike Cuyler Goodwill, is reflective. While her own father has metamorphosed several times without wasting time on nostalgia for past selves or "his lost country," Daisy feels that Magnus Flett, who has gone back to the Orkney Islands looking for his own home and memorized Charlotte Bronte's *Jane Eyre* in an effort to discover what his wife missed in him, is "the suffering modern man," a wanderer like herself, "with an orphan's heart and a wistful longing for refuge." Daisy is not only absent from the narrative but also present in the narrative, as Magnus Flett, at 115, is still—barely—alive when Daisy finds him in Stromness.

The Stone Diaries is a rewriting of the story of the erasure of women's lives, especially those of her mother's generation, that Shields has been re-telling since the Aunt Violet poems. But in its length and thickness—in Daisy's long life and wide travels and the plethora of documents and viewpoints that construct her—it is also a story about the instability of identity and the unreliability of the means by which people perceive it. The family trees, newspaper clippings, and especially photographs that give the book the appearance of a "real" biography or autobiography also call attention to its constructedness. (Where did she get these photographs? Who are they really of?) The images of stone (Daisy's birthright, solid, carved, enduring) and flowers (her vocation, fragile, grown, transient) that run through the novel and come together in the rare fossils of early plant life that Victoria and her colleague are looking for in the Orkneys form the warp and weft of an identity that is both solid and fragile, both constructed and real, both present and not yet found.

The Stone Diaries catapulted Carol Shields to literary celebrity. Before *The Stone Diaries,* only four of Shields's nine previous novels had been published in the United States. As soon as *The Stone Diaries* began winning prizes—it was short-listed for the Booker Prize in 1993—Viking Penguin began publishing the backlist, and Shields's subsequent books have been published in the United States the same year as in Canada. By 1995, *The Stone Diaries* had won the Canadian Governor General's Award, the National Book Critics Circle Award, and the Pulitzer Prize (as well as the McNally Robinson Award for Manitoba Book of the Year, the Canadian Booksellers Association Prize, the French *Prix de Lire,* and a place on the shortlist for the *Prix Femina étranger*). Film productions of *The Stone Diaries* and *The Republic of Love* as well as *Swann* were announced (though only *Swann* had appeared by 2000). When Penguin published Shields's first two novels in the wake of this success, they were reviewed as precursors to *The Stone Diaries.* And when *Larry's Party* was published in both Canada and the United States in 1997, it came into a different world from any of its predecessors.

Larry's Party addresses the explicit question that focuses the dinner party conversation in the last chapter, "what is it like to be part of the company of men at the end of our millennium?"—when social change of all sorts, but especially gender upheaval, has upset the old foundations of men's lives. But it also asks the question implicit in Larry's progress from floral arts graduate of Red River College and employee of Flowerfolks in Winnipeg at age twenty-six to internationally known designer of garden mazes at forty-six: How does art come out of common clay? In effect, *Larry's Party* joins the two halves of *Happenstance.* Like Jack Bowman, Larry has to adjust to the women in his life outgrowing the selves he married. His first wife Dorrie, who he always thought was a little dumb ("She actually thinks *flower* college is *college,*") moves up from clerk-receptionist at Manitoba Motors to salesperson, and after he leaves her, to CEO of a greeting card company. His second wife Beth, a graduate student when they meet, finishes her dissertation, takes a job as head of Women's Studies at the University of Sussex, and decides she does not want to be married anymore. Like Jack's, too, Larry's life is defined by accident. As Jack attributes his relatively happy and comfortable situation to "happenstance," Larry's life is directed by mistakes. He took floral arts because the college sent him the wrong brochure, married Dorrie because she got pregnant, got into mazes because he felt happy being lost in the Hampton Court maze he and Dorrie were taken to on the honeymoon tour of England his parents gave them for a wedding present. Unlike Jack, however, whose life remains static, Larry moves on, too. Like Brenda, he begins to make art to furnish his own home, in his case a maze in his own yard on Lipton Street in Winnipeg, and gradually learns about maze designs, soil, climate, shrub varieties, and how to put them all together to suit a particular location and client. As Brenda appropriates the guestroom for a workroom and begins to sell her quilts for wall hangings instead of bedcovers, Larry quits his flower shop job and takes a maze-designing commission in Chicago. As Brenda becomes reflective about quilting, Larry learns how to think about mazes, their defining characteristics, histories, purposes, famous examples, and connection to his life.

The connection is both multi-dimensional and simple. "A maze is a puzzle. . . . designed to deceive travelers who seek a promised goal." Larry's life is a puzzle to himself, which he keeps trying to figure out by reading the signs around him and gratefully storing the explanations others provide. He keeps a dictionary under the counter at Flowerfolks to unlock the secrets of words. He's "grateful, grateful," to Sally Wolsche, who in initiating him into sex "had taken his puny, unamplified self and unlocked the door to his body and to that greater mystery of where he stood on the planet." A maze is a way of getting lost so one can be found. Larry is willing to go down unknown paths and take wrong turns. When his son asks him a worldly riddle he cannot answer, he feels "a stab of love" as he watches "his son watching him—a grown man who stumbled,

fell into error, got lost, made a fool of himself, but was willing, at least, to be rescued," and thinks, "Something good was bound to come of this." Every maze has a goal at the center, but the goal is not the point, only the enticement to the journey. The culmination of Larry's life "so far," the party that brings together his sister, his two ex-wives, his current woman friend, his latest clients, and a new acquaintance, celebrates the journey and takes Larry back, as a maze also does, to his beginning, as he and Dorrie, both matured by their separate journeys, rediscover their love for each other. In *Larry's Party,* as well as *The Stone Diaries* and *The Republic of Love,* Shields opens out the focus on domesticity in her early novels to the quest for home.

The structure of *Larry's Party* is simultaneously chronological and synchronic. Each chapter—"Larry's Love, 1978," "Larry's Words, 1983," "Larry's Penis, 1986," and so on—is an associative essay on an aspect of Larry's identity that subsumes some life event—divorce, marriage, his first commission—as a maze does its goal. The book is like the CAT scan his father undergoes and the chapters are slices of his life, "brilliantly dyed and intricately detailed," that reproduce the same constants, "his work, his friends, his family, his son, his love for his two wives, his bodily organs," from different perspectives as he grows older. This structure replicates the way Larry assimilates the story of how his mother killed her mother-in-law (with improperly canned runner beans), and the way we assimilate stories generally, "in small pieces, by installments as it were." Each return to Larry's transcendent moment in the maze at Hampton Court, his first maze on Lipton Street, and his marriage to Dorrie, thickens their implications. With this structure Shields finds a conduit from the inner life of the character to the mind of the reader, a way to represent the unknowable other.

Larry's Party is risky in its repetition, its ubiquitous metaphor, and its romantic ending. Most critics mentioned one or more of these risks as slight flaws overwhelmed by the novel's generosity, its acute rendering of the disequilibrium of the contemporary world, and its transformation of artifice into the experience of an inner life. The novel was named a Notable Book of 1997 by the *New York Times* and won the 1998 Orange Prize for fiction written by women and published in Britain.

The life stories of Larry Weller and Daisy Goodwill fulfill Shields's statement to Eleanor Wachtel that biography is "the only story we've got." When Shields and her husband moved from their six-bedroom home in Winnipeg to a two-bedroom apartment, Shields gave the materials for her own biography to the National Library of Canada, a gesture she represents, characteristically, as a housecleaning move. In the fall of 1998, she was diagnosed with breast cancer. The following fall, when the cancer was in remission, writer colleagues paid public tribute to her work and her personal generosity in a program that opened the International Festival of Authors in Toronto. As the new millennium opened, Shields was at work on an actual biography, of Jane Austen. It is "part of a series that isn't trying to compete with professional biographers," she explained to Leslie Forbes. "Each book is really a history of one author's reading of another." She also published her third collection of short stories, *Dressing Up for the Carnival* (2000), which includes some stories her editor did not think fit in *The Orange Fish,* and three written after her mastectomy. Many reflect on writing and the writing life. One of the new stories, "A Scarf," stages an awkward meeting and reconciliation between two old friends who seem to represent aspects of Shields's writing persona, the "sunny" winner of a slightly embarrassing prize honoring literary accessibility and the unrecognized writer of "stuff" that "is off-centre and steers a random course."

Selected Bibliography

WORKS OF CAROL SHIELDS

NOVELS AND SHORT STORIES
Quotations, except from *Dressing Up for the Carnival,* are from American editions.
Small Ceremonies. Toronto: McGraw-Hill Ryerson, 1976; New York: Penguin, 1996.
The Box Garden. Toronto: McGraw-Hill Ryerson, 1977; New York: Penguin, 1996.
Happenstance. Toronto: McGraw-Hill Ryerson, 1980. *Happenstance: Two Novels in One About a Marriage in Transition: The Husband's Story.* New York: Penguin, 1994.
A Fairly Conventional Woman. Toronto: McGraw-Hill Ryerson, 1982. *Happenstance: Two Novels in One About a Marriage in Transition: The Wife's Story.* New York: Penguin, 1994.
Various Miracles. Toronto: Stoddart, 1985; New York: Penguin, 1989.
Swann: A Mystery. Toronto: Stoddart, 1987; *Swann.* New York: Viking Penguin, 1989.
The Orange Fish. Toronto: Random House of Canada, 1989; New York: Viking Penguin, 1990.
A Celibate Season. With Blanche Howard. Regina, Sask.: Coteau, 1991; New York: Penguin, 1999.
The Republic of Love. Toronto: Random House of Canada, 1992; New York: Viking Penguin, 1992.
The Stone Diaries. Toronto: Random House of Canada, 1993; New York: Viking Penguin, 1994.
Larry's Party. Toronto: Random House of Canada, 1997; New York: Viking Penguin, 1997.
Dressing Up For the Carnival. Toronto: Random House of Canada, 2000; New York: Viking Penguin, 2000.

POETRY AND PLAYS
Intersect: Poems. Ottawa: Borealis Press, 1974.
Departures and Arrivals. Winnipeg, Man.: Blizzard, 1990.
Thirteen Hands: A Play in Two Acts. Winnipeg, Man.: Blizzard, 1993.
Coming to Canada: Poems. Edited and with an introduction by Christopher Levenson. Ottawa: Carleton University Press, 1992. (Republished by Carleton in 1995 as *Coming to Canada,* with 11 poems each

from *Others* and *Intersect,* 33 new poems, and a new introduction by Christopher Levenson.)

Fashion, Power, Guilt, and the Charity of Families. With Catherine Shields. Winnipeg, Man.: Blizzard, 1995.

Anniversary. With Dave Williamson. Winnipeg, Man.: Blizzard, 1998.

ESSAYS AND CRITICISM

Susanna Moodie: Voice and Vision. Ottawa: Borealis, 1977.

" 'Thinking Back Through Our Mothers': Tradition in Canadian Women's Writing." In *Re(Dis)covering Our Foremothers: Nineteenth-Century Canadian Women Writers.* Edited by Lorraine McMullen. Ottawa: University of Ottawa Press, 1990. Pp. 9–13.

"Jane Austen Images of the Body: No Fingers, No Toes." *Persuasions* 13:132–137 (December 1991).

"Encounter." In *Without A Guide: Contemporary Women's Travel Adventures.* Edited by Katherine Govier. St. Paul, Minn.: Hungry Mind, 1994. Pp. 225–228.

"Travelwarp." In *Writing Away: The PEN Canada Travel Anthology.* Edited by Constance Rooke. Toronto: McClelland & Stewart, 1994. Pp. 276–280.

"Framing the Structure of a Novel." *The Writer* 111: 3–7 (1998). Online. Infotrac. (February 21, 2000).

"Giving your literary papers away." *Quill & Quire* 64, 11:43 (November 1998).

"Opting for Invention over the Injury of Invasions." *New York Times,* April 10, 2000, pp. E1–E2. (In occasional series, Writers on Writing.)

CRITICAL AND BIOGRAPHICAL STUDIES

Armstrong, Isobel. "Designs for Living." Review of *Happenstance: The Husband's Story; The Wife's Story. Times Literary Supplement,* March 1, 1991, p. 21

Atwood, Margaret. "In Praise of Shields: Hilarious Surfaces, Ominous Depths." *The National Post,* October 22, 1999, p. A19.

Besner, Neil, and G. N. L. Jonasson, eds. *Carol Shields.* Special issue of *Prairie Fire* 16, no. 1:5–192 (1995).

Giardini, Anne. "Reading My Mother." *Prairie Fire* 16, no. 1:6–12 (1995).

Gom, Leona. "Stone and Flowers." *Prairie Fire* 16, no. 1:22–27 (1995).

Hall, Susan Grove. "The Duality of the Artist/Crafter in Carol Shields's Novels." *Kentucky Philological Review* 12:42–47 (March 1997).

Hammill, Faye. "Carol Shields's 'Native Genre' and the Figure of the Canadian Author." *Journal of Commonwealth Literature* 31, no. 2:87–99 (1996).

Helwig, Maggie. "Constructing Ourselves For Others." Review of *Swann: A Mystery. The Canadian Forum* 67:48–49 (February/March 1988).

Howard, Blanche. "Collaborating with Carol." *Prairie Fire* 16, no. 1:71–78 (1995).

Ings, Katharine Nicholson. "Illuminating the Moment: Verbal Tableaux in Carol Shields's Poetry." *Prairie Fire* 16, no. 1:168–173 (1995).

Johnson, Chris. "Ordinary Pleasures (and Terrors): The Plays of Carol Shields." *Prairie Fire* 16, no. 1: 161–167 (1995).

Klinkenborg, Verlyn. "A Maze Makes Sense From Above." Review of *Larry's Party. New York Times Book Review,* September 7, 1997, p. 7.

Mellor, Winifred M. " 'The Simple Container of Our Existence': Narrative Ambiguity in Carol Shields's *The Stone Diaries.*" *Studies in Canadian Literature* 20, no. 2:97–110 (1995).

Nodelman, Perry. "Living in the Republic of Love: Carol Shields's Winnipeg." *Prairie Fire* 16, no. 1: 40–55 (1995).

Parini, Jay. "Men and Women, Forever Misaligned." Review of *The Stone Diaries. New York Times Book Review,* March 27, 1994, pp. 3, 14.

Pool, Gail. "Imagination's Invisible Ink." Review of *Happenstance: Two Novels in One About a Marriage in Transition* and *The Stone Diaries. Women's Review of Books,* May 1994, p. 20.

Rosborough, Linda. "Three Shields books set to become movies." *Globe and Mail,* August 25, 1995, p. C4

Rubins, Josh. "They All Want a Piece of the Legend." Review of *Various Miracles* and *Swann. New York Times Book Review,* August 6, 1989, p. 11.

"Shields of Honour." *Globe and Mail,* October 23, 1999, p. D4–D5.

Sigurdson, Norman. "Carol Shields: Raising Everyday Lives to the Level of Art." Review of *Swann: A Mystery. Quill & Quire* 53, no. 11:21 (November 1987).

Slethaug, Gordon E. " 'The Coded Dots of Life': Carol Shields's Diaries and Stones." *Canadian Literature* 156:59–81 (Spring 1998).

Sweeney, Susan Elizabeth. "Formal Strategies in a Female Narrative Tradition: The Case of *Swann: A Mystery.*" In *Anxious Power: Reading, Writing, and Ambivalence in Narrative by Women.* Edited by Carol J. Singley and Susan Elizabeth Sweeney. Albany, N.Y.: SUNY Press, 1993. Pp. 19–32.

Thomas, Clara. "Reassembling Fragments: Susanna Moodie, Carol Shields, and Mary Swann." In *Inside the Poem: Essays in Honour of Donald Stephens.* Edited by W. H. New. Toronto: Oxford University Press, 1992. Pp. 196–204.

———. "Stories Like Sonnets: 'Mrs. Turner Cutting the Grass.' " *Prairie Fire* 16, no. 1:79–83 (1995).

Thompson, Kent. "Reticence in Carol Shields." *Room of One's Own* 13, nos. 1 & 2:69–76 (1989).

Vauthier, Simone. " 'They say miracles are past' but they are wrong." *Prairie Fire* 16, no. 1:84–104 (1995).

Wachtel, Eleanor, ed. *Carol Shields.* Special issue of *Room of One's Own* 13, nos. 1 & 2:2–150 (1989).

Williamson, Dave. "Collaborating With Carol." *Prairie Fire* 20, no. 1:123–125 (1999).

INTERVIEWS

Anderson, Marjorie. "Interview with Carol Shields." *Prairie Fire* 16, no. 1:139–150 (1995).

Burgess, Linda. "A Subject Worthy of Her Talent: An Interview with Carol Shields." *Windsor Review* 28, no. 2:34–43 (1995).

De Roo, Harvey. "A Little Like Flying: An Interview with Carol Shields." *West Coast Review* 23, no. 3: 38–56 (1988).

Forbes, Leslie. "More Spice Than Nice." *Globe and Mail,* February 26, 2000, pp. D2–D3.

Hollenberg, Donna Krolik. "An Interview With Carol Shields." *Contemporary Literature* 39, no. 3:339–355 (1998).

Ross, Val. "Unsung Lives of Girls, Women Carol Shields's Strong Suit." *Globe and Mail,* April 29, 1995, p. C17.

Thomas, Joan. "An Epistolary Interview with Carol Shields." *Prairie Fire* 16, no. 1:121–137 (1995).

Wachtel, Eleanor. "Interview with Carol Shields." *Room of One's Own* 13, nos. 1 & 2:5–45 (1989).

FILM BASED ON THE WORKS OF CAROL SHIELDS

Swann. Screenplay by David Young. Directed by Anna Benson Gyles. Greenpoint Films, Majestic Films, Norstar Entertainment Inc., and Shaftesbury Films, 1996.

—SUSAN L. BLAKE

Tobias Wolff

1945—

AT THE CONCLUSION of Tobias Wolff's memoir *In Pharaoh's Army: Memories of the Lost War* (1994), the paratrooper trainee Hugh Pierce stands poised in the doorway of a C-130 turboprop. As Pierce prepares to jump, he sings in falsetto and dances within the otherwise orderly formation of men progressing towards the doorway. In this remembered construction, Wolff trails Pierce in the line, bearing grateful, if uneasy, witness to his friend's levity. Thousands of feet above Fort Benning, Georgia—with only the enormous uncertainty of the jump beneath them—the rest of the soldiers are nervous and quiet. Pierce is the exception. Wolff writes: "He laughs at the look on my face, then turns and takes his place in the door, and jumps, and is gone." The book has ended, the image has vanished, and the idea of Pierce has been spoken but not analyzed. Roland Barthes' dictum from *S/Z: An Essay* that, "beauty cannot really be explained . . . it stands out, repeats itself, but it does not describe itself," has been realized to its fullest extent in this passage. Wolff allows the image itself to serve its purpose; the act of remembering what has vanished becomes the most important part of the artist's work. Any analysis of the memory is left out of the work and the remembrance stands by itself as a complete story.

Pierce is the primary tragic figure of *In Pharaoh's Army*. Through Pierce's death shortly after his arrival in Vietnam in 1966, Wolff presents the familiar archetype of a vital and vigorous life sadly truncated by war. In this first-person narrative, this particular tragedy is culled from the war's litany of tragedies and given importance, primacy. Pierce's story rises from the stories of countless dead American soldiers—many of whom Wolff sees, knows, and remembers—and takes a position at the forefront of the memoir. This is, of course, to be expected. He was a close friend of Wolff's, someone whom Wolff imagines, "would have been one of them, another godfather for my children, another bighearted man for them to admire and stay up late listening to." But Pierce's importance shifts the focus of the memoir. Though events and actions form the body of the tale, its pith and emotional center lie somewhere else. It lies with what is absent, with the idea of a dead soldier, and with the way that memory can haunt and persist long after a moment of action has passed. This is the condition endemic of modern, self-conscious, self-remembering man. It is also, according to Anton Chekhov—one of Wolff's foremost influences—what the writer must simply describe. "It is not the writer's job to solve problems," Chekhov writes, "his only job is to be an impartial witness." This will be a familiar argument to the reader of Wolff, an argument that holds as most important the recording vision, the observant gaze, and the carefully detailed image.

John Keegan's statement in *The Face of Battle,* that the study of warfare is the study of human collapse because "it is towards the disintegration of human groups that battle is directed," cannot be underestimated or ignored. Much of the first part of *In Pharaoh's Army* involves the story of Wolff's trip along a rural road between U.S. military installations in the Mekong River Delta on Thanksgiving Day in 1967. There are no mileage markers for the journey from Lieutenant Wolff's base at My Tho to Dong Tam, his eventual destination. The distance stretches, elongates, and becomes discursive. As it will in much of Wolff's subsequent writing, the physical landscape of the place he is in—in this case rural Vietnam—dramatically affects the inner landscape of his self. Because he is a writer, and because he is a writer obsessed with personal memory, the uncertain territory through which he drives becomes a departure point for inquiries into the self.

The images presented by memory, then, serve not only as independent structures, but also as points of departure for further trips into self-disclosure. The trauma of war's isolation, the hardship it enforces on the psyche—which must concentrate solely on survival—eventually leads to the act of writing. Wolff writes as a means of escaping the force of memory. He tunnels. On that Thanksgiving in 1967, he traverses a physical tunnel—the road with its absolute boundaries and impregnable borders of farmland. Yet the physical tunneling leads to a clearing of the self, a space in which this deeper destination reveals more images, and parallel revelations about feeling.

The trip is made in order to procure a television set; Wolff and his assistant, Sergeant Benet, have decided that they want to watch the two-hour Thanksgiving Day episode of *Bonanza* on a large color television. Over the first ten months of their stay in My Tho as adjuncts to a base composed entirely of South Vietnamese soldiers, the two Americans have steadfastly refused any degree of acculturation. They have resolved to "live like Americans," and have spent much of their time bartering for goods. They have acquired a sizable stash of things. They compile "electric lights, a TV, a stereo, a stove, a refrigerator, and a generator to keep it all running." In this process, Wolff surrounds himself with as many American consumer goods as possible. Alienated, lonely, and bored—a frightened soldier performing a doomed task in a doomed war—Wolff cannot strip himself of the things to which he has become accustomed. His response to immersion in a foreign culture is to refuse the immersion. He builds a barrier of possessions between himself and the larger Vietnamese society. "Given the chance," he writes, "I'd have lived smack in the middle of a minefield twenty miles wide."

Wolff feels besieged. He is what will become a familiar character for the reader of Wolff: the lonely man who is, because of circumstances, separated from the remainder of the world in which he lives. In Vietnam the isolation and separation occurs because of physical danger. "If I ran over a touch-fused 105 shell it wouldn't make any difference how fast I was going," Wolff writes of the prospects of negotiating the road to Dong Tam. "I'd seen a two-and-a-half-ton truck blown right off the road by one of those, just a few vehicles ahead of me in a convoy coming back from Saigon." Even these many years later, relating his Vietnamese tour in memoir form, Wolff is preoccupied by the moments at which he came close to death. With great precision he relays the instances in which he nearly died; these "Close Calls" comprise the fourth section of the book.

Two of the moments at which Wolff's own mortality intrudes into his consciousness are explained by machinery, by the vagaries of warfare. On one occasion the support ropes snap off a Howitzer he is attaching to the underside of a Chinook helicopter. The gun plummets seventy feet from the sky and nearly crushes him; he happens to look up at the right moment and scurries clear of danger. On another occasion Wolff attends Easter services at a Catholic Church in the Mekong Delta. He is on a mission in the field, and after the Mass he takes advantage of a pause in operations to drive with Sergeant Benet to the local market to buy fresh vegetables. Even though the service has occurred several years after the Vatican has resolved to abrogate the Latin Mass, the priest still uses the unfamiliar language. The looping, foreign lexicon—the same in Vietnam as had been for centuries around the world—tricks Wolff into a sense of security. "Without marking the change in myself, I had begun to let go a little, lulled from the state of paranoid watchfulness I'd been in since my first night off the plane." This relaxation nearly costs Wolff his life. The moment at which the tunnel of paranoia and cultural detritus relents, its space around the self is replaced by violent aggression. An unseen hand rolls a live grenade underneath his jeep. It fails to detonate and he is spared, but his besieged mind encloses itself further within the fortifications of his American enclave.

This enclosure of the self within comfortable goods is an understandable response to the fear through which Wolff must live each day. Wolff comes to the Army as a step in his search for the structure and possibility for valor that his childhood has lacked. He enlists as the culmination of many years of searching for "legitimacy," for some validation of his self by the larger apparatus of society. "The men I'd respected when I was growing up had all served, and most of the writers I looked up to—Norman Mailer, Irwin Shaw, James Hones, Erich Maria Remarque, and of course Hemingway, to whom I turned for guidance in all things—[had also served]." His desire to live a life similar to those lived by his heroes is a boy's wish, the culmination of a childhood in which idols and exemplars have been extremely few. *In Pharaoh's Army* satisfies the particulars for this type of memoir—it is a sol-

dier/writer's explication of self, a renegade individualist's appraisal of his country's army and this army's most recent extended war. Yet it also tells the story of a child who, driven by the absence of his father, seeks formal approval for his life. A young Wolff enlists to satisfy the yearning for respectability and authority that his father never supplied.

After he has spent a year in Vietnam, Wolff returns to California and civilian life. His discharge pay amounts to a year's salary, and he goes to visit his father on this money, intent on coming to terms with the figure whose absence, in many ways, drove him to the war. The novelist and critic Geoffrey Wolff—Tobias Wolff's older brother—has also written a memoir, entitled *The Duke of Deception,* which documents their father and his steady lying, desertion, and mischievous abuse of the law. This man—a middle-class, Jewish engineer—was not able to live with his own faith or his average economic position. He fled from his family and instated himself in a dominion of lies on the Southern California coast. His protection of his true identity through an insulating layer of interference is not unlike the process that the younger Wolff has undergone in Vietnam.

Thus, when the son has stripped off the second, defensive skin, and returned once again to civilian life, he flees to his father, intent on showing him what he has learned. Wolff has also gone to visit his dad immediately prior to leaving for Vietnam. These visits—the bookends of his active duty in the military—are extreme contrasts. The first time, Wolff appears unexpectedly. About to embark on his Vietnamese tour, Wolff is unable to reconcile his paternal relationship. "Of course I'd been a jackass to surprise him, but it went beyond that," Wolff writes. "It had to do with the whole of our history. He must have wondered where we stood in all this, what I'd forgiven, what I held against him, what I held against myself." Through the process of fighting, though the lessons learned or unlearned in Vietnam, Wolff begins to accept his father. It is one of the few instances of clear linear progress in the work. He returns to California and spends a week with his father. Though nothing conscious has changed, no puzzle has been overtly worked out in the intervening pages, the two men now are able to coexist. "So we gave it another try," the narrative states, "and this time we got it right." He allows his father to tell his stories. He comes to forgive his eccentricities, and in a way, to accept them. Yet this acceptance comes at the price of the rigid infrastructure of formal father-son relations.

Wolff writes, "I had come back to Manhattan Beach, I surely understood even then, because there could no longer be any question of judgement between my father and me." He spends several weeks in California, reconciling with his father, concocting plans to stay and enroll in community college. Then, after a particularly miserable date, he calls his ex-girlfriend Vera in Washington D.C., the city where his brother and mother are also living. He hangs up the phone shaking; hearing Vera's voice has reminded him of their love. He aches for another chance at making their relationship work. Having partially mended one relationship, he seeks to fix another. This effort will, of course, lead to failure and, more importantly, prompt him to leave his father. Yet it is important, in many ways, to note that Wolff attempts reconciliation with his father, following in part what John Stoltenberg has termed, in his important work *Refusing to Be A Man,* the desire of the son to "belong to the father for the rest of his natural life."

On the night before Wolff's departure, the two men go to dinner. He has still not informed his father of his decision and, late in the meal, he breaks the news. His father tries bravely to shrug off the sorrow of his son's departure. He realizes that, much like the reader of the text, he will be left with only memory, and the sorrow of a partial presence. "He tried to smile but couldn't, his very flesh failed him, and that was the closest I came

to changing my mind." They calm their roiling emotions with promises of return. Yet there is, in the sadness of passed time, an awareness of actuality that Wolff inserts into the text. "I meant it when I said I'd be back but it sounded like a bald-faced lie, as if the truth was already known to both of us that I would not be back and that he would live alone and die alone, as he did, two years later." Though mutual reparations have been paid, there is not a sense of complete peace between the two of them. After his father dies, Wolff feels something akin to guilt, but he accepts it as a part of his self. This self is, in turn, the substance of the book's revelations. Through the war, Wolff has come closer to the truth of his paternal relationship. Through visiting his father, Wolff has come closer to what he perceives as the truth about his own life. It is a harmony of spheres towards which he moves; through writing about his life, he endeavors to fashion it into a beauty of accordance and concordance.

WOLFF'S CHILDHOOD

It is this beauty, this realization of "who he is" towards which Wolff is constantly striving. It is this tension between the past and the present that gives his memoir its primary tautness. Born in Birmingham, Alabama to Arthur "Duke" and Caroline Wolff on June 19, 1945, Tobias Wolff had a turbulent childhood. Even while he delves into the past, into the *was* of his time in Vietnam, he is forever explicating the less chronological, less linear development of his mind, a development begun, in earnest, in his boyhood. Though Wolff is acutely self-conscious at all points within his works of autobiography, there is the sense that this consciousness takes its shape more fully through the process of writing. As Peter J. Bailey writes of *This Boy's Life: A Memoir* (1989), Wolff's revelatory memoir about his childhood: "It is in the unresolved tension between truth and lie, self and imposture, autobiography and fiction, that the book finds a structuring dichotomy worthy of and concordant with the finest literary fiction." This, then, is a *buildungsroman* of the first order, a nonfictional novel of education that can be assessed independently of *In Pharaoh's Army*.

First published in 1989, *This Boy's Life* can be credited with touching off the avalanche of first-person autobiography that now comprises such a flowering and prodigious genre in American literature. Wolff writes about himself, plain and simple, focusing on the ignoble trials of his youth. *This Boy's Life* contains the components that have become so familiar to the modern reader: the abusive family life, the trials of poverty, and the eventual triumph of the literary artist. Wolff tells the story of a young boy whose father leaves his family, disappearing to California without warning. The text begins with a paean to the open road, to the freedom of a mother traveling with her son, to the joy of movement and the vitality of flight. Like a long string following the tradition of real and fictional protagonists of American literature—a list of names ranging from Jack Kerouac's Neal Cassady to John Steinbeck's Tom Joad to Saul Bellow's young Charlie Citrine—the Wolffs migrate by car in search of a better future, in pursuit of a change in luck. "Everything was going to change when we got out West," Wolff details, and the innocence of the statement foreshadows that this will be a troubled text, a story of displacement and hardship.

Indeed, the opening tribute has its grisly side. The mother and son are free—heading for what they believe will be a better life—but they have had car trouble while crossing the Continental Divide. Here Wolff is traveling with his mother, the feminine presence preventing this story from becoming, in the words of the critic Nina Baym, a "melodrama of beset manhood," one of the many that she identifies in her 1985 essay "Melodramas of Beset Manhood" as dotting the history of American literature. While they are waiting on the side of the road for the their radiator to cool, a large truck roars by them, out of control, having just lost its brakes. By the time they reach the site of its accident—the truck has plummeted over the edge of a cliff—a large crowd has gathered to watch the burning cab, which is lying upside-down in a gully many thousands of feet below. The driver has died and Wolff's mother becomes protective of her son. "For the rest of the day she kept looking over at me, touching me, brushing back my hair. I saw that the time was right to make my play for souvenirs." The twist Wolff puts on the end of this scene prompts a sense of repulsion. It is an instance of a son using his own mother's love as a means towards the acquisition of material possessions—trinkets and souvenirs that she could not otherwise afford to purchase for him.

Manipulation, whether it is through lying or through physical violence, figures prominently in *This Boy's Life*. Wolff and his mother settle in Utah, where she hopes to make a fortune working in the uranium mines. Instead, her abusive ex-boyfriend—whom the mother and son had originally set out to escape—appears on her doorstep, having tracked their route. Work is not as plentiful as Wolff's mother had hoped—they nearly starve as she looks for a job—and the boyfriend, Roy, only complicates matters. He loiters about the house and drains the resources from the family. He drinks and exhibits violent behavior, living primarily on a small disability check he receives from the Veterans Administration. "When he wasn't hunting or fishing or checking up on my mother," Wolff writes, "he sat at the kitchen table with a cigarette in his mouth and squinted at *The Shooter's Bible* through the smoke that veiled his face." Young Wolff has no ability to control his surroundings.

Though Wolff willingly secedes this control to his mother, whom he loves, Roy seizes this control from him. Roy's presence intrudes upon the solitude of the boy's domestic life; he is a burning, uncomfortable, and powerfully smoky reminder of the violence of men. Powerless against this virulent male presence, the young Wolff begins to lie, to shape the truth of his environment through story. In his work, *Stories of Resilience in Childhood,* Daniel Challener traces this storytelling to Wolff's desire to move away from masculinity and towards the feminine presence of his mother. "After Toby has mastered the physical act of writing, her influence is not solely limited to the initial task-specific neuro-muscular training she has given him." Wolff is escaping from the neuro-muscular training of his manifestly male body, and creating a story-life where he can identify with all things female. While Wolff stops short of the revelatory confessions of works such as Edmund White's *A Boy's Own Story,* he does detail, with great and submerged energy, an individual struggle away from the ordinary constraints of gender.

Before this process can develop fully, however, the family is uprooted again. There is no verbal warning for Wolff before his mother decides to flee, to leave Utah and migrate north to Seattle. Instead he comes home from school early, having skipped archery practice, to find her packing his suitcase. They are leaving, she says. Does he have any suggestions? She has decided their ultimate destination already, but with this semblance of democratic intent, Wolff's mother indicates that she understands that he deserves some voice in the matter, even if the fulfillment of his wishes does not occur. Wolff is not unhappy to flee even farther towards the continent's corner. "I was glad to be once more on the run," the young boy asserts, "and glad that I would have her to myself again." As the decision is made to leave, however, Wolff is telling a lie about his whereabouts. His archery practice has not been canceled, as he asserts. The lie that he has constructed segues smoothly into the projected path of departure for mother and son. Whether objective truth is as-

serted becomes meaningless; all that matters is that which fuels movement, departure, and travel. The reader becomes aware that this is a memoir about the interrelationship of fact and fiction, about the ways in which one can mix with and lead to the other.

Later in the text, when Wolff is established in another loveless household and has further developed his propensity for lying, he forges applications to East Coast boarding schools, hoping to gain whatever support he lacks in his hopeless hometown of Concrete, Washington. He steals stationery from the principal's office of Concrete High, and creates the complete admissions package for himself—recommendation letters, transcripts, and evidence of extracurriculars. None of what he writes is true. Like many children of abusive homes, Wolff finds that his self-confidence is wrecked; he lacks the respect for his own intellectual abilities that is necessary for academic success. Yet he obtains a strange sense of truth from the act of lying about his own qualifications. "I felt full of things that had to be said, full of stifled truth . . . It was truth known only to me, but I believed in it more than I believed in the facts arrayed against it." He will be rejected from a list of the more prestigious academies—Deerfield, Choate, Exeter, Andover, St. Paul's—but will garner a scholarship to Hill, a boarding school where he will matriculate and, eventually, from which he will be expelled. Though he does not know it, Wolff is fulfilling the legacy of his father. Expelled from Deerfield many years before, the elder Wolff is buoyed by the idea of his son applying to the boarding academies.

While Wolff's father is absent, the role of father in his life is filled by a string of abusive surrogates. First there is Roy, the boyfriend from whom his mother finally manages to flee when she moves to Seattle. Yet it is difficult for a single mother to raise her son—both monetarily and socially—and she soon allows a cavalcade of suitors into her life. This is a difficult time for Wolff; he sees his mother's self-reliance eroded by the necessities of family life. He has violent friends, and feels immersed in a destructive culture, one that is teaching him to hate, in a way, his own circumstances. Anchored in front of the relatively new technology of television, watching a purportedly educational documentary about the American conquest of the Third Reich during World War II, Wolff feels the indoctrination slipping its fibers into him. "These shows instructed us further in the faith we were already beginning to hold: that victims are contemptible, no matter how much people pretend otherwise; that it is more fun to be inside than outside, to be arrogant than to be kind, to be with a crowd than to be alone." The writer's craft, of course, is at odds with this type of belief. In order to perform his work, the adult Wolff requires solitude, exclusion, and concentrated reflection.

Eventually, Wolff's mother settles on a prospective husband—Dwight, an initially charming, if somewhat unsettling man from Concrete, Washington, a small town enclosed on all sides by the Mount Baker-Snoqualmie National Forest in northwestern Washington. Though Wolff's mother is reluctant to give up her own freedom, she believes that her son will benefit from the presence of a father-figure in his life. She is already disturbed by what she has gathered from his counselors at school; he lies constantly, lapses in and out of trouble, and fails to achieve to the limits of his academic potential. She decides that Wolff will live with Dwight in Concrete over late winter and early spring and, if all goes well, she will move from the city in the summer and join the makeshift family. "I thought I had no choice," he writes of the moment when he is asked for his approval of the plan, "so I gave it." Dwight has three children from a previous marriage; Wolff is anxious as the date of his departure approaches. He feels that he has been forced to leave Seattle.

The feeling of helplessness and the sensation of being a victim do not desert him.

ABUSE AND ESCAPE

Once Dwight has the young Wolff in his purview, he changes completely. He betrays himself for what he is—a foul, violent, alcohol-dependent mechanic, living a meager existence far from the limits of acceptable society. With barely restrained anger, Wolff recounts Dwight's attempts to change the boy's flippant approach to family life. "Dwight made a study of me," he writes, relating, through this terminology, his sense of being the subject of an experiment, rather than a self-controlling individual. Wolff continues: "He thought about me during the day while he grunted over the engines of trucks and generators, and in the evening while he sat heavy-lidded at the kitchen table with a pint of Old Crow and a package of Camels to support him in his deliberations." Smoke and alcohol are the hallmarks of his character, and he wields a despotic, violent control over the young Wolff. The backlash can be felt in every sentence of the text of *This Boy's Life,* which contains a dedication to Dwight. "My first stepfather used to say that what I didn't know would fill a book. Well, here it is." Indeed, Wolff has accomplished a remarkable task: he has taken the victim—the utterly powerless little boy who is ruled by the bitter stepfather—and empowered him. He has given retributive force to his art, and through his art has claimed retribution.

The catalog of brutalities is long. As Bailey notes, "Wolff wrote an autobiography that reads like a novel because of his control over the material and his conviction that the dividing line between fiction and autobiography is a tenuous, ethereal one." To this end, Wolff is remarkably fluent with the placement of the story's vignettes and with the revelation of the information that will amount to the sense of protracted conversation that the work provides. Immediately upon leaving Seattle and the protection of his mother, Wolff must endure his future stepfather's verbal abuse. Coming around the corner of a rural mountain road, Dwight runs over a beaver, swerving his car into the oncoming lanes in order to hit it. He immediately stops and pushes Wolff out of the car. He demands that Wolff pick up the carcass of the animal, and, when the boy fails to respond, Dwight heaves the blood-soaked beast into the trunk. Halfway home they stop at a tavern, where Wolff must wait in the January-cold car while Dwight goes inside and gets drunk. "Dwight came out of the tavern a long time after he went in, at least as long a time as we'd spent getting there from Seattle, and gunned the car out of the lot." He is drunk; the car fishtails; Wolff complains that he's feeling sick. "Sick to your stomach?" Dwight replies. "A hotshot like you?" His aggression is mindless and total. As soon as they arrive in Concrete, Wolff learns that it will be his job to shuck hundreds of bags of horse chestnuts that have been languishing in the cellar. This will be brutal work, and will last months; it is Dwight's way of teaching the boy discipline. "My fingers were crazed with cuts and scratches," Wolff writes. "Even worse, the broken husks bled a juice that made my hands stink and turned them orange." Dwight refuses to allow Wolff to wear gloves, because of his belief that gloves are effeminate, and would insulate the boy from the true spirit of the labor.

Eventually, Wolff's mother comes to join him. Immediately after the wedding, however, she falls into a deep depression. "She slept late, something she has never done before, and when I came home for lunch I sometimes still found her in her bathrobe, sitting at the kitchen table and staring dazedly down the bright white tunnel of the house." Then, gradually, she rebounds. Fiercely independent, she joins the Parent Teacher Association and the Gun Club, becoming that so-

ciety's first female member. She tries to turn the six people living in the run-down house in Concrete into a family. Her success, of course, is limited at best. Dwight's only son soon leaves home, and his two daughters detest their father. Dwight lies around the house, works lazily at his job as a mechanic, ineptly hunts and fishes, and verbally abuses everyone who is close to him. Finally, he steals all of the money that Wolff has been saving through his paper route, over one thousand dollars, the result of over three years of delivering papers. This becomes one of the final acts of a doomed marriage; with Wolff's acceptance at the East Coast boarding school assured, Wolff's mother leaves Dwight and goes to Washington D.C. The story is not over, though. Dwight trails her to D.C. and tries to strangle her in the lobby of the hotel where she is living. She barely escapes with her life, obtains a restraining order, and Dwight is forced to leave for Seattle. Wolff never sees him again.

Wolff's two autobiographical books then, do tell a sequential and chronologically progressive narrative. They accomplish this through the presentation of individual moments of memory that eventually broaden out, through their buried connections, into a narrative tapestry. "When we are green," Wolff writes in the conclusion to *This Boy's Life,* "still half-created, we believe that our dreams are rights, that the world is disposed to act in our best interests, and that falling and dying are for quitters." All around him, in these two remarkable books, Wolff sees people close to him fail and suffer and die. His most profound lesson—an appreciation for his own blessed luck—comes to him only gradually. Once it is in place, however, he consecrates the beauty of his writing to its altar. This memoir of a violent youth has an ending that is similar to the ending of *In Pharaoh's Army.* Again it is an image, a moment when he is driving with a friend along a deserted mountain road in the summer. They have been drinking, and the recklessness of youth is strong within them. "It was a good night to sing and we sang for all we were worth, as if we'd been saved." The belief in salvation—in this instance a purely secular redemption of drinking, speed, and song—is the most important thing that Wolff can communicate. Again, it is a wordless image conveyed through words, a goal that is often elusive for the nonfiction writer, who is often tied to storytelling and the explanation of factual circumstances.

THE FICTION

Wolff's fiction, however, in the words of James Hannah, has a habit of "entering the story in medias res, in the middle of things." Hannah asserts that Wolff's style consists of repeated punctures of brilliance. He believes that these brilliant moments, however, frequently lead to conclusions that lack resolution. This is the poet's approach, and it applies well to Wolff's most anthologized story, "Hunters in the Snow." First published in *TriQuarterly Magazine* in 1980—the year Wolff began his seventeen-year tenure as the Writer-In-Residence at Syracuse University, a tenure that would end with his move to Stanford University in 1998—"Hunters" will be familiar to the thorough reader of Wolff. Its chief concern—the brutality of ordinary people in ordinary circumstances—arises repeatedly throughout the body of Wolff's work. "Hunters" was later published in Wolff's *In the Garden of the North American Martyrs* (1981).

"Tub had been waiting an hour in the falling snow," it begins, and the story lurches forward, already in motion. Three friends—Kenny, Tub, and Frank—are hunting in eastern Washington, in the snow-covered hills that surround Spokane. They have been hunting all day without luck when they come to a set of tracks. It is near dusk, and they hurry to follow the trail, which leads onto the property of a farmer. Kenny goes to the farmhouse to obtain permission to hunt on the

family's property. He gets permission but with one condition: he must shoot the farmer's dog, which is old and sick and dying. All of this happens unbeknownst to the reader; the narration remains outside with Frank and Tub. When Kenny comes back outside, the three men immediately begin to follow the trail. It dies after a matter of moments, and Kenny, in mock-frustration shoots a fence post. "I hate that post," he says, immediately before he shoots it.

Kenny is an angry man; his personality clashes with Frank, whose "hippie-bullshit" and new-age vocabulary stress what he terms 'the forces' of hunting. He also has difficulties with Tub, who is enormously obese and whom he teases mercilessly and relentlessly. When Kenny follows his mock-execution of the post with shootings of the tree and then, shockingly, the dog that the reader does not know he is supposed to kill, both Tub and Frank are horrified. His humor misunderstood, Kenny looks at Tub and declares: "I hate you." Tub shoots him in the stomach; the wound is dire but not immediately fatal; Kenny falls sadly to the ground, holding his wound closed with his hands.

Ignoring Kenny's pathetic pleas—which include a desperate request for aspirin to ease the pain—the two men take their time getting directions to the hospital, which they ultimately forget in the farmhouse. They return to the scene of the shooting to find Kenny jackknifed over the rear gate of the truck, dazed by pain and a loss of blood. They put him on boards in the bed of the truck and then drive away—exposing the dying man to the cold winter wind. They are all abusive to each other, and their treatment of Kenny—treatment that leads directly to his death by hypothermia on the boards in the rear of the truck—shocks and appalls the reader. The two men stop to get food on their way to the hospital—a destination to which they will never arrive—and, over flapjacks, Frank tells Tub that he is having an affair with his fifteen-year-old babysitter.

While Kenny is dying in the truck, the focus of the story shifts to the drama between Frank and Tub. Frank confesses his indecent lust and worries about the fate of his marriage, and Tub admits that he is obese not because of a gland problem, as he had previously claimed, but because of overeating. At its conclusion, it cuts back to Kenny, who, as the truck meanders along the country roads of rural Washington, is repeating to himself the doomed mantra: "I'm going to the hospital." Only later, through a blood-soaked admission, will Kenny's friends learn that his act was not simply brutal violence.

Much of this story does not come with a willful amorality, but rather an amorality that comes from simple poor decisions and general ignorance. The third-person narration frees Wolff from the compulsion of providing a likable protagonist. This will be a pattern that repeats itself throughout his fictional oeuvre. Expectations are raised and deflated on a regular basis; the heroic is notable only because of its absence. Even the stories that follow innocence and youth focus primarily on the ways in which this innocence can be corrupted. By the end of "Hunters in the Snow," Kenny, the most violent and least likable of the three characters, has become the chief point of empathy. He is something of a Wolff archetype: he is lonely, marginal, and utterly doomed by his circumstances. This is similar to the powerless figure of *This Boy's Life*— the young boy, reasserting and inventing himself, again and again, through the craft of fiction.

Another doomed and lonely character is the young boy, Eugene, who functions as the center of "Smokers," first published in *Atlanta Monthly* in 1980. This story is set at Choate, where the chief concerns of the protagonist—a nameless first-person narrator—are mostly to do with social activities, rather than academics. As a conspicuous outsider, branded as such by the fact that he wears, "a green Alpine hat with feathers stuck in the brim," Eugene's appearance is analogous

to Wolff's inner, conflicted self. Much of the story is concerned with the narrator's less-than-successful attempts to integrate himself into the society of the more privileged boys at the boarding school. Even as he fails, he must watch Eugene—feather-cap and all—make a respectable reputation for himself. The reader cannot help but be reminded of *This Boy's Life,* where a young Tobias goes to Seattle to take the entrance exams for Deerfield, Choate, and all the other East Coast academies. Determined to "solve the class problem by changing classes," Wolff observes the ways that the other boys dress, act, and speak, pretending that "I belonged here, that these handsome old buildings, webbed with vines of actual ivy to which a few brown leaves still clung, were my home."

In "Smokers," Eugene gets kicked out of school for smoking, an accusation that is not based on fact. His roommate, Talbot Nevin, is a privileged member of the school's aristocracy, a boy whose family has endowed the school with a hockey rink, a library, and a lecture series. "Talbot Nevin's father had driven his car to second place in the Monaco Grand Prix two years earlier, and celebrity magazines often featured a picture of him with someone like Jill St. John and a caption underneath quoting them as saying, " 'We're just good friends.' " Eugene gets along well with his roommate, and this angers the unnamed narrator, who desperately wants to count Talbot among his friends. It is Talbot's smoking—discovered by its vestigial odor after he has left the room—which prompts Eugene's undeserved notice of dismissal. Eugene, the extremely amiable and unique student, is made to suffer for the rule breaking of the school's aristocratic pupils. The narrator of the story, however, was in the room with Talbot immediately prior to the discovery of the lingering smoke. Though he has the opportunity to turn Talbot in, he refuses it in order to have a chance of rooming with a member of the Nevin family. He hides his motivations from even himself. "The problem was, if I told the dean about Talbot he would find out about me, too." He resolves to keep his secret and then excuses it. "If you wanted to get technical about it, he was guilty as charged a hundred times over. It wasn't as if some great injustice had been done." Innocence is unfairly victimized; there is no resolution in favor of morality or fair play. Of this victimization and imperfection, Wolff himself says in his contribution to *Passion and Craft: Conversations with Notable Writers:* "Many of the characters are somewhat self-deceived, as most of us are in one way or another." Self-deception has become the hallmark of a series of his characters, all of which are encountered in a seemingly random arc of plot.

This randomness of chance carries over from story to story within *In the Garden of the North American Martyrs,* Wolff's first full-length collection of stories, published in 1981 by The Ecco Press. In these pieces Wolff occasionally presses against the boundaries of what it means to tell a story, to extract a work of fiction from crucial moments within the lives of its characters. In "Wingfield," the shortest story in the collection, the bulk of its beginning is an introduction of the title character, a young soldier from North Carolina whose "voice oozed out of him thick and slow and sweet," a perfect Southern drawl. Wingfield is a narcoleptic, the reader learns, an innocent boy-man who is constantly falling asleep. Wolff then presents two stories that concern Wingfield's life and how it intersects with the life of the main character, again a first-person narrator. Without pausing between stories or introducing any explicit connection between them, Wolff's narrator tells of a practice operation in a forest, in which two companies of men assume opposing sides in a battle for territory. Wolff's narrator's group executes a nighttime raid on the other group of men, surprising them as they loaf in front of their fires in the cold night air. He catches Wingfield on watch, and creeps up behind him.

"With hatred and contempt and joy I took him from behind, and as I drew it across his throat I was wishing that my finger was a knife." The hatred is not pure hatred; rather, it is corrupted by joy, and is made more repulsive by the presence of enjoyment in violence.

This violence foretells the fate of American soldiers throughout Vietnam later in the war, a fate that, more often than not, seems utterly random. The soldiers storm the camp, firing into the tents with simulated weapons, massacring all of the unprepared soldiers. "It was exactly the same thing that happened to us a year and three months later," Wolff's narrator recounts, "as we slept beside a canal in the Mekong Delta, a few kilometers from Ben Tré." A member of the narrator's division who is transferred to the hospital for malaria immediately prior to the canal attack, a man named Parker, forms the core of the story's third section. Parker writes to the narrator after they have both returned stateside; Parker does not know that almost everyone in the division was killed, and Wolff's narrator ignores his letters. "Then," he rationalizes, "he would lose only one friend instead of twenty-six." After ten years—at a point close to the date of the story's narration—Parker shows up at the narrator's house. He has come for an accounting; he has comes to hear what happened to the members of his division. The meeting is solemn. "Parker asked the question he'd come to ask and then sat back and waited while I spoke name after name into the night." The names of the dead hang in the air between the men, rising from their entombment and nearly sacred departure.

As Parker leaves he passes a bit of information on to the narrator: Wingfield has survived the war—Parker has seen him recently at a train station in Charlotte. Stunned, the narrator watches his old friend's car depart. He takes a bottle of wine out onto the lawn and begins drinking. This drinking, however, is no small matter. He obliterates all sense of his self, and submerges himself entirely in alcohol. "I drank to the snoring earth, to the closed eye of the moon, to the trees that nodded and sighed: until, already dreaming, I fell back upon the blanket." Almost clumsily, nature is snoring, its eyes are symbolically closed, it nods and sighs, indifferent. Through his heavy drinking, the narrator tries to assert that the world is void of reason, that it is actually based entirely on chance and luck. The soldiers who are most unfit for battle still have a chance to survive; other more vigilant or skilled individuals are not as lucky. Wolff's topos has been irreversibly skewed by the experience of war. Reality becomes dream-like, a narcoleptic necessity. The possibility of a normal, outwardly sane existence is transformed into a dream. Ernest Hemingway's legacy of implication is masterfully carried out here. The narrator takes the escape from war's brutality that was taken by so many members of the Lost Generation—the willful and purposeful loss of both will and purpose.

"Wingfield," however, extends the moment of the story beyond the traditional boundaries of the genre. The internal progress of the story's protagonist continues through a series of seemingly unrelated occurrences that are bound together only by the presence of Wingfield. Yet the combination of these three instances brings about a tremendous change in the mind of the story's narrator. Though nothing actually happens in the story—all of its tragedies and joys are located in the past—the movement of the story is tremendously fluid. In a 1996 interview with Joan Smith, Wolff has discussed his affinity for movement of this sort within the stories of Chekhov. In the interview, Wolff describes a moment in Chekhov where a "brute" of a soldier who has died unredeemed, is being buried at sea. Chekhov describes the tragedy of the event, Wolff says, but does not stop there. He takes the focus away from the body of the man bobbing in the sea and "moves the vision back up to the sea and the sky where just at that moment the sun is breaking

through the clouds and he talks about the light dancing on the water—and I'm trying to get this right—'with a sort of joy for which there is no word in the language of men.' " Here, in a path that is similar to the one taken in "Wingfield," the boundary of the story is extended. The primary difference with Wolff, however, is that the progression is often external rather than internal; the subconscious is his staked-out territory. A work that takes this area—the human mind—and applies this extension technique is "Bullet In the Brain."

"Bullet In the Brain," appears as the concluding work in Tobias Wolff's collection, *The Night In Question: Stories* (1996). In it, the application of this Chekhovian pattern of attention can be easily perceived. This story also provides Wolff with a platform for one of the more enjoyable tasks for any writer—the butchery, in print, of a book critic. This piece tells the story of the death of the critic Anders, an older man, whose submersion in irony leads to his own death. In the first part of this story, Anders has the misfortune of coming to his bank as it is being robbed. Wolff plays with the notions of plot and cliché—the criminals behave exactly like Hollywood sketches of bank robbers, wearing ski masks and speaking in thick, thug-like accents. Anders cannot help but notice this instance of life imitating bad art. He is so occupied by the idea of this irony that he cannot control himself; he becomes, quite unintentionally, engaged in a verbal sparring match with one of the thieves. This power struggle leads to his death; the criminal—who does not understand Anders' ironic laughter or his smirking references to John Woo's movie *The Killers*—shoots him in the head.

Wolff, of course, does not stop there. "The bullet smashed Anders' skull and ploughed through his brain and exited behind his right ear, scattering shards of bone into the cerebral cortex, the corpus callosum, back toward the basal ganglia, and down into the thalamus." This specificity of medical vocabulary is perhaps Wolff's way of atoning for what is about to occur: he is about to foray from the world of the observable into the realm of thought. He describes the pattern of Anders' thoughts as he is dying. The two most important ideological tenets of this story—extension of a story's moment in time, coupled with the randomness of life's chaotic wash of memories—become its artistic focus. Wolff describes some of the most important occurrences in Anders' life, the moments of joy or suffering, and then tells the reader that, in his moment of death, these important memories are not what Anders remembers. Rather, Wolff asserts, Anders remembers an afternoon in his childhood of playing baseball and the appearance on the sandlot of a cousin of one of his friends, an uneducated boy from Mississippi. Wolff lingers on the description of this afternoon of baseball, focusing on each detail as if he were trying desperately to elongate the limited time span with which he is working. "The bullet is already in the brain," he writes, "it won't be outrun forever . . . In the end it will do its work and leave the troubled skull behind, dragging its comet's tail of memory and hope and talent and love into the marble hall of commerce." This is a departure from Wolff's usual tone; here he seems to have taken on the role of gnostic, describing for the reader, people's fate as individuals, marked, as they all are, for death's marble hall, its emotionless entombment.

ISOLATION AND IMAGE

The first lesson of the soldier—that death in the field can be quick, merciless, and entirely random—is thoroughly applied in the body of Wolff's fiction, written, as it is, from the field of living. Anders is a lonely man. Wolff has experienced profound isolation—both in his childhood and in the battlefields of Vietnam—and many of his characters reflect this primacy of the

individual, this intense solitude. Another war story that extends this " 'live alone, die alone' " philosophy also comes from *The Night In Question.* This work, "The Other Miller," encompasses many of the elements that the reader will witness in other parts of Wolff's fictional work. In it, a young protagonist—he is close to twenty years old—has joined the army because of a feud with his mother. This unusually intimate relationship with the maternal figure is a theme developed in *This Boy's Life,* where a young Tobias develops much of his self-respect and identity through his adventures—wild and country-spanning—with his mother. The central figure of "The Other Miller" also has this bond. In the absence of his father—he died in an army training accident at Fort Benning—Miller has developed an uncommon, almost erotic bond with his mother. He is in high school; she is struggling to support them both; they spend all of their time together, and Miller becomes attached to this way of living. Eventually, though, his mother falls in love again, and makes plans to get married. Miller, of course, feels threatened by this new masculine presence in her life. He does not understand how his mother can ignore what they have. He remembers, "The two of them drinking their coffee together and talking about different things, or maybe not talking at all—maybe just sitting in the kitchen while the room got dark around them, until the telephone rang or the dog started whining to get out." Miller resolves to break up the wedding.

When Miller fails, his life becomes turmoil and despair. He joins the army as a means of retribution, leaving before he earns his high school diploma. His mother tries calling and writing him during his first year of enlistment, but he does not respond or answer the telephone. When the action of the story opens, Miller's commander has just pulled him from his division's training maneuvers and told him that his mother has died. To Miller, who has not yet seen the truth of the soldier's life—that the body, the whole of existence, is frailty—this news is not understandable. He greets it by laughing, internally, and thanking his good luck at missing the miserable weather of maneuvers. He refuses to accept the news of his mother's death. He is certain that he has been confused with the other man named Miller in the company. He jokes with the men who are there to take him from maneuvers to his base, horrifying them utterly. In the course of their questioning, however, he realizes that in order to continue in life, he must heal the broken relationship with his mother. "This was supposed to be her punishment," he thinks, "but somehow it has become his own." He resolves to come home and solve the differences between them.

The naive reader, operating at the lingual level of the text, works with the assumption that Miller is correct, that his mother has indeed not died. Wolff constructs the patterning of the story so that, near its conclusion, it sweeps inward, into Miller's thoughts. Sitting in the back of the jeep that will bear him back to base, he begins reflecting on death and the impermanence of the individual. These reflections give way to a fantasy of the moment at which he will return home, and there the narration removes itself from his control. In a voice that the reader cannot reliably identify, the camera of the scene moves back and captures Miller entering his house and walking into a crowd of people and a miasma of perfume. Phil Dove, the man his mother has married, is there, as is a crowd of people—the mourners at a wake. Dove ushers him into the house with a grieved salutation, and the horror of Miller's mother's death—which until now has been in question—becomes real. The story ends abruptly, without any further explanation.

The image has again supplanted a conscious explication of plot. Indeed, this story, when thrown into the body of Wolff's work, evinces a movement away from plot and towards the loaded image—that is, the image with symbolic or psychological resonance. A well-developed example of this comes from Wolff's second collection of stories, *Back In The World,* first published by Houghton Mifflin in 1985. "Say Yes" is the shortest story in the collection—six pages in total—but it is also Wolff's closest approach to the solitary image. The body of the story concerns a suburban couple living in a house on El Camino Real, a snake-like street of strip malls that passes by Stanford University, where Wolff was a Stegner Fellow from 1975 to 1976, three years after the completion of his undergraduate degree at Oxford University. The husband and wife have an argument and, at its conclusion, vaguely dissatisfied, the husband walks outside with the trash from the kitchen. He sees the traffic on the street, and something moves within his mind. He feels an urgency rise from the understanding of his own mortality. "In another thirty years or so they would both be dead." He can no longer rationalize the argument he has just had. "He thought of the years they had spent together and how close they were and how well they knew each other, and his throat tightened so that he could hardly breathe." He returns to the house and finds his wife in the bathroom; he lies in bed and waits for her to appear. When she does, she demands that he extinguish the light. He does and she rustles towards him in the darkness, completely unseen. Even those that people love, even those whom they hold closest, Wolff is arguing, are nothing but strangers to each other when they are laid bare before the image of mortality.

This message, implicit in much of his short fiction, would seem to be at odds with the text of Wolff's novella, *The Barracks Thief.* First published in 1984, *The Barracks Thief* is an adventurous exercise in changing perspective—it shifts between first- and third-person narration in a manner that is as much puzzle as pattern. Through the protagonist's first-person recollections form the bulk of the work, Wolff still provides the reader with the missing parts of the story, with the vignettes that the narrator was not there to see. The story that *The Barracks Thief* tells is predictably gruesome. Tormented by the death of his father and his own repressed sexuality, the character Lewis begins to steal the wallets of the other soldiers in his barracks. He desperately needs the money in order to satisfy a debt he owes to an alcoholic hooker. Eventually he is caught and given a dishonorable discharge, but not before he topples the entire barracks into turmoil and brings aspersions of guilt onto the narrator.

Though Wolff's short fiction and nonfiction are rather dissimilar, thematic concerns do unite many of his texts. These are the stories of personal loneliness, of the individual besieged by violence, mortality, or an uncaring social system. Many of the subjects of his fiction—boarding school, the army, the intricacies of the relationship between a mother and son—can be traced directly to the occurrences of his life. Wolff claims a scrupulous honesty in his depiction of his childhood and tour of duty; this attempt at honesty translates into a simplicity of style and an accessibility to his inner life. The psychological torments of his fictional characters, however, are often walled within their selves; they choose poorly and do so based on reasons that are not evident to the reader. Though both fiction and nonfiction engage in a highly controlled form of discourse—a discourse that has its nouns and verbs housed in a series of clear images—this discourse is often invisible in all but its most outward components. Perhaps this is part of the explanation for James Hannah's observation that there is "almost no conventional scholarly criticism of Tobias Wolff's work." Though there is a tremendous body of reviewers' commentary—ranging from Mona Simpson to Anatole Broyard—a large portion of his work remains beyond the critical eye.

In the work "Our Story Begins," one of the middle pieces of *Back In the World,* the young writer-protagonist imagines himself "kneeling in the prow of that boat, lamp in hand, intent on the light shining just there before him." Wolff's life path has been circuitous and brutal, full of stren-uous trial and personal adversity. The characters of his fiction are often lampless—lacking in even the smallest illumination to guide them through their daily lives. Yet this lack of light gives them a distinct commonality. In his interview with Joan Smith, Wolff said of his fictional characters: "Though these stories are all different, the people in them breathe the same moral and spiritual atmosphere." Though he has been severely tested, Wolff's art has risen from the bleak structure of his past—the oxygen-poor atmosphere of poverty and hardship—to delineate both its own world and to explain the details of his childhood. Literature has become an extension of the life, and the life, in its past, has become delineated by literature. Through his work, Wolff seeks out the most vivid image, presents it, and allows it to stand on it own. Like the jumper in the door of the airplane, he slips into the text of the work and is gone. His residue, the spiral of the work's symbolic and conceptual meaning, lingers behind, in the language of the printed page.

Selected Bibliography

WORKS OF TOBIAS WOLFF

NOVELS AND SHORT STORIES
Ugly Rumours: A Novel. London: Allen & Unwin, 1975.
In the Garden of the North American Martyrs. New York: Ecco Press: 1981.
The Barracks Thief. New York: Ecco Press, 1984.
Back in the World. Boston: Houghton Mifflin, 1985.
The Night in Question: Stories. New York: Knopf, 1996.

NONFICTION
This Boy's Life: A Memoir. New York: Atlantic Monthly Press, 1989.
In Pharaoh's Army: Memories of the Lost War. New York: Knopf, 1994.

CRITICAL AND BIOGRAPHICAL STUDIES

Allen, Brooke. "Scheherazade's Exhaustion: The Work of Writers John Barth, William Trevor, and Tobias Wolff." *The New Criterion* 15:51–57 (November 1996).

Bailey, Peter J. "Why Not Tell the Truth? The Autobiographies of Three Fiction Writers." *Critique: Studies in Contemporary Fiction* 32, no. 4:211–223 (Summer 1991).

Barboni, Patrizia. *Dirty Realism: Raymond Carver, Tobias Wolff, Richard Ford.* Bologna, Italy: University of Bologna, 1994.

Challener, Daniel. *Stories of Resilience In Childhood: The Narratives of Maya Angelou, Maxine Hong Kingston, Richard Rodriguez, John Edgar Wideman, and Tobias Wolff.* New York: Garland, 1997.

DePietro, Thomas. "Minimalists, Moralists, and Manhattanites." *Hudson Review* 39:487–494 (Autumn 1986).

Halpert, Sam, ed. . . . *When We Talk About Raymond Carver.* Layton, Utah: Peregrine Smith, 1991.

Hannah, James. *Tobias Wolff: A Study of the Short Fiction.* New York: Twayne, 1996.

Keegan, John. *The Face of Battle.* New York: The Viking Press, 1976.

Kelly, Colm L. "Affirming the Indeterminable: Deconstruction, Sociology, and Tobias Wolff's 'Say Yes.' " *Mosaic* 32:149–166 (March 1999).

Lyons, Bonnie, and Bill Oliver. *Passion and Craft: Conversations with Notable Writers.* Champaign, Ill.: University of Illinois Press, 1998.

Wolff, Geoffrey. *The Duke of Deception.* New York: Penguin, 1986.

Woodruff, Jay. *A Piece of Work: Five Writers Discuss Their Revisions.* Iowa City: Iowa University Press, 1993.

INTERVIEWS

Bonetti, Kay. *Interview: Tobias Wolff.* Columbia, Mo.: American Audio Prose Library, 1985.

Burke, Michael D. *Interview: Tobias Wolff.* San Francisco: FM Five, 1986.

Smith, Joan. *Interview: Tobias Wolff. Salon Magazine* www.salon.com/dec96/interview961216.html (December 16–20, 1996).

FILM BASED ON THE WORKS OF TOBIAS WOLFF

This Boy's Life. Screenplay by Robert Getchell and Tobias Wolff. Directed by Michael Caton-Jones. Warner Bros. 1993.

—PAULS TOUTONGHI

Index

Index

*Arabic numbers printed in bold-face type refer
to extended treatment of a subject.*

A Complete Listing of Authors in
American Writers

Sandburg, Carl   Volume 3
Santayana, George   Volume 3
Schwartz, Delmore   Supplement II
Sexton, Anne   Supplement II
Shapiro, Karl   Supplement II
Shepard, Sam   Supplement III
Shields, Carol   Supplement VII
Silko, Leslie Marmon   Supplement IV
Simon, Neil   Supplement IV
Sinclair,Upton   Supplement V
Singer, Isaac Bashevis   Volume 4
Smiley, Jane   Supplement VI
Snodgrass, W. D.   Supplement VI
Sontag, Susan   Supplement III
Stegner, Wallace   Supplement IV
Stein, Gertrude   Volume 4
Steinbeck, John   Volume 4
Stevens, Wallace   Volume 4
Stevens, Wallace   Retrospective Supplement I
Stone, Robert   Supplement V
Stowe, Harriet Beecher   Supplement I
Strand, Mark   Supplement IV
Styron, William   Volume 4
Swenson, May   Supplement IV
Tate, Allen   Volume 4
Taylor, Edward   Volume 4
Taylor, Peter   Supplement V
Thoreau, Henry David   Volume 4
Thurber, James   Supplement I
Toomer, Jean   Supplement III
Trilling, Lionel   Supplement III
Twain, Mark   Volume 4
Tyler, Anne   Supplement IV

Updike, John   Volume 4
Updike, John   Retrospective Supplement I
Van Vechten, Carl   Supplement II
Veblen, Thorstein   Supplement I
Vidal, Gore   Supplement IV
Vonnegut, Kurt   Supplement II
Walker, Alice   Supplement III
Warren, Robert Penn   Volume 4
Welty, Eudora   Volume 4
Welty, Eudora   Retrospective Supplement I
West, Nathanael   Volume 4
Wharton, Edith   Volume 4
Wharton, Edith   Retrospective Supplement I
White, E. B.   Supplement I
Whitman, Walt   Volume 4
Whitman, Walt   Retrospective Supplement I
Whittier, John Greenleaf   Supplement I
Wilbur, Richard   Supplement III
Wilder, Thornton   Volume 4
Williams, Tennessee   Volume 4
Williams, William Carlos   Volume 4
Williams, William Carlos   Retrospective
   Supplement I
Wilson, Edmund   Volume 4
Winters, Yvor   Supplement II
Wolfe, Thomas   Volume 4
Wolfe, Tom   Supplement III
Wolff, Tobias   Supplement VII
Wright, Charles   Supplement V
Wright, James   Supplement III
Wright, Richard   Volume 4
Wylie, Elinor   Supplement I
Zukofsky, Louis   Supplement III

BELMONT UNIVERSITY LIBRARY